Selected Readings in Econometrics from *Econometrica*

Selected Readings in

Econometrics

from *Econometrica*

edited by

John W. Hooper and Marc Nerlove

The M.I.T. Press

Cambridge, Massachusetts, and London, England

PREFACE

THE PURPOSE of this volume is to present in a convenient form certain articles, originally published in *Econometrica*, which we think have played a major role in the development of econometrics. We hope that this collection of representative articles will prove useful to students and professional practitioners of econometrics as a reference work, and that it will serve to suggest the growth, development, and changing emphasis of the subject over the past thirty years.

In order to delimit the scope of the present volume, we restricted these selections to articles whose content was primarily concerned with statistical methods or applications of statistical methods to economic models. A similar volume of theoretical readings is planned. Within our chosen limits, we sought a balance between articles in econometric methodology and those in econometric applications. In addition, we have attempted to obtain a historically representative list of papers which have had, and in most cases continue to have, a considerable impact on the development of econometrics. It is for this reason that we did not consider any papers published after 1964; we felt that insufficient time had elapsed to enable us to obtain sufficient perspective from which to judge their long-run importance.

One indisputable fact which one learns from the study of economics is that preference functions can, and do usually, vary enormously among different individuals. For this reason we should not expect any other two individuals, even those adopting our chosen constraints, to select an identical list of articles. Indeed, at times we have experienced some difficulty in aggregating our two choices into one consistent preference order. From our own give-and-take and compromise, we hope that a useful selection has emerged, and that our choices will not prove too idiosyncratic.

Many people have given us useful comments and criticisms on various versions of our "list," and we particularly want to thank Zvi Griliches, Lawrence Klein, Edmond Malinvaud, S. H. Nerlove, Henri Theil, and Jan Tinbergen for their thoughtful comments. In addition, we wish to thank Joseph Stiglitz for his services as general editor of this volume. Of course, none of these persons should be held responsible for our ultimate selection of papers; as much as we would wish to implicate them, it would hardly be fair to do so.

J. W. H.
M. N.

CONTENTS

vii

Selected Readings in Econometrics from *Econometrica*

Econometrica, Vol. 1, 3 (July 1933)

CAN STOCK MARKET FORECASTERS FORECAST?

BY ALFRED COWLES 3RD

A paper read before a joint meeting of the Econometric Society and the
American Statistical Association, Cincinnati, Ohio, December 31, 1932

INTRODUCTION

THIS paper presents results of analyses of the forecasting efforts of 45
professional agencies which have attempted, either to select specific
common stocks which should prove superior in investment merit to the
general run of equities, or to predict the future movements of the stock
market itself. The paper falls into two main parts. The first deals with
the attempts of two groups, 20 fire insurance companies and 16 financial services, to foretell which specific securities would prove most
profitable. The second part deals with the efforts of 25 financial publications to foretell the future course of the stock market. Various statistical tests of these results are given.

These investigations were instituted five years ago as a means of
testing the success of applied economics in the investment field. It
seemed a plausible assumption that if we could demonstrate the existence in individuals or organizations of the ability to foretell the elusive
fluctuations, either of particular stocks, or of stocks in general, this
might lead to the identification of economic theories or statistical practices whose soundness had been established by successful prediction.

The forecasters include well-known organizations in the different
fields represented, many of which are large and well financed, employ-
ing economists and statisticians of unquestioned ability. The names of
these organizations are omitted, since their publication would be likely
to invite wholesale controversy over the interpretation of their records.
Some of the forecasters seem to have taken a page from the book of
the Delphic Oracle, expressing their prophecies in terms susceptible of
more than one construction. It would frequently be possible, therefore,
for an editor, after the event, to present a plausible challenge of our
interpretation. Most of the forecasts appear through the medium of
weekly publications and each of these has been read and recorded on
the day it became available to us, which in practically every case was
before the event. In this way certain possible elements of bias have
been eliminated. It was impossible that hindsight could influence our
judgment, either in the selection of publications for analysis or in the
interpretations placed on their forecasts. In the case of the fire insurance companies, however, the analyses were made annually, based on
the transactions reported in *Kimber's Record of Insurance Company
Security Purchases*. The companies were selected as fairly representa-

1

tive of their class. The analysis of the 26-year forecasting record of William Peter Hamilton, former editor of the *Wall Street Journal*, also falls in a different category, in that it was undertaken because of the reputation for successful forecasting which he had established over a long period of years.

FORECASTING THE COURSE OF INDIVIDUAL STOCK PRICES

We turn first to the records of two groups, the financial services and the fire insurance companies, which have attempted to select individual stocks that would prove more profitable for investment than the average issue. The first part of this section deals with the records, over the $4\frac{1}{2}$ years ending July, 1932, of 16 leading financial services which have made a practice of regularly submitting to their subscribers selected lists of common stocks for investment. Our analysis includes about 7,500 separate recommendations, requiring approximately 75,000 entries. The first step was to record each week the name and price of each stock recommended for purchase or sale by each service. Next came the tabulation of the advice to sell or cover the commitment previously advised. Reiterated advice was not considered, action being assumed to have been taken as of the date when the recommendation was first published. The percentage gain or loss on each such transaction was recorded and, in a parallel column, the gain or loss of the stock market for the identical period. A balance was struck every six months which summarized 'the total results secured by each service as compared with the action of the stock market. Proper corrections were, of course, made to offset the effect of changes in capital structure resulting from the issue of rights, stock dividends, etc. Since a tendency existed among some services to emphasize their conspicuously successful stock recommendations and ignore more unfortunate commitments, we adopted a practice of automatically dropping a stock from the list six months after it had been last recommended, when specific advice to sell was not given.

A redistribution of funds in equal amounts among all stocks recommended has been assumed for each service at the beginning of every six months' period analyzed. It could be maintained, of course, that this equalizing process should take place as often as once a week, but this would increase the labor of computation to overwhelming proportions. Provisional experiments demonstrated that it would yield conclusions practically identical with those secured by the shorter method. Compounding the successive six months' records gives the percentage by which each service's recommendations have exceeded, or fallen behind, the stock market, as shown in Table I.

Only six of the 16 services achieved any success. To arrive at an average performance, the record of each service was reduced to an effective annual rate which was then weighted in accordance with the length of the period represented. The average annual effective rate of all the services, thus arrived at, is −1.43 per cent.

TABLE I
RESULTS OF COMMITMENTS IN STOCKS RECOMMENDED BY 16 FINANCIAL SERVICES (RELATED TO MARKET AVERAGES)

Service	Weeks	Per cent
1.	234	+20.8
2.	234	+17.2
3.	234	+15.2
4.	234	+12.3
5.	234	+ 8.4
6.	26	+ 6.1
7.	52	0.
8.	104	− 0.5
9.	234	− 1.9
10.	52	− 2.2
11.	52	− 3.0
12.	52	− 8.3
13.	78	−16.1
14.	104	−28.2
15.	104	−31.2
16.	156	−33.0

PROBABILITY TESTS

In an attempt to determine whether the service having the best record achieved its result through skill or chance, we resorted to the theories of compound and inverse probability. Our conclusion is thus rendered consistent by obtaining approximately the same answer in two different ways.

With the aid of various checks, involving 1250 computations of the action of individual stocks selected at random, we derived a formula, A.D. $(t) = 5.42 + 1.5t$ (A.D. = average deviation, t, in units of 4 weeks, ≥ 1), representing the deviation, for all periods from one month up to one year, of the average individual stock from the average of all stocks.

Service Number 1, for the 9 six months' periods from January 1, 1928 to July 1, 1932, was successful 7 times and unsuccessful 2 times. With the aid of the table referred to, the averages of "chances in 1000 to do worse" for the 7 periods in which it was successful and the 2 periods in which it was unsuccessful were found to be 842 and 66 respectively. By the theory of direct probabilities, the probability of a single service being right at least 7 times in 9 is equal to the sum of the first 3 terms of the binomial $(\frac{1}{2}+\frac{1}{2})^9$.

$$p = 1/2^9 + 9/2^9 + 36/2^9 = 46/512 = .090$$

The probability that a single service could in 9 predictions be 7 times on the positive side and in these 7 forecasts equal the achievement of Service Number 1 is,

$$P = .090 \times (1 - .842) = .014$$

However, the record of the best service is marred by its failure in the two negative cases. The average of the two chances to do worse in these cases is .066. We then have,

$$Q = (7/9) \times .842 + 2/9 \times .066 = .670$$

as the probability of a single random service having a record worse than that of Service Number 1. We therefore conclude that the probability that a random service can, first, be on the right side of the market 7 times out of 9, and second, equal in performance the record of Service Number 1, is

$$P = .090 \times (1 - .670) = .030.$$

This means that in 16 services we should expect to find $16 \times .030 = .48$ services which will equal the record of Service Number 1. That is to say, the chance is even that we should get at least one service as good as Number 1.

Because of the assumptions implied in this computation, we shall argue this another way. We shall assume that the probability that a service for its total forecast shall be on the positive side of the market is $1/2$. Then the estimate of its success must be made by a different evaluation of Q. For this purpose we shall adopt a formula suggested by Bayes' rule in inverse probability in which the weights .910 and .090 instead of 7/9 and 2/9 are used. We get

$$Q = \frac{.910\,(.842)}{.910\,(.842) + (.090)\,(.934)} = .901$$

Hence, if a service was on the right side of the market, the probability of its achieving the success of Service Number 1 would be $1-Q$. Thus the compound probability would be

$$P = 1/2\,(1 - .901) = .050.$$

Among the 16 services the probability of the most successful one equalling the record of Service Number 1 would be $P = 16 \times .050 = .80$, that is to say, we should expect to get among 16 random services about one service which would equal Number 1. Since this answer is quite consistent with our previous answer, our analysis suggests the conclusion that the record of Service Number 1 could not be definitely attributed to skill.

TWENTY FIRE INSURANCE COMPANIES

The second analysis deals with the common stock investments, from 1928 to 1931 inclusive, of 20 of our leading fire insurance companies. Its significance lies in the fact that these companies are representative of a class of common stock investor which has had long years of experience and large amounts of capital at its disposal. Fire insurance dates from the Great London Fire of 1666, and active investment in stocks developed during the nineteenth century. The fire insurance companies are much older hands at the business of investment than either the financial services, which are a twentieth century product, or American investment trusts, which are largely a development of the last few years. The investment policies of these companies are based on the accumulated knowledge of successive boards of directors whose judgment might be presumed, over the years, to have been well above that of the average investor. The 20 companies which were selected for analysis hold assets totalling several hundred million dollars, and seem a fair sample of their kind.

Fire insurance companies carry between 20 and 30 per cent of their total investments in common stocks. Their average turnover amounts to only some 5 per cent a year. For this reason it was thought best to confine our analysis to the record of the actual purchases and sales made during the period under examination, rather than to compute the record of the entire common stock portfolio. To simplify the labor, all items of stock purchased were given equal weights, regardless of the amounts involved. While the conclusion does not exactly reflect the actual investment results secured by these companies, it should, however, provide a satisfactory test of the success of these organizations in selecting stocks which performed better than the average.

The method employed in the analysis is essentially the same as that used in the case of the investment services. A second purchase of an item was omitted from the record unless a sale of this item intervened. A record of the sale of an item, of course, determined the date as of which it was dropped from the list. Also, any item of which there had been no purchase recorded for 12 months was automatically considered sold.

The compounded records of the 20 companies for the 4-year period are shown in Table II.

Six of the companies show evidence of success, and the average of the 20 is -4.72 per cent. The average record of the companies in the stocks which they selected for investment fell below the average of the stock market at the effective annual rate of 1.20 per cent. A comparable result could have been achieved through a purely random selection of stocks. The analysis of the fire insurance companies' records thus confirms the results secured in appraising the records of the financial services.

TABLE II

RESULTS OF COMMITMENTS IN STOCKS MADE BY TWENTY FIRE INSURANCE
COMPANIES (RELATED TO STOCK MARKET AVERAGES)

All companies 1928–31, inc.

Company	Per cent
1.	+27.35
2.	+25.11
3.	+18.34
4.	+10.38
5.	+10.12
6.	+ 3.20
7.	− 2.06
8.	− 3.63
9.	− 5.06
10.	− 6.67
11.	−10.44
12.	−10.55
13.	−11.76
14.	−12.92
15.	−13.82
16.	−14.96
17.	−18.03
18.	−21.89
19.	−23.44
20.	−33.72

FORECASTING THE STOCK MARKET ACCORDING TO THE DOW THEORY

Having dealt with the efficiency of two great groups of professionals, fire insurance companies and financial services, in selecting common stocks for investment, we turn now to a consideration of skill in predicting the course of the stock market as a whole. This section also is in two principal sub-divisions. First we consider the record of William Peter Hamilton.

This analysis was undertaken because several decades of editorials in the country's leading financial newspaper have built up a great popular following for the Dow Theory, of which Hamilton was the principal sponsor. The Dow Theory was the creation of Charles H. Dow, founder of the Dow Jones financial news service, founder and editor of the *Wall Street Journal*. After Dow's death in 1902 Hamilton succeeded him as editor of the *Wall Street Journal*, continuing in this position until his death in December, 1929.

During 26 years of his incumbency Hamilton wrote 255 editorials which presented forecasts for the stock market based on the Dow Theory. These were sufficiently definite to permit scoring as bullish, bearish, or doubtful. This we did by a majority vote of five readers. When doubtful we assumed that he abstained from trading. When bullish it was assumed that he bought equal dollar amounts of the stocks included in the Dow Jones railroad and industrial averages, and sold them only when he became bearish or doubtful. When bearish we assumed that he sold short equal dollar amounts of these stocks and covered only when he became doubtful or bullish. The percentage gain or loss on each such transaction has been calculated, and the results compounded through the 26 years. Since the Dow Jones averages have only recently been corrected to offset the effect of stock rights, stock dividends, and stock splits, such adjustments have been made for all the previous years on the basis of tables published by Dwight C. Rose in his book *Investment Management*. Corrections have also been made to allow for the effect of brokerage charges, cash dividends, and the interest presumably earned by Hamilton's funds when they were not in the stock market. The fully adjusted figures were then reduced to an effective annual rate of gain which is presented as a measure of the result accomplished.

From December 1903 to December 1929, Hamilton, through the application of his forecasts to the stocks composing the Dow Jones industrial averages, would have earned a return, including dividend and interest income, of 12 per cent per annum. In the same period the stocks composing the industrial averages showed a return of 15.5 per cent per annum. Hamilton therefore failed by an appreciable margin to gain as much through his forecasting as he would have made by a continuous outright investment in the stocks composing the industrial averages. He exceeded by a wide margin, however, a supposedly normal investment return of about 5 per cent. Applying his forecasts to the stocks composing the Dow Jones railroad averages, the result is an annual gain of 5.7 per cent while the railroad averages themselves show a return of 7.7 per cent.

Hamilton was long of stocks 55 per cent, short 16 per cent, and out of the market 29 per cent, of the 26 years under review. Counting only changes of position, he made bullish forecasts 29 times. Applying these to the industrial averages, 16 were profitable, 13 unprofitable. He announced bearish forecasts 23 times, 10 were profitable, 13 unprofitable. He advised 38 times that funds be withdrawn from the stock market, 19 of these withdrawals being profitable, 19 unprofitable. In all, 45 of his changes of position were unsuccessful, 45 successful. The application of the forecasts to the railroad averages confirms these conclusions except that in this case 41 changes of position were successful and 49 unsuccessful. For the period from 1909 to 1914 inclusive, when the industrial averages displayed what, in effect, was a horizontal trend, his hypothetical fund shrank 7.8 per cent per annum below what it would have been if loaned at 5 per cent interest. The result of applying his forecasts to the railroad averages deserves attention in view of the fact that this group displayed an almost horizontal secular trend for the 26 years under consideration. His average annual gain of 5.7 per cent in this group would have been approximately equalled, in the case of a continuous outright investment, by the dividend income.

STOCK MARKET FORECASTS OF TWENTY-FOUR FINANCIAL PUBLICATIONS

For the analysis of other results secured in forecasting the course of the stock market, we selected during the period from January 1, 1928, to June 1, 1932, 24 publications (among which were 18 professional financial services, 4 financial weeklies, one bank letter, and one investment house letter). More than 3,300 forecasts were tabulated. The method used has been for each reader to ask himself the question, "In the light of what this particular bulletin says, would one be led to buy stocks with all the funds at his disposal, or place a portion only of his funds in stocks, or withdraw entirely from the market?" The reader graded the advice in each instance by means of one of nine possible entries, namely 100 per cent of funds in the market, $87\frac{1}{2}$, 75, $62\frac{1}{2}$, 50, $37\frac{1}{2}$, 25, $12\frac{1}{2}$, or 0 per cent. The great majority of forecasters confine themselves to general discussions of the investment situation, leaving to the reader the decision as to what proportion of his funds he shall place in the market. The tabulation, therefore, cannot be mathematically conclusive. Our method, in general, has been to have the vote of three readers of competent intelligence determine the interpretation of each forecast. Marginal commitments have not been incorporated in our tabulations because in no case have they been advised by any of the forecasters. Similarly, short commitments are not in general assumed because, of the entire 24 forecasters, only one recommended them. His record has been computed on a special basis.

The tabulated forecasts have been tested in the light of the actual fluctuations of the stock market as reflected by the Standard Statistics Company index of 90 representative stocks. If a forecast is 100 per cent bullish and the market rises 10 per cent in the subsequent week, the forecaster is scored as $+10$ per cent. If the forecaster, after weighing the favorable and unfavorable factors, leaves the decision hanging in the balance, the score is $+5$ per cent or one-half of the market advance. This is on the assumption that the investor, being in doubt as to the future course of the market and being, by definition, committed to common stocks as a possible investment medium, would be led to adopt a hedged position with half of his funds in stocks and half in reserve. If the forecast is 100 per cent bearish, the score is zero, regardless of the subsequent action of the market, on the assumption that, under such conditions, the investor would withdraw all of his funds from stocks. On the other hand, if the forecast is 100 per cent bullish and the market drops 10 per cent in the ensuing week, the score is − 10 per cent. If the forecast is doubtful when the market drops 10 per cent, the score is − 5 per cent. The compounding of all these weekly scores for the period covered gives a cumulative record for each forecaster. This permits comparisons which reveal relative success and average performance. While it may be thought that accurate week-to-week forecasting is a hopeless ideal, it should be emphasized that our analysis of weekly results also measures accurately the efficiency of long swing forecasts.

A figure representing the average of all possible forecasting results for the period was arrived at by compounding one-half of every weekly percentage change in the level of the stock market. The final scores given below for the 24 forecasters were computed by dividing the actual performance of each by the average of all possible results referred to above, and subtracting 100.

TABLE III

RESULTS OF STOCK MARKET FORECASTS

Forecaster	Weeks	Per cent
1.	105	+72.4
2.	230	+31.5
3.	230	+28.3
4.	21	+24.2
5.	157	+ 9.0
6.	53	+ 3.0
7.	126	+ 2.4
8.	53	+ 1.3
9.	105	− 1.7
10.	157	− 2.1
11.	230	− 3.6
12.	43	− 6.0
13.	53	− 6.7
14.	131	− 6.9
15.	230	−12.5
16.	230	−13.5
17.	53	−17.2
18.	230	−21.5
19.	69	−29.4
20.	230	−33.0
21.	230	−35.3
22.	230	−41.5
23.	157	−45.3
24.	230	−49.1

The records show that only one-third of the list met with any success. In order to derive a significant average of the performance of the

10 ECONOMETRICA

entire group the results listed above have been reduced to effective
annual rates, and each has been given a weight to conform with the
length of the record analysed. After these adjustments, we are enabled
to conclude that the average forecasting agency fell approximately
4 per cent per annum below a record representing the average of all
performances achievable by pure chance. This would seem to indicate
that, in general, these stock market forecasters failed to accomplish
their objective. The most that can be said in extenuation is that the
long-continued decline in securities has been, naturally, a handicap to
a group which, taking warning from the experience of Cassandra, usually seems constrained to look on the bright side. During the 4½ year
period under analysis the number of weeks in which the stock market
declined almost exactly equalled the number of weeks in which advances were recorded, and the total amount of the declines considerably exceeded the total amount of the advances. Yet we recorded
during this period 2035 bullish, 804 bearish, and 479 doubtful forecasts. Further, we note that in 1928, the only year the market showed
a net gain, the excess of bullish over bearish forecasts was smaller than
in any succeeding year. Taking a glaring example, in the rising market
of 1928 the ratio of bullish to bearish forecasts was only four to three.
In 1931, when the market declined 54 per cent, there were sixteen
bullish forecasts to every three bearish.

STATISTICAL INTERPRETATIONS OF RESULTS

In an attempt to illuminate the problem of whether the records of all
these forecasters lay within the limits of pure chance, we compiled
24 records, identical with those of the 24 forecasters as to the total
period covered, but having purely fortuitous advices applied to random
intervals within these perids. For example, to compile a purely chance
record to compare with the actual record of a forecaster whose operations covered 230 weeks from January 1, 1928, to June 1, 1932, we first
determined the average number of changes of advice for such a period,
which was 33. Cards numbered from 1 to 229 were shuffled, drawn, re-
shuffled, drawn, in all 33 times. Thus 33 random dates were selected
as of which forecasts were to be changed. The investment policies
which were to apply to the intervals between those dates were derived
in similar fortuitous fashion, by drawing 33 times from nine cards on
each of which a different one of the nine possible investment policies
was noted.

It only remained to relate these random advices to a stock market
index, cumulate the results, relate them, as we had done with the
records of the actual forecasters, to the average of all chances for the
period, and subtract 100. Thus we had a list of 24 purely chance fore-

casting records, shown in Table IV, to compare with the records of the actual prophets.

TABLE IV

RESULTS OF RANDOM FORECASTS

Forecaster	Weeks	Per cent
1.	230	+71.1
2.	230	+37.2
3.	230	+24.2
4.	157	+19.1
5.	230	+13.2
6.	105	+ 9.2
7.	230	+ 2.7
8.	53	+ 2.5
9.	131	+ 1.3
10.	230	+ 1.1
11.	53	− .1
12.	54	− .6
13.	157	− 2.5
14.	230	− 4.6
15.	43	− 5.4
16.	53	− 6.1
17.	230	−10.5
18.	21	−10.9
19.	157	−11.0
20.	105	−13.0
21.	230	−13.1
22.	230	−14.2
23.	69	−18.7
24.	126	−27.1

For easy comparison of the two groups we have prepared Figure 1 showing all the records, actual and hypothetical. The chart indicates that where forecasting agencies made gains, even the greatest of these lay within limits equalled by the best of our 24 imaginary records representing random action at random intervals. But the extremer losses of the forecasters tended to exceed the losses registered by the least successful of our 24 records of purely chance operations.

In any attempt at interpreting the significance of the performances of the various stock market forecasters we are embarrased by our inability to determine how often economic developments occur of sufficient importance to justify the revision of forecasts. This is tantamount to admitting that we do not know the true number of independent cases, or items, in the time series representing the various forecasting records. In these circumstances, probable errors for correlation coefficients, or for normal distributions, cannot constitute very exact measures of probability. We do know, however, since we are dealing with weekly publications, that the maximum possible number of forecasting opportunities is 52 a year. We also know that forecasts, on the average, undergo some degree of revision about 7 times a year. The correlation coefficients and probable errors, which constitute one of our tests of probability, have been worked out on both of these bases.

The record of Forecaster Number 1 was available to us for a period of only two years, during which he did not once change his advice. We therefore omitted his record from consideration in our statistical interpretation on the ground that inferences based on it would be relatively inconclusive. For the correlation test therefore, Forecasters Number 2, 3, 22 and 24 were chosen as representing the best and the worst whose records covered the entire period under analysis. The weekly forecasts of each of these four were correlated with the first differences

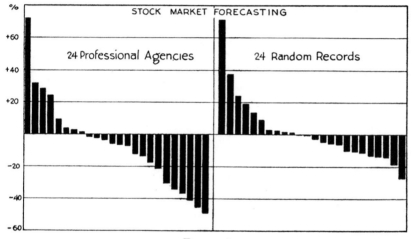

Figure 1

of the logarithms of the stock market averages over $4\frac{1}{2}$ years. Forecaster Number 2 had a correlation coefficient of .151; Forecaster Number 3, of .197; and Forecasters Number 22 and 24, of $-.124$ and $-.132$ respectively. The probable error of the best correlation coefficient, with $n = 230$, was .043. The difference in r between Forecasters Numbers 2 and 3 is about equal to this probable error, and $r = .197$ is greater than 4 times the probable error of .043. We have interpreted these data by the use of R. A. Fisher's technique, where $z = \tan h^{-1}r$. The best correlation $r = .197$, $n = 230$, was first compared with a theoretical $r = .000$, $n = 230$; and then compared with $r = -.132$, $n = 230$, that is the lowest correlation coefficient.

	r	z	$n-3$	$1/n-3$
1st sample	.197	.200	227	.00441
2nd sample	.000	.000	227	.00441
	Difference	.200		Sum	.00882

$$2\sqrt{.00882} = .188$$

.188 is to be compared with .200. Since these figures are approximately equal, the presumption of skill is slight although the presumption does exist because of the fact that .188 is less than .200, the difference between the two values for z. Using R. A. Fisher's technique in the second case, that is, comparing the best correlation coefficient $r = .197$ with the lowest correlation coefficient $r = -.132$, seems to indicate that there is a real difference between the two samples. If another sample were taken from each of these two forecasters, we should expect to find a similar difference between them in favor of the first forecaster within the limits of the probable error.

We then computed correlation coefficients and probable errors for the data arrived at by taking as our items the periods during which each forecast was in force. We thus had 30 items for Forecaster Number 2, which equalled the number of changes he made in his forecasts, instead of the 230 items which represented the number of weeks for which his record was tabulated. On this basis Forecaster Number 2 had a correlation coefficient of .479; Forecaster Number 3 had a correlation coefficient of .245; and Forecasters Number 22 and 24 had correlation coefficients of $-.513$ and $-.206$ respectively. The probable error of the best correlation coefficient, with $n = 30$, was found to be .095. Thus $r = .479$ was about five times the probable error of .095. The best random forecast had $r = .356 \pm .102$, when his changes of position were taken as the items of the series. When the number of weeks (230), over which his random record extends, was used, and this record correlated with the first differences of the logarithms of the stock market averages, $r = .125 \pm .044$.

Deductions as to the significance of the relationships of the various correlation coefficients to the probable errors are rendered inconclusive, not only by our inability to identify the true number of independent cases in each series, but also by the fact that we have not computed a sufficient number of the correlation coefficients to enable us to determine the character of their distribution.

Having thus experimented with various correlation tests we then resorted to measuring the spread of the performances of the individual forecasters by means of frequency distributions of the percentage weekly gains and losses of each of six forecasters divided by the average result of all possible forecasts. The six chosen were two of the best actual records, two of the worst actual records, and the best and almost the worst random records. The series thus arrived at were each distributed into several classes ranging from 92.50 per cent to 108.50 per cent; these frequencies were plotted and appeared to be reasonably normal. (See Figure 2.) Averages of each of the percentage frequency distributions were computed and compared with a theoretical average

14 ECONOMETRICA

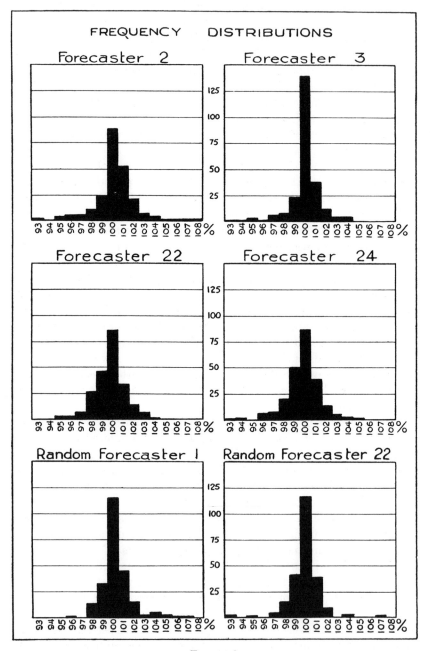

FIGURE 2

of 100, which represented the average of all random frequency distributions. The probable error of the latter was found to be .086. Forecasters Number 2 and 3 showed averages of 100.098 and 100.103 respectively; each deviating from the theoretical average by amounts which were slightly greater than the probable error .086, but considerably less than twice this probable error. Forecasters Number 22 and 24 had averages of 99.674 and 99.711 respectively; less than the theoretical average by .326 and .289. Each of these differences was more than three, and less than four, times greater than the probable error .086. When a similar frequency distribution is made for the best purely random forecaster, it is found that the average was equal to 100.213, which is greater than that of Forecasters 2 and 3. The deviation from the theoretical average lies within three times the probable error of this theoretical average.

SUMMARY

1. Sixteen financial services, in making some 7500 recommendations of individual common stocks for investment during the period from January 1, 1928, to July 1, 1932, compiled an average record that was worse than that of the average common stock by 1.43 per cent annually. Statistical tests of the best individual records failed to demonstrate that they exhibited skill, and indicated that they more probably were results of chance.

2. Twenty fire insurance companies in making a similar selection of securities during the years 1928 to 1931, inclusive, achieved an average record 1.20 per cent annually worse than that of the general run of stocks. The best of these records, since it is not very much more impressive than the record of the most successful of the sixteen financial services, fails to exhibit definitely the existence of any skill in investment.

3. William Peter Hamilton, editor of the *Wall Street Journal*, publishing forecasts of the stock market based on the Dow Theory over a period of 26 years, from 1904 to 1929, inclusive, achieved a result better than what would ordinarily be regarded as a normal investment return, but poorer than the result of a continuous outright investment in representative common stocks for this period. On 90 occasions he announced changes in the outlook for the market. Forty-five of these predictions were successful and 45 unsuccessful.

4. Twenty-four financial publications engaged in forecasting the stock market during the 4½ years from January 1, 1928, to June 1, 1932, failed as a group by 4 per cent per annum to achieve a result as good as the average of all purely random performances. A review of the various statistical tests, applied to the records for this period, of these 24 fore-

casters, indicates that the most successful records are little, if any, better than what might be expected to result from pure chance. There is some evidence, on the other hand, to indicate that the least successful records are worse than what could reasonably be attributed to chance.

Cowles Commission for Research in Economics

Econometrica, Vol. 1, 4 (October 1933)

PARTIAL TIME REGRESSIONS AS COMPARED WITH INDIVIDUAL TRENDS

By RAGNAR FRISCH AND FREDERICK V. WAUGH[1]

I. INTRODUCTION

THERE are in common use two methods of handling linear trend in correlation analysis of time series data; first, to base the analysis on *deviations* from trends fitted separately to each original series; and, second, to base the analysis on the original series without trend elimination, but instead to introduce *time* itself as one of the variables in a multiple correlation analysis. The first method may be called the individual trend method and the latter the partial time regression method.

There are certain misconceptions about the relative value of the two methods and about the kinds of statistical results that are obtained by the two methods. The following simple example illustrates the situation. Suppose we are studying the relation of sugar consumption to sugar prices. We have data representing total annual consumption and price for several consecutive years. There may be a strong upward trend in consumption due to population increase or to some other factor that changes or shifts the demand curve. If we want to study only the relation of consumption to price, naturally we must eliminate the trend from the consumption before using the data to measure demand elasticity.

But, suppose that, during the period studied, there has been a persistent tendency in sugar prices to decline and that this has caused a long-time increase in consumption. This fact may be just what we want to express when we speak of the relation of sugar consumption to price. This long-time connection between consumption and price may be even more important for our problem than the short-time connection. If so, we must not, of course, eliminate trends from the variables before proceeding to the analysis. On the contrary, in this case the trend variation in price and the trend variation in consumption must be left in the material and *should be allowed to influence the regression coefficient* between consumption and price.

A common idea seems to be that this can be obtained by using the partial time regression method instead of the individual trend method. This is false. The possibility of determining the long time relation

[1] Mr. Waugh is a fellow of the Social Science Research Council and the present study was made in connection with research in Europe made possible by his fellowship.

considered in the above example does not depend on which of the two methods is used, but on a certain criterion regarding the variability type of the material at hand (the criterion is discussed below). The partial trend regression method can *never*, indeed, achieve anything which the individual trend method cannot, because the two methods lead by definition to *identically* the same results. They differ only in the technique of computation used in order to arrive at the results.

This illustrates one of several misconceptions that exist in this field, but there are also others; the various misunderstandings may be briefly classified into the following three points:

1. The significance of the regression coefficients as determined by the two methods. In particular, there exists a misconception as to the meaning of these coefficients as approximations to the underlying "true" relationship between the variables.

2. The significance of the correlation coefficients as determined by the two methods.

3. The significance of the trends. This last question is of particular interest from the point of view of forecasting.

Before proceeding to a more systematic discussion of these points we shall, by quotations from well known statisticians, illustrate the nature of the misunderstandings.

II. QUOTATIONS

The following are excerpts from an article by Bradford B. Smith "The Error of Eliminating Secular Trends and Seasonal Variation before Correlating Time Series," in the *Journal of the American Statistical Association*, December, 1925. He says:

Should these two series, dependent and independent, chance to have approximately similar trend or seasonal movements, and should these latter be extracted from the two series prior to their correlation, one might under the name of seasonal and trend extract much of the variation by which the two were related, and thus obscure their true relationship. The unconsidered practice of eliminating trend and seasonal from series prior to their correlation is to be looked upon askance, therefore. It is often a serious error.

The escape from this predicament involves no new theoretical consideration. . . . All that is necessary is to remember that fundamentally a numerical description of passage of time is merely taken to represent the magnitude of the combined effect of otherwise unmeasured factors and then this series of "magnitudes" is treated precisely as any other independent factor. [In Bradford Smith's paper "time" is treated as a factor in a multiple regression equation and partial coefficients of regression are obtained to indicate the relation of the dependent variable to this trend and to the other factors]. . . . In following this practice, as often occurs, proper methods go hand in hand with better results. On theoretical considerations, correlation coefficients secured by *simultaneous*, or multiple, correlation methods will be as high or higher, and never less, than those resulting from any possible sequence of *consecutive* elimination of the influence of independent factors from the dependent, of which current methods of eliminating seasonal variations *before* correlating are an example. In actual trials of the two methods the writer has found that the simultaneous solution for trend and seasonal regression curves and curves for other factors always give markedly higher correlations. . . .

Mordecai Ezekiel in his book *Preisvoraussage bei landwirtschaft-lichen Erzeugnissen* published in the series of the Frankfurter Gesellschaft für Konjunkturforschung, 1930, says (page 23):— "Oft wird es notwendig sein, den zusammengesetzten Einfluss dieser Kräfte, die mit dem Kalender variieren, zu messen; . . . allerdings ohne dass man dabei der stets vorhandenen Gefahr unterliegen darf, den Einflusz von zeitlich variienden Faktoren Veränderungen zuzuschreiben, die in Wirklichkeit auf andere Ursachen zurückzerfuhren sind. Aus dieser Grunde wird der Einflusz der zeitlich variierden Faktoren am besten durch eine Bestemmung des Trends in der Relation und nicht durch Feststellung desselben bein jeden eizelnen Faktor gewessen."

III. WHAT IS THE "TRUE" RELATIONSHIP

Proceeding now to a more exact statement of the problem, we must first consider the meaning of a "true" relationship, and in what sense such a "true" relationship can be approximated by various empirical methods.

When comparing the results of different methods in time series analysis one must keep clearly in mind the *object* of the analysis. It must be specified which sort of influence it is desired to eliminate, and which sort to preserve. Unless this is specified it has no meaning to say that a certain method will yield a "truer" relationship than another.

Such an expression has a meaning only if it is referred to a given theoretical framework. An empirically determined relation is "true" if it approximates fairly well a certain well-defined *theoretical* relationship, assumed to represent the nature of the phenomenon studied. There does not seem to be any other way of giving a meaning to the expression "a true relationship." For clearness of statement we must therefore first define the nature of the *a priori* relationship that is taken as the ideal.

Let us express this in mathematical terms. We consider a number of variables $x_0, x_1, \cdots, x_n$, the last of them, i.e., x_n, denoting time. We conceive *a priori* of a relation that expresses x_0 in terms of the other variables, if, for simplicity, the relation is assumed linear, it may be written

$$(3.1) \qquad x_0 = \beta_{01\cdot2\cdots n}\cdot x_1 + \cdots + \beta_{0n\cdot12\cdots n-1}\cdot x_n$$

where the β's are constants and the variables are measured from their respective means. Each of the constants in (3.1) is conceived so as to represent an *independent* influence on x_0, for instance, the constant $\beta_{0n\cdot12}\cdots{}_{n-1}$ represents the independent influence which time may exert directly on x_0, regardless of the particular way in which the other variables $x_1\cdots x_{n-1}$ happen to evolve. A theoretical relation postulated *a priori* in this way we may call a *structural* relation. The coefficient $\beta_{0n\cdot12}\cdots{}_{n-1}$ in (3.1) we may call the partial, structural coefficient between x_0 and time.

Besides the structural relation (3.1) postulated by theory we shall now consider certain relations obtained by the classical statistical procedures. First we consider the regression of x_0 on the other variables, determined by the usual partial regression method, i.e. the relation

$$(3.2) \qquad x_0 = b_{01\cdot2\cdots n}\cdot x_1 + \cdots + b_{0n\cdot12\cdots n-1}\cdot x_n$$

where the b's are the usual regression coefficients, $b_{0n\cdot12}\cdots{}_{n-1}$ we may call the partial trend coefficient of x_0.

On the other hand we may fit to each variable a straight line trend, i.e., a trend of the form

$$x_i = b_{in}x_n.$$

The coefficients b_{in} we call the individual trend coefficient of x_i $(i=0,1\cdots n)$. Further we consider the deviations

$$x'_i = x_i - b_{in}x_n$$

and determine the regression of x'_0 on $x_1'\cdots x'_{n-1}$.

This relation is of the form

$$(3.3) \qquad x_0' = b'_{01\cdot2\cdots n-1}\cdot x_1' + \cdots + b'_{0,n-1\cdot1\cdots n-2}\cdot x'_{n-1}.$$

The coefficients b' in (3.3) we call the deviation-from-trend coefficients, or shorter the b' coefficients, and the coefficients b in (3.2) we call the time-as-a-variable coefficients, or shorter the b coefficients.

The first question we want to raise is: Will the b' coefficients be significant expressions for the structural coefficients, i.e., for the β coefficients? If not, will the b coefficients be more significant expressions for the β coefficients? On this point the misunderstanding seems to be particularly great. The belief seems to exist—the quotations given indicate this—that if trends are present in the variables $x_1\cdots x_{n-1}$ the coefficient b' will not measure correctly the β, but the coefficient b will. This is entirely wrong. The correct answer is this: If the material at hand satisfies a certain variability condition, then either the b' or the b may be taken as approximations to the β, while if this variability condition is not fulfilled, neither the b' nor the b will represent the β. The b and the b' are always identical, the two methods only represent different ways of computing the same magnitudes.

The variability condition envisaged is this: Each variable x must contain (beside the linear trend and beside the irregularities that are not systematically connected with x_0) an independent non-linear component. In other words, the deviation of x_i from its linear trend must be *significant* from the point of view of the connection between x_i and x_0. And, furthermore, this fluctuation must not be linearly dependent on the deviations of the other variables from their linear trends.

This means that if the relation between x_0 and the other variables is assumed linear, it is *by definition impossible to discriminate* between that part of a linear trend in x_0 that is caused by linear trends in the other variables and that part which is caused independently by the flow of time. Either we have to leave both these parts of the linear x_0 trend in the data, or we have to eliminate both parts. In the first case the regression coefficients between x_0 and the other variables will be influenced amongst other factors by whatever independent linear shift there has been in x_0 over the period studied. In the second case this linear shift is eliminated but at the same time all long-time (linear) relations between x_0 and the other variables are eliminated, so that the regression coefficients between x_0 and the other variables will be determined only by the short time fluctuations.

These criteria are consequences of the considerations developed by one of the present authors in an earlier publication.[2] We shall not give any formal proof of these criteria here. We shall confine ourselves to showing that the coefficients b and b' are identical by definition. This will of course be sufficient to exhibit the fallacy of the belief that anything more can be accomplished by the partial trend regression method than by the method of individual trends.

IV. THE IDENTITY OF THE REGRESSIONS DETERMINED BY THE INDIVIDUAL TREND METHOD AND THE PARTIAL TIME REGRESSION METHOD

We consider first the case of two variables (with time as the third variable). Let there be observed a set of values $x^{(1)}$, $x^{(2)} \cdots$ and $y^{(1)}$, $y^{(2)} \cdots$ of the two variables x and y at the points of time $t = t^{(1)}$, $t^{(2)} \cdots$, and let these values be expressed as deviations from their respective means. That is to say, we have $\sum x = 0$, $\sum y = 0$, $\sum t = 0$, where the summations are extended to all the observations.

The moments of the variables we denote

---

[2] Ragnar Frisch: "Correlation and Scatter in Statistical Variables," *Nordic Statistical Journal*, August 1929, pp. 36—103.

$$(4.1) \quad \begin{array}{lll} m_{xx} = \Sigma x^2 & m_{yy} = \Sigma y^2 & m_{tt} = \Sigma t^2 \\ m_{xy} = \Sigma xy & m_{xt} = \Sigma xt & m_{yt} = \Sigma yt. \end{array}$$

Let us first measure the relation of y to x by the individual trend method. If linear trends are fitted separately to x and y by the ordinary least squares procedure, the regression coefficient of x on t is m_{xt}/m_{tt} and the regression coefficient of y on t is m_{yt}/m_{tt}. If the deviations from trend are denoted x' and y' we consequently have

$$(4.2) \qquad x' = x - \frac{m_{xt}}{m_{tt}} \cdot t$$

$$(4.3) \qquad y' = y - \frac{m_{yt}}{m_{tt}} \cdot t$$

and the regression coefficient of y' on x' is

$$(4.4) \qquad b_{y'x'} = \frac{\Sigma \left(x - \dfrac{m_{xt}}{m_{tt}} \cdot t \right) \cdot \left(y - \dfrac{m_{yt}}{m_{tt}} \cdot t \right)}{\Sigma \left(x - \dfrac{m_{xt}}{m_{tt}} \cdot t \right)^2}$$

Expanding this we get

$$(4.5) \qquad b_{y'x'} = \frac{m_{tt}m_{xy} - m_{xt}m_{yt}}{m_{tt}m_{xx} - m_{xt}^2}.$$

Now let the data be analysed by the partial time regression method with y as the dependent variable and x and t as the independent variables. The regression coefficients of y on x and t are then found by the solution of the following simultaneous equations:

$$(4.6) \qquad \begin{array}{l} m_{xx}b_{yx \cdot t} + m_{xt}b_{yt \cdot x} = m_{xy} \\ m_{xt}b_{yx \cdot t} + m_{tt}b_{yt \cdot x} = m_{ty}. \end{array}$$

Multiplying the second equation by m_{xt}/m_{tt} and subtracting from the first we get

$$(4.7) \qquad m_{xx} - \frac{m_{xt}^2}{m_{tt}} b_{yx \cdot t} = m_{xy} - \frac{m_{xt}m_{yt}}{m_{tt}}$$

that is

$$(4.8) \qquad b_{yx \cdot t} = \frac{m_{tt}m_{xy} - m_{xt}m_{yt}}{m_{tt}m_{xx} - m_{xt}^2}.$$

Similarly we obtain

$$(4.9) \qquad b_{yt \cdot x} = \frac{m_{xx}m_{yt} - m_{xy}m_{xt}}{m_{tt}m_{xx} - m_{xt}^2}.$$

But (4.8) is identically the same as (4.5).

Furthermore, (4.9) is identically the same as the coefficient one would get in *estimating* y by the individual trend method. Indeed, if at the point of time t, the independent variable had the value x, then the estimated value y of the dependent variable would be determined as follows. First one would determine the trend value of y as $m_{yt}/m_{tt} \cdot t$, and to this one would add (4.5) times the estimate of deviation from trend in x, which is equal to $(x - m_{xt}/m_{tt} \cdot t)$. The total estimate of y would consequently be

$$(4.10) \qquad y = \left(x - \frac{m_{xt}}{m_{tt}} \cdot t \right) \cdot \frac{m_{tt}m_{xy} - m_{xt}m_{yt}}{m_{tt}m_{xx} - m_{xt}^2} + \frac{m_{yt}}{m_{tt}} \cdot t$$

which reduces to

$$(4.11) \qquad y = \frac{m_{tt}m_{xy} - m_{xt}m_{yt}}{m_{tt}m_{xx} - m_{xt}^2} \cdot x + \frac{m_{xx}m_{yt} - m_{xy}m_{xt}}{m_{tt}m_{xx} - m_{xt}^2} \cdot t.$$

The coefficient of x in this expression is identical with (4.8) and the coefficient of t is identical with (4.9). Therefore *the regression equations given by the two methods are identical.*

A Numerical Example

These results can easily be checked by setting up a simple problem and solving it by the two methods. The following computations may serve as an example.

Observed data			Moments about the mean		
x	t	y			
-5	-3	$+6$	$m_{xx} = 68$	$m_{xt} = 41$	$m_{xy} = -84$
-3	-2	$+5$		$m_{tt} = 28$	$m_{ty} = -60$
-2	-1	$+1$		Trend coefficients	
$+2$	0	$+2$			
$+1$	$+1$	-3		$b_{xt} = \dfrac{41}{28} = 1.464$	
$+4$	$+2$	-5			
$+3$	$+3$	-6		$b_{yt} = \dfrac{-60}{28} = 2.143$	

By the individual trend method we consequently get:

Trend values		Deviations	
Of x	Of y	x'	y'
-4.393	$+6.429$	$-.607$	$-.429$
-2.929	$+4.286$	$-.071$	$+.714$
-1.464	$+2.143$	$-.536$	-1.143
0.000	0.000	$+2.000$	$+2.000$
$+1.464$	-2.143	$-.464$	$-.857$
$+2.929$	-4.286	$+1.071$	$-.714$
$+4.393$	-6.429	-1.393	$+.429$

$$b_{y'x'} = \frac{m_{x'y'}}{m_{x'x'}} = \frac{3.858}{7.964} = 0.484.$$

And by the method of partial time regression we get:

$$68\,b_{yx.t} + 41\,b_{yt.x} = -84$$
$$41\,b_{yx.t} + 28\,b_{yt.x} = -60$$

$$\overline{60.036\,b_{yx.t} + 41\,b_{yt.x} = -87.857}$$

$$7.964\,b_{yx.t} = 3.857$$

$$b_{yx.t} = 0.484 \quad \text{(The same value as } b_{y'x'}\text{)}$$

Consider now the n variables $x_0 \cdots x_{n-1}$ and let time be an $(n+1)$th variable x_n. Let all the variables be measured from their means so that $\sum x_i = 0$ $(i = 0, 1 \cdots n)$ where $\sum$ denotes a summation over all the observations. Let $m_{ij} = \sum x_i x_j$ be the moment of the variable x_i with x_j. The regression of the variable x_k on all the others is the linear equation obtained by replacing the row $m_{k0}, m_{k1} \cdots m_{kn}$ in the moment determinant by $x_0, x_1 \cdots, x_n$ and equating the result to 0. In particular, if x_0 is selected as the dependent variable, the regression will be

$$(4.12) \qquad \begin{vmatrix} x_0 & x_1 & \cdots & x_n \\ m_{01} & m_{11} & \cdots & m_{1n} \\ \cdot & \cdot & \cdots & \cdot \\ m_{n0} & m_{n1} & \cdots & m_{nn} \end{vmatrix} = 0.$$

On the other hand, if we fit to x_i $(i = 0, 1 \cdots n-1)$ by least squares a straight line in x_n, we obtain the equation $x_i = m_{in}/m_{nn} \cdot x_n$, so that the deviations from trend will be

$$(4.13) \qquad x_i' = x_i - \frac{m_{in}}{m_{nn}} \cdot x_n.$$

The regression of x_0' on $x_1' \cdots x_{n-1}'$ is consequently

(4.14)
$$\begin{vmatrix} x'_0 & x'_1 & \ldots x'_{n-1} \\ m'_{10} & m'_{11} & \ldots m'_{1,n-1} \\ \cdots & \cdots & \cdots \\ m'_{n-1,0} & m'_{n-1,1} & \ldots m'_{n-1,n-1} \end{vmatrix} = 0$$

where $m'_{ij} = \sum x_i' x_j'$ are the moments of the deviations. We proposed first to show that the regression coefficient of x_0 on x_i $(i = 1, 2 \cdots n-1)$ in (4.12) is identically the same as the coefficient of x'_0 on x'_i in (4.14).

By virtue of (4.13) the moments of the deviations are expressed in terms of the original moments thus:

(4.15)
$$m'_{ij} = m_{ij} - \frac{m_{in}m_{nj}}{m_{nn}} \qquad (i, j = 0, 1 \cdots n)\cdot$$

Obviously $m'_{ij} = 0$ whenever $i = n$ or $j = n$, or both $i = n$ and $j = n$.

We subtract from the row m_{i0}, $m_{i1} \cdots m_{in}$ $(i = 1, 2 \cdots n-1)$ in (4.12) m_{in}/m_{nn} times the last row. The resulting expression will be the determinant obtained from (4.12) by replacing all the moments m by m' except those in the last row. In particular, the moments in the last column thus obtained will be zero, except the last element of the last column which is maintained equal to m_{nn}.

In other words (4.12) takes the form

(4.16)
$$\begin{vmatrix} x_0 & x_1 & \cdots x_{n-1} & x_n \\ m'_{10} & m'_{11} & \cdots m'_{1,n-1} & 0 \\ \cdots & \cdots & \cdots & \cdots \\ m'_{n-1,0} & m_{n-1,1} & \cdots m'_{n-1,n-1} & 0 \\ m_{n0} & m_{n1} & \cdots m_{n,n-1} & m_{nn} \end{vmatrix} = 0.$$

But the determinant (4.14) may be enlarged to

(4.17)
$$\begin{vmatrix} x_0' & x_1' & \cdots x'_{n-1} & 0 \\ m'_{10} & m'_{11} & \cdots m'_{1,n-1} & 0 \\ \cdots & \cdots & \cdots & \cdots \\ m'_{n-1,0} & m'_{n-1,1} & \cdots m'_{n-1,n-1} & 0 \\ c_0 & c_1 & \cdots c_{n-1} & 1 \end{vmatrix} = 0$$

where $c_0, c_1 \cdots c_{n-1}$ is a set of arbitrary numbers, for instance m_{n0}, $m_{n1} \cdots m_{n,n-1}$. This shows that when we write (4.12) and (4.14) in the forms

(4.18)
$$a_0 x_0 + a_1 x_1 + \cdots + a_n x_n = 0$$

and

(4.19) $a_0'x_0' + a_1'x_1' + \cdots + a'_{n-1}x'_{n-1} = 0$

then the first n coefficients $a_0 \cdots a_{n-1}$ in (4.18) will be proportional to the coefficients $a_0' \cdots a'_{n-1}$ in (4.19). Indeed, the a-coefficients will simply be equal to m_{nn} times the a'-coefficients. We consequently have

(4.20) $b_{0i.12\cdots n} = b'_{0i.12\cdots n-1}$ $(i = 1.2 \cdots n - 1)$

where b and b' are the coefficients of (3.2) and (3.3) respectively.

Furthermore it is clear that we can take the regression equation (3.3) as a starting point, insert here the values $x_i' = x_i - b_{in}x_n$ and thus get a regression expressing x_0 in terms of $x_1 \cdots x_n$. This latter regression is identical with the regression (3.2). This follows from (4.20) and from the well known fact that

(4.21) $b_{0n} = b_{01.2\cdots n}b_{1n} + b_{02.13\cdots n}b_{2n} + \cdots + b_{0n.12\cdots n-1}b_{nn}(b_{nn} = 1)$.

Thus the complete regression equation determined by the partial time regression method and the method of individual trends are identical, (3.2) and (3.3) are only two ways of writing the same equation. This also has a bearing on the meaning of trends as a means of forecasting, this aspect of the problem we shall take up in Section 6.

The way in which we pass from (4.12) to (4.16) is in reality nothing but an application of the Gaussian algorithm for solving the normal equations.[3]

This throws an interesting light on the connection between (4.14) and (4.16) and also on the nature of the Gaussian algorithm itself. It shows that the Gaussian algorithm simply consists in this: First one fits to all the variables, except x_n, a "trend" which is linear in x_n. Then to the deviations from trend in all the remaining variables one fits a new "trend" which is linear in the deviation x'_{n-1}, and so on. In this way one finally gets down to a two-variable problem. And this successive fitting of *individual* trends is identical with the determination of a simultaneous partial regression. *The identity of these two processess is just the basis of the Gaussian algorithm.*

V. THE CORRELATION COEFFICIENTS OBTAINED BY THE TWO METHODS

Another misunderstanding seems to be that the higher correlation coefficients obtained by the partial time regression method than by the individual trend method is an expression of the superiority of the first of

---

[3] Most of the "new" schemes for solving the normal equations that are developed from time to time are nothing but unessential modifications of the Gaussian algorithm. This applies, for instance, to the Doolittle method.

these two methods. The fact that a comparison of correlation coefficients in this case can lead to a belief in the "superiority" of a method that is by definition identical with the "inferior" method, is a striking example of the perfectly imaginary character of much of the reasoning that is currently based on correlation coefficients.

A coefficient of multiple correlation showing the total relationship between one variable such as prices and two others such as consumption and time, must *by its very definition* always be as high as or higher than the gross correlation between price and consumption expressed as deviations from their respective trends, in other words we always have by definition

$$(5.1) \qquad r^2_{y.zt} \geqq r^2_{z'y'}.$$

Indeed it is easy to verify that

$$(5.2) \qquad r^2_{y.zt} = 1 - \frac{\Delta_{zyt}}{\Delta_{zt}}$$

$$(5.3) \qquad r^2_{z'y'} = 1 - \frac{\Delta_{zyt}}{\Delta_{zt}\Delta_{yt}}$$

where Δ_{zt}, Δ_{yt} and Δ_{zyt} denote the correlation determinants in the sets zt, yt and zyt respectively. These are positive definite determinants lying between 0 and 1. Any of them is equal to 1 when, and only when, all the variables in the set are uncorrelated.[4] The formulae (5.2) and (5.3) show that $r^2_{y.zt}$ is always larger than $r^2_{z'y'}$ *no matter what the data are* (provided only that they consist of real numbers). The only exception is the limiting case $r^2_{y.zt} = r^2_{z'y'}$ which occurs when, and only when, y and t are uncorrelated (disregarding the case where there exists a mathematically exact linear relationship in the set zyt). But that is not all. There is a *great* discrepancy between $r^2_{y.zt}$ and $r^2_{z'y'}$ when and only when nearly all the variation in y can be represented simply by a linear trend. From (5.2) and (5.3) we get indeed

$$(5.4) \qquad \frac{1 - r^2_{y.zt}}{1 - r^2_{z'y'}} = \Delta_{yt} = 1 - r^2_{yt}.$$

In other words the only thing that a comparison between $r^2_{y.zt}$ and $r^2_{z'y'}$ can tell us *is whether y has a pronounced trend or not*. The comparison does not tell anything about the nature of this trend: whether it is due to a variation in x or to some other cause. It has no meaning as an indication of a "better result," it does not tell us anything about whether the b coefficients or the b' coefficients are the better approxima-

---

[4] See for instance "Correlation and Scatter."

tions to the "true" β coefficients (as implied for instance in the quotation from Bradford Smith).

Since the comparison of $r_{y \cdot zt}$ and $r_{x'y'}$ indicates only whether y has a pronounced trend or not, and since this fact will be revealed immediately from the plot of y, the computation of these correlations in the present problem will in our opinion serve no significant purpose. It is only a play with formulae which at best is superfluous, but at worst is dangerous, because it may lead to wholly unwarranted conclusions, such as, for example, the conclusion about the "superiority" of the time regression method.

Some concrete examples may illustrate this. In such studies as those concerned with consumption as a function of prices, price as a function of supply, or acreage as a function of previous price, *it is always possible to obtain high coefficients of multiple correlation by including in the simultaneous analysis such factors as time, population, etc.*, whenever the period studied is one of considerable change in one of these factors.

One of the authors of the present article once published[5] the results of certain studies of the relation of vegetable prices to quality, based on several hundred observations which indicated total correlations of about 0.70 between certain qualities and the deviation of prices from the daily quotation on the market. He was criticized in a review by Dr. Bean who claimed that the correlation coefficients were too low to be significant. The critic remarked that he had found from experience that correlations of at least 0.90 were necessary for significant results in price analysis: and well he might, because he was working with annual data of supplies and prices covering from eight to ten observations and using multiple curvilinear correlation methods, including in the analysis such factors as trend. In the case of the study of quality, it would have been an easy matter to raise the coefficient of multiple correlation high enough to suit such a critic, indeed it could have been raised practically as near to unity as one pleased by the simple expedient of including as an independent factor in the analysis the daily quotation for standard quality. This was avoided in order to get a truer statement of the actual relation between quality and price.

We do not wish to object to the various results obtained by Dr. Bean, but we do want to point out the uselessness of comparing results of time series analyses merely on the basis of multiple correlation coefficients.

VI. THE MEANING OF THE TRENDS

In the structural relation (3.1) each variable exerts an *independent* influence on x_0. Hence, if trends are present in $x_1 \cdots x_{n-1}$, this will

---

[5] F. V. Waugh: *Quality as a Determinant of Vegetable Prices.* New York, 1929.

contribute towards the total trend in x_0. This total trend in x_0 may be looked upon as made up of the indirect trends produced by the trends in $x_1 \cdots x_{n-1}$ and of the partial trend caused by the last term in (3.1). Let us express this mathematically remembering the fundamental distinction between the structural coefficients β and the empirically determined regression coefficients b. If x_i is expressed in the form

$$x_i = x_i' + \beta_{in}x_n \qquad (x_n = \text{time}) \qquad (i = 1, 2 \cdots n)$$

where β_{in} is a constant and x_i' the deviation from trend in x_i, then (3.1) may be written in the form

$$(6.1) \qquad x_0 = \beta_{01.2\ldots_n}x_1' + \cdots + \beta_{0,n-1.12\ldots_n}x'_{n-1} + \beta_{0n}x_n$$

where the coefficient β_{0n} is equal to

$$(6.2) \qquad \beta_{0n} = \beta_{01.2\ldots_n}\beta_{1n} + \beta_{02.13\ldots_n}\beta_{2n} + \cdots + \beta_{0,n-1.12\ldots_n}\beta_{n-1,n}$$
$$+ \beta_{0n.12\ldots_{n-1}}.$$

β_{0n} is the *total* structural trend coefficient for x_0, β_{in} are the *individual* structural trend coefficients for the variables $x_i \cdots x_{n-1}$; the products $\beta_{0i.12\ldots n} \cdot \beta_{in}$ are the *indirect* trend coefficients in x_0; and $\beta_{0n.12\ldots n-1}$ the *partial* (and direct) trend coefficient in x_0.

If, in the material at hand, the deviations $x'_1 \cdots x'_{n-1}$ from (linear) trends exhibit systematic, linearly independent variations, the structural coefficients β in (3.1) may be determined by the data, the empirically determined regression coefficients b may then be taken as approximations to the structural coefficients β with the same subscripts.

Consequently if the coefficients $b_{0i.12\ldots n}$, and the individual coefficients b_{in} $(i = 1 \cdot 2 \cdots n)$ $(b_{nn} = 1)$, are determined empirically we have (on the assumption that the x'-s deviate significantly from linear trends) representations for all the terms in the right member of (6.2), we may consequently say that we also have determined empirically an approximation to the *total* trend coefficient for x_0. Let b_{0*} be the total trend coefficient thus determined by inserting b for β in the right member of (6.2). In other words, b_{0*} is defined as the composite effect of the trends in $x_1 \cdots x_{n-1}$ and the partial trend of x_0, these latter trends being determined by the usual regression procedure.

We may of course also consider the *individual* trend coefficient for x_0 just as for the other variables. If this individual coefficient is determined by the usual regression procedure, i.e. as the coefficient b_{0n} *it becomes just equal to* b_{0*}. This simply follows from (4.21). And from (4.20) it follows that we get exactly the same determination of b_{0*} whether in the right member of (6.2) we use b_{in}' as approximations to β_{in} or we use b_{in}.

We may express this by saying that the partial trend coefficient for x_0 may be determined either by the partial time regression method directly as the usual coefficient $b_{0n \cdot 12 \ \cdots \ n-1}$ or it may be determined as the difference between total trend in x_0 and the trends in x_0 that are ascribed to the influence of the various independent factors, *these latter being determined by the individual trend method.* Also, with respect to the interpretation of the trends, the two methods yield consequently exactly the same results, the only difference being a difference in the technique of computation. The fact here discussed is of course only another aspect of the fact proved in Section 4, namely that the complete regression equations determined by the two methods are identical.

The above conclusion may be illustrated by the case of two variables x and y with time t as a third variable. The partial trend coefficient in y is $b_{yt \cdot x}$, and the trend effect in y computed by the individual trend method is equal to $b_{yt} - b_{xt} \cdot b_{y'x'}$, i.e., total trend in y minus indirect trend in y attributed to the fact that y depends on x, this latter dependence being determined by the individual trend method. But according to the general formula (4.21) we just have $b_{yt \cdot x} = b_{yt} - b_{xt}b_{y'x'}$. This checks in the numerical example in Section 4 since $-2.143 - (1.464) \cdot (0.484) = -2.852$.

How do these considerations affect the use of trends in forecasting? There are three possible procedures for extrapolating a trend into the future: (1) we can project the total trend observed in x_0, simply using the angular coefficient b_{0n}; (2) we can project the partial trend observed in x_0, namely the trend defined by the coefficient $b_{0n \cdot 12 \ \ldots \ n-1}$; or (3) we can make what we may call a *composition forecast* of the trend in x_0 by forecasting each of the variables $x_1 \cdots x_{n-1}$ and from these forecasts and the relation between x_0 and $x_1 \cdots x_{n-1}$ and the partial trend in x_0, build up a total forecast of the trend in x_0.

If we are to make such a composition forecast of x_0 we must make individual forecasts of $x_1 \cdots x_{n-1}$ and also of the partial trend in x_0. If each of these forecasts is made by the usual regression methods on the basis of the information contained in the material at hand, *the composition forecast of the trend in x_0 will be exactly the same as the direct mechanical projection of the total trend of x_0.* This follows immediately from the above considerations (see in particular formulae (4.21)). In other words the whole process of determining partial regression coefficients in this case is an entirely unnecessary roundabout calculation. This is another aspect of the identity between partial time regression and the individual trend method.

The only reason for using a composition forecast instead of a mechanical projection of the total observed trend in x_0 is to make it possible to utilize some *other information* regarding the probable future trends of the variable $x_1 \cdots x_{n-1}$. Instead of assuming that all the variables, $x_1 \cdots x_{n-1}$, will continue their growth at the average rate observed in the material, we may, for instance, assume that one of them is going to remain stationary at the level it had at the end of the period studied, or we may assume that its growth rate will become less, etc. If such specific guesses are made about the variables $x_1 \cdots x_{n-1}$, the composition forecast for x_0 using the regression (3.2) will not, of course, be identical with the direct mechanical forecast.

To illustrate the difference between a direct mechanical forecast of the total trend and a composition forecast, let x_0 be the consumption of sugar. If we fit a trend line to sugar consumption over the interval of time for which we have observations, and simply project this line into the future, we are assuming that the trends in population, sugar prices, and other factors influencing sugar consumption, will continue at the same rate that we have observed in the past. In some cases such an assumption is admissable, and in others it is not. For example, prices may have dropped so low during the period studied that further declines are very improbable, so that in forecasting the trend of sugar consumption we must reckon with a probable change in the trend of sugar prices which will, in turn, influence the total trend of consumption. To forecast the trend of consumption in this case, we need to know more than its average rate of increase in the past; we need also to know how much of this increase was due to the decrease in prices, so as to be able to say what the trend would have been had prices remained at a level corresponding to that expected in the future. In other words we must use a composition forecast with more or less plausible guesses regarding the future trends of the variables which influence sugar consumption.

Or, to take another example, if x_0 is the yield of potatoes, and $x_1 \cdots x_{n-1}$ represent weather data such as rainfall and temperature, in many cases we have no reason for expecting a real trend in the weather data, and probably can make no better forecast than to assume that the weather factors will vary around averages based on past observations. In this case the trend in x_0 which we would project would be the partial trend $b_{0n.12 \ldots n-1}$, which as we have shown is the same as the total trend in x_0 minus the trend in x_0 attributed to the factors $x_1 \cdots x_{n-1}$. The projection of this partial trend may, then, be considered as one form of the composition forecast in which we forecast that the various independent factors will not continue their observed rate of growth but will vary around their observed average.

Statistical Seminar, University of Norway

Econometrica, Vol. 11, 1 (January 1943)

THE STATISTICAL IMPLICATIONS OF A SYSTEM OF SIMULTANEOUS EQUATIONS

By Trygve Haavelmo

1. INTRODUCTION

Measurement of parameters occurring in theoretical equation systems is one of the most important problems of econometrics. If our equations were exact in the *observable* economic variables involved, this problem would not be one of statistics, but a purely mathematical one of solving a certain system of "observational" equations, having the parameters in question as unknowns. This might itself present complicated and interesting problems, such as the problem of whether or not there is a one-to-one correspondence between each system of values of the parameters and the corresponding set of all values of the variables satisfying the equation system. For example, if we have, simultaneously, a demand curve and a supply curve, the set of possible observations might be just one single intersection point, and knowing that only would not, in general, permit us to draw any inference regarding the slope of either curve.

Real statistical problems arise if the equations in question contain certain stochastical elements ("unexplained residuals"), in addition to the variables that are given or directly observable. And some such element must, in fact, be present in any equation which shall be applicable to actual observations (unless the equation in question is a trivial identity). In other words, if we consider a set of related economic variables, it is, in general, not possible to express any one of the variables as an exact function of the other variables only. There will be an "unexplained rest," and, for statistical purposes, certain stochastical properties must be ascribed to this rest, a priori. Personally I think that economic theorists have, in general, paid too little attention to such stochastical formulation of economic theories. For the necessity of introducing "error terms" in economic relations is not merely a result of statistical errors of measurement. It is as much a result of the very nature of economic behavior, its dependence upon an enormous number of factors, as compared with those which we can account for, explicitly, in our theories. We need a stochastical formulation to make simplified relations elastic enough for applications.

This is, perhaps, generally realized among econometricians. But they frequently fail to consider, in full, the *statistical* implications of assuming a system of such stochastical equations to be *simultaneously fulfilled* by the data. More specifically, if one assumes that the economic variables considered satisfy, simultaneously, several stochastic relations, it is usually *not* a satisfactory method to try to determine each of the equations separately from the data, without regard to the restrictions which the *other* equations might impose upon the same variables. That this is so is almost self-evident, for in order to prescribe a meaningful method of fitting an equation to the data, it is necessary to define the stochastical properties of *all* the variables involved (e.g., that some of them are given time series, or remain constant, etc.). Otherwise, we shall not know the meaning of the statistical results obtained. Furthermore, the stochastical properties ascribed to the variables in *one* of the equations should, naturally, not contradict those that are implied by the *other* equations. For example, suppose that X and Y are two variables satisfying the following two stochastical relations

$$(1.1) \qquad Y = aX + \epsilon_1,$$

$$(1.2) \qquad X = bY + \epsilon_2,$$

where ϵ_1 and ϵ_2 are assumed to be two normally and independently distributed random variables with zero means and variances equal to σ_1^2 and σ_2^2 respectively. Then, from the first equation alone, one might perhaps think that the expected value of Y, *given* X, should be equal to aX [because $E(\epsilon_1)=0$]. But if ϵ_1 and ϵ_2 are independent, as assumed, the statement $E(Y|X)=aX$ leads to a contradiction. That is seen as follows: X and Y are linear functions of ϵ_1 and ϵ_2, viz.,

$$(1.3) \qquad Y = \frac{\epsilon_1 + a\epsilon_2}{1 - ab},$$

$$(1.4) \qquad X = \frac{b\epsilon_1 + \epsilon_2}{1 - ab}.$$

Therefore, X and Y are jointly normally distributed with means equal to zero. If ρ_{XY} be the correlation coefficient between X and Y, and σ_X^2, σ_Y^2 their variances, one obtains

$$(1.5) \qquad E(Y|X) = \frac{\sigma_Y}{\sigma_X} \rho_{XY}X = \frac{b\sigma_1^2 + a\sigma_2^2}{b^2\sigma_1^2 + \sigma_2^2} X,$$

the right-hand side of which is, in general, different from aX.

The example above suggests the following rule for clarifying the joint distribution properties (of the observational variables), which a system of stochastical equations implies: In a system [such as (1.1)–(1.2)] of equations, involving certain specified (but not observable) stochastical variables (such as ϵ_1 and ϵ_2), the *observable* variables involved (such as X and Y) may be considered as transformations of the specified stochastical ones (the ϵ's). Therefore, the specification of the distribution of these theoretical variables (the ϵ's) permits us, usually, to calculate the joint distribution of the observable variables, or certain properties of this distribution. This *joint* distribution should be studied to clarify the stochastical relationship, which the equation system implies with respect to the observable variables.

Instead of going further into this problem in general, it will, I think, be more explicit and more suggestive for further work in this field, to argue along a particular, simple example.

2. A MODEL AND ITS MEANING

Let us consider the following simplified *tableau économique*, assuming all prices constant:

1. The propensity to consume. Assume that if the group of all consumers in the society were repeatedly furnished with the total income, or purchasing power, r per year, they would, on the average or "normally," spend a total amount $\bar{u}$ for consumption per year, equal to

$$(2.1) \qquad \bar{u} = \alpha r + \beta,$$

where α and β are constants. The amount, u, *actually* spent each year might differ from $\bar{u}$. Suppose that the amount actually spent would be given by

$$(2.2) \qquad u = \alpha r + \beta + x,$$

where x is a certain random residual with mean value = zero, irrespective of the value given to r.

2. The propensity to invest. Assume that, if the group of all (private) investors in the society (the fact that they are also consumers being immaterial) were repeatedly confronted with an increase, δ, over last year, in the demand for consumption goods, they would, on the average, invest an amount, $\bar{v}$, given by

$$(2.3) \qquad \bar{v} = \kappa \cdot \delta$$

(the "acceleration principle"), where κ is a constant. The amount, v, actually invested each year, for a given δ, might differ from $\bar{v}$. Suppose that the amount, v, actually invested each year would be given by

$$(2.4) \qquad v = \kappa \delta + y,$$

where y is a certain random residual with mean value = zero, irrespective of the value ascribed to δ.

It is on purpose that we have used different letters u and δ for "consumption" in the two schemes above. For in the process of constructing each of the two schemes one does not have in mind the fact that the variables in one of them are restricted, simultaneously, by the other. Each of the two schemes represent a hypothetical splitting of the real economic world into two separate spheres of action, the consumer action and the producer action. It would require controlled experiments to bring about the real counterparts to one or the other of the two schemes. Actually, in a closed economy, each year's increase, δ, in the demand for consumption goods, would be the result, $u_t - u_{t-1}$, of consumers' action, and this action would, in turn, be dependent on the amount of investment, because of the "closed market" identity, $r_t = u_t + v_t$.

Now, if we assume that: 1. whatever be the value of r, u is given by (2.2), and 2. whatever be the value of δ, v is given by (2.4); then the two equations will also hold if we impose $\delta = \delta_t = u_t - u_{t-1}$, and $r_t = u_t + v_t$.

Our two theoretical schemes (2.2) and (2.4), taken together, thus lead us to believe that the data for consumption u and investment v (or their sum r) which the market mechanism actually produces will satisfy the joint system

$$(2.5) \qquad\qquad u_t = \alpha r_t + \beta + x_t,$$

$$(2.6) \qquad\qquad v_t = \kappa(u_t - u_{t-1}) + y_t,$$

$$(2.7) \qquad\qquad r_t = u_t + v_t,$$

where x_t and y_t are certain residuals as explained above. (The actual data which we consider as the real counterparts to the theoretical variables might deviate from these theoretical variables by reason of purely statistical errors of measurements. But this we shall neglect in the analysis which follows. It is not essential for our arguments.)

The economic meaning of the joint system (2.5)–(2.7) might then be described as follows: During the year t, whatever be the "would-be" normal consumption $\alpha r_t + \beta$, the individuals choose to add a certain (positive or negative) amount, x_t, to this normal consumption, depending on a complex of factors not explicitly introduced in the theory. And similarly for the investment relation (2.6).

Now, in order that the system above be of any use for the purpose of making forecasts or some other type of inference, we need some information about two things, namely, 1. the numerical values of α, β, κ, and 2. some properties of the residual variables x and y. Usually, pure economic theory does not say anything about these things. And as long as that is the case, the equations (2.5)–(2.7) do not impose any restriction whatsoever upon the observed series of u and v (or r). For we might choose α, β, κ, at pleasure, and take (2.5) and (2.6) as definitions of the residuals x and y, since these variables are not observable anyhow. To talk about estimation of α, β, and κ without ascribing, a priori, certain properties to x and y has, therefore, no sense. The theory must first be given a statistical formulation.

3. STATISTICAL FORMULATION OF THE THEORY, AND THE PROBLEMS OF ESTIMATION

Instead of trying to give a precise statistical formulation of their economic models, many economists seem to prefer a procedure as follows: They assume, taking our example, that the observed series for u_t, v_t, and r_t satisfy the relations $u_t = \alpha r_t + \beta$, $v = \kappa(u_t - u_{t-1})$, "apart from some small deviations, x_t and y_t, which vary up and down around zero." Then they proceed to "estimate" α, β, κ, from the time series observed, first, by minimizing $\sum_t (u_t - \alpha r_t - \beta)^2$ with respect to α and β, next, by minimizing $\sum_t [v_t - \kappa(u_t - u_{t-1})]^2$ with respect to κ. [This procedure we shall call, for short, "the least-squares method applied to the equations (2.5) and (2.6) separately."]

Without further specification of the model, this procedure has no foundation, and that for two main reasons. First, the notion that one can operate with some vague idea about "small errors" without introducing the concepts of stochastical variables and probability distributions, is, I think, based upon an illusion. For, since the errors are not just constants, one has to introduce some more complex notion of "small" or "large" than just the numerical values of the individual errors. Since it is usually agreed that the errors are "on the whole small" when individual errors are large only on *rare* occasions, we are led to consider, not only the size of each individual error, but also the *frequency* with which errors of a certain size occur. And so forth. If one really tries to dig down to a clear, objective formulation of the notions of "small irregular errors," or the like, one will discover, I think, that we have, at least for the time being, no other practical instrument for such a formulation than those of random variables and probability distributions. Nor is there any loss of generality involved in the application of these analytical instruments, for any variable may be "probabilized," provided we allow sufficiently complicated distribution functions.

Next, many economists, after admitting that one must introduce the notions of probability and random variables, think that the statistical specification job is done when they have stated that: For each point of time, t, x_t is a certain random variable with a certain probability distribution, and similarly for y_t. Usually it is assumed that the variables x and y have the same distribution for all values of t. To make the statement more precise: Suppose we consider N different points of time, $t=1, 2, \cdots, N$, assuming that, for $t=0$, u_0 is a given constant. Then we consider $2N$ random variables, $x_1, x_2, \cdots, x_N, y_1, y_2, \cdots, y_N$. The specification mentioned above amounts to specifying only the *marginal* probability law for each of the $2N$ random variables. The usual specification of these probability laws is that each of the N x's has the same distribution, p_x say, with mean value = zero and finite variance, σ_x^2, and that each of the N y's has the same distribution, p_y say, with mean value = zero and finite variance σ_y^2. Some people go further, assuming, e.g., that p_x and p_y are normal distributions, to be "quite sure" that the least-squares method applied to the two equations (2.5) and (2.6) separately as indicated above, will be all right. In fact, the specification described is far from any justification for this least-squares procedure. And it is easy to see why that is so.

Let ξ_{1t} and ξ_{2t}, $t=1, 2, \cdots, N$, be $2N$ observable variables connected by a relation $\xi_{1t} = k_1\xi_{2t} + k_0 + \eta_t$, where k_1 and k_0 are constants, and where η_t, $t=1, 2, \cdots, N$, are N nonobservable random variables. An essential condition for using the numbers k_1^* and k_0^* which minimizes $\sum_{t=1}^{N}(\xi_{1t} - k_1^*\xi_{2t} - k_0^*)^2$ as estimates of k_1 and k_0 (although this condition alone does not insure "best" estimates) is that

$$E(\xi_{1t} \mid \xi_{2t}) = k_1\xi_{2t} + k_0, \qquad t = 1, 2, \cdots, N.$$

Therefore, in order that the least-squares procedure applied to (2.5) and (2.6) separately should be justified, we should have to have

(3.1) $\qquad E(u_t \mid r_t) = \alpha r_t + \beta, \qquad E(v_t \mid u_t - u_{t-1}) = \kappa(u_t - u_{t-1}).$

But if we impose this, we impose at the same time a restriction upon the *joint* distribution of the x's and the y's. More explicitly, let $p(x_t, y_t)$ be the joint probability law of x_t and y_t, and consider, for a given u_{t-1}, the distribution, $p_1(u_t, v_t)$ say, of the two variables u_t and v_t. The transformations (2.5)–(2.6) give at once

(3.2) $\quad p_1(u_t, v_t) = [1 - (1+\kappa)\alpha]p\{[u_t - \alpha(u_t+v_t) - \beta], [v_t - \kappa(u_t - u_{t-1})]\}$

as the relation between p and p_1. A restriction, such as (3.1), upon p_1 is then, evidently, also a restriction upon p. Specification of the marginal distributions of x_t and y_t such that $E(x_t) = 0$, $E(y_t) = 0$, does not insure the relationships (3.1), because it does not specify $p(x_t, y_t)$, hence it does not specify $p_1(u_t, v_t)$, and, therefore, it does not suffice to draw the conclusions (3.1).

Suppose, for example, that x_t and y_t are jointly normally distributed, independent, and such that $E(x_t) = E(y_t) = 0$. Then, since the transformations (2.5) and (2.6) are linear, we know at once that u_t and r_t,

u_{t-1} being given, must be jointly normally distributed, and we know also that, for example, $E(u_t | r_t)$ must be a linear function, say $Ar_t + B$, of r_t. What is this linear function? If ρ be the correlation coefficient of u_t and r_t, and $\sigma_u{}^2$, $\sigma_r{}^2$ their variances, then the constant A, for example, is given by

$$(3.3) \qquad\qquad A = \frac{\sigma_u}{\sigma_r}\rho.$$

From (2.5) and (2.6) one can easily calculate $\sigma_u{}^2$, $\sigma_r{}^2$, and ρ directly. One obtains

$$(3.4) \qquad\qquad \sigma_u{}^2 = \frac{\sigma_z{}^2 + \alpha^2\sigma_y{}^2}{[1 - (1 + \kappa)\alpha]^2},$$

$$(3.5) \qquad\qquad \sigma_r{}^2 = \frac{(1 + \kappa)^2\sigma_z{}^2 + \sigma_y{}^2}{[1 - (1 + \kappa)\alpha]^2},$$

$$(3.6) \qquad\qquad \rho = \frac{(1 + \kappa)\sigma_z{}^2 + \alpha\sigma_y{}^2}{\sqrt{[(1 + \kappa)^2\sigma_z{}^2 + \sigma_y{}^2][\sigma_z{}^2 + \alpha^2\sigma_y{}^2]}}.$$

From (3.4), (3.5), and (3.6) one gets

$$(3.7) \qquad\qquad A = \frac{(1 + \kappa)\sigma_z{}^2 + \alpha\sigma_y{}^2}{(1 + \kappa)^2\sigma_z{}^2 + \sigma_y{}^2}.$$

If, therefore, the first equation in (3.1) should be true under these assumptions about the distribution of x_t and y_t, we should have to have $A \equiv \alpha$, for all values of the parameters involved, and that is, evidently, not true. Thus, the assumption we have made about $p(x_t, y_t)$ and the assumptions (3.1) would, in general, be inconsistent.

The essential lesson of these considerations is this: When one has to do with a system, such as (2.5)–(2.7), this system should, for statistical purposes, be considered as a system of transformations, by which to derive the joint probability distribution of the *observable* variables from the specified distribution of the error terms. And then, to avoid inconsistencies, like the ones indicated above, all formulae for estimating the parameters involved should be derived on the basis of this joint probability law of all the observable variables involved in the system. (This, I think, is obvious to statisticians, but it is overlooked in the work of most economists who construct dynamic models to be fitted to economic data.)

The correct procedure for estimating α, β, κ, in our system (2.5)–(2.7) can be formulated precisely as follows: Let $x_1, x_2, \cdots, x_N, y_1, y_2, \cdots, y_N$ be $2N$ random variables whose joint probability law, say

$$(3.8) \qquad\qquad f(x_1, x_2, \cdots, x_N, y_1, y_2, \cdots, y_N),$$

is specified, except, perhaps, for a certain number of unknown parameters (such as σ_x or σ_y above). And assume that u_0 is a given constant (initial condition). Then the joint probability law, say f^*, of the $2N$ observable random variables $u_1, u_2, \cdots, u_N, r_1, r_2, \cdots, r_N$, is given by

$$
\begin{aligned}
(3.9) \quad & f^*(u_1, u_2, \cdots, u_N, r_1, r_2, \cdots, r_N) \\
& = [1 - (1 + \kappa)\alpha]^N f(x_1, x_2, \cdots, x_N, y_1, y_2, \cdots, y_N).
\end{aligned}
$$

The problem of estimating α, β, κ, is, therefore, the problem of estimating the parameters of this joint probability law, on the basis of a sample point $(u_1, r_1, u_2, r_2, \cdots, u_N, r_N)$. The method of estimation will depend on the form of f.

If f is such that the method of maximum likelihood applied to (3.9) can be shown to give good (if not the "best") estimates of the parameters, these estimates have a great technical advantage besides, namely that of being invariant for transformations of the parameters. That is, a function of the maximum-likelihood estimates of α, β, κ, as derived from (3.9) is equal to the maximum-likelihood estimate of that function. In particular, if we have the maximum-likelihood estimates, $\alpha^\circ, \beta^\circ, \kappa^\circ$, say,[1] of α, β, κ, we have also the maximum-likelihood estimates of functions of α, β, κ, appearing as coefficients in equations derived by combining (2.5), (2.6), and (2.7), simply by substitution of $\alpha^\circ, \beta^\circ, \kappa^\circ$, in these functions. For other methods of estimation such a procedure would, in general, not be permissible.

As an illustration suppose that, in the system (2.5)–(2.7), u_0 is a given constant, while $x_1, x_2, \cdots, x_N, y_1, y_2, \cdots, y_N$ are $2N$ normally and independently distributed random variables with zero means and variance equal to σ_x^2 for all the x's, and equal to σ_y^2 for all the y's. Then the maximum-likelihood estimates, $\alpha^\circ, \beta^\circ, \kappa^\circ, \sigma^\circ{}_x^2, \sigma^\circ{}_y^2$, of the parameters are given by

$$
(3.10) \quad \sum_{t=1}^{N} \left\{ [u_t - \alpha^\circ r_t - \beta^\circ][r_t + (1 + \kappa^\circ)(\beta^\circ - u_t)] \right\} = 0,
$$

$$
(3.11) \quad \sum_{t=1}^{N} \left\{ [v_t - \kappa^\circ u_t + \kappa^\circ u_{t-1}][(1 - \alpha^\circ)(u_t - u_{t-1}) - \alpha^\circ v_t] \right\} = 0,
$$

$$
(3.12) \quad \sum_{t=1}^{N} u_t - \alpha^\circ \sum_{t=1}^{N} r_t - N\beta^\circ = 0,
$$

$$
(3.13) \quad \sum_{t=1}^{N} (u_t - \alpha^\circ r_t - \beta^\circ)^2 = N\sigma^\circ{}_x^2
$$

[1] These somewhat unusual notations for maximum-likelihood estimates have been necessitated for purely typographical reasons.—MANAGING EDITOR.

$$(3.14) \qquad \sum_{t=1}^{N} [v_t - \kappa^\circ(u_t - u_{t-1})]^2 = N\sigma^\circ_y{}^2.$$

If, for example, one wants the maximum-likelihood estimate of the constant A in (3.7), one has only to introduce the solutions α°, κ°, $\sigma^\circ_x{}^2$, $\sigma^\circ_y{}^2$, of the system above in the expression (3.7).

The formulae (3.10)–(3.12) above are particular instances of an easily established general rule, which may be stated as follows:

Consider m observable economic time series, say $w_{1t}, w_{2t}, \cdots, w_{mt}$, satisfying a system of m linear lag equations of the following type:

$$(3.15) \qquad \sum_{i=0}^{\omega} a_{k1,i} w_{1,t-i} + \sum_{i=0}^{\omega} a_{k2,i} w_{2,t-i} + \cdots$$

$$+ \sum_{i=0}^{\omega} a_{km,i} w_{m,t-i} + a_{k0,0} = \epsilon_{k,t},$$

$$t = 1, 2, \cdots, N > \omega, \; k = 1, 2, \cdots, m,$$

or, for short, denoting the left-hand side by $L_{k,t}$,

$$(3.15') \qquad L_{k,t} = \epsilon_{k,t}, \qquad \begin{aligned} t &= 1, 2, \cdots, N, \\ k &= 1, 2, \cdots, m, \end{aligned}$$

where, in each of the m equations, one of the coefficients $a_{k1,0}, a_{k2,0}, \cdots, a_{km,0}$ (the coefficient of the "dependent variable") is equal to -1 by definition, and where the mN random variables $\epsilon_{k,t}$ are independently and normally distributed variables with zero means and variances σ_k^2, $k=1, 2, \cdots, m$, which are independent of t. ω denotes the largest lag occurring in the system (3.15). Many of the coefficients a may, of course, be zero. All those a's which are not either equal to zero or equal to -1 by definition, are assumed to be unknown parameters to be estimated. Let the quantities $w_{j,t}$ for $t=0, -1, -2, \cdots, -\omega$, $j=1, 2, \cdots, m$ (i.e., the initial conditions) be $given$ $constants$. Then the system (3.15) represents a linear transformation of the mN random variables $\epsilon_{k,t}$, $k=1, 2, \cdots, m$, $t=1, 2, \cdots, N$, in terms of the observable random variables w. Assume that the transformation is nonsingular, and let J be its Jacobian. J will, in general, be a function of the parameters a. The maximum-likelihood estimates, a°, of the unknown parameters a are then the solutions of a system of "normal equations" obtained by setting

$$(3.16) \qquad \frac{1}{N} \frac{\partial |J^\circ|}{\partial a^\circ_{kj,i}} \cdot \sum_{t=1}^{N} L^{\circ 2}_{k,t} - |J^\circ| \cdot \sum_{t=1}^{N} L^\circ_{k,t} \frac{\partial L^\circ_{k,t}}{\partial a^\circ_{kj,i}} = 0$$

for all those a's, and those only, which are not either equal to zero or equal to -1 by definition.

If, therefore, the Jacobian is independent of the a's, the method reduces to that of fitting each equation separately, by the least-squares method in the usual way, as explained previously. Also, if the Jacobian is independent of the coefficients of *some* of the equations, these particular equations may likewise be fitted, separately, by the ordinary least-squares method.

4. EQUATIONS OF PREDICTION VERSUS EQUATIONS OF THEORY

The economist may have two different purposes in mind when he constructs a model like (2.5)–(2.7).

First, he may consider himself in the same position as an astronomer; he cannot interfere with the actual course of events. So he sets up the system (2.5)–(2.7) as a tentative description of the economy. If he finds that it fits the past, he hopes that it will fit the future. On that basis he wants to make predictions, assuming that no one will interfere with the game.

Next, he may consider himself as having the power to change certain aspects of the economy in the future. If then the system (2.5)–(2.7) has worked in the past, he may be interested in knowing it as an aid in judging the effect of his intended future planning, because he thinks that certain elements of the old system will remain invariant. For example, he might think that consumers will continue to respond in the same way to income, no matter from what sources their income originates. Even if his future planning would change the investment relation (2.6), the consumption relation (2.5) might remain true. He might be interested in the consumption relation only, but in order to estimate it from past observations, he has to set up the investment equation (2.6) too. For the fact that this equation, by assumption, was active during the past, in addition to (2.5), has implications for the statistical material available—and, hence, for the technique to be used—for estimating the consumption relation (2.5) from the observations. This we discussed in the preceding section.

Let us first consider certain problems of prediction in our model (2.5)–(2.7). Assume that we know the true values of α, β, κ, and that, for simplicity, x_t and y_t are normally and independently distributed with zero means and variances equal to σ_x^2 and σ_y^2 respectively, and that their distribution is independent of *past* values of u, r, x, and y. Consider u_{t-1} as a given quantity, and consider the following problems of prediction:

1. To predict u_t from past observations.
2. To predict v_t from past observations.

3. To predict u_t when r_t and past observations are given.

4. To predict v_t when u_t and past observations are given.

As the best prediction of a variable we choose its expected value. Since, by assumption, u_t and v_t are jointly normally distributed, the conditional expectations in question can be obtained very easily from the transformations (2.5)–(2.6), using standard formulae associated with the normal distribution. For the four prediction formulae required above, one obtains then, in the same order:

$$(4.1) \qquad E(u_t|u_{t-1}) = -\frac{\alpha \kappa}{1-(1+\kappa)\alpha}u_{t-1} + \frac{\beta}{1-(1+\kappa)\alpha},$$

$$(4.2) \qquad E(v_t|u_{t-1}) = -\frac{(1-\alpha)\kappa}{1-(1+\kappa)\alpha}u_{t-1} + \frac{\kappa\beta}{1-(1+\kappa)\alpha},$$

$$(4.3) \qquad \begin{aligned} E(u_t|r_t, u_{t-1}) &= \frac{(1+\kappa)\sigma_z{}^2 + \alpha\sigma_y{}^2}{(1+\kappa)^2\sigma_z{}^2 + \sigma_y{}^2}r_t + \frac{(1+\kappa)\kappa\sigma_z{}^2}{(1+\kappa)^2\sigma_z{}^2 + \sigma_y{}^2}u_{t-1} \\ &\quad + \frac{\beta\sigma_y{}^2}{(1+\kappa)^2\sigma_z{}^2 + \sigma_y{}^2}, \end{aligned}$$

$$(4.4) \qquad \begin{aligned} E(v_t|u_t, u_{t-1}) &= \frac{\kappa\sigma_z{}^2 + \alpha(1-\alpha)\sigma_y{}^2}{\sigma_z{}^2 + \alpha^2\sigma_y{}^2}u_t - \frac{\kappa\sigma_z{}^2}{\sigma_z{}^2+\alpha^2\sigma_y{}^2}u_{t-1} \\ &\quad - \frac{\alpha\beta\sigma_y{}^2}{\sigma_z{}^2 + \alpha^2\sigma_y{}^2}. \end{aligned}$$

It is worth noticing that *none* of these formulae are the same as those obtained by omitting the error terms x and y in equations (2.5), (2.6). For prediction purposes the original equations of the system have no practical significance, they play only the role of theoretical tools by which to derive the prediction equations.

What *is* then the significance of the theoretical equations obtained by omitting the error terms in (2.5) and (2.6)? To see that, let us consider, not a problem of passive predictions, but a problem of government planning.

Assume that the Government decides, through public spending, taxation, etc., to keep income, r_t, at a given level, and that consumption u_t and private investment v_t continue to be given by (2.5) and (2.6), the only change in the system being that, instead of (2.7), we now have

$$(2.7') \qquad\qquad r_t = u_t + v_t + g_t,$$

where g_t is Government expenditure, so adjusted as to keep r constant, whatever be u and v, as given by (2.5) and (2.6). (2.7') then does not impose any new restriction upon u and v, beyond that which is expressed by (2.5)–(2.6). Then, from (2.5) and (2.6) it is readily seen that

(4.5) $$E(u_t|r_t) = \alpha r_t + \beta,$$

(4.6) $$E(v_t|u_t - u_{t-1}) = \kappa(u_t - u_{t-1}).$$

That is, to predict consumption u_t and private investment v_t under the Government policy expressed by (2.7′) we may use the "theoretical" equations obtained from (2.5) and (2.6) by omitting the error terms x_t and y_t. This is only natural, because now the Government is, in fact, performing "experiments" of the type we had in mind when constructing each of the two equations (2.5) and (2.6).

University Institute of Economics
  Oslo

Econometrica, Vol. 11, 2 (April 1943)

THE DEMAND FOR DURABLE GOODS

By CHARLES F. ROOS and VICTOR S. VON SZELISKI

I. THE GENERAL THEORY OF DURABLE-GOODS DEMAND

Demand as an Explanation of Sales

THIS PAPER essays a systemization of the procedure of demand analysis with special reference to durable goods. The first section takes up the demand for durable goods in general, and the two following give more detailed consideration to the demand for durable consumer and durable producer goods (capital goods), respectively. The first topic is of an analytical nature: the setting of the demand problem in relation to the economic mechanism as a whole, what is to be accepted as an explanation of demand, what the elements of the explanation may be, what are the general characteristics of demand functions.

The demand for a product may be said to be explained (and the demand problem solved) when a relationship has been obtained connecting the quantity of a commodity sold with a factor or factors at least formally independent of the quantity sold. This requirement is less exacting than that for an explanation in the natural sciences, where, according to P. W. Bridgman,

... the essence of an explanation consists in reducing a situation to elements with which we are so familiar that we accept them as a matter of course, so that our curiosity rests.[1]

Few of the elements or concepts which economists are attempting to fit together into satisfactory working theories are accepted by many "as a matter of course." In the present state of science it had better be said that the elements of explanation are simply factors about which we agree not to ask embarrassing questions for the time being, and if "our curiosity rests," it is more apt to be on account of a printer's deadline than because of a feeling of complete mental satisfaction. Many parts of the structure of economics will doubtless be torn down and rebuilt in new form with new building materials and new types of interconnecting members.

A root reason why it is difficult to make progress in building up an economic science is the lack of facts with which to direct and fertilize

---

[1] Bridgman, *Logic of Modern Physics*, New York, 1928, p. 37.

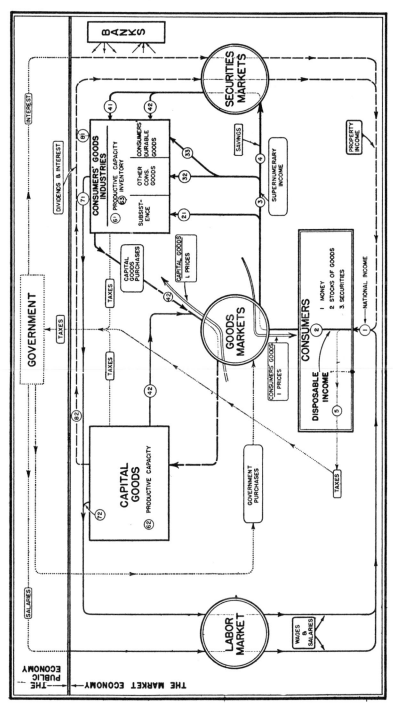

FIGURE 1.—Principal money flows in an exchange economy.

the logic. In the natural sciences logical method and induction (experimental method) go hand in hand and direct and support each other. Such is far from being the case in economics. The chief present opportunity for carrying out a scientific procedure in economics seems to be by the use of statistical induction and correlation analysis. This correlation technique is a sort of combination of the method of differences and the method of concomitant variations of logic, with several independent variables instead of just one.

Various studies[2] show that as far as fitting data to curves is concerned one can obtain many different formulations or explanations. The data themselves do not point to a particular demand function; they are neutral and will obligingly "confirm" widely disparate analyses. The significance of any analysis therefore depends more on economic logic than on statistical techniques as such. As G. C. Evans has so aptly remarked:

... when we find this feeling for hypothesis and definition and, in addition, become involved in chains of deductive reasoning, we are driven to a characteristic method of construction and analysis which we may call the mathematical method.

It is not a question as to whether mathematics is desirable or not in such a subject. We are in fact forced to adopt the mathematical method as a condition of further progress.[3]

Henry Schultz has extended us the good advice that

As economists we will do well to study the implications of Professor Bridgman's distinction between concepts which are defined in terms of *operations* and those which are defined in terms of *properties* of things.[4]

In following this advice we shall first describe the groups and institutions and the flows in the economic mechanism which are of major usefulness for explaining demand problems. These are outlined in the accompanying diagram, Figure 1, which will also be useful for orienting the two later studies.

The two main groups are:

    I. Consumers (individuals),

    II. Producers.

For purposes of this exposition at least four types of producers need to be distinguished: enterprises producing consumer goods (and services), enterprises producing capital goods, banks, and the government. Government should be classified separately, because it does not operate under the market economy (and in a study of demand we are necessarily

[2] See, for instance, *Dynamics of Automobile Demand*, General Motors Corporation, New York, 1939, pp. 30–31.

[3] G. C. Evans, *Mathematical Introduction to Economics*, New York, 1930, p. 113.

[4] Henry Schultz, *The Theory and Measurement of Demand*, University of Chicago Press, 1938, page 11.

studying a phenomenon of the *market*). Government and flows associated with it are represented by dots in the flow diagram. Certain activities of the government, such as the post office, municipal power, etc., should, however, be classified with enterprises.

Consumer-goods enterprises will be subclassified as:
1. Producers of necessities,[5]
2. Producers of durable consumer goods (nonnecessary),
3. Others.

There are three markets: the labor market, the goods market (which may be divided into a capital-goods market and a consumer-goods market, though such a separation is largely formal), and a securities market, which includes the market for new securities.

Now consider the money flows between these groups. As the total flow is circular, any point may be selected as a starting point. Let us start with consumer income. This is the line (1) at the bottom of the chart, flowing toward the consumers' rectangle. Direct personal taxes are drawn off to the left. These pass out of the domain of the market economy to government and are shown as a dotted line. Only the balance, disposable income, line (2), is spent within the market economy, and it, rather than income (1), is the purchasing power with which we should be concerned in demand studies of durable goods. [When (2) leaves the consumers' rectangle, it may also be called disposable outlay.]

Subsistence living costs (21) are the first subtraction from this stream; these are minimum expenditures for food, clothing and shelter, fuel and light, etc., reckoned at about $200 per capita with living costs as of 1923 = 100[6] and varying above or below $200 per capita with the cost of living. The balance (3) is called supernumerary income and may be regarded as the amount available for expenditure for goods above the necessity class and for savings. Part of the supernumerary income is spent for durable consumer goods (33), part for other consumer goods (32) or for extra quality in necessary goods, and part is saved (4). This last is invested, part (42) in capital-goods companies. Total receipts of consumer-goods companies are receipts for goods sold, plus net new investment (41).

Outlays of these companies are: taxes (shown as the dotted line leaving the market economy), expenditures for capital goods (42) which pass through the goods market and enter the capital-goods rectangle, wages (71), and property income (81), dividends, interest, and rents.

Government expenditures enter the market economy through the

[5] The difficulty of defining necessities is recognized.
[6] *The Dynamics of Automobile Demand*, published by General Motors Corp., 1939, page 41.

labor market as salaries, through the securities market as interest, and through the goods market as direct purchases of public works, navy vessels, paper, office equipment, etc. They constitute, with disposable income (2) and capital-goods purchases (42), the total purchasing power entering the goods market.

Detailed explanation of the rest of the diagram is unnecessary. The rectangle for banks has been drawn off to one side. It is possible to disregard the banks in much of the analysis of demand. But whenever they act in an inflationary or deflationary manner, they affect the functioning of the economy in an important way: they supply money to the government, to enterprises, and to individuals in inflation and absorb it in deflation.

When changes in the money supply and hoarding are ruled out, the flow of money is wholly cyclic; there is a balance of inflow and outflow between the main groups in the economy. If we postulate such a balance, it has certain implications for our choice of demand functions.

The diagram shows money flows only; it will be understood that corresponding to each money flow there is a reverse flow of goods, man power, or securities.[7]

We are now ready to consider what demand is as an object of statistical study. It is concerned with the flow of goods (including services) through the goods-market countering consumers' expenditures (2), capital-goods expenditures (42), and sometimes government expenditures. More particularly we are concerned with statistical observations measuring the quantity of flow—pointer readings, as Eddington would call them.[8] The "demand" for these goods has been explained when numerical connections have been established between these pointer readings and other readings obtained in measuring factors which we are pleased to regard as "elements" for purposes of explanation, e.g., in establishing an equation:

$$y = f(x_1, x_2, x_3, \cdots, x_n),$$

where y is the quantity ordered or purchased (consumer takings) and x_1, x_2, etc. are the elements of explanation. The observed y's are counts, sometimes of dollar values, sometimes of physical quantities, passing through the goods[9] market within certain time intervals.

---

[7] Taxes excepted. It is, of course, possible to regard taxes as payment for government services and protection, thus maintaining a neat logical symmetry. However, what is the best way to regard taxes and government services need not be settled here.

[8] Eddington, *The Nature of the Physical World*, page 252; "The whole subject-matter of exact science consists of pointer-readings and similar indications."

[9] In practice, it is not often possible to measure the movement of goods at this point in the cyclic flow. Sometimes it is necessary to use consumption of a raw

Variables Entering a Demand Function

Now, what factors shall be taken as the x's? Historically, the demand function was first taken to be a function of a single variable, the price of the commodity in question. Such simple determination of demand is, of course, contrary to everyday experience.[10] So Walras was led to formulate the general equation:

$$y = f(p_1, p_2, p_3, \cdots, p_n),$$

where the p's are the prices of all commodities, and one of the writers generalized this to include other variables as well as a function of time. The simplest such generalization is:

$$y = f(p_1, p_2, \cdots, t),$$

where t is time or any other parameter.

Now let us place these variables on our diagram. The prices p are numbers attached to goods as they stand in the market place, in the circle called the "Goods Market." The y's are counts of quantities moving through the Goods circle. The Walras equation, then, explains the y's in the circle by the p's in the circle. When we introduce a time element t in the demand equation, we must recognize that the t stands nowhere—it represents systematic changes which occur over a period of time and which are not attributed to any named variable.

Is this scheme of explanation satisfactory? The following points may be noted: (1) Choice of prices as elements of the explanation is proper. Prices are certainly formally independent of quantities and so serve excellently as elements of explanation. (2) It would be desirable, however, to choose some elements of explanation having their *locus* (so to speak) *outside of* the Goods Market, otherwise a study of demand is "introvert," and never gets outside the market place. It is only by establishing more distant connections, e.g., with consumers' income, that we can link up the various parts of the economy and form an integrated picture of its functioning. (3) It is further desirable, however, to choose some elements lying *upstream* from the goods market, because such elements are related to consumers' takings as cause and effect. Economic flows of the type here described are cyclic and unidirectional. Human volition enters every linkage and determines that the cause-effect direction shall be one way and not another.[11] For ex-

---

material as a measure of consumer takings (e.g., mill consumption of cotton), or imports (e.g., tea), or "disappearance" (e.g., factory production of butter adjusted for changes in stocks). The point at which an economic flow is measured should always be carefully stated. See Appendix I of *Patterns of Resource Use*, published by the National Resources Committee, Washington, D. C., 1939.

[10] Schultz, *op. cit.*, page 9.

[11] Theoretically and in the abstract, economic men act so as to increase utility. Utility thus gives direction to events somewhat as entropy does in physics.

ample, automobiles purchased are effects of consumer income. Automobile purchases cause consumer income only by progressing around the circle the long way, with the arrow points, by determining automobile production, which in turn brings about activities in the steel industry, etc., and both of which result in outpayments of wages, taxes, and property income, which eventually complete the closed path back to consumers.[12]

Thus, the explanatory elements which we use in a consumer-goods demand study are to be sought in the goods market (prices, inventory, etc.) or upstream in the consumers' rectangle. In the passenger-car demand study which will be described later the following variables were used as explanatory factors: (1) consumers' disposable income, (2) consumers' stocks of cars in operation or usable, (3) price of automobiles, (4) replacement pressure (a quantity derived from the age distribution of the car stock), (5) cost of living. The probable effects of certain other variables were discussed, such as (6) operating costs, (7) price of used cars, and (8) financing terms.[13] In a residential-building demand study these were used: (1) building need (a function of the number of consumers, existing buildings, and families), (2) consumer income, (3) net rents (a function of gross rents, occupancy, and real-estate taxes), (4) foreclosures, and (5) building costs. All these variables satisfy the above requirements.

An important point of departure in each study above described from the usual demand study for a perishable good is the introduction of such factors as consumers' stocks and replacement pressure or foreclosures which are neither prices nor present production. These factors are functionals[14] and not the simple function used in classical studies.

[12] Not a few analysts use production as an explanatory variable for consumer-goods demand. See, for example, *Patterns of Resource Use.* Justification of this procedure depends on the fact that, empirically, production as measured, say, by the Federal Reserve Board Index of Production is highly correlated with consumer income. A good deal of consumer income originates in manufacturing and mining. But the connection of production with aggregate consumer income is not strong enough to permit the indiscriminate use of the former as proxy for the latter. That portion of income originating in government, or in new industries, such as airplane manufacture, is not closely correlated with the FRB Index. Another cause of divergence is the building and depletion of inventories and imports and exports of monetary metals. Hence, while the variable may be suitable for getting a statistical fit, it does not aid much in forming a closely knit explanation of the functioning of the economy.

[13] Introduction of financing terms requires connecting the banks into the circuit (not shown on diagram).

[14] A functional is a function of a curve. The area under a curve is a simple example of a functional. A function depends upon a point value; a functional depends upon all points of the curve in a range.

Any one or all of these functionals of economics can be expressed as functions of time. Therefore, we can write $y = f(p_1, p_2, \cdots, p_n, t)$ with perfect generality. However, here as in many other cases, generality such as this loses the sharpness of delineation so desirable in obtaining explanations.

Relationship among the Variables

The independent variables have been discussed, and attention may now be turned to the functions which connect them. The demand functions with which we actually deal in applied economics are the results of performing certain statistical operations on the quantity, price, and other data of the problem. They summarize and describe the mass behavior of consumers in respect to a particular commodity under a range of conditions. Differing statistical procedures will yield different demand functions. The concept is, therefore, not precise; it is relative to the procedure selected for obtaining it which, therefore, must always be specified in sufficient detail.

What these demand functions have in common with the demand schedules of abstract economics is a problem for the economic logician. It may be possible to look upon the statistical demand functions as aggregates of the demand function of individuals. These latter may be discontinuous, have several points of inflection, regions of sharp curvature, etc., which disappear in the process of summation. It is certain that the above statistical functions imply nothing with respect to choices of individuals as such and do not even require that individuals know what their own demand schedules are, or what their behavior will be under specified circumstances.

Choice of the functional form to be fitted to the data—that is, selecting a hypothesis for testing—is a thorny problem. The economist has not much to guide him in this respect in making this selection; he is not in the position of the physicist who has a vast range of accurately verified theory to help him in his hypothesis making. Abstract economic theory has no such precision in its concepts,[15] as has physics; and, therefore, the mathematical economist cannot declare a particular formula as uniquely appropriate for describing a given economic phenomenon.

But this partial agnosticism which one must accept at this stage of development in economic science does not justify one in selecting some ready-to-hand formula and plunging ahead with a least-squares determination; careful analysis will suggest, if not a particular functional form, at least the general characteristics which would make a function appropriate. See, for example, the authors' derivation of a demand

---

[15] Consider, for example, the diversity of views concerning the content of national income.

function for passenger-car sales,[16] and Schultz's discussion[17] of the "integrability condition" which imposed important restrictions on the demand function for commodities of related demand.[18]

Relations between the Demand Functions

The next stage, which, however, is not likely to be attempted on any exact scale for many years, is an integration of demand functions so as to give a unified and consistent picture of the functioning of the entire consumer area in the flow diagram discussed earlier.[19] When this is reached, the requirement that the value of commodities consumed equals consumers' disposable income may be imposed (as long as the system is closed—provided that money is not being supplied from banks, gold imports, etc.).

Let subscripts 1, 2, $\cdots$, n denote the goods, services, and securities on which money is spent. Suppose that the demand function for each is of the form:

$$y_i = y(p_i, \cdots, I, \cdots),$$

where y_i is the quantity taken of the ith commodity or unit of manpower or security issue, p_i is its price, and I is disposable income. The dollar value of the purchase is $p_i y_i$. As long as the system is closed, it is clear that

$$I(t) = \sum p_i(t) \cdot y_i(t);$$

consumers' disposable income equals consumers' outlay. This is an equation of constraint that must apply to any wide view of the situation. The function y_i should, for greatest accuracy, be such as can satisfy the above equality identically. This is a restriction that is by no means easy to apply, but it can generally be disregarded in studying individual commodities.[20]

---

[16] *The Dynamics of Automobile Demand, op. cit.*, page 32.

[17] Schultz, *op. cit.*, pages 575–580.

[18] It is usually reasonable to choose the demand function so that it takes the value 0 when the income factor is 0. This does not mean that people starve if their monetary income drops to zero; they may become self-sufficient or live in some type of rationing economy. It does mean that they do not acquire consumable goods by *monetary exchange*. This condition is in effect an additional and exact observation well outside the range of observed data, which will often contribute materially to the accuracy of the demand function, on the slope of which it will have considerable influence. It is also reasonable to ask that the demand function should remain finite and approach an upper limit as price approaches zero. Not even free goods are consumed in infinite amounts. The popular form

$$y = A p^{-\alpha}$$

does not satisfy this requirement.

[19] A courageous attempt along these lines is presented in *Patterns of Resource Use*, published by the National Resources Committee, Washington, D. C., 1939.

[20] In fact, in practice it must be disregarded.

Some Business-Cycle Aspects of Demand

The preceding section has discussed the demand function for durable goods from the standpoint of the "simultaneous" relations of quantities consumed y with a number of other variables. We now turn to an examination of the sequential relations among these factors, principally the question of cyclic variation in the demand for durable goods.

Writers on business cycles who emphasize overinvestment, i.e., excessive capital-goods orders, to go back to sources, are of the following classes:

(A) Wicksellian school, which believes that monetary forces operating under a particular form of credit organization produce the disequilibrium between the lower and higher stages of production. Among the writers in this school are Hayek, Machlup, Mises, Robbins, and Wicksell.

(B) Writers who stress inventions, discoveries, the opening of new markets, etc.—that is, circumstances which provide new investment opportunities. Included in this school are Cassel, Hansen, Schumpeter, and Spiethoff.

(C) Writers who hold that changes in the production of consumer goods give rise, for technological reasons, to much more violent fluctuations in the production of producer goods in general and fixed capital equipment in particular. Important writers in this group are Aftalion, Bickerdike, Carver, Pigou, J. M. Clark, and R. F. Harrod.

Through many of the writings there is a story on the relation of interest rates to investment which is about as follows for a closed economy:

... the boom is brought about by discrepancy between the natural [money supply–money demand] rate and the money [or market] rate of interest. ... As soon as prices begin to rise, the process tends to become cumulative for the reason that there is a twofold causal connection between interest rates and the price level. ... If prices rise and people expect them to continue to rise, they become more eager to borrow and the demand for credit becomes stronger. Falling prices have the contrary effect. ...

... The ability of the banks to create credit makes the total supply elastic. A considerable increase in the demand will be met without much rise in the interest rate, though the supply of voluntary saving may not have increased very much. ...

... A credit expansion ensues, prices rise, and the rise in prices raises profits. ... if the banks persist in maintaining the same rate of interest, the gap between the equilibrium rate and the market rate will be even wider than before, and the amount of credit expansion required even greater. Prices rise higher still, profits are raised, and the vicious spiral of inflation continues. ...

If a part of current income is being saved,—i.e., if not all income is devoted to buying consumers' goods—the demand for consumers' goods falls off and factors of production are made available. ...

... the necessary condition is that the demand for consumers' goods does not rise *pari passu* with the creation of credit and the rise in demand for capital goods. ...

... by the artificial lowering of the interest rate, the economy is lured into long round-about methods of production which cannot be maintained permanently. The structure of production becomes, so to speak, top-heavy.[21]

Another group, in which we may place Hayek, Machlup, Mises, Robbins, and Strigl, maintains that if once the boom has been allowed to develop and to give rise to maladjustments, the price has to be paid in the shape of a deflation.

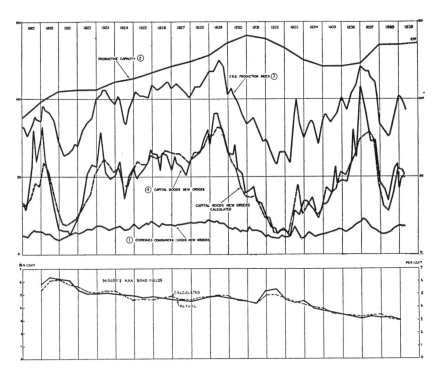

FIGURE 2.—Indexes of capital goods, and Moody's Aaa bond yields.

Some of the above contentions have foundation in fact; others are not supported; and still others can be shown to be false. Hence, it is desirable to reconsider the problem.

Figure 2 shows the course of interest rates in the United States, both actual and "natural," and capital-goods new orders for 1919 to date. The interest rate is the yield on Aaa bonds (Moody's Investors Service). The "natural" interest rate is a derived curve calculated from the relation of certain money-supply factors or liquidity assets[22] to the factors

[21] Haberler, Gottfried, *Prosperity and Depression*, Geneva, 1937, pp. 33–41.
[22] C. F. Roos & Victor S. Von Szeliski, "Determination of Interest Rates," *Journal of Political Economy*, Vol. 50, August, 1942.

representing demand for money. The former include adjusted demand deposits of Federal Reserve member banks, government deposits, time deposits, interbank deposits, nonmember and other Federal Reserve accounts, short-term government bonds, and the capital account of banks. The demand side includes government demand, business demand, security-market demand, and bank demand.

The "natural" rate in Figure 2 is a statistical construction. It is the moving intersection point of functions of money in existence and of money in use, these functions being determined so that the intersection point will approximate the market rate in the least-squares sense. If it be premised that the disequilibria between natural and market rates described in the above quotation can persist for not more than, say, two years, and that they balance out in the long run the quotation marks may be removed from "natural." This is an open question.

First of all, it appears from this study that the interest rate in the United States is to a large extent a consequence of independent monetary variables and a natural consequence of earlier economic conditions. It hardly seems to be a prime cause of capital-goods demand. Notice that in late 1919 and early 1920 capital-goods orders continued to rise in the face of a sharply rising interest rate.

The high interest rates of 1920 seem to be a consequence of the heavy capital-goods orders and inventory buying in 1919. They may also have been one cause of the drastic decline in capital-goods orders in 1920, but was not this latter development more a consequence of the completion of the reconversion program?

A rise in the rate in 1922 and 1923 occurred only after capital-goods orders had increased materially. From 1923 to early 1928 the interest rate declined while capital-goods orders remained relatively steady and during this period the market rate was sometimes above and sometimes below the "natural" rate. Late in 1927 capital-goods orders began a sharp increase which continued into 1929. Interest rates followed upward several months later. In 1929 capital-goods orders turned down following declines in consumer-goods orders and residential building.

It is clear, therefore, that a rise in interest rates occurs at the top of the boom and a decline in interest rates at or before the bottom of the depression. But, as we shall see, in each case a condition calling for a change in the direction of business has already been set up. In fact, a fairly satisfactory explanation of the business or capital-goods cycle can be obtained if the interest rate is ignored.

This is not a denial that rates at which money is actually offered and terms of lending play a part in determining the volume of economic activity. It merely says that linkages may be established part way around the flow circuit in Figure 1, connecting capital-goods orders with factors which business men do take into account in planning their capital expenditures, and that the interest-rate factor need not be linked in.

The writers doubt that published interest rates are representative of the scales of offers of and demand for money that relate to capital-goods financing. Published interest-rate statistics relate to very specialized and selected types of loans. Long-term bond yields relate to *seasoned* securities, and these yields may or may not reflect the cost of capital for new ventures. Since yields in seasoned securities often fall during depressions, at the very time when business risks are increasing, published yield averages may actually have an inverse correlation with the cost of financing capital expansions. The cost which businesses have to pay for capital is affected by a multitude of terms that are part of the legal instruments relating to the loan or financing. The SEC report on unseasoned securities during 1933–39 showed that costs of underwriting were from 10 to 40 per cent of the cash proceeds. Federal Reserve Board studies of interest rates on loans show wide variations. Hence, the exclusion of interest rates from the studies here presented shows only that current yields on seasoned bonds are not closely related to capital-goods activity.

For a determination of the demand for capital goods that ignores the interest rate one needs an index of combined consumer-goods new orders representing the expected use of plant and an index measuring industrial capacity. Such measures can be defined as follows:

Combined Consumer-Goods New Orders (1) is a weighted average of the physical volume of new orders for consumer goods and for durable consumer goods. About 1300 companies are represented in recent years. The weights are based upon the U. S. Census of Manufactures. It is a comprehensive index and as such is a measure of the seasonally corrected replacement demand for capital goods.

Productive Capacity (2) represents the industrial capacity output in terms of the Federal Reserve Board Production Index (3). Since actual capacity depends on prices, hours of work, management, and many other factors, a completely definitive measure of capacity cannot be constructed. However, an index derived by cumulating the deflated dollar value of equipment installations and deducting depreciation and obsolescence in accordance with an approximate life table of industrial equipment is useful for indicating the general economic level of capacity.

Capital-Goods New Orders (Calculated) (4) is a series derived from Combined Consumer-Goods New Orders (1) and the spread between Productive Capacity and the Federal Reserve Board Index of Production by the formula:

Capital-Goods New Orders = (Constant) × (Consumer-Goods Orders)
+ (Constant) × (Capacity − FRB Produc-
tion).

This may be taken to be the Demand for Capital Goods.

The fitted curve is seen to indicate very well both the level and the direction of capital-goods orders.[23] One point that stands out is that neither series shows a consistent lead over the other. During the depression that began in 1920, Capital-Goods New Orders declined a little ahead of Demand. In the recovery the Demand led throughout 1921. In 1922 and early 1923 Capital-Goods New Orders took the lead. This last movement, probably reflecting confidence, culminated in a decline that began early in 1923. In the 1924 recovery both series started upward at about the same time, although there is some evidence that the upturn in Capital Goods began as a rebound from an abnormally low level. From 1925 to the end of 1927 the Demand usually led. Then in 1928 Capital-Goods Orders began to run ahead of Demand. By the end of the first quarter of 1929 Orders were declining and during the third quarter were below Demand. In the fourth quarter Demand declined more rapidly than Orders and in general this situation prevailed until the fourth quarter of 1932. Then, as a rule, Demand remained ahead of Capital-Goods Orders until the third quarter of 1935 when the Supreme Court decision outlawing NRA seems to have been associated with returning confidence and a rapid rise in Capital-Goods Orders. In the second quarter of 1936 Capital-Goods Orders began to rise faster than Demand and in the fourth quarter of 1936 and the first quarter of 1937 an excess of orders comparable to the excesses of 1919, 1923, and 1929 were placed.

The boom is characterized chiefly by a temporary squeeze between rapidly rising orders and inflexible productive capacity. This seems to set various forces of adjustment into motion. While inventory in consumer-goods lines is being worked down, production of consumer-goods declines, capacity is excessive, and capital-goods orders decline materially. To explain completely the business cycle one still needs to explain consumer-goods orders. The durable-goods section of such orders will be explained in the next section of this paper. At present the other seems to be simply an inventory cycle brought about by a succession of random events and influenced particularly by the rate of change of money supply.

The small residuals mentioned correlate very well with the variations

[23] For various reasons one need not expect this relation to hold during World War II. In particular, armaments are produced in large volume by the capital-goods industries, and priorities will prevent capital-goods demand by civilian industries from asserting itself.

in yield on high-grade bonds and, hence, the fit will be materially improved except for a trend factor by introducing the interest factor. One then obtains a series that characteristically leads Capital-Goods New Orders and gives also the level of orders to be expected.

II. THE DEMAND FOR DURABLE CONSUMER GOODS

This part deals with the special problem of demand for durable consumer goods as illustrated by demand functions for passenger automobiles and residential building.[24] Two principal topics will be discussed, the content of demand functions and what these functions contribute toward an understanding of the cyclic fluctuations in demand, which are now receiving so much attention.

Demand Functions for Durable Consumer Goods

The important steps in deriving demand functions are selection of the independent factors and selection of the function which summarizes their relation to the predictant. Selection of the factors is largely a

TABLE 1

FACTORS USED IN PASSENGER-CAR AND RESIDENTIAL-BUILDING DEMAND
STUDIES

	New Passenger Cars	Residential Building
Factors Associated with Commodities	Price (Used-Car Prices) (Operating Costs) Cost of Living (Financing Terms) Durability	Gross Rents Occupancy Real-Estate Taxes Construction Cost Foreclosures
Factors Associated with Consumers	Consumers' Car Stock Pressure for Replacement Consumer Income Number of Families Population	Building Need (a function of number of families, marriages, etc.) Consumer Income
Other Factors	(Highway Mileage and Service Facilities)	Interest Rates Time Trend

matter of imagination and being sufficiently acquainted with the industry. In general, the variables that are useful in demand studies are of two types, those associated with the consumers of the commodity and those describing the commodity itself. Table 1 lists those used in the

[24] "Factors Governing Changes in Domestic Automobile Demand," Roos and Von Szeliski, pp. 20–95 of *Dynamics of Automobile Demand*, published by General Motors Corp.

"Factors Influencing Residential Building," Roos and Von Szeliski, pp. 69–110 of *Dynamic Economics*, Principia Press.

passenger-car and residential-building studies. The items in parentheses were discussed, but not introduced formally into the demand equations. In terms of the flow diagram presented earlier, the first group of factors is to be thought of as located in the circle called "The Goods Market," while the second group is located in the consumers' rectangle at the bottom of the diagram. Some of the items which condition consumer decisions are listed there as cash, securities, and commodity stocks.

The above variables were not all used as independent: consumer income and subsistence living costs for the population were combined into *supernumerary income*, and price and durability were combined to give *replacement cost*, so that the fitting of the formula of automobile demand actually involved only six variables: supernumerary income, the number of families, consumers' car stocks, pressure for replacement, price, and replacement cost. In the case of residential building the factors, rent, occupancy, taxes, construction cost, and interest rates, were combined. The first four may be combined into a measure of the net rate of return on a residential-real-estate investment:

$$\text{Rate of Return} = \frac{\text{Rent} \times \text{Occupancy} - \text{Taxes}}{\text{Construction Cost}}.$$

The numerator, divided by interest rates, gives capitalized value of rentals. The ratio of capitalized value to cost may be called *incentive*. Thus, the statistical analysis of the building study resolves into the fitting of only four variables and a time trend to the observed number of residential units constructed: incentive, foreclosures, need, and income. Foreclosures may, as a matter of fact, be eliminated without much affecting the agreement of actual and calculated values.

The passenger-car-sales equation finally arrived at was:

$$\text{Sales} = \left(\frac{\text{Supernumerary}}{\text{Income}}\right)^{1.2} (\text{Price})^{-0.65} \left\{ 0.0254C(M - C) \right.$$

$$\left. + 0.65\left(\frac{\text{Replacement}}{\text{Pressure}}\right)\right\}.$$

The parts of the equation represented by letters are cars in operation, C, the potential new owners $(M-C)$, in which M is the maximum ownership or "saturation level" (a function of number of families, income, and operating costs), and replacement pressure, which is the expectancy of car scrappage from a life table. Sales vary with the 1.2th power of the income factor, supernumerary income, and the -0.65th power of price.[25]

[25] As income and price also appear in the factor M, these exponents do not show the separate effects of the variables.

These demand functions are a far cry from those suggested in the premathematical period of economics, when price was treated as the factor of chief importance. As a matter of fact, variations in the price of passenger cars account for only a small portion of the fluctuations in passenger-car sales. Most of the variation is due to the factors associated with consumers: their income and the number of cars in operation.

Another way of classifying the variables for demand analyses is into general variables such as consumer income, cost of living, and the interest rate, which may apply for any number of commodities, and specific variables, such as price, quality, stock, operating characteristics, etc., pertaining to the particular commodity under investigation.

What variables control in each individual case can only be determined by analysis. One should, of course, pay heed to the rule of not introducing into an explanation more independent variables than are strictly necessary, and one would wish to keep the economic system neatly closed, as the flow diagram is drawn. However, in a field for investigation as complicated as the modern economy, it would be well for the time being to work out the demand functions for each industry as a fresh task, using whatever variables appear necessary, whether they be economic factors, or political, sociological, or psychological. When demand studies shall have been made for a wider variety of goods, it will be time to organize and integrate them and work them into a more compact and economical system.

Cyclic Variations in the Demand for Consumers' Goods

The equations given for passenger-car and residential-building demand provide no clue to how cyclical variations in total production originate. But they do show how cyclical variation in or disequilibrium among the independent variables, such as income or price, is transmitted to automobile sales, how small-amplitude cycles in income, etc. and certain differences in phase between the independent factors produce large-amplitude swings in sales. The process by which these cycles become magnified is generally characteristic of durable goods.

First, it should be noted that supernumerary income itself has cycles in magnified form. The factor is:

$$\frac{\text{Supernumerary}}{\text{Income}} = \frac{\text{Consumer}}{\text{Income}} - \frac{\text{Direct Per-}}{\text{sonal Taxes}} - \frac{\text{Necessary Liv-}}{\text{ing Costs.}}$$

Direct personal taxes are chiefly income, gift, and estate taxes. These go up and down with the business cycle, but the important fact to note is that they normally lag behind consumer income. Thus, when the latter flattens out after a rise, taxes continue to advance. Necessary living costs also lag; retail prices of even sensitive commodities like food and clothing tend to respond more slowly to business-cycle influences, while the lag in rents, because of their contractual nature, is very pronounced. Thus, when consumer income flattens out after a cyclical rise, taxes and living costs continue to advance and supernumerary income may thus actually decline; it is pinched or squeezed between consumer income on the one hand, and taxes and living costs on the other. The year 1937 furnished a very clear illustration of this squeezing process, which was accentuated by a raising of tax rates, a sharp upward acceleration of the price level, due mostly to labor-union activities, and monetary deflation by the Federal Reserve Board.

An analogous sequence of events occurs at the bottom of the cycle; supernumerary income turns up more sharply than consumer income, because taxes and living costs generally continue to fall after the turn. Variation in demand for consumer durable goods may, therefore, be explained in part by the phase difference between incomes and prices.

The potential-new-owners term, $M - C$, is one of the most important in the equation. It is the difference between the actual car stock and the maximum-ownership level or the number of cars which consumers would maintain on their current income under current prices. The maximum-ownership level M is thought of as constantly changing with the economic status of consumers and other factors, and consumers are assumed to be continuously adjusting the number of their cars toward the maximum-ownership level as a current objective. While the objective is above the number of cars in operation, car sales will be high, but if the maximum-ownership level falls below cars in operation (owing, say, to a drop in income), and the potential-new-owners term $M - C$ becomes negative, car sales will actually be less than replacement requirements. In the early growth stage of the automobile industry there was little danger of this happening. Ten-per-cent drops in the maximum-ownership level still left a large potential market for automobile sales, but when consumers' stocks finally approached the saturation level, a ten-per-cent drop in the latter became sufficient to wipe out the new-owners market and start liquidation of consumers' car stocks. This factor of potential new car owners will be of primary importance in determining postwar demand.

The sensitivity of car sales to income fluctuations is best illustrated by partial differentiation of a demand function. Differentiation of a function like the above shows that a 1-per-cent change in supernumerary income produced a change of about 1.5 per cent under conditions as of 1920 and a change of 2.8 per cent under the more saturated conditions of 1937.[26] This increasing sensitivity of automobile sales relative

[26] *Dynamics of Automobile Demand*, p. 92.

to the income factor as a function of the degree of saturation of the market is an important conclusion in regard to durable-goods demand, and emphasizes the importance of avoiding disturbance of consumer confidence.

The year 1937 again affords a fine illustration. The car-population stocks had been built up almost to the maximum-ownership level, stimulated in part by the drastic easing of installment terms in 1935–1938 and the soldiers' bonus. Then came the moderate drop in consumer income. This was magnified into a somewhat more abrupt drop in supernumerary income, as already described. The maximum-ownership level fell and the consumers found themselves with more cars than they cared to maintain. So they bought only 1,850,000 cars in the 1938-model year, compared to 3,750,000 in the 1937-model year.

The above formulation has its affinities with the "acceleration principle," associated with the names of J. M. Clark, Mitchell, Kuznets, Harrod, Pigou, and others. Both describe the same mechanism and, in broad outline, the views as to the causal relationships are the same. (See for example, *Prosperity and Depression*, by Gottfried Haberler, pp. 80–88.) But whereas the present formulation makes use of the difference between current stocks, C, and the maximum stocks sustainable, M,

$$S = f(M - C),$$

the acceleration principle is generally translated into mathematics as a function of the primary demand and its time derivative:

$$S = f\left(I, \frac{dI}{dt}\right).$$

(For an example of the latter, see *Dynamics of Automobile Demand*, page 12.) The former is believed to have its advantages: it introduces explicitly the variable which in the verbal statements of the acceleration theory is assigned due importance, viz., consumer stocks. It makes use of a varying maximum-ownership level as a separate concept; it avoids the need of auxiliary explanations for applying the acceleration principle to cases where there is unused capacity; and it avoids the assumption of a constant ratio between primary demand and the stock of (consumers') capital goods.[27] Moreover, the maximum-ownership level is traced and related explicitly to the factors which determine it, the number of families, per capita real income, and durability. The quantity M in the above formulas is:

[27] Qualifications discussed by Haberler on p. 91 of his *Prosperity and Depression*.

$$M = \left(\begin{matrix}\text{Number of} \\ \text{Families}\end{matrix}\right) \times \left\{0.5000\right.$$

$$+ 0.000544 \times \left(\begin{matrix}\text{Real Supernumerary} \\ \text{Income per Capita}\end{matrix}\right)\right\} \times (\text{Durability})^{0.3}.$$

The maximum-ownership level is, of course, not a directly observed quantity, but if we are willing to accept sales formulas like the above, we can "observe" it indirectly, and compare it with the calculated values.[28]

The same process of expansion and contraction of a maximum-ownership level occurs in residential building. When incomes fall, people "double up" and a surplus of housing ensues. This is aggravated by an increase of houses coming on the market through foreclosure.

The above demand equation also offers some evidence on the "echo" theory, which is that the demand pattern of a durable good tends to repeat after a lapse of n years, if n is the average useful life of the good. The variable "replacement pressure" represents this tendency. However, replacement pressure is itself a fairly smooth line, because the scrapping of cars put into service in one year is spread out over a considerable period, and thus the scrapping curve itself smooths out the prior pattern considerably. In addition to this, the factor receives a weight of only 0.65 in the formula, which shows that quite apart from the smoothing effect of the scrapping curve, 35 per cent of the prior pattern tends to disappear. The echo theory, therefore, is of secondary importance as an explanatory principle.

III. THE DEMAND FOR CAPITAL GOODS AS ILLUSTRATED BY ELECTRICAL EQUIPMENT

Investigation of the nature of the demand for capital goods has long been pursued by economists, probably because the production of this type of goods fluctuates so violently with changes in business activity. Perusal of previous studies of capital goods reveals that an astonishing number and variety of theories, conclusions, and explanations have, in the past, won followers among economists; this leads one to but a single *sure* conclusion, namely, that the problem is a difficult one.

The wide divergence of opinion has been chiefly on the question of what relationship exists between the demand for consumer goods and the demand for capital goods. Is capital goods the pivotal segment of the economy, i.e., do the changes in capital goods, with their wide swings, inaugurate changes in consumer goods? Does the relationship, whatever it is, have the same function in both the upside and the downside of the business cycle? Is expansion in capital goods made at the

[28] See pp. 55–58 of *Dynamics of Automobile Demand.*

expense of consumer goods and vice versa, as was once thought? Or do consumer goods and capital goods expand and contract together, the demand for capital goods being *derived from* the demand for consumer goods?

Historical data, which incidentally were not readily available to the earlier writers, give an affirmative answer to only the last of the above questions. It does indeed seem that consumer goods and capital goods expand and contract together. And, as Dr. Moulton has pointed out in *The Formation of Capital*, the concept that demand for capital goods is derived from demand for consumer goods is entirely tenable.

"The available . . . evidence supports the view that growth of capital is directly related to the demand for consumption goods. In the first place, changes in the direction of business activity in most cases appears to have begun with factors affecting the consumption side of the economic picture. In the second place, the growth of new capital is adjusted to the rate of expansion of consumptive demand . . . [29]

Accordingly, this study of the demand for electrical equipment by the public utilities has been made along the lines of the above tenets—that expansion of capital equipment is directly dependent upon the demand for the end product, electric power.[30]

This is another way of saying that the utilities add to (or decrease) their productive capacity when the demand for electricity increases (or decreases); they *do not* expand capacity *in order* to create a demand. It seems logical that this effect of consumption on capital expansion exists not only for utility electrical equipment but throughout the economy, because a reasonable expectation of greater profits *in the near future* is the final criterion of plant enlargement.[31]

The use of utility equipment to illustrate the nature of the demand for capital goods has certain advantages: (1) The consumption good and the capital good are on consecutive levels in the modern complicated process of roundabout production, thus making less difficult the determination of their relationship; (2) the problem is not complicated by inventories of the consumptive product. These advantages of simplicity are, by their very nature, also disadvantages which cause electrical equipment to be an atypical capital good. But, for that matter, what instrument of production is *typical* of capital goods in general? In the subsequent analysis the demand for utility electrical equipment

[29] Moulton, H. G., *The Formation of Capital*, The Brookings Institute, 1935, p. 158.

[30] Electricity is not, of course, wholly a consumer's good.

[31] The federal government, a nonprofit organization, was operating on the reverse principal in its electric-power policies. The plan apparently was to make large quantities of electricity available to the public at a low price and so encourage an increase in demand.

seems to have no indigenous characteristics which make the above concept less applicable to such equipment than to most other capital goods.

In proceeding to the specific case of utility equipment, it becomes evident that the effect of consumption upon capital expansion may be more closely approximated if another factor, generating capacity, is introduced. The stimulus to expand capital equipment arises, as stated above, from increases in consumption, but this stimulus is conditioned by the proximity of production to capacity. That is, when the amount of unused capacity is abnormally large, the need for plant expansion is diminished.

In view of these considerations it should be possible to calculate the demand for utility equipment from a formula of the type:

$$\frac{\text{Utility}}{\text{Equipment}} = \left(\frac{\text{Constant}}{\text{Power Production}}\right)^x - \text{Constant (Capacity}$$

$$- \text{ Power Production} + \text{Constant} + \text{Time Trend}).$$

The dependent variable or predictant is an index number with $1933 = 100$. It represents volume of generating and transmission equipment manufactured. The series was prepared from basic data reported by the Census of Manufactures, supplemented by some of the Institute of Applied Econometrics new-orders work, information supplied by the large electrical companies and electrical trade organizations, and, for 1920–1933, from Simon Kuznets' work.[32]

The independent variables, power production and power capacity, are data reported by the Federal Power Commission. Production in KWH is for calendar years, and capacity in KW is as of January 1st of each year. The reported capacity figures have been multiplied by 8,760, the number of hours in a year, to convert them into KWH, comparable to the production series.

The equation is, in a sense, a hybrid in that the units of measurement are not strictly comparable; production and capacity are in KWH, while utility equipment is an index number representing volume of apparatus. It would be preferable to have utility equipment in KWH also, but much apparatus (power switching equipment, panel boards, etc.) cannot be reduced to KWH, and those items with known KW (turbines, generators, etc.) are available for only a few years. However, comparison of the available KW data with the series used in this study indicates that the two are closely correlated.

The unknown constants can be readily obtained from the data. The results of a computation are shown on the Figures 3–6. From Figure 3

---

[32] Kuznets, Simon, *Commodity Flow and Capital Formation*, National Bureau of Economic Research, New York, 1938.

one can see that the fit, as a whole, considering that only two independent variables are used, is satisfactory. Note that the agreement between actual and calculated is less good in the period 1921–1926 than from 1927 on. This can be explained by the fact that in the 1920's, when the industry was expanding rapidly, much of the new capacity was not installed in the most strategic geographic areas. Thus, the errors in management's judgment caused some equipment to be installed where the economic need was not justified.

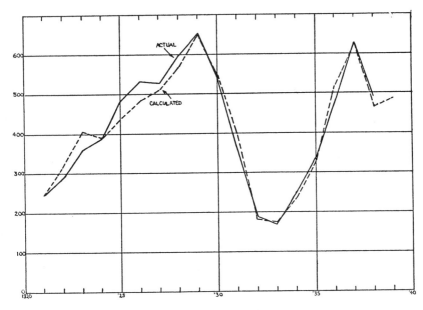

FIGURE 3.—Utility equipment (deflated).

For example, in 1922 the rate of increase of capacity increased from $4\frac{1}{2}$ per cent per year to $9\frac{1}{2}$ per cent, while the rate of increase of production declined from $19\frac{1}{2}$ per cent to 6 per cent. This apparent excess of capacity caused calculated utility equipment to decline in 1924, while the actual data show a rise. During 1923 new equipment was installed in areas where greater demand for electricity did not occur; but the excess capacity in these regions did not remove the real necessity for expansion in other parts of the country. Purchases exceeded actual equipment.

Figure 4 shows the effect of power production on manufactures of utility electrical equipment, with the influence of the other factors removed. The residuals are small, the largest being in 1931 when the utilities purchased even less than the small amount indicated by the retarded consumption.

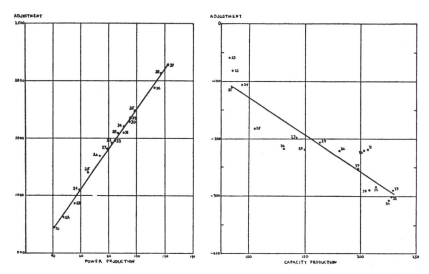

FIGURE 4.—Utility Equipment.   FIGURE 5.—Utility Equipment.

Figure 5 shows the effect of the difference between capacity and production of manufactures of utility equipment. The slope is, of course, negative, since the more unused capacity there is, the less equipment will be installed, other things being equal.

The time trend, Figure 6, is significant. Its downward slope represents (1) the increasing efficiency of generating apparatus, (2) more interconnections of power systems, thus removing the necessity of

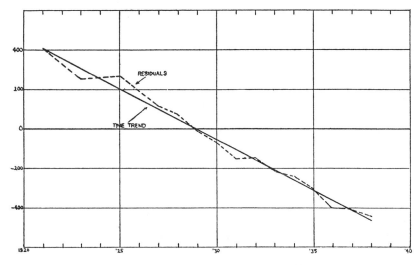

FIGURE 6.—Utility Equipment and Time.

maintaining so much excess capacity, (3) the trend of the country as a whole toward a higher load factor.[33]

Because central-station equipment is extremely durable, replacement requirements, as a demand factor, have not been treated in this study, except insofar as replacements may be measured by actual power production. Depreciation from use is negligible; practically all replacements are made for reasons of obsolescence. Hence, since replacement purchases may be deferred for long periods, demand can be greatly affected by money-market conditions and the relationship between the utilities and the government.

SUMMARY

Disposable income, that is, income less direct personal taxes, is spent within the market economy and it, rather than income, is the purchasing power with which we should be concerned in demand studies. Subsistence living costs are the first subtraction from this stream of disposable income; these are minimum expenditures for food, clothing and shelter, fuel and light. They may be taken as $200 per capita with living costs as of 1923 = 100 and varying above and below $200 per capita with cost of living. The balance has been called supernumerary income and may be regarded as the amount available for expenditures for goods above the necessity class and for savings.

Demand for goods may be considered as the flow of goods through the goods market countering consumers' expenditures, capital-goods expenditures, and sometimes government expenditures. By relating demand to expenditures of disposable income, it is possible to link up the various parts of the economy into a complete flow circuit and form an integrated picture of its functioning. For example, automobile purchases are effects of income, i.e., automobile purchases cause consumer income only by progressing around the circuit and starting automobile production, which in turn brings about activities in the steel and coal industries, textile industries, and in transportation. Therefore, a satisfactory explanation of passenger-car demand can be based upon (1) consumers' disposable income, (2) cost of living, (3) consumers' stocks of cars in operation or usable, (4) replacement pressure (a quantity derived from the age distribution of the car stock), and (5) the price of automobiles.

The following factors explain residential-building demand: (1) building need (a function of the number of consumers, existing buildings, and families), (2) disposable income, (3) net rents (a function of gross rents, occupancy, and real-estate taxes), (4) foreclosures, and (5) building costs.

[33] The seasonal peaks are steadily diminishing.

An important point of departure in each study from the usual demand study for a perishable good is the introduction of such factors as consumers' stocks and replacement pressure or foreclosures, which are neither prices nor present production.

The demand for capital goods can be expressed as a function of consumer-goods new orders and the spread or divergence between productive capacity and an index of production such as the Federal Reserve Board index. The shortage of capacity relative to incoming orders is a characteristic feature of the boom stage of the cycle; it leads business men to place excessive orders for capital goods. After the boom, liquidation of the consumer-goods inventory takes place as orders for consumer goods decrease. Meanwhile the new capacity has come into production and business men find it excessive in relation to the shrinking demand for consumer goods.

A fairly satisfactory explanation of the business or capital-goods cycle can be obtained if the interest rate is ignored. This is not a denial that rates at which money is actually offered and terms of lending play a part in determining the volume of economic activity. Published interest rates are probably not representative of the scales of offers of and demand for money that relate to capital-goods financing. The exclusion of interest rates on loans shows only that the current yields on seasoned bonds are not closely related to capital-goods activity.

Institute of Applied Econometrics

Econometrica, Vol. 11, 3-4 (July-October 1943)

ON THE STATISTICAL TREATMENT OF LINEAR STOCHASTIC DIFFERENCE EQUATIONS

By H. B. Mann and A. Wald

INTRODUCTION

THE VALUES OF a great many variables important in the study of economics depend on the values previously assumed by these variables. For example present prices of a certain set of commodities may depend on the prices of these commodities in previous time periods, etc.

Such a relationship is usually described by a set of stochastic difference equations. Thus if $x_{1t}, \cdots, x_{rt}$ are the values of the variables $x_1, \cdots, x_r$ at the time t we should have equations of the following type:

$$\phi_i(x_{1t}, \cdots, x_{rt}, x_{1,t-1}, \cdots, x_{r,t-1}, \cdots, x_{1,t-p}, \cdots, x_{r,t-p},$$

$$\epsilon_{1t}, \cdots, \epsilon_{rt}) = 0 \qquad (i = 1, 2 \cdots, r),$$

where $\epsilon_{1t}, \cdots, \epsilon_{rt}$ are random variables representing the effect of errors and disturbing factors. In practice mostly linear functions ϕ_i are considered.

In the case $r = 1$ we have a single equation of the form

(1) $$x_t + \alpha_1 x_{t-1} + \cdots + \alpha_p x_{t-p} + \alpha_0 = \epsilon_t.$$

The ϵ_t's are usually assumed to be independently distributed random variables with mean 0 and to have the same distribution for each value of t.

Ordinarily some or all of the coefficients $\alpha_1, \cdots, \alpha_p, \alpha_0$ in equation (1) are unknown. Also the distribution of ϵ_t will usually involve a finite number of unknown parameters. Thus we have to deal with the following statistical problem: On the basis of the observed values of x_t for a finite number of time points t we want to set up statistical estimates for the unknown α's and for some of the unknown parameters of the distribution of ϵ_t. In addition to the problem of estimation we may also have the problem of predicting future values of x_t on the basis of previously observed values. The problems of estimation and prediction are closely connected. In fact, if a_i are functions of the observations which are used as statistical estimates of α_i and if the distributions of a_i and ϵ_t are known, then the future values $x_{t+1}, x_{t+2}, \cdots, x_{t+j}$ may be predicted on the basis of equation (1) by substituting a_i for α_i and zero for ϵ_t. The distribution of these predicted values can be derived from the distribution of the a_i and ϵ_t. Hence the fundamental problem is to derive estimates of the α_i and then to study the joint distribution of these estimates.

In estimating the values of unknown parameters the method of maximum likelihood is widely used and has been shown to have certain optimum properties at least in the case when the observations are independent of each other. This method consists of the following procedure: Let $f(x, \theta_1, \cdots, \theta_p)$ be the elementary probability law of the random variable x. Assume that a sample of N independent observations $x_1, x_2, \cdots, x_N$ is drawn. Then the joint elementary probability law of $x_1, x_2, \cdots, x_N$ is given by $f(x_1, \theta_1, \cdots, \theta_p)f(x_2, \theta_1, \cdots, \theta_p) \cdots f(x_N, \theta_1, \cdots, \theta_p) = F(x_1, x_2, \cdots, x_N, \theta_1, \cdots, \theta_p)$. The values $\bar{\theta}_1, \cdots, \bar{\theta}_p$ of the parameters $\theta_1, \cdots, \theta_p$ for which F is maximized are called the maximum-likelihood estimates of $\theta_1, \cdots, \theta_p$. J. L. Doob [1][1] proved that under certain restrictive conditions on the elementary probability law $f(x, \theta_1, \cdots, \theta_p)$ the maximum-likelihood estimate is consistent and its limit distribution normal.

However, in the case of a linear stochastic difference equation we cannot use these results of the general theory of the maximum-likelihood estimate, since the observations are not independent of each other. Nevertheless, by formally applying the maximum-likelihood method we shall obtain certain functions of the observations which will be shown to be consistent estimates of the α's. We shall also show that these estimates are in the limit normally distributed.

The authors believe that the maximum-likelihood estimates of the α's have the same optimum properties that they are known to possess in the case of independent observations. However, no rigorous proof of this statement has as yet been given.

In the case of a single equation we shall be led, as we shall see later, to the ordinary least-squares procedure. However, the least-squares procedure is not generally applicable to the case of a system of equations with several variables; it may lead to inconsistent estimates. T. Haavelmo [2] pointed out this fact in his extensive discussion of the statistical problems connected with systems of stochastic difference equations. The problem of the exact distribution of the maximum-likelihood estimate of the coefficient of a single linear stochastic difference equation with $p=1$ under the assumption that the population value of this coefficient is zero has been treated by R. L. Anderson [3], T. Koopmans [4], and others. It appears from T. Koopmans' paper that this distribution is difficult to derive and cumbersome to handle.

[1] Numbers in brackets refer to references listed at end of this article.

In this paper we deal with the general problem of estimating the coefficients of linear stochastic difference equations but confine ourselves to the distribution of the maximum-likelihood estimates obtained from large samples. It is shown that the maximum-likelihood estimates are consistent and their limit distributions normal.

We shall give now some definitions and notations which will be used throughout this paper.

For any statement A we shall denote by $P(A)$ the probability that A is true.

Let $\{x_N\}$ be a sequence of random variables. We shall write $\mathrm{plim}_{N\to\infty}\, x_N = a$ to mean that the probability limit of x_N equals a, i.e., that $\lim_{N\to\infty} P(|x_N - a| \leqq \epsilon) = 1$ for every positive ϵ.

Let $t_N(x_1, \cdots, x_N)$ be an estimate of the parameter θ computed from N observations $x_1, \cdots, x_N$. We call t_N a consistent estimate of θ if $\mathrm{plim}_{N\to\infty}\, t_N = \theta$.

For any random variable x the symbol $E(x)$ will denote the expected value of x, and $\sigma(x)$ the standard deviation of x.

PART I

THE CASE OF A SINGLE EQUATION

1. Assumptions Underlying the Statistical Analysis

Let x_t be a variable depending on t where t can take only integral values.

Assumption I. x_t satisfies the equation

$$(1') \qquad x_t = \alpha_1 x_{t-1} + \alpha_2 x_{t-2} + \cdots + \alpha_p x_{t-p} + \alpha_0 + \epsilon_t,$$

where the α's are known or unknown constants, the random variables $\epsilon_1, \epsilon_2, \cdots$, ad inf. are independently distributed, each having the same distribution, and $E(\epsilon_t) = 0$.

Assumption II. All roots of the equation in ρ

$$(2) \qquad \rho^p - \alpha_1 \rho^{p-1} \cdots - \alpha_p = 0$$

are <1 in absolute value.

Since by assumption 1 is not a root of (2), we must have

$$(3) \qquad 1 - \alpha_1 - \cdots - \alpha_p \neq 0.$$

Assumption II implies, as we shall show, that $\lim_{t\to\infty} E(x_t)$ and $\lim_{t\to\infty} E(x_t^2)$ exist and are finite. On the other hand if $\lim_{t\to\infty} E(x_t)$ and $\lim_{t\to\infty} E(x_t^2)$ exist, then the roots of equation (2) are smaller than 1 in absolute value.

Assumption III. All moments of the ϵ_t exist and are finite.

2. The Maximum-Likelihood Estimates of the α's

If the variables ϵ_t are normally distributed with mean 0 and variance σ^2 then the joint probability distribution of $\epsilon_1, \cdots, \epsilon_N$ is given by

$$\frac{1}{(2\pi)^{N/2}\sigma^N} \exp\left(-\frac{1}{2\sigma^2}\sum_{t=1}^{N}\epsilon_t^2\right) d\epsilon_1 \cdots d\epsilon_N$$

$$(4) \quad = \frac{1}{(2\pi)^{N/2}\sigma^N}$$

$$\cdot \exp\left(-\frac{1}{2\sigma^2}\sum_{t=1}^{N}(x_t-\alpha_1 x_{t-1}-\cdots-\alpha_p x_{t-p}-\alpha_0)^2\right) d\epsilon_1 \cdots d\epsilon_N.$$

We have $dx_t/d\epsilon_t=1$, $dx_{t-i}/d\epsilon_t=0$ for $i>0$. Hence it follows from (4) that the joint probability density of $x_1, \cdots, x_N$ is given by

$$(4') \quad \frac{1}{(2\pi)^{N/2}\sigma^N} \exp\left[-\frac{1}{2\sigma^2}\sum_{t=1}^{N}(x_t-\alpha_1 x_{t-1}-\cdots\right.$$

$$\left.- \alpha_p x_{t-p}-\alpha_0)^2\right] dx_1 \cdots dx_N.$$

To obtain the maximum-likelihood estimates of $\alpha_1, \cdots, \alpha_p, \alpha_0, \sigma^2$ we have to maximize (4') or its logarithm with respect to $\alpha_1, \cdots, \alpha_p, \alpha_0, \sigma^2$. This leads to the following equations:

$$\sum_{t=1}^{N} x_t x_{t-j} - \sum_{i=1}^{p} a_i \sum_{t=1}^{N} x_{t-i}x_{t-j} - a_0 \sum_{t=1}^{N} x_{t-j} = 0 \quad (j=1,\cdots,p),$$

$$(5) \quad \sum_{t=1}^{N} x_t - \sum_{i=1}^{p} a_i \sum_{t=1}^{N} x_{t-i} - Na_0 = 0,$$

$$s^2 = \frac{1}{N}\sum_{t=1}^{N}(x_t - a_1 x_{t-1} - \cdots - a_p x_{t-p} - a_0)^2,$$

where $a_1, \cdots, a_p, a_0, s^2$ are the maximum-likelihood estimates of $\alpha_1, \cdots, \alpha_p, \alpha_0, \sigma^2$ respectively.[2]

In deriving the large-sample distributions of these maximum-likelihood estimates we shall not assume normality of the distribution of ϵ_t. If the quantities $x_1, \cdots, x_N$ were independently distributed, then it would follow from known results that our estimates of the $\alpha_i, \alpha_0, \sigma^2$ are consistent. Since $x_1, \cdots, x_N$ are obviously not independ-

[2] We shall refer to the solutions of (5) as maximum-likelihood estimates also in the case when the ϵ_t are not normally distributed. The phrase maximum-likelihood estimate is then to be considered only as an abbreviation and the reader should not be misled by it into thinking that we assume a normal distribution of the ϵ_t.

ent, we have to prove this property of our estimates. We shall prove even more. We shall prove that $\sqrt{N}(a_i - \alpha_i)$, $(i = 0, 1, \cdots, p)$, are in the limit normally distributed with 0 mean and finite covariance matrix. The essential point in this proof is the fact that under our assumptions the stochastic limits $\text{plim}_{N \to \infty} \sum_{t=1}^{N} x_{t-i} x_{t-j}/N$ and $\text{plim}_{N \to \infty} \sum_{t=1}^{N} x_{t-i}/N$ exist and are finite. We shall prove this point in the next section.

3. *Proof of the Existence of* $\text{plim}_{N \to \infty} \sum_{t=1}^{N} x_{t-i} x_{t-j}/N$ *and* $\text{plim}_{N \to \infty} \sum_{t=1}^{N} x_{t-i}/N$

From (1) it follows that x_t is a linear function of $\epsilon_\tau (\tau = 1, \cdots, t)$. Hence we may write

(6) $$x_t = \phi_0(t) + \phi_1(t)\epsilon_1 + \cdots + \phi_t(t)\epsilon_t.$$

But then we have from (1)

$$\phi_0(t) + \phi_1(t)\epsilon_1 + \cdots + \phi_t(t)\epsilon_t$$
$$= \alpha_0 + \alpha_1[\phi_0(t-1) + \phi_1(t-1)\epsilon_1 + \cdots + \phi_{t-1}(t-1)\epsilon_{t-1}]$$
$$+ \alpha_2[\phi_0(t-2) + \cdots + \phi_{t-2}(t-2)\epsilon_{t-2}]$$
$$+ \alpha_p[\phi_0(t-p) + \cdots + \phi_{t-p}(t-p)\epsilon_{t-p}]$$
$$+ \epsilon_t.$$

This is an identity in $\epsilon_\tau(\tau = 1, \cdots, t)$ and therefore we must have

$$\phi_0(t) = \alpha_0 + \alpha_1\phi_0(t-1) + \cdots + \alpha_p\phi_0(t-p),$$
$$\phi_\tau(t) = \alpha_1\phi_\tau(t-1) + \cdots + \alpha_p\phi_\tau(t-p) \quad (\tau = 1, \cdots, t-p),$$
$$\phi_\tau(t) = \alpha_1\phi_\tau(t-1) + \cdots + \alpha_i\phi_\tau(t-i)$$
$$(\tau = t - i; i = 1, \cdots, p-1),$$
$$\phi_t(t) = 1,$$
$$\phi_t(t-h) = 0 \qquad\qquad\qquad (h > 0).$$

This gives a system of difference equations for $\phi_\tau(t)$ and $\phi_0(t)$:

$$\phi_0(t) = \alpha_0 + \alpha_1\phi_0(t-1) + \cdots + \alpha_p\phi_0(t-p) \qquad (t > 0),$$
$$\phi_\tau(t) = \alpha_1\phi_\tau(t-1) + \cdots + \alpha_p\phi_\tau(t-p) \qquad (t > \tau > 0),$$

satisfying the initial conditions

(7)
$$\phi_\tau(\tau) = 1, \quad \phi_\tau(\tau-1) = 0, \cdots, \phi_\tau(\tau-p+1) = 0,$$
$$\phi_0(0) = x_0, \quad \phi_0(-1) = x_{-1}, \cdots, \phi_0(-p+1) = x_{-p+1}.$$

Solving first the homogeneous difference equations we obtain

(8) $$\phi_\tau(t) = P_{1\tau}(t)\rho_1{}^t + \cdots + P_{l\tau}(t)\rho_l{}^t \qquad (\tau > 0),$$

where $\rho_1, \cdots, \rho_l$ are the roots of the equation

$$\rho^p = \alpha_1 \rho^{p-1} + \cdots + \alpha_{p-1}\rho + \alpha_p$$

and $P_{ir}(t)$ is a polynomial in t whose degree is one less than the multiplicity of the root ρ_i. Since according to (3) $1 - \alpha_1 - \cdots - \alpha_p \neq 0$, the solution of the nonhomogeneous equation is given by

$$(9) \qquad \phi_0(t) = P_1(t)\rho_1{}^t + \cdots + P_l(t)\rho_l{}^t + c,$$

where

$$c = \alpha/(1 - \alpha_1 - \cdots - \alpha_p).$$

The expressions $P_{1r}(t), \cdots, P_{lr}(t)$ can easily be determined from the initial conditions (7). In fact we have the following initial conditions:

$$1 = \sum_{i=1}^{l} P_{ir}(\tau)\rho_i{}^\tau,$$

$$0 = \sum_{i=1}^{l} P_{ir}(\tau - j)\rho_i{}^{\tau-j} \quad (j = 1, \cdots, p-1; \tau = 1, 2, \cdots, \text{ad inf.}).$$

It is known that the polynomials $P_{ir}(t)$ are uniquely determined by the initial conditions and by the condition that the degree of $P_{ir}(t)$ is one less than the multiplicity of the root ρ_i. Let

$$P_{ir}^*(t) = P_{i1}(t - \tau + 1)/\rho_i{}^{\tau-1} \qquad (\tau = 2, 3, \cdots).$$

Obviously the degree of $P_{ir}^*(t)$ is the same as that of $P_{i1}(t)$ and consequently is one less than the multiplicity of the root ρ_i. By substituting $P_{ir}^*(t)$ for $P_{ir}(t)$ in the initial conditions, it can easily be verified that the initial conditions are satisfied. Since the initial conditions determine uniquely the polynomials $P_{ir}(t)$ we must have

$$P_{ir}(t) = P_{ir}^*(t) = P_{i1}(t - \tau + 1)/\rho_i{}^{\tau-1} \qquad (\tau = 2, 3, \cdots).$$

For the sake of simplicity we shall carry our proofs out only for the case when all roots are different. The proof in the more general case is completely analogous.

We then have

$$(10) \qquad \phi_0(t) = \sum_{i=1}^{p} \mu_i \rho_i{}^t + c,$$

$$(11) \qquad \phi_\tau(t) = \sum_{i=1}^{p} \lambda_i \rho_i{}^{t-\tau+1},$$

where μ_i, λ_i are constants.

Let δ_{ij} denote the Kronecker δ; i.e., $\delta_{ij}=0$ if $i \neq j$ and $\delta_{ij}=1$ if $i=j$. Since the covariance $\sigma_{\epsilon_\tau \epsilon_{\tau'}}$ is equal to $\delta_{\tau\tau'}\, \sigma^2$ where σ^2 is the variance of ϵ_τ we obtain from (6), (10), and (11)

$$E\left(\sum_{t=1}^{N} x_t x_{t-i}/N\right) = \frac{\sigma^2}{N} \sum_{t=1}^{N} \sum_{\tau=1}^{t} \phi_\tau(t)\phi_\tau(t-i)$$

$$+ \frac{1}{N} \sum_{t=1}^{N} \phi_0(t)\phi_0(t-i)$$

$$(12) \qquad = \frac{\sigma^2}{N} \sum_{t=1}^{N} \sum_{\tau=1}^{t-i} \sum_{\alpha=1}^{p} \sum_{\beta=1}^{p} \lambda_\alpha \lambda_\beta \rho_\alpha{}^{t-\tau+1} \rho_\beta{}^{t-\tau-i+1}$$

$$+ \frac{1}{N} \sum_{t=1}^{N} \sum_{\alpha=1}^{p} \sum_{\beta=1}^{p} \mu_\alpha \mu_\beta \rho_\alpha{}^{t} \rho_\beta{}^{t-i}$$

$$+ \frac{c}{N}\left(\sum_{t=1}^{N} \sum_{\alpha=1}^{p} \mu_\alpha \rho_\alpha{}^{t} + \sum_{t=1}^{N} \sum_{\alpha=1}^{p} \mu_\alpha \rho_\alpha{}^{t-i}\right)$$

$$+ c^2.$$

Since $|\rho_\alpha| < 1$ $(\alpha = 1, \cdots, p)$ we certainly have

$$(13) \qquad \lim_{N\to\infty} \frac{c}{N}\left[\sum_{t=1}^{N} \sum_{\alpha=1}^{p} (\mu_\alpha \rho_\alpha{}^{t} + \mu_\alpha \rho_\alpha{}^{t-i})\right] = 0,$$

$$\lim_{N\to\infty} \frac{1}{N} \sum_{t=1}^{N} \sum_{\alpha=1}^{p} \sum_{\beta=1}^{p} \mu_\alpha \mu_\beta \rho_\alpha{}^{t} \rho_\beta{}^{t-i} = 0.$$

Furthermore it is clear that

$$(14) \qquad \lim_{t\to\infty} \sum_{\tau=1}^{t-i} \lambda_\alpha \lambda_\beta \rho_\alpha{}^{t-\tau+1} \rho_\beta{}^{t-\tau-i+1} = \lambda_\alpha \lambda_\beta \rho_\alpha \rho_\beta{}^{-i+1} \sum_{m=i}^{\infty} (\rho_\alpha \rho_\beta)^m$$

$$= \lambda_\alpha \lambda_\beta \rho_\alpha{}^{i+1} \rho_\beta / (1 - \rho_\alpha \rho_\beta).$$

From (14) it follows that

$$(15) \qquad \lim_{N\to\infty} \frac{\sigma^2}{N} \sum_{t=1}^{N} \sum_{\tau=1}^{t-i} \sum_{\alpha=1}^{p} \sum_{\beta=1}^{p} \lambda_\alpha \lambda_\beta \rho_\alpha{}^{t-\tau+1} \rho_\beta{}^{t-\tau-i+1}$$

$$= \sigma^2 \sum_{\alpha=1}^{p} \sum_{\beta=1}^{p} \lambda_\alpha \lambda_\beta \rho_\alpha{}^{i+1} \rho_\beta / (1 - \rho_\alpha \rho_\beta).$$

From (12), (13), and (15) we obtain

$$(16) \qquad \lim_{N\to\infty} \sum_{t=1}^{N} x_t x_{t-i}/N = \sigma^2 \sum_{\alpha=1}^{p} \sum_{\beta=1}^{p} \lambda_\alpha \lambda_\beta \rho_\alpha{}^{i+1} \rho_\beta / (1 - \rho_\alpha \rho_\beta) + c^2.$$

In a similar way it can be shown that

$$(16') \qquad \lim_{t\to\infty} E(x_t x_{t-i}) = \sigma^2 \sum_{\alpha=1}^{p} \sum_{\beta=1}^{p} \lambda_\alpha \lambda_\beta \rho_\alpha{}^{i+1} \rho_\beta / (1 - \rho_\alpha \rho_\beta) + c^2.$$

Now we shall show that the variance of $\sum_{t=1}^{N} x_t x_{t-i}/N$ is of order $1/N$. We have

(17)
$$\sum_{t=1}^{N} x_t x_{t-i} = \sum_{t=1}^{N} [x_t - \phi_0(t)][x_{t-i} - \phi_0(t-i)]$$
$$+ \sum_{t=1}^{N} x_t \phi_0(t-i) + \sum_{t=1}^{N} \phi_0(t) x_{t-i}$$
$$- \sum_{t=1}^{N} \phi_0(t) \phi_0(t-i).$$

We shall first show that the variance of $\sum_{t=1}^{N} [x_t - \phi_0(t)][x_{t-1} - \phi_0(t-i)]/N$ is of order $1/N$.

From (6) it follows that

$$E\left[\sum_{t=1}^{N} [x_t - \phi_0(t)][x_{t-i} - \phi_0(t-i)] \right]^2 / N^2$$

$$= \frac{1}{N^2} E\left[\sum_{t=1}^{N} \sum_{\tau=1}^{t} \sum_{\tau'=1}^{t-i} \phi_\tau(t) \phi_{\tau'}(t-i) \epsilon_\tau \epsilon_{\tau'} \right]^2$$

$$= \frac{1}{N^2} \sum_{t=1}^{N} \sum_{\tau=1}^{t} \sum_{\tau'=1}^{t-i} \sum_{t'=1}^{N} \sum_{\tau''=1}^{t'} \sum_{\tau'''=1}^{t'-i} \phi_\tau(t) \phi_{\tau'}(t-i) \phi_{\tau''}(t') \phi_{\tau'''}(t'-i)$$
$$\cdot E(\epsilon_\tau \epsilon_{\tau'} \epsilon_{\tau''} \epsilon_{\tau'''}).$$

But $E(\epsilon_\tau \epsilon_{\tau'} \epsilon_{\tau''} \epsilon_{\tau'''})$ is different from 0 only if either $\tau = \tau'$ and $\tau'' = \tau'''$ or $\tau = \tau''$ and $\tau' = \tau'''$, or $\tau = \tau'''$ and $\tau' = \tau''$. Moreover $E(\epsilon_\tau \epsilon_{\tau'} \epsilon_{\tau''} \epsilon_{\tau'''})$ is equal to the fourth moment μ_4 of ϵ_t if $\tau = \tau' = \tau'' = \tau'''$ and is equal to σ^4 or 0 if two of the ϵ's are different. Hence we obtain

$$E\left\{ \sum_{t=1}^{N} [x_t - \phi_0(t)][x_{t-i} - \phi_0(t-i)]/N \right\}^2$$

$$= \frac{1}{N^2}\left[\sigma^4 \sum_{t=1}^{N} \sum_{\tau=1}^{t-i} \sum_{t'=1}^{N} \sum_{\tau'=1}^{t'-i} \phi_\tau(t) \phi_\tau(t-i) \phi_{\tau'}(t') \phi_{\tau'}(t'-i) \right.$$

$$+ \sigma^4 \sum_{t=1}^{N} \sum_{t'=1}^{N} \sum_{\tau=1}^{\min(t,t')} \sum_{\tau'=1}^{\min(t,t'-i)} \phi_\tau(t) \phi_{\tau'}(t-i) \phi_\tau(t') \phi_{\tau'}(t'-i)$$

$$+ \sigma^4 \sum_{t=1}^{N} \sum_{t'=1}^{N} \sum_{\tau=1}^{\min(t,t'-i)} \sum_{\tau'=1}^{\min(t-i,t')} \phi_\tau(t) \phi_{\tau'}(t-i) \phi_{\tau'}(t') \phi_\tau(t'-i)$$

$$\left. + (\mu_4 - 3\sigma^4) \sum_{t=1}^{N} \sum_{t'=1}^{N} \sum_{\tau=1}^{\min(t-i,t'-i)} \phi_\tau(t) \phi_\tau(t-i) \phi_\tau(t') \phi_\tau(t'-i) \right].$$

Since

$$\left[E\left\{ \sum_{t=1}^{N} [x_t - \phi_0(t)][x_{t-i} - \phi_0(t-i)/N] \right\} \right]^2$$

$$= \frac{\sigma^4}{N^2} \sum_{t=1}^{N} \sum_{t'=1}^{N} \sum_{\tau=1}^{t-i} \sum_{\tau'=1}^{t'-i} \phi_\tau(t)\phi_\tau(t-i)\phi_{\tau'}(t')\phi_{\tau'}(t'-i),$$

we have

$$\sigma^2 \left\{ \sum_{t=1}^{N} [x_t - \phi_0(t)][x_{t-i} - \phi_0(t-i)]/N \right\}$$

(18)

$$= \frac{1}{N^2} [(\mu_4 - 3\sigma^4)d + \sigma^4(b+c)],$$

where

$$(19) \quad d = \sum_{t=1}^{N} \sum_{t'=1}^{N} \sum_{\tau=1}^{\min\,(t-i,\,t'-i)} \phi_\tau(t)\phi_\tau(t-i)\phi_\tau(t')\phi_\tau(t'-i),$$

$$(20) \quad b = \sum_{t=1}^{N} \sum_{t'=1}^{N} \sum_{\tau=1}^{\min\,(t,\,t')} \sum_{\tau'=1}^{\min\,(t,\,t'-i)} \phi_\tau(t)\phi_{\tau'}(t-i)\phi_\tau(t')\phi_{\tau'}(t'-i),$$

$$(21) \quad c = \sum_{t=1}^{N} \sum_{\tau'=1}^{N} \sum_{\tau=1}^{\min\,(t,\,t'-i)} \sum_{\tau'=1}^{\min\,(t',\,t-i)} \phi_\tau(t)\phi_{\tau'}(t-i)\phi_{\tau'}(t')\phi_\tau(t'-i).$$

We have

$$|\phi_\tau(t)| = \left| \sum_{\alpha=1}^{p} \lambda_\alpha \rho_\alpha^{t-\tau+1} \right| \leq M\rho^{t-\tau+1}$$

where

$$M = \sum_{\alpha=1}^{p} |\lambda_\alpha|, \quad \rho = \max |\rho_\alpha|.$$

Hence

$$|d|,\,|b|,\,|c| \leq \sum_{t=1}^{N} \sum_{t'=1}^{N} \sum_{\tau=1}^{\min\,(t,\,t')} \sum_{\tau'=1}^{\min\,(t,\,t')} \rho^{-2i} M^4 \rho^{t+t'-2\tau+2} \rho^{t+t'-2\tau'+2}$$

$$\leq \sum_{t=1}^{N} \sum_{t'=1}^{N} \frac{\rho^{-2i}}{(1-\rho^2)^2} M^4 (\rho^2)^{t-\min\,(t,\,t')} (\rho^2)^{t'-\min\,(t,\,t')}$$

$$\leq M' \sum_{t=1}^{N} \left[\sum_{t'=1}^{t} (\rho^2)^{t-t'} + \sum_{t'=t+1}^{N} (\rho^2)^{t'-t} \right]$$

$$\leq M'N(1+\rho^2)/(1-\rho^2) \leq M''N,$$

where M'' is independent of N. Hence

$$\sigma^2 \left\{ \sum_{t=1}^{N} [x_t - \phi_0(t)][x_{t-i} - \phi_0(t-i)]/N \right\} \leq M'''N/N^2 = M'''/N,$$

where M''' is independent of N.

In analogous manner we can show that the variances of $\sum_{t=1}^{N} x_t \phi_0(t-i)/N$, $\sum_{t=1}^{N} \phi_0(t) x_{t-i}/N$ are of the order $1/N$. Hence from (17) we see that also the variance of $\sum_{t=1}^{N} x_t x_{t-i}/N$ is of the order $1/N$.

Since we have shown that $\lim E[\sum_{t=1}^{N} x_{t-i} x_{t-j}/N]$ exists and that the variance of $\sum_{t=1}^{N} x_{t-i} x_{t-j}/N$ is of order $1/N$, it follows from Tchebycheff's inequality that

$$P(|\textstyle\sum_{t=1}^{N} x_{t-i} x_{t-j}/N - E\sum_{t=1}^{N} x_{t-i} x_{t-j}/N| > \epsilon) \leqq M'''/\epsilon^2 N.$$

Hence if we put $\lim E[\sum_{t=1}^{N} x_{t-j} x_{t-j}/N] = D_{ij}$, we must have

$$\operatorname*{plim}_{N\to\infty} \sum_{t=1}^{N} x_{t-i} x_{t-j}/N = D_{ij}.$$

Now we shall prove that

$$(22) \qquad \operatorname*{plim}_{N\to\infty} \sum_{t=1}^{N} x_t/N = \lim_{N\to\infty} E\left(\sum_{t=1}^{N} x_t/N \right) = \lim_{t\to\infty} E(x_t) = c.$$

Since

$$x_t = \phi_0(t) + \phi_1(t)\epsilon_1 + \cdots + \phi_t(t)\epsilon_t$$

we have that

$$\lim_{t\to\infty} E(x_t) = \lim_{t\to\infty} \phi_0(t) = c.$$

Furthermore we see that

$$\lim_{N\to\infty} E\left(\sum_{t=1}^{N} x_t/N \right) = \lim_{N\to\infty} \sum_{t=1}^{N} \phi_0(t)/N = c.$$

Hence in order to prove (22) we have merely to show that $\sigma^2(\sum x_t/N)$ is of order $1/N$. In fact we have

$$\sum_{t=1}^{N} x_t/N = \sum_{t=1}^{N} \phi_0(t)/N + \sum_{t=1}^{N} [\phi_1(t)/N]\epsilon_1 + \cdots + \sum_{t=1}^{N} [\phi_t(t)/N]\epsilon_t.$$

Hence

$$\sigma^2\left(\sum_{t=1}^{N} x_t/N \right) = \frac{\sigma^2}{N^2}\left\{\left[\sum_{t=1}^{N} \phi_1(t) \right]^2 + \cdots + \left[\sum_{t=1}^{N} \phi_t(t) \right]^2\right\}.$$

We have proved that

$$|\phi_\tau(t)| \leqq M\rho^{t-\tau+1}$$

where M is a fixed positive constant. Hence $\sum_{t=1}^{N} \phi_\tau(t)$ is a bounded function of τ and N. From this it follows that $\sigma^2(\sum_{t=1}^{N} x_t/N)$ is of order $1/N$. Hence (22) is proved.

4. Proof of the Consistency of the Maximum-likelihood Estimates a_i, a_0, s^2

We put

$$y_i = \frac{1}{\sqrt{N}} \sum_{t=1}^{N} (x_t - \alpha_1 x_{t-1} - \cdots - \alpha_p x_{t-p} - \alpha_0) x_{t-i},$$

$$y_0 = \frac{1}{\sqrt{N}} \sum_{t=1}^{N} (x_t - \alpha_1 x_{t-1} - \cdots - \alpha_p x_{t-p} - \alpha_0).$$

Then because of (5) we have

$$(23) \quad y_i = \sum_{j=1}^{p} \sqrt{N} (a_j - \alpha_j) \sum_{t=1}^{N} x_{t-i} x_{t-j}/N + \sqrt{N} (a_0 - \alpha_0) \sum_{t=1}^{N} x_{t-i}/N$$

$$(i = 1, \cdots, p),$$

$$y_0 = \sum_{j=1}^{p} \sqrt{N} (a_j - \alpha_j) \sum_{t=1}^{N} x_{t-j}/N + \sqrt{N} (a_0 - \alpha_0).$$

But

$$(24) \quad \begin{aligned} y_i &= \frac{1}{\sqrt{N}} \sum_{t=1}^{N} \epsilon_t x_{t-i}, \\[2mm] y_0 &= \frac{1}{\sqrt{N}} \sum_{t=1}^{N} \epsilon_t. \end{aligned}$$

Since ϵ_r is independent of x_{t-i} we can easily show that

$$(25) \quad \begin{aligned} E(y_i) &= 0 & (i = 0, 1, \cdots, p), \\[2mm] E(y_i y_j) &= \sigma^2 E\left(\sum_{t=1}^{N} x_{t-i} x_{t-j}/N \right) & (i, j = 1, \cdots, p), \\[2mm] E(y_i y_0) &= \sigma^2 E\left(\sum_{t=1}^{N} x_{t-i}/N \right) & (i = 1, \cdots, p), \\[2mm] E(y_0^2) &= \sigma^2. \end{aligned}$$

We put $\sum_{t=1}^{N} x_{t-i} x_{t-j}/N = D_{ijN}$, $\sum_{t=1}^{N} x_{t-i}/N = D_{i0N} = D_{0iN}$. Let furthermore $D_{00N} = 1$. Then equations (23) can be written

$$(26) \quad y_i = \sum_{j=0}^{p} \sqrt{N} (a_j - \alpha_j) D_{ijN} \qquad (i = 0, 1, \cdots, p).$$

Denoting the constant c by $D_{0i} = D_{i0}$ $(i = 1, \cdots, p)$ and putting D_{00} equal to 1, we have

$$(27) \quad \operatorname*{plim}_{N \to \infty} D_{ijN} = D_{ij} \qquad (i, j = 0, 1, \cdots, p).$$

Now we shall show that the determinant value D of the matrix $\|D_{ij}\|(i, j=0, 1, \cdots, p)$ is different from 0. Consider the expected value

(28) $$E[(b_1 x_{t-1} + \cdots + b_p x_{t-p} + b_0)^2],$$

where $b_1, \cdots, b_p, b_0$ are arbitrary real values subject to the restriction $\sum_{i=0}^{p} b_i^2 \neq 0$. Since for any t' the conditional variance of $x_{t'}$, given $x_{t'-1}, \cdots, x_{t'-p}$, is equal to $\sigma^2 > 0$, we see that the expected value (28), as well as the limit value of (28) when $t \to \infty$, must be positive for arbitrary values $b_0, \cdots, b_p$ subject to the restriction $\sum_{i=0}^{p} b_i^2 \neq 0$. But this is possible only if the matrix $\|D_{ij}\|(i, j, = 0, 1, \cdots, p)$ is positive definite. Hence we have proved that $D > 0$.

From (25) we see that $E(y_i) = 0$ and that the covariance matrix of the random variables $y_0, y_1 \cdots, y_p$ is a bounded function of N. Hence from (26), (27), and the fact that $D > 0$ it follows easily that $\lim E\sqrt{N}(a_j - \alpha_j) = 0$, $(j = 0, 1, \cdots, p)$ and that the covariance matrix of the variates $\sqrt{N}(a_0 - \alpha_0)$, $\sqrt{N}(a_1 - \alpha_1)$, $\cdots$, $\sqrt{N}(a_p - \alpha_p)$ is a bounded function of N. Thus we must have

$$\text{plim } a_j = \alpha_j \qquad\qquad (j = 0, 1, \cdots, p).$$

We now proceed to prove the consistency of the estimate s^2 of σ^2. We have

$$s^2 = \frac{1}{N} \sum_{t=1}^{N} (x_t - a_1 x_{t-1} - \cdots - a_p x_{t-p} - a_0)^2$$

$$= \frac{1}{N} \left(\sum_{t=1}^{N} x_t^2 - a_1 \sum_{t=1}^{N} x_t x_{t-1} - \cdots - a_p \sum_{t=1}^{N} x_t x_{t-p} - a_0 \sum_{t=1}^{N} x_t \right)$$

(29)
$$- \frac{1}{N} \sum_{i=1}^{p} a_i \left(\sum_{t=1}^{N} x_t x_{t-i} - a_1 \sum_{t=1}^{N} x_{t-1} x_{t-i} - \cdots \right.$$

$$\left. - a_p \sum_{t=1}^{N} x_{t-p} x_{t-i} - a_0 \sum_{t=1}^{N} x_{t-i} \right)$$

$$- \frac{1}{N} a_0 \left(\sum_{t=1}^{N} x_t - a_1 \sum_{t=1}^{N} x_{t-1} - \cdots - a_p \sum_{t=1}^{N} x_{t-p} - N a_0 \right).$$

Hence on account of (5) we have

(30)
$$s^2 = \sum_{t=1}^{N} x_t^2/N - a_1 \sum_{t=1}^{N} x_t x_{t-1}/N - \cdots$$

$$- a_p \sum_{t=1}^{N} x_t x_{t-p}/N - a_0 \sum_{t=1}^{N} x_t/N.$$

Since the expressions $\sum_{t=1}^{N} x_t x_{t-j}/N$ and $\sum_{t=1}^{N} x_t/N$ converge stochastically to their limit expectations and since $\mathrm{plim}_{N\to\infty} a_i = \alpha_i$, we see that the stochastic limit of the right-hand side of (30) is not changed if we replace a_i by $\alpha_i(i=0, 1, \cdots, p)$. Since the right-hand side of (30) is identically equal to

$$(31) \qquad \frac{1}{N} \sum_{t=1}^{N} (x_t - a_1 x_{t-1} - \cdots - a_p x_{t-p} - a_0)^2,$$

the stochastic limit of (31) is not changed if we replace a_i by $\alpha_i(i=0, 1, \cdots, p)$. Then from (29) it follows that

$$\mathrm{plim}_{N\to\infty} s^2 = \mathrm{plim}_{N\to\infty} \frac{1}{N} \sum_{t=1}^{N} (x_t - \alpha_1 x_{t-1} - \cdots - \alpha_p x_{t-p} - \alpha_0)^2$$

$$= \mathrm{plim}_{N\to\infty} \frac{1}{N} \sum_{t=1}^{N} \epsilon_t^2 = \sigma^2.$$

5. Large-Sample Distribution of the Maximum-Likelihood Estimates

Now we shall derive the limit distribution of the maximum-likelihood estimates $a_i(i=0, 1, \cdots, p)$. For this purpose we shall show first that the variates $y_0, y_1, \cdots, y_p$ have a joint normal distribution in the limit. For proving the latter statement we need the following lemma.

Lemma 1. Let $\{x_n\}$ *be a sequence of random variables such that* $\lim_{n\to\infty} P(x_n \leq t) = F(t)$. *Let* $\{z_n^i\}$ $(i=1, 2, \cdots,$ *ad inf.) be a sequence of sequences of random variables such that* $\lim_{n\to\infty} E(z_n^i)^2 = \epsilon_i$ *and* $\lim_{i\to\infty} \epsilon_i = 0$. *Then for every* $\delta > 0$ *there exists an integer* $\bar{\imath}$ *such that*

$$F(t - \delta) - \delta \leq \lim_{n\to\infty} P(x_n + z_n^i \leq t) \leq F(t + \delta) + \delta \qquad (i > \bar{\imath}).$$

Proof: We have

$$P(x_n + z_n^i \leq t) \geq P(x_n \leq t - \delta \ \& \ z_n^i \leq \delta) \geq P(x_n \leq t - \delta) - P(z_n^i \geq \delta)$$

and

$$P(x_n \leq t + \delta) \geq P(x_n + z_n^i \leq t \ \& \ z_n^i \geq -\delta) \geq P(x_n + z_n^i \leq t) - P(z_n^i \leq -\delta).$$

But by choosing i and n sufficiently large we can make the probabilities $P(z_n^i \geq \delta)$ and $P(z_n^i \leq -\delta)$ less than δ and obtain our lemma by letting n approach infinity.

We have by (24)

$$y_i = \sum_{t=1}^{N} \epsilon_t x_{t-i}/\sqrt{N} \quad (i = 1, \cdots, p), \qquad y_0 = \sum_{t=1}^{N} \epsilon_t/\sqrt{N}.$$

We put

$$x_t = x_t' + x_t'',$$

where

$$(32) \qquad \begin{aligned} x_t' &= \epsilon_t + \phi_{t-1}(t)\epsilon_{t-1} + \cdots + \phi_{t'+1}(t)\epsilon_{t'+1}, \\ x_t'' &= \phi_{t'}'(t)\epsilon_{t'} + \cdots + \phi_1(t)\epsilon_1, \\ t' &= t - d \end{aligned} \qquad\qquad (d > 0).$$

We have

$$(33) \qquad |\phi_i(t)| = |\lambda_1\rho_1^{t-i+1} + \cdots + \lambda_p\rho_p^{t-i+1}| \leq pM\rho^{t-i+1},$$

where $M = \max(|\lambda_1|, |\lambda_2|, \cdots, |\lambda_p|)$ and $\rho = \max(|\rho_1|, \cdots, |\rho_p|)$. Hence

$$(34) \qquad \begin{aligned} E(x_t'')^2 &= \sigma^2 \sum_{i=1}^{t-d} \phi_i^2(t) \leq p^2 M^2 \sigma^2 (\rho^{2t} + \rho^{2(t-1)} + \cdots + \rho^{2(d+1)}) \\ &\leq \frac{p^2 M^2 \sigma^2 \rho^{2(d+1)}}{1 - \rho^2}. \end{aligned}$$

We put

$$y_i = y_i' + y_i'',$$

where

$$y_i' = \sum_{t=1}^{N} x_{t-i}'\epsilon_t/\sqrt{N}, \quad y_i'' = \sum_{t=1}^{N} x_{t-i}''\epsilon_t/\sqrt{N} \quad (i = 1, \cdots, p).$$

Then

$$\sigma^2(y_i'') = \sum_{t=1}^{N} E(x_{t-i}'')^2/N\sigma^2 \leq p^2 M^2 \sigma^2 (\rho^2)^{d+1}/(1 - \rho^2).$$

By choosing d sufficiently large we can make $\sigma^2(y_i'') = E(y_i'')^2$ as small as we wish. But then, by Lemma 1, the distribution of y_i' differs arbitrarily little from the distribution of y_i. Hence if we can prove that y_i' is in the limit normally distributed for any d, then also y_i must be in the limit normally distributed.

We shall show now that y_i' is in the limit normally distributed. We put $d+i+1 = d^*$ and let n be an integer $> 2d^*$.

Suppose that $N = kn + m$ where k is a positive integer and $0 \leqq m < n$. Denote $\sum_{t=jn+1}^{(j+1)n-d^*-1} x_t'_{-i} \epsilon_t$ by b_{j+1} and $\sum_{(j+1)n-d^*}^{(j+1)n} x_t'_{-i} \epsilon_t$ by a_{j+1} $(j = 0, \cdots, k-1)$. Then we have

$$\sqrt{N}\, y_i' = \sum_{j=1}^{k} (b_j + a_j) + \sum_{kn+1}^{kn+m} x_t'_{-i}\epsilon_t.$$

Evidently for any fixed n the limit distribution of $(1/\sqrt{N}) \sum_{j=1}^{k}(b_j + a_j)$ when $N \to \infty$ is the same as the distribution of y_i. Hence we have merely to show that $(1/N)\sum_{j=1}^{k}(b_j + a_j)$ is in the limit normally distributed. It can be seen that for any value τ the variate ϵ_τ does not occur in both b_i and b_j if $i \neq j$. Hence $b_1, \cdots, b_k$ are independently distributed. Similarly we see that $a_1, \cdots, a_k$ are independent. We have

$$(35) \qquad \sigma^2(a_j) = \sigma^2 \sum_{jn-d^*}^{jn} E(x_{t-i}')^2, \qquad \sigma^2(b_j) = \sigma^2 \sum_{(j-1)n+1}^{jn-d^*-1} E(x_{t-i}')^2.$$

As we have shown $\lim E(x_{t-i})^2$ exists. Since according to (34) $E(x_{t-i})^2$ differs from $E(x'_{t-i})^2$ by an arbitrarily small quantity we have that

$$(36) \qquad \sigma^2(a_j)/\sigma^2(b_j) \leq M(d^* + 1)/n,$$

where M is a fixed constant independent of j, d^*, and n. By choosing n sufficiently large we can make this ratio arbitrarily small. Since $a_1, \cdots, a_k$ are independent of each other and also $b_1, \cdots, b_k$ are independent of each other, it follows from (36) that

$$(37) \qquad \frac{\sigma^2 \left(\sum_{j=1}^{k} a_j \right)}{\sigma^2 \left(\sum_{j=1}^{k} b_j \right)} = \sum_{j=1}^{k} \sigma^2(a_j) / \sum_{j=1}^{k} \sigma^2(b_j) \leqq M(d^* + 1)/n.$$

It can be seen from (35) that $\sum_{j=1}^{k}\sigma^2(b_j)/N$ is a bounded function of N. Hence it follows from Lemma 1 that the limit distribution of $(1/\sqrt{N})\sum_{j=1}^{k}(a_j + b_j)$ is the same as the limit distribution of $(1/\sqrt{N}) \sum_{j=1}^{k} b_j$. Thus the limit distribution of y_i is the same as the limit distribution of $(1/\sqrt{N})\sum b_j$. From the definition of b_j it follows that b_j is a quadratic function of the ϵ_t's, the number of terms and the coefficients being bounded functions of j. Hence since ϵ_t has finite moments by assumption, the third absolute moment of b_j is a bounded function of j. Furthermore $\sigma^2(b_j)$ converges to a finite positive limit with $j \to \infty$. The b_j's therefore fulfil the Liapounoff conditions and the distribution of $\sum_{j=1}^{k} b_j/\sqrt{N}$ approaches a normal distribution. Hence we have proved that y_i is in the limit normally distributed.

The proof carried through for each y_i can be carried through in exactly the same manner for every linear combination.

$$y = \gamma_1 y_1 + \cdots + \gamma_k y_k + \gamma_0 y_0.$$

Since the moments of ϵ_i are finite by assumption, we see that the moments of any linear combination $\sum_{i=0}^{p} \gamma_i y_i$ converge with $N \to \infty$ to the moments of a normal distribution. The fact that $y_0, y_1, \cdots, y_p$ have in the limit a joint normal distribution follows from the following lemma.

Lemma 2. Let $Y_1^{(n)}, \cdots, Y_k^{(n)}$ be k sequences of random variables such that for any set of coefficients $\gamma_1, \cdots, \gamma_k$ for which $\sum \gamma_i^2 \neq 0$ the moments of $\gamma_1 Y_1^{(n)} + \cdots + \gamma_k Y_k^{(n)}$ converge with $n \to \infty$ to the moments of a normal distribution with 0 mean and finite variance. Then the joint limiting distribution of the variates $Y_1^{(n)}, \cdots, Y_k^{(n)}$ is a multivariate normal distribution.

This lemma can be proved as follows: There exists a linear transformation

$$\bar{Y}_i^{(n)} = \sum_{j=1}^{k} \gamma_{ij} Y_j^{(n)} \qquad (i = 1, \cdots, k)$$

such that the covariance matrix of $\bar{Y}_1^{(n)}, \cdots, \bar{Y}_k^{(n)}$ converges with $n \to \infty$ to the unit matrix. Then it follows from the assumptions of our lemma that the moments of

$$\gamma_1 \bar{Y}_1^{(n)} + \cdots + \gamma_k \bar{Y}_k^{(n)} / \sqrt{\gamma_1^2 + \cdots + \gamma_k^2}$$

converge to the moments of a normal distribution with zero mean and unit variance for arbitrary values $\gamma_1, \cdots, \gamma_k$ subject to the restrictions $\sum \gamma_j^2 \neq 0$. Hence for any positive integer r we have

$$\lim_{n \to \infty} E\left(\sum_{i=1}^{k} \gamma_i \bar{Y}_i^{(n)} / \sqrt{\gamma_1^2 + \cdots + \gamma_k^2} \right)^r$$

$$(38) \qquad = \lim_{n \to \infty} \left[\frac{1}{\sqrt{\sum_{i=1}^{k} \gamma_i^2}} \right]^r \sum_{l_1 + \cdots + l_k = r} r! / l_1! l_2! \cdots l_k! \gamma_1^{l_1} \cdots \gamma_k^{l_k}$$

$$\cdot E[(\bar{Y}_1^{(n)})^{l_1} \cdots (\bar{Y}_k^{(n)})^{l_k}] = \mu_r$$

where μ_r denotes the rth moment of the normal distribution with 0 mean and unit variance.

Since (38) must be fulfilled identically in $\gamma_1, \cdots, \gamma_k$ we must have

$$\lim_{n \to \infty} E\{(\bar{Y}_1^{(n)})^{l_1} \cdots (\bar{Y}_k^{(n)})^{l_k}\} = \mu_{l_1} \mu_{l_2} \cdots \mu_{l_k}.$$

Hence the variates $\bar{Y}_1^{(n)}, \cdots, \bar{Y}_k^{(n)}$ are in the limit normally and independently distributed. From this it follows that the joint limiting distribution of $Y_1^{(n)}, \cdots, Y_k^{(n)}$ is a multivariate normal distribution and Lemma 2 is proved.

Thus we have arrived at the important result that $y_0, \cdots, y_p$ have in the limit a joint normal distribution with zero means and finite covariance matrix.

From (25) we see that the covariance matrix of the variates $y_0, y_1, \cdots, y_p$ is given by

$$(39) \qquad \|\sigma(y_iy_j)\| = \sigma^2\|E(D_{ijN})\| \qquad (i, j = 0, 1, \cdots, p).$$

Since $\operatorname{plim}_{N\to\infty} s^2 = \sigma^2$ and since $\operatorname{plim}_{N\to\infty}[D_{ijN} - E(D_{ijN})] = 0$ we have that

$$(40) \qquad \operatorname*{plim}_{N\to\infty} \left[\sigma(y_iy_j) - s^2 D_{ijN}\right] = 0.$$

Let $\|c_{ijN}\|$ be equal to $\|D_{ijN}\|^{-1}$. Then we obtain from (26)

$$(41) \qquad \sqrt{N}\,(a_i - \alpha_i) = \sum_{j=0}^{p} c_{ijN} y_j \qquad (i = 0, \cdots, p).$$

Let $\|c_{ij}\| = \|D_{ij}\|^{-1}$. Since $\operatorname{plim}_{N\to\infty} D_{ijN} = D_{ij}$ and since the matrix $\|D_{ij}\|$ is positive definite, we see that the limit distribution of $\sum_{j=0}^{p} c_{ijN} y_j$ is the same as the limit distribution of $\sum_{j=0}^{p} c_{ij} y_j$. From this and (41) it follows that the joint limiting distribution of $\sqrt{N}(a_j - \alpha_j)(j = 0, 1, \cdots, p)$ is a multivariate normal distribution with 0 means and finite covariance matrix.

Denote $\sqrt{N}(a_i - \alpha_i)$ by $\xi_i (i = 0, \cdots, p)$. We shall calculate the limiting covariance matrix of the variates $\xi_0, \cdots, \xi_p$.[3]

Since $\operatorname{plim}_{N\to\infty} c_{ijN} = c_{ij}$, it follows from (41) that

$$(42) \qquad \begin{aligned} \operatorname*{plim}_{N\to\infty} \sigma\,(\xi_i\xi_j) &= \operatorname*{plim}_{N\to\infty} \sum_{l=0}^{p}\sum_{k=0}^{p} c_{ik}c_{jl}\sigma(y_iy_j) \\ &= \sum_{l=0}^{p}\sum_{k=0}^{p} c_{ik}c_{jl}D_{kl}\sigma^2. \end{aligned}$$

Since $\|c_{ij}\| = \|D_{ij}\|^{-1}$ and since $D_{ij} = D_{ji}$ we have that

$$\sum_{l=0}^{p}\sum_{k=0}^{p} c_{ik}c_{jl}D_{kl} = c_{ij}.$$

Hence we obtain from (42)

$$(43) \qquad \operatorname*{plim}_{N\to\infty} \sigma(\xi_i\xi_j) = c_{ij}\sigma^2 = \operatorname*{plim}_{N\to\infty} s^2 c_{ijN}.$$

Our results can be summarized in the following

[3] That $\lim \sigma\,(\xi_i, \xi_j)$ is actually the covariance of the limit distribution of ξ_i, ξ_j follows from the proof of lemma 2. [Added in 1970 by H. B. Mann. — The Editors.]

Theorem. Let $\xi_i = \sqrt{N}(a_i - \alpha_i)$ $(i=0, \cdots, p)$ *where* a_i *is the maximum-likelihood estimate of* α_i. *Furthermore let* $D_{ijN} = \sum_{t=1}^{N} x_{t-i} x_{t-j}/N$ $\cdot (i, j=1, \cdots, p)$, $D_{i0N} = D_{0iN} = \sum_{t=1}^{N} x_{t-i}/N$ $(i=1, \cdots, p)$, $D_{00N} = 1$, *and* $\|c_{ijN}\| = \|D_{ijN}\|^{-1}(i, j=0, \cdots, p)$. *Finally let* s^2 *be the maximum-likelihood estimate of* σ^2. *The joint limiting distribution of* $\xi_0, \xi_1, \cdots, \xi_p$ *is a multivariate normal distribution with* 0 *means and finite covariance matrix. The limiting value of the covariance between* ξ_i *and* ξ_j *is equal to the stochastic limit of* $s^2 c_{ijN}$.

For large N we can replace the covariance between ξ_i and ξ_j by the quantity $s^2 c_{ijN}$ which can be calculated from the observations. Thus we see that the joint limiting distribution of the estimates $a_i(i=0, \cdots, p)$ is the same as the distribution we should obtain from the classical regression theory if x_t is considered as the dependent variable and $x_{t-1}, \cdots, x_{t-p}$ as the independent variables.

In other words a single stochastic difference equation in one variable can be treated for large N as a classical regression problem where x_t is the dependent variable and $x_{t-1}, \cdots, x_{t-p}$ are the independent variables.

6. *Estimation and Prediction*

On the basis of the joint limiting distribution of the maximum-likelihood estimates $a_0, a_1, \cdots, a_p$ we can carry out tests of significance or derive confidence regions for the unknown coefficients $\alpha_0, \cdots, \alpha_p$ provided that N is large. If we want to test the hypothesis that, for a given i, $\alpha_i = \alpha_i^0$ where α_i^0 is some specified value, we proceed as follows: We form the ratio

(44) $$\sqrt{N} (a_i - \alpha_i^0)/s\sqrt{c_{iiN}}.$$

This ratio is in the limit normally distributed with zero mean and unit variance if the hypothesis to be tested is true. We decide to reject the hypothesis under consideration if the ratio (44) has an absolute value which exceeds the critical value d_0 corresponding to the chosen level of significance. If we choose 5 per cent as the level of significance then $d_0 = 1.96$.

A confidence interval for the unknown coefficient α_i is obtained as follows: Consider the inequality

(45) $$\sqrt{N} (a_i - \alpha_i)/s\sqrt{c_{iiN}} \leqq d_0.$$

The set of all values α_i which are not rejected on the basis of the observations, i.e., the set of all values α_i which satisfy (45), forms a confidence interval for the unknown coefficient α_i.

Now suppose that we want to test the values of several coefficients α_i simultaneously. More precisely, we want to test the hypothesis that $\alpha_{1'} = \alpha_{1'}^0, \cdots, \alpha_{q'} = \alpha_{q'}^0$, where $1' < \cdots < q'$ are nonnegative integers

$\leq p$ and $\alpha_{1'}{}^0, \cdots, \alpha_{q'}{}^0$ are some given specified values. The proper large-sample test procedure can be carried out as follows: We form the expression

$$(46) \qquad T^2 = \frac{1}{s^2} \sum_{j=1}^{q} \sum_{i=1}^{q} N(a_{i'} - \alpha_{i'})(a_{j'} - \alpha_{j'})c_{i'j'N}^*,$$

where

$$(47) \qquad \|c_{i'j'N}^*\| = \|c_{i'j'N}\|^{-1} \qquad (i, j = 1, \cdots, q).$$

The expression (46) has in the limit the χ^2-distribution with q degrees of freedom. We reject the hypothesis under consideration if the expression (45) exceeds the critical value χ_0^2 of the χ^2-distribution corresponding to the chosen level of significance.

A confidence region for the unknown parameters $\alpha_{1'}, \cdots, \alpha_{q'}$ is given by the set of all points $(\alpha_{1'}{}^0, \cdots, \alpha_{q'}{}^0)$ which satisfy the inequality

$$(48) \qquad T^2 \leq \chi_0^2.$$

The region defined by the inequality (48) is an ellipsoid with the center at the point $(a_{1'}, \cdots, a_{q'})$.

If $q = p+1$ then $1' = 0$, $2' = 1$, $\cdots$, $q' = p$ and the expression (46) goes over into

$$(49) \qquad \frac{1}{s^2} \sum_{j=0}^{p} \sum_{i=0}^{p} N(a_i - \alpha_i{}^0)(a_j - \alpha_j{}^0)D_{ijN}.$$

As a problem of prediction let us consider the following simple case: Suppose we want to predict the future value x_{t+1} on the basis of the past observed values $x_1, \cdots, x_t$. It is clear that the conditional expected value of x_{t+1} given $x_1, \cdots, x_t$ is equal to

$$(50) \quad E(x_{t+1}/x_1, \cdots, x_t) = \alpha_1 x_t + \alpha_2 x_{t-1} + \cdots + \alpha_p x_{t-p+1} + \alpha_0.$$

Hence the expression

$$(51) \qquad X_{t+1} = a_1 x_t + a_2 x_{t-1} + \cdots + a_p x_{t-p+1} + a_0$$

can be used as a point estimate of x_{t+1}. If N is large, the sampling variance of a_i can be neglected as compared with the variance σ^2 of ϵ_t. Hence for large N we can say that the distribution of

$$x_{t+1} - (a_1 x_t + a_2 x_{t-1} + \cdots + a_p x_{t-p+1} + a_0)$$

is the same distribution as that of ϵ_{t+1}. Thus we obtain confidence limits for x_{t+1} by setting confidence limits for ϵ_{t+1}. The problem of predicting $x_{t+h}(h > 1)$ on the basis of $x_1, \cdots, x_t$ can be treated in a similar way provided that h is small. If h is large the sampling variation of the maximum-likelihood estimates $a_0, a_1 \cdots, a_p$ cannot be neglected in setting up confidence limits for x_{t+h}.

PART II

THE CASE OF SEVERAL EQUATIONS IN
SEVERAL VARIABLES

1. *Assumptions Underlying the Statistical Analysis*

Let $x_{1t}, \cdots, x_{rt}$ be a set of r random variables depending on t where t can take only integral values.

Assumption I_2. The set of variables $x_{1t}, \cdots, x_{rt}$ satisfies the system of linear stochastic difference equations

$$(52) \qquad \sum_{j=1}^{r} \sum_{k=0}^{p_{ij}} \alpha_{ijk} x_{j,t-k} + \alpha_i = \epsilon_{it} \qquad (i = 1, \cdots, r),$$

where p_{ij} is the highest lag in the variable x_{jt} occurring in the ith equation, the α's are known or unknown constants, the random vectors $(\epsilon_{11}, \cdots, \epsilon_{r1})$, $(\epsilon_{12}, \cdots, \epsilon_{r2})$, $\cdots$ ad inf. are independently distributed each having the same distribution and $E(\epsilon_{it}) = 0$ for all values of i and t.

Since the joint distribution of the variates $\epsilon_{1t}, \cdots, \epsilon_{rt}$ does not depend on t the covariance between ϵ_{it} and ϵ_{jt} also does not depend on t. We shall denote this covariance by σ_{ij}.

Assumption II_2. The determinant value $|\sigma_{ij}|$ of the matrix $\|\sigma_{ij}\|$ $(j, i = 1, \cdots, r)$ is not equal to 0.

Assumption III_2. All moments of ϵ_{it} are finite.

Assumption IV_2. Denote $\sum_{k=0}^{p_{ij}} \alpha_{ijk}\rho^{-k}$ by $b_{ij}(\rho)$ and let $|b_{ij}(\rho)|$ be the determinant value of the matrix $\|b_{ij}(\rho)\|(i, j = 1, \cdots, r)$. It is assumed that all roots of the equation

$$(53) \qquad |b_{ij}(\rho)| = 0$$

are smaller than 1 in absolute value.

2. *Application of the Maximum-Likelihood Method*

If the variables $\epsilon_{1t}, \cdots, \epsilon_{rt}$ have a joint normal distribution then the joint distribution of the $\epsilon_{it}(i=1, \cdots, r; t=1, \cdots, N)$ is given by

$$\frac{C}{|\sigma_{ij}|^{N/2}} \exp\left(-\frac{1}{2} \sum_{t=1}^{N} \sum_{i=1}^{r} \sum_{j=1}^{r} \sigma^{ij} L_{it} L_{jt}\right) d\epsilon_{11} \cdots d\epsilon_{1t} \cdots d\epsilon_{r1} \cdots d\epsilon_{rt},$$

where C is a constant,

$$L_{it} = \epsilon_{it} = \sum_{j=1}^{r} \sum_{k=0}^{p_{ij}} \alpha_{ijk} x_{j,t-k} + \alpha_i,$$

and

$$\|\sigma^{ij}\| = \|\sigma_{ij}\|^{-1} \qquad (i, j = 1, \cdots, r).$$

We have $\partial \epsilon_{i\alpha}/\partial x_{j\alpha} = \alpha_{ij0}$, $\partial \epsilon_{i\alpha}/\partial x_{j\beta} = 0$ for $\beta > \alpha$. Hence the joint distribution of the $x_{it}(i = 1, \cdots, r; t = 1, \cdots, N)$ is given by

$$(54) \qquad P = (C/\mid \sigma_{ij} \mid^{N/2}) J^N \exp\left(-\frac{1}{2} \sum_{t=1}^{N} \sum_{i=1}^{r} \sum_{j=1}^{r} \sigma^{ij} L_{it} L_{jt}\right)$$

$$\cdot\, dx_{11} \cdots dx_{1N} \cdots dx_{r1} \cdots dx_{rN},$$

where $J = \mid \alpha_{ij0} \mid$.

Put $\sum_{t=1}^{N} L_{it} L_{jt} = Q_{ij}$, then

$$\log P = N \log J + \log C + (N/2) \log \mid \sigma^{ij} \mid - (1/2) \sum_{i=1}^{r} \sum_{j=1}^{r} \sigma^{ij} Q_{ij}.$$

Maximizing $\log P$ with respect to α_{ijk} and σ^{ij} we obtain the following system of equations:

$$(55) \qquad (N/J)(\partial J/\partial \alpha_{ijk}) - \frac{1}{2} \sum_{l=1}^{r} \sigma^{il} \partial Q_{il}/\partial \alpha_{ijk} = 0$$

$$(i = 1, \cdots, r; k = 1, \cdots, p_{ij}),$$

$$\|\sigma_{ij}\| = \|Q_{ij}/N\|.$$

Let us denote $(1/N)(\sum_{t=1}^{N} x_{it}, {}_{t-k} x_{j,t-l})$ by D_{ikjlN}. Just as in the case of a single equation the essential point in our considerations will be the fact that

$$\plim_{N \to \infty} (D_{ijklN} - E(D_{ikjlN})) = 0$$

and that $\lim_{N \to \infty} E(D_{ikjlN})$ exists and is finite. In the next section we shall outline a proof of this fact. This proof is very similar to the proof given in the case of one equation and we shall discuss only those parts of it in which the generalization from the case of a single equation is not immediately obvious.

3. Proof of the Existence of $\plim_{N \to \infty} \sum_{t=1}^{N} x_{i,t-k} x_{j,t-l}/N$

It follows from (52) that x_{it} is a linear function of $\epsilon_{jr}(j = 1, \cdots, r; \tau = 1, \cdots, t)$. Hence

$$(56) \qquad x_{it} = \phi_i(t) + \sum_{\tau=1}^{t} \sum_{j=1}^{r} \phi_{ij\tau}(t) \epsilon_{jr}.$$

Substituting this in (52) we obtain

$$\sum_{j=1}^{r} \sum_{k=0}^{p_{ij}} \alpha_{ijk}\phi_i(t-k) + \sum_{j=1}^{r} \sum_{k=0}^{p_{ij}} \sum_{l=1}^{r} \sum_{\tau=1}^{t} \alpha_{ijk}\phi_{jl\tau}(t-k)\epsilon_{l\tau} + \alpha_i = \epsilon_{it}.$$

This is an identity in the ϵ_{ji}'s. Hence we must have

$$\sum_{j=1}^{r} \sum_{k=0}^{p_{ij}} \alpha_{ijk}\phi_j(t-k) + \alpha_i = 0 \qquad (i = 1, \cdots, r),$$

$$\sum_{j=1}^{r} \sum_{k=0}^{p_{ij}} \alpha_{ijk}\phi_{jl\tau}(t-k) = 0 \qquad (t > \tau; i, l = 1, \cdots, r),$$

(57)

$$\sum_{j=1}^{r} \sum_{k=0}^{p_{ij}} \alpha_{ijk}\phi_{jit}(t-k) = 1,$$

$$\sum_{j=1}^{r} \sum_{k=0}^{p_{ij}} \alpha_{ijk}\phi_{jlt}(t-k) = 0 \qquad (l \neq i).$$

Since according to (56)

$$\phi_{ij\tau}(t) = 0 \qquad (\tau > t; i, j = 1, \cdots, r),$$

we have that

(58)
$$\phi_{jlt}(t-k) = 0 \qquad (k = 1, \cdots, p_{ij}).$$

From (58) and the last two equations in (57) we obtain

$$\sum_{j=1}^{r} \alpha_{ij0}\phi_{jit}(t) = 1,$$

(59)

$$\sum_{j=1}^{r} \alpha_{ij0}\phi_{jlt}(t) = 0 \qquad (l \neq i).$$

It is clear that functions $\phi_{ij\tau}(t)$ satisfying the equations (57) and (58) exist. For the sake of simplicity we shall assume that all roots of the equation (53) are distinct. It is known from general mathematical theory that the solution of the system of linear difference equations (57) must then be of the form:

$$\phi_{ij\tau}(t) = \lambda_{1j\tau}A_{1i}\rho_1^t + \cdots + \lambda_{\pi j\tau}A_{\pi i}\rho_\pi^t,$$
$$\phi_i(t) = \lambda_1 A_{1i}\rho_1^t + \cdots + \lambda_\pi A_{\pi i}\rho_\pi^t + c_i,$$

where the ρ_i are the solutions in ρ of the equation (53), the $A_{\beta i}$ are not all equal to zero and satisfy the systems of equations

$$\sum_{j=1}^{r} A_{\beta j}b_{ij}(\rho_\beta) = 0 \qquad (i = 1, \cdots, r),$$

the constants c_i are the solutions of the system of equations

$$\sum_{j=1}^{r} \sum_{k=0}^{p_{ij}} \alpha_{ijk} c_j = - \alpha_i \qquad (i = 1, \cdots, r).$$

(The determinant of the latter system is equal to $|b_{ij}(1)|$ which is unequal to 0 by Assumption IV_2) and the $\lambda_{\beta jr}$ and λ_β are constants. From the equations (57), (58), (59) it follows in a similar way to that for the case of a single equation that

$$\lambda_{\beta jr} = \lambda_{\beta j1}/\rho_\beta^{r-1}.$$

Writing $\lambda_{\beta j}$ instead of $\lambda_{\beta j1}$ we therefore have

$$\lambda_{\beta jr} = \lambda_{\beta j}/\rho_\beta^{r-1}.$$

Hence we have

(60) $$\phi_{ijr}(t) = \lambda_{1j} A_{1i} \rho_1^{t-r+1} + \cdots + \lambda_{rj} A_{ri} \rho_r^{t-r+1}.$$

Using (60) we can show in complete analogy to the case of a single equation that $\text{plim}_{N \to \infty}[\sum_{t=1}^{N} x_{i,t-k} x_{j,t-l}/N - E(\sum_{t=1}^{N} x_{i,t-k} x_{j,t-l}/N)]=0$ and that $\lim_{N \to \infty} E(\sum_{t=1}^{N} x_{i,t-k} x_{j,t-l}/N)=\lim_{t \to \infty} E(x_{i,t-k} x_{j,t-l})$. Denote this limit expected value by D_{ikjl}. Then we have

(61) $$\text{plim}_{N \to \infty} D_{ikjlN} = D_{ikjl} \qquad (i, j = 1, \cdots, r).$$

Similarly it can be seen that

(62) $$\text{plim}_{N \to \infty} \sum_{t=1}^{N} x_{it}/N = \lim_{N \to \infty} E\left(\sum_{t=1}^{N} x_{it}/N \right) = \lim_{t \to \infty} E(x_{it}) = c_i$$

$$(i = 1, \cdots, r).$$

4. Treatment of the Equation (52) when $\|\alpha_{ij0}\|$ Is Equal to the Unit Matrix and $\sigma_{ij}=0$ for $i \neq j$

First we shall treat the equations (52) in the special case when $\|\alpha_{ij0}\| (i, j=1, \cdots, r)$ is equal to the unit matrix, i.e., $\alpha_{ij0}=0$ if $i \neq j$ and $\alpha_{ii0}=1$, and $\sigma_{ij}=0$ for $i \neq j$. The reason for discussing this special case separately is that it is an important one in applications and the results are very simple. The statistical treatment of such a system of equations can be reduced to the case of a single equation. In the special case under consideration the Jacobian is equal to 1 and the system of equations (55) reduces to

(63) $$\partial Q_{ii}/\partial \alpha_{ijk} = 0, \qquad \sigma_{ii} = Q_{ii}/N \qquad (i = 1, \cdots, r).$$

Hence we can proceed exactly as in the case of a single equation and prove the consistency of the maximum-likelihood estimates a_{ijk}, a_i, and s_{ii} of α_{ijk}, α_i, and σ_{ii} respectively. Furthermore we can prove in a way analogous to the case of a single equation that the variates $\sqrt{N}(a_{ijk}-\alpha_{ijk})$ and $\sqrt{N}(a_i-\alpha_i)(i, j=1, \cdots, r)(k=1, \cdots, p_{ij})$ have in the limit a joint normal distribution with zero means and finite covariance matrix.

Now we shall derive the limit covariance matrix of the variates $\sqrt{N}(a_{ijk}-\alpha_{ijk})$, $\sqrt{N}(a_i-\alpha_i)(i, j=1, \cdots, r; k=1, \cdots, p_{ij})$. For the sake of convenience we introduce the following notations: The variable x_{0t} is identically equal to 1, i.e., for all values of t, x_{0t} is equal to 1. The symbols α_{i01} and a_{i01} will stand for α_i and a_i respectively. The value of p_{i0} is defined to be equal to 1. The symbols D_{ikjlN} and D_{ikjl} have been previously defined only for positive values of i and j. Now we shall extend this definition to include the cases when i or j or both are equal to zero. We put

(64)
$$\sum_{t=1}^{N} x_{i,t-k}x_{j,t-l}/N = D_{ikjlN},$$

$$\lim_{N\to\infty} E\left(\sum_{t=1}^{N} x_{i,t-k}x_{j,t-l}/N \right) = D_{ikjl} \qquad (i, j = 0, \cdots, r).$$

It is clear that

(65)
$$D_{0k0lN} = D_{0k0l} = 1.$$

From (62) it follows that

(66)
$$D_{ik0l} = D_{0lik} = c_i \qquad (i = 1, \cdots, r).$$

We put

(67)
$$\sqrt{N}\,y_{ijk} = \tfrac{1}{2}\partial Q_{ii}/\partial\alpha_{ijk} = \sum_{t=1}^{N} \epsilon_{it}x_{j,t-k}$$

$$(i = 1, \cdots, r; j = 0, \cdots, r; k = 1, \cdots, p_{ij}).$$

According to (63) we have

(68)
$$\sum_{t=1}^{N} x_{j,t-k}\left(x_{it} + \sum_{l=1}^{p_{im}}\sum_{m=0}^{r} a_{iml}x_{m,t-l} \right) = 0$$
$$(i = 1, \cdots, r; j = 0, \cdots, r).$$

From (67) and (68) we obtain

(69)
$$\sqrt{N}\,y_{ijk} = \sum_{t=1}^{N} x_{j,t-k}\left[\sum_{l=1}^{p_{im}}\sum_{m=0}^{r} (a_{iml} - \alpha_{iml})x_{m,t-l} \right].$$

Let ξ_{ijk} be equal to $\sqrt{N}(a_{ijk}-\alpha_{ijk})$. Then we obtain from (69)

$$
\begin{aligned}
(70) \quad y_{ijk} &= \sum_{l=1}^{p_{im}} \sum_{m=0}^{r} \xi_{iml} \left(\sum_{t=1}^{N} x_{j,t-k} x_{m,t-l}/N \right) \\
&= \sum_{l=1}^{p_{im}} \sum_{m=0}^{r} D_{jkmlN} \xi_{iml} \qquad (i = 1, \cdots, r; j = 0, \cdots, r).
\end{aligned}
$$

In order to obtain the limit covariance matrix of the variates ξ_{ijk} we need to know the limit covariance matrix of the variates y_{ijk}. First we show that the covariance between y_{ijk} and $y_{i'j'k'}$ is zero if $i \neq i'$. In fact, since $E(y_{ijk}) = 0$, we have

$$
\begin{aligned}
(71) \quad \sigma(y_{ijk} y_{i'j'k'}) &= E(y_{ijk} y_{i'j'k'}) = \frac{1}{N} \sum_{t=1}^{N} E(\epsilon_{it} \epsilon_{i't}) E(x_{j,t-k} x_{j',t-k'}) \\
&= \sigma_{ii'} E \left(\sum_{t=1}^{N} x_{j,t-k} x_{j',t-k'}/N \right).
\end{aligned}
$$

Since $\sigma_{ii'} = 0$ for $i \neq i'$, we obtain from (71)

$$
(72) \qquad (y_{ijk} y_{i'j'k'}) = 0 \quad \text{for} \quad i \neq i'.
$$

If $i = i'$ it follows from (71) that

$$
(73) \qquad \lim_{N \to \infty} \sigma(y_{ijk} y_{ij'k'}) = \sigma_{ii} D_{jkj'k'}.
$$

Denote by m_i the number of different pairs (j, k) for which y_{ijk} is defined. For a given value i we can arrange the m_i pairs (j, k) in an ordered sequence. We shall denote y_{ijk} by y_{iu} where (j, k) is the uth pair in the ordered sequence. Similarly, we shall denote $D_{jkj'k'N}$ by $D_{uu'N}$ and $D_{jkj'k'}$ by $D_{uu'}$ respectively where (j, k) is the uth element and (j', k') the u'th element in the ordered sequence. Then equations (70) and (73) can be written

$$
(74) \qquad y_{iu} = \sum_{v=1}^{m_i} D_{uvN} \xi_{iv}
$$

and

$$
(75) \qquad \lim_{N \to \infty} \sigma(y_{iu} y_{iu'}) = \sigma_{ii} D_{uu'}.
$$

Let

$$
\| C_{uu'N} \| = \| D_{uu'N} \|^{-1}, \quad \| C_{uu'} \| = \| D_{uu'} \|^{-1} \quad (u, u' = 1, \cdots, m_i).
$$

Then it can be shown on the basis of (74) and (75) and the relation $\operatorname{plim}_{N \to \infty} D_{uvN} = D_{uv}$ that

$$
(76) \qquad \lim_{N \to \infty} \sigma(\xi_{iu} \xi_{iv}) = \sigma_{ii} C_{uv} = \operatorname*{plim}_{N \to \infty} s_{ii} C_{uvN}.
$$

The proof of (76) is entirely analogous to that of (43) in the case of a single equation and is therefore omitted. Since $\sigma(y_{ijk}y_{i'j'k'}) = 0$ for $i \neq i'$ we obtain

$$(77) \qquad \lim_{N \to \infty} \sigma(\xi_{iu}\xi_{i'v}) = 0 \quad \text{for} \quad i \neq i'.$$

Thus (76) and (77) furnish the complete limit covariance matrix of the variables ξ_{ijk}.

Knowing that the joint limiting distribution of the variates ξ_{ijk} is a multivariate normal distribution with zero means and covariance matrix given by (76) and (77), tests of significance, derivation of confidence regions, and prediction of future values can be carried out in the same way as has been shown in the case of a single equation.

Frequently some of the coefficients α_{ijk} are known a priori to have some particular values. All of our results in this section can be extended without any difficulty to this case. Suppose that the coefficients α_{ijk} are classified into two groups. The first group contains all the coefficients α_{ijk} which are unknown and the second group contains those which have values known a priori. For any α_{ijk} in the second group we put $a_{ijk} = \alpha_{ijk}$. The variates y_{ijk} are defined only for those triples (i, j, k) for which α_{ijk} lies in the first group. Then all our results remain valid.

5. *Treatment of the Equations* (52) *when* $\|\alpha_{ij0}\|$ *Is Equal to the Unit Matrix and Nothing Is Known about the Covariance Matrix* $\|\sigma_{ij}\|$

We shall consider the following special case: The matrix $\|\alpha_{ij0}\|$ is equal to the unit matrix and p_{ij} has the same value for all pairs (i, j), i.e., $p_{ij} = p$ (say). It is furthermore assumed that all coefficients $\alpha_{ijk}(k > 0)$ and all covariances σ_{ij} are unknown. Then the Jacobian J is equal to 1 and the system of equations (55) reduces to

$$(78) \qquad \sum_{l=1}^{r} \sigma^{il} \partial Q_{il}/\partial \alpha_{ijk} = 0; \qquad \sigma_{ij} = Q_{ij}/N.$$

Denote $\sum_{t=1}^{N} x_{j,t-k}L_l$ by M_{jkl}. Then it follows from (78) that

$$(79) \qquad \sum_{l=1}^{r} \sigma^{il} M_{jkl} = 0 \quad (i = 1, \cdots, r; j = 1, \cdots, r; k = 1, \cdots, p).$$

For fixed values of j and k the equations (79) form a system of r homogeneous linear equations in $M_{jk1}, \cdots, M_{jkr}$. Since the determinant $|\sigma^{il}|$ of these equations is different from 0, the equations (79) are equivalent to

$$M_{jkl} = 0 \qquad (l = 1, \cdots, r).$$

Thus (78) can be written as

$$\text{(80)} \qquad \partial Q_{il}/\partial \alpha_{ijk} = M_{jkl} = 0; \qquad \sigma_{ij} = Q_{ij}/N.$$

In deriving the equations (80) we made use of the assumptions that $p_{ij}=p$ and that all coefficients α_{ijk} are unknown. Otherwise it would not have been true that for any fixed values j, k the equations (79) hold for all values of i, i.e., for $i=1, 2, \cdots, r$.

Since the maximum-likelihood estimates are solutions of the equations (80), the joint limiting distribution of the maximum-likelihood estimates can be derived in the same way as it has been done in the special case discussed in the previous section. Thus we shall merely give the results.

The symbols D_{ikjlN} and D_{ikjl} are defined as in the previous section. We arrange the pairs (m, n) $(m=1, \cdots, r; n=1, \cdots, p)$ in an ordered sequence. We shall denote a_{ijk} and α_{ijk} by a_{iu} and α_{iu} respectively if (j, k) is the uth pair in the ordered sequence. Similarly we shall denote D_{ikjlN} and D_{ikjl} by D_{uvN} and D_{uv} respectively if (i, k) is the uth and (j, l) the vth pair in the ordered sequence. Let

$$\|C_{uvN}\| = \|D_{uvN}\|^{-1} \quad \text{and} \quad \|C_{uv}\| = \|D_{uv}\|^{-1}.$$

The joint limiting distribution of the variates $\sqrt{N}(a_{iu}-\alpha_{iu})=\xi_{iu}$ $(u=1, \cdots, rp; i=1, \cdots, r)$ is a multivariate normal distribution with zero means and finite covariance matrix. The limit covariance of ξ_{iu} and ξ_{jv} is equal to $\sigma_{ij}C_{uv}$. Since $\text{plim}_{N\to\infty}s_{ij}C_{uvN}=\sigma_{ij}C_{uv}$, for large N we can replace the unknown value $\sigma_{ij}C_{uv}$ by the observed value $s_{ij}C_{uvN}$.

On the basis of the joint normal distribution of the maximum-likelihood estimates ξ_{ijk} we can carry out tests of significance or derive confidence regions for the unknown coefficients α_{ijk} in the usual manner.

We want to make a few remarks concerning the process of prediction, since this differs in some respects from the case when $\sigma_{ij}=0$ for $i\neq j$. If we want to predict the value of x_{it} on the basis of the values $x_{j\tau}$ $(j=1, \cdots, r; \tau=1, \cdots, t-1)$ then the process of prediction can be carried out in the same way as in the case when $\sigma_{ij}=0$ for $i\neq j$. A somewhat different situation arises, however, if we want to predict $x_{1t}, \cdots, x_{qt}(q<r)$ on the basis of $x_{q+1,t}, \cdots, x_{rt}$ and all previously observed values $x_{j\tau}(j=1, \cdots, r; \tau<t)$. For this purpose we need the conditional distribution of $x_{1t}, \cdots, x_{qt}$ given $x_{q+1,t}, \cdots, x_{rt}$ and $x_{j\tau}(j=1, \cdots, r; \tau<t)$. Let $M_{it}=x_{it}+\sum_{j=1}^{r}\sum_{k=1}^{p}a_{ijk}x_{jt-k}+a_i$. Since in the subpopulation considered $x_{it}-M_{it}$ is a fixed constant, our problem is equivalent to the problem of predicting $M_{1t}, \cdots, M_{qt}$ when the values of $M_{q+1,t}, \cdots, M_{rt}$ and $x_{j\tau}(\tau<t)$ are given. Since for large N the sampling variance of the maximum-likelihood estimates a_{ijk} can be neglected as

compared to the variance σ_{ii} of x_{it} the joint distribution of the variates $\epsilon_{1t}, \cdots, \epsilon_{rt}$ is the same as the joint limiting distribution of $M_{1t}, \cdots, M_{rt}$. Thus the problem of predicting $M_{1t}, \cdots, M_{qt}$ can be reduced to the problem of predicting $\epsilon_{1t}, \cdots, \epsilon_{qt}$ when $\epsilon_{q+1,t}, \cdots, \epsilon_{rt}$ are given. We assume that $\epsilon_{1t}, \cdots, \epsilon_{rt}$ have a joint normal distribution. Let

$$(81) \qquad \|\sigma_{ij}^*\| = \|\sigma_{ij}\|^{-1} \qquad (i, j = q+1, \cdots, r);$$

then for any index $m \leqq q$ the conditional expected value of ϵ_{mt} given $\epsilon_{q+1,t}, \cdots, \epsilon_{rt}$ is known to be equal to

$$(82) \qquad E(\epsilon_{mt} \mid \epsilon_{q+1,t}, \cdots, \epsilon_{rt}) = \sum_{v=q+1}^{r} \sum_{u=q+1}^{r} \sigma_{uv}^* \sigma_{mv} \epsilon_{ut}.$$

Let

$$(83) \qquad \|\bar{\sigma}_{ij}\| = \|\sigma^{ij}\|^{-1} \qquad (i, j = 1, \cdots, q).$$

It is known that the conditional covariance matrix of $\epsilon_{1t}, \cdots, \epsilon_{qt}$ given $\epsilon_{q+1,t}, \cdots, \epsilon_{rt}$ is equal to $\|\bar{\sigma}_{ij}\|\,(i, j = 1, \cdots, q)$. Thus

$$E_{mt} = \sum_{v=q+1}^{r} \sum_{u=q+1}^{r} \sigma_{uv}^* \sigma_{mv} \epsilon_{ut}$$

can be used as a point estimate of ϵ_{mt}. A confidence interval for ϵ_{mt} is given by $E_{mt} \pm \lambda \sqrt{\bar{\sigma}_{mm}}$ where λ is a constant corresponding to the confidence coefficient we wish to have. For large N we can replace σ_{ij} by its estimate s_{ij} and ϵ_{it} can be replaced by M_{it}. Thus we arrive at the following results: For large N we can use

$$E_{mt}' = \sum_{v=q+1}^{r} \sum_{u=q+1}^{r} s_{uv}^* s_{mv} M_{ut}$$

as a point estimate for M_{mt}. A confidence interval for M_{mt} is given by $E_{mt}' \pm \lambda \sqrt{\bar{s}_{mm}}$ where λ is a constant determined so that the confidence coefficient should have the required magnitude.

6. The General Case

In Sections 4 and 5 we have considered the special case when $\|\alpha_{ij0}\|$ is equal to the unit matrix. Here we shall deal with the general case.

The treatment of the general case presents a number of difficulties which do not arise in the special cases discussed before. Suppose that in the equations (52) all coefficients $\alpha_{ijk}(i, j = 1, \cdots, r; k = 1, \cdots, p_{ij})$, $\alpha_i(i = 1, \cdots, r)$ and all covariances σ_{ij} are unknown. Assume furthermore that p_{ij} has the same value for all indices (i, j), i.e., $p_{ij} = p$ (say). Then it is not possible to have consistent estimates for all the parameters $\alpha_{ijk}, \alpha_i, \sigma_{ij}$. This can be seen as follows: Let $\|\lambda_{uv}\|$ $(u, v = 1, \cdots,$

r) be an r-rowed square matrix with nonvanishing determinant. Let furthermore

$$\bar{\alpha}_{ujk} = \sum_{v=1}^{r} \lambda_{uv}\alpha_{vjk}, \quad \bar{\alpha}_u = \sum_{v=1}^{r} \lambda_{uv}\alpha_v,$$

$$\bar{\epsilon}_{ut} = \sum_{v=1}^{r} \lambda_{uv}\epsilon_{vt}.$$

Then the system of equations

$$(84) \qquad \sum_{j=1}^{r} \sum_{k=0}^{p} \bar{\alpha}_{ujk}x_{j,t-k} + \bar{\alpha}_u = \bar{\epsilon}_{ut} \qquad (u = 1, \cdots, r)$$

is equivalent to the system (52). The random variables $\bar{\epsilon}_{ut}$ satisfy all the assumptions made concerning the random variables ϵ_{ut}. Thus, on the basis of the observed values $x_{1\tau}, \cdots, r_{r\tau}(\tau=1, \cdots, N)$ it is not possible to distinguish the system (84) from (52). On the other hand the coefficients $\bar{\alpha}_{ijk}$, $\bar{\alpha}_i$ in (84) are different from the coefficients α_{ijk}, α_i in (52). Hence it is impossible to have consistent estimates for all the unknown parameters α_{ijk}, α_i, and σ_{ij}.

In all that follows we shall assume that the determinant value $|\alpha_{ij0}|$ of the matrix $\|\alpha_{ij0}\|(i, j=1, \cdots, r)$ is different from zero. Then the system of equations (52) can be brought to the following reduced form:

$$(85) \qquad x_{it} + \sum_{j=1}^{r} \sum_{k=1}^{p_{ij}} \alpha_{ijk}^{*}x_{j,t-k} + \alpha_i^{*} = \epsilon_{it}^{*} \qquad (i = 1, \cdots, r),$$

where α_{ijk}^{*} is a linear function of $\alpha_{1jk}, \cdots, \alpha_{rjk}$; a_i^{*} is a linear function of $\alpha_1, \cdots, \alpha_r$, and ϵ_{it}^{*} is a linear function of $\epsilon_{1t}, \cdots, \epsilon_{rt}$. Denote the covariance of ϵ_{it}^{*} and ϵ_{jt}^{*} by σ_{ij}^{*}. Of course, the parameters α_{ijk}^{*}, α_i^{*}, σ_{ij}^{*} depend also on the coefficients α_{ij0}. It follows from the result obtained in Section 5 that the parameters α_{ijk}^{*}, α_i^{*}, and σ_{ij}^{*} can be estimated from the observations. Since the system (85) is equivalent to (52), it is clear that the observations cannot yield any additional information as to the values of the parameters α_{ij0}, α_{ijk} $(k=1, \cdots, p_{ij})$, α_i, and σ_{ij} beyond that contained in the estimates of the parameters α_{ijk}^{*}, α_i^{*}, and σ_{ij}^{*}. While the parameters α_{ijk}, α_i, and $\sigma_{ij}(i, j=1, \cdots, r$; $k=0, 1, \cdots, p_{ij})$ determine uniquely the values of α_{ijk}^{*} $(k>0)$, α_i^{*}, and σ_{ij}^{*}, the converse is not true. Thus it is impossible to have estimates of all the parameters α_{ijk}, α_i, and σ_{ij} on the basis of the observations alone. However, if we have some a priori knowledge as to the values of α_{ijk}, α_i, and σ_{ij}, for instance, if we know that some of the coefficients α_{ijk}, α_i are equal to 0, then it may be possible to estimate all the unknown parameters in the original system (52). In order that we should be able to estimate all the unknown parameters in this system, it is necessary and sufficient that the values of the parameters α_{ijk}^*, α_i^*, and σ_{ij}^*, together with the available a priori knowledge, should determine uniquely the values of all the parameters α_{ijk} $(i, j = 1, \cdots, r; k = 0, 1 \cdots, p_{ij})$, α_i, and σ_{ij}.

Since (85) is equivalent to (52), we can discard the system (52) and treat the system (85). A definite advantage is gained by this procedure if there is no a priori knowledge whatsoever as to the values of α_{ijk}, α_i, and σ_{ij}, or if the a priori knowledge available does not imply any restrictions as to the values of α_{ijk}^* $(i, j = 1, \cdots, r; k = 1, \cdots, p_{ij} = p)$, α_i^*, σ_{ij}^*. For in this case we have to deal with the special situation discussed in Section 5 and the statistical treatment of (85) does not present any difficulties. If, however, the available a priori knowledge implies certain restrictions as to the values of the parameters α_{ijk}^*, α_i^*, and σ_{ij}^*, then the statistical treatment of (85) may be just as involved as that of (52) and no advantage is gained. In such cases it may even be preferable to treat the equations in their original form (52), since usually the coefficients in (52) have immediate meaning in economic theory, while the coefficients in (85) derive their significance merely from the fact that they are certain functions of the coefficients in (52).

In some practical cases one may find it perhaps worth while to discard the available a priori knowledge and to treat the equations (85) as if the parameters α_{ijk}^*, α_i^*, σ_{ij}^* were not subject to any restrictions. By doing so we decrease the efficiency of our statistical procedure but we gain in simplicity. In all that follows we shall assume that the available a priori knowledge implies restrictions as to the values of α_{ijk}^*, α_i^*, and σ_{ij}^* and that we are not willing to discard this information in order to gain in simplicity. Furthermore we assume that this a priori knowledge and the values of α_{ijk}^*, α_i^*, and σ_{ij}^* uniquely determine all the parameters α_{ijk}, α_i, and σ_{ij}. Since in such cases no advantage is gained by treating (85) instead of (52), we shall treat the equations in the original form (52). A frequent form of a priori knowledge is the following: It is known that ϵ_{it} is independent of ϵ_{jt} for $i \neq j$ and the values of some of the coefficients α_{ijk}, α_i are known to be zero. We shall restrict ourselves to the case when the a priori knowledge is of the type described above. There is no loss of generality in assuming that $\sigma_{ii} = 1$, since this can always be achieved by multiplying the equations (52) by a constant factor. Then of course we cannot assume that $\alpha_{ii0} = 1$. On the basis of these assumptions we shall procede to prove the consistency of the maximum-likelihood estimates and to derive their joint limiting distribution.

A. Consistency of the maximum-likelihood estimates. Let a_{ijk}, a_i be the maximum-likelihood estimates of the unknown coefficients α_{ijk} and α_i respectively. For triples (i, j, k) for which α_{ijk} is known to be zero we shall put $a_{ijk} = \alpha_{ijk} = 0$. Similarly $a_i = \alpha_i = 0$ if the value of α_i is a priori known to be zero. We bring the equations (52) into the reduced form

$$(86) \qquad x_{it} + \sum_{j=1}^{r} \sum_{k=1}^{P} \alpha_{ijk}^* x_{j,t-k} + \alpha_i^* = \epsilon_{it}^* \qquad (i = 1, \cdots, r),$$

where P is the maximum of the integers p_{ij}. Denote the covariance of ϵ_{it}^* and ϵ_{jt}^* by σ_{ij}^*. Our a priori knowledge imposes certain restrictions on the parameters α_{ijk}^*, α_i^*, and σ_{ij}^*. Denote by a_{ijk}^*, a_i^*, and s_{ij}^* the maximum-likelihood estimates of α_{ijk}^*, α_i^*, and σ_{ij}^* respectively calculated under the restrictions imposed by the a priori knowledge. Since according to our assumption the parameters α_{ijk}^*, α_i^*, and σ_{ij}^* together with the a priori knowledge determine uniquely the coefficients α_{ijk} and α_i the consistency of the estimates a_{ijk} and a_i is proved if we prove the consistency of the estimates a_{ijk}^*, a_i^*, and s_{ij}^*. Denote by a_{ijk}', a_i', and s_{ij}' the maximum-likelihood estimates we should obtain if the parameters α_{ijk}^*, α_i^*, and σ_{ij}^* were not subject to any restrictions. Let

$$p = \frac{1}{(2\pi)^{rN/2} |\sigma_{ij}^*|^{N/2}} \exp \left[-\frac{1}{2} \sum_{j=1}^{r} \sum_{i=1}^{r} \sum_{t=1}^{N} \sigma^{*ij} L_{it} L_{jt} \right],$$

where $L_{it} = x_{it} + \sum_{j=1}^{r} \sum_{k=1}^{P} \alpha_{ijk}^* x_{j,t-k} + \alpha_i^*$. Denote by p_0 the value of p at the true values of the parameters α_{ijk}^*, α_i^*, and σ_{ij}^*. Let p^* be the value of p if we substitute a_{ijk}^*, a_i^*, and s_{ij}^* for α_{ijk}^*, α_i^*, and σ_{ij}^* respectively. Finally denote by p' the value of p we obtain if we replace α_{ijk}^*, α_i^*, and σ_{ij}^* by a_{ijk}', a_i', and s_{ij}' respectively. Then we obviously have

$$(87) \qquad \log p_0 \leqq \log p^* \leqq \log p'.$$

From our results in Section 5 it follows that a_{ijk}', a_i', and s_{ij}' converge stochastically to α_{ijk}^*, α_i^*, and σ_{ij}^* respectively. From this and the fact that $(1/N) \sum_{t=1}^{N} x_{i,t-k} x_{j,t-l}$ converges stochastically to a fixed constant D_{ikjl} we easily obtain

$$(88) \qquad \text{plim } [(\log p_0)/N - (\log p')/N] = 0.$$

From (87) and (88) it follows that

$$(89) \qquad \text{plim } [(\log p^*)/N - (\log p')/N] = 0.$$

Let $\bar{p}$ be the expression we obtain from p if we replace $(1/N) \sum_{t=1}^{N} x_{i,t-k} x_{j,t-l}$ by its stochastic limit D_{ikjl}. Let $\bar{a}_{ijk}^*$, $\bar{a}_i^*$, and $\bar{s}_{ij}^*$

be the maximum-likelihood estimates we obtain instead of a_{ijk}^*, a_i^* and s_{ij}^* if we replace p by $\bar{p}$. The symbols $\bar{a}_{ijk}'$, $\bar{a}_i'$, and $\bar{s}_{ij}'$ are similarly defined. Then we obviously have

$$(90) \quad \text{plim } (\bar{a}_{ijk}' - \alpha_{ijk}^*) = \text{plim } (\bar{a}_i' - \alpha_i^*) = \text{plim } (\bar{s}_{ij}' - \sigma_{ij}^*) = 0,$$

$$(91) \quad \text{plim } (\bar{a}_{ijk}^* - a_{ijk}^*) = \text{plim } (\bar{a}_i^* - a_i^*) = \text{plim } (\bar{s}_{ij}^* - s_{ij}^*) = 0,$$

and, on account of (89),

$$(92) \qquad\qquad \text{plim } (\log \bar{p}^* - \log \bar{p}')/N = 0.$$

Since $\bar{a}_{ijk}'$, $\bar{a}_i'$, and s_{ij}' are unique solutions of the maximum-likelihood equations, the value of $\bar{p}$ is less than $\bar{p}'$ for any set of parameter values α_{ijk}^*, α_i^*, σ_{ij}^* which are not equal to the maximum-likelihood estimates. From this, (92), and the fact that $(\log \bar{p})/N$ does not depend on N, it follows that

$$(93) \quad \text{plim } (\bar{a}_{ijk}^* - \bar{a}_{ijk}') = \text{plim } (\bar{a}_i^* - \bar{a}_i') = \text{plim } (\bar{s}_{ij} - \bar{s}_{ij}') = 0.$$

The consistency of a_{ijk}^*, a_i^*, and s_{ij}^* follows from (90), (91), and (93). Hence the consistency of the estimates a_{ijk} and a_i is proved.

B. *Limiting distribution of the maximum-likelihood estimates.* It will be convenient to denote α_i by α_{i00} and a_i by a_{i00}. Furthermore we put $x_{0t}=1$ for all values of t. Then equations (52) can be written

$$(94) \qquad \sum_{j=0}^{r} \sum_{k=0}^{p_{ij}} \alpha_{ijk} x_{j,t-k} = \epsilon_{it} \qquad (i = 1, \cdots, r),$$

where $p_{i0}=0$. Denote by J the determinant value of the matrix $|\alpha_{ij0}|$ $(i, j=1, \cdots, r)$. Then the maximum-likelihood estimates a_{ijk} are roots of the equation

$$(95) \qquad (N \partial J/\partial \alpha_{ijk})/J - \left(\sum_{j=0}^{r} \sum_{l=0}^{p_{ij}} \sum_{t=1}^{N} \alpha_{ijl} x_{j,t-l} \right) x_{j,t-k} = 0.$$

The equations (95) are formed for all triples (i, j, k) for which a_{ijk} is unknown. For $k>0$ we have $\partial J/\partial \alpha_{ijk}=0$. Also for $j=k=0$ the derivative $\partial J/\partial \alpha_{ijk}$ is zero.

We put

$$(96) \quad y_{ijk} = (\sqrt{N}\, \partial J/\partial \alpha_{ijk})/J - \left(\sum_{j=0}^{r} \sum_{l=0}^{p_{ij}} \sum_{t=1}^{N} \alpha_{ijl} x_{j,t-l} \right) x_{j,t-k}/\sqrt{N},$$

where y_{ijk} is defined only for triples (i, j, k) for which α_{ijk} is unknown. In order to derive the joint limiting distribution of the maximum-likelihood estimates a_{ijk} we need to know the joint limiting distribution of the variates y_{ijk}. It can be shown that the joint limiting distribution of the variates y_{ijk} is a multivariate normal distribution. The proof of this statement is entirely analogous to that given in the case of a single equation and is therefore omitted. Thus for specifying completely the limiting distribution of the variates y_{ijk}, we merely need to know the limiting mean values and covariances of the variates y_{ijk}. First we show that

$$(97) \qquad\qquad E(y_{ijk}) = 0.$$

From (96) it follows that

$$(98) \qquad\qquad y_{ijk} = \sqrt{N}\, \partial J/\partial \alpha_{ijk} - \frac{1}{\sqrt{N}} \sum_{t=1}^{N} \epsilon_{it} x_{j,t-k}.$$

Since $\partial J/\partial \alpha_{ijk} = 0$ for $k > 0$ and since $E(\epsilon_{it} x_{j,t-k}) = 0$ for $k > 0$, equation (97) is proved for $k > 0$. For $j = k = 0$ we have $\partial J/\partial \alpha_{ijk} = 0$ and $E(\epsilon_{it} x_{0t}) = E(\epsilon_{it}) = 0$. Hence we see that (97) holds also when $j = k = 0$. Thus equation (97) is completely proved if we show that it holds when $j > 0$ and $k = 0$. Let $\|\alpha^{ij}\| = \|\alpha_{ij0}\|^{-1}(i,\ j = 1, \cdots, r)$. Then $(1/J)(\partial J/\partial \alpha_{ij0}) = \alpha^{ji}$ and from (98) we obtain

$$(98') \qquad\qquad y_{ij0} = \sqrt{N}\, \alpha^{ji} - \frac{1}{\sqrt{N}} \sum_{t=1}^{N} E(\epsilon_{it} x_{jt}).$$

Hence

$$(99) \qquad\qquad E(y_{ij0}) = \sqrt{N}\, \alpha^{ji} - \frac{1}{\sqrt{N}} \sum_{t=1}^{N} E(\epsilon_{it} x_{jt}).$$

Since the covariance matrix of the variates $\epsilon_{1t}, \cdots, \epsilon_{rt}$ is the unit matrix it can easily be shown that

$$(100) \qquad\qquad E(\epsilon_{it} x_{jt}) = \alpha^{ji}.$$

From (99) and (100) we obtain $E(y_{ij0}) = 0$. Hence (97) is proved in all cases.

Now we shall derive the limiting covariance matrix of the variates y_{ijk}. We have

$$\sigma(y_{ijk} y_{lmn}) = \frac{1}{N} E\left\{ \left[(N/J)(\partial J/\partial \alpha_{ijk}) - \sum_{t=1}^{N} \epsilon_{it} x_{j,t-k} \right] \right.$$

$$(101)$$

$$\left. \cdot \left[(N/J)(\partial J/\partial \alpha_{lmn}) - \sum_{t=1}^{N} \epsilon_{lt} x_{m,t-n} \right] \right\}.$$

From (97) it follows that

$$E\left[(N/J)(\partial J/\partial \alpha_{ijk}) - \sum_{t=1}^{N} \epsilon_{it} x_{j,t-k} \right]$$

$$(102)$$

$$= E\left[(N/J)(\partial J/\partial \alpha_{lmn}) - \sum_{t=1}^{N} \epsilon_{lt} x_{m,t-n} \right] = 0.$$

From (101) and (102) we easily obtain

(103)
$$\sigma(y_{ijk}y_{lmn}) = \frac{1}{N}\left[E\left(\sum_{t=1}^{N} \epsilon_{it}x_{j,t-k}\right)\left(\sum_{t=1}^{N} \epsilon_{lt}x_{m,t-n}\right) \right.$$
$$\left. - (N^2/J^2)(\partial J/\partial\alpha_{ijk})(\partial J/\partial\alpha_{lmn}) \right].$$

We shall denote $(1/N)\sum_{t=1}^{N}x_{j,t-k}x_{m,t-n}$ by D_{jkmnN} and plim D_{jkmnN} by D_{jkmn}. Furthermore we denote $E(D_{jkmnN})$ by B_{jkmnN}. We obviously have

(104)
$$\text{plim } B_{jkmnN} = D_{jkmn}.$$

In order to evaluate the right-hand side of (103) we shall distinguish different cases.

Case I. $k>0$ *and* $n>0$. In this case we have

(105)
$$\sigma(y_{ijk}y_{lmn}) = \frac{1}{N} E\left[\sum_{t=1}^{N}\sum_{t'=1}^{N} \epsilon_{it}x_{j,t-k}\epsilon_{lt'}x_{m,t'-n} \right].$$

Since

$$E(\epsilon_{it}x_{j,t-k}\epsilon_{lt'}x_{mt'-n}) = 0 \quad \text{for} \quad t \neq t',$$

we obtain

(106)
$$\sigma(y_{ijk}y_{lmn}) = \frac{1}{N} E\left[\sum_{t=1}^{N} \epsilon_{it}\epsilon_{lt}x_{j,t-k}x_{m,t-n} \right]$$
$$= E(\epsilon_{it}\epsilon_{lt})E\left(\frac{1}{N}\sum_{t=1}^{N} x_{j,t-k}x_{m,t-n} \right) = \delta_{il}B_{jkmnN},$$

where δ_{il} is the Kronecker δ, i.e., $\delta_{il}=0$ for $i\neq l$ and $\delta_{ii}=1$.

Case II. $k=0$ *and* $n>0$. In this case we have

(107)
$$\sigma(y_{ij0}y_{lmn}) = \frac{1}{N} E\left[\sum_{t'=1}^{N}\sum_{t=1}^{N} \epsilon_{it}\epsilon_{lt'}x_{jt}x_{m,t'-n} \right].$$

We have

(108)
$$E(\epsilon_{it}\epsilon_{lt'}x_{jt}x_{m,t'-n}) = E\left[\epsilon_{it}\epsilon_{lt'}(x_{jt} - \alpha^{ji}\epsilon_{it})x_{m,t'-n} \right]$$
$$+ \alpha^{ji}E(\epsilon_{it}^{2}\epsilon_{lt'}x_{m,t'-n}).$$

We shall prove that the right-hand side of (108) is equal to 0 if $t \neq t'$. This is clearly true when $t'>t$. If $t>t'$ then ϵ_{it} is independent of $\epsilon_{lt'}$ and of $x_{m,t'-n}$. Since ϵ_{it} is independent of $(x_{jt}-\alpha^{ji}\epsilon_{it})$, we see that the right-hand side of (108) is equal to zero if $t>t'$. Hence we have

$$\text{(109)} \quad \sigma(y_{ij0}y_{lmn}) = \frac{1}{N} E\left\{ \sum_{t=1}^{N} \epsilon_{it}\epsilon_{lt}(x_{jt} \quad \alpha^{ji}\epsilon_{it})x_{m,t-n} \right.$$
$$\left. + \alpha^{ji}\sum_{t=1}^{N} E(\epsilon_{it}{}^{2}\epsilon_{lt}x_{m,t-n}) \right\}.$$

If $l \neq i$ then ϵ_{it} is independent of the set of variates ϵ_{lt}, $(x_{jt}-\alpha^{ji}\epsilon_{it})$, and $x_{m,t-n}$. From this it follows easily that the right-hand side of (109) is zero for $l \neq i$. We have

$$\text{(110)} \quad \begin{aligned} E\left[\epsilon_{it}{}^{2}(x_{jt} - \alpha^{ji}\epsilon_{it})x_{m,t-n}\right] &= E(\epsilon_{it}{}^{2})E\left[(x_{jt} - \alpha^{ji}\epsilon_{it})x_{m,t-n}\right] \\ &= E(x_{jt}x_{m,t-n}). \end{aligned}$$

Furthermore we have

$$\text{(111)} \quad E(\epsilon_{it}{}^{3}x_{m,t-n}) = E(\epsilon_{it}{}^{3})E(x_{m,t-n}) = \mu_{3}{}^{(i)}E(x_{m,t-n}),$$

where $\mu_{3}{}^{(i)}$ denotes the third moment of ϵ_{it}. From (109), (110), and (111) we obtain

$$\text{(112)} \quad \sigma(y_{ij0}y_{lmn}) = B_{j0mnN} + \mu_{3}{}^{(i)}\alpha^{ji}B_{00mnN}.$$

Thus our final result can be summarized in the equation

$$\text{(113)} \quad \sigma(y_{ij0}y_{lmn}) = \delta_{il}(B_{j0mnN} + \alpha^{ji}\mu_{3}{}^{(i)}B_{00mnN}),$$

where δ_{il} is the Kronecker delta.

Case III. $k>0$ and $n=0$. The results in this case can be obtained from those in Case II by interchanging the pairs (j, k) and (m, n). Thus we have

$$\text{(114)} \quad \sigma(y_{ijk}y_{lm0}) = \delta_{il}(B_{m0jkN} + \alpha^{mi}\mu_{3}{}^{(i)}B_{00jkN}).$$

Case IV. $k=n=0$. For treating this case we shall break it down into four subcases IV_1–IV_4

Subcase IV_1. $j>0$, $m>0$, $k=n=0$. In this case we have on account of (97)

$$E(y_{ij0}y_{lm0}) = E\left[(y_{ij0} - \sqrt{N}\,\alpha^{ji})(y_{lm0} - \sqrt{N}\,\alpha^{ml})\right] - N\alpha^{ji}\alpha^{ml}.$$

Hence on account of (98') we obtain

$$\text{(114')} \quad \sigma(y_{ij0}y_{lm0}) = E\left[\frac{1}{N}\sum_{t=1}^{N}\sum_{t'=1}^{N}\epsilon_{it}\epsilon_{lt'}x_{jt}x_{mt'}\right] - N\alpha^{ji}\alpha^{ml}.$$

We have the identity

$$\text{(115)} \quad \begin{aligned} E(\epsilon_{it}\epsilon_{lt'}x_{jt}x_{mt'}) &= E\left[\epsilon_{it}\epsilon_{lt'}(x_{jt} - \alpha^{ji}\epsilon_{it})(x_{mt'} - \alpha^{ml}\epsilon_{lt'})\right] \\ &\quad + \alpha^{ji}E\left[\epsilon_{lt'}\epsilon_{it}{}^{2}(x_{mt'} - \alpha^{ml}\epsilon_{lt'})\right] \\ &\quad + \alpha^{ml}E\left[\epsilon_{lt'}{}^{2}\epsilon_{it}(x_{jt} - \alpha^{ji}\epsilon_{it})\right] \\ &\quad + \alpha^{ml}\alpha^{ji}E(\epsilon_{lt'}{}^{2}\epsilon_{it}{}^{2}). \end{aligned}$$

From (59) it follows that $\phi_{jit}(t) = \alpha^{ji}$. Hence according to (56) $x_{jt} - \alpha^{ji}\epsilon_{it}$ is independent of ϵ_{it}. We shall frequently use this fact in the following derivations.

If t is different from t', say $t > t'$, then ϵ_{it} is independent of the set of variables $\epsilon_{lt'}$, $(x_{jt} - \alpha^{ji}\epsilon_{it})$ and $(x_{mt'} - \alpha^{ml}\epsilon_{lt'})$. Hence since $E(\epsilon_{it}) = 0$ we have

$$E\left[\epsilon_{it}\epsilon_{lt'}(x_{jt} - \alpha^{ji}\epsilon_{it})(x_{mt'} - \alpha^{ml}\epsilon_{lt'})\right]$$
$$= E(\epsilon_{it})E\left[\epsilon_{lt'}(x_{jt} - \alpha^{ji}\epsilon_{it})(x_{mt'} - \alpha^{ml}\epsilon_{lt'})\right] = 0.$$

Similarly for $t' > t$

$$E\left[\epsilon_{it}\epsilon_{lt'}(x_{jt} - \alpha^{ji}\epsilon_{it})(x_{mt'} - \alpha^{ml}\epsilon_{lt'})\right]$$
$$= E(\epsilon_{lt'})E\left[\epsilon_{it}(x_{jt} - \alpha^{ji}\epsilon_{it})(x_{mt'} - \alpha^{ml}\epsilon_{lt'})\right] = 0.$$

Hence

(116) $\quad E\left[\epsilon_{it}\epsilon_{lt'}(x_{jt} - \alpha^{ji}\epsilon_{it})(x_{mt'} - \alpha^{ml}\epsilon_{lt'})\right] = 0 \qquad (t \neq t').$

On account of the independence of ϵ_{ut} and $(x_{vt} - \alpha^{vu}\epsilon_{ut})$ $(v = 1, \cdots, r; u = 1, \cdots, r)$ we obtain

(117) $E\left[\epsilon_{lt'}\epsilon_{it}^2(x_{mt'} - \alpha^{ml}\epsilon_{lt'})\right] = E\left[\epsilon_{lt'}^2\epsilon_{it}(x_{jt} - \alpha^{ji}\epsilon_{it})\right] = 0 \ (t \neq t').$

Furthermore we have, because of $E(\epsilon_{lt'}^2) = 1$,

$$E(\epsilon_{lt'}^2\epsilon_{it}^2) = E(\epsilon_{lt'}^2)E(\epsilon_{it}^2) = 1.$$

Hence on account of (115), (116), (117) we have

(118) $\qquad\qquad E(\epsilon_{it}\epsilon_{lt'}x_{jt}x_{mt'}) = \alpha^{ml}\alpha^{ji} \qquad\qquad (t \neq t').$

For $t = t'$ we use the identity

(119)
$$\begin{aligned} E(\epsilon_{it}\epsilon_{lt}x_{jt}x_{mt}) &= E\left[\epsilon_{it}\epsilon_{lt}(x_{jt} - \alpha^{ji}\epsilon_{it})(x_{mt} - \alpha^{mi}\epsilon_{it})\right] \\ &+ \alpha^{ji}E\left[\epsilon_{it}^2\epsilon_{lt}(x_{mt} - \alpha^{mi}\epsilon_{it})\right] \\ &+ \alpha^{mi}E\left[\epsilon_{it}^2\epsilon_{lt}(x_{jt} - \alpha^{ji}\epsilon_{it})\right] \\ &+ \alpha^{ji}\alpha^{mi}E(\epsilon_{it}^3\epsilon_{lt}). \end{aligned}$$

Since ϵ_{it} is independent of $(x_{jt} - \alpha^{ji}\epsilon_{it})$, $(x_{mt} - \alpha^{mi}\epsilon_{it})$, and of ϵ_{lt} if $i \neq l$, we have, for $i \neq l$,

$$E\left[\epsilon_{it}\epsilon_{lt}(x_{jt} - \alpha^{ji}\epsilon_{it})(x_{mt} - \alpha^{mi}\epsilon_{it})\right]$$
$$= E(\epsilon_{it})E\left[\epsilon_{lt}(x_{jt} - \alpha^{ji}\epsilon_{it})(x_{mt} - \alpha^{mi}\epsilon_{it})\right]$$
$$= 0,$$

$$E\left[\epsilon_{it}^2\epsilon_{lt}(x_{mt} - \alpha^{mi}\epsilon_{it})\right] = E(\epsilon_{it}^2)E\left[\epsilon_{lt}(x_{mt} - \alpha^{mi}\epsilon_{it})\right]$$

(120) $\qquad\qquad = E\left[\epsilon_{lt}(x_{mt} - \alpha^{mi}\epsilon_{it})\right],$

$$E\left[\epsilon_{it}^2\epsilon_{lt}(x_{jt} - \alpha^{ji}\epsilon_{it})\right] = E(\epsilon_{it}^2)E\left[\epsilon_{lt}(x_{jt} - \alpha^{ji}\epsilon_{it})\right]$$
$$= E\left[\epsilon_{lt}(x_{jt} - \alpha^{ji}\epsilon_{it})\right],$$

$$E(\epsilon_{it}^3\epsilon_{lt}) = 0 \qquad\qquad (i \neq l).$$

Hence we have on account of (100), (119), and (120)

$$E(\epsilon_{it}\epsilon_{lt}x_{jt}x_{mt}) = \alpha^{ji}E\big[\epsilon_{lt}(x_{mt} - \alpha^{mi}\epsilon_{it})\big] + \alpha^{mi}E\big[\epsilon_{lt}(x_{jt} - \alpha^{ii}\epsilon_{it})\big]$$

(121)
$$= \alpha^{ji}E(\epsilon_{lt}x_{mt}) + \alpha^{mi}E(\epsilon_{lt}x_{jt})$$

$$= \alpha^{ji}\alpha^{ml} + \alpha^{mi}\alpha^{jl} \qquad\qquad (i \neq 1).$$

From (121) and (118) we see that for $i \neq l$ in the double sum on the right-hand side of (114') the term $\alpha^{ji}\alpha^{ml}$ occurs N^2 times, the term $\alpha^{mi}\alpha^{jl}$ N times. Hence we obtain

(122) $$\sigma(y_{ij0}y_{lm0}) = \alpha^{mi}\alpha^{jl} \quad \text{for} \quad i \neq 1.$$

For $i = l$ we have

$$E\big[\epsilon_{it}^2(x_{jt} - \alpha^{ii}\epsilon_{it})(x_{mt} - \alpha^{mi}\epsilon_{it})\big]$$

$$= E(\epsilon_{it}^2)E\big[(x_{jt} - \alpha^{ii}\epsilon_{it})(x_{mt} - \alpha^{mi}\epsilon_{it})\big]$$

(123)
$$= E\big[(x_{jt} - \alpha^{ii}\epsilon_{it})(x_{mt} - \alpha^{mi}\epsilon_{it})\big]$$

$$= E\big[x_{jt}(x_{mt} - \alpha^{mi}\epsilon_{it})\big] = E(x_{jt}x_{mt}) - \alpha^{mi}E(\epsilon_{it}x_{jt})$$

$$= E(x_{jt}x_{mt}) - \alpha^{ji}\alpha^{mi}.$$

Furthermore we have

(124) $$E\big[\epsilon_{it}^3(x_{mt} - \alpha^{mi}\epsilon_{it})\big] = E(\epsilon_{it}^3)E\big[(x_{mt} - \alpha^{mi}\epsilon_{it})\big] = \mu_3^{(i)}E(x_{mt}),$$

where $\mu_3^{(i)} = E(\epsilon_{it}^3)$. Similarly we obtain

(125) $$E\big[\epsilon_{it}^3(x_{jt} - \alpha^{ii}\epsilon_{it})\big] = E(\epsilon_{it}^3)E(x_{jt} - \alpha^{mi}\epsilon_{it}) = \mu_3^{(i)}E(x_{jt}).$$

Putting $E(\epsilon_{it}^4) = \mu_4^{(i)}$ we finally obtain from (119), (123), (124), and (125)

(126)
$$E(\epsilon_{it}^2x_{jt}x_{mt}) = E(x_{jt}x_{mt}) + \mu_3^{(i)}\big[\alpha^{ji}E(x_{mt}) + \alpha^{mi}E(x_{jt})\big]$$
$$+ (\mu_4^{(i)} - 1)\alpha^{ji}\alpha^{mi}.$$

Hence from (114), (118), and (126) we obtain

$$\sigma(y_{ij0}y_{im0}) = \frac{1}{N}\sum_{t=1}^{N} E(x_{jt}x_{mt})$$

(127)
$$+ \mu_3^{(i)}\bigg[\alpha^{ji}\sum_{t=1}^{N} E(x_{mt})/N + \alpha^{mi}\sum_{t=1}^{N} E(x_{jt})/N\bigg]$$

$$+ (\mu_4^{(i)} - 2)\alpha^{ji}\alpha^{mi}$$

$$= B_{j0m0N} + \mu_3^{(i)}(\alpha^{ji}B_{m000N} + \alpha^{mi}B_{j000N})$$

$$+ (\mu_4^{(i)} - 2)\alpha^{ji}\alpha^{mi}.$$

We can summarize our result as follows:

$$(128) \quad \begin{aligned} \sigma(y_{ij0}y_{lm0}) &= \alpha^{il}\alpha^{mi} + \delta_{il}[B_{j0m0N} + \mu_3{}^{(i)}\alpha^{jl}B_{m00N} \\ &\quad + \mu_3{}^{(l)}\alpha^{mi}B_{j000N} + (\mu_4{}^{(i)} - 3)\alpha^{il}\alpha^{mi}] \end{aligned}$$
$$(j > 0,\ m > 0),$$

where δ_{ij} denotes the Kronecker delta.

Subcase IV_2. $j>0$, $m=0$. In this case we have from (98)

$$(129) \quad \begin{aligned} \sigma(y_{ij0}y_{l00}) &= E\left[\frac{1}{N}\sum_{t=1}^{N}\sum_{t'=1}^{N}\epsilon_{it}\epsilon_{lt'}x_{jt}\right] - \alpha^{ii}E\left[\sum_{t=1}^{N}\epsilon_{lt}\right] \\ &= E\left[\frac{1}{N}\sum_{t=1}^{N}\sum_{t'=1}^{N}\epsilon_{it}\epsilon_{lt'}x_{jt}\right]. \end{aligned}$$

We have the identity

$$(130) \quad E(\epsilon_{lt'}\epsilon_{it}x_{jt}) = E\left[\epsilon_{lt'}\epsilon_{it}(x_{jt} - \alpha^{ii}\epsilon_{it})\right] + \alpha^{ii}E(\epsilon_{it}{}^2\epsilon_{lt'}).$$

We see from (130) that $E(\epsilon_{lt'}\epsilon_{it}x_{jt})=0$ if $i\neq l$ or $t\neq t'$, since then the set of variables $\epsilon_{lt'}$, ϵ_{it}, $(x_{jt}-\alpha^{ii}\epsilon_{it})$ are independent of each other. We furthermore have from (130) and the fact that $E(\epsilon_{it}{}^2)=1$

$$(131) \quad E(\epsilon_{it}{}^2 x_{jt}) = E(x_{jt}) + \alpha^{ii}\mu_3{}^{(i)},$$

where $\mu_3{}^{(i)}$ is the third moment of ϵ_{it}. Hence we have

$$(132) \quad \begin{aligned} \sigma(y_{ij0}y_{l00}) &= \delta_{il}\left(\sum_{t=1}^{N} E(x_{jt})/N + \alpha^{ii}\mu_3{}^{(i)}\right) \\ &= \delta_{il}(B_{j000N} + \alpha^{ii}\mu_3{}^{(i)}). \end{aligned}$$

Subcase IV_3. $j=0$, $m>0$. In this case we have

$$(133) \quad \sigma(y_{i00}y_{lm0}) = \sigma(y_{lm0}y_{i00}).$$

Hence from (132) and (133) we see that

$$(134) \quad \sigma(y_{i00}y_{lm0}) = \delta_{il}(B_{m000N} + \alpha^{mi}\mu_3{}^{(l)}).$$

Subcase IV_4. $j=m=0$. In this case we obtain from (98)

$$(135) \quad \sigma(y_{i00}y_{l00}) = E\left(\frac{1}{N}\sum_{t=1}^{N}\sum_{t'=1}^{N}\epsilon_{it}\epsilon_{lt'}\right).$$

Because of the independence of ϵ_{it}, $\epsilon_{lt'}$ for $i\neq l$ or $t\neq t'$ and because of $E(\epsilon_{it}{}^2)=1$ we have

$$(136) \quad E(\epsilon_{it}\epsilon_{lt'}) = \delta_{il}\delta_{tt'}.$$

From (135) and (136) we obtain

(137) $\sigma(y_{i00}y_{l00}) = \delta_{il}.$

Summarizing our results we have

$$(138) \quad \sigma(y_{ijk}y_{lmn}) = \begin{cases} \delta_{il}B_{jkmnN} & \text{if } k > 0, n > 0, \\ \delta_{il}(B_{j0mnN} + \alpha^{ji}\mu_3{}^{(i)}B_{00mnN}) & \text{if } k = 0, n > 0, \\ \delta_{il}(B_{m0jkN} + \alpha^{mi}\mu_3{}^{(i)}B_{00jkN}) & \text{if } k > 0, n = 0, \\ \alpha^{il}\alpha^{mi} + \delta_{il}[B_{j0m0N} + \mu_3{}^{(i)}\alpha^{il}B_{m000N} \\ \quad + \mu_3{}^{(l)}\alpha^{mi}B_{j000N} + (\mu_4{}^{(i)} - 3)\alpha^{il}\alpha^{mi}] \\ \qquad \text{if } k = 0, n = 0, j > 0, k > 0, \\ \delta_{il}(B_{j000N} + \alpha^{ji}\mu_3{}^{(i)}) & \text{if } j > 0, m = k = n = 0, \\ \delta_{il}(B_{m000N} + \alpha^{mi}\mu_3{}^{(i)}) & \text{if } m > 0, j = k = n = 0, \\ \delta_{il} & \text{if } j = k = m = n = 0. \end{cases}$$

Since according to (104) $\operatorname{plim}_{N \to \infty}B_{jkmnN} = D_{jkmn} = \operatorname{plim}_{N \to \infty}D_{jkmnN}$, we have

(139) $\displaystyle\operatorname*{plim}_{N \to \infty} (B_{jkmnN} - D_{jkmnN}) = 0.$

Hence the limit covariance matrix of the variates y_{ijk} is not changed if we replace in (138) B_{jkmnN} by D_{jkmnN}. Furthermore because of $\operatorname{plim}_{N \to \infty}a_{ijk} = \alpha_{ijk}$, we can in (138) replace the parameters α_{ij0} by their consistent estimates a_{ij0}. Finally the moments $\mu_3{}^{(i)}$, $\mu_4{}^{(i)}$ can also be replaced by consistent sample estimates if they are not a priori known. Hence all quantities occuring on the right-hand side of (138) can be replaced by sample estimates without changing the limiting values of the covariances of the variates y_{ijk}. The limit covariance matrix of the y_{ijk} can be obtained from (138) by replacing B_{jkmnN} by its stochastic limit D_{jkmn}.

From the limit covariance matrix of the $y_{ijk}(i = 1, \cdots, r; j = 0, \cdots, r; k = 0, \cdots, p_{ij})$ we shall derive the limit covariance matrix of the quantities $\sqrt{N}(a_{ijk} - \alpha_{ijk})(i = 1, \cdots, r; j = 0, \cdots, r; k = 0, \cdots, p_{ij})$.

We shall denote by a^{ji} the value we obtain if we replace in the expression α^{ji} the parameters α_{ij0} by their estimates a_{ij0}. We furthermore put $\alpha^{ij0} = \alpha^{ij}, a^{ij0} = a^{ij}(i, j = 1, \cdots, r)$, $\alpha^{i0k} = \alpha^{0ik} = a^{i0k} = a^{0ik} = 0$ and $\alpha^{ijk} = a^{ijk} = 0$ for $k > 0$. Then from (55) and (96) we obtain

$$(140) \quad y_{ijk} = \sum_{l=0}^{r}\sum_{m=0}^{p_{il}}\sqrt{N}\,(a_{ilm} - \alpha_{ilm})D_{jklmN} - \sqrt{N}\,(a^{jik} - \alpha^{jik}).$$

Since plim $a_{ijk} = \alpha_{ijk}$, we can for large N replace $a^{ji0} - \alpha^{ji0}$ by the linear term of its Taylor expansion. Thus we obtain

$$
(140') \quad
\begin{aligned}
y_{ijk} &= \sum_{l=1}^{r} \sum_{m=1}^{p_{il}} \sqrt{N}\,(a_{ilm} - \alpha_{ilm}) D_{jklmN} \\
&\quad + \sum_{u=1}^{r} \sum_{v=1}^{r} (\partial \alpha^{jik}/\partial \alpha_{uvk}) \sqrt{N}\,(a_{uvk} - \alpha_{uvk}).
\end{aligned}
$$

For large N we can replace $\partial \alpha^{jik}/\partial \alpha_{uvk}$ by $\partial a^{jik}/\partial a_{uvk}$. Thus finally we can write

$$
(140'') \quad
\begin{aligned}
y_{ijk} &= \sum_{l=1}^{r} \sum_{m=1}^{p_{il}} \sqrt{N}\,(a_{ilm} - \alpha_{ilm}) D_{jklmN} \\
&\quad + \sum_{u=1}^{r} \sum_{v=1}^{r} (\partial a^{jik}/\partial a_{uvk}) \sqrt{N}\,(a_{uvk} - \alpha_{uvk}).
\end{aligned}
$$

We shall now enumerate the triples (i, j, k) for which α_{ijk} is unknown and write $y_u = y_{ijk}$ if (i, j, k) is the uth triple in our enumeration. We furthermore put $\xi_u = \sqrt{N}(a_{ijk} - \alpha_{ijk})$ if (i, j, k) is the uth triple in our enumeration. Let there be h triples (i, j, k). Then we have from $(140'')$

$$
(141) \qquad\qquad y_u = \sum_{u'=1}^{h} b_{uu'N} \xi_{u'},
$$

where $b_{uu'N}$ may be determined from $(140'')$. We shall now further assume that the distribution of the ϵ_{it} is such that $\mathrm{plim}_{N \to \infty} |b_{uu'N}|$ is different from 0. As we shall show later this is always the case if the ϵ_{it} are normally and independently distributed.

We put $\|b_{uu'N}\|^{-1} = \|c_{uu'N}\|$. Then

$$
\xi_u = \sum_{u'=1}^{r} c_{uu'N} y_{u'}.
$$

Hence for large N

$$
\sigma(\xi_u \xi_v) = E\left[\sum_{u'=1}^{h} \sum_{v'=1}^{h} c_{uu'N} c_{vv'N} y_{u'} y_{v'}\right] = \sum_{u'=1}^{h} \sum_{v'=1}^{h} c_{uu'N} \sigma(y_{u'} y_{v'}) c_{vv'N}.
$$

The above equation can be written as the following matrix equation

$$
(142) \qquad\qquad \|\sigma(\xi_u \xi_v)\| = \|c_{uvN}\|\, \|\sigma(y_u y_v)\|\, \|c_{uvN}\|^t,
$$

where $\|c_{uvN}\|^t$ is the transposed matrix of $\|c_{uvN}\|$. The coefficients c_{uvN} do not involve any unknown parameters; they can be calculated from the observations. As mentioned before the formula (142) is valid only for large N. More precisely, the difference between the right-hand side expression in (142) and the exact value of the covariance between ξ_u and ξ_v converges stochastically to zero.

If we know a priori that the ϵ_{it} are normally and independently distributed with means zero and variances 1, the limit covariance matrix of the variables ξ_u can be considerably simplified. According to (54) the probability density p of the variables $x_{1t}, \cdots, x_{rt}$ is given by

$$(143) \qquad p = \frac{J^N}{(2\pi)^{rN/2}} \exp\left(-\frac{1}{2} \sum_{i=1}^{r} L_{it}^2\right),$$

where

$$L_{it} = \sum_{i=1}^{r} \sum_{j=0}^{r} \sum_{k=0}^{p_{ij}} \alpha_{ijk} x_{j,t-k}.$$

We have

$$(144) \qquad \sqrt{N}\, y_u = \partial \log p / \partial \alpha_u.$$

Hence, writing dx for $dx_{11}, \cdots, dx_{r1}, \cdots, dx_{1N}, \cdots, dx_{rN}$, we have

$$(145) \qquad \begin{aligned} E(y_u) &= \frac{1}{\sqrt{N}} \int_R (\partial \log p / \partial \alpha_u) p\, dx \\ &= \frac{1}{\sqrt{N}} \int_R [(\partial p / \partial \alpha_u)/p]p\, dx = \int_R (\partial p / \partial \alpha_u)\, dx, \end{aligned}$$

where the symbol $\int_R$ denotes the integral over the whole space. Since $\int_R p\, dx = 1$ identically in $\alpha_u(u=1, \cdots, h)$ we must have

$$(146) \qquad \int_R (\partial p / \partial \alpha_u)\, dx = 0.$$

From (145) and (146) we obtain

$$(147) \qquad E(y_u) = 0.$$

Furthermore we have from (144)

$$(148) \qquad N\sigma(y_u y_v) = E\left[(\partial \log p / \partial \alpha_u)(\partial \log p / \partial \alpha_v)\right].$$

We shall prove that

$$(149) \qquad E\left[(\partial \log p / \partial \alpha_u)(\partial \log p / \partial \alpha_v)\right] = -E(\partial^2 \log p / \partial \alpha_u \partial \alpha_v).$$

We start from the equation

$$(150) \qquad \int_R (\partial \log p / \partial \alpha_u) p\, dx = 0.$$

Differentiating (150) with respect to α_v we obtain

(151) $\int_R [(\partial^2 \log p/\partial\alpha_u\partial\alpha_v)p + (\partial \log p/\partial\alpha_u)(\partial p/\partial\alpha_v)]dx = 0.$

Since

(152) $\partial p/\partial\alpha_v = [(\partial p/\partial\alpha_v)/p]p = (\partial \log p/\partial\alpha_v)p,$

(149) follows from (151) and (152). Hence we obtain

(153) $N\sigma(y_u y_v) = -E(\partial^2 \log p/\partial\alpha_u\partial\alpha_v).$

It can be shown that the results in (153) check with those in (138) if we put $\mu_3^{(i)} = (\mu_4^{(i)} - 3) = 0$ and use the identity $\partial\alpha^{ji}/\partial\alpha_{lm0} = -\alpha^{mi}\alpha^{jl}$.

Expanding $\partial \log p/\partial\alpha_u$ into a Taylor series around $a_u(u=1, \cdots, h)$ and putting $\xi_u = \sqrt{N}(a_u - \alpha_u)$ we obtain

(154)
$$\sqrt{N}\, y_u = \partial \log p/\partial\alpha_u = (\partial \log p/\partial\alpha_u)_{\alpha_x = a_x (x=1, \cdots, h)}$$
$$+ \sum_{v=1}^{h} \frac{1}{\sqrt{N}} (\partial^2 \log p/\partial\alpha_u\partial\alpha_v)_{\alpha_x = \bar{a}_y (x=1, \cdots, h)}\xi_v.$$

where $\bar{a}_x$ is a value between a_x and $\alpha_x(x=1, \cdots, h)$. Since the quantities a_x have been determined so that

(155) $(\partial \log p/\partial\alpha_u)_{\alpha_x = \bar{a}_x (x=1, \cdots, h)} = 0,$

we obtain from (154) and (155)

(156) $y_u = -\sum_{v=1}^{h} \frac{1}{\sqrt{N}} (\partial^2 \log p/\partial\alpha_u\partial\alpha_v)_{\alpha_x = \bar{a}_x (x=1, \cdots, h)}\xi_v.$

Since plim $a_u = \alpha_u$ the limit covariance matrix of the variates ξ_u is not changed if in (156) we replace $(1/N)(\partial^2 \log p/\partial\alpha_u\partial\alpha_v)_{\alpha_x = \bar{a}_x (x=1, \ldots, h)}$ by $(1/N)(\partial^2 \log p/\alpha_u\partial\alpha_v)$ taken at the point α_x $(x=1, \cdots, h)$. Moreover, since $(1/N)(\partial^2 \log p/\partial\alpha_u\partial\alpha_v)$ can be shown to converge to its limit expectation, we may replace $(1/N)(\partial^2 \log p/\partial\alpha_u\partial\alpha_v)$ by its expectation. Hence on account of (153)

(157) $y_u = -\sum_{v=1}^{h} \frac{1}{N} E(\partial^2 \log p/\partial\alpha_u\partial\alpha_v)\xi_v = \sum_{v=1}^{h} \sigma(y_u y_v)\xi_v.$

Equation (157) implies that the covariance matrix of the variates ξ_u is equal to the inverse of the covariance matrix of the variates y_u. Since (157) is valid only in the limit, we can merely state that the limit covariance matrix of the variates ξ_u is equal to the inverse of the limit covariance matrix of the variates y_u.

7. *Examples*

In his paper "The Statistical Implications of a System of Simultaneous Equations," [2] T. Haavelmo discussed the following system of equations:

$$(158) \qquad Y = aX + \epsilon_1, \qquad X = bY + \epsilon_2,$$

where ϵ_1, ϵ_2 are assumed to be normally and independently distributed with mean 0. Bringing this system to the form (85), which we shall call the reduced form, Haavelmo obtains

$$(159) \qquad Y = \epsilon_1{}^*, \qquad X = \epsilon_2{}^*,$$

where
$$\epsilon_1{}^* = (\epsilon_1 + a\epsilon_2)/(1 - ab), \qquad \epsilon_2{}^* = (b\epsilon_1 + \epsilon_2)/(1 - ab).$$

In the form (158) 4 parameters are unknown, namely a, b, $\sigma_1{}^2$, $\sigma_2{}^2$, where $\sigma_1{}^2$ and $\sigma_2{}^2$ are the variances of ϵ_1 and ϵ_2 respectively. From the reduced form (159) we can see that we can estimate not more than three parameters namely $E(X^2)$, $E(Y^2)$, $E(XY)$. Hence it is impossible to estimate *all* unknown parameters in the system (158) with any method, whatever the number of observations.

We can see this easily directly as follows: The system (158) is equivalent to

$$(160) \qquad \begin{aligned} Y &= X(1 - a)/(1 - b) + (\epsilon_1 + \epsilon_2)/(1 - b) = a^*X + \epsilon_1, \\ X &= Y(1 + b)/(1 + a) + (\epsilon_2 - \epsilon_1)/(1 + a) = b^*Y + \epsilon_2', \end{aligned}$$

where again ϵ_1', ϵ_2' are normally and independently distributed. The coefficients in (160), $a^* = (1-a)/(1-b)$, $b^* = (1+b)/(1+a)$, are certainly different from the coefficients in (158). Moreover the variance of ϵ_1' and ϵ_2' are different from the variances of ϵ_1 and ϵ_2 respectively. Hence it is clear that a and b as well as $\sigma_1{}^2$ and $\sigma_2{}^2$ cannot be estimated from any sample and from the conditions (158) alone.

If we should have the additional knowledge that $\sigma_1{}^2 = \sigma_2{}^2 = \sigma^2$ then (158) would uniquely determine the parameters a, b, and σ^2. The number of unknown parameters is then three, that is to say, the same as the number of unknown parameters in the reduced form. The unreduced form, however, does not offer any advantage over the reduced form. We should therefore also in this case prefer to solve the equations in the reduced form.

Haavelmo then discussed an economic model which leads to the following system of difference equations:

$$(161) \qquad \begin{aligned} u_t &= \alpha r_t + \beta + \epsilon_{1t}, \\ v_t &= k(u_t - u_{t-1}) + \epsilon_{2t}, \\ r_t &= u_t + v_t, \end{aligned}$$

where ϵ_{1t}, ϵ_{2t} are assumed to be independently and normally distributed with mean 0. Eliminating the third of the equations (161) we obtain

(162)
$$(1 - \alpha)u_t - \alpha v_t - \beta = \epsilon_{1t},$$
$$v_t - ku_t + ku_{t-1} = \epsilon_{2t}.$$

The reduced form of the system (162) is given by

(163)
$$u_t + \alpha_{11}u_{t-1} + \alpha_1 = \epsilon_{1t}^*,$$
$$v_t + \alpha_{21}u_{t-1} + \alpha_2 = \epsilon_{2t}^*,$$

where α_{11}, α_{21}, α_1, α_2, and the parameters σ_{11}^*, σ_{22}^*, σ_{12}^* can be expressed in terms of the five parameters of the system (161), i.e.,

$$\alpha_{11} = \alpha k/(1-\alpha-\alpha k), \quad \alpha_{21} = (1-\alpha)k/(1-\alpha-\alpha k), \quad \alpha_1 = -\beta/(1-\alpha-\alpha k),$$
$$\alpha_2 = -\alpha k/(1-\alpha-\alpha k), \quad \sigma_{11}^* = (\sigma_1^2 + \alpha^2\sigma_2^2)/(1-\alpha-\alpha k)^2,$$
$$\sigma_{12}^* = [k\sigma_1^2 + \alpha(1-\alpha)\sigma_2^2]/(1-\alpha-\alpha k)^2,$$
$$\sigma_{22}^* = [k^2\sigma_1^2 + (1-\alpha)^2\sigma_2^2]/(1-\alpha-\alpha k)^2.$$

In this case we can estimate the 7 parameters α_{11}, α_{21}, α_1, α_2, σ_{11}^*, σ_{12}^*, σ_{22}^* from the sample. The number of unknown parameters in the original form is 5, namely α, k, β, σ_1^2, σ_2^2. Hence by using the reduced form and estimating the 7 parameters as if they were not subject to any restrictions we should throw away some information and lose in efficiency.

SUMMARY

In the first part of this paper the statistical treatment of a single stochastic difference equation

(A)
$$x_t = \alpha_1 x_{t-1} + \alpha_2 x_{t-2} + \cdots + \alpha_p x_{t-p} + \epsilon_t$$

is discussed where $\alpha_1, \cdots, \alpha_p$, and α_0 are constant coefficients and $\epsilon_1, \epsilon_2, \cdots$, are random variables. It is assumed that $\epsilon_1, \epsilon_2, \cdots$, are independently distributed each having the same distribution and $E(\epsilon_t) = 0$. Furthermore it is assumed that all moments of ϵ_t are finite and that the roots of the equation in ρ

$$\rho^p - \alpha_1\rho^{p-1} - \cdots - \alpha_p = 0$$

are less than 1 in absolute value. Suppose that the value of x_t has been observed for $t = 1-p, 1-p+1, \cdots, N$. As statistical estimates of the coefficients $\alpha_1, \cdots, \alpha_p$, α_0 the values $a_1, \cdots, a_p$, a_0 are used for which

$$\sum_{t=1}^{N} (x_t - \alpha_1 x_{t-1} - \cdots - \alpha_p x_{t-p} - \alpha_0)^2$$

becomes a minimum. The estimates $a_1, \cdots, a_p, a_0$ are the maximum-likelihood estimates of $\alpha_1, \cdots, \alpha_p, \alpha_0$, respectively, if ϵ_t is normally distributed. Although it is not assumed that the distribution of ϵ_t is normal, the estimates $a_1, \cdots, a_p, a_0$ are referred to as maximum-likelihood estimates and the joint limiting distribution of these estimates is derived.

Our main result in Part I can be summarized as follows: For large N the stochastic difference equation (A) can be treated in exactly the same way as a classical regression problem where x_t is the dependent variable and $x_{t-1}, \cdots, x_{t-p}$ are the independent variables. That is to say, the estimates of the coefficients $\alpha_1, \cdots, \alpha_p, \alpha_0$, as well as the joint limiting distribution of these estimates, are the same as if (A) were treated as a classical regression problem. Hence, the joint limiting distribution of $\sqrt{N}(a_1 - \alpha_1), \cdots, \sqrt{N}(a_p - \alpha_p)$, and $\sqrt{N}(a_0 - \alpha_0)$ is a multivariate normal distribution with zero means and a finite covariance matrix. The covariance between $\xi_i = \sqrt{N}(a_i - \alpha_i)$ and $\xi_j = \sqrt{N}(a_j - \alpha_j)$ $(i, j = 0, 1, \cdots, p)$ can be obtained as follows: Denote $(1/N)\sum_{t=1}^{N} x_{t-i} x_{t-j}$ by $D_{ijN}(i, j = 1, \cdots, p), (1/N)\sum_{t=1}^{N} x_{t-i}$ by $D_{i0N} = D_{0iN}$ and let $D_{00N} = 1$. Furthermore let $\|c_{ijN}\| = \|D_{ijN}\|^{-1}(i, j = 0, 1, \cdots, p)$ and $s^2 = (1/N)\sum_{t=1}^{N}(x_t - a_1 x_{t-1} - \cdots - a_p x_{t-p} - a_0)^2$. Then the limit covariance between ξ_i and ξ_j is equal to the stochastic limit of $s^2 c_{ijN}$. Thus, for large N the covariance of ξ_i and ξ_j can be replaced by the quantity $s^2 c_{ijN}$ which can be calculated from the observations.

The second part of the paper deals with a system of r difference equations

(B)
$$\sum_{j=1}^{r} \sum_{k=0}^{p_{ij}} \alpha_{ijk} x_{j,t-k} + \alpha_i = \epsilon_{it},$$

where p_{ij} is the highest lag in the variable x_{jt} occurring in the ith equation, the α's are known or unknown constants, the random vectors $(\epsilon_{11}, \cdots, \epsilon_{r1}), (\epsilon_{12}, \cdots, \epsilon_{r2}), \cdots$, are independently distributed each having the same distribution, and $E(\epsilon_{it}) = 0$ for all values of i and t. It is assumed that ϵ_{it} has finite moments and that the roots of the equation in ρ

$$\begin{vmatrix} b_{11}(\rho) & \cdots & b_{1r}(\rho) \\ \cdot & \cdots & \cdot \\ b_{r1}(\rho) & \cdots & b_{rr}(\rho) \end{vmatrix} = 0$$

are smaller than 1 in absolute value. The expression $b_{ij}(\rho)$ is given by $\sum_{k=1}^{p_{ij}} \alpha_{ijk}\rho^{-k}$.

The maximum-likelihood estimates of α_{ijk} and α_i are derived under the assumption that the joint distribution of $\epsilon_{1t}, \cdots, \epsilon_{rt}$ is normal.

Denote these maximum-likelihood estimates by a_{ijk} and a_i respectively. The joint limiting distribution of these estimates is derived without assuming normality of the distribution of ϵ_{it}. To summarize the results obtained, we distinguish 3 different cases.

Case A. The matrix $\|\alpha_{ij0}\|$ *is equal to the unit matrix and* $\sigma(\epsilon_{it}\epsilon_{jt}) = 0$ *for* $i \neq j$. In this case the maximum-likelihood estimates a_{ijk} and a_i are those values of α_{ijk} and α_i for which the sum of squares

$$\sum_{t=1}^{N} \sum_{i=1}^{r} \left[\sum_{j=1}^{r} \sum_{k=0}^{p_{ij}} (\alpha_{ijk} x_{j,t-k} + \alpha_i) \right]^2$$

becomes a minimum, i.e., the maximum-likelihood estimates are equal to the least-squares estimates. The joint limiting distributing of $\xi_{ijk} = \sqrt{N}(a_{ijk} - \alpha_{ijk})$ and $\xi_i = \sqrt{N}(a_i - \alpha_i)$ is a multivariate normal distribution with zero means and finite covariance matrix.

To give the explicit formulas for the covariances, the following notations are introduced: The variable x_{0t} is identically equal to 1. The symbols a_{i00}, α_{i00}, ξ_{i00} will stand for a_i, α_i, and ξ_i respectively. Furthermore, we put

$$p_{i0} = 0, \qquad D_{ikjlN} = \frac{1}{N} \sum_{t=1}^{N} x_{it-k} x_{jt-l},$$

$$Q_{il} = \left(\sum_{j=0}^{r} \sum_{k=0}^{p_{ij}} \alpha_{ijk} x_{j,t-k} \right) \left(\sum_{j=0}^{r} \sum_{k=0}^{p_{ij}} \alpha_{ljk} x_{j,t-k} \right),$$

and $\overline{Q}_{il}$ is obtained from Q_{il} by substituting a_{ijk} for α_{ijk}. For any given value i $(i = 1, \cdots, r)$ denote by m_i the number of different pairs (j, k) for which a_{ijk} is defined, i.e., for which α_{ijk} is unknown. Then we denote ξ_{ijk} by ξ_{iu} if (j, k) is the uth element in this sequence. Similarly we denote D_{iklmN} by $D_{uvN}{}^{(i)}$ if (j, k) is the uth element and (l, m) the vth element in this sequence (the superscript i is used because the ordered sequence of pairs (j, k) may depend on i). Let $\|c_{uvN}{}^{(i)}\| = \|D_{uvN}{}^{(i)}\|^{-1}$ $(u, v = 1, \cdots, m_i)$. The limit covariance between ξ_{iu} and ξ_{lv} is zero if $i \neq l$ The limit covariance between ξ_{iu} and ξ_{iv} is equal to the stochastic limit of $(\overline{Q}_{ii}/N)C_{uvN}{}^{(i)}$. Thus, for large N the covariance of ξ_{iu} and ξ_{iv} can be replaced by $(\overline{Q}_{ii}/N)C_{uvN}{}^{(i)}$ which can be calculated from the observations.

Case B. Here we consider the case in which $\|\alpha_{ij0}\|$ is the unit matrix and nothing is known about the covariance matrix $\|\sigma_{ij}\|$ of the variates $\epsilon_{it}, \cdots, \epsilon_{rt}$. It is furthermore assumed that p_{ij} has the same value p for all pairs (i, j) $(i, j = 1, \cdots, r)$ and that all coefficients $\alpha_{ijk}(k > 0)$ and α_i are unknown. We shall use the notations introduced in Case A. The maximum-likelihood estimates $a_{ijk}(i = 1, \cdots, r; \; j = 0, \cdots, r)$ are again equal to the least-squares estimates. The joint limiting distribution of the variates $\xi_{ijk} = \sqrt{N}(a_{ijk} - \alpha_{ijk})$ is a multivariate normal distribution with zero means and finite covariance matrix. To express the covariances, we arrange the pairs $(0, 0)$ and $(j, k)(j=1, \cdots, r; k=1, \cdots, p)$ in an ordered sequence. Denote D_{ijklN} by D_{uvN} if (i, k) is the uth and (j, l) the vth element in the ordered sequence. Similarly we denote ξ_{ijk} by ξ_{iu} if (j, k) is the uth element of the ordered sequence. Then the limit covariance between ξ_{iu} and ξ_{jv} is equal to the stochastic limit of $(\overline{Q}_{ij}/N)C_{uvN}$ where $\|C_{uvN}\| = \|D_{uvN}\|^{-1}$.

Case C. Here we deal with the general case in which $\|\alpha_{ij0}\|$ is not equal to the unit matrix. The treatment of the general case presents a number of difficulties which do not arise in the special cases A and B. Suppose that all coefficients α_{ijk} and α_i in equation (B) are unknown and that nothing is known about the covariance matrix $\|\sigma_{ij}\|$ of the variates $\epsilon_{1t}, \cdots, \epsilon_{rt}$. Suppose furthermore that p_{ij} has the same value for all pairs $(i, j)(i, j = 1, \cdots, r)$. Then it is not possible to have consistent estimates for all parameters α_{ijk}, α_i, and σ_{ij}. Let

$$\text{(C)} \qquad x_{it} + \sum_{j=1}^{r} \sum_{k=1}^{p_{ij}} \alpha_{ijk}^* x_{j,t-k} + \alpha_i^* = \epsilon_{it}^*$$

be the reduced form of the equations (B). Then the coefficient α_{ijk}^* is a linear function of $\alpha_{ijk}, \cdots, \alpha_{rjk}$; α_i^* is a linear function of $\alpha_1, \cdots, \alpha_r$, and ϵ_{it}^* is a linear function of $\epsilon_{1t}, \cdots, \epsilon_{rt}$. Denote the covariance of ϵ_{it}^* and ϵ_{jt}^* by σ_{ij}^*. Of course, α_{ijk}^*, α_i^*, and σ_{ij}^* depend also on α_{ij0}. It has been shown that the observations x_{it} cannot yield any additional information as to the values α_{ijk}, α_i, and σ_{ij} beyond that contained in the estimates of the parameters α_{ijk}^*, α_i^*, and σ_{ij}^*.

If there is no a priori knowledge whatsoever as to the values α_{ijk}, α_i, and σ_{ij}, or if the a priori knowledge available does not imply any restrictions on the values of α_{ijk}^*, α_i^*, and σ_{ij}^*, then it is best to treat the difference equations in the reduced form (C), i.e., to estimate α_{ijk}^*, α_i^*, and σ_{ij}^*. Since the reduced equations (C) satisfy all conditions of Case B, the procedure described in Case B can be applied. If, however, the available a priori knowledge implies certain restrictions on the values of the parameters α_{ijk}^*, α_i^*, and σ_{ij}^*, then the statistical treatment of the reduced equations (C) may be just as involved as that of the original system (B) and no advantage is gained. In some practical cases one may find it worth while to discard the available a priori knowledge and to treat the reduced equations (C) as if the parameters α_{ijk}^*, α_i^*, and σ_{ij}^* were not subject to any restrictions. By doing so we decrease the efficiency of our statistical procedure, but we gain in simplicity. In some cases the gain in simplicity may compensate for the loss in efficiency.

If the a priori knowledge implies restrictions on the parameters α_{ijk}^*, α_i^*, and σ_{ij}^*, and if we are not willing to discard the available information, then it seems preferable to treat the equations in the original form (B). A frequent form of the a priori knowledge is the following: It is known that $\epsilon_{1t}, \cdots, \epsilon_{rt}$ are independently distributed and the values of some of the coefficients α_{ijk}, α_i are known to be zero. The treatment of the equations (B) is carried out in the case when the a priori knowledge is of the type described above. Furthermore it is assumed that this a priori knowledge and the parameters α_{ijk}^*, α_i^*, and σ_{ij}^* uniquely determine all parameters α_{ijk}, α_i, and σ_{ij}. Finally it is assumed that $\sigma^2(\epsilon_{it}) = 1$, since this can always be achieved by multiplying the equations (B) by a constant factor. Under these conditions the joint limiting distribution of the maximum-likelihood estimates of α_{ijk} and α_i is derived. While the distribution of the maximum-likelihood estimates is derived without assuming normality of the distribution of ϵ_{it}, the results become much simpler if the distribution of ϵ_{it} is normal. We shall summarize here merely the results obtained under the assumption of normality of the distribution of ϵ_{it}. Denote α_i by α_{i00}, a_i by a_{i00} and let $\xi_{ijk} = \sqrt{N}(a_{ijk} - \alpha_{ijk})$. Arrange the triples (i, j, k) for which α_{ijk} is unknown in an ordered sequence. Denote α_{ijk}, a_{ijk}, and ξ_{ijk} by α_u, a_u, and ξ_u, respectively, if (i, j, k) is the uth triple in the ordered sequence. Let p be the joint probability density of the variates $x_{11}, \cdots, x_{rN}$ and let $\bar{p}$ be the expression we obtain from p if we replace α_u by a_u. Then our results can be summarized as follows: The joint limiting distribution of the variates ξ_u is a multivariate normal distribution with zero means and finite covariance matrix. The limit value of the covariance matrix $\|\sigma(\xi_u \xi_v)\|$ is equal to the stochastic

limit of $\left\| -\dfrac{1}{N}\dfrac{\partial^2 \log \bar{p}}{\partial a_u \partial a_v} \right\|^{-1}$. Hence, for large N the matrix $\|\sigma(\xi_u \xi_v)\|$ can

be replaced by $\left\| -\dfrac{1}{N}\dfrac{\partial^2 \log \bar{p}}{\partial a_u \partial a_v} \right\|^{-1}$. The quantity $\dfrac{\partial^2 \log \bar{p}}{\partial a_u \partial a_v}$ can be cal-

culated from the observations.

Columbia University

REFERENCES

[1] J. L. Doob, "Probability and Statistics," *Transactions of the American Mathematical Society*, Vol. 36, 1934, pp. 759-775.

[2] T. Haavelmo, "The Statistical Implications of a System of Simultaneous Equations," Econometrica, Vol. 11, January, 1943, pp. 1-12.

[3] R. L. Anderson, "Distribution of the Serial Correlation Coefficient," *Annals of Mathematical Statistics*, Vol. 13, March, 1942, pp. 1-13.

[4] Tjalling Koopmans, "Serial Correlation and Quadratic Forms in Normal Variables," *Annals of Mathematics Statistics*, Vol. 13, March, 1942, pp. 14-33.

Econometrica, Vol. 15, 2 (April 1947)

THE USE OF ECONOMETRIC MODELS AS A GUIDE TO ECONOMIC POLICY*

By Lawrence R. Klein

It is desirable to provide tools of analysis suited for public economic policy that are, as much as possible, independent of the personal judgments of a particular investigator. Econometric models are put forth in this scientific spirit, because these models, if fully developed and properly used, eventually should lead all investigators to the same conclusions, independent of their personal whims. The usual experience in the field of economic policy is that there are about as many types of advice as there are advisors (sometimes even more!).

Statistical models of the working of the economy are not proposed as magic formulas which divulge all the secrets of the complex real world in a single equation. The statistical models attempt to provide as much information about future or other unknown phenomena as can be gleaned from the historical records of observable and measurable facts. To the extent to which people maintain their past behavior patterns in the future, the statistical models provide information about the quantitative properties of economic variables in the future. However, econometricians do not operate in a vacuum; their methods are not purely mechanical in the sense that they do nothing but substitute in formulas. Any information of a qualitative nature that is available should be used by the econometrician in drawing inferences about the real world from his models. For example, suppose that an econometrician is called upon to forecast next year's level of employment and suppose further that this econometrician knows that war will break out next year. Would the econometrician merely substitute into his equations of peacetime behavior patterns in order to forecast employment in a period during which there will be war? Obviously, any qualitative information (e.g., the outbreak of war next year) must be taken into account in order to make a proper forecast.

The nonstatistical economist has only qualitative information from which to make judgments. The statistical economist has this same qualitative information plus a thorough knowledge of historically developed behavior patterns; hence it may be said that the latter is better equipped.

* It must be emphasized that the forecasts for fiscal year 1947 in this paper were all made during the week of November 10, 1946.

This paper was presented at the meeting of the Econometric Society at Atlantic City, January 25, 1947. It will be reprinted as Cowles Commission Papers, New Series, No. 23.

TYPES OF POLICIES

The ideas that grew out of the discussion on the Full Employment Bill showed clearly the close relationship between forecasting and economic policy. As the Bill was originally drafted, it called for a periodic forecast of the deflationary or inflationary gap. A predicted deflationary gap would call for one type of policy and a predicted inflationary gap for another type of policy. Thus the first step in carrying out the provisions of the Bill is to make a forecast. The success of the public policy will depend vitally on the accuracy of the forecast. An important use of econometric models, as will be demonstrated below, is to make forecasts.

The second step in the implementation of a Full Employment Bill is to wipe out the forecasted deflationary or inflationary gap. This step will also have to be quantitative. How much employment will be created by an x-per-cent cut in taxes? By how much will prices be expected to rise if government expenditures rise by a known amount with constant tax rates? These are only a sample of the types of questions that must be answered in order to decide among alternative policies. It is evident that the answers to such questions depend upon consumer and business spending-saving habits. The statistical approach is to examine the spending-saving habits of past periods in order to get some idea of the pattern of future habits.

Suppose that the population's habits are going to change in a known way. We may want to know the effect of this change upon the entire system. If we have econometric models, we can often predict the results of such changes. An example can easily be given. If it is known that the introduction of a social security program will raise the marginal propensity to consume by y per cent because people will be more certain of the future, the quantitative effects of the program can be estimated in advance from statistical models. The estimate may very well have some influence on the decision whether or not to adopt the social-security scheme.

A similar use of models arises in the study of the effects of technological change. A change in the technique of production can often be translated into an exact quantitative change in some of the parameters of the production function that has been statistically determined from data which referred to the old process of production. It is possible to calculate the change in several relevant variables of the system such as employment, output, wages, prices, etc., as a result of the technological change, provided we have an appropriate econometric model. On the basis of the limited number of observations available for testing different economic models from which to form policy decisions, it is not yet possible to select an unique model. More than one model are consistent with the observations. In this paper we shall present three plausible models, and methods of forming policy will be studied with each alternative. The reader is free to choose among the models, all of which rest on different hypotheses. Other models, in addition to those presented here, have also been studied by the author, but they are not demonstrated in order to avoid repetition.

MODEL I—EXOGENOUS INVESTMENT

A simple model in which there is little possibility of confusion is useful to demonstrate some very specific applications of econometric models in policy formation.

The following variables comprise the system:

C = consumer expenditures measured in billions of current dollars.

$\mathcal{I}'$ = gross private capital formation measured in billions of current dollars.

G = government expenditures on goods and services measured in billions of current dollars.

Υ = disposable income measured in billions of current dollars.

$G\mathcal{NP}$ = gross national product measured in billions of current dollars (expenditure concept).[1]

$\mathcal{T}$ = government receipts+corporate savings+business reserves − transfer payments − inventory profits, all measured in billions of current dollars.

p = cost-of-living index, 1935–1939:1.00.

N = population of the continental United States measured in billions of persons.

u = normally distributed random disturbance.

The economic model connecting these variables is:

$$(1.1) \qquad \frac{C}{pN} = \alpha_0 + \alpha_1 \frac{\Upsilon}{pN} + \alpha_2 \left(\frac{\Upsilon}{pN}\right)_{-1} + u,$$

$$(1.2) \qquad G\mathcal{NP} = C + \mathcal{I}' + G,$$

$$(1.3) \qquad \Upsilon + \mathcal{T} = G\mathcal{NP}.$$

Equation (1.1) is an economic-behavior equation which relates consumer spending to income, current and past. Since this is an equation

---

[1] Gross national product may be computed directly as the sum of consumer, business, and government spending (expenditure concept) or as the sum of income payments to factors of production and indirect taxes plus business reserves (income concept). The two measures should be equal but there is now a sizeable discrepancy of about $5 billion in the official estimates. The symbol $G\mathcal{NP}$ will refer everywhere in this paper to the expenditure concept.

of economic behavior, it is subject to random disturbance. Equations
(1.2) and (1.3) are definitions. They hold exactly and are not subject
to random disturbance.

The endogenous variables are C/pN, GNP/pN, and Υ/pN. The
exogenous variables are $\mathcal{J}'/pN$, G/pN, $\mathcal{C}/pN$. There is some question
whether the truly exogenous variables of capital formation, govern-
ment spending, and taxation, should be aggregates in current dollars
or per capita variables in constant dollars. For the statistical estimation of the parameters of the system we shall proceed as though $\mathcal{J}'/pN$,
G/pN, and $\mathcal{C}/pN$ are the exogenous variables rather than $\mathcal{J}'$, G, and
$\mathcal{C}$, although the most correct solution is far from obvious.

Haavelmo[2] has shown that the system (1.1)–(1.3) may be solved to
get

$$(1.4)\quad \frac{\Upsilon}{pN}=\frac{\alpha_0}{1-\alpha_1}+\frac{\alpha_2}{1-\alpha_1}\left(\frac{\Upsilon}{pN}\right)_{-1}+\frac{1}{1-\alpha_1}\left(\frac{\mathcal{J}'+G-\mathcal{C}}{pN}\right)+\frac{1}{1-\alpha_1}\,u,$$

and that the parameters of this latter equation can be consistently
estimated by the method of least squares if we make the assumptions
that we have made about endogenous and exogenous variables. It will
be observed that a knowledge of the estimates of the parameters of
(1.4) leads to a knowledge of the estimates of the parameters of (1.1).
Statistical estimates of (1.4) yield the results

$$(1.5)\quad \frac{\Upsilon}{pN}=202.54+\underset{(0.12)}{0.37}\left(\frac{\Upsilon}{pN}\right)_{-1}+\underset{(0.28)}{2.39}\,\frac{\mathcal{J}'+G-\mathcal{C}}{pN},$$

$$S=\$21.21,\qquad \delta^2/S^2=1.14.$$

The numbers in parentheses below the coefficients are standard errors;
S = square root of the estimate of the variance of $u/(1-\alpha_1)$; δ^2/S^2 = the
ratio of the mean-square successive difference to the variance of the
residuals. The distribution of this ratio has been tabulated,[3] and we
conclude that the probability is slightly less than 3 per cent that we
could get a sample value for δ^2/S^2 as small as 1.14 if the population
values of the u's were independent in time (i.e., nonautocorrelated).
The sample value of δ^2/S^2 is slightly less than the size usually required
(the value corresponding to the 5-per-cent significance level) in order

---

[2] T. Haavelmo, "Methods of Measuring the Marginal Propensity to Consume,"
Journal of the American Statistical Association, Vol. 42, March, 1947, pp. 105–122.

[3] J. von Neumann, "Distribution of the Ratio of the Mean Square Successive
Difference to the Variance," *Annals of Mathematical Statistics*, Vol. 12, pp. 367–
395; B. I. Hart and J. von Neumann, "Tabulation of the Probabilities for the
Ratio of the Mean Square Successive Difference to the Variance," *Annals of
Mathematical Statistics*, Vol. 13, pp. 207–214.

to be confident that the disturbances are random. The statistical methods assume that the disturbances are nonautocorrelated, and this assumption is not quite fulfilled in (1.5), although this is clearly a borderline case.

The numerical values of (1.5) imply the following numerical results for an estimate of (1.1):

$$(1.6) \qquad \frac{C}{pN} = 84.74 + 0.58 \frac{\Upsilon}{pN} + 0.15 \left(\frac{\Upsilon}{pN} \right)_{-1}.$$

Provided the relevant information concerning the size of $\mathcal{I}'$, $\mathcal{G}$, $\mathcal{T}$ is known in advance, equation (1.5) can be used to make forecasts. We generally know, in advance, the size of $\mathcal{G}$ and $\mathcal{T}$. Government expenditures are fixed by the budgets that are adopted by federal, state, and local governments; hence we can assign a definite value of $\mathcal{G}$. It is not possible to assign an unique value of $\mathcal{T}$ because the observed value of $\mathcal{T}$ depends upon the level of income. We estimated the parameters of (1.4) as though $\mathcal{T}$ were an exogenous variable but there is an error committeed in this approach. $\mathcal{T}$, in fact, is a function of Υ or $\mathcal{GNP}$, and the parameters of this function are the exogenous elements. One of the major elements of $\mathcal{T}$ is taxes. Taxes vary with income, but the government autonomously sets the tax rates. The parameters of the function connecting $\mathcal{T}$ and $\mathcal{GNP}$ are averages of these tax rates. In practice, we proceed as follows:[4] We assume several hypothetical values of $\mathcal{GNP}$ and estimate according to existing laws on taxes, unemployment compensation, etc., the corresponding values of $\mathcal{T}$. We then determine from these hypothetical values of $\mathcal{T}$ and $\mathcal{GNP}$ a relation of the form:

$$(1.7) \qquad \mathcal{T} = \beta_0 + \beta_1(\mathcal{GNP}).$$

This could also be written as:

$$\mathcal{GNP} - \Upsilon = \beta_0 + \beta_1(\mathcal{GNP}),$$
$$\Upsilon = -\beta_0 + (1 - \beta_1)(\mathcal{GNP}),$$

or

$$\mathcal{T} = \beta_0 + \beta_1(\Upsilon + \mathcal{T}),$$
$$\mathcal{T} = \frac{\beta_0}{1 - \beta_1} + \frac{\beta_1}{1 - \beta_1} \Upsilon,$$

since $\mathcal{GNP} = \Upsilon + \mathcal{T}$. It is assumed that equation (1.7) is exact and not subject to a random disturbance.

[4] See pp. 119–120 below for a more detailed discussion.

Since population (N) changes very slowly, it is not difficult to assign a numerical value to this variable for a few months or a year in advance. The remaining variables that are necessary in order to forecast Υ or $\mathcal{GNP}$ are Υ_{-1}, p_{-1}, N_{-1}, p, and $\mathcal{I}'$. The lagged variables are known from historically recorded observations, but the other two variables are not known in advance with the same certainty that we know $\mathcal{G}$, $\mathcal{T}$, or N in advance. Government agencies survey business firms in order to find out what the latter *intend* to spend on plant, equipment, and inventories. In this way, there is an attempt to assign a known value to $\mathcal{I}'$, but such attempts are not entirely satisfactory because businessmen are in no way committed to spend what they intend to spend. At best, we can solve the system of equations for Υ, given $\mathcal{G}$, β_0, β_1, N, p_{-1}, Υ_{-1}, N_{-1}, in terms of p and $\mathcal{I}'$. For the fiscal year 1947 we assign the values:

$\mathcal{G} = \$32.8$ billion,
$\mathcal{T} = -39.52 + 0.61\Upsilon$,
$\Upsilon_{-1} = \$138.7$ billion,
$p_{-1} = 1.30$,
$N_{-1} = 0.140$.

Substituting these numerical values into (1.5), we get:

(1.8) $$\Upsilon = 70.32 + 27.51p + 0.97\mathcal{I}'.$$

For any pair of values corresponding to p and $\mathcal{I}'$, there results a definite forecast of Υ. However, an error must be attached to this forecast. The quantity $u/(1-\alpha_1)$ in (1.4) fluctuates about its mean (zero) and thereby causes the observed value of Υ/pN to deviate from the value calculated from (1.5). On top of this error caused by the disturbance $u/(1-\alpha_L)$, there is another error resulting from the fact that we do not know the exact values of the parameters, α_0, α_1, α_2. The numerical (point) estimates given in (1.5) are subject to error, and only a range is known which encloses these parameters with a specified probability. A combination of the errors in the estimates of the parameters α_0, α_1, α_2, and the disturbances u provides a range of error for any forecasts from this model.

Hotelling[5] has given a very clear exposition of the theory underlying errors in prediction. Hotelling's formula applied to our problem gives:

(1.9)   estimate of variance of forecast

$$= S^2 + S_{11}\left(\frac{\overset{*}{\Upsilon}}{pN}\right)^2_{-1} + 2S_{12}\left(\frac{\overset{*}{\Upsilon}}{pN}\right)_{-1}\frac{\overset{*}{\mathcal{I}'} + \overset{*}{\mathcal{G}} - \mathcal{T}}{pN}$$

[5] Harold Hotelling, "Problems of Prediction," *The American Journal of Sociology*, Vol. 48, 1942, pp. 61–76.

$$+ S_{22}\left(\frac{\mathscr{G}' + \overset{*}{\mathscr{G}} - \mathscr{C}}{pN}\right)^2 + S^2\frac{1}{20},$$

where

S_{11} = estimate of the variance of $\dfrac{\alpha_2}{1 - \alpha_1}$,

S_{12} = estimate of the covariance of $\dfrac{\alpha_2}{1 - \alpha_1}$ with $\dfrac{1}{1 - \alpha_1}$,

S_{22} = estimate of the variance of $\dfrac{1}{1 - \alpha_1}$,

and the * sign denotes deviations from the sample mean. The numerical values of the estimated variance of forecast depend upon the values assigned to the predetermined and exogenous variables.

In carrying out the computations for (1.9), the value used for $\mathscr{C}$ was the value obtained by substituting the point estimate of Υ into $\mathscr{C} = -39.52 + 0.61\Upsilon$. However, since there is an interval of error to be attached to Υ, it is not obvious that the correct value of $\mathscr{C}$ for (1.9) can be estimated from the point estimates of Υ. But it happens that the error committed by this procedure is negligible. This can be seen as follows: (1) Solve for the forecast error as a function of $\mathscr{C}$. (2) Solve for $\mathscr{C}$ as a function of the point estimate of Υ and the error attached to the point estimate of Υ. (3) Substitute $\mathscr{C}$ from step 2 into (1.9). This gives one equation in one unknown variable, namely, the error of forecast. (4) The error attached to $\mathscr{C}$ may be positive or negative. Choose that sign which gives the largest possible range of forecast error and solve the equation from step 3 for the error of forecast. We find that the error of forecast obtained by computing $\mathscr{C}$ from the point estimate of Υ alone is not different (in billions of dollars) from the worst possible error obtained by taking account of an error in $\mathscr{C}$.

We shall denote the expression in (1.9) by $S_F{}^2$. Probability theory tells us that there is somewhat less[6] than a 70-per-cent chance that the true value of Υ/pN will be in the range

$$\left[-S_F + \left(\frac{\Upsilon}{pN}\right)^0, \left(\frac{\Upsilon}{pN}\right)^0 + S_F\right],$$

where $(\Upsilon/pN)^0$ is the value of Υ/pN forecast from (1.5). If we want a

[6] The value of t for the 30-per-cent significance level and 17 degrees of freedom is 1.069. The significance level corresponding to $t = 1$ is slightly larger than 30 per cent but is not given in all tables.

larger probability of being correct, we must widen the range of forecast. In general, our forecast will be of the form:

$$(1.10) \qquad \left(\frac{\Upsilon}{pN}\right)^0 \pm t_\alpha S_F,$$

where t_α is taken from the table of the t-distribution at the αth significance level.

The ranges of error in Table I refer to errors in the forecast of Υ and $\mathcal{GNP}$ in current prices. Forecasts in constant dollars lead to much smaller ranges because the forecast equation (1.5) is in constant dollars, and when we multiply both sides of this equation by p to get forecasts in current prices, the forecast error is also multiplied by p, which is greater than unity during the present period. It is evident that the percentage error is the same for forecasts of disposable income in current or constant dollars. It should be pointed out, further, that the ranges of error are calculated from (1.10) under the condition that $t_\alpha = 1$.

TABLE I

FORECASTS FOR FISCAL 1947: MODEL I

Disposable Income (Υ)

Price Index p	Gross Capital Formation ($\mathcal{I}'$)					
	30	32	34	36	38	40
1.35	137 ± 6	139 ± 6	140 ± 6	142 ± 6	144 ± 6	146 ± 6
1.40	138 ± 7	140 ± 7	142 ± 7	144 ± 6	146 ± 6	148 ± 6
1.45	139 ± 7	141 ± 7	143 ± 7	145 ± 7	147 ± 7	149 ± 7
1.50	141 ± 8	143 ± 7	145 ± 7	147 ± 7	148 ± 7	150 ± 7

Gross National Product ($\mathcal{GNP}$)

Price Index p	Gross Capital Formation ($\mathcal{I}'$)					
	30	32	34	36	38	40
1.35	181 ± 10	184 ± 10	187 ± 10	190 ± 10	193 ± 10	196 ± 10
1.40	183 ± 11	186 ± 11	189 ± 11	192 ± 10	195 ± 10	198 ± 10
1.45	185 ± 11	188 ± 11	191 ± 11	194 ± 11	198 ± 11	201 ± 11
1.50	187 ± 13	190 ± 11	194 ± 11	197 ± 11	200 ± 11	203 ± 11

The forecasts presented thus far refer to fiscal year 1947, but, at this writing (November, 1946) part of this fiscal year has already elapsed. If we subtract what has already been observed for fiscal 1947 from the values in the tables, we have a forecast of the remainder of fiscal 1947, an unobserved period.

Table I tells us that the present price level (1.43–1.45) and volume of capital formation (32–34) imply a value of $\mathcal{GNP}$ for fiscal 1947 at about the present annual rate. If prices and private capital formation do not fall, the current rate of national product will be maintained, i.e., national product will not fall or rise appreciably in the first half of calendar 1947. If price and capital formation fall, $\mathcal{GNP}$ is likely to fall in calendar 1947 and if prices and capital formation rise, $\mathcal{GNP}$ is likely to rise in calendar 1947. Later we shall attempt to forecast the behavior of capital formation in a model where this variable is endogenous.

It is easy to see how other types of policy decisions could be made on the basis of this model. Various levels of government spending can be inserted into the numerical system. Each value of $\mathcal{G}$ will lead to a different set of values for Υ and $\mathcal{GNP}$, hence we can judge the quantitative effects of government spending on income and national product. Similarly it is possible to calculate the effects of changes in tax rates by altering the numerical estimates of β_0 or β_1 depending upon the type of tax change under consideration. A different set of values for β_0 and β_1 will generate a different set of values of forecasted Υ and $\mathcal{GNP}$. The change in the forecast as a consequence of the change in the tax laws, gives an evaluation of some of the important implications of the tax policies.

There are many steps involved in the computation of (1.7) and it is not entirely correct to assume that this equation is not subject to random error. The computation of the values of the parameters involves several approximations and the linear form of the equation is, in itself, an approximation; hence it would be desirable to attach an error to the estimate of (1.7), but this has not yet been done. We shall outline the steps involved in estimating the parameters of (1.7) in order that the various sources of error can be properly exposed:

1. Assume an arbitrary value of $\mathcal{GNP}$.
2. Subtract from $\mathcal{GNP}$, government interest and wage-salary payments, to get privately produced $\mathcal{GNP}$.
3. Estimate corporate profits before taxes as a function of private $\mathcal{GNP}$.
4. Apply existing tax rates to the estimated corporate profits before taxes to get corporate taxes.

5. From corporate profits after taxes estimate the distribution between dividends and corporate savings.

6. For the hypothetical level of GNP and existing tax rates for other business taxes, estimate the volume of other business taxes (not corporate taxes).

7. For the hypothetical level of GNP, estimate the total business reserves (depreciation, depletion, capital outlays charged to current expense).

8. For the hypothetical level of GNP, estimate the profit or loss on inventory revaluation.

9. From GNP subtract corporate taxes, other business taxes, business reserves, and the negative of inventory profits. The result is a hypothetical level of national income corresponding to a a hypothetical GNP.

10. Calculate transfer payments estimated at existing benefit rates for the assumed level of national income.

11. Compute the contributions to social insurance funds by applying existing rates to the hypothetical national income.

12. To national income add transfer payments and subtract the sum of corporate savings and contributions to social insurance funds. The result is income payments to individuals.

13. Apply existing personal tax rates to income payments to get personal tax and nontax payments to government.

14. Subtract personal tax and nontax payments from income payments to get disposable income.

It is obvious that all tax payments (personal, corporate, and other business) depend upon the distribution of income among taxpaying units as well as upon the sum of individual incomes. However, assuming little change in income distribution, it is possible to estimate approximately the tax revenues corresponding to any particular level of income. But it should be noted that this is an approximation and not an exact relation. However, there are other steps at which the approximations are less exact and subject to much wider errors. Steps 3 and 5 involve some estimates on which there undoubtedly could be improvement. Step 3 makes use of a behavior equation which should be part of the economic model and which should be subject to random disturbance. From past data, the regression of corporate profits on private GNP is obtained, and this regression is used to estimate corporate profits corresponding to the assumed hypothetical levels of total and private GNP. The use of simple least-squares correlations between corporate profits and private GNP can fortunately be justified, although many investigators have been using this correlation in the steps outlined above without knowing why it is correct. The models which the author has constructed, have often contained the wage-bill as a linear function of the value of private output. The best relation also makes use of a trend and lagged as well as current output. It has been found in several cases that the least-squares regression of wages on private output is practically the same as the relation obtained by the use of more satisfactory methods of statistical estimation that are known to be consistent (i.e., roughly unbiased in large samples). Since the sum of wages and profits is approximately equal to the value of private output, it is also true that the least-squares regression of profits on output will not differ appreciably from a consistent estimate of the true relation between these two variables. But no matter how correct we find the statistical estimates to be, the equation used in step 3 is an equation of economic behavior and is subject to random disturbance.

Step 5 also involves the use of an economic-behavior equation, and unfortunately this equation is not nearly as well established as that used in step 3. In step 5, it is necessary to split net corporate profits after taxes into two components, dividends and corporate savings. How do boards of directors decide upon their dividend policies? No simple economic theory seems to have been adequately developed to explain the behavior pattern of corporate directors. Tinbergen[7] has advanced a relation that is consistent with the observed data. He found that dividends are a linear function of net corporate income, current and lagged, and the accumulated surplus lagged. Until a theory of dividend distribution is more definitively established we shall have to work with Tinbergen's relation, but here, also, the relation is subject to error (probably a wide error), and consequently another inexactness is introduced into the model. In making up the table of the relationship between disposable income and assumed levels of $\mathcal{GNP}$, we should insert the latest observed figure of dividends corresponding to the observed levels of $\mathcal{GNP}$ and net corporate profits, and then from Tinbergen's formula calculate the change in the absolute level of dividends associated with any assumed change in the absolute level of net corporate profits. This procedure should be adopted because the lagged value of surplus (the other variable in Tinbergen's equation) is predetermined for our problem and does not vary with the different hypothetical levels of $\mathcal{GNP}$.

Finally, step 8 involves some very questionable relationships. Ordinarily, inventory revaluation might not be large, but in periods of rapidly changing prices, the capital gains (or losses) on stocks of goods

[7] J. Tinbergen, *Statistical Testing of Business Cycle Theories, Part II, Business Cycles in the United States of America, 1919–1932*, League of Nations, Geneva, 1939, pp. 115–116.

are large and play an important role in determining the level of effective demand. Inventory profits are especially large now, and cannot be neglected. For any hypothetical level of $G\mathcal{NP}$, a figure for inventory revaluation must be estimated. Any estimates are subject to a large error. No systematic relationship has been used for the evaluation of this item other than some informed guesses as to future developments in the labor situation that will serve to determine wage rates and thus prices (assuming a fixed profit margin).

Forecasts from econometric models undoubtedly can be greatly improved, and one of the first points of attacks should be on the relationship between disposable income and $G\mathcal{NP}$. In the estimation of the parameters of the models, it has usually been assumed that the difference, $G\mathcal{NP} - \Upsilon = \mathcal{C}$, is exogenous, but the above discussion has shown this to be an incorrect assumption. At best, we can assume that tax rates, unemployment compensation rates, pensions, government interest payments, and the like are exogenous. Further work is called for here.

MODEL II—EXOGENOUS INVESTMENT AND LIQUIDITY

Let us modify Model I by the addition of one new variable to the system, namely cash balances. One of the most frequently-heard explanations of the present boom is that private economic units have emerged from the War with large accumulations of liquid assets that cause people to spend at an abnormally high rate. This hypothesis can be tested from the data to see whether or not the total private holdings of liquid assets influenced spending habits in the past. Since we could not split total private holdings of cash balances for all past years into personal holdings and business holdings, we used the total private holdings of cash balances as the appropriate variable. For the pre-war years in which total balances have been split into private and business categories, there is a close linear relationship between the two components;[8] so it seems that the total can be used as an index of either type in a linear system. The consumption function will now be written as

$$(2.1) \quad \frac{C}{pN} = \alpha_0' + \alpha_1' \frac{\Upsilon}{pN} + \alpha_2' \left(\frac{\Upsilon}{pN} \right)_{-1} + \alpha_3' \left(\frac{\mathcal{M}}{pN} \right)_{-1} + u',$$

where $\mathcal{M}_{-1}$ = currency outside banks+demand deposits adjusted+time deposits of the middle of the preceding year measured in billions of current dollars.

[8] See S. Shapiro, "The Distribution of Deposits and Currency in the United States, 1929–1939," *Journal of the American Statistical Association*, Vol. 38, 1943, pp. 438–444.

All the other equations of the system are unchanged. The forecast equation which is obtained by solving for Υ/pN in terms of predetermined and exogenous variables is

$$
(2.2) \quad \frac{\Upsilon}{pN} = \frac{\alpha_0'}{1 - \alpha_1'} + \frac{\alpha_2'}{1 - \alpha_1'}\left(\frac{\Upsilon}{pN}\right)_{-1} + \frac{1}{1 - \alpha_1'}\frac{\mathcal{J}' + G - \mathcal{C}}{pN}
$$
$$
+ \frac{\alpha_3'}{1 - \alpha_1'}\left(\frac{\mathcal{M}}{pN}\right)_{-1} + \frac{1}{1 - \alpha_1'}u'.
$$

The statistical estimate of (2.2) is

$$
(2.3) \quad \frac{\Upsilon}{pN} = 186.53 + \underset{(0.13)}{0.30}\left(\frac{\Upsilon}{pN}\right)_{-1} + \underset{(0.34)}{2.36}\frac{\mathcal{J}' + G - \mathcal{C}}{pN} + \underset{(0.10)}{0.13}\left(\frac{\mathcal{M}}{pN}\right)_{-1},
$$

$$
S = \$20.69, \qquad \delta^2/S^2 = 1.28.
$$

The statistic δ^2/S^2, in this model, is large enough so that we cannot reject the hypothesis that the u's are nonautocorrelated at the 5-percent level of significance.

From the estimates of the parameters of (2.2), we can derive estimates of the parameters of (2.1). They are

$$
(2.4) \quad \frac{\mathcal{C}}{pN} = 79.04 + 0.58\frac{\Upsilon}{pN} + 0.13\left(\frac{\Upsilon}{pN}\right)_{-1} + 0.06\left(\frac{\mathcal{M}}{pN}\right)_{-1}
$$

If to the estimates of the predetermined and exogenous variables used in Model I for fiscal 1947, we add the estimate $\mathcal{M}_{-1} = \$175.4$ billion, the resulting forecast equation,

$$
(2.5) \quad \Upsilon = 69.96 + 31.13p + 0.97\mathcal{J}',
$$

is obtained. Corresponding to Table I used in conjunction with Model I, we now have Table II which gives the forecasts obtained from Model II. In spite of the fact that the coefficient of $(\mathcal{M}/pN)_{-1}$ is small in (2.3), the value of this variable is so high now that the forecasted $\mathcal{GNP}$ is raised considerably as compared with Model I. But the standard error of the coefficient of $(\mathcal{M}/pN)_{-1}$ is very large. As a matter of fact, the standard error of the coefficient of $(\mathcal{M}/pN)_{-1}$ in (2.3) is sufficiently large that we cannot reject the hypothesis that the true value of the parameter is zero. The past data do not contradict the hypothesis that spending habits are not influenced by the holding of liquid assets. In estimating the error of forecast, however, it is not sufficient to look at the estimated standard error of the coefficient of $(\mathcal{M}/pN)_{-1}$ without taking into consideration the covariance of this coefficient and the other coefficients of the forecast equation. The ap-

TABLE II

FORECASTS FOR FISCAL 1947: MODEL II

Disposable Income (Υ)

Price Index p	Gross Capital Formation ($\mathcal{I}'$)					
	30	32	34	36	38	40
1.35	141 ± 7	143 ± 7	145 ± 7	147 ± 7	149 ± 6	151 ± 6
1.40	143 ± 8	145 ± 7	147 ± 7	148 ± 7	150 ± 7	152 ± 7
1.45	144 ± 9	146 ± 9	148 ± 8	150 ± 8	152 ± 8	154 ± 8
1.50	146 ± 10	148 ± 9	150 ± 9	152 ± 9	154 ± 9	155 ± 8

Gross National Product ($\mathcal{GNP}$)

Price Index p	Gross Capital Formation ($\mathcal{I}'$)					
	30	32	34	36	38	40
1.35	188 ± 11	191 ± 11	194 ± 11	197 ± 11	200 ± 11	203 ± 10
1.40	190 ± 13	193 ± 11	196 ± 11	199 ± 11	203 ± 11	206 ± 11
1.45	193 ± 15	196 ± 15	199 ± 13	202 ± 13	205 ± 13	208 ± 13
1.50	195 ± 16	198 ± 15	201 ± 15	204 ± 15	208 ± 15	211 ± 13

plication of Hotelling's formula for the estimate of the variance of the forecast explicitly takes into account the covariances as well as the variances of the parameters. The range of error attached to the forecasts of Model II is larger than the corresponding range for Model I, but the former range is not as much larger as one might hastily conclude from looking at the variance alone. A 70-per-cent probability of being correct requires a range of $\pm\$13$ to $\$15$ billion for forecasts of $\mathcal{GNP}$ in Model II; whereas the range for the same probability level in Model I is about $\pm\$11$ billion.

Equation (2.3) might be used to answer another type of question that is important in policy formation. In the presence of unemployment what is the effect, on the level of income, of deficit spending with a constant real money supply, or of an increase in the real money supply with a constant deficit? To simplify the problem, let us try to answer these questions for the equilibrium situation, i.e., the situation in which all variables assume their equilibrium values. In equilibrium we have:

$$\frac{\Upsilon}{pN} = \left(\frac{\Upsilon}{pN}\right)_{-1} = \left(\frac{\Upsilon}{pN}\right)^0, \quad \frac{\mathfrak{M}}{pN} = \left(\frac{\mathfrak{M}}{pN}\right)_{-1} = \left(\frac{\mathfrak{M}}{pN}\right)^0,$$

and

$$\frac{\mathcal{I}' + \mathcal{G} - \mathfrak{C}}{pN} = \left(\frac{\mathcal{I}' + \mathcal{G} - \mathfrak{C}}{pN}\right)_{-1} = \left(\frac{\mathcal{I}' + \mathcal{G} - \mathfrak{C}}{pN}\right)^0.$$

The equilibrium solution for (2.3) becomes:

$$(2.6) \quad \left(\frac{\Upsilon}{pN}\right)^0 = 266.87 + 3.37\left(\frac{\mathcal{I}' + \mathcal{G} - \mathfrak{C}}{pN}\right)^0 + 0.19\left(\frac{\mathfrak{M}}{pN}\right)^0,$$

assuming the point estimates for the parameters to be correct. From (2.6) we can calculate the following two multipliers: (1) An extra dollar of deficit spending (with a constant money supply) creates $3.37 additional disposable income; (2) an extra dollar of money supplied (with a constant deficit) creates $0.19 additional disposable income.

MODEL III—ENDOGENOUS INVESTMENT

The forecasts made from the first two models were, of course, contingent upon the correct choice of exogenous variables, of which some of the principal ones were government spending, government receipts and transfers, and private capital formation. There is little that can be done to improve upon the assumed levels of government variables for purposes of prediction, but we may be able to make considerable improvement in the estimation of private capital formation. If the latter variable is assumed to be exogenous, our only known method for the estimation of this variable is to survey businessmen and ask them what they *intend* to spend in the future on capital goods. However, if we assume that business decisions are endogenous variables, we can study the historical records to attempt to discover the laws of business behavior. Model III will be one in which definite behavior patterns are assumed for many more variables in the system than was the case for Models I and II. In this paper, we shall not attempt to present a theoretical justification for all the equations of Model III, but we shall write explicitly all the equations. In a subsequent publication, there will be a lengthy justification for the model on theoretical grounds. At present, we shall merely attempt to show how such models can be used in forecasting.

In forecasting, especially under the conditions of November, 1946, certain equations of the complete model are suppressed because of government controls or other reasons. The full set of equations will be presented and the suppressions will be pointed out for the applications.

The notation is as follows:

I = net investment in private producers' plant and equipment, measured in billions of 1934 dollars.

q = price index of private producer's plant and equipment, 1934: 1.00.

p = price index of output as a whole, 1934:1.00.

X = output of the private sector of the economy, exclusive of housing services, measured in billions of 1934 dollars.

$\mathcal{E}$ = excise taxes, measured in billions of current dollars.

K = end-of-year stock of private producers' plant and equipment, measured in billions of 1934 dollars.

H = end-of-year stock of inventories, measured in billions of 1934 dollars.

$\mathcal{W}_1$ = private wage-salary bill, measured in billions of current dollars.

Y = disposable income, measured in billions of 1934 dollars.

C = consumer expenditures, measured in billions of 1934 dollars.

D_1 = gross construction expenditures on owner-occupied, single-family, nonfarm residences, measured in billions of 1934 dollars.

r = index of rents, 1934:1.00.

q_1 = index of construction costs, 1934:1.00.

ΔF = thousands of new nonfarm families.[9]

D_2 = gross construction expenditures on rented, nonfarm residences, measured in billions of 1934 dollars.

i = average corporate-bond yield.

v = percentage of nonfarm housing units occupied at the end of the year.

N^s = millions of available nonfarm housing units at the end of the year.

$\mathcal{M}_1$ = demand deposits adjusted and currency outside banks averaged during the year, measured in billions of current dollars.

$\mathcal{M}_2$ = time deposits, averaged during the year, measured in billions of current dollars.

$\mathcal{E}_r$ = excess reserves, averaged during the year, measured in millions of current dollars.

T = government revenues+corporate savings−transfer payments −government interest payments−inventory profits, all measured in billions of 1934 dollars.

[9] In what follows, we shall adopt the convention, $\Delta x = x - x_{-1}$ for any variable x.

G = government expenditures on goods and services—government interest payments+net exports+net investment of nonprofit institutions, all measured in billions of 1934 dollars.

D_3 = gross construction expenditures on farm residences, measured in billions of 1934 dollars.

D'' = depreciation of all residences (farm and nonfarm) measured in billions of 1934 dollars.

W_2 = government wage-salary bill, measured in billions of current dollars.

R_1 = nonfarm rentals, paid and imputed, measured in billions of current dollars.

R_2 = farm rentals, paid and imputed, measured in billions of current dollars.

u_2 = estimate of the disturbances in the inventory-demand equation.

The equations are:

$$I = 2.18 + 0.13 \; \frac{pX - \mathcal{E}}{q} + 0.04 \left(\frac{pX - \mathcal{E}}{q} \right)_{-1} - 0.09 K_{-1},$$

(3.1) $S = 0.49, \qquad \delta^2/S^2 = 1.50$

(demand for private producers' plant and equipment);

$$H = 0.79 + 4.17p + 0.11(X - \Delta H) + 0.50 H_{-1},$$

(3.2) $S = 0.61, \qquad \delta^2/S^2 = 2.17$

(demand for inventories);

$$\Delta X = 2.99 - 4.25(u_2)_{-1} + 75.09 \Delta p,$$

(3.3) $S = 5.98, \qquad \delta^2/S^2 = 1.69$

(output adjustment equation);

$$W_1 = 5.03 + 0.42(pX - \mathcal{E}) + 0.17(pX - \mathcal{E})_{-1} + 0.17(t - 1931),$$

(3.4) $S = 1.00, \qquad \delta^2/S^2 = 1.86$

(equation of the demand for labor);

$$D_1 = -9.03 + 3.74 \left(\frac{r}{q_1} \right) + 0.02(Y + Y_{-1} + Y_{-2}) + 0.0043 \Delta F$$

(3.5)

$$S = 0.21, \qquad \delta^2/S^2 = 2.26$$

(demand for new owner-occupied nonfarm residences);

(3.6)
$$D_2 = -2.14 + 2.81r_{-1} + 0.02(q_1)_{-1} - 0.44(q_1)_{-2} + 0.0016(\Delta F)_{-1} - 0.18i,$$

$$S = 0.26, \quad \delta^2/S^2 = 2.07$$

(demand for new rented nonfarm residences);

(3.7)
$$v = 178.01 + 0.29Y - 2.62r + 1.42(t - 1931) - 3.76N^s,$$

$$S = 0.79, \quad \delta^2/S^2 = 1.52$$

(demand for nonfarm dwelling space);

(3.8)
$$\Delta r = -2.15 + 0.02v_{-1} + 0.00071Y + 0.17\,\frac{1}{r_{-1}}$$

$$S = 0.03, \quad \delta^2/S^2 = 1.04$$

(rent adjustment equation);

(3.9)
$$C = 11.87 + 0.73Y + 0.04(t - 1931),$$

$$S = 1.36, \quad \delta^2/S^2 = 1.20$$

(demand for consumer goods);

(3.10)
$$\mathcal{M}_1 = 8.45 + 0.24p(Y + T) + 0.03p(Y + T)(t - 1931) - 1.43(t - 1931),$$

$$S = 1.20, \quad \delta^2/S^2 = 1.33$$

(demand for active cash balances);

(3.11)
$$\mathcal{M}_2 = 15.37 + 0.28i - 1.90i_{-1} + 0.74(\mathcal{M}_2)_{-1} - 0.18(t - 1931),$$

$$S = 0.67 \quad \delta^2/S^2 = 1.49$$

(demand for idle cash balances);

(3.12)
$$\Delta i = 2.00 - 0.17\mathcal{E}_r - 0.37i_{-1} - 0.0052(t - 1931),$$

$$S = 0.47 \quad \delta^2/S^2 = 1.77$$

(interest-rate adjustment equation);

(3.13)
$$Y + T = I + \Delta H + C + D_1 + D_2 + D_3 - D'' + G$$

(definition of net national product);

$$(3.14) \qquad X = \frac{p(Y + T) - \mathcal{W}_2 - \mathcal{R}_1 - \mathcal{R}_2}{p}$$

(definition of privately produced output exclusive of housing services);

$$3.15) \qquad \Delta K = I$$

(definition of net investment);

$$(3.16) \qquad \mathcal{R}_1 = 0.278r \left(\frac{vN^s}{100} + \frac{v_{-1}N^s_{-1}}{100} \right) \frac{1}{2}$$

(definition of total nonfarm rent payments, paid and imputed).

All parameters have been estimated for the period 1922–1941, except for (3.6), (3.10), (3.11), (3.12), when the period is 1921–1941. The method of statistical estimation employed is called the "method of reduced forms" and is one of the methods suited for obtaining consistent estimates of parameters in systems of simultaneous economic equations. This method has been developed by T. W. Anderson, Jr., M. A. Girshick, and H. Rubin.[10]

It should be pointed out that the parameter 0.278 in equation (3.16) is known a priori. This equation is a definition and is not a behavior equation with unknown parameters to be estimated from the observed data. Since r is an index number while $\mathcal{R}_1$ is in billions of dollars, it is necessary to multiply the right-hand side of (3.16) by the base-year value of average rental payments.

The forecasts for fiscal 1947 will be made from equations (3.1), (3.2), (3.5), (3.6), (3.9), (3.13), and (3.14). Equation (3.3), if left in the system, would give us enough equations to determine the general level of prices, p, but this equation is not very well established as can be seen by the very large estimate of the variance of the disturbance. We can probably do best to assign a particular value to the price level which will be determined by other considerations, as will be explained later. Equation (3.4) is omitted because we have no direct need for the de-

[10] A paper on the method of reduced forms was presented by Anderson at the August, 1946, meeting of the Institute of Mathematical Statistics, Ithaca, N. Y. A joint paper by Anderson and Rubin will soon be forthcoming. See also M. A. Girshick and Trygve Haavelmo, "Statistical Analysis of the Demand for Food: Examples of Simultaneous Estimation of Structural Equations," in this issue of ECONOMETRICA, Vol. 15, April, 1947, pp. 79–110.

termination of $\mathcal{W}_1$ in the system. However, if it were required to forecast $\mathcal{W}_1$ as well as $p(Y+T)$, we should have to include (3.4). Implicitly, an equation like (3.4) will be used to determine the relation between T and Y for the step in which it is required to estimate corporate profits for each assumed level of $\mathcal{GNP}$. This estimate corresponds to step 3 on page 119 above. Equations (3.7) and (3.8) are suppressed for this calculation because the present level of rents is not determined in a free market as is assumed in these two equations. The specific assumptions pertaining to rent control will be stated below. Equations (3.10) and (3.11) are omitted because it is not desired to know the values of $\mathcal{M}_1$ and $\mathcal{M}_2$ for our forecasts. If we were interested in forecasting the demand for cash balances as well as the level of income and output we should need to make use of demand relations for cash, but for the present problem we can omit some of the equations referring to the money market. Equation (3.11), furthermore, does not fit the postwar data, and would be very poor for purposes of prediction. In the postwar situation, for observed values of i, i_{-1}, $(\mathcal{M}_2)_{-1}$, and t, the demand for idle balances, as estimated by (3.11), is much less than the observed value. There are several possible explanations for this phenomenon, but one tempting explanation is the following: The Keynesian hypothesis that the demand for idle balances has very large (practically infinite) interest-elasticity at low interest rates requires a highly nonlinear form for the liquidity-preference equation (3.11). In the prewar years, the linear equation fits the data well, but now we are getting so close to "minimum" interest rates that the equation must be made very nonlinear in the region of present observations. There are several nonlinear functions that would fit the prewar data as well as (3.11) does and also fit the postwar observations very closely. Other explanations have to do with shifts (permanent or temporary) in the function, but, in any case, equation (3.11) is not satisfactory for prediction as it now stands. Fortunately, we are not attempting to estimate the demand for cash, so that (3.11) may be disregarded for the calculation in this paper. Finally, we shall also omit equation (3.12), which serves to determine the interest rate as a function of exogenous or predetermined variables. This equation also does not fit the postwar facts very closely and we can probably do better to assign the present rate of bond yields in equation (3.6), rather than attempt to estimate it from (3.12). During the war, the government and the central banking system made various manipulations in the money market to control the rate of interest, which may account for the fact that equation (3.12) appears not to hold very closely now.

Model III is an improvement over Models I and II in the sense that more variables that are not known accurately in advance are made endogenous and can be estimated from the model, but Model III is still far from being complete. The most glaring deficiency is in equations to determine the various price levels. To a certain extent, this deficiency is a result of the fact that there are not sufficiently detailed data available to construct, from past observations, a model that contains certain market adjustment equations necessary for the determination of price levels. Equation (3.8) is an example of the type of equation that is needed to determine a specific price level.

Instead of using behavior equations of the mathematical model to determine the levels of various prices, we have made use of certain information outside the model in order to assign specific values to p, q, q_1, r, etc. Our basic assumption in quantitative terms is that average prices (except rent) in fiscal 1947 will be about 10 per cent above those observed for fiscal 1946. Our reasoning is that prices will probably not fall by very much, if at all, in the latter part of the fiscal year because basic wage rates will not be permitted to fall. The latter observation follows from personal judgments (generally accepted) that collective bargaining in the early part of calendar 1947 will bring about some basic wage increases. Regardless of the level of prices assumed (within reason) the model leads to deflationary forecasts, i.e., falling production and employment, in the early part of calendar 1947; therefore we do not assume runaway price increases. However, the big increases of prices that occurred since the removal of OPA in the first half of fiscal 1947 will not be wiped out by the events of the second half of the fiscal year. There will probably be some price increase, on the average, for the fiscal year. In line with past experience since the end of the war when there have been similar rounds of wage and price increases, we assume a 10-per-cent change. In Tables I and II, it can be seen by how much small variations in the price index lead to variations in the forecasts of national product. This method of assuming a side relation between prices and wages, where the latter are estimated by guesses as to the outcome of collective bargaining, is not satisfactory, and work must be done in order to improve the model by the introduction of more price-formation equations.

In Table III are presented all the values assigned to predetermined or exogenous variables. In the appendix, the reader will find a detailed description of all the time series used in the estimation of the parameters of Model III and all the steps involved in the calculation of the values inserted in Table III. It is essential to study carefully the steps involved in the construction of the series in order to know how to calculate the values of Table III:

TABLE III

ASSUMPTIONS AND INITIAL CONDITIONS FOR MODEL III (FISCAL YEARS)

	Fiscal 1947	Fiscal 1946	Fiscal 1945
$\mathcal{E}$	5.5	7.3	
K_{-1}	114.3		
p	1.55	1.42	
H_{-1}	27.9		
r	1.20	1.15	
Y		100.	103.
q_1	2.00	1.825	1.69
i	2.8	2.765	
D_2	0.3		
D''	2.0		
G	21.4	36.3	
$\mathcal{W}_2$	16.2	24.75	
$\mathcal{R}_1 + \mathcal{R}_2$	12.4	11.8	
ΔF	500.	800.	
$p(Y+T)$		173.35	
q	1.50	1.36	

It is not possible to assign a specific value to the variable T because this variable will change with changing income. From our knowledge of existing tax rates, unemployment compensation rates, etc., we obtain by the same methods that were used for (1.7):

$$(3.17) \qquad T = - \frac{29.475}{p} + 0.385\,(Y + T).$$

A word of explanation is required about (3.17). The variable T is defined above as government revenues+corporate savings−transfer payments−government interest payments−inventory profits. Actually in the determination of the parameters from the data of the interwar period, inventory profits or losses were not subtracted from T, although, perhaps, they should have been. For the prediction in fiscal 1947 it does not seem correct to neglect inventory profits because they are so large. The consumption function (3.9) probably understates rather than overstates the consumption corresponding to a particular level of disposable income. The inclusion of inventory profits in Y (their exclusion in T) helps to explain the high levels of consumption; therefore Model III is interpreted as including inventory profits in Y, although this item was neglected in the past. Except for a couple of years in the interwar period, inventory profits were sufficiently small so that they would not have had an important influence on the numerical estimates of the parameters.[11]

Equations (3.1), (3.2), (3.5), (3.6), (3.9), (3.13), (3.14), (3.17) and the assumptions in Table III, lead to the following results:

$$Y = \$ \ 83.3 \text{ billion.}$$
$$Y + T = \ 104.5,$$
$$p(Y + T) = \ 162.0,$$
$$\mathcal{GNP} = \ 177.5.^{12,13}$$

The error to be attached to this forecast is not known exactly. In Models I and II, the statistical methods employed enabled us to determine the errors in forecasting that result from the variation of the disturbance and from the sampling fluctuations involved in the determination of the parameters of the forecasting equation, but we are not able to calculate both types of error in Model III. In the latter model we can calculate the error resulting from the variations in the disturbances but we do not have estimates of the other types of error,

[11] There is no error in this procedure if the marginal propensity to consume out of inventory profits is the same as the marginal propensity to consume out of other disposable income. If the two marginal propensities differ, the correct estimate for the model should be a weighted average of the two. The weight attached to inventory profits for the past observation will be small if inventory profits were a small percentage of disposable income, as was the case. The error is undoubtedly negligible.

[12] There are definite correction factors that lead from the variable $p(Y+T)$ to the official government figures on $\mathcal{GNP}$. The exact series used for $p(Y+T)$ are given in the appendix so that the reader can determine exactly the relationship between this variable and the official figures of $\mathcal{GNP}$. If we add government interest+depreciation and depletion−net imputed rents on owner-occupied nonfarm residences to $p(Y+T)$ we get $\mathcal{GNP}$.

[13] It appears now (April, 1947) that the assumption of 10-per-cent price increases is a low estimate. If the assumptions are modified by allowing a greater price increase, say 15 or 20 per cent, the forecasted level of $\mathcal{GNP}$ and the range of error will be raised.

i.e., that type which results from the fact that we have only a finite sample to determine the parameters of the model. The size of the first type of error, however, gives a rough guide as to the accuracy of the results. The estimated square root of the variance of the disturbances involved in forecasting disposable income (constant dollars) is about $3 billion, the same as for Models I and II. If the sampling fluctuations lead to an error of the same relative size in all models, we can say that the estimates of $\mathcal{GNP}$ from Model III should lie in a range $\pm\$13$ billion with a 70-per-cent probability.

It is instructive to examine the past record of Model III. In the spring of 1946, a list of exogenous and predetermined variables was prepared for the calendar year 1946 corresponding to the values given in Table III for fiscal 1946. At the time of the actual forecast, "reduced form" estimates of the parameters of Model III were not available; hence single-equation, least-squares estimates were used to make the forecasts. The estimated parameters obtained by the latter method are not appreciably different in this case from those obtained by the former method.

We shall now present a table of the assumptions actually used in the forecasts made in the spring of 1946 and substitute them into Model III. The comparison between actual and forecasted results will then show how well the prewar model fits the postwar data. The relation between T and Y that was used is given by

$$(3.18) \qquad T = -\frac{42.4003}{p} + 0.440(Y + T).$$

The values in Table IV and (3.18) may not be the same as observed values.

Equations (3.1), (3.2), (3.5), (3.6), (3.9), (3.13), (3.14), (3.18), and the assumptions lead to the following results

$$Y = \$\ 95.8 \text{ billion,}$$
$$Y + T = \ 121.6,$$
$$p(Y + T) = \ 186.0,$$
$$\mathcal{GNP} = \ 201.$$

If an error of $\pm\$13$ billion is attached to this forecast of $\mathcal{GNP}$, the range will certainly include the observed value.[14]

Equation (3.18) was used in the spring of 1946 as the best available estimate, but it may not agree with observations. If we substitute

[14] *The Economic Report of the President to the Congress* (Jan. 8, 1947) estimates $\mathcal{GNP}$ at $194 billion for 1946.

(3.17), which was computed more recently for fiscal 1947, for (3.18), the forecasted point estimate of $\mathcal{GNP}$ is reduced to $191 billion.

THE FORECAST

What is the interpretation of these numerical results? Models I and III, the most reliable systems, state that $\mathcal{GNP}$ will, at best, maintain its present level and is likely to fall during the remainder of fiscal 1947. Model I states that the current rate of capital formation and price level will just maintain $\mathcal{GNP}$ during the rest of the fiscal year, but if we try to estimate capital formation from the structure of the system,

TABLE IV

ASSUMPTIONS AND INITIAL CONDITIONS FOR MODEL III (CALENDAR YEARS)

	Calendar 1946	Calendar 1945	Calendar 1944
$\mathcal{E}$	7.8	7.0	
K_{-1}	111.4		
p	1.53	1.38	
H_{-1}	27.4		
r	1.16	1.15	
Y		102.5	105.
q_1	1.89	1.72	1.62
i	2.7	2.87	
D_3	0.3		
D''	2.0		
G	23.6		
$\mathcal{W}_2$	19.5	30.6	
$\mathcal{R}_1 + \mathcal{R}_2$	12.0	12.0	
ΔF	821.	691.	
$p(Y+T)$		183.	
q	1.46	1.33	

as in Model III, we find that $G\mathcal{NP}$ is likely to fall. If there arc any sizeable disturbances in these models, now, they are likely to be positive, i.e., on the side of abnormal spending. If our past estimates of the disturbances are used as a guide, we can say that $G\mathcal{NP}$ is likely to be in the range \$177.5 billion to \$190.5 billion[15] in the first half of 1947. The models point to a turning point for real income during fiscal 1947.

NEGLECT OF SUPPLY FACTORS?

Models like those of this paper have often been criticized for including only the demand side of the national market to the neglect of the supply side. This type of criticism has been especially prevalent in the recent months because it is often stated that demand is temporarily insatiable and the only limitation on the expansion of income during the postwar transition is the ability to supply goods. How can models composed exclusively of demand factors be useful in making predictions during such a period?

This criticism appears wrong, immediately, to those actively engaged in the construction of econometric models because we know that it is exhaustive to say that the economy can be decomposed into three groups, say, households, business firms, and government, and then to include the behavior pattern of these three groups in our models. What can we have neglected? The very simplest models, such as Model I, are deceptive because all the variables of this model are classified as demand variables. We have the demand by households for consumer goods, the demand by business firms for producer goods, and the demand by government for its goods and services. Where is supply? The difficulty lies in the fact that there are some equations that are imbedded within the business demand for producer goods and cover up the supply side even though it is nonetheless present. Business firms demand capital in order to produce goods that they supply to the market. Once we know the *demand* by business firms for factors of production, we know how much business firms will *supply* to the market because there is a technical relation connecting the output of business firms to their input of productive factors. The technical relationship, the production function, has been, so to speak, solved out of the system in constructing the models, but it has not been neglected.

A very simple example will make these points clear. Let us use Model I with the additional variable N_E = total number of employees, w = wage rate, and K_{-1} = total stock of fixed capital available at the beginning of the period. The complete set of equations is:

---

[15] Or in a corresponding higher range for assumed price increases greater than 10 per cent.

$$(4.1) \qquad \frac{C}{pN} = \alpha_0 + \alpha_1 \frac{\Upsilon}{pN} + \alpha_2 \left(\frac{\Upsilon}{pN} \right)_{-1} + u_1,$$

$$(4.2) \qquad \mathcal{GNP} = C + \mathcal{I}' + G,$$

$$(4.3) \qquad \mathcal{GNP} = \Upsilon + T,$$

$$(4.4) \qquad \frac{\mathcal{I}'}{pN} = \text{exogenous},$$

$$(4.5) \qquad \frac{G}{pN} = \text{exogenous},$$

$$(4.6) \qquad \frac{T}{pN} = \text{exogenous},$$

$$(4.7) \qquad \frac{\mathcal{GNP}}{p} = f\left(N_E, \frac{\mathcal{I}'}{p}, K_{-1} \right) + u_2,$$

$$(4.8) \qquad \frac{wN_E}{p} = \gamma_0 + \gamma_1 \frac{\mathcal{GNP}}{p} + \gamma_2 \left(\frac{\mathcal{GNP}}{p} \right)_{-1} + u_3,$$

$$(4.9) \qquad \Delta K = \frac{\mathcal{I}'}{p} - \text{depreciation}.$$

In this model, we can determine the demand for factors of production by business firms, their output or supply of goods, and real wages. This model might be called a model of effective demand, yet the production functions and demand for factors of production are part of the system. Equation (4.4) is the demand equation of business firms for producer goods; equation (4.7) is the technical input-output relation for business firms; and equation (4.8) is the demand equation of business firms for labor. It happens that the structure of the system is such that (4.1)–(4.6), as a unit, are sufficient to determine the level of output, but this does not mean that supply conditions are neglected.

There is a supply variable that is omitted from this model, namely, the supply of labor, or the labor force. The variable N_E represents the total demand for labor by business firms. Knowing N_E and the labor force, we can determine the amount of unemployment; however, the models have not been criticized for leaving the supply of labor out of account. The critics had the supply of commodities in mind rather than the supply of labor.

It is obvious that if the model forecast extraordinarily high levels of national product at present prices, say $\mathcal{GNP} = \$225$ billion, this forecast, in real terms, must be discarded because it exceeds our present capacity to supply goods. In the event that the exogenous and lagged variables are such that levels of national product exceeding our capacity are forecast, all that we can say is that real output will be at its maximum level and prices will rise. The exact rise in prices cannot be forecast with any confidence from the models of this paper, however. It is possible to construct models in which there are enough equations to determine prices as well as output, although satisfactory statistical estimates of such equations are still lacking.

THE USEFULNESS OF ECONOMETRIC MODELS

Those engaged in the construction of econometric models know only too well the limitations on these models. The ranges of error associated with forecasts at reasonable probability levels are larger than will be required for many problems. In several cases we shall find that the plus-minus bands of error include both inflation and deflation or yes and no. That part of the error associated with sampling fluctuations can be improved upon. We can get more data and better data, both of which give additional information and help to establish the parameters of the system with a greater degree of accuracy. For example, if we could get good quarterly observations for all series used in this paper over the entire interwar period we should have more information from which to estimate the parameters of the system. There would not be four times as much information, but there would be much more information.

It is, of course, important to know what we cannot do in order that we do not fool ourselves, but our results are not purely negative. They show clearly, in this paper, that the probability is high that national product will fall in the latter part of the present fiscal year. This forecast can be made in spite of the fact that the range of error is fairly wide, say $10 or $15 billion. From Model II, we deduce that deficit spending has a higher multiplier effect than is the case for an easy-money policy. This deduction follows in spite of the fact that the parameters of the model are subject to considerable error. In the recent past (fiscal 1946 and calendar 1946), Model III has shown that there would probably be an inflationary gap rather than a deflationary gap. Not only was this forecast definite, but it was also correct.

Even if a forecast from a model includes the joint possibilities of inflation and deflation, the forecast may be very useful in policy formation. Suppose that a particular value of GNP, call it $(GNP)^0$, represents neither inflation nor deflation. Suppose further that the forecast is that GNP will be in the range $[-\epsilon_1+(GNP)^0,(GNP)^0+\epsilon_2]$ with (high) probability, p^0. If $0<\epsilon_1<\epsilon_2$, there is a greater chance for inflation than for deflation. Government agencies that are prepared to combat inflation should be given greater powers than the agencies that are prepared to combat deflation, although both agencies should be given some powers because there is a possibility that either one may be needed. In the other case where $0 < \epsilon_2 < \epsilon_1$, the greater powers should be given to the anti-deflationary agency. In both examples, the amounts to be given each type of agency will depend upon the exact sizes of ϵ_1 and ϵ_2. But the principle of action is obvious.

The above type of policy is applicable only in the case in which the costs of preparing for inflation, or for deflation, or for both, are negligible. If there is a cost attached to the carrying out of policies, such as the cost of diverting resources to precautionary government activities, a different type of calculation must be made. If the cost of preparing for inflation when the true situation is deflation, the costs of preparing for deflation when the true situation is inflation, and the costs of preparing for the correct situation are known in advance, it is also possible to advise the government on a correct choice of alternative policies even though the forecast interval covers both inflation and deflation simultaneously.

Cowles Commission for Research in Economics
The University of Chicago

(See Appendix beginning on following page.)

APPENDIX ON DATA

MODELS I AND II: TIME SERIES

	C	g'	G	Y	GNP	U	p	N	M
1921	50.5	9.2	8.5	52.8	68.2	15.4	1.277	0.1085	37.8
1922	52.0	10.0	7.9	57.0	69.9	12.9	1.197	.1101	39.0
1923	57.8	15.3	8.5	66.1	81.6	15.5	1.219	.1120	42.7
1924	60.9	12.3	8.8	66.7	82.0	15.3	1.222	.1141	44.5
1925	63.0	15.7	9.3	70.6	88.0	17.4	1.254	.1158	48.3
1926	66.3	16.4	9.5	73.2	92.3	19.1	1.264	.1174	50.6
1927	66.0	14.9	10.0	73.5	90.9	17.4	1.240	.1190	52.2
1928	68.8	14.3	10.6	75.4	93.7	18.3	1.226	.1205	54.7
1929	70.8	17.6	11.0	79.6	99.4	19.8	1.225	.1218	55.2
1930	64.9	12.1	11.2	70.7	88.2	17.5	1.194	.1238	54.4
1931	54.2	6.4	11.5	59.6	72.1	12.5	1.087	.1248	52.9
1932	43.0	2.2	10.2	45.6	55.4	9.8	0.976	.1256	45.4
1933	42.4	3.3	9.1	44.5	54.8	10.3	0.924	.1263	41.7
1934	47.7	5.3	10.8	51.0	63.8	12.8	0.957	.1271	46.0
1935	52.2	6.7	11.9	56.3	70.8	14.5	0.981	.1280	49.9
1936	59.1	10.0	12.6	65.2	81.7	16.5	0.991	.1289	55.1
1937	62.5	11.6	13.6	69.2	87.7	18.5	1.027	.1296	57.3
1938	58.5	7.7	14.4	62.9	80.6	17.7	1.008	.1307	56.6
1939	61.7	10.9	16.0	67.7	88.6	20.9	0.994	.1317	60.9
1940	65.7	14.8	16.7	72.9	97.1	24.2	1.002	.1328	67.0
1941	74.6	19.1	26.5	88.7	120.2	31.5	1.052	0.1340	74.2

C = Consumer expenditures on goods and services, measured in billions of current dollars, U. S. Department of Commerce.

g' = Private gross capital formation, measured in billions of current dollars, U. S. Department of Commerce.

G = Government expenditures for goods and services, measured in billions of current dollars, U. S. Department of Commerce.

Y = Disposable income, measured in billions of current dollars, U. S. Department of Commerce

GNP = Gross national product measured in billions of current dollars, U. S. partment of Commerce.

$U = GNP - Y$.

p = Cost-of-living index, 1935–1939:1.00, U. S. Bureau of Labor Statistics.

N = Population of the continental United States, measured in billions of persons, U. S. Bureau of the Census.

M = Total deposits adjusted and currency outside banks, measured in billions of current dollars on June 30 of each year, Board of Governors of the Federal Reserve System.

MODEL III: TIME SERIES

	C	I	q	ΔH	D_1	q_1	D_2	D_3	D''	G	$Y+T$
1920	39.8	1.1	1.459	2.4	0.4	1.758	0.5	0.2	2.0	4.7	47.1
1921	41.9	0.1	1.169	0.1	0.8	1.342	0.5	0.1	1.9	6.7	48.3
1922	45.0	0.6	1.067	0.6	1.3	1.242	1.0	0.2	1.9	6.3	53.0
1923	49.2	2.0	1.173	2.1	1.3	1.391	1.4	0.2	2.0	5.9	60.1
1924	50.6	1.6	1.154	−0.2	1.5	1.379	1.7	0.2	2.0	6.9	60.2
1925	52.6	2.4	1.133	0.7	1.7	1.348	1.8	0.2	2.0	6.9	64.2
1926	55.1	2.5	1.132	1.2	1.5	1.348	1.9	0.2	2.1	7.0	67.3
1927	56.2	2.2	1.130	0.2	1.4	1.348	1.8	0.2	2.1	8.1	68.0
1928	57.3	2.0	1.118	−0.3	1.4	1.348	1.6	0.2	2.2	8.3	68.2
1929	57.8	2.8	1.139	1.3	1.0	1.348	1.7	0.2	2.2	8.4	71.0
1930	55.0	1.6	1.092	−0.3	0.8	1.242	0.6	0.2	2.2	9.7	65.4
1931	50.9	−0.7	1.016	−2.1	0.7	1.106	0.6	0.1	2.2	10.9	58.2
1932	45.6	−2.2	0.944	−2.7	0.4	0.963	0.2	0.1	2.1	10.3	49.6
1933	46.5	−2.7	0.926	−0.8	0.3	0.932	0.1	0.1	2.1	9.3	50.7
1934	48.7	−1.6	1.000	−0.1	0.4	1.000	0.2	0.1	2.0	10.0	55.7
1935	51.3	−0.6	1.013	0.2	0.7	1.006	0.2	0.2	2.0	10.5	60.5
1936	57.7	0.5	1.034	2.0	0.9	1.056	0.4	0.2	2.0	10.4	70.1
1937	58.7	1.4	1.129	1.0	0.8	1.230	0.5	0.2	2.0	11.1	71.7
1938	57.5	−0.4	1.133	−1.2	0.9	1.236	0.5	0.2	2.0	13.1	68.6
1939	61.6	0.2	1.131	0.9	1.1	1.242	0.8	0.2	2.0	14.5	77.3
1940	65.0	1.2	1ʹ.159	1.7	1.3	1.267	0.8	0.2	2.0	15.5	83.7
1941	69.7	1.3	1.222	3.0	1.6	1.354	0.7	0.3	2.0	22.4	96.9

C: Consumption measured in billions of 1934 dollars:

$$C = \frac{(1) + (2)}{(3)}.$$

(1) = Consumer expenditures, Mary S. Painter, "Estimates of Gross National Product, 1919–1928," *Federal Reserve Bulletin*, Vol. 31, September, 1945, pp. 872–873. Official data of the U. S. Department of Commerce are given in this article for the period 1929–1941.

(2) = Imputed net rents on owner-occupied residences, S. Kuznets, *National Income and Its Composition*, Vol. II, p. 735. These data are given for 1919–1938. For 1939, 1940, 1941 the estimates for gross imputed rent have been extended by Kuznets' method (estimated number of owner-occupied units multiplied by average monthly rental; converted to net rents by use of free-hand regression between net and gross imputed rents, 1933–1938):

> 1939:$1.5 billion,
> 1940:$1.5 billion,
> 1941:$1.6 billion.

(3) = Price index implicit in the adjustment of consumers' outlay, 1934:1.00.

MODEL III: TIME SERIES (*continued*)

Y	p	$\mathcal{W}_2$	$\mathcal{W}_1$	$\mathcal{R}_1$	$\mathcal{R}_2$	r	ΔF	v^*	N^*	i	$\mathcal{M}_1$
1920	42.3	1.611	3.5	41.4	6.5	0.9	1.279	612	99.1	19.0	7.08	23.7
1921	44.2	1.317	3.6	32.0	8.1	0.8	1.468	561	100.4	19.4	7.04	20.8
1922	47.0	1.251	3.6	34.1	8.4	0.7	1.512	582	100.7	19.9	5.95	21.4
1923	53.7	1.281	3.7	40.6	9.3	0.8	1.551	630	100.1	20.7	6.04	22.7
1924	53.7	1.267	3.9	40.1	10.1	0.8	1.606	515	98.8	21.5	5.80	23.5
1925	56.6	1.294	4.1	41.6	10.2	0.8	1.612	529	97.6	22.3	5.47	25.2
1926	59.3	1.293	4.3	44.3	10.0	0.8	1.596	542	96.4	23.1	5.21	25.7
1927	60.1	1.260	4.5	44.3	10.1	0.8	1.571	465	95.2	23.9	4.97	25.8
1928	59.5	1.267	4.7	45.8	10.0	0.8	1.534	419	94.3	24.6	4.94	26.3
1929	61.9	1.259	5.0	48.1	10.4	0.8	1.498	474	93.4	25.3	5.21	26.4
1930	60.1	1.211	5.1	43.1	10.0	0.8	1.457	306	92.7	25.8	5.09	25.3
1931	56.6	1.088	5.2	35.4	9.3	0.8	1.380	234	92.0	26.2	5.81	23.3
1932	49.2	0.966	5.1	26.6	8.2	0.7	1.238	112	91.1	26.4	6.87	20.8
1933	46.2	0.931	5.2	24.6	7.2	0.6	1.067	380	92.5	26.6	5.89	19.8
1934	50.4	1.000	6.0	28.5	6.9	0.6	1.000	553	94.1	26.7	4.96	21.4
1935	54.0	1.040	6.3	31.2	7.0	0.6	0.998	551	95.2	27.0	4.46	25.1
1936	63.5	1.047	7.7	35.3	7.2	0.6	1.021	572	95.7	27.4	3.87	29.0
1937	62.6	1.096	7.3	41.0	7.7	0.6	1.069	585	95.8	27.9	3.94	30.4
1938	60.2	1.047	8.1	37.0	8.0	0.6	1.103	456	95.8	28.5	4.19	30.4
1939	67.6	1.035	8.1	40.0	8.2	0.6	1.105	520	95.8	29.2	3.77	33.8
1940	72.3	1.049	8.4	44.0	8.5	0.7	1.108	508	96.3	30.1	3.55	39.0
1941	82.9	1.121	9.5	55.1	9.0	0.7	1.122	518	97.2	31.0	3.34	45.5

* A figure greater than 100 indicates that demand exceeds physical supply.

S. Kuznets, *op. cit.*, Vol. I, p. 145, col. 3, converted to 1934 base year. These data are given for 1919–1938. For 1939, 1940, 1941 the estimates have been extended by Kuznets' method (weighted average of Bureau of Labor Statistics cost-of-living index and U. S. Department of Agriculture index of prices paid by farmers for subsistence, weights being proportionate to ratio of urban and rural populations respectively):
1939:1.026,
1940:1.034,
1941:1.093.

I: Net Investment in private producers' plant and equipment, measured in billions of 1934 dollars.

$$I = \frac{(4)}{(5)} + \frac{(6)}{(7)} - \frac{(8)}{(9)} - \frac{(10)}{(7)} .$$

(4) = Gross expenditures on private producers' nonagricultural plant and equipment, G. Terborgh, *Federal Reserve Bulletin*, Vol. 25, September, 1939, p. 732; Vol. 26, February, 1940, p. 116; F. Dirks, *Federal Reserve Bulletin*, Vol. 28, April, 1942, p. 318.

MODEL III: TIME SERIES (concluded)

	$\mathcal{M}_2$	$\mathcal{E}_r$	K	H	$\mathcal{E}$	u_2	X
1920	15.8	28	97.2	22.1	0.6	0.52	40.3
1921	16.6	29	97.3	22.2	0.6	−0.45	47.8
1922	17.4	64	97.9	22.8	0.6	−0.10	52.5
1923	19.7	35	99.9	24.9	0.6	0.95	59.6
1924	21.3	16	101.5	24.7	0.6	−0.51	59.7
1925	23.1	11	103.9	25.4	0.7	−0.17	63.7
1926	24.7	−35	106.4	26.6	0.7	0.40	66.7
1927	26.4	5	108.6	26.8	0.8	−0.05	67.4
1928	28.2	13	110.6	26.5	0.9	−0.54	67.5
1929	28.5	43	113.4	27.8	1.0	0.82	70.2
1930	28.6	55	115.0	27.5	1.1	0.53	64.5
1931	27.9	89	114.3	25.4	1.2	−0.28	57.1
1932	25.1	256	112.1	22.7	1.4	−0.48	48.1
1933	22.6	528	109.4	21.9	1.8	0.35	48.8
1934	22.6	1564	107.8	21.8	2.2	−0.09	53.5
1935	23.8	2469	107.2	22.0	2.6	−0.48	58.0
1936	24.8	2512	107.7	24.0	3.0	0.55	67.2
1937	25.8	1220	109.1	25.0	3.2	0.06	68.8
1938	26.3	2522	108.7	23.8	3.3	−1.30	65.4
1939	26.7	4392	108.9	24.7	3.5	−0.47	73.9
1940	27.4	6326	110.1	26.4	3.9	0.13	80.0
1941	27.8	5324	111.4	29.4	4.5	0.68	92.9

(5) = Price index of business capital goods, 1934:1.00, S. Fabricant, *Capital Consumption and Adjustment*, pp. 178–197, converted to 1934 base year. These data are for 1919–1935. The figures for 1936–1941 have been supplied by Fabricant in private correspondence.

(6) = Expenditures on farm buildings (excluding dwellings) +expenditures on farm machinery +expenditures on farm trucks +40 per cent of expenditures on farm automobiles other than trucks, *Net Farm Income and Parity Report*, U.S. Department of Agriculture, 1943, p. 27.

(7) = Price index of farm capital goods, 1934:1.00. Weighted average of indexes of prices paid for building materials, farm machinery, and motor vehicles. The weights are proportional to constant-dollar expenditures on farm buildings (excluding dwellings), on farm machinery, and on trucks +40 per cent of other motor vehicles respectively. *Agricultural Statistics*, 1943, p. 394, *Income Parity for Agriculture*, U.S. Department of Agriculture, Part III, Section 4, p. 11.

(8) = Depreciation charges on private producers' nonagricultural plant and equipment, - S. Fabricant, *op. cit.*, pp. 260–261. These data are used for 1919–1928. J. Mosak, "Forecasting Postwar Demand: III," ECONOMETRICA, Vol. 13, 1945, pp. 45–53. These data are used for 1929–1941.

(9) = Price index underlying business depreciation charges, 1934 base, S. Fabricant, *op. cit.*, p. 183, converted to 1934 base year. These data are for 1919–1935. The figures for 1936–1941 have been supplied by S. Fabricant in private correspondence.

(10) = Depreciation charges on farm plant and equipment (exclusive of dwellings); calculated at replacement costs. *Net Farm Income and Parity Report*, U.S. Department of Agriculture, 1943, p. 23, and *Income Parity for Agriculture*, U.S. Department of Agriculture, Part II, Section 5, p. 24.

q: Price index of private producers' plant and equipment. 1934:1.00.

$$q = (5)\,\frac{(4)}{(4)+(6)} + (7)\,\frac{(6)}{(4)+(6)}\,.$$

ΔH: Net change in inventories, measured in billions of 1934 dollars.

$$\Delta H = \frac{(11)}{(12)}\,.$$

(11) = Net inventory change, Mary S. Painter, *loc. cit.*

(12) = Wholesale price index, 1934:1.00, Supplement to the *Survey of Current Business*, 1942, p. 18, converted to 1934 base year.

D_1: Gross construction expenditures on owner-occupied, single-family, nonfarm residences, measured in billions of 1934 dollars.

$$D_1 = \frac{(13)\cdot 1.18\cdot 1.126\cdot (14)\cdot 0.63 + (15)\cdot 0.23}{(16)}\,.$$

(13) = Average permit valuation of single-family, nonfarm residences, Bureau of Labor Statistics, *The Construction Industry in the United States*, Bulletin 786, table 11, p. 21.

    1.18 = Correction for undervaluation of building permits, taken from D. Wickens, *Residential Real Estate*.

    1.126 = ratio of the average rental value of owner-occupied, single-family, nonfarm residences (constructed 1935–1940) to the average rental value of all single-family nonfarm residences (constructed 1935–1940), *Census of Housing*, 1940, Vol. III, Part I, table A4.

(14) = Number of single-family, nonfarm dwelling units constructed annually, Bureau of Labor Statistics, *op. cit.*, table 18, p. 35.

    0.63 = Fraction of single-family, nonfarm dwelling units constructed 1935–1940, that were owner-occupied in 1940, *Census of Housing*, *loc. cit.*

(15) = Expenditures for alterations, additions, and repairs, Twentieth Century Fund, *American Housing*, table 12, p. 367. These data are for 1919–1940. For 1941 it was assumed that maintenance was the same percentage of total housing expenditures as in 1940.

    0.23 = 0.32·0.357/0.524, where 0.32 = the ratio of owner-occupied single-family, nonfarm dwelling units to total nonfarm dwelling units in 1940; 0.357 = the fraction of repairs estimated by the U.S. Department of Commerce to be attributable to owner-occupied, nonfarm residences (average of 1930 and 1940 figures); 0.524 = the ratio of owner-occupied nonfarm units to total nonfarm units, 1930.

(16) = American Appraisal Co. index of construction costs (national average), 1934:1.00, Supplement to the *Survey of Current Business*, 1942, p. 25, converted to 1934 base year.

q_1: Index of constuction costs, 1934:1.00.

$$q_1 = (16).$$

D_2: Gross construction expenditures on rented, nonfarm residences, measured in billions of 1934 dollars.

$$D_2 = \frac{(17)}{(16)} - D_1.$$

(17) = Gross construction expenditures on private nonfarm residences, Bureau of Labor Statistics, *op. cit.*, table 1, p. 4.

D_3: Gross construction expenditures on farm residences, measured in billions of 1934 dollars.

$$D_3 = \frac{(18)}{(19)}.$$

(18) = Gross construction expenditures on farm residences, Bureau of Labor Statistics, *op. cit.*, table 1, p. 4.

(19) = Index of farm construction costs, 1934:1.00, *Income Parity for Agriculture*, Part II, Section 5, p. 27. These data are for 1919–1940. The 1941 figure was taken from a freehand regression between (19) and the index of the cost of building materials taken from *Agricultural Prices*, Feb. 29, 1944, col. 7, p. 25. All indexes are converted to 1934 base year.

D'': Depreciation of all residences (farm and nonfarm), measured in billions of 1934 dollars.

$$D'' = \left[67.6 - \sum_{i=t+1}^{1933} (D_1 + D_2 + D_3)_i + \sum_{i=t+1}^{1933} D_i'' \right] \frac{0.03}{0.97}$$

$$- (D_1 + D_2 + D_3)_t \frac{0.015}{0.97}, \qquad t < 1933,$$

$$D'' = 67.6 \frac{0.03}{0.97} - (D_1 + D_2 + D_3)_t \frac{0.015}{0.97}, \qquad t = 1933,$$

$$D'' = 67.6(0.03) + (D_1 + D_2 + D_3)_t(0.015), \qquad t = 1934,$$

$$D'' = (67.6)(0.97)^{t-1934}(0.03)$$

$$+ \sum_{i=1934}^{t-1} (D_1 + D_2 + D_3)_i(0.985)(0.97)^{i-1-1934} \quad (0.03)$$

$$+ (D_1 + D_2 + D_3)_t(0.015), \qquad t > 1934.$$

67.6 = The estimated value, Jan. 1, 1934, of the stock of residential dwellings in the U.S. It is 80 per cent of Wickens' (*Residential Real Estate*, table A8, p. 93) figure for the value of nonfarm land and dwellings plus 14.3 per cent of the value of total farm real estate, *Net Farm Income and Parity Report*, U.S. Department of Agriculture, 1943, table 18, p. 29. The figures of 80 per cent and 14.3 per cent are taken as the proportions of nonfarm residential and farm real estate respectively that are represented by dwellings alone.

G: Government expenditures for goods and services (exclusive of government interest payments) plus net exports plus net investment of nonprofit institutions, all measured in billions of 1934 dollars.

$$G = \frac{(20) - (21) - (22)}{(23)} + \frac{(22)}{(16)} + \frac{(24)}{(12)} + \frac{(25) - 0.1}{(16)}.$$

(20) = Government expenditures for goods and services, Mary S. Painter, *loc. cit.*

(21) = Government interest payments, S. Kuznets, *op. cit.*, Vol. II, p. 813. These data for 1919–1928. J. Mosak, *op. cit.*, p. 51. These data are for 1929–1941.

(22) = Public construction expenditures, including work-relief construction, Bureau of Labor Statistics, *op. cit.*, table 1, p. 4. and *Statistical Abstract of the United States*, 1942, p. 992.

(23) = Index of wholesale prices of nonfarm products, 1934:1.00, *Agricultural Statistics*, 1942, p. 649, converted to 1934 base year.

(24) = Net exports and monetary use of gold and silver, Mary S. Painter, *loc. cit.*

(25) = Gross construction expenditures by nonprofit institutions, G. Terborgh, *loc. cit.*, and F. Dirks, *loc. cit.*

0.1 = Annual depreciation charges attributed to the plant of nonprofit institutions. This figure is about 3 per cent of the 1934, end-of-year, stock of capital owned by these institutions.

$Y+T$: Net national product, measured in billions of 1934 dollars.

$$Y + T = C + I + \Delta H + D_1 + D_2 + D_3 - D'' + G.$$

Y: Disposable income, measured in billions of 1934 dollars.

$$Y = \frac{(1)+(2)+(4)+(6)-\dfrac{(8)}{(9)}(5)-(10)+(11)+(17)+(18)-(16)D'' +(20)+(24)+(25)-0.1-(26)-(27)-(28)+(29)}{(3)}.$$

(26) = Federal government receipts, *Annual Report of the Secretary of the Treasury*.

(27) = State and local government receipts, National Industrial Conference Board, *Economic Almanac*, 1944–1945, p. 102. These data are given for fiscal years and are converted to a calendar-year basis by taking a two-year moving average of a three-year moving average.

(28) = Net corporate savings, M. Hoffenberg, "Estimates of National Output, Distributed Income, Consumer Spending, Saving and Capital Formation," *Review of Economic Statistics*, Vol. 25, May, 1943, p. 156 (Commerce estimates).

(29) = Transfer payments, *Survey of Current Business*, Vol. 22, May, 1942, p. 12, and August, 1943, p. 13. These data are for 1929–1941. The data for 1919–1928 are set at a constant rate of $0.7 billion per annum. This constant figure is justified on the grounds that veterans' payments by the federal government were stable at $0.4 billion for the entire period of the 1920's and that state relief expenditures were also stable at $0.1 billion for the same period. The remaining transfer payments, those of local governments, were assumed to be stable also. Hence the figure of $0.7 billion, observed for 1929 and 1930, was extended to the previous years.

p: Price index of output as a whole, 1934:1.00

$$p = \frac{(1)+(2)+(4)+(6)-\dfrac{(8)}{(9)}(5)-(10)+(11)+(17)+(18)-(16)D'' +(20)-(21)+(24)+(25)-0.1}{Y+T}.$$

$\mathcal{W}_1$: Private wage-salary bill, measured in billions of current dollars.

$$\mathcal{W}_1 = (30) - (31).$$

(30) = Total employee compensation, M. Hoffenberg, *loc. cit.* (Commerce estimates).

(31) = Government wages and salaries, including work-relief wages, *Survey of Current Business*, March, 1943, p. 22. These data are for 1929–1941.

The figures for 1919–1928 are estimated from a freehand regression between the U. S. Department of Commerce estimates (1929–1938) and Kuznets' estimates (1929–1938). See S. Kuznets, *op. cit.*, Vol. II, p. 811. Kuznets' figures are known for 1919–1928; hence the corresponding commerce figures can be estimated from the regression.

W_2: Government wage-salary bill, measured in billions of current dollars.

$$W_2 = (31).$$

R_1: Nonfarm rentals, paid and imputed, measured in billions of current dollars.

$$R_1 = (32).$$

(*32*) = Gross nonfarm rentals, paid and imputed, for residential dwellings, special release. U. S. Department of Commerce, 1929–1941. Estimated 1921–1928 from free-hand regression between Commerce Department gross rentals (1929–1938) and Barger's data on gross rentals (1929–1938). See H. Barger, *Outlay and Income in the United States, 1921–1938.* pp. 226–227. Barger's figures are known for 1921–1928; hence the corresponding Commerce figures can be estimated from the regression. Estimated 1919, 1920 from

$$R_1 = 0.278r \left(\frac{vN^s}{100} + \frac{v_{-1}N_{-1}{}^s}{100} \right) \frac{1}{2}.$$

See below for definitions of v and N^s.

R_2: Farm rentals, paid and imputed, measured in billions of current dollars.

$$R_2 = (33).$$

(*33*) = Gross rentals, paid and imputed, for farm dwellings, *Agricultural Statistics,* 1942, p. 660.

r: Index of rents, 1934:1.00.

$$r = (34).$$

(*34*) = Rent component of Bureau of Labor Statistics cost-of-living index, 1934:1.00, converted to 1934 base year, *Statistical Abstract of the United States,* 1943, pp. 404–405.

ΔF: Thousands of new nonfarm families.

$$\Delta F = (35).$$

(*35*) = Annual number of families added in nonfarm areas, Twentieth Century Fund, *op. cit.*, table 40, p. 418. These data are for 1919–1939. For 1940 and 1941, the data are the first differences in the beginning-of-the-year number of families given in the *Statistical Abstract of the United States,* 1943, table 40, p. 46, multiplied by 0.795, the ratio of nonfarm families to all families in 1940.

v: Percentage of nonfarm housing units occupied at the end of the year.

$$v = (36), \qquad\qquad 1919\text{–}1927,$$
$$v = (37), \qquad\qquad 1928\text{–}1941.$$

(*36*) = Ratio of nonfarm families to available nonfarm dwelling units. L. Chawner, *Residential Building,* Housing Monograph Series, No. 1, table VI, p. 16.

(*37*) = Percentage of urban dwelling units occupied, K. Johnson, "Residential Vacancies in Wartime United States," *Survey of Current Business,* Vol. 22, December, 1942, table 1, p. 19.

N^e: Millions of available nonfarm dwelling units at the end of the year.

$$N^e = 24.6 - \sum_{i-t+1}^{1928} \Delta(38)_i, \qquad t = 1919\text{--}1927,$$

$$N^e = (39), \qquad\qquad\qquad 1928\text{--}1941.$$

(38) = Available nonfarm dwelling units, at the end of the year, L. Chawner, *op. cit.*, table VI, p. 16.

24.6 = Available nonfarm dwelling units on January 1, 1929, "Dwelling Units in the United States, 1929–1942," special release of the United States Department of Commerce.

(39) = Available nonfarm dwelling units, at the end of the year, "Dwelling Units in the United States, 1929–1942."

i: Average corporate-bond yield.

$$i = (40).$$

(40) = Average corporate-bond yield, Board of Governors of the Federal Reserve System, *Banking and Monetary Statistics*, p. 468.

$\mathcal{M}_1$: Demand deposits adjusted plus currency outside banks, averaged during the year, measured in billions of current dollars.

$$\mathcal{M}_1 = (41).$$

(41) = Demand deposits adjusted plus currency outside banks, average of beginning-, middle-, and end-of-the-year figures (except 1919–1923, for which middle-of-year figures are used), Board of Governors of the Federal Reserve System, *op. cit.*, p. 34.

$\mathcal{M}_2$: Time deposits, averaged during the year, measured in billions of current dollars.

$$\mathcal{M}_2 = (42).$$

(42) = Time deposits, average of beginning-, middle-, and end-of-year figures (except 1919–1923, for which middle-of-year figures are used), Board of Governors of the Federal Reserve System, *op. cit.*, p. 34.

$\mathcal{E}_r$: Excess reserves, averaged during the year, measured in millions of current dollars.

$$\mathcal{E}_r = (43), \qquad\qquad 1919\text{--}1928,$$

$$\mathcal{E}_r = (44), \qquad\qquad 1929\text{--}1941.$$

(43) = Member bank, excess reserve balances, call dates, Board of Governors of the Federal Reserve System, *op. cit.*, p. 395.

(44) = Member bank, excess reserve balances, annual averages of daily figures, Board of Governors of the Federal Reserve System, *op. cit.*, p. 368.

K: End-of-year stock of private producers' plant and equipment measured in billions of 1934 dollars.

$$K = 107.8 - \sum_{i-t+1}^{1934} I_i, \qquad t < 1934,$$

$$K = 107.8, \qquad\qquad\qquad 1934,$$

$$K = 107.8 + \sum_{i-1935}^{t} I_i, \qquad t > 1934.$$

107.8 = End-of-1934 stock of private producers' plant and equipment. Net capital assets, excluding land, for corporations, end-of-1934, are taken from S. Fabricant, *op. cit.*, p. 271. These data are converted to estimates for both corporate and noncorporate enterprises by dividing the figure for each industry by the ratio of corporate output to total output. These ratios are:

Mining and Quarrying	0.96,
Manufacturing	0.92,
Construction	0.60,
Transportation and Public Utilities	1.00,
Trade	0.63,
Service	0.30,
Finance and Real Estate	0.84.

These ratios are found in *The Structure of the American Economy*, National Resources Planning Board, pp. 375–376. The capital for the service industries is corrected by subtracting the capital of nonprofit institutions. Agricultural capital, exclusive of livestock, land, and dwellings is taken from *The Structure of the American Economy*, p. 377.

H: End-of-year stock of inventories, measured in billions of 1934 dollars.

$$H = 21.8 - \sum_{i=t+1}^{1934} (\Delta H)_i, \qquad t < 1934,$$

$$H = 21.8, \qquad\qquad\qquad 1934,$$

$$H = 21.8 + \sum_{i=1935}^{t} (\Delta H)_i. \qquad t > 1934.$$

21.8 = End-of-1934 stock of inventories.

Business inventories, end of 1934	$17,913 million
Less: Inventories of Agricultural Corporations	196
	$17,717
Plus: Total agricultural inventories	4,087
	$21,804

Business inventories and inventories of agricultural corporations come from *Survey of Current Business*, Vol. 22, September, 1942, p. 18. Agricultural inventories come from *Agricultural Statistics*, 1942 (value of crops for sale, plus value of livestock).

$\mathcal{E}:$ Excise taxes, measured in billions of current dollars.

$$\mathcal{E} = (45).$$

(45) = State sales taxes plus state insurance taxes plus state public utility taxes plus federal taxes on alcoholic beverages, tobacco, and motor fuel, plus other manufacturers' excises. *Federal, State, and Local Government Fiscal Relations*, Senate Document no. 79, 78th Congress, first session, 1943, pp. 320, 337, 340–343. Fiscal-year data are converted to calendar-year data by taking a two-year moving average of a three-year moving average.

COMPUTATION OF PREDETERMINED AND EXOGENOUS VARIABLES USED IN MODEL III

$\mathcal{E}:$ The components of $\mathcal{E}$ that represent federal taxes can be obtained from the *Treasury Bulletin* for past months, and those components that represent state and local taxes can be obtained from the *Statistical Abstract* for recent years. There is little variation in the state and local taxes so they have been set arbitrarily at the levels given by the latest observations in the *Statistical Abstract*. The sum of the components of $\mathcal{E} = \$7.3$ billion for fiscal 1946. A figure this large for fiscal 1947 is not consistent with the levels of $\mathcal{GNP}$ generated by the model for that period; i.e., present tax rates would not yield taxes as high as those of last year if $\mathcal{GNP}$ falls from last year's level. By successive approximations, we obtained assumptions of falling excise taxes and falling $\mathcal{GNP}$ that are consistent with each other at current tax rates. The variable $\mathcal{E}$ does not, by itself, play an important role in the model, however, and a slight error in the assumed value of $\mathcal{E}$ will have a negligible result on the forecast.

K_{-1}: Expenditures on private producers' plant and equipment during the war years (since Pearl Harbor) approximately, though not quite, balanced depreciation charges. It was assumed that the stock of capital in plant and equipment could be set at \$111.0 billion for the beginning of fiscal 1946. This figure is in 1934 dollars. Net investment in 1934 dollars for fiscal 1946 has been estimated at \$2.3 billion, which brings the stock of private capital up to \$113.3 billion for the beginning of fiscal 1947. To this figure we add approximately \$1 billion to account for the transfer of surplus property, in the form of producers' plant, from the public to the private sector of the economy. (See *8th Report* by the Director of War Mobilization and Reconversion, Oct. 1, 1946, p. 69.)

p: From the published observations for fiscal 1946, we calculated, according to the definitions used in Model III, $p(Y+T)$ and $Y+T$. The ratio of these two quantities gives p. We have assumed approximately a 10-per-cent rise from fiscal 1946 to fiscal 1947 for this variable.

H_{-1}: To our figure for year-end inventories in 1941, we added the net annual change, in 1934 dollars, up to the end of 1945. There are also data for the first half of 1946, which were added in 1934 dollars. The result was the stock of inventories existing at the beginning of fiscal 1947, \$27.9 billion.

r: It was assumed that strict rent controls would be maintained throughout the first half of the fiscal year and would be relaxed to permit an increase in the ceilings by 10 to 15 per cent during the second half of the fiscal year. We placed the average increase for the year at 5 points in the index.

Y_{-1}, Y_{-2}: The difference between the Commerce Department definition of disposable income and the definition used in Model III is equal to net imputed rents on owner-occupied residences. The sum of \$2 billion was added to the Commerce estimates for fiscal 1945 and for fiscal 1946 to get disposable income in current dollars. The price index of consumer goods was then used as a deflator to get disposable income in 1934 dollars. The price index is a weighted average of the cost-of-living index and the index of prices paid by farmers, the weights being 0.77 and 0.23 respectively. These weights are the percentages of the population in nonfarm and farm areas respectively.

q_1: For fiscal 1945 and fiscal 1946, the index of construction costs was taken from the observations (American Appraisal Co., national average), transformed to a 1934 base. A 10-per-cent increase was assumed for fiscal 1947 as compared with fiscal 1946.

i: The average corporate-bond yield, which changes very slowly, was kept at its present level.

D_3:   Farm residential construction was put at its peacetime maximum. This figure is very small and can have little influence on the final result.

D'':   Depreciation of residences has been at a nearly constant rate over the last two decades. Small changes in the stock of housing will cause very small changes in depreciation. Maximum building rates will not change this figure (in tenths of billions) for a few years. The latest prewar rates were extended to fiscal 1946 and fiscal 1947.

G: For fiscal 1946, it is possible to use observed values of government spending, (excluding interest), foreign trade, and net investment of nonprofit institutions, all properly deflated. For fiscal 1947 we used official government forecasts of expenditures (excluding interest) and the foreign balance. The assumed wholesale price index (10 per cent above fiscal 1946) was used as a deflator. The net investment of nonprofit institutions was put at its prewar maximum; however, this figure has a negligible effect on the final result.

W_2:   Government wages and salaries are known for fiscal 1946. Official forecasts were used for fiscal 1947.

$R_1 + R_2$ Assuming an increase in the number of housing units and in the level of rents, we should find an increase in total rentals. A 5-per-cent increase from the observations of fiscal 1946 was assumed for fiscal 1947.

ΔF: The net increase in the number of families (farm and nonfarm) has been forecast for calendar years in the *Statistical Abstract of the United States, 1944–45,* p. 49. The percentage of all families that will be in nonfarm areas is set at 82.7 per cent (see National Housing Agency, *Housing Needs,* November, 1944) The 1946 forecast was used unchanged (except for rounding off) for fiscal 1946. The forecast for calendar 1947 was revised upward in order to apply to fiscal 1947 since the latter year will catch some of the demobilization while the former will not. The upward revision was from about 416 thousand families to 500 thousand families.

$p(Y + T)$:   The observed value of net national product in current dollars for fiscal 1946 was formed from the sum:

        Consumer expenditures
+ $2 billion imputed net rents
+ net change in inventories
+ construction
+ private producers' equipment
+ government expenditures
+ net exports
− $11 billion depreciation
− $5.3 billion government interest payments.

q: For fiscal 1946 we calculated q from the ratio of expenditures on producers' plant and equipment in current dollars to expenditures in 1934 dollars. The latter figure was obtained by deflating equipment expenditures by the wholesale price index of machinery and plant expenditures by the construction cost index. We assumed a 10-per-cent increase in q from fiscal 1946 to fiscal 1947.

Econometrica, Vol. 17, 2 (April 1949)

IDENTIFICATION PROBLEMS IN ECONOMIC MODEL CONSTRUCTION[1]

By Tjalling C. Koopmans

Statistical inference, from observations to economic behavior parameters, can be made in two steps: inference from the observations to the parameters of the assumed joint distribution of the observations, and inference from that distribution to the parameters of the structural equations describing economic behavior. The latter problem of inference, described by the term "identification problem," is discussed in this article in an expository manner, drawing on other more original work for concepts and theorems, and using a number of examples drawn partly from econometric literature.

1. INTRODUCTION

THE CONSTRUCTION of dynamic economic models has become an important tool for the analysis of economic fluctuations and for related problems of policy. In these models, macro-economic variables are thought of as determined by a *complete system of equations*. The meaning of the term "complete" is discussed more fully below. At present it may suffice to describe a complete system as one in which there are as many equations as endogenous variables, that is, variables whose formation is to be "explained" by the equations. The equations are usually of, at most, four kinds: equations of economic behavior, institutional rules, technological laws of transformation, and identities. We shall use the term structural equations to comprise all four types of equations.

Systems of structural equations may be composed entirely on the basis of economic "theory." By this term we shall understand the combination of (a) principles of economic behavior derived from general observation—partly introspective, partly through interview or experience—of the motives of economic decisions, (b) knowledge of legal and institutional rules restricting individual behavior (tax schedules, price controls, reserve requirements, etc.), (c) technological knowledge, and (d) carefully constructed definitions of variables. Alternatively, a structural equation system may be determined on the dual basis of such "theory" combined with systematically collected statistical data for the relevant variables for a given period and country or other unit. In this article we shall discuss certain problems that arise out of model construction in the second case.

[1] I am indebted to present and former Cowles Commission staff members and to my students for valuable critical comments regarding contents and presentation of this article. An earlier version of this paper was presented before the Chicago Meeting of the Econometric Society in December 1947. [This article was reprinted, with the addition of a sixth example, in Section 2, as Chapter II of *Studies in Econometric Method*, edited by William C. Hood and Tjalling C. Koopmans (New York: John Wiley & Sons, 1953). — The Editors.]

160   TJALLING C. KOOPMANS

Where statistical data are used as one of the foundation stones on which the equation system is erected, the modern methods of statistical inference are an indispensable instrument. However, without economic "theory" as another foundation stone, it is impossible to make such statistical inference apply directly to the equations of economic behavior which are most relevant to analysis and to policy discussion. Statistical inference unsupported by economic theory applies to whatever statistical regularities and stable relationships can be discerned in the data.[2] Such purely empirical relationships when discernible are likely to be due to the presence and persistence of the underlying structural relationships, and (if so) could be deduced from a knowledge of the latter. However, the direction of this deduction cannot be reversed—from the empirical to the structural relationships—except possibly with the help of a theory which specifies the form of the structural relationships, the variables which enter into each, and any further details supported by prior observation or deduction therefrom. The more detailed these specifications are made in the model, the greater scope is thereby given to statistical inference from the data to the structural equations. We propose to study the limits to which statistical inference, from the data to the structural equations (other than definitions), is subject, and the manner in which these limits depend on the support received from economic theory.

This problem has attracted recurrent discussion in econometric literature, with varying terminology and degree of abstraction. Reference is made to Pigou [16], Henry Schultz [17, especially Chapter II, Section IIIc], Frisch [4, 5], Marschak [15, especially Sections IV and V], Haavelmo [6, especially Chapter V]. An attempt to systematize the terminology and to formalize the treatment of the problem has been made over the past few years by various authors connected in one way or another with the Cowles Commission for Research in Economics. Since the purpose of this article is expository, I shall draw freely on the work by Koopmans and Rubin [14], Wald [18], Hurwicz [7, 8], Koopmans and Reiersöl [13], without specific acknowledgement in each case. We shall proceed by discussing a sequence of examples, all drawn from econometrics, rather than by a formal logical presentation, which can be found in references [14], [7] and [13].

2. CONCEPTS AND EXAMPLES

The *first example*, already frequently discussed, is that of a competitive market for a single commodity, of which the price p and the quantity q are determined through the intersection of two rectilinear schedules, of demand and supply respectively, with instantaneous response of quantity

[2] See T. C. Koopmans [12].

to price in both cases. For definiteness' sake, we shall think of observations as applying to successive periods in time. We shall further assume that the slope coefficients α and γ of the demand and supply schedules respectively are constant through time, but that the levels of the two schedules are subject to not directly observable shifts from an equilibrium level. The structural equations can then be written as:

$$(1) \quad \begin{cases} (1d) & q + \alpha p + \epsilon = u \quad \text{(demand)} \\ (1s) & q + \gamma p + \eta = v \quad \text{(supply)}. \end{cases}$$

Concerning the shift variables u and v we shall assume that they are random drawings from a stable joint probability distribution with mean values equal to zero:

$$(2) \qquad \phi(u, v), \qquad \mathcal{E}u = 0, \qquad \mathcal{E}v = 0.$$

We shall introduce a few terms which we shall use with corresponding meaning in all examples. The not directly observable shift variables u, v are called *latent variables*, as distinct from the *observed variables*, p, q. We shall further distinguish *structure* and *model*. By a structure we mean the combination of a specific set of structural equations (1) (such as is obtained by giving specific numerical values to α, γ, ϵ, η) and a specific distribution function (2) of the latent variables (for instance a normal distribution with specific, numerically given, variances and covariance). By a model we mean only a specification of the form of the structural equations (for instance their linearity and a designation of the variables occurring in each equation), and of a class of functions to which the distribution function of the latent variables belongs (for instance, the class of all normal bivariate distributions with zero means). More abstractly, a model can be defined as a set of structures. For a useful analysis, the model will be chosen so as to incorporate relevant a priori knowledge or hypotheses as to the economic behavior to be described. For instance, the model here discussed can often be narrowed down by the usual specification of a downward sloping demand curve and an upward sloping supply curve:

$$(3) \qquad \alpha > 0, \qquad \gamma < 0.$$

Let us assume for the sake of argument that the observations are produced by a structure, to be called the "true" structure, which is contained in (permitted by) the model. In order to exclude all questions of sampling variability (which are a matter for later separate inquiry), let us further make the unrealistic assumption that the number of observations produced by this structure can be increased indefinitely. What inferences can be drawn from these observations toward the "true" structure?

A simple reflection shows that in our present example neither the "true" demand schedule nor the "true" supply schedule can be determined from any number of observations. To put the matter geometrically, let each of the two identical scatter diagrams in Figures 1A and 1B represent the jointly observed values of p and q. A structure compatible with these observations can be obtained as follows: Select arbitrarily "presumptive" slope coefficients α and γ of the demand and supply schedules. Through each point $S(p, q)$ of the scatter diagrams draw two straight lines with slopes given by these coefficients. The presumptive

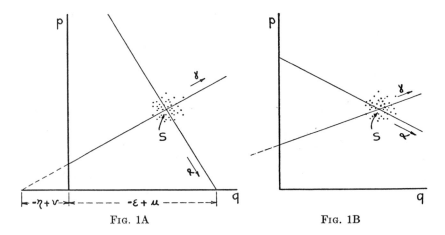

Fig. 1A   Fig. 1B

demand and supply schedules will intersect the quantity axis at distances $-\epsilon + u$ and $-\eta + v$ from the origin, *provided* the presumptive slope coefficients α and γ are the "true" ones. We shall assume this to be the case in Figure 1A. In that case the values of ϵ and η can be found from the consideration that the averages of u and v in a sufficiently large sample of observations are practically equal to zero.

However, nothing in the situation considered permits us to distinguish the "true" slopes α, γ (as shown in Figure 1A) from any other presumptive slopes (as illustrated in Figure 1B). Any arbitrary set of slope coefficients α, γ (supplemented by corresponding values ϵ, η of the intercepts) represents another, statistically just as acceptable, hypothesis concerning the formation of the observed variables.

Let us formulate the same remark algebraically in preparation for further examples in more dimensions. Let the numerical values of the "true" parameters $\alpha, \gamma, \epsilon, \eta$ in (1) be known to an individual who, taking delight in fraud, multiplies the demand equation (1d) by 2/3, the supply equation (1s) by 1/3, and adds the result to form an equation

$$(4d) \qquad q + \frac{2\alpha + \gamma}{3}\, p + \frac{2\epsilon + \eta}{3} = u',$$

which he proclaims to be the demand equation. This equation is actually different from the "true" demand equation (1d) because (3) implies $\alpha \neq \gamma$. Similarly he multiplies the same equations by 2/5 and 3/5 respectively, say, to produce an equation

$$(4s) \qquad q + \frac{2\alpha + 3\gamma}{5}\, p + \frac{2\epsilon + 3\eta}{5} = v',$$

different from the "true" supply equation (1s), but which he presents as if it were the supply equation. If our prankster takes care to select his multipliers in such a manner as not to violate the sign rules (3) imposed by the model, the deceit cannot be discovered by statistical analysis of any number of observations.[3] For the equations (4), being derived from (1), are satisfied by all data that satisfy the "true" equations (1). Moreover, being of the same form as the equations (1), the equations (4) are equally acceptable a priori.

Our *second example* differs from the first only in that the model specifies a supply equation containing in addition an exogenous variable. To be definite, we shall think of the supply of an agricultural product as affected by the rainfall r during a critical period of crop growth[4] or crop gathering. This variable is called exogenous to our model to express the plausible hypothesis that rainfall r, while affecting the market of the commodity concerned, is not itself affected thereby. Put in mathematical terms, this hypothesis specifies that the disturbances u and v in

$$(5) \quad \begin{cases} (5d) & q + \alpha p \qquad\quad + \epsilon = u \quad \text{(demand)} \\ (5s) & q + \gamma p + \delta r + \eta = v \quad \text{(supply)} \end{cases}$$

are statistically independent[5] of the values assumed by r.

It will be seen at a glance that the supply equation still cannot be determined from a sample of any size. If, starting from "true" structural equations (5) we multiply by $-1/2$ and $3/2$, say, and add the results to obtain a pretended supply equation,

$$(6s) \qquad q + \frac{3\gamma - \alpha}{2}\, p + \frac{3\delta}{2}\, r + \frac{3\eta - \epsilon}{2} = v'$$

[3] The deceit could be discovered if the model were to specify a property (e.g., independence) of the disturbances u and v, which is not shared by $u' = (2u + v)/3$ and $v' = (2u + 3v)/5$. We have not made such a specification.

[4] With respect to this example, the assumption of a linear relationship can be maintained only if we think of a certain limited range of variation in rainfall. Another difficulty with the example is that for most agricultural products, the effect of price on supply is delayed instead of instantaneous, as here assumed. A practically instantaneous effect can, however, be expected in the gathering of wild fruits of nature.

[5] It is immaterial for this definition whether the exogenous variable is regarded as a given function of time—a concept perhaps applicable to a variable set by government policy—or as itself a random variable determined by some other

of the same prescribed form as (5s), any data will satisfy this equation (6s) as well as they satisfy the two equations (5).

A similar reasoning can *not* be applied to the demand equation in the present model. Any attempt to construct another pretended demand equation by a linear combination involving the supply equation (5s) would introduce into that pretended demand equation the variable r which by the hypotheses underlying the model does not belong in it.

It might be thought that, if r has the properties of a random variable, its presence in the pretended demand equation might be concealed because its "contribution" cannot be distinguished from the random disturbance in that equation. To be specific, if $4/3$ and $-1/3$ are arbitrarily selected multipliers, the disturbance in the pretended demand equation might be thought to take the form

$$u' = \frac{4u - v}{3} - \frac{\delta}{3} r.$$

This, however, would violate the specification that r is exogenous and that therefore r and u' are to be statistically independent as well as r and (u, v). The relevance of the exogenous character of r to our present discussion is clearly illustrated by this remark.

Our analysis of the second example suggests (and below we shall cite a theorem establishing proof) that a sufficiently large sample does indeed contain information with regard to the parameters α, ϵ of the demand equation (it being understood that such information is conditional upon the validity of the model). It can already be seen that there must be the following exception to the foregoing statement. If in fact (although the model does not require it) rainfall has no influence on supply, that is, if in the "true" structure $\delta = 0$, then any number of observations must necessarily be compatible with the model (1), and hence does not convey information with regard to either the demand equation or the supply equation.

As a *third example* we consider a model obtained from the preceding one

---

structure involving probability distributions—a concept applicable particularly to weather variables. It should further be noted that we postulate independence between r and (u, v), not between r and (p, q), although we wish to express that r "is not affected by" p and q. The meaning to be given to the latter phrase is that in other equations explaining the formation of r the variables (p, q) do not enter. Precisely this is implied in the statistical independence of r and (u, v), because (p, q) is, by virtue of (5), statistically dependent on (u, v), and any role of (p, q) in the determination of r would therefore create statistical dependence between r and (u, v). On the other hand, the postulated statistical independence between r and (u, v) is entirely compatible with the obvious influence, by virtue of (5), of r on (p, q).

by the inclusion in the demand equation of consumers' income i as an additional exogenous variable. We assume the exogenous character of consumers' income merely for reasons of exposition, and in full awareness of the fact that actually price and quantity on any market do affect income directly to some extent, while furthermore the disturbances u and v affecting the market under consideration may well be correlated with similar disturbances in several other markets which together have a considerably larger effect on consumers' income.

The structural equations are now

$$(7) \quad \begin{cases} (7\mathrm{d}) & q + \alpha p + \beta i \quad\quad\quad + \epsilon = u \quad \text{(demand)} \\ (7\mathrm{s}) & q + \gamma p \quad\quad + \delta r + \eta = v \quad \text{(supply)}. \end{cases}$$

Since each of the two equations now excludes a variable specified for the other equation, neither of them can be replaced by a different linear combination of the two without altering its form. This suggests, and proof is cited below, that from a sufficiently large sample of observations, the demand equation can be accurately determined provided rainfall actually affects supply ($\delta \neq 0$), and the supply equation can be determined provided consumers' income actually affects demand ($\beta \neq 0$).

The *fourth example* is designed to show that situations may occur in which some but not all parameters of a structural equation can be determined from sufficiently many observations. Let the demand equation contain both this year's income i_0 and last year's income i_{-1}, but let the supply equation not contain any variable absent from the demand equation:

$$(8) \quad \begin{cases} (8\mathrm{d}) & q + \alpha p + \beta_0 i_0 + \beta_{-1} i_{-1} + \epsilon = u \\ (8\mathrm{s}) & q + \gamma p \quad\quad\quad\quad + \eta = v. \end{cases}$$

Now obviously we cannot determine either α or ϵ, because linear combinations of the equations (8) can be constructed which have the same form as (8d) but other[6] values α' and ϵ' for the coefficients α and ϵ. However, as long as (8d) enters with some nonvanishing weight into such a linear combination, the ratio β_{-1}/β_0 is not affected by the substitution of that linear combination for the "true" demand equation. Thus, if the present model is correct, the observations contain information with respect to the relative importance of present and past income to demand, whereas they are silent on the price elasticity of demand.

The *fifth example* shows that an assumption regarding the joint distribution of the disturbances u and v, where justified, may open the door to a determination of a structural equation which is otherwise indeterminate. Returning to the equation system (5) of our second example, we shall now make the model specify in addition that the

[6] As regards ϵ' this is true whenever $\epsilon \neq \eta$. As regards α' it is safeguarded by (3).

disturbances u in demand and v in supply are statistically independent. Remembering our previous statement that the demand equation can already be determined without the help of such an assumption, it is clear that in attempting to construct a "pretended" supply equation, no linear combination of the "true" demand and supply equations (5), other than the "true" supply equation (5s) itself, can be found which preserves the required independence of disturbances in the two equations. Writing λ and $1 - \lambda$ for the multipliers used in forming such a linear combination, the disturbance in the pretended supply equation would be

(9) $$v' = \lambda u + (1 - \lambda)v.$$

Since u and v are by assumption independent, the disturbance v' of the pretended supply equation is independent of the disturbance u in the demand equation already found determinable, if and only if $\lambda = 0$, i.e., if the pretended supply equation coincides with the "true" one.

We emphasize again the expository character of the foregoing examples. It has already been indicated that the income variable i is not truly exogenous. By assuming it to be so, we have held down the size of the equation system underlying our discussion, and we may as a result have precluded ourselves from seeing indeterminacies that could come to light only by a study of all relationships participating in the formation of the variables involved. It will therefore be necessary to develop criteria by which indeterminacies of the coefficients of larger equation systems can be detected. Before discussing such criteria for linear systems, we shall formalize a few of the concepts used or to be used.

3. THE IDENTIFICATION OF STRUCTURAL PARAMETERS

In our discussion we have used the phrase "a parameter that can be determined from a sufficient number of observations." We shall now define this concept more sharply, and give it the name *identifiability* of a parameter. Instead of reasoning, as before, from "a sufficiently large number of observations" we shall base our discussion on a hypothetical knowledge of the probability distribution of the observations, as defined more fully below. It is clear that exact knowledge of this probability distribution cannot be derived from any finite number of observations. Such knowledge is the limit approachable but not attainable by extended observation. By hypothesizing nevertheless the full availability of such knowledge, we obtain a clear separation between problems of statistical inference arising from the variability of finite samples, and problems of identification in which we explore the limits to which inference even from an infinite number of observations is subject.

A *structure* has been defined as the combination of a distribution of latent variables and a complete set of structural equations. By a *complete set of equations* we mean a set of as many equations as there are endogenous variables. Each endogenous variable may occur with or without time lags, and should occur without lag in at least one equation. Also, the set should be such as to permit unique determination of the nonlagged values of the endogenous variables from those of the lagged endogenous, the exogenous, and the latent variables. Finally, by *endogenous variables* we mean observed variables which are not exogenous, i.e., variables which are not known or assumed to be statistically independent of the latent variables, and whose occurrence in one or more equations of the set is necessary on grounds of "theory."

It follows from these definitions that, for any specific set of values of the exogenous variables, the distribution of the latent variables (i.e., one of the two components of a given structure) entails or generates, through the structural equations (i.e., the other component of the given structure), a probability distribution of the endogenous variables. The latter distribution is, of course, conditional upon the specified values of the exogenous variables for each time point of observation. This conditional distribution, regarded again as a function of all specified values of exogenous variables, shall be the hypothetical datum for our discussion of identification problems.

We shall call two structures S and S' (observationally) *equivalent* (or indistinguishable) if the two conditional distributions of endogenous variables generated by S and S' are identical for all possible values of the exogenous variables. We shall call a structure S permitted by the model (uniquely) *identifiable* within that model if there is no other equivalent structure S' contained in the model. Although the proof has not yet been completely indicated, it may be stated in illustration that in our third example almost all structures permitted by the model are identifiable. The only exceptions are those with either $\beta = 0$ or $\delta = 0$ (or both). In the first and second examples, however, no structure is identifiable, although in the second example, we have stated that the demand equation by itself is determinate. To cover such cases we shall say that a certain parameter θ of a structure S is uniquely *identifiable* within a model, if that parameter has the same value for all structures S' equivalent to S, contained in the model. Finally, a *structural equation* is said to be *identifiable* if all its parameters are identifiable.

This completes the formal definitions with which we shall operate. They can be summarized in the statement that anything is called identifiable, the knowledge of which is implied in the knowledge of the distribution of the endogenous variables, given the model (which is accepted as valid). We now proceed to a discussion of the application of this concept to linear models of the kind illustrated by our examples.

4. IDENTIFIABILITY CRITERIA IN LINEAR MODELS

In our discussion of these examples, it has been possible to conclude that a certain structural equation is not identifiable whenever we are able to construct a different equation, obtained by linear combination of some or all structural equations, which likewise meets the specifications of the model. In the opposite case, where we could show that no such different linear combination exists, we could not yet conclude definitely that the equation involved is identifiable. Could other operations than linear combination, perhaps be used to derive equations of the same form?

We shall now cite a theorem which establishes that no such other operations can exist. The theorem relates to models specifying a complete set of structural equations as defined above, and in which a given set of endogenous and exogenous variables enters linearly. Any time lags with which these variables may occur are supposed to be integral multiples of the time interval between successive observations. Furthermore the exogenous variables (considered as different variables whenever they occur with a different time lag) are assumed not to be linearly dependent, i.e., in the functional sense.[7] Finally, although simultaneous disturbances in different structural equations are permitted to be correlated, it is assumed that any disturbances operating in different time units (whether in the same or in different structural equations) are statistically independent.

Suppose the model does not specify anything beyond what has been stated. That is, no restrictions are specified yet that exclude some of the variables from specific equations. Obviously, with respect to such a broad model, not a single structural equation is identifiable. However, a theorem has been proved [14] to the effect that, given a structure S within that model, any structure S' in the model, equivalent to S, can be derived from S by replacing each equation by some linear combination of some or all equations of S.

It will be clear that this theorem remains true if the model is narrowed down by excluding certain variables from certain equations, or by other restrictions on the parameters. Thus, whenever in our examples we have concluded that different linear combinations of the same form prescribed for a structural equation did not exist, we have therewith established the identifiability of that equation. More in general, the analysis of the identifiability of a structural equation in a linear model consists in a

---

[7] The criteria of identifiability to be stated would require amended formulation if certain identities involving endogenous variables would be such that each variable occuring in them also occurs, in some equation of the complete set, with a time lag, and if this time lag were the same for all such variables. In this case, a complication arises from linear (functional) dependence among lagged endogenous (and possibly exogenous) variables.

study of the possibility to produce a different equation of the same prescribed form by linear combination of all equations. If this is shown to be impossible, the equation in question is thereby proved to be identifiable. To find criteria for the identifiability of a structural equation in a linear model is therefore a straightforward mathematical problem, to which the solution has been given elsewhere [14]. Here we shall state without proof what the criteria are.

A *necessary condition* for the identifiability of a structural equation within a given linear model is that the number[8] of variables excluded from that equation (more generally: the number of linear restrictions on the parameters of that equation) be at least equal to the number (G, say) of structural equations less one. This is known as the *order condition* of identifiability. A *necessary and sufficient condition* for the identifiability of a structural equation within a linear model, restricted only by the exclusion of certain variables from certain equations, is that we can form at least one nonvanishing determinant of order $G - 1$ out of those coefficients, properly arranged, with which the variables excluded from that structural equation appear in the $G - 1$ other structural equations. This is known as the *rank condition* of identifiability.

The application of these criteria to the foregoing examples is straightforward. In all cases considered, the number of structural equations is $G = 2$. Therefore, any of the equations involved can be identifiable through exclusion of variables only if at least $G - 1 = 1$ variable is excluded from it by the model. If this is so, the equation is identifiable provided at least one of the variables so excluded occurs in the other equation with nonvanishing coefficient (a determinant of order 1 equals the value of its one and only element). For instance, the conclusion already reached at the end of the discussion of our second example is now confirmed: The identifiability of the demand equation (5d) is only then safeguarded by the exclusion of the variable r from that equation if $\delta \neq 0$, that is, if that variable not only possibly but actually occurs in the supply equation.

5. THE STATISTICAL TEST OF A PRIORI UNCERTAIN IDENTIFIABILITY

The example just quoted shows that the identifiability of one structural parameter, θ, say, may depend on the value of another structural parameter, η, say. In such situations, which are of frequent occurrence, the identifiability of θ cannot be settled by a priori reasoning from the model alone. On the other hand, the identifiability of θ cannot escape all analysis because of possible nonidentifiability of η. As is argued more fully elsewhere [13], since the identifiability of any parameter is a

[8] Again counting lagged variables as separate variables.

property of the distribution of the observations, it is subject to some suitable statistical test, of which the degree of conclusiveness tends to certainty as the number of observations increases indefinitely. The validity of this important conclusion is not limited to linear models.

In the case of a linear model as described in Section 4, the present statement can also be demonstrated explicitly by equivalent reformulation of the rank criterion for identifiability in terms of identifiable parameters only. By the *reduced form* of a complete set of linear structural equations as described in Section 4, we mean the form obtained by solving for each of the *dependent* (i.e., nonlagged endogenous) variables, in terms of the *predetermined* (i.e., exogenous or lagged endogenous) variables, and in terms of transformed disturbances (which are linear functions of the disturbances in the original structural equations). It has been argued more fully elsewhere [**14**, Section 3.1.6], that the coefficients of the equations of the reduced form are parameters of the joint distribution of the observations, and as such are always identifiable.

It may be stated briefly without proof that the following rank criterion for identifiability of a given structural equation, in terms of coefficients of the reduced form, is equivalent to that stated in Section 4 above: Consider only those equations of the reduced form that solve for dependent variables, specified by the model as occurring in (strictly: as not excluded from) the structural equation in question. Let the number of the equations so obtained be H, where $H \leqslant G$. Now form the matrix Π^{**} of the coefficients, in these H equations, of those predetermined variables that are excluded by the model from the structural equation involved. A necessary and sufficient condition for the identifiability of that structural equation is that the rank of Π^{**} be equal to $H - 1$. A direct proof of the equivalence of the two identification criteria will be published in due course.

6. IDENTIFICATION THROUGH DISAGGREGATION AND INTRODUCTION OF SPECIFIC EXPLANATORY VARIABLES

As a further exercise in the application of these criteria, we shall consider a question which has already been the subject of a discussion between Ezekiel [**2, 3**] and Klein [**9, 10**]. The question is whether identifiability of the investment equation can be attained by the subdivision of the investment variable into separate categories of investment. In the discussion referred to, which took place before the concepts and terminology employed in this article were developed, questions of identifiability were discussed alongside with questions regarding the merit of particular economic assumptions incorporated in the model, and with questions of the statistical method of estimating parameters that have been recognized as identifiable. In the present context, we shall avoid the latter two groups of problems and concentrate on the formal analysis of identifiability, accepting a certain model as economically valid for purposes of discussion.

As a starting point we shall consider a simple model expressing the crudest elements of Keynesian theory. The variables are, in money amounts,

(10)
$$\begin{cases} S & \text{savings} \\ I & \text{investment} \\ Y & \text{income} \\ Y_{-1} & \text{income lagged one year.} \end{cases}$$

The structural equations are:

(11)
$$\begin{cases} \text{(11id)} & S - I & = 0 \\ \text{(11S)} & S \quad - \alpha_1 Y - \alpha_2 Y_{-1} - \alpha_0 = u \\ \text{(11I)} & I - \beta_1 Y - \beta_2 Y_{-1} - \beta_0 = v. \end{cases}$$

Of these, the first is the well-known savings-investment identity arising from Keynes's definitions of these concepts.[9] The second is a behavior equation of consumers, indicating that the money amount of their savings (income not spent for consumption) is determined by present and past income, subject to a random disturbance u. The third is a behavior equation of entrepreneurs, indicating that the money amount of investment is determined by present and past income, subject to a random disturbance v.

Since the identity (11id) is fully given a priori, no question of identifiability arises with respect to the first equation. In both the second and third equations, only one variable is excluded which appears in another equation of the model, and no other restrictions on the coefficients are stated.[10] Hence both of these equations already fail to meet the necessary order criterion of identifiability. This could be expected because the two equations connect the same savings-investment variable with the same two income variables, and therefore can not be distinguished statistically.

[9] These definitions include in investment all increases in inventory, including undesired inventories remaining in the hands of manufacturers or dealers as a result of falling demand. In principle, therefore, the "investment" equation should include a term or terms explaining such inventory changes. The absence of such terms from (11) and from later elaborations thereof may be taken as expressing the "theory" that for annual figures, say, such changes can be regarded as random. Alternatively, investment may be defined so as to exclude undesired inventory changes, and (11id) may be interpreted as an "equilibrium condition," expressing the randomness of such changes by replacing the zero in the right hand member by a disturbance w. The obvious need for refinement in this crude "theory" does not preclude its use for illustrative purposes.

[10] The normalization requirement that the variables S and I shall have coefficients $+1$ in (11S) and (11I) respectively does not restrict the relationships involved but merely serves to give a common level to coefficients which otherwise would be subject to arbitrary proportional variation.

Ezekiel attempts to obtain identifiability of the structure by a refinement of the model as a result of subdivision of aggregate investment I
into the following four components:

(12a) $\begin{cases} I_1 \text{ investment in plant and equipment} \\ I_2 \text{ investment in housing} \\ I_3 \text{ temporary investment: changes in consumers' credit and in} \\ \quad \text{business inventories} \\ I_4 \text{ quasi-investment: net contributions from foreign trade and} \\ \quad \text{the government budget.} \end{cases}$

If each of these components were to be related to the same set of explanatory variables as occurs in (11), the disaggregation would be of no
help toward identification. Therefore, for each of the four types of
investment decisions, Ezekiel introduces a separate explanatory equation,
either explicitly or by implication in his verbal comments. In attempting
to formulate these explanations in terms of a complete set of behavior
equations, we shall introduce two more variables:

(12b) $\begin{cases} H \text{ semi-independent cyclical component of housing investment} \\ E \text{ exogenous component of quasi-investment.} \end{cases}$

In addition, linear and quadratic functions of time are introduced as
trend terms in some equations by Ezekiel. For purposes of the present
discussion, we may as well disregard such trend terms, because they
would help toward identification only if they could be excluded a priori
from some of the equations while being included in others—a position
advocated neither by Ezekiel nor by the present author.

With these qualifications, "Ezekiel's model" can be interpreted as
follows:

(13) $\begin{cases} \text{(13id)} \quad S - I_1 - I_2 - I_3 - I_4 & = 0 \\ \text{(13S)} \quad S \qquad\qquad\quad - \alpha_1 Y - \alpha_2 Y_{-1} & - \alpha_0 = u \\ \text{(13I}_1\text{)} \quad\quad I_1 \qquad\quad - \beta_1 Y - \beta_2 Y_{-1} & - \beta_0 = v_1 \\ \text{(13I}_2\text{)} \qquad\quad I_2 \qquad - \gamma_1 Y - \gamma_2 Y_{-1} - H & - \gamma_0 = v_2 \\ \text{(13I}_3\text{)} \qquad\qquad\quad I_3 \quad - \delta_1 Y + \delta_1 Y_{-1} & - \delta_0 = v_3 \\ \text{(13I}_4\text{)} \qquad\qquad\qquad\quad I_4 - \epsilon_1 Y - \epsilon_2 Y_{-1} & - E - \epsilon_0 = v_4 \end{cases}$

(13id) is the savings-investment identity. (13S) repeats (11S), and
(13I$_1$) is modeled after (11I). More specific explanations are introduced
for the three remaining types of investment decisions.

Housing investment decisions I_2 are explained partly on the basis of
income[11] Y, partly on the basis of a "semi-independent housing cycle" H.

[11] We have added a term with Y_{-1} because the exclusion of such a term could
hardly be made the basis for a claim of identifiability.

In Ezekiel's treatment H is not an independently observed variable, but a smooth long cycle fitted to I. We share Klein's objection [9, p. 255] to this procedure, but do not think that his proposal to substitute a linear function of time for H does justice to Ezekiel's argument. The latter definitely thinks of H as produced largely by a long-cycle mechanism peculiar to the housing market, and quotes in support of this view a study by Derksen [1] in which this mechanism is analyzed. Derksen constructs an equation explaining residential construction in terms of the rent level, the rate of change of income, the level of building cost in the recent past, and growth in the number of families; he further explains the rent level in terms of income, the number of families, and the stock of dwelling units (all of these subject to substantial time lags). The stock of dwelling units, in its turn, represents an accumulation of past construction diminished by depreciation or demolition. Again accepting without inquiry the economic assumptions involved in these explanations, the point to be made is that H in $(13I_2)$ can be thought to represent specific observable exogenous and *past* endogenous variables.

Temporary investment I_3 is related by Ezekiel to the rate of change in income. Quasi-investment I_4 is related by him partly to income[12] (especially via government revenue, imports), partly to exogenous factors underlying exports and government expenditure where used as an instrument of policy. The variable E in $(13I_4)$ is therefore similar to H in that it can be thought to represent observable exogenous or past endogenous variables.

It cannot be said that this interpretation of the variables H and E establishes the completeness of the set of equations (13) in the sense defined above. The variable H has been found to depend on the past values of certain indubitably endogenous variables (building cost, rent level) of which the present values do not occur in the equation system (13), and which therefore remain unexplained by (13). The reader is asked to accept what could be proved explicitly: that incompleteness of this kind does not invalidate the criteria of identifiability indicated.[13]

Let us then apply our criteria of identifiability to the behavior equations in (13). In each of these, the number of excluded variables is at least 5, i.e., at least the necessary number for identifiability in a model of 6 equations. In order to apply the rank criterion for the identifiability of the savings equation (13S), say, we must consider the matrix

[12] We have again added a term with Y_{-1} on grounds similar to those stated with respect to $(13I_2)$.

[13] Provided, as indicated in footnote 7, there is no linear functional relationship between the exogenous and lagged endogenous variables occurring in (13).

$$
\begin{array}{cccccc}
(I_1) & (I_2) & (I_3) & (I_4) & (H) & (E)
\end{array}
$$

(14)
$$
\begin{bmatrix}
-1 & -1 & -1 & -1 & 0 & 0 \\
1 & 0 & 0 & 0 & 0 & 0 \\
0 & 1 & 0 & 0 & -1 & 0 \\
0 & 0 & 1 & 0 & 0 & 0 \\
0 & 0 & 0 & 1 & 0 & -1
\end{bmatrix}
$$

There are several ways in which a nonvanishing determinant of order 5 can be selected from this matrix. One particular way is to take the columns labeled I_1, I_2, I_3, H, E. It follows that if the present model is valid, the savings equation is indeed identifiable.

It is easily seen that the same conclusion applies to the equations explaining investment decisions of the types I_1 and I_3. Let us now inspect the rank criterion matrix for the identifiability of $(13I_2)$:

$$
\begin{array}{ccccc}
(S) & (I_1) & (I_3) & (I_4) & (E)
\end{array}
$$

(15)
$$
\begin{bmatrix}
1 & -1 & -1 & -1 & 0 \\
1 & 0 & 0 & 0 & 0 \\
0 & 1 & 0 & 0 & 0 \\
0 & 0 & 1 & 0 & 0 \\
0 & 0 & 0 & 1 & -1
\end{bmatrix}
$$

Again the determinant value of this square matrix of order 5 is different from zero. Hence the housing equation is identifiable. A similar analysis leads to the same conclusion regarding the equation $(13I_4)$ for quasi-investment.

It may be emphasized again that identifiability was attained not through the mere subdivision of total investment, but as a result of the introduction of specific explanatory variables applicable to some but not all components of investment.[14] Whenever such specific variables are available in sufficient number and variety of occurence, on good grounds of economic theory as defined above, the door has been opened in princi-

[14] In fact, more specific detail was introduced than the minimum necessary to produce identifiability. Starting again from (11), identifiability can already be obtained if it is possible to break off from investment I some observable exogenous component, like public works expenditure P (supposing that to be exogenous for the sake of argument). Writing $Q = I - P$ for the remainder of investment, (11) is then modified to read

(11a)
$$
\begin{cases}
S - Q - P & = 0 \\
S \quad - \alpha_1 Y - \alpha_2 Y_{-1} - \alpha_0 = u \\
Q \quad - \beta_1 Y - \beta_2 Y_{-1} - \beta_0 = v,
\end{cases}
$$

of which each equation meets our criteria of identifiability. The intent of this remark is largely formal, because (11a) is not as defensible a "theory" as (13).

ple to statistical inference regarding behavior parameters—inference conditional upon the assumptions derived from "theory."

How wide the door has been opened, i.e., how much accuracy of estimation can be attained from given data, is of course a matter depending on many circumstances, and to be explored separately by the appropriate procedures of statistical inference.[15] In the present case, the extent to which the exclusion of H and/or E from certain equations contributes to the reliability of estimates of their parameters depends very much on whether or not there are pronounced differences in the time-paths of the three *predetermined variables* Y_{-1}, H, E, i.e., the variables determined either exogenously or in earlier time units. These time-paths represent in a way the basic patterns of movement in the economic model considered, such that the time-paths of all other variables are linear combinations of these three paths, modified by disturbances. If the three basic paths are sufficiently distinct, conditions are favorable for estimation of identifiable parameters. If there is considerable similarity between any two of them, or even if there is only a considerable multiple correlation between the three, conditions are adverse.

7. IMPLICATIONS OF THE CHOICE OF THE MODEL

It has already been stressed repeatedly that any statistical inference regarding identifiable parameters of economic behavior is conditional upon the validity of the model. This throws great weight on a correct choice of the model. We shall not attempt to make more than a few tentative remarks about the considerations governing this choice.[16]

It is an important question to what extent certain aspects of a model of the kind considered above are themselves subject to statistical test. For instance, in the model (13) we have specified linearity of each equation, independence of disturbances in successive time units, time lags which are an integral multiple of the chosen unit of time, as well as exclusions of specific variables from specific equations. It is often possible to subject one particular aspect or set of specifications of the model to a statistical test which is conditional upon the validity of the remaining

---

[15] We are not concerned here with an evaluation of the particular estimation procedures applied by Ezekiel.

[16] In an earlier article [11] I have attempted, in a somewhat different terminology, to discuss that problem. That article needs rewriting in the light of subsequent developments in econometrics. It unnecessarily clings to the view that each structural equation represents a causal process in which one single dependent variable is determined by the action upon it of all other variables in the equation. Moreover, use of the concept of identifiability will contribute to sharper formulation and treatment of the problem of the choice of a model. However, the most serious defect of the article, in my view, cannot yet be corrected. It arises from the fact that we do not yet have a satisfactory statistical theory of choice among several alternative hypotheses.

specifications. This is, for instance, the case with respect to the exclusion of any variable from any equation whenever the equation involved is identifiable even without that exclusion. However, at least *four* difficulties arise which point to the need for further fundamental research on the principles of statistical inference.

In the *first* place, on a given basis of maintained hypotheses (not subjected to test) there may be several alternative hypotheses to be tested. For instance, if there are two variables whose exclusion, either jointly or individually, from a given equation is not essential to its identifiability, it is possible to test separately (a) the exclusion of the first variable, or (b) of the second variable, or (c) of both variables simultaneously, as against (d) the exclusion of neither variable. However, instead of three separate tests, of (a) against (d), (b) against (d), and (c) against (d), we need a procedure permitting selection of one of the four alternatives (a), (b), (c), (d). An extension of current theory with regard to the testing of hypotheses, which is concerned mainly with choices between two alternatives, is therefore needed.

Secondly, if certain specifications of a model can be tested given all other specifications, it is usually possible in many different ways to choose the set of "other" specifications which is not subjected to test. It may not be possible to choose the minimum set of untested specifications in any way so that strong a priori confidence in the untested specifications exists. Even in such a case, it may nevertheless happen that for any choice of the set of untested specifications, the additional specifications that are confirmed by test also inspire some degree of a priori confidence. In such a case, the model as a whole is more firmly established than any selected minimum set of untested specifications. However, current theory of statistical inference provides no means of giving quantitative expression to such partial and indirect confirmation of anticipation by observation.

Thirdly, if the choice of the model is influenced by the same data from which the structural parameters are estimated, the estimated sampling variances of these estimated parameters do not have that direct relation to the reliability of the estimated parameters which they would have if the estimation were based on a model of which the validity is given a priori with certainty.

Finally, the research worker who constructs a model does not really believe that reality is exactly described by a "true" structure contained in the model. Linearity, discrete time lags, are obviously only approximations. At best, the model builder hopes to construct a model that contains a structure which approximates reality to a degree sufficient for the practical purposes of the investigation. The tests of current statistical theory are formulated as an (uncertain) choice, from two or more sets of structures (single or composite hypotheses), of that one which contains the "true" structure. Instead we need to choose the simplest possible set—in some sense—which contains a structure sufficiently approximative—in some sense—to economic reality.

8. FOR WHAT PURPOSES IS IDENTIFICATION NECESSARY?

The question should finally be considered why it is at all desirable to postulate a structure behind the probability distribution of the variables and thus to become involved in the sometimes difficult problems of identifiability. If we regard as the main objective of scientific inquiry to make prediction possible and its reliability ascertainable, why do we need more than a knowledge of the probability distribution of the variables to permit prediction of one variable on the basis of known (or hypothetical) simultaneous or earlier values of other variables?

The answer to this question is implicit in Haavelmo's discussion of the degree of permanence of economic laws [6, see p. 30] and has been formulated explicitly by Hurwicz [8]. Knowledge of the probability distribution is in fact sufficient whenever there is no change in the structural parameters between the period of observation from which such knowledge is derived and the period to which the prediction applies. However, in many practical situations it is required to predict the values of one or more economic variables, either under changes in structure that come about independently of the economist's advice, or under hypothetical changes in structural parameters that can be brought about through policy based in part on the prediction made. In the first case knowledge may, and in the second case it is likely to, be available as to the effect of such structural change on the parameters. An example of the first case is a well-established change in consumers' preferences. An example of the second case is a change in the average level or in the progression of income tax rates.

In such cases, the "new" distribution of the variables on the basis of which predictions are to be constructed can only be derived from the "old" distribution prevailing before the structural change, if the known structural change can be applied to identifiable structural parameters, i.e., parameters of which knowledge is implied in a knowledge of the "old" distribution combined with the a priori considerations that have entered into the model.

Cowles Commission for Research in Economics

REFERENCES

[1] J. B. D. DERKSEN, "Long Cycles in Residential Building: An Explanation." ECONOMETRICA, Vol. 8, April 1940, pp. 97–116.

[2] M. EZEKIEL, "Saving, Consumption and Investment," *American Economic Review*, Vol. 32, March 1942, pp. 22–49; June 1942, pp. 272–307.

[3] M. EZEKIEL, "The Statistical Determination of the Investment Schedule," ECONOMETRICA, Vol. 12, January 1944, pp. 89–90.

[4] R. FRISCH, *Pitfalls in the Statistical Construction of Demand and Supply Curves*, Veröffentlichungen der Frankfurter Gesellschaft für Konjunkturforschung, Neue Folge, Heft 5, Leipzig, 1933.

[5] R. FRISCH, "Statistical versus Theoretical Relations in Economic Macrodynamics," Mimeographed document prepared for a League of Nations conference concerning Tinbergen's work, 1938.

[6] T. HAAVELMO, "The Probability Approach in Econometrics," ECONOMETRICA, Vol. 12, Supplement, 1944, also Cowles Commission Paper, New Series, No. 4.

[7] L. HURWICZ, "Generalization of the Concept of Identification," in *Statistical Inference in Dynamic Economic Models*, Cowles Commission Monograph 10, New York, John Wiley and Sons. (forthcoming).

[8] L. HURWICZ, "Prediction and Least-Squares," in *Statistical Inference in Dynamic Economic Models*, Cowles Commission Monograph 10, New York, John Wiley and Sons. (forthcoming).

[9] L. KLEIN, "Pitfalls in the Statistical Determination of the Investment Schedule," ECONOMETRICA, Vol. 11, July–October 1943, pp. 246–258.

[10] L. KLEIN, "The Statistical Determination of the Investment Schedule: A Reply," ECONOMETRICA, Vol. 12, January 1944, pp. 91–92.

[11] T. C. KOOPMANS, "The Logic of Econometric Business Cycle Research," *Journal of Political Economy*, Vol. 49, 1941, pp. 157–181.

[12] T. C. KOOPMANS, "Measurement Without Theory," *The Review of Economic Statistics*, Vol. 29, No. 3, August 1947, pp. 161–172, also Cowles Commission Paper, New Series, No. 25.

[13] T. C. KOOPMANS and O. REIERSOL, "Identification as a Problem in Inference," to be published.

[14] T. C. KOOPMANS, H. RUBIN and R. B. LEIPNIK, "Measuring the Equation Systems of Dynamic Economics," in *Statistical Inference in Dynamic Economic Models*, Cowles Commission Monograph 10, New York, John Wiley and Sons. (forthcoming).

[15] J. MARSCHAK, "Economic Interdependence and Statistical Analysis," in *Studies in Mathematical Economics and Econometrics*, in memory of Henry Schultz, Chicago, The University of Chicago Press, 1942, pp. 135–150.

[16] A. C. PIGOU, "A Method of Determining the Numerical Values of Elasticities of Demand," *Economic Journal*, Vol. 20, 1910, pp. 636–640, reprinted as Appendix II in *Economics of Welfare*.

[17] HENRY SCHULTZ, *Theory and Measurement of Demand*, Chicago, The University of Chicago Press, 1938.

[18] A. WALD, "Note on the Identification of Economic Relations," in *Statistical Inference in Dynamic Economic Models*, Cowles Commission Monograph 10, New York, John Wiley and Sons. (forthcoming).

Econometrica, Vol. 20, 1 (January 1952)

OVERCAPACITY AND THE ACCELERATION PRINCIPLE[1]

By Hollis B. Chenery

The paper traces the effect of economies of scale on investment behavior.

I. Starting with a given production function and forecast of demand, it is shown that there is an optimum relation between capacity and output that is a function of the economy of scale, the discount rate, the planning period, and the rate of increase in demand. Graphical solutions are given showing the effect of these parameters on the optimum amount of overcapacity.

II. Using these results, a formula for predicting investment is derived by successive modifications in the acceleration principle. The differences in cyclical behavior between this "capacity principle" and the acceleration principle are shown to depend on two parameters, the reaction coefficient and the optimum overcapacity.

III. Although the effect of excess capacity in a whole industry will not necessarily be the same as for a firm, capacity series for six industries are analyzed to compare the predictions given by the two hypotheses. For the four industries having suitable structural characteristics, the capacity formula gives much better results than the accelerator, while in the other two cases the latter gives better predictions.

MOST empirical work on investment behavior has been based on statistical inference from time series covering whole industries. In these studies investment has been correlated with changes in demand (the acceleration principle), profits, the interest rate, etc. Because of the well-known limitations on time series analysis, these studies have not been able to get at the underlying structural relations leading to the observed results even though they have demonstrated certain correlations. In order to gain a better understanding of investment behavior, therefore, there is a need for structural analysis by more direct methods.

The present paper investigates the effect of technology on investment behavior. The most significant aspects of technology in this regard are the economies of scale which occur in various productive processes. Preliminary investigations show that economies of scale are quite pronounced in most of the basic industries, which are also the industries

[1] I am indebted to Richard M. Goodwin, Robert Solow, Thomas Schelling, and Carl Kaysen for their helpful suggestions, particularly on the mathematical formulation of Sections I and II. Most of the paper was presented at Professor Leontief's seminar at Harvard University in 1948. Statistical assistance was provided by the Harvard Research Project on the Structure of the American Economy.

179

which have a high ratio of capital to output.[2] The principal explanation
of investment behavior now in use, the acceleration principle, ignores
economies of scale and the indivisibilities on which they are based. The
main body of this study, therefore, is concerned with deriving a formula
for investment behavior from a more generalized type of production
function than the oversimplified one required by the acceleration principle. The statistical work presented here is of secondary importance
because much approximation is involved in applying hypotheses derived
for the behavior of firms to aggregate data for whole industries, and the
problem of aggregation has not been investigated.

The procedure may be outlined as follows. First, the reaction of a
profit-maximizing entrepreneur to an expected secular rise in demand
is analyzed, taking price and the production function of the firm as
given. For this purpose an actual production function derived in an
earlier paper and showing considerable economies of scale is taken as a
starting point. It is shown that when economies of scale exist, excess
capacity will occur even with perfect forecasting; this may be called
"optimum" overcapacity. The degree of overcapacity is expressed as a
function of the properties of the production function, the planning
period, and the discount rate.

In the second section, the reaction of the entrepreneur to cyclical
fluctuations in demand is analyzed, assuming on the basis of the earlier
results that his aim is to maintain the "optimum" degree of overcapacity in the long run. In this case, unplanned overcapacity also arises
from cyclical fluctuations. A general relation between investment,
output, and capacity is formulated, including the usual accelerator
formula as a special case.

In the final section, results of a preliminary statistical test based on
capacity series for six industries are given. The accelerator and capacity
hypotheses are put in comparable form with equal degrees of freedom.
A structural analysis suggests that aggregation is only valid in some of
the industries which were selected with regard to the capacity explanation, and in these cases a considerable improvement over the accelerator
is shown. The hypothesis could be tested more accurately from estimates
of the production functions involved and from time series for individual
firms if this type of data were available.

I. DETERMINATION OF "OPTIMUM" OVERCAPACITY

The decision to increase the capacity of a plant or to build a new one
is based on estimates of the most profitable output to be produced

[2] See my "Process and Production Functions from Engineering Data," in Wassily
W. Leontief (ed.), *Studies in the Structure of the American Economy* [New York:
Oxford University Press, 1953].

throughout the foreseeable future. The entrepreneur may be thought of as trying to equate the discounted marginal revenue and marginal cost over a given planning period. Output and investment decisions are thus assumed to be made together and to be interdependent. They may, however, be separated in many cases without loss of accuracy. If demand is inelastic with respect to price, variations in marginal cost will have little effect on the output forecast. Even if demand has some elasticity there may be other reasons, such as the desire to maintain a certain share of the market or an obligation to serve the public, which will cause producers to ignore the possibility of output variation due to price changes. For simplicity, I shall assume here that the estimate of output is made prior to the investment decision and shall only take up the latter.

If the firm has decided on the rate of increase of demand (and hence its expected total revenue) for planning purposes, profits will be maximized by an investment program which minimizes the total cost of production over the period. More distant profits and costs would have to be discounted at the appropriate interest rate. Since total revenue is taken as given, the optimum plan is one which minimizes discounted total costs. If no allowance is made for risk, expected profits depend only on expected price, the discount rate, and expected costs. With a production function involving economies of scale, the cost will vary according to the size of equipment and other factors affecting the scale of operation.

The discounted net profit can be expressed mathematically as follows:

$$(1) \qquad \pi = \sum_{t=1}^{t=n} \frac{(PX_t - C_t)}{(1 + r)^t} = R - \sum_{t=1}^{t=n} \frac{C_t(S, X)}{(1 + r)^t},$$

where R represents discounted total revenue; π, discounted net profit; C_t, total cost at time t; P, price (assumed constant); r, discount rate; S, index of scale of plant[3]; X_t, output (demand) at time t; and n, planning period. If we assume all parameters[4] fixed except S, the scale of plant to be built, profit becomes only a function of S. A necessary condition for maximum discounted net profit is that the (discounted)

[3] The index of scale may be thought of as the size of equipment installed, but it should in some cases include the type of process chosen, relations among processes, etc.

[4] For simplicity, I shall assume that the discount rate includes the total anticipated effect of risk and uncertainty on the present value of future income. The planning period, the expected rate of increase in output, and the discount rate therefore comprise all the nontechnological parameters.

sum of the derivatives of total cost with respect to scale of plant be
zero (assuming a continuous function):

$$(2) \qquad \frac{d\pi}{dS} = \sum_{t=1}^{t=n} \left[\frac{-1}{(1+r)^t} \frac{dC_t}{dS} \right] = 0.$$

Let us now consider a specific example of a function showing the
variation in cost over time for different equipment sizes. Figure 1 shows
the total cost functions which can be derived from the production function for natural gas transmission.[5] The "plant" in question consists of
two major processes, the compression of gas in a pumping station and
its expansion as it flows through a pipe of large diameter. The combination of processes is such that it is possible to increase output by adding
more compressors while keeping the same pipeline. In more general
terms, the total production function consists of two processes which can
be combined in varying proportions to produce a given output. The
pipe is an indivisible factor which determines the size of the plant. The
other process, pumping, requires several units of equipment, and their
indivisibility is not important. Since pipe costs are twice as important
as pumping costs and pipe is the indivisible element, we may take the
size of pipe (when the optimum amount of pumping is installed) as an
index of the scale[6] of the plant.

In Figure 1 the long-run cost curve resulting from an optimum combination of factors for a given output is labelled C_L. The functions
resulting from fixing the pipe size (scale of plant) and varying other
factors (amount of pumping equipment, etc.) will be called "intermediate" cost functions.[7] It is possible to move along the intermediate
cost curves only as long as demand is expanding. A contraction of
demand will involve a movement along a "plant" curve (not shown)
where the only important variable is fuel consumption. These curves
are linear and almost horizontal, with a slope given by the variable
cost.

If we start with a given size of pipeline, say 50,000,000 cubic feet per
day at "rated" capacity,[8] continued addition of pumping equipment

[5] See my "Engineering Production Functions," *Quarterly Journal of Economics*,
Vol. 63, November, 1949, pp. 507–531. The production function is derived from
the engineering formulae for the design of pipelines.

[6] The "scale" of operations is in general determined from the size of one or
more indivisible units of plant or equipment—e.g., a blast furnace, a cement
kiln, a special-purpose machine tool. It is not synonymous with the capacity of
the plant when these indivisible units are duplicated.

[7] See my "Engineering Production Functions," *ibid.*, p. 521.

[8] In Figure 1 the "capacity" of a given size of pipe is shown by the point of
tangency between the intermediate cost curves and the long-run cost curves. For
example, $S = 50$ represents 18-inch pipe under the assumed conditions.

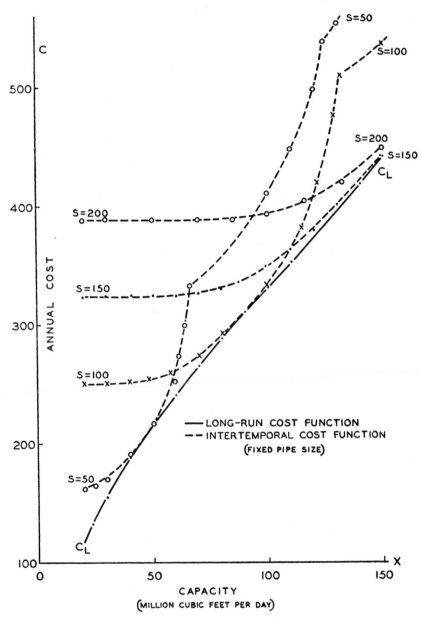

FIGURE 1—Intertemporal cost functions (natural gas pipeline).

will become more costly per unit of extra capacity realized. At some point it will be economical to duplicate the pipeline rather than raise the capacity of the existing one. It can be shown that profit maximization will require installation of about the same scale[9] of plant (pipe) as previously existed. The output at which it pays to install a second parallel line is indicated by the intersection of the cost curves for one and two pipes. Similar reasoning applies to the transition from two to three, and so forth. On the assumption that the size of unit installed is unchanged, therefore, we can draw a series of curves representing the variation of cost over time if output always *increases*. These will be called intertemporal cost curves.

Two characteristics of the production function determine the shape of these intertemporal cost functions: the elasticity of output with respect to cost (scale coefficient) and the substitutability of one process for another (process flexibility). It is convenient to separate their effects. Let us first assume no flexibility and ignore the variable costs since they are very small. The intertemporal cost function would then consist of a series of stair steps since additional capacity would only be obtainable by duplicating the plant. The size of plant chosen initially determines the cost function over time. For analytical convenience in determining optimum plant sizes we can replace the discontinuous function by a straight line through the mid-points of the stair steps. Such functions for three different sizes of plant are shown in Figure 2.[10]

The long-run cost function of the gas pipeline (Figure 1) has almost constant elasticity of output with respect to cost over most of its range. Because of this property, the curve can be very closely approximated by the following type of formula:

$$(3) \qquad C_L = bS^{1/\psi},$$

where C_L represents total cost; S, capacity of plant (pipeline); ψ, scale coefficient (1.5); and b, constant (72). The parameter ψ makes a convenient index of the economy of scale. The formula for the linear approximation to the intertemporal cost curve for any size of plant (Figure 2) can be derived from this long-run curve:

$$C_t = a_1 + \frac{a_2 S}{2} + a_2 t \Delta X,$$

$$a_2 = \frac{C_L - a_1}{S},$$

$$(4) \qquad C_t = \frac{a_1}{2} + \frac{b}{2} S^{1/\psi} + b t S^{(1/\psi)-1} \Delta X - \frac{a_1 t \Delta X}{S},$$

[9] It is exactly the same size if the demand at time 0 is 0.

[10] The same long-run cost curve is used in Figure 2 as in Figure 1 so that an estimate can be made later of the effect of process flexibility.

where C_t represents total cost at time t; ΔX, annual increment to output; a_1, the portion of total cost which does not depend on output; and a_2, slope of line.

The timing of investment in any plant having the cost function of equation (4) can now be determined by applying the conditions for profit maximization derived in equation (2).[11] Two parameters are involved, the planning period and the discount rate. I shall assume that expected

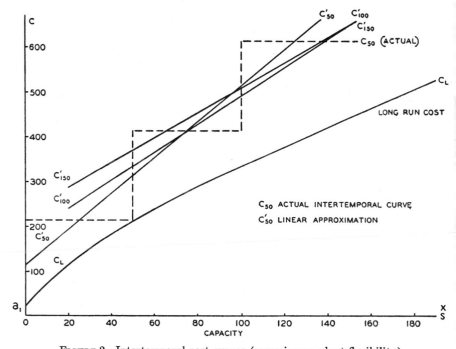

FIGURE 2—Intertemporal cost curves (assuming no plant flexibility).

increments to output are constant over time and that there is no demand at time 0 (i.e., that existing plants are able to meet the present demand). The scale of plant which will maximize profits under these assumptions can conveniently be related to the rate of growth of output

[11] Differentiating equation (4) with respect to S gives

$$\frac{dC_t}{dS} = \frac{b}{2\psi} S^{(1/\psi)-1} + b\,[(1/\psi)-1]\,\Delta X t S^{(1/\psi)-2} + \frac{a_1 t \Delta X}{S^2}.$$

For the cost curve of equation (3) this gives

$$\frac{dC_t}{dS} = 24 S^{-0.333} - 24 t S^{-1.33} + \frac{18t}{S^2}.$$

Figures 3 and 4 were derived by substituting these values in equation (2) and solving for various values of ψ, r, and n.

by taking the annual increment in output as the unit of capacity (i.e., $\Delta X = 1$). A scale of five, for example, means a plant size of five times the annual increment. For different discount rates we can then determine the optimum scale for each planning period. The results of this calculation are shown in Figures 3a and 3b.

Since I have taken a cost curve with a constant scale coefficient, it is possible to represent the effect of changes in the production function merely by varying the scale coefficient. Curves are plotted in Figures 3a and 3b for values of the scale coefficient higher and lower than those observed in the pipeline (1.5), for constant values of the two parameters (a_1 and b) in the cost function, and for two values of the discount rate.

Figures 4 and 5 show the effect of variations in the discount rate and the scale coefficient when the planning period is given. Figure 5 is of greatest interest here because it illustrates the effect of the production function, represented by the scale coefficient, on the optimum scale. It shows that, whatever the discount rate, the optimum size of equipment to be installed increases very rapidly as the economy of scale increases. For the pipeline case (assuming $n = 30$) a discount rate of ten percent would lead to the installation of a pipe size equal to seven times the annual increment in demand. A rise in the discount rate to twenty percent would reduce this figure to five and one half, while with no discount it would pay to build fourteen years ahead.

We can now revert to the actual cost curves of Figure 1 and take up the effect of process flexibility—i.e., the possibility of varying the amount of pumping capacity attached to the same pipe. Since this possibility reduces the cost of excess pipe capacity, it will increase the profitability of building pipe capacity ahead of demand. We can determine the optimum scale of pipeline corresponding to each planning period as before, using graphical methods. The result is plotted in Figure 3a. It shows that the possibility of installing only the principal process at first and then adding the rest of the plant as demand grows increases the optimum scale by about 75%.

This type of analysis may be extended to any number of processes. A productive plant may be broken up into the units which have to be installed at the same time and the optimum scale of each determined separately.[12]

---

[12] Paul Clark has found that such a procedure is followed in planning the installation of telephone equipment; the optimum scale varies from twenty-five years for cables to two years for switchboards. See his chapter in *Studies in the Structure of the American Economy, op. cit.*

This variation in the capacity of the different pieces of equipment which are combined at a given time makes the definition of the "capacity" of a plant a rather arbitrary matter. It may refer to the plant as presently installed, or it may be considered to be the output of the principal process or processes if the others were expanded the necessary amount. The second alternative is used here. If we

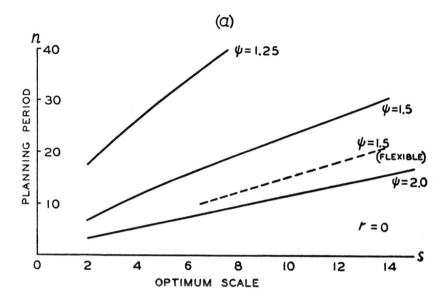

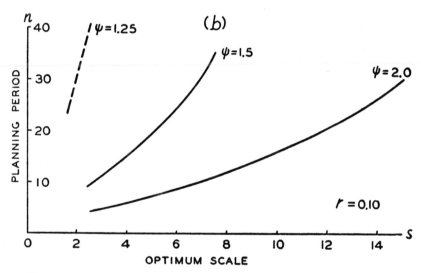

FIGURE 3—Effect on optimum scale of variation in the planning period.

The principal result of this section has been to show that with moderate economies of scale[13] ($\psi = 1.25$ to 1.5) and plausible values of the

---

measure steel capacity by blast furnaces or electric capacity by generators installed, for example, we adopt this method since the rest of the equipment may not be adequate to operate at the same level.

[13] For estimates of economies of scale in several other industrial processes, see my "Process and Production Functions from Engineering Data," *op. cit.*

discount rate and the planning period, one would expect to find plants built to take care of demand a number of years ahead. From the graph-

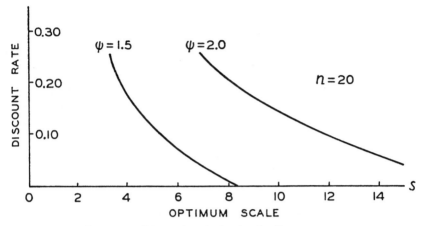

FIGURE 4—Effect of variation in the discount rate.

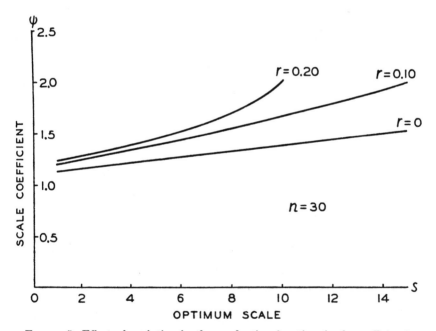

FIGURE 5—Effect of variation in the production function (scale coefficient).

ical solutions in Figures 3, 4, and 5, five to ten years would be a con-servative estimate. This would be increased for flexible processes such as the pipeline case given in Figure 1.

In predicting investment behavior it is more useful to apply these results to industry groups than to individual plants and firms. The above analysis was based on the assumptions of a single firm and given locational factors.[14] The introduction of more than one firm would cause no change in the aggregate result as long as each could predict its share of the market. The entry of new firms might upset this assumption and cause a larger amount of excess capacity or a drop in price unless the likelihood of new entries was taken account of in the predictions of other firms. The theory is not applicable to perfectly competitive industries in its present form since it assumes that demand for the output of individual plants is inelastic at any given moment.

As a preliminary estimate it may be concluded that the factors determining excess capacity for individual plants or firms will apply to groups of plants and firms having similar production functions and markets characterized by some degree of monopoly. These conditions will be examined further in Section III.

II. VARIATIONS IN OUTPUT AND CAPACITY

The next problem is to adapt the excess capacity hypothesis, derived from an expectation of a steady increase in output, to explain reactions of investment[15] to fluctuating demand.

The substitution of an expectation of fluctuating output for a steady secular rise affects all the parameters in equation (2) to some extent. The discount of future income will probably be increased. The planning period, n, may become shorter (its effect is the same as a rise in the discount rate). There will be a higher premium placed on flexible production techniques, which usually involve selection of a production function with somewhat less economy of scale. But the basic calculation of the entrepreneur is essentially the same. The change in the parameters will merely reduce the optimum degree of overcapacity. The estimates of future demand which firms make, however, will vary more with fluctuating conditions and cause a greater dispersion in the reactions of the various firms in an industry.

The results of the previous analysis can best be used to formulate a more general form of the acceleration principle by introducing successive modifications in the basic idea. The acceleration principle is derived from the assumption that the value of capital must have a constant

---

[14] Changes in locational factors due to technological changes or new sources of supply may cause additional variation in capacity. These are best discussed for individual industries and in any case must be treated as exogenous factors.

[15] Although the intention is ultimately to explain fluctuations in investment, the formulation will be restricted, as before, to changes in the stock of capital goods as measured by their capacity.

190   HOLLIS B. CHENERY

ratio to the output.[16] This leads to the following formula for net investment[17] induced by changes in output:
Assume that $K = \beta X$. Then

(5) $$I_t = \frac{\Delta K}{\Delta t} = \beta \frac{\Delta X}{\Delta t},$$

where K represents capital stock; X, output; I, rate of net investment; β, accelerator constant (capital per unit of output); and t, time.

Two modifications have been suggested to make this simple version more realistic. It is plausible to introduce a lag in the reaction to represent the average interval between the change in the demand and the new investment which it evokes.[18] Furthermore, it must be a distributed lag because entrepreneurs take past as well as current changes in output as an indication of future demand. If there is some overcapacity, we can also assume that the investment induced by a given change in demand will be less than the amount required to provide an equal amount of new capacity. This hypothesis can be formulated as follows:

(6) $$\Delta K_{t+\theta} = K_{t+\theta} - K_{t+\theta-1} = b\beta(X_t - X_{t-1}),$$

where b is a reaction coefficient and θ is the lag between output changes and investment.

J. Tinbergen and others have applied similar equations to various time series to test the acceleration principle. The results have been disappointing in most cases and have led Tinbergen to conclude that "the acceleration principle cannot help very much in the explanation of the details in real investment fluctuations, with the possible exception of railway rolling stock."[19]

Equation (6) does not allow for the chief discrepancy between the simple accelerator assumption and observed behavior: the fact that capital is not and cannot be contracted as rapidly as it expands. In each industry there is a technological limit to the rate at which capital is retired which depends on its durability, rate of obsolescence, and so

[16] A good discussion of the acceleration principle is found in G. Haberler, *Prosperity and Depression*, 3rd ed., New York: United Nations, 1946, pp. 85–105.
[17] Throughout the present discussion investment will be thought of in physical terms since this is the real basis for the acceleration principle.
[18] The precise magnitude of the lag will depend on the series used to measure investment. If financial data are used it will be shorter than if investment is measured by the actual completion of new capacity.
[19] J. Tinbergen, "Statistical Evidence on the Acceleration Principle," *Economica*, Vol. 5 (New Series), May, 1938, p. 176. See also his *Statistical Testing of Business-Cycle Theories*, Vol. I, Geneva: League of Nations, 1939, Chapter V; and Jan Tinbergen and J. J. Polak, *The Dynamics of Business Cycles*, Chicago: University of Chicago Press, 1950, pp. 164–166.

forth.[20] Unless we limit the acceleration principle to periods of full utilization of capacity, it will forecast too rapid a decrease of capacity in a downswing and too rapid an increase in recovery. When a single regression line is fitted to data for a whole cycle, an average value for the accelerator emerges which does not describe any part of the period accurately.[21]

In order to take account of the possible variation in the ratio of capital to output, the underlying hypothesis may be formulated in a different way. If we start with a period of equilibrium, when capital and output have their "normal" relationship[22] (with a suitable lag), we may write $K_t = \beta X_{t-\theta}$, as before. Instead of taking investment in any period as proportional to the change in output, however, it may be assumed to be proportional to the deviation of actual output from "normal" output, K_t/β. This results in the following formula:

$$(7) \qquad \Delta K_{t+\theta} = b(\beta X_t - K_t).$$

If the value of the reaction coefficient, b, is 1 (and $\theta = 1$), then equation (7) will give the same predictions as equation (6) because capacity will always keep up with output and the ratio between them will be maintained. However, any other value of b will cause quite a different type of variation because equation (7) takes account of the degree of over- or undercapacity (which the accelerator ignores). Equation (7) results in a "pursuit curve" or feedback mechanism in which entrepreneurs are trying to balance capacity against output but do not invest (or disinvest) the whole amount necessary to do so in any one period.

By a different line of reasoning R. M. Goodwin has developed an equation similar to equation (7), which he calls a "flexible accelerator."[23]

[20] Simon Kuznets, in "The Relation between Capital Goods and Finished Products in the Business Cycle," *Economic Essays in Honor of Wesley Clair Mitchell*, New York: Columbia University Press, 1935, pp. 209–267, has pointed out the inevitability of overcapacity in industries where the ratio of capital to output is large, and the correlation between the capital intensity and the expected overcapacity. It is for these industries, where induced investment may be very large, that a modification of the simple accelerator is most needed.

[21] The prediction can be improved by using a lower value of b for negative changes in output, but the general bias still remains.

[22] This "normal" output represents the capacity of the industry (under stationary conditions) in the sense of the most profitable output, but not in the sense of maximum output with given plant.

[23] Richard M. Goodwin, "Secular and Cyclical Aspects of the Multiplier and the Accelerator," in *Income, Employment, and Public Policy* (Essays in Honor of Alvin H. Hansen), New York: W. W. Norton and Co., 1948, p. 120. His equation is differential in form and has no lag. He says of it: "It implies that there is an asymptotic approach to any persisting equilibrium level of capital; it is simply a flexible form of the accelerator." After we had discovered the similarity in our formulations, he suggested the vector analysis that is used below.

He interprets the coefficient b as the reciprocal of the number of years over which entrepreneurs plan to make up the deficiency in investment. Its magnitude may be expected to depend on the factors underlying entrepreneurs' expectations: the past rate of growth of demand, the amplitude of cyclical fluctuations that have been experienced, and so forth. However, the introduction of the stock of capital in conjunction with the reaction coefficient has a more fundamental effect than merely making the accelerator flexible. It changes the simple dependence of investment on the rate of change in demand, it alters the phase relations between investment and output over the cycle, and it does not require that the amplitude of fluctuations in gross investment be larger than those in output.[24] A more general type of accelerator-multiplier relation can be developed using this formulation, as Goodwin has shown.

Equation (7) remedies two of the major deficiencies of the acceleration principle. It does not require that firms invest an amount sufficient to keep up with changes in demand period by period, and it allows for the amount by which they fail to do so in predicting the investment of future periods. It still assumes, however, that the aim of entrepreneurs is to operate at full capacity[25] in each period.

In Section I it was shown that if firms seek to minimize the cost of production over time they will on the average build ahead of demand (when there are economies of scale) and will have a normal degree of

[24] J. M. Clark, in his original version of the acceleration principle ("Business Acceleration and the Law of Demand," *Journal of Political Economy*, Vol. 25, March, 1917, pp. 217–235), summarized the chief effects of the acceleration principle as follows:

"1. The demand for enlarging the means of production (including stocks of finished goods on the way to the consumer) varies, not with the volume of demand for the finished product, but rather with the acceleration of that demand, allowance being made for the fact that the equipment cannot be adjusted as rapidly as demand changes and so may be unusually scarce or redundant to start with in any given period. . . .

"2. The total demand for producers' goods tends to vary more sharply than the demand for finished products, the intensification being in proportion to the average life of the goods in question.

"3. The maximum and minimum points in the demand for producers' goods tend to precede the maximum and minimum points in the demand for the finished products, the effect being that the change may appear to precede its own cause."

While Clark did not subscribe to the rigid form of the accelerator which has been used in statistical verifications of the principle, the rigid form used by most authors makes the second and third points necessary rather than merely tendencies. For the more general version in equation (7), these statements are only true of certain values of the parameter b (see Appendix to Section II).

[25] By capacity is meant the point of tangency of the plant curve and the long-run cost curve.

overcapacity. It is easy to modify equation (7) to take care of this probability. The increase in capital stock may be assumed to be proportional to the difference between the amount of capital needed for current output (βX_t) and the optimum degree of utilization of present capital (λK_t). This will make the more general version of equation (7) read

$$(8) \qquad \Delta K_{t+\theta} = b(\beta X_t - \lambda K_t),$$

where λ is the optimum degree of utilization of plant, or "capacity factor."

The optimum degree of overcapacity was previously expressed in terms of the annual increment in demand—i.e., the slope of the forecast trend line. If demand increases at a constant relative rate (instead of the constant absolute rate used for simplicity before), the optimum degree of overcapacity will be a constant[26] proportion $(1 - \lambda)$ of total capacity. When the production function is known and the parameters r and n can be estimated, the value of λ can be determined directly by the methods of Section I.

The effect of introducing λ in equation (8) is to change the amplitude of variation in K for a given variation in X (see Figures 7 and 8). The phase relations between K and X are unchanged.

As long as we confine ourselves to changes in capacity, b and λ are the only significant parameters. The accelerator coefficient β is equal to 1 when capital is measured in terms of capacity and may be omitted. The value of b may be expected to vary according as X_t is greater or less than normal output, λK_t. Where X_t is less than normal output, a lower value of b may be expected because the movement is against the trend and because of technological limitations on a decrease in capital stock.[27]

The value of λ is likely to affect the entrepreneur's response to changes in demand, as measured by b. If large economies of scale make a low capacity factor normal in the industry, the value of b is likely to be low also because the need to expand is less urgent. In other words, an industry with a good reason for maintaining excess capacity also has a good reason to react slowly to changes in demand.[28] It should be noted

[26] As long as the scale coefficient, ψ, is constant. For types of production function other than equation (3), λ may vary with the absolute size of plant.

[27] It may be argued that the rate of disinvestment should be proportional to total capacity rather than to the excess of capacity over "normal." This would be true if disinvestment were a purely technological phenomenon which occurred whenever there was excess capacity. In fact, however, it is likely to depend more on expectations about the duration of the slump in demand. Technology merely sets an upper limit to the value of b for disinvestment.

[28] The outstanding case is the steel industry, which is discussed below.

that the capacity factor does not change with the increase in demand unless the scale coefficient of the production function varies with plant size. However, the absolute size of plants which it pays to build will vary.

APPENDIX TO SECTION II

Before applying equation (8) to time series analysis, we can usefully study the effect of the parameters b and λ on the timing and magnitude of investment in hypothetical cases.[29] To illustrate the effect of different values of these parameters, let us take a sinusoidal output pattern[30] and rewrite equation (8) in differential form:

(9) $bX_t = bX_0 \sin \omega t = (dK/dt)_{t+\theta} + b\lambda K_t$.

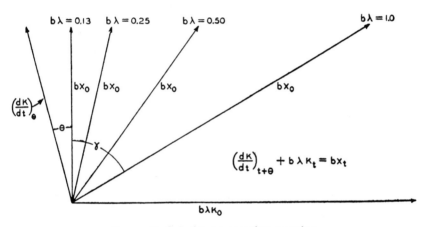

FIGURE 6—Solution to capacity equation.

Goodwin has suggested a convenient graphical method for showing the phase relations and the magnitude of the dependent variables in such oscillatory mechanisms by the use of rotating vectors.[31] Equation (9) is represented in Figure 6 by three vectors such that bX is the vectorial sum of $(dK/dt)_\theta$ and $b\lambda K_0$. Since X is assumed to have a sinusoidal form, the other variables have a similar oscillation over time and their magnitudes can be determined.[32] The vectors represent the maximum value of each variable, while their values at any time are given by their vertical components. The effect of variations in the parameters b and λ can

---

[29] It should be remembered that λ in turn is a function of the planning period (n), discount rate (r), and economy of scale (ψ) as shown in Section I. For simplicity, b will be assumed to have the same value for positive and negative deviations.

[30] Since any variation in output can be decomposed into the sum of a series of sine waves, the results are not limited to the wave form considered here.

[31] Goodwin, *op. cit.*, pp. 122–123.

[32] The solution (for which I am indebted to Goodwin) may be indicated as

be determined graphically, since K and dK/dt must always remain perpendicular and in fixed proportions to each other. From this vector diagram an equation can be written for γ, the angle by which the peak of investment leads peak output:

(10)
$$\tan \gamma = \frac{b\lambda - \omega \sin \theta}{\omega \cos \theta},$$

where ω represents angular velocity and θ represents lag.

The effect of the parameters is now apparent. Since in the diagram the investment vector dK/dt is kept constant, any decrease in either b or λ from their maximum values of 1 will decrease the vector $b\lambda K$. This will have the effect of shortening the time by which investment leads output. For very low values of b and λ it is even possible for the peak of investment to be reached after the peak in output if the lag, θ, is appreciable. For the lag chosen here, one-half year out of a twelve-year cycle, this is true for values of $b\lambda$ less than 0.13. (In the steel and cement industries, the statistically determined value of this product is below that figure.)

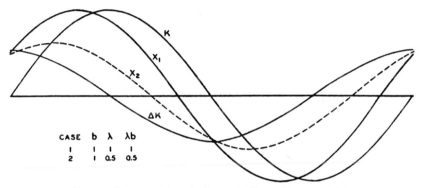

CASE	b	λ	λb
I	I	I	I
2	I	0.5	0.5

FIGURE 7—Examples of phase relations, Cases 1 and 2.

Graphical representations of the cycles which result from equation (9) are easily made by rotating the vectors and measuring their vertical components at each time period. Figures 7 and 8 show cycles for three values of $b\lambda$. Since the variation in capital has been taken as given in the four cases shown there, only the output curve is different for the different values of the parameters. In Cases 2 and 3 the phase relations are shown to depend only on the product $b\lambda$. Lower

---

follows: The output $X_0 \sin \omega t$, may be thought of as the imaginary part of the expression:
$$X_t = X_0 e^{i\omega t} = X_0(\cos \omega t + i \sin \omega t).$$

The equation can be solved by determining first the complex solution and then taking only the imaginary part. The other magnitudes required are
$$K_t = K_0 e^{i\omega(t+\theta)}, \qquad dK/dt = i\omega K_t .$$

This means that dK/dt is always at right angles to K_t and bears a fixed proportion to it. A decrease in either b or λ will therefore increase the ratio of dK/dt to $b\lambda K$.

In Figure 6, dK/dt is kept constant and the magnitude of bx_0 and $b\lambda K_0$ are determined for various values of the parameters.

values of λ decrease the amplitude of output variation required to produce a given capital variation (comparing Case 2 to Case 1), while lower values of *b* increase it (comparing Case 3 to Case 1, and Case 4 to Case 2). Case 4 represents the value of *b*λ at which investment and output are in phase for the value of the lag chosen.

In the next section it is shown that *b* may range from 0.07 to 0.91, while plausible values of λ are between 0.50 and 0.80. Realistic types of phase relations are shown by Cases 1, 2, and 4.

III. SOME EMPIRICAL TESTS

To test the usefulness of the capacity principle, six industries have been selected which conform in varying degrees to the assumptions on which the principle is based. They are steel ingot production, electric generation, portland cement, zinc refining (electrolytic), petroleum refining, and paper and paperboard. All are basic industries in the early

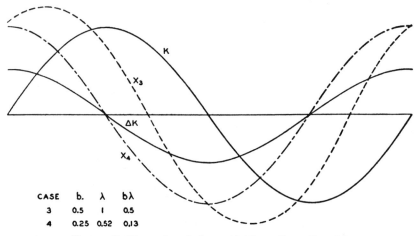

CASE	b.	λ	bλ
3	0.5	1	0.5
4	0.25	0.52	0.13

FIGURE 8—Examples of phase relations, Cases 3 and 4.

stages of production. It would also be desirable to test the principle on industries in the later stages of production, but capacity data on such industries are either nonexistent or hard to interpret because of the variety of products made. It seems, therefore, that tests on an industry-wide basis must be limited to the earlier stages. The six industries were chosen mainly because of the availability of capacity data.

A. *Procedure.*[33] It was thought desirable to use as uniform a statistical procedure as possible rather than to try to improve the results for each case by individual variations. Therefore, an interval of two years for the increment in capacity was used for all series. The capacity and acceleration principles were made comparable by putting each in the form of a percentage ratio, which is the form that has usually been used

---

[33] The procedure is described more fully in the Statistical Appendix.

in testing the accelerator. An unexplained constant was added to the accelerator to allow for other sources of investment and to give it as many degrees of freedom as the capacity formula. A constant already exists in the capacity principle. The degree of normal or planned overcapacity cannot be distinguished statistically from overcapacity resulting from locational shifts or technological change.

The two formulae to be compared are the following:

Capacity principle:

$$(11) \qquad \frac{\Delta K_{t+\theta}}{K_{t+\theta-2}} = b\left(\frac{X_t}{K_t}\right) - b\lambda,$$

Acceleration principle:

$$(12) \qquad \frac{\Delta K_{t+\theta}}{K_{t+\theta-2}} = b\left(\frac{\Delta X_t}{X_t}\right) + C.$$

In each case the lag that gave the best correlation was used. It was found that a change in the lag had little effect on the regression coefficient b and rarely changed the coefficient of correlation more than five points for a six-months change. The other two parameters in each formula were determined by simple correlation. The results are shown in the Table below and in Figures 9–14.

B. *Structural factors.* Before examining the statistical results it is useful to compare the six industries on the basis of their known structural characteristics. Technologically, they all process bulk materials, produce homogeneous products (except paper), and are subject to substantial economies of scale. However, these economies vary considerably. In order of the importance of economies of scale, the industries would stand roughly as follows: steel, electricity, zinc, cement, petroleum, paper. The capital intensity, or investment per dollar of output, is in about the same order. For these reasons one would expect that there would be more normal overcapacity and a slower reaction to change in demand in steel and electricity than in petroleum and paper, if demand conditions were comparable.

Locational factors also vary considerably among the six industries. The number of plants in all the industries is relatively small. Cement has the highest transport costs relative to its value, while petroleum and paper have the lowest. Plants in the latter industries may be able to operate at a higher capacity in the face of market shifts through their ability to reach a wider market.

Demand factors varied greatly during the period considered. The annual growth rates (see the Table) were very high for electricity and petroleum, moderate for zinc and paper, and very low for steel and cement. (The degree of cyclical variation in demand was in the reverse order.) If entry is not hampered by large capital requirements, an expanding demand may attract new firms even if there is already over-capacity in the industry, particularly if technological change gives them some advantage over older plants.[34] This possibility favors the accelerator explanation over the capacity formula. On the other hand, if expan-

STATISTICAL RESULTS[a]

Industry[b]	CAPACITY PRINCIPLE						
	N	θ	λ	b_1	r_1	$b\lambda$	Annual Growth Rate (1922–1939)
Electric power	20	1	0.27	0.915	0.89	0.24	8.8%
Steel	19	1.5	0.35	0.071	0.87	0.025	1.3%
Portland cement	19	1	0.41	0.193	0.91	0.08	0.5%
Zinc	15	0	0.41	0.362	0.69	0.147	3.8%
Petroleum refining	15	0	0.57	0.650	0.70	0.45	7.1%
Paper and paperboard	11	1	0.63	0.210	0.65	0.13	2.8%

	ACCELERATION PRINCIPLE					
	N	θ	b_2	r_2	C	$r_1 - r_2$
Electric power	20	0	0.546	0.71	0.039	0.18
Steel	18	2	0.024	0.38	0.032	0.49
Portland cement	19	2	0.148	0.45	0.056	0.46
Zinc	15	1	0.015	0.04	0.094	0.65
Petroleum refining	20	0	0.513	0.84	0.028	−0.14
Paper and paperboard	10	1	0.179	0.69	0.045	−0.04

Symbols: N represents number of observations; θ, lag (between midpoints of periods); λ, normal capacity factor; b, reaction coefficient; r, coefficient of correlation; and C, unexplained constant.

[a] Most of the statistical work summarized here was done by Mr. Irwin Leff.
[b] Industries are listed in inverse order of magnitude of the parameter λ.

sion of capacity is made almost entirely by firms already in the industry, they may be expected to take more account of the existing degree of excess capacity.

The capacity principle may be thought of as applying particularly to oligopolies and industries with high capital intensities, while the accel-

[34] Technological change and shifts in location of markets or resources may lead to the installation of new capacity before the old capital is retired. This is more likely to happen in an expanding market and hence will upset the capacity principle more than the accelerator, which ignores excess capacity.

OVERCAPACITY AND ACCELERATION PRINCIPLE

erator more nearly fits competitive markets and production functions permitting lower capital coefficients. Steel, cement, electricity, and zinc fall in the former categories, while paper and petroleum refining are more nearly in the latter.

C. *Statistical comparisons.* On an over-all basis, the capacity principle showed reasonable success (a coefficient of correlation greater than 0.65) for all the industries tested, while the accelerator was quite inadequate (r less than 0.50) in half of them. However, in two cases, petroleum and paper, the accelerator was slightly better than the capacity explanation. Some of the reasons why this might be expected have been indicated above.

The relation between the growth rate and the reaction coefficient, b, is of particular interest. The correlation between the two is very high; the rank of the six industries on both bases is almost identical. The electric industry, which has the highest rate of growth, invests about 91% of the indicated discrepancy in capacity each year. The cement and steel industries, with very low rates of growth, invested only 19% and 7%, respectively.

It is impossible to determine the actual value of the normal degree of overcapacity, λ, statistically. The fact that there may be some net investment due to locational shifts or changes in market conditions, even though the industry as a whole is below its normal output level, makes the determined values of λ too low in each case.[35] A rough correction may be applied by determining the output-capacity ratio at which the industry invests 1% of total capacity[36] (instead of the zero point). On this basis, the normal capacity factors range from 46% in cement and zinc to 68% for paper.[37, 38] These are probably considerably lower than the value of "optimum overcapacity" described earlier,[39] but there is no way to segregate (in the data available) the obsolete capacity which is maintained only for periods of maximum output.

The characteristic defect as well as the merits of the acceleration principle are also shown by these results. Despite the use of an optimum

[35] If λ could be estimated from the production function, an additional constant could be added to take care of these unexplained factors.

[36] That is, by assuming that exogenous factors caused an increase in capacity of one percent per year on the average over the period considered.

[37] Electricity is a special case since it must supply an instantaneous instead of an annual demand, and the capacity factor is of course much lower. It cannot be interpreted in the same way as the degree of utilization of capacity in the other industries.

[38] Instead of from 35% to 63% as shown in the Table.

[39] Building ahead of demand five to ten years would, as deduced in Section I, give values of λ of 0.55 to 0.90 if applied to the observed growth rates for the whole period. (The *expected* growth rates of the entrepreneurs may well have been different from those which occurred.)

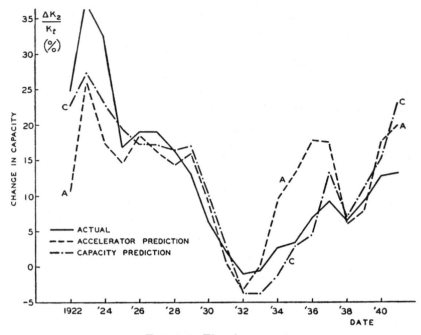

FIGURE 9—Electric power.

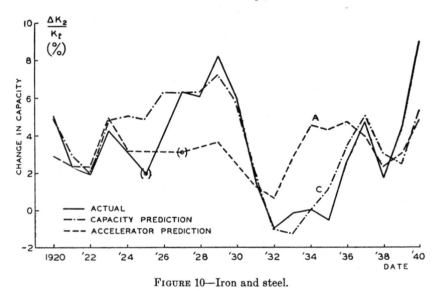

FIGURE 10—Iron and steel.

lag, the predicted value of investment was in every case far too high after the depression, when overcapacity existed. The predicted peak in investment usually occurs one or two years too soon because of the fixed timing which the accelerator requires (see Case 1, Figure 7). The timing of peaks and troughs given by the capacity principle is usually better. The advantages of the accelerator formulation are shown in the case of petroleum, where the existence of substantial amounts of obsolete refining capacity in the early twenties does not affect the accelerator predictions although it spoils the capacity principle during this period. More accurate data on the type as well as total amount of capacity would be necessary to make the capacity principle work in such a case.[40]

Both principles would be improved by introducing different values for the reaction coefficient for negative predictions. The interpretation given to a decrease in demand in an industry with a long-run upward

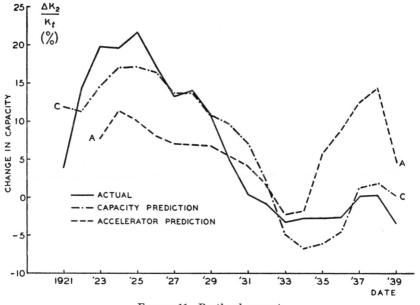

FIGURE 11—Portland cement.

trend is quite different from the reaction to an increase, and the cost calculation is quite different. The fewness of negative observations did not permit the determination of a separate regression for these points, but the correlation coefficient would have been considerably improved in most cases by omitting them. (For steel, electricity, and cement the correlation coefficient becomes 0.94 or higher for the capacity explanation.)

[40] The capacity prediction is not plotted in Figure 13 for the years 1922–1925 for this reason, but it would have shown considerably lower values than the actual increases if the available data had been used. For the remaining years it is considerably better than the accelerator forecast.

IV. CONCLUSIONS

The difference between the capacity and the accelerator explanations lies in the assumption made about the effect of excess capacity. This preliminary statistical work suggests that the two principles are suited

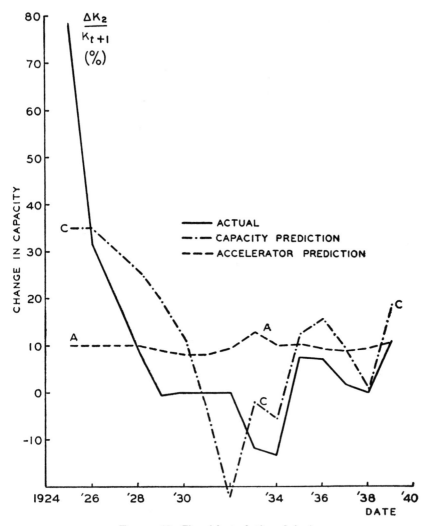

FIGURE 12—Zinc (electrolytic refining).

to different types of industry and that both may be useful for more detailed empirical work on investment. Since the technological structure is the most important factor differentiating the cases to which they are applicable, a careful analysis of the productive conditions of the firm or industry should precede the choice of a formula for statistical work.

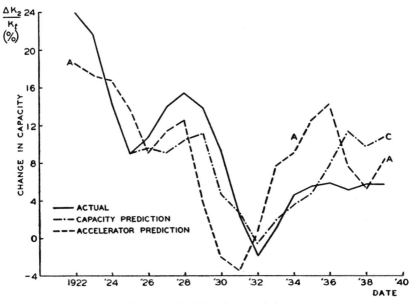

FIGURE 13—Petroleum refining.

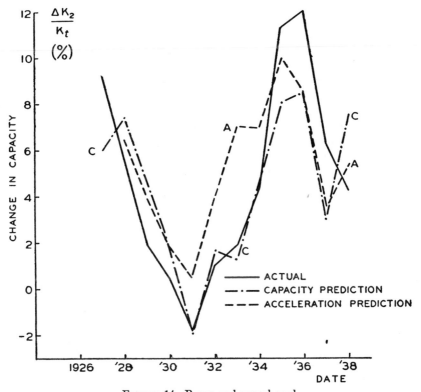

FIGURE 14—Paper and paperboard.

The capacity principle gave its best results[41] in two cases where the accelerator was at its worst: steel and cement. Similarly, the accelerator principle gave the best results for paper and petroleum, where the capacity formula was at its worst. For industry studies, therefore, they may be alternative formulations. The lower the value of the product $b\lambda$, the more likely is the capacity principle to give better results. In most cases b is correlated with λ, making excess capacity the clue to the selection.

If an analysis of changes in capacity could be made for firms instead of industries, the capacity formulation would include the accelerator because the disturbing influences of new firms and locational shifts could be eliminated. If some weight could be given to the differences in efficiency of plants, the capacity principle would probably provide a more accurate method of prediction in all cases in which "capacity" is a meaningful concept.

It should be emphasized that the results of this series of tests in no way "prove" the validity of the particular overcapacity explanation given in Section I; various reasons can be given for the existence of overcapacity in an industry even though the firms do not intentionally build ahead of demand. The results do show, however, that once overcapacity exists it is taken into account in further investment and hence should be embodied in whatever equation is used to predict fluctuations in investment.

Economic Cooperation Administration, Rome

STATISTICAL APPENDIX

The general procedure employed in the statistical analysis has already been indicated, but several special problems require further mention. Most of them are typical of the analysis of economic time series; here I shall only indicate my reasons for choosing among the alternative methods of handling the data.

First, there is the problem of the meaning of the "capacity" series used. On theoretical grounds it is preferable to use capacity installed rather than monetary expenditure as a measure of investment because it eliminates two problems: the separation of replacement and maintenance from net investment and the variation in capital-output ratios due to technological change and price variation. Both the accelerator and the capacity principle refer to physical additions to productive capacity; only by assuming the accelerator coefficient to be constant do they apply equally to monetary expenditure.

While it is obviously preferable to use a physical measure of capacity, there remains the problem of what the published series represent. In general they come

---

[41] A. S. Manne, in "Some Notes on the Acceleration Principle," *Review of Economic Statistics*, Vol. 27, May, 1945, pp. 93–99, found that the capacity factor gave a better prediction than the accelerator for freight cars but did not suggest an explanation of this result.

from trade association statistics or from government reports. What little information is available on the subject indicates that the term "capacity" means the amount that could be produced under normal operating conditions with the existing physical plant. This may not represent the most efficient use of plant, either economically or technologically (although the economic criterion is probably closer to being satisfied), nor does it represent the technological maximum. From the point of view of statistical analysis, however, the important requirement is that the capacity be reported on the same basis from year to year. In at least one case, the steel series in 1926, the definition of capacity was changed by the Iron and Steel Institute, and the data show a discontinuity which cannot be corrected. The consistency of the other capacity series has not been investigated.

In several industries it is apparent that removing a trend from the data would improve the results. A trend could arise from several sources; the reaction to a given capacity factor may change over time because of a changing expectation of the future, or a change in the underlying technology may make a different utilization of capacity more desirable. It is clear that the latter case prevailed in the electric industry, where increasing interconnection during the period made it possible to operate with less reserve capacity. Therefore, a linear trend has been removed from the published "plant factor" series to represent a changing "normal" load. In petroleum, a change in the reaction to a given excess demand is also observable after 1935, but this appears to be a psychological phenomenon. No trend correction was made in this case because it would have removed the predictive value of the principle unless it could have been estimated from other sources.

The way in which the capacity principle is formulated raises the possibility of securing spurious correlations[42] because the term K_t appears on both sides of the equation. This possibility exists whether the absolute form [equation (8)] is fitted or whether both sides are divided by K_t, as was actually done. It was decided to use the latter formula [equation (11)] for two reasons. The existence of a pronounced trend in some of the series makes it necessary to decide which hypothesis will give the better distribution of errors. Although there would be no difference in the result if the correlation were perfect, the scatter of points about the regression line and the slope which is determined depend on whether relative or absolute capacity differences are used. The relative form reduces the disturbing effects of growth in output, which makes the absolute increments become larger. The relative form is also easier to analyze because λ can be determined from the constant term in the simple regression rather than by multiple correlation. Where the correlation is good, as in electric power, tests of both methods show little difference. In the relative form, a rough test for the existence of spurious correlation can be made by comparing the series $1/K$ to the other two series being correlated. Since in most cases capacity increases steadily with only minor reversals, the occurrence of K in the denominator of both sides appears to have little effect on the correlation.

The time interval of two years for the increments in capacity and output was chosen to fit the majority of series. Since the value of b is less than 0.5 on an annual basis for most series and the observed lags vary from six months to two years, it seems logical to expect the effect of a given deviation from normal capacity to be better measured over the succeeding two-year period than over one

[42] See G. Udny Yule and M. G. Kendall, *An Introduction to the Theory of Statistics*, 13th ed., London: Charles Griffin and Co., 1947, p. 300, for a brief discussion of spurious correlation.

year. As in the case of the lags, however, the effect of varying the time interval
is only to change the correlation coefficient slightly but not the slope of the regression line. (In the plotted results of Figures 9–14, the two-year increments in
capacity are plotted opposite the beginning of the period although the lags are
measured from the middle of the period over which the change is taken.)

SOURCES OF DATA.[43] 1. *Electric power.* Federal Power Commission (new series).
The Commission's computation of the "plant factor" for the whole industry was
used rather than the ratio of X/K computed from the data because the former
represents a weighted average.

   2. *Paper and paperboard.* Bureau of the Census, U. S. Department of Commerce, Biennial Reports on Forest Products, 1928–1941. (Capacity is computed
on the basis of 310 days of operation.)

   3. *Zinc (electrolytic refineries).* Yearbook, American Bureau of Metal Statistics,
1920–1947. (The number of refineries increased from one to four during the period,
causing some discontinuities.)

   4. *Petroleum refining.* Petroleum Data Book, Petroleum Engineer Publishing
Co., Dallas, Texas. (The capacity data represent total capacity including shut-
downs and plants being built; the latter inclusion may account for the absence
of observed lag.)

   5. *Portland cement.* Portland Cement Association, *Cement and Concrete Reference Book*, 1941.

   6. *Steel (ingots and steel for casting).* American Iron and Steel Institute, *Annual
Statistical Report*, 1945. (Series changed in 1926.)

[43] [The data are not reprinted here, but may be found in the original article.—
The Editors.]

Econometrica, Vol. 20, 3 (July 1952)

HABIT PERSISTENCE AND LAGS IN CONSUMER BEHAVIOUR[1]

By T. M. Brown

The nature of consumer demand is explored after an initial demonstration of the presence of lagged influences. Experimentation with various alternative hypotheses leads to the development of a habit "hysteresis" or habit persistence theory of the causal basis of the lag. A theory of the time relationships of this lag on consumer behaviour is also suggested. The consumer theory finally selected is fitted to the observed Canadian data by first building around it a small macromodel of the economy followed by simultaneous estimation of parameters. The goodness of fit is studied of first, the individual equations and then of the model treated as a whole. Finally, short-run and long-run multipliers are estimated for the complete model.

I. INTRODUCTION

Previous research on the form of a consumer demand equation which would adequately explain the Canadian observed data had clearly demonstrated that *lagged* values of some of the variables involved exert an important influence on current consumer behaviour. The presence of lags means that the full reaction of consumers to changes in income does not occur immediately but instead takes place gradually. This means that in estimating the multiplier effect of certain impulses, such as changes in exogenous demands, one must consider the period of time within which the multiplier effect is to be considered. The accumulated effect will presumably increase with time, and will approach some equilibrium value asymptotically.

The purpose of this project was to probe the nature of consumer demand with special reference to lagged influences, and then to use the results of this research to distinguish between a short-run and a long-run marginal propensity to consume. From these it would then be possible to estimate short-run and long-run multipliers. These are of importance to the economist estimating the repercussion effects of various possible future exogenous developments, or of various alternative policies. In some cases, as for example in matters of employment and inflation, it may be the short-run or intra-year repercussions that are of supreme importance. In other cases the long-range view may be the

[1] The writer is indebted to Dr. L. R. Klein and to Mr. S. J. May for giving helpful comments on various drafts of this work.

desired one and then the long-run, inter-year multiplier may be what
is needed. It is evident then, if there are lags in consumer behaviour,
that no single multiplier or repercussion table can adequately serve for
all problems. Ideally for each problem the *time* within which the cumulative effects of certain changes are to be estimated should be decided
upon, and then the multipliers and repercussion tables estimated to suit
that particular time period.

The first phase of the work that follows is to test for the existence of
lags in the consumption function, and then to probe for a form of the
function which will be in agreement with general observations of economic behaviour, and which will also give a close fit to the observed
data.

II. RESEARCH ON THE FORM OF THE CONSUMPTION FUNCTION

In this project all variables are aggregative over the whole economy
and are in billions of constant dollars of the period 1935–1939. The data
used for the original research was developed for internal research only.
Recently, however, comparable data (with the sole exception of the
separation of *disposable* income into wage and nonwage components)
have been published [2]. The observations used in the analysis were
for the years 1926–1941 and 1946–1949, inclusive. Thus, those war
years in which it was believed that there had been a considerable change
in the structure of consumer behaviour, were excluded from the analysis.

The experimental work was carried out by testing as many plausible
hypotheses as could be discovered or devised as the work proceeded.
The testing at this stage was done mainly by classical single-equation
least-squares. But each equation that lent itself to such treatment was
converted to a complete and just identified model, by the addition of
an accounting identity, and its coefficients were then estimated again
by maximum–likelihood. The method used followed the procedure outlined by Dr. Trygve Haavelmo [6].

The first hypothesis tested was the most simple and direct: Consumption is a linear function of total disposable income:

(1) $C = a_0 + a_1 Y + u,$

where u is a random disturbance or residual. It turned out that this
equation fit the data very poorly, for the residuals were both large and
serially correlated. (The von Neumann [7] ratio[2] δ^2/S^2, was .728 indicating positive serial correlation.) The time pattern of the residuals from

---

[2] For a sample of residuals of size 18, the probability is 5 per cent or less that
the sample came from a population which is nonautocorrelated, if the von Neumann ratio falls outside a band of values extending from 1.20 to 3.04.

this hypothesis however told an interesting story, and it now appears from hindsight that the form of the equation finally selected could almost have been deduced from this first equation and its residuals. The time series of these residuals is shown in graphical form in the Figure.

The first aspect of the residuals that strikes the eye in the time graph below is that they are distinctly nonrandom in time. They display a clear cyclical pattern that is in some way related to the business cycle.

We might describe the pattern of these residuals as follows: During the late 1920's while income was rising the residuals were negative, but decreasing in absolute value. In the early 1930's while income was declining the residuals became positive and increasing. After 1933 income increased steadily to 1941, except for one reversal in the year 1938, while the residuals declined steadily but with one reversal in the same year, 1938.

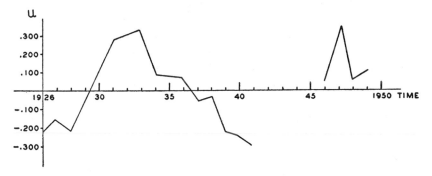

From 1926 to 1941 the story is clear: When income is rising, consumer expenditure lags behind the simple relationship (1), and we have negative residuals; when income is falling, once again consumer expenditures lag behind and we have positive residuals. Thus, during these years consumer demand appeared to be related in some way to the income (or to some similar cyclical variable) of a *previous* period.

In the postwar period the residuals would have been negative if they had followed the prewar relationship, since this was a period of rising income. But the residuals of this period turned out to be distinctly positive indicating that either the prewar relationship had changed, or that some new influence had been superimposed on it. The latter suggestion appeared quite plausible since it was well-known that consumers had deferred their wants and needs (mainly for durables) during the war, and had at the same time, through saving, accumulated large stocks of liquid assets. We could accordingly expect considerable consumer spending out of these past savings, in the early postwar period. And this particular type of spending would be related to the level of consumers'

210 T. M. BROWN

deferred wants and liquid assets, rather than (directly) to either current or lagged levels of income. Thus it seemed that the postwar experience might be explained by adding to the equation the liquid asset holdings of households. Since data did not exist for this variable a temporary alternative device was attempted, following some success in the use of this device by Dr. William C. Hood. The method was to shift the whole consumer demand equation upward in the postwar period by the use of a "shift variable" (A^c). A^c was given a value zero during all of the prewar years and unity for each of the postwar years. This method had been previously used by Dr. A. R. Prest [11] who termed the variable a "discontinuity variate," and who made use of it whenever a demand equation appeared to have shifted upward or downward to a greater extent than could be explained by the price and income variables in the equation.

It was believed that the use of the shift variable A^c would enable the equation to adjust itself to the extent of the upward deferred demand, liquid asset shift, and at the same time enable the other parameters of the equation to adjust properly to their true structural values.[3]

Let us return now to the basic relationship between consumer demand, current disposable income, and some lagged cyclical variable such as disposable income. The simplest linear relationship of this sort to try would be one in which the total disposable income of the previous year, Y_{-1}, is added as an additional variable to (1). This gives us:

$$(2) \qquad C = a_0 + a_1 Y + a_2 Y_{-1} + u.$$

This hypothesis suggests that consumers are slow to adjust to current income changes because of some inertia in their reactions to these changes. The statistical goodness of fit of this hypothesis was much better than that for (1).

It may help to sharpen the analysis if we attempt to develop a theory explaining this inertia. The work of Professor Franco Modigliani [10] and Professor J. S. Duesenberry [3] is very closely related to this problem, and suggests the hypothesis that the inertia mentioned above is due to consumers' memories of the highest previous level of disposable income which they have attained ($\overset{\circ}{Y}$) in the past. Presumably they try to maintain the standard of this peak year, until some higher level is reached

[3] There is now some doubt in the writer's mind, however, about the advisability of having used the shift variable for all of the postwar years. If it was truly operative in only 1946 and 1947, say, then the use of it for 1946–49, inclusive, would tend to weaken the influence of some of the other variables in the equation. Some of the residuals suggest that such may be the case, but further research on this point is necessary.

which sets a new standard. If we express this hypothesis in linear form
we have:

(3) $$C = a_0 + a_1 Y + a_2 \overset{*}{Y} + u.$$

This hypothesis implies that from 1928 to 1939 the only variation in
(3) occurred in the variable Y, and that the influence of $\overset{*}{Y}_{1928}$ persisted
constant and undiminished throughout all of this period. It hardly
seems likely on a priori grounds that this is the best hypothesis of the
lag effect in consumer behaviour, yet in the statistical testing this hypothesis produced an equation which "explained" the observed data
very closely.

A third hypothesis which had gradually suggested itself was that the
lag effect in consumer demand was produced by the consumption *habits*
which people formed as a result of past consumption. The habits, cus-
toms, standards, and levels associated with real consumption previously
enjoyed become "impressed" on the human physiological and psychological systems and this produces an inertia or "hysteresis" in consumer
behaviour. Because of this inertia, consumer demand reacts to changes
in consumer income with a certain slowness, and thus past real consumption exerts a stabilizing effect on current consumption. In order to test
the agreement of this hypothesis with the observed data it is evident
that it is not previous income, but rather *previous real consumption actually experienced* (C_{-t}), which will be the appropriate lagged variable.

This immediately raises the question of the appropriate time (t) that
real consumption should be lagged in the consumer behaviour equation.
We might assume that the "habit persistence" effect induced on current
behaviour by past consumption would be strongest when t is small and
gradually die away as t becomes larger. Another way of expressing this
hypothesis would be to say that the habit persistence effect is continuous, and is an inverse function of time. This would suggest that we could
use whatever time lag the data permitted and get the strongest lag effect
for the shortest possible lag, and the weakest lag effect for the longest
lag, permitted by the data.[4] Since the present project was carried out
with annual observations, and since one of the purposes was to discover
the intra-year marginal propensity to consume, a lag of one year was used.

We may now summarize this hypothesis in a form in which it can be
tested with the observed data:

(4) $$C = a_0 + a_1 Y + a_2 C_{-1} + u.$$

The statistical fit here was quite good.

Instead of assuming a continuous, inverse linear time relationship for

---

[4] Rough testing of this hypothesis provided good support for it.

the lag effect of past consumption on present consumption, we might assume a discontinuous time relationship of the type suggested in the work of Modigliani [10] and Duesenberry [3] mentioned above. The hypothesis would then be worded that the habit persistence effect is produced by the *highest previous level of real consumption experienced.* This effect persists undiminished until a higher level produces a new standard. We may represent this hypothesis in equation form, ready for statistical testing, as follows:

(5) $C = a_0 + a_1 Y + a_2 \overset{\circ}{C} + u.$

The statistical goodness of fit of this hypothesis was also high.

Another type of hypothesis which suggested itself in the course of the project was that the marginal propensity to consume was not constant over the business cycle, but tended to expand in the buoyancy of the upswing, and contract in the depression of the downswing. The simplest way of expressing this hypothesis is:

(6) $\dfrac{dC}{dY} = c_1 + c_2 Y,$

then

(7) $C = c_0 + c_1 Y + c_2 \dfrac{Y^2}{2} + u.$

We may think of (7) as the long-run consumption function which curves upward in a parabola. Tangents to this parabola may then act as a family of short-run consumption functions, to which the long-run function is the envelope.

The fit to this hypothesis was discovered to be considerably improved by using lagged income in the basic hypothesis. Thus:

(6a) $\dfrac{dC}{dY} = c_1 + c_2 Y_{-1},$

(7a) $C = c_0 + c_1 Y + c_2 Y Y_{-1} + u.$

In the statistical testing of the above seven hypotheses, it was found that all of them, except (1), gave rather good explanations of consumer behaviour in the period studied. The shift variable A^c was added to each of the hypotheses as the testing proceeded and this in each case improved the fit. At this stage of the testing one of the hypotheses was just slightly better than any of the others on the basis of statistical goodness of fit. This was the Modigliani–Duesenberry hypothesis [(3) above] with A^c added.

The next phase of the experimental work was to follow the lead of Dr. L. R. Klein in separating total income into wage and nonwage components. Klein had made this separation of gross income, as distinct from disposable income, in his analysis of the United States economy [8], on the grounds that the marginal propensity to consume from wage income should be significantly larger than that from property and enterprise income. It so happened that it was possible with the Canadian data to make an estimated separation of *disposable* income into its wage and nonwage components,[5] Y_w and Y_π , respectively, where $Y = Y_w + Y_\pi$. Klein has pointed out to the writer that he prefers this separation of income because it gives more information and because there are significant differences between the marginal propensity to consume out of wage and nonwage income. He has also stated that he is not sure that this separation will improve the predictive power of the equation.

Each of the linear hypotheses above was now tested with the statistical data with the variable Y replaced by the two separate variables Y_w and Y_π . In this phase of the testing the Modigliani–Duesenberry type hypothesis broke down by showing a larger marginal propensity to consume from disposable nonwage than from disposable wage income. However the somewhat similar hypothesis using the highest previous level of real consumption (C) gave quite satisfactory results. But it was the habit persistence hypothesis with the continuous time lag (i.e., using C_{-1} as the lagged variable) that produced the best all-round result from the point of view of economic rationale and statistical goodness of fit.

Thus the form of the best linear hypothesis of consumer behaviour which the research presented was able to discover, at the stage of the development outlined here, was:

(8) $$C = a_0 + a_1 Y_w + a_2 Y_\pi + a_3 C_{-1} + a_4 A^c + u.$$

When the parameters of this equation were estimated using single-equation least-squares, the following numerical results were obtained:

(8a) $C = 0.9138 + 0.5929\ Y_w + 0.3419\ Y_\pi$
$\qquad$ (5.5) $\quad$ (8.1) $\qquad$ (5.8)
$$+ 0.2000\ C_{-1} + 0.6958\ A^c + u.$$
$\qquad$ (2.8) $\qquad$ (5.1)

Goodness of fit statistics for this equation are as follows: (1) The numbers in parenthesis under each parameter represent the number of times the parameter contains its own standard error. (2) $\overline{S}$ = the standard error of estimate of the equation, corrected for degrees of freedom, 0.063 billion constant dollars. (3) $\overline{S}/\overline{C} \times 100$ = coefficient of variation of the equation = 1.5% ($\overline{C}$ = mean value of dependent variable C). (4)

[5] This separation has not as yet been published.

214 T. M. BROWN

$\delta^2/S^2 = 3.3$ (Cf. J. von Neumann [7]) (The time pattern of the residuals tended to be *saw-toothed*, that is, to have a certain degree of negative autocorrelation.) (5) $(1 - \overline{S}^2/\sigma^{-2}) \times 100 =$ coefficient of determination, or percentage of variance of dependent variable explained by the equation = 99.8%.

This concludes the outline of the experimental *probing* for the form of the consumer demand equation which included the observed lag effects. The next phase of the work was to estimate the parameters of the equation (8) selected, now using the simultaneous estimation techniques.

III. SIMULTANEOUS ESTIMATION OF PARAMETERS

The consumer demand equation (8) above and the associated identity $Y = Y_w + Y_\pi$ contain a total of four endogenous variables C, Y, Y_w, and Y_π. In order to fit equation (8) by simultaneous methods it is necessary to work with a complete equation system, that is, one in which each endogenous variable can be solved in terms of predetermined variables only. (It is not necessary to estimate all of the parameters in the complete system. Dr. T. W. Anderson (see [9, pp. 311–322]) outlines the estimation of the parameters of a single equation only within the framework of the simultaneous estimation techniques.) In order to build a complete model around the consumption function (8) and the identity $Y = Y_w + Y_\pi$, it is evident that we must add two further equations which contain no additional endogenous variables.

There is one further identity inherent in the system and it is of the form $C + I = Y$. I is of the nature of net investment and in this small model we shall treat it as exogenous (cf. Haavelmo [6, pp. 105–107]). More precisely, since Y is the total disposable income of the private sector of the economy, I may be designated as equal to the total spending offsets to the savings of the private sector of the economy. We accordingly use the symbol S_0 in place of I in what follows and define S_0 as equal to net home investment, plus net foreign investment, plus the government deficit. In the *ex post* sense we always have, of course, $S_0 = Y - C$.

This exhausts the identities inherent in our system, and we must accordingly add one more behaviour (hence stochastic) equation to the system to make it complete. This equation must explain either Y_w or Y_π, and will accordingly require a theory of the distribution of national product into factor shares (preferably disposable factor shares).

Since wage income is contractual while a large part of nonwage income is residual in its nature (profits), it was decided to explain Y_w in the model and then treat Y_π as a residual. The distribution theory required had already been worked out in a form suitable for econometric estimation by Klein.[6] In his analysis the theory became a demand for labor

---

[6] See for example [8, pp. 21, 65].

equation representing the behaviour of firms maximizing profits by demanding labour up to the point where its marginal cost equals its marginal product. His equation in our symbdʻls, becomes:

(9) $W = b_0 + b_1 (Y + S_1) + b_2 (Y + S_1)_{-1} + b_3 t + u,$

where W represents the real contractual wage bill. $(Y + S_1)$ represents real GNP (Gross National Product), and t represents time in units of one year.

Equation (9) represents labour's share of national product before the redistribution effects of government taxes and transfers. But the effective share of wage-salary earners is, of course, their share after taxes and transfers, that is, as represented by our symbol Y_w. Also since it is Y_w which occurs in (8) it would simplify our model, by eliminating any need for net wage and nonwage tax (transfer) variables, if (9) could be cast into a form where it explained Y_w instead of W. To do so would imply a hypothesis that labour and management, when engaged in the bargaining process, think to some extent in terms of *disposable* factor shares. This is not an unreasonable hypothesis and when tested by single equation methods, surprisingly enough, yielded a slightly better fitting equation than the original (9).

The complete model designed for enabling the simultaneous fitting of the consumer demand equation (8) can now be set out:

(8) $C = a_0 + a_1 Y_w + a_2 Y_\pi + a_3 C_{-1} + a_4 A^c + u_1,$

(9a) $Y_w = b_0 + b_1(Y + S_1) + b_2(Y + S_1)_{-1} + b_3 t + u_2,$

(10) $Y = Y_w + Y_\pi,$

(11) $(Y + S_1) = C + S_0 + S_1,$

where S_1 represents $T + D - J + \frac{1}{2}R$; T = government disposable income, which equals total taxes from, less total transfers to, the private sector of the economy; D = depreciation allowances; J = inventory valuation adjustment; $\frac{1}{2}R$ = residual error of estimate on GNP side of national accounts; t = calendar year $- 1926$; S_0 = total spending offsets to the savings of the private sector = net home investment + net foreign investment + the government deficit $- R$; $S_0 + S_1$ = government spending + gross private domestic investment + net foreign investment $- \frac{1}{2}R$.

Each of the two stochastic behaviour equations in this model is over-identified. The complete consumer behaviour model above was estimated simultaneously by the "limited-information maximum-likelihood" method.[7] The estimated model is presented in Table I.

---

[7] As outlined in papers by Drs. M. A. Girshick and Trygve Haavelmo [5]; Drs. Bronfenbrenner and Herman Chernoff [1]; and Dr. T. W. Anderson Jr., Cowles Commission Monograph No. 10 [9].

TABLE I

The Consumer Behaviour Model with Associated Goodness of
Fit Statistics

Equations	Statistics Associated with Variance of Random Variable			
	$\bar{S}$	$\dfrac{\bar{S}}{\bar{Y}} \times 100^a$	$\dfrac{\delta^2}{S^2}$	$\left(1 - \dfrac{\bar{S}^2}{\sigma^2}\right) \times 100$

(8) $C = 0.8962 + 0.6061\, Y_w + 0.2828\, Y_\pi$
       (4.8)   (7.4)   (4.2)
      $+ 0.2171\, C_{-1} + 0.6910\, A^c + u_1$
       (2.8)   (4.8)
	0.066	1.6%	2.8	99.5%

(9a) $Y_w = 0.3407 + 0.1723\,(Y+S_1)$
       (3.7)   (3.6)
      $+ 0.2215\,(Y+S_1)_{-1} + 0.03491\, t + u_2$
       (5.0)   (7.2)
	0.069	2.3	1.8	99.4

(10) $Y = Y_w + Y_\pi$	0.0	0.0		100.0
(11) $(Y+S_1) = C + S_0 + S_1$	0.0	0.0		100.0

a In this context Y means the appropriate endogenous variable.

IV. GOODNESS OF FIT

(a) *Individual equations.* Many of the details about the goodness of
fit of the model can be ascertained by examination of the various statistics in Table I. However in order to attempt to complete the picture,
certain further details are presented here.

In the fitting process the assumptions are made that the residuals
u_1 and u_2 are nonautocorrelated, and also that they are uncorrelated
with the predetermined variables. Let us examine the first of these
assumptions. The timegraphs of u_1 and u_2 present a general appearance
of randomness in time, although the graph of u_1 is slightly *saw-toothed*
and hence is, to some extent, negatively autocorrelated. The value of
the von Neumann ratio (2.8), although it does not refute the hypothesis
that the residuals are random in time at the five per cent significance
level (see footnote 2), does indicate a degree of negative serial correlation. To check on the degree of this negative correlation the coefficient
of correlation (r) of u with u_{-1} was calculated for u_1. Its value came out
to be -0.318. For sixteen degrees of freedom a correlation coefficient
of 0.4683 (0.4555 for seventeen degrees of freedom) or greater rejects
the hypothesis of lack of correlation at the five per cent significance
level (see Fisher [4, p. 204]). Thus at the five per cent significance level
the hypothesis of nonautocorrelation is not rejected. The corresponding
coefficient of correlation for u_2 was 0.093.

To check the validity of the second assumption a correlation table
was drawn up between the residuals and the predetermined variables.

This table shows that the second assumption above is satisfactorily met in the model.

TABLE II

CORRELATIONS BETWEEN RESIDUALS AND PREDETERMINED VARIABLES

	C_{-1}	$(Y+S_1)_{-1}$	A^c	t	S_1	S_0
u_1	0.0022	0.0245	0.0023	-0.0449	0.0476	0.0002
u_2	0.0109	0.0010	0.1013	0.0013	-0.0906	-0.0160

An examination of the residuals to check for any unusual items reveals a large value of u_2 for 1934 ($+6.2\%$ of the observed value for that year), and of u_1 for 1947 ($+2.4\%$ of the observed value). No explanation for the 1934 value of u_2 suggests itself, but the 1947 value of u_1 seems relatively easy to explain. Presumably 1947 was the first postwar year in which supply conditions made it possible for consumers to "let themselves go" on the purchase of durables.

(b) *Complete model.* The residuals analysed in the previous section were obtained by inserting observed values for a particular year of *all* variables on the right-hand side of each equation and subtracting the computed value of the variable being explained from its observed value. Such residuals are associated with a particular structural equation only, and may be designated as *partial* residuals (u_p). Suppose now that we insert observed values of the *predetermined* variables only, for the particular year, into the model. Then we can obtain a solution vector for the endogenous variables which, on subtraction from the corresponding observation vector, gives us a random variable or residual vector. We now have a residual for each of the four endogenous variables. It is evident that these new residuals are different from the partial residuals and are related to the model as a whole in simultaneous solution, rather than just to individual equations. Let us designate these new residuals as *total* residuals (u_s).

Let Y' be the vector of endogenous variables and Z' be the vector of predetermined variables in the model. Then the model with *estimated* structure can be designated as

(12) $$\hat{\beta}Y' + \hat{\Gamma}Z' + \hat{\epsilon}' = u'_p,$$

or as

(12a) $$BY' + CZ' + E' = u'_p.$$

In order to obtain forecasts from the model or to estimate the total residuals, it is necessary to solve for the endogenous variables in terms of the predetermined variables. This is known as converting the model to *reduced form* but it is a special kind of reduced form, in terms of the *estimated* structure.[8] Let us call this the *forecast reduced form* of the model. In symbols, the forecast reduced form becomes

$$(13) \qquad Y' = -B^{-1}CZ' - B^{-1}E' + B^{-1}u'_p \ .$$

It is evident from the above definitions and equation (13) that $B^{-1}u'_p = u'_s$. Thus we see the relationship between the partial residuals and the total residuals, and the identity between the forecast reduced form residuals and the total residuals.

Total residuals were calculated for the consumer behaviour model and the goodness of fit of the complete model studied from them. It was found that the total residuals followed the same general patterns as the partial residuals but tended to be larger. A table showing statistics associated with the variance of the total residuals of the model is now presented.

TABLE III

STATISTICS ASSOCIATED WITH VARIANCE OF TOTAL RESIDUALS OF
CONSUMER BEHAVIOUR MODEL

Endogenous Variable	$\bar{S}_s$	$\dfrac{\bar{S}_s}{\bar{Y}} \times 100^a$	$\dfrac{\delta^2}{S_s^2}$	$\left(1 - \dfrac{\bar{S}^2}{\sigma^2}\right) \times 100$
		%		%
C	0.104	*2.5*	2.8	*99.5*
Y_w	0.078	*2.6*	1.8	*99.6*
Y_π	0.095	*6.1*	2.6	*98.4*
$(Y + S_1)$	0.104	*1.8*	2.8	*99.8*

a In this context Y means the appropriate endogenous variable.

In this table we have variance statistics for each of the four endogenous variables, whereas in Table I such statistics were available for only two of the endogenous variables. The high relative variability of nonwage income is in conformity with general observations on the volatility of this type of income.

V. MULTIPLIERS

(a) *Short-run analysis.* The analysis has suggested that the shorter the time period within which we are working the smaller will be the marginal propensity to consume from increments to income within the time period, and the stronger will be the effects of previous consumption habits. As we lengthen the time period of the analysis from say one month to one year and then to several years we would expect the marginal propensity to consume to increase and the lag effects to decrease. Thus the shorter the time period the smaller the multiplier effects within

8 As distinct from the regression of each Y on all Z's.

that time period will be, and conversely the longer the time period the greater the multiplier effects.

In our consumer behaviour model presented above we can readily estimate the short-run, intra-year marginal propensity to consume and then various short-run, intra-year multipliers by treating all the lagged variables in the analysis as constants. In the model we let Gross National Product $(GNP) = Y_4$. Then $Y_4 = Y + S_1 = C + S_0 + S_1$. Let $GNE - C = E$. Then $E = S_0 + S_1$. (It should be recalled that both S_0 and S_1 are treated as exogenous in the present model.) Thus E can be treated as the total exogenous demand acting on our model economy, and then C is the total endogenous demand.

Let us assume now that we wish to study the short-run or intra-year effects of changes in exogenous demand on the model. In the short-run all changes in E must occur in S_0, since we assume that both T and D remain fixed.

Then $\Delta E = \Delta S_0$, $Y_4 = Y + S_1$, and $\Delta Y_4 = \Delta Y$. Thus $(dY_4/dE) = (dY/dS_0)$ and $(dC/dY_4) = (dC/dY)$.

$$(14) \qquad Y_4 = C + E; \qquad 1 = \frac{dC}{dY_4} + \frac{dE}{dY_4},$$

$$(15) \qquad \frac{dY_4}{dE} = \frac{1}{1 - \dfrac{dC}{dY_4}} = \frac{1}{1 - \dfrac{dC}{dY}}.$$

From equation (8) we have

$$(16) \qquad \frac{dC}{dY} = a_1 \frac{dY_w}{dY} + a_2 \frac{dY_\pi}{dY}.$$

From (10),

$$(17) \qquad 1 = \frac{dY_w}{dY} + \frac{dY_\pi}{dY}.$$

Hence

$$(18) \qquad \frac{dC}{dY} = (a_1 - a_2) \frac{dY_w}{dY} + a_2.$$

From (9a),

$$(19) \qquad \frac{dY_w}{dY} = b_1.$$

Hence

$$(20) \qquad \frac{dC}{dY} = b_1(a_1 - a_2) + a_2.$$

Thus in our consumer behaviour model the short-run marginal propensity to consume involves three parameters from two different equations.

The short-run multiplier effects of exogenous demand on the endogenous variables of the model can now be readily set out. From equation
(15) we have

$$(21) \qquad \frac{dY_4}{dE} = \frac{dY}{dE} \qquad = \frac{1}{1 - b_1(a_1 - a_2) - a_2}$$

$$(22) \qquad \frac{dC}{dE} = \frac{dC}{dY} \cdot \frac{dY}{dE} = \frac{b_1(a_1 - a_2) + a_2}{1 - b_1(a_1 - a_2) - a_2}$$

$$(23) \qquad \frac{dY_w}{dE} = \frac{dY_w}{dY} \cdot \frac{dY}{dE} = \frac{b_1}{1 - b_1(a_1 - a_2) - a_2}$$

$$(24) \qquad \frac{dY_\pi}{dE} = \frac{dY_\pi}{dY} \cdot \frac{dY}{dE} = \frac{1 - b_1}{1 - b_1(a_1 - a_2) - a_2}.$$

The short-run, intra-year marginal propensity to consume and multipliers are now tabulated in numerical form:

$$\frac{dC}{dY} = 0.3385,$$

$$\frac{dY_4}{dE} = \frac{dY}{dS_0} = 1.512, \qquad \frac{dC}{dE} = \frac{dC}{dS_0} = 0.5118;$$

(25)

$$\frac{dY_w}{dE} = 0.2605,$$

$$\frac{dY_\pi}{dE} = 1.251.$$

We expect these values to be low since they represent only the short-run,
as distinct from the total, effect of exogenous demand impulses.

In the above analysis we have dealt with the multiplier effects of a
change in S_0 only. However, in a forecast from a base year to the next
consecutive year changes will occur in all of the predetermined variables. It is useful to know the effect of the change in each predetermined
variable on each endogenous variable, and it turns out that it is very
easy to obtain the full array of such multipliers. Equation (13) above
may be rewritten as

$$(13a) \qquad\qquad Y' = P(1Z)' + u'_s,$$

where P is the matrix of the forecast reduced form parameters. The
multiplier effect of any Z on any Y in this system is given by $\partial Y_i/\partial Z_k$

$(i = 1, 2, 3, 4; k = 1, 2, \cdots , 6)$. It is evident that the matrix of all such multipliers is given by P, and we may symbolize this result by the equation:

(26)
$$\frac{\partial Y'}{\partial(1Z)} = P.$$

Thus the complete multiplier matrix is identical with the matrix of forecast reduced form parameters and this matrix is now presented:

	1	C_{-1}	A^c	$(Y + S_1)_{-1}$	$t/10$	S_1	S_0
C	1.521	0.3282	1.045	0.1082	0.1706	0.08420	0.5118
Y_w	0.6028	0.05655	0.1800	0.2401	0.3785	0.1868	0.2605
Y_π	0.9185	0.2717	0.8646	−0.1319	−0.2079	−0.1026	1.251
Y_4	1.521	0.3282	1.045	0.1082	0.1706	1.084	1.512

We would expect the multipliers in (25) above to appear in this overall multiplier matrix, and we find them in the last column.

(b) *Long-run analysis.* Consider the consumption function in the form

(27)
$$C = a_0 + a_1 Y + a_2 C_{-1} + a_3 A^c + u.$$

Allowing for only short-run effects, we have $dC/dY = a_1$. From the above computations (25) and the original equation (8) we may now write:

(27a) $C = 0.8962 + 0.3385Y + 0.2171C_{-1} + 0.6910A^c + u.$

Taking the lagged variable into the calculations and giving it full play, we are able to calculate the value of dC/dY at a stationary or equilibrium point [8, pp. 77–80]. It becomes $d\bar{C}/d\bar{Y} = a_1/1 - a_2$. Using the values in (27a) we get $d\bar{C}/d\bar{Y} = 0.4324$. Then the long-run multiplier is

$$\frac{d\bar{Y}_4}{dE} = \frac{1}{1 - \dfrac{d\bar{C}}{d\bar{Y}}} = 1.762,$$

where it is again assumed that S_1 is held constant. This value seems to be somewhat low and it is felt that this may be the result of leaving the shift variable effective in too many of the postwar years.

The long-run multiplier was also estimated directly through fitting equation form (27) with maximum-likelihood estimates in a small just identified model using the method in Haavelmo [6]. This gave:

(27b) $C = 0.9113 + 0.4048Y + 0.3157\ C_{-1} + 0.6835\ A^c + u,$

$Y = C + S_0.$

The residuals in this equation were random in time, and the coefficient of variation was 1.8 per cent. Computation of stationary values of the long-run marginal propensity to consume and the multiplier for this model gave:

$$\frac{d\bar{C}}{d\bar{Y}} = .5916 \quad \text{and} \quad \frac{d\bar{Y}}{dS_0} = 2.449.$$

VI. CONCLUSIONS

The present analysis may serve to point the way for further experimentation on some of the problems raised. For example, if estimates of the liquid asset holdings of households can be completed back to 1926, this variable should be used in the consumer demand equation to replace the shift variable. Failing this, more study should be directed to the problem of determining the correct years in which to make the shift variable active. For example, it may be possible to discover at least the years during which household holdings of liquid assets were higher than "normal" after adjustment for price changes and also for changes in either population or the volume of output.

It does seem possible to conclude that there is a definite lag or inertia to consumers' responses to current income changes. Two main theories have been raised in the attempt to reach the causes behind this inertia. One has followed the theories of Modigliani and Duesenberry, and explains the inertia in terms of consumers' memories of past heights or peaks of real income. The second theory followed the approach that past real consumption patterns and levels form consumer habits which persist long enough to slow down the effects of current income changes on current consumption. This theory assumes that the decline of the effect of past habits is continuous over time, rather than discontinuous as the Modigliani-Duesenberry hypothesis suggests. Thus the habits from any real consumption vector experienced die away continuously as the time period between it and the present increases. As each new real consumption vector occurs it becomes the most recent, and hence the strongest habit-forming experience; but it, itself, has been influenced by earlier consumption experience and habits. Any level of actual consumption then represents the cumulation of all past experience, and hence a single lag of only one time period seems to be all that is required.

A corollary of this latter theory is that the economist must consider the *time period* within which multiplier effects via the marginal propensity to consume are to be studied. The marginal propensity to consume and hence the multiplier effects should increase up to some long-run stationary value as the time period is lengthened.

The growing availability of quarterly data, although their use introduces problems of serial correlation and seasonality, may enable further testing of the above theories.

Ottawa, Canada

REFERENCES

[1] BRONFENBRENNER, JEAN AND HERMAN CHERNOFF, "Computational Methods Used in Limited Information Treatment of a Set of Linear Stochastic Difference Equations," Cowles Commission Discussion Paper: Statistics, No. 328, 21 pp.
[2] DOMINION BUREAU OF STATISTICS, "National Accounts, Income, and Expenditure, 1926–1950," Ottawa, Canada, December, 1951, 127 pp.
[3] DUESENBERRY, J. S., *Income, Saving and the Theory of Consumer Behavior*, Cambridge, Mass., Harvard University Press, 1949, 128 pp.
[4] FISHER, R. A., *Statistical Methods for Research Workers*, Ninth ed., Edinburgh and London: Oliver and Boyd, 1944, 239 pp.
[5] GIRSHICK, M. A., AND TRYGVE HAAVELMO, "Statistical Analysis of the Demand for Food: Examples of Simultaneous Estimation of Structural Equations," ECONOMETRICA, Vol. 15, April, 1947, pp. 79–110.
[6] HAAVELMO, TRYGVE, "Methods of Measuring the Marginal Propensity to Consume," *Journal of the American Statistical Association*, Vol. 42, March, 1947, pp. 105–122.
[7] HART, B. I. AND J. VON NEUMANN, "Tabulation of the Probabilities for the Ratio of the Mean Square Successive Difference to the Variance," *Annals of Mathematical Statistics*, Vol. 13, June, 1942, pp. 207–214.
[8] KLEIN, LAWRENCE R., *Economic Fluctuations in the United States, 1921–1941*, Cowles Commission Monograph No. 11, New York: John Wiley and Sons, 1950, 174 pp.
[9] KOOPMANS, TJALLING C., ed., *Statistical Inference in Dynamic Economic Models*, Cowles Commission Monograph No. 10, New York: John Wiley and Sons, 1950, 438 pp.
[10] MODIGLIANI, FRANCO, *Fluctuations in the Saving-Income Ratio: A Problem in Economic Forecasting*, Studies in Income and Wealth (Conference on Research in Income and Wealth). Vol. 11. New York: National Bureau of Economic Research, 1949, pp. 371–438.
[11] PREST, A. R., "Some Experiments in Demand Analysis," *The Review of Economics and Statistics*, Vol. 31, February, 1949, pp. 33–49.

Econometrica, Vol. 25, 1 (January 1957)

A GENERALIZED CLASSICAL METHOD OF LINEAR ESTIMATION OF COEFFICIENTS IN A STRUCTURAL EQUATION[1]

By R. L. Basmann[2]

The classical method of least-squares estimation of the coefficients α in the (matrix) equation $y = Z\alpha + e$ yields estimators $\hat{\alpha} = Ay = \alpha + Ae$. This method, however, employs only one of a class of transformation matrices, A, which yield this result; namely, the special case where $A = (Z'Z)^{-1}Z'$. As is well known, the consistency of the estimators, $\hat{\alpha}$, requires that all of the variables whose sample values are represented as elements of the matrix Z be asymptotically uncorrelated with the error terms, e. In recent years some rather elaborate methods of obtaining consistent and otherwise optimal estimators of the coefficients α have been developed. In this paper we present a straightforward generalization of classical linear estimation which leads to estimates of α which possess optimal properties equivalent to those of existing limited-information single-equation estimators, and which is pedagogically simpler and less expensive to apply.[3]

LET IT BE required to estimate the coefficients α_1 in the equation

$$(1) \qquad\qquad y_1 = Z\alpha_1 + e,$$

where

$$y_1 = \text{col. } (y_{11}, y_{21}, \cdots, y_{N1}),$$

$$Z = [z_{th}], \qquad\qquad t = 1, 2, \cdots, N; \qquad h = 1, 2, \cdots, n;$$

$$\alpha_1 = \text{col. } (\alpha_{11}, \alpha_{12}, \cdots, \alpha_{1n}),$$

$$-\infty < \alpha_{1i} < \infty,$$

$$e_1 = \text{col. } (e_{11}, e_{21}, \cdots, e_{N1}).$$

The elements of y_1 and Z denote sample values of continuous real variables which have first been divided by the square-root of the number, N, of observa-

[1] Journal Paper No. J-2844 of the Iowa Agricultural Experiment Station, Ames, Iowa. Project No. 1200.

[2] The author is indebted to Professors Gerhard Tintner, Herman Wold, and Trygve Haavelmo, to Mr. Leif Johansen and Mr. Arthur Goldberger for their advice and criticisms. Responsibility for any errors found in this article belongs to the author alone.

[3] After submitting this article for publication, the author discovered Professor H. Theil's earlier mimeographed essay, *Estimation and Simultaneous Correlation in Complete Equation Systems*, The Hague: Centraal Planbureau, 1953. The present author's generalization of classical linear estimation leads to estimators precisely equivalent to Professor Theil's "raw second round" estimators, one of several types discussed by him. Professor Theil's methods are to be discussed in Klein's forthcoming article, "On the Interpretation of Theil's Method of Estimating Economic Relationships," in *Metroeconomica*, Vol. 8, 1956. Also cf. R. Radner and F. Bobkoski, "Some Recent Work of H. Theil on Estimation in Systems of Simultaneous Equations," (mimeographed) Cowles Commission Discussion Paper. Stat. No. 385. May 28, 1954, 10 pp.

tions in the sample, and the elements of e_1 denote random errors in the equation. We assume that

$$(2) \qquad \sum_{t=1}^{N} z_{\text{th}}^2 > 0, \qquad \text{as } N \to \infty \qquad \text{for all } h.$$

The errors in the equation, e_1, are presumed to have the following properties:

$$(3a) \qquad E(e_1) = 0,$$

$$(3b) \qquad E(e_1 e_1') = I_N \omega_{11}/N < \infty,$$

where ω_{11} = constant denotes the variance of the errors, (say) e_1'', which have been divided by $\sqrt{N}$ to form e_1 ;

$$(3c) \qquad E\,(e_{s1} e_{t1}) = 0 \qquad \text{for all } s \neq t.$$

We construct estimators, $\hat{\alpha}_1$, of α_1, linear in the elements of y_1 and e_1 as follows: let

$$(4) \qquad \hat{\alpha}_1 = A y_1 = \alpha_1 + A e_1 ,$$

A thus being an n-row, N-column matrix such that

$$(5) \qquad AZ = I_n .$$

Let C denote an N-row, N-column matrix such that

$$(6) \qquad C'C = C' = C,$$

i.e., the matrix C is idempotent.[4] Then, using C, we construct

$$(7) \qquad A = [(CZ)'(CZ)]^{-1}(CZ)'.$$

It is easy to see that from (6) it follows that

$$(8) \qquad (CZ)'(CZ) = (CZ)'Z,$$

a matrix which we shall hereafter denote by S, and thus

$$(9) \qquad AZ = S^{-1}(CZ)'Z = I_n$$

as required by (5). Using the matrix A defined by (7), we obtain from (4) the linear estimators

$$(10) \qquad \hat{\alpha}_1 = [(CZ)'(CZ)]^{-1}(CZ)'y_1$$
$$= S^{-1}(CZ)'y_1$$
$$= \alpha_1 + S^{-1}(CZ)'e_1 .$$

[4] A. C. Aitken, *Determinants and Matrices*, London: Oliver and Boyd, 1949, p. 97.

The problem of finding *consistent* estimators of α_1 involves the construction of the idempotent matrix C such that

(11) $$\text{Plim } S^{-1}(CZ)'e_1 = [\text{Plim } S^{-1}][\text{Plim } (CZ)'e_1] = 0$$

where Plim $S^{-1} \neq 0$ and is finite; that is, such that

(12) $$\text{Plim } (CZ)'e_1 = 0.$$

The particular construction adopted as the matrix C depends on the assumed presence or non-presence of correlation between the variables (column vectors) of Z and the errors, e_1.

In the special classical case (Gauss-Markoff)[5] it is assumed that

(13) $$E(z_{tj}e_{t1}) = 0 \qquad \text{for all } j = 1, 2, \cdots, n.$$

From this assumption it clearly follows that

(14) $$E(Z'e_1) = 0;$$

and from (2), (3b), and (3c)

(15) $$E(Z'e_1)(Z'e_1)' = (Z'Z)I_N\omega_{11}/N \to 0 \text{ as } N \to \infty.$$

Consequently,[6]

(16) $$\text{Plim } (Z'e_1) = 0.$$

Thus the special idempotent matrix $C = Z(Z'Z)^{-1}Z'$, or its equivalent $C = I_N$, meets all the requirements for the construction of the matrix C. Letting $C = I_N$, we obtain from (10) the *consistent* linear estimators

(17) $$\hat{\alpha}_1 = \alpha_1 + (Z'Z)^{-1}Z'e_1$$

which we recognize as classical least-squares estimators. In addition to being *consistent*, the estimators (17) are "best" linear *unbiased*.[7]

If equation (1) is interpreted as one equation of a system of simultaneous structural equations,[8] the matrix Z represents the sample values of endogenous (except, of course, for y_1) and exogenous variables actually present in the equation. Let there be m endogenous variables and p exogenous variables present in equation (1), where

$$n = m + p - 1.$$

[5] Cf. H. Wold and L. Juréen, *Demand Analysis*, New York; John Wiley, 1953, pp. 208–209, and O. Kempthorne, *Design and Analysis of Experiments*, New York: John Wiley, 1952, Appendix, Ch. 5.

[6] S. S. Wilks, *Mathematical Statistics*, Princeton: Princeton University Press, 1950, pp. 133–134.

[7] Cf. H. Wold and L. Juréen, *op. cit.*, p. 208.

[8] Cf. G. Tintner, *Econometrics*, New York: John Wiley, 1952, pp. 155 ff.

Partition[9] the matrix Z according to the endogenous-exogenous classification of the variables.

$$(18) \qquad Z = [Y_1 : X_1]$$

where

$$Y_1 = [y_{th}], \qquad\qquad h = 2, 3, \cdots, m;$$

$$X_1 = [x_{tk}], \qquad\qquad k = 1, 2, \cdots, p.$$

Partition the vector α_1 conformably to the partition of Z:

$$(19) \qquad \alpha_1 = \text{col. } (\beta_1 : \gamma_1).$$

In terms of the new notation, equation (1) is expressed as

$$(20) \qquad y_1 = Y_1\beta_1 + X_1\gamma_1 + e_1 .$$

Included in the system of structural equations, but not in the equation (20) to be estimated, let there be $q - p$ additional *exogenous* variables with sample values denoted by

$$(21) \qquad X_2 = [x_{tj}], \qquad j = p + 1, p + 2, \cdots, q,$$

where

$$(22) \qquad q - p \geqslant m - 1.$$

The relation (22) expresses a *necessary* condition for identification of equation (20).[10]

Assume

$$(23) \qquad y_{ti} = \sum_{k=1}^{q} x_{tk}\pi_{ik} + \eta_{ti} = \mu_{ti} + \eta_{ti}, \qquad i = 1, 2, \cdots, m,$$

$$-\infty < \pi_{ik} < \infty,$$

where

$$(24) \qquad E(\eta_{ti}) = 0;$$

$$(25) \qquad E(x_{tk}\eta_{ti}) = 0, \qquad\qquad \text{for all } i, k;$$

$$(26) \qquad E(\eta_{ti}^2\eta_{tj}^2) < \infty, \qquad\qquad i, j = 1, 2, \cdots, m;$$

$$(27) \qquad E(\eta_{ti}\eta_{tj}) = \sigma_{ij}/N.$$

The relation (26) implies

$$(28) \qquad \sigma_{ij} \text{ is finite;}$$

[9] Cf. A. C. Aitken, *op. cit.*, pp. 21–25.
[10] Cf. G. Tintner, *op. cit.*, pp. 155–157. Let there be g equations. Then (22) implies that at least $g - 1$ endogenous and exogenous variables are excluded from (20).

(29) $$E[(\sum_t y_{ti} y_{tj})^2] \to 0 \text{ as } N \to \infty$$

The relation (29) and the relation (2) imply that

(30) $$\text{Plim} \sum_t y_{ti} y_{tj} = \sigma_{ij} + \text{Plim} \sum_t \mu_{ti} \mu_{tj}$$

is finite and, in general, non-zero.

Taking advantage of the non-correlation property (25) and the stochastic convergence (30), we can construct out of the sample observations on only the exogenous variables the matrix C which satisfies (6), (11), and (12); that is, which yields through (10) consistent linear estimators of the coefficients α. On grounds of efficiency we use all the exogenous variables in the construction of C. Let

(31) $$C = X(X'X)^{-1}X',$$

where

$$X = [X_1 : X_2].$$

It is easy to verify that the matrix C as defined by (31) is idempotent as required by (6). Let

(32) $$Y_1^* = CY_1 = X(X'X)^{-1}X'Y_1 .$$

Then

(33) $$CZ = X(X'X)^{-1}X'[Y_1 : X_1] = [Y_1^* : X_1];$$

and, according to (8),

(34) $$S = \begin{bmatrix} Y_1^{*'} Y_1^* & Y_1^{*'} X_1 \\ \hline X_1' Y_1^* & X_1' X_1 \end{bmatrix}.$$

Since the matrix C is idempotent, the equations (9) and (10) are satisfied, and we have from the latter

(35) $$\hat{\alpha}_1 = \begin{bmatrix} \hat{\beta}_1 \\ \hat{\gamma}_1 \end{bmatrix} = \begin{bmatrix} \beta_1 + M_{11}^{-1}[Y_1^{*'} e_1 - Y_1^{*'} X_1 (X_1' X_1)^{-1}(X_1' e_1)] \\ \gamma_1 + M_{22}^{-1}[X_1' e_1 - X_1' Y_1^* (Y_1^{*'} Y_1^*)^{-1}(X'_1 e_1)] \end{bmatrix},$$

where

$$M_{11} = Y_1^{*'} Y_1^* - Y_1^{*'} X_1 (X_1' X_1)^{-1} X_1' Y_1^* ,$$

$$M_{22} = X_1' X_1 - X_1' Y_1^* (Y_1^{*'} Y_1^*)^{-1} Y_1^{*'} X_1 .$$

By the stochastic convergence (30) the elements of the matrix S defined by (34) and the elements of the matrix

(36) $$(CZ)' e_1 = [Y_1^* : X_1]' e_1$$

have finite expectations, and their variances converge to zero as $N \to \infty$. The same is true of the elements of the matrices M_{11} and M_{22} which appear in the inverse matrix S^{-1}. By a theorem due to Slutsky[11, 12]

$$(37) \qquad \text{Plim } S^{-1}(Y_1^*:X_1)'e_1 = [\text{Plim } S]^{-1} \text{Plim } (Y_1^*:X_1)'e_1$$

which shows that the first relation of equation (11) is satisfied by the construction of C according to (31). By the same theorem we have

$$(38) \qquad \text{Plim } X_1'e_1 = 0,$$

and

$$(39) \qquad \text{Plim } Y_1^{*'}e_1 = [\text{Plim } Y_1'X(X'X)^{-1}][\text{Plim } X'e_1] = 0.$$

Thus, the construction (31) also satisfies the requirement (12). It follows that

$$(40) \qquad \text{Plim } \hat{\alpha}_1 = \alpha_1$$

where the estimators $\hat{\alpha}_1$ are defined by (35).

Furthermore, by the same considerations, we have for the limiting variances and covariances of the estimators (45)

$$(41) \qquad \text{Plim } N(\hat{\alpha}_1 - \alpha_1)(\hat{\alpha}_1 - \alpha_1)' = \text{Plim } [S^{-1}(CZ)'(Ne_1e_1')(CZ)S^{-1}]$$

$$(42) \qquad = \omega_{11} \text{Plim } S^{-1}.$$

It should be clear from (42) how consistent estimators of the variances and covariances of $\hat{\alpha}_1$ are constructed.

Let $\alpha_1^* = By_1 = \alpha_1 + Be_1$ denote linear estimators of α_1 such that $BZ = I_n$ and there hold sufficient[13] conditions for the consistency of α_1^*. For instance, choose B such that the rows of $B - S^{-1}(CZ)'$ are orthogonal to any $m + p - 1$ columns of X. Then

$$(43) \quad \text{Plim } N(\alpha_1^* - \alpha_1)(\alpha_1^* - \alpha_1)' = \text{Plim } B(Ne_1e_1')B'$$

$$= \omega_{11} \text{Plim } [S^{-1} + \{B - S^{-1}(CZ)'\}$$

$$\{B - S^{-1}(CZ)'\}']$$

$$> \text{Plim } N(\hat{\alpha}_1 - \alpha_1)(\hat{\alpha}_1 - \alpha_1)'.$$

We interpret the relation (43) as follows: The estimators $\hat{\alpha}_1$ defined by (35) are "best" linear consistent estimators of α_1 in equation (20).

The method of estimation proposed here is thus a simple, straightforward generalization of the classical method of least-squares. If one replaces Y_1 in equation (20) by Y_1^* defined by (32), the estimators (35) are easily obtained

[11] Cf. E. Slutsky, "Über stochastische Asymptoten und Grenzwerte," *Metron*, Vol. 5, 1925, pp. 3–89, esp. p. 78.

[12] Cf. H. Cramér, *Mathematical Methods of Statistics*, Uppsala: Almquist and Wiksells, 1945, pp. 254–255.

[13] Cf. S. S. Wilks, *op. cit.*, pp. 133–134.

by applying the method of least-squares directly to the transformed equation.[14] Large-sample estimates of the variance-covariance matrix elements are obtained in exactly the same way as the corresponding estimates are obtained by least-squares computations.

The estimators (35) have precisely the same asymptotic variances as single-equation estimators obtained by application of the *least-variance ratio principle*.[15] The latter are obtained by choosing those magnitudes of $\tilde{\beta}_1$ and

$$(44) \qquad \tilde{\gamma}_1 = (X_1'X_1)^{-1}X_1'(y_1 - Y_1\tilde{\beta}_1)$$

for which the ratio

$$(45) \qquad l = \frac{G_1(\tilde{\beta}_1) - G_2(\tilde{\beta}_1)}{G_2(\tilde{\beta}_1)}$$

is a minimum, where

$$(46) \qquad G_1(\tilde{\beta}_1) = (y_1 - Y_1\tilde{\beta}_1)'[I_N - X_1(X_1'X_1)^{-1}X_1'](y_1 - Y_1\tilde{\beta}_1)$$

$$(47) \quad G_2(\tilde{\beta}_1) = (y_1 - Y_1\tilde{\beta}_1)'[I_N - X(X'X)^{-1}X'](y_1 - Y_1\tilde{\beta}_1) \leqslant G_1(\tilde{\beta}_1).$$

Let l_1 denote this minimum ratio.

The limiting variance-covariance matrix of the estimators $\tilde{\beta}_1$ is given by

$$(48) \qquad \text{Plim} \left[{}_{11}R_{\Delta\Delta} - \frac{l_1}{G_2(\tilde{\beta}_1)} \, {}_{11}\{(\overline{W}_{\Delta\Delta}\dot{b}_\Delta)(\overline{W}_{\Delta\Delta}b_\Delta)'\} \right]^{-1} \omega_{11}$$

in terms of the Chernoff-Divinsky notation.[16] We are concerned here only with the matrix ${}_{11}R_{\Delta\Delta}$ which is, in terms of our notation, M_{11} defined in connection with (35). By the Slutsky theorem alluded to above,

$$(49) \qquad \text{Plim } G_1(\tilde{\beta}_1) = \text{Plim } G_2(\tilde{\beta}_1).$$

By (45), the limiting variance-covariance matrix (48) reduces to

$$(50) \qquad \text{Plim } N(\tilde{\beta}_1 - \beta_1)(\tilde{\beta}_1 - \beta_1)' = \omega_{11} \text{ Plim } M_{11}^{-1}.$$

Consequently, by (44)

$$(51) \qquad \text{Plim } N(\tilde{\alpha}_1 - \alpha_1)(\tilde{\alpha}_1 - \alpha_1)' = \omega_{11} \text{ Plim } S^{-1}$$

$$= \text{Plim } N(\hat{\alpha}_1 - \alpha_1)(\hat{\alpha}_1 - \alpha_1)'.$$

Northwestern University

[14] Cf. H. Theil, *op. cit.*, pp. 15 ff.

[15] Cf. T. W. Anderson and H. Rubin, "Estimation of the Parameters of a Single Equation in a Complete System of Stochastic Equations," *Annals of Mathematical Statistics*, Vol. 20, 1949, pp. 46–63, and ———, "Asymptotic Properties of Estimators of Parameters in a Complete System of Stochastic Equations," *loc. cit.*, Vol. 21, 1950, pp. 570–582.

[16] H. Chernoff and N. Divinsky, "The Computation of Maximum-likelihood Estimates of Linear Structural Equations," in W. C. Hood and T. C. Koopmans, *Studies in Econometric Method*, New York: John Wiley, 1953, pp. 242–245.

Econometrica, Vol. 25, 4 (October 1957)

HYBRID CORN: AN EXPLORATION IN THE ECONOMICS OF TECHNOLOGICAL CHANGE [1]

By Zvi Griliches

This is a study of factors responsible for the wide cross-sectional differences in the past and current rates of use of hybrid seed corn in the United States.

Logistic growth functions are fitted to the data by states and crop reporting districts, reducing differences among areas to differences in estimates of the three parameters of the logistic: *origins*, *slopes*, and *ceilings*.

The lag in the development of adaptable hybrids for particular areas and the lag in the entry of seed producers into these areas (differences in *origins*) are explained on the basis of varying profitability of entry, "profitability" being a function of market density, and innovation and marketing cost.

Differences in the long-run equilibrium use of hybrid corn (*ceilings*) and in the rates of approach to that equilibrium (*slopes*) are explained, at least in part, by differences in the profitability of the shift from open pollinated to hybrid varieties in different parts of the country.

The results are summarized and the conclusion is drawn that the process of innovation, the process of adapting and distributing a particular invention to different markets and the rate at which it is accepted by entrepreneurs are amenable to economic analysis.

1. INTRODUCTION

THE WORK presented in this paper is an attempt to understand a body of data: the percentage of all corn acreage planted with hybrid seed, by states and by years. By concentrating on a single, major, well defined, and reasonably well recorded development—hybrid corn—we may hope to learn something about the ways in which technological change is generated and propagated in U. S. agriculture.

The idea of hybrid corn dates back to the beginning of this century and its first application on a substantial commercial scale to the early thirties. Since

[1] This research was begun during my tenure as a Research Training Fellow of the Social Science Research Council. It has been supported by the Office of Agricultural Economics Research at the University of Chicago and is being supported by a generous grant from the National Science Foundation. I am indebted to Professor T. W. Schultz for arousing my interest in this problem and for encouraging me in my work, to Professors H. G. Lewis and A. C. Harberger for their valuable advice and guidance, and to the members of the Public Finance Workshop and other members of the Department of Economics at the University of Chicago, both faculty and students, for their suggestions and criticisms. I owe to the generosity of the Field Crop Statistics Branch of the Agricultural Marketing Service a large part of the unpublished data used in this paper. I also want to acknowledge and thank the people directly connected with hybrid corn, both in the Agricultural Experiment Stations and in the private seed companies, for their complete cooperation. This article is based on my unpublished Ph.D. dissertation, "Hybrid Corn: An Exploration in Economics of Technological Change," on file at the University of Chicago Library.

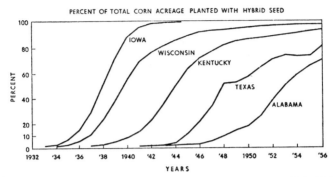

FIGURE 1.—Percentage of Total Corn Acreage Planted with Hybrid Seed.
Source: U.S.D.A., *Agricultural Statistics*, various years.

then it has spread rapidly throughout the Corn Belt and the rest of the nation.[2]
There have been, however, marked geographic differences in this development
(see Figure 1). Hybrid corn was the invention of a method of inventing, a method
of breeding superior corn for specific localities.[3] It was not a single invention
immediately adaptable everywhere. The actual breeding of adaptable hybrids
had to be done separately for each area. Hence, besides the differences in the
rate of adoption of hybrids by farmers—the "acceptance" problem—we have
also to explain the lag in the development of adaptable hybrids for specific
areas—the "availability" problem.

In the following sections I shall first outline a method used to summarize the
data. Essentially it will consist of fitting trend functions (the logistic) to the
data, reducing thereby the differences among areas to differences in the values

[2] A popular history of hybrid corn can be found in A. R. Crabb, *The Hybrid Corn Makers:
Prophets of Plenty*, Rutgers University Press, 1948. See also F. D. Richey, "The Lay of the
Corn Huckster," *Journal of Heredity*, 39(1), 1946, 10–17; P. C. Mangelsdorf, "The History
of Hybrid Corn," *loc. cit.*, 39, 1948, 177–180; G. F. Sprague, "The Experimental Basis for
Hybrid Maize," *Biological Reviews*, 21, 1946, 101–120; M. T. Jenkins, "Corn Improve-
ment," *U. S. Department of Agriculture Yearbook*, 1936, 455–522; and H. A. Wallace and
W. L. Brown, *Corn and Its Early Fathers*, Michigan State University Press, 1956.

[3] "Hybrid corn is the product of a controlled, systematic crossing of specially selected
parental strains called 'inbred lines.' These inbred lines are developed by inbreeding,
or self-pollinating, for a period of four or more years. Accompanying inbreeding is a rigid
selection for the elimination of those inbreds carrying poor heredity, and which, for one
reason or another, fail to meet the established standards." "[The inbred lines] are of little
value in themselves for they are inferior to open-pollinated varieties in vigor and yield.
When two unrelated inbred lines are crossed, however, the vigor is restored. *Some* of these
hybrids prove to be markedly superior to the original varieties. The development of hybrid
corn, therefore, is a complicated process of continued self-pollination accompanied by selection of the most vigorous and otherwise desirable plants. These superior lines are then used
in making hybrids." First quote is from N. P. Neal and A. M. Strommen, "Wisconsin Corn
Hybrids," Wisconsin Agricultural Experiment Station, Bulletin 476, February, 1948, p. 4;
and the second quote is from R. W. Jugenheimer, "Hybrid Corn in Kansas," Kansas Agricultural Experiment Station, Circular 196, February, 1939, pp. 3–4. See also the references
in the previous footnotes.

of a few parameters. Then I will present a model rationalizing these differences and illustrate it with computational results. Finally, I shall draw some conclusions on the basis of these results and other accumulated information.

2. THE METHOD AND THE MODEL

A graphical survey of the data by states and crop reporting districts along the lines of Figure 1 led to the conclusion that nothing would be gained by trying to explain each observation separately, as if it had no antecedent.[4] It became obvious that the observations are not points of equilibrium which may or may not change over time, but points on an adjustment path, moving more or less consistently towards a new equilibrium position. Hence we should phrase our questions in terms of the beginning of the movement, its rate, and its destination. This led to the decision to fit some simple trend functions to the data and concentrate on the explanation of the cross-sectional differences in the estimates of their parameters.

The choice of a particular algebraic form for the trend function is somewhat arbitrary. As the data are markedly S-shaped, several simple S-shaped functions were considered. The cumulative normal and the logistic are used most widely for such purposes. As there is almost no difference between the two over the usual range of data,[5] the logistic was chosen because it is simpler to fit and in our context easier to interpret. While there are some good reasons why an adjustment process should follow a path which is akin to the logistic, I do not want to argue the relative merits of the various S-curves.[6] In this work the growth curves serve as a summary device, perhaps somewhat more sophisticated than a simple average, but which should be treated in the same spirit.

---

[4] This conclusion was also supported by the results of an attempt to fit a model in which the year-to-year changes in the percentage planted to hybrid seed were to be explained by year-to-year changes in the price of corn, price of hybrid seed, the superiority of hybrids in the previous year or two, etc. The trend in the data was so strong that, within the framework of this particular model, it left nothing of significance for the "economic" variables to explain.

[5] For a comparison, see C. P. Winsor, "A Comparison of Certain Symmetrical Growth Curves," *Journal of the Washington Academy of Sciences*, 22, 1932, 73–84, and J. Aitchison and J. A. C. Brown, *The Lognormal Distribution*, Cambridge University Press, 1957, pp. 72–75.

[6] It may be worthwhile to indicate why it is reasonable that the development should have followed an S-shaped growth curve. The dependent variable can vary only between 0 and 100 per cent. If we consider the development to be an adjustment process, the simplest reasonable time-path between 0 and 100 per cent is an ogive. While the supply of seed can increase exponentially, the market for seed is limited by the total amount of corn planted, and that will act as a damping factor. Also, if we interpret the behavior of farmers in the face of this new, uncertain development as if they were engaged in sequential decision making, the ASN curve will be bell-shaped, and the cumulative will again be S-shaped. See also H. Hotelling, "Edgeworth's Taxation Paradox and the Nature of Demand and Supply Curves," *Journal of Political Economy*, 40, October, 1932. The argument for the logistic is given by R. Pearl, *Studies in Human Biology*, Baltimore, 1924, 558–583, and S. Kuznets, *Secular Movements in Production and Prices*, Houghton Mifflin, Boston, 1930, 59–69.

The logistic growth curve is defined by $P = K/1 + e^{-(a+bt)}$, where P is the percentage planted with hybrid seed, K the ceiling or equilibrium value, t the time variable, b the rate of growth coefficient, and a the constant of integration which positions the curve on the time scale. Several features of this curve are of interest: It is asymptotic to 0 and K, symmetric around the inflection point, and the first derivative with respect to time is given by $dP/dt = -b \, (P/K) (K - P)$.[7] The rate of growth is proportional to the growth already achieved and to the distance from the ceiling. It is this last property that makes the logistic useful in so many diverse fields.[8]

There are several methods of estimating the parameters of the logistic.[9] The method chosen involves the transformation of the logistic into an equation linear in a and b. By dividing both sides of the logistic by $K - P$ and taking the logarithm, we get its linear transform, $\log_e [P/(K-P)] = a + bt$, allowing us to estimate the parameters directly by least squares.[10] The value of K, the ceiling, was estimated crudely by plotting the percentage planted to hybrid seed on logistic graph paper and varying K until the resulting graph approximated a straight line. After adjusting for differences in K, the logistic was fitted to the data covering approximately the transition from 5 to 95 per cent of the ceiling. The observations below 5 and above 95 per cent of the ceiling value were discarded because they are liable to very large percentage errors and would have had very little weight anyway in any reasonable weighting scheme. The period included in the analysis, however, accounts for the bulk of the changes in the data.

The procedure outlined above was used to calculate the parameters of the

[7] For a more detailed description of the logistic and its properties, see Pearl, *op. cit.*

[8] Perhaps the simplest interpretation of the logistic is given by A. Lotka, *Elements of Physical Biology*, Williams and Wilkins, Baltimore, 1925, p. 65. We are interested in the general adjustment function, $dP/dt = F(P)$. Using a Taylor Series approximation and disregarding all the higher terms beyond the quadratic we get a function whose integral is the logistic. The logistic is the integral of the quadratic approximation to the adjustment function.

[9] See Pearl, *op. cit.*; H. T. Davis, *The Theory of Econometrics*, Principia Press, 1941, Chapter II; and G. Tintner, *Econometrics*, John Wiley & Sons, 1952, 208–211, and the literature cited there.

[10] This is a simplification of a method proposed by Joseph Berkson. Berkson's method is equivalent to weighted least squares regression of the same transform with $P(K - P)$ as weights. J. Berkson, "A Statistically Precise and Relatively Simple Method of Estimating the Bioassay with Quantal Response, Based on the Logistic Function," *Journal of the American Statistical Association*, 48 (1953), 565–599, and "Maximum Likelihood and Minimum Chi-square Estimates of the Logistic Function," *loc. cit.*, 50 (1955), 130–162. Berkson proposed this procedure in the context of bio-assay. It is not clear, however, whether the bio-assay model is applicable in our context, nor is it obvious, even in bio-assay, what system of weights is optional. See also J. Berkson, "Estimation by Least Squares and by Maximum Likelihood," *Proceedings of the Third Berkeley Symposium on Mathematical Statistics*, Vol. I, University of California Press, 1–11. Hence no weights were used. In view of the excellent fits obtained, it is doubtful whether alternative weighting systems would have made much difference.

logistic for 31 states and for 132 crop reporting districts within these states.[11] The states used account for almost all of the corn grown in the U.S. (all states except the West and New England). Out of a total of 249 crop reporting districts only those were used for which other data by crop reporting districts were readily available. Districts with negligible amounts of corn and unreliable estimates of hybrid corn acreage were also left out.[12]

The results of these calculations are presented in Tables I and II. Table I summarizes the state results, Table II the results by crop reporting districts. Time is measured from 1940, and $(-2.2-a)/b$ indicates the date at which the function passed through the 10 per cent value. This date will be identified below with the date of *origin* of the development. Several things are noteworthy about these figures: the high r^2's indicate the excellent fits obtained.[13] The b's, representing the slope of the transform or the rate of adjustment, are rather uniform, becoming lower as we move towards the fringes of the Corn Belt. The values of $(-2.2-a)/b$, the dates of *origin*, indicate that the development started in the heart of the Corn Belt and spread, rather regularly, towards its fringes.[14] The ceiling—K—also declines as we move away from the Corn Belt.

In this section we have succeeded in reducing a large mass of data to three sets of variables—*origins*, *slopes*, and *ceilings*. "Thus on the basis of three numbers we are prepared, in principle, to answer all the questions the original data sheet can answer provided that the questions do not get down to the level of a single cell . . . . . This is saying a great deal."[15]

The economic interpretation of the differences in the estimated coefficients will be developed in the following sections. The values of the different parameters are not necessarily independent of each other, but for simplicity will be considered separately. Variations in the date of origin will be identified with supply factors, variations in slopes with factors affecting the rate of acceptance

[11] Each state is usually divided into nine crop reporting districts numbered in the following fashion:

$$
\begin{array}{c}
\text{N} \\
1 \quad 2 \quad 3 \\
\text{W} \quad 4 \quad 5 \quad 6 \quad \text{E} \\
7 \quad 8 \quad 9 \\
\text{S}
\end{array}
$$

[12] It should be noted that the sum of logistics is not usually a logistic. However, the logistic is also valid for an aggregate, as long as the components are similar in their development. See L. J. Reed and R. Pearl, "On the Summation of Logistic Curves," *Journal of the Royal Statistical Society*, 90 (New Series), 1927, 729–746. How good the approximation is in fact is indicated by the results below.

[13] These r^2's should be taken with a grain of salt. They are the r^2's of the transform rather than of the original function and give less weight to the deviations in the center. Also, they do not take into account the excluded extreme values. Nevertheless, an examination of the original data indicates that they are not a figment of the fitting procedure.

[14] *Origin* is measured from 1940. Hence, the *origin* in Iowa is placed approximately in 1936, and in Georgia in 1948.

[15] R. R. Bush and F. Mosteller, *Stochastic Models for Learning*, John Wiley and Sons, New York, 1955, p. 335.

TABLE I
Hybrid Corn Logistic Trend Functions by States

States	Origin $\frac{-2.2-a}{b}$	Rate of acceptance b	Ceiling K	r^2
N.Y.	−.89	.36	.95	.99
N.J.	−1.48	.54	.98	.90
Pa.	−1.29	.48	.95	.98
Ohio	−3.35	.69	1.00	.97
Ind.	−3.13	.91	1.00	.99
Ill.	−4.46	.79	1.00	.99
Mich.	−1.44	.68	.90	.98
Wisc.	−3.52	.69	.91	.99
Minn.	−3.06	.79	.94	.99
Iowa	−4.34	1.02	1.00	.99
Mo.	−3.32	.57	.98	.98
N.D.	−.65	.43	.65	.96
S.D.	−.40	.42	.85	.95
Neb.	−.60	.62	.97	.99
Kan.	.42	.45	.94	.97
Del.	.21	.47	.99	.98
Md.	−.73	.55	.98	.97
Va.	1.60	.50	.92	.97
W. Va.	−.23	.39	.85	.98
N.C.	5.14	.35	.80	.89
S.C.	5.72	.43	.60	.96
Ga.	7.92	.50	.80	.99
Fla.	2.89	.38	.90	.93
Ky.	.08	.59	.90	.99
Tenn.	2.65	.34	.80	.97
Ala.	7.84	.51	.80	.99
Miss.	4.75	.36	.60	.98
Ark.	1.46	.41	.78	.99
La.	4.89	.45	.53	.99
Okla.	3.57	.56	.80	.98
Tex.	3.64	.55	.78	.98

Notes: $P = \frac{K}{1+e^{-(a+bt)}}$; $\log_e\left(\frac{P}{K-P}\right) = a + bt$; $t_{1940} = 0$; $N = -6$ to 16; Max $S_b = .06$; Origin = Date of 10 per cent $= \frac{-2.2-a}{b}$, measured from 1940, e.g., $-4.0 = 1936, +7.0 = 1947$; Rate of acceptance = Slope = b; and Ceiling = K

by farmers, and variations in ceilings with demand factors affecting the long-run equilibrium position. In each case we shall consider briefly the implicit identification problem.

3. THE SUPPLY OF A NEW TECHNIQUE

There is no unique way of defining the data of *origin* or of "availability." Hybrid corn was not a single development. Various experimental hybrids were tried until superior hybrids emerged. After a while, these were again superseded by newer hybrids. Nor is there a unique way of defining *origin* with respect to growth curve. The logistic is asymptotic to zero; it does not have a "beginning." Nevertheless, it is most important to distinguish between the lag in "availability" and the lag in "acceptance." It does not make sense to blame the Southern farmers for being slow in acceptance, unless one has taken into account the fact that no satisfactory hybrids were available to them before the middle nineteen-forties.

I shall use the date at which an area began to plant 10 per cent of its ceiling acreage with hybrid seed as the date of *origin*.[16] The 10 per cent date was chosen as an indicator that the development had passed the experimental stage and that superior hybrids were available to farmers in commercial quantities. The reasonableness of this definition has been borne out by a survey of yield tests in various states and it has been supported by conversations with various people associated with developments in hybrid corn in the experiment stations and private seed companies.[17]

"Availability" is the result of the behavior of agricultural experiment stations and private seed companies. If we include the growers of station hybrids in the general term "commercial seed producers," then availability is the direct result of the actions of seed producers with the experiment stations affecting it through the provision of free research results and foundation stocks. The activities of the experiment stations serve to reduce the cost of innovation facing the seed producers but the entry decisions are still their own. The date at which adaptable hybrids became available in an area is viewed as the result of seed producers ranking different areas according to the expected profitability of entry and deciding their actions on this basis.[18] The relative profitability of entry into an area will depend on the size of the eventual market in that area, marketing cost, the cost of innovating for that area, and (given a positive rate of interest) the expected rate of acceptance.[19]

It is extremely difficult to define "market size" operationally. The definition

[16] The date at which the fitted logistic passes through 10 per cent is given by $Y = (-2.2 - a)/b$. As the variation of b is small relative to that of a, small changes in the definition of Y will be in the nature of an additive constant and will rarely change the ranking of the data of *origin* in different areas.

[17] This is essentially a definition of "commercial" availability. An attempt was made to measure the date of "technical" availability by going through yield tests and other official publications and noting the first year in which hybrids clearly outyielded the open pollinated varieties. The rank correlation between this technical definition and the "10 per cent" definition was .93. The average lag between the technical and the commercial availability was approximately 2 years. Also, preliminary explorations with 1 and 5 per cent definitions, and with the rank of an area rather than the absolute date, indicated that the results are not very sensitive to changes in definition.

[18] Implicitly, we have assumed here that the lag between the entry decision and actual availability is approximately constant or at least independent of other variables under analysis.

[19] Throughout the paper it is assumed that the price of hybrid seed is given and approximately uniform in different areas. This is a very close approximation to reality and a result of a very elastic long-run supply curve of seed.

TABLE II
Hybrid Corn Logistic Trend Functions by Crop Reporting Districts*

State and C. R. District	Origin	Rate of Acceptance	Ceiling	r^2	State and C. R. District	Origin	Rate of Acceptance	Ceiling	r^2
Pa. 1	.15	.41	.85	.99	Wisc. 5	−2.54	.61	.90	.98
2	1.16	.49	.90	.99	6	−3.03	.87	.78	.99
3	.76	.46	.91	.98	7	−4.16	.89	.98	.99
4	.44	.47	.92	.99	8	−3.55	.88	.95	.99
5	.11	.62	.95	.98	9	−3.21	.72	.95	.98
6	−1.02	.55	.95	.99					
7	−.63	.40	.90	.98	Minn. 7	−3.08	1.36	1.00	.99
8	−1.04	.54	.96	.99	8	−3.66	1.14	1.00	.99
9	−2.35	.60	.98	.97	9	−3.04	1.01	1.00	.99
Ohio 1	−3.22	1.25	1.00	.99	Iowa 1	−4.39	1.01	1.00	.99
2	−2.73	.99	1.00	.98	2	−4.78	1.05	1.00	.99
3	−1.77	.75	.95	.98	3	−4.46	1.00	1.00	.99
4	−3.00	.90	1.00	.98	4	−3.71	1.12	1.00	.99
5	−3.19	.77	1.00	.98	5	−4.70	1.13	1.00	.99
6	−3.14	.69	.95	.94	6	−5.15	1.09	1.00	.99
7	−2.69	.88	1.00	.98	7	−2.74	1.25	1.00	.99
8	−1.78	.60	.95	.99	8	−3.61	1.07	1.00	.99
9	−1.80	.73	.95	.97	9	−4.15	1.10	1.00	.99
Ind. 1	−3.82	1.15	1.00	.99	Mo. 1	−1.37	1.19	1.00	.97
2	−3.60	1.10	1.00	.99	2	−1.33	1.15	1.00	.95
3	−3.12	1.15	1.00	.99	3	−1.27	1.15	1.00	.96
4	−3.24	.95	1.00	.99	4	−1.51	.66	.95	.98
5	−2.85	1.07	1.00	.99	5	−.64	.78	.93	.99
6	−2.63	1.12	1.00	.99	6	−1.11	.72	.97	.97
7	−1.67	.87	1.00	.96	7	.16	.46	.90	.99
8	−1.57	.82	1.00	.98	8	.63	.63	.87	.99
9	−1.88	.76	1.00	.98	9	−.94	.64	.97	.99
Ill. 1	−4.81	1.13	1.00	.99	N.D. 9	.40	.74	.85	.96
3	−4.59	.98	1.00	.99					
4	−4.16	1.08	1.00	.99	S.D. 3	−.53	.57	.90	.99
4a	−2.65	1.09	1.00	.99	6	−.71	.85	.93	.99
5	−4.68	1.17	1.00	.99	9	−1.72	.75	.95	.99
6	−4.25	1.18	1.00	.99					
6a	−2.46	.91	1.00	.99	Neb. 3	−2.48	.90	1.00	.99
7	−.81	.64	1.00	.97	5	.36	.82	.93	.99
9	−.58	.78	1.00	.97	6	−2.18	.85	1.00	.99
					7	2.33	.90	.95	.99
Mich. 7	−1.12	.77	.92	.97	8	1.60	.94	.95	.99
8	−1.04	.89	.92	.98	9	−.77	.91	1.00	.97
9	−1.70	.78	.92	.98					
					Kan. 1	2.68	.41	.95	.95
Wisc. 1	−2.17	.81	.85	.99	2	1.52	.66	1.00	.98
2	−2.22	.97	.70	.99	3	−.88	.72	1.00	.99
3	−2.42	.93	.60	.99	6	−.88	.68	.92	.99
4	−3.24	.67	.95	.96	9	.73	.41	.95	.99

TABLE II—*Continued*

State and C. R. District	Origin	Rate of Acceptance	Ceiling	r^2	State and C. R. District	Origin	Rate of Acceptance	Ceiling	r^2
Md. 1	2.92	.37	.97	.94	Ala. 1	7.73	.56	.60	.98
2	−1.12	.64	1.00	.97	2	6.33	.57	.99	.99
8	.88	.48	.98	.98	2a	8.80	.45	.90	.97
9	.40	.60	1.00	.93	3	7.68	.54	.95	.98
					4	7.45	.42	.50	.95
Va. 2	.87	.68	1.00	.99	5	8.08	.49	.70	.95
4	1.51	.61	.98	.93	6	8.15	.39	.60	.95
5	2.37	.68	.95	.99	7	7.84	.58	.85	.97
6	2.06	.63	.97	.96	8	8.24	.45	.70	.97
7	1.21	.29	.80	.85	9	8.53	.55	.90	.99
8	2.18	.40	.85	.90					
9	1.04	.50	.95	.96	Ark. 1	.41	.37	.75	.97
					2	1.98	.40	.82	.98
Ky. 1	.67	.89	.95	.97	3	.68	.50	.85	.99
2	−.42	.72	.98	.99	4	2.24	.42	.77	.94
3	.49	.61	.90	.97	5	1.89	.35	.85	.95
4	−.36	.83	.92	.99	6	1.54	.35	.80	.99
5	−.77	.78	.90	.99	7	1.66	.32	.55	.93
6	1.94	.62	.60	.98	8	2.41	.37	.70	.92
					9	1.88	.33	.85	.99
Tenn. 1	.76	.29	.85	.97					
2	1.88	.33	.55	.99	Okla. 3	2.61	.49	.80	.97
3	2.64	.39	.70	.97	5	3.62	.55	.90	.97
4	2.53	.43	.75	.96	6	3.17	.52	.88	.93
5	3.43	.35	.80	.91	7	4.05	.39	.80	.97
6	2.94	.33	.70	.95	8	4.85	.67	.90	.98
					9	4.08	.52	.75	.95

* I am indebted to the Field Crop Statistics Branch of the Agricultural Marketing Service for the unpublished data by crop reporting districts.

is not independent of marketing cost or of the particular characteristics of the innovation (the area of adaptability of a particular hybrid) and is complicated by the arbitrariness of the political subdivisions used as the geographic units of analysis. The problem of the "right" geographic unit of analysis, however, will be postponed to the end of this section. As an approximation to the size of the market I used the average corn acreage in the area at about the time of the date of entry, adjusted for differences in ceilings. That is, the average corn acreage was multiplied by .9 if that was the estimate of the fraction of the corn acreage which would be ultimately planted with hybrid seed. Because the political subdivisions are of various and sundry sizes, to make them more comparable the adjusted corn acreage was divided by total land in farms. The resulting variable —X_1 = (Average corn acreage) $\times K \div$ Total land in farms—is a measure of "market density" rather than of "market size."[20] If the areas are not too different

[20] Differences in seeding rates have been disregarded here. There is, however, some evidence that the results would have been somewhat better if X_1 were adjusted for these differences.

in size and in the range of adaptability of their hybrids, market density will closely approximate a relevant measure of market size. Also, in its own right, it is important as a measure of marketing cost, the relative cost of selling a given supply of seed in different areas. Under the name of "market potential," such a variable was, in fact, used by at least one major seed company in its decision making process. The importance of a variable of this sort was strongly emphasized, in private conversations, by executives of the major seed companies.

The importance of marketing cost is underscored by the striking differences in marketing methods of hybrid seed in different parts of the country. While almost 90 per cent of all the seed in the Corn Belt is sold by individual salesmen who call on each farmer, almost all of the seed in the South is sold through stores where the farmer must come and get it. The small size of the corn acreage per farm, the relative isolation of the small farm, and the large proportion of corn on noncommercial farms make the type of marketing used in the Corn Belt prohibitively expensive in the South. The cost of selling a given amount of seed is quite different in various parts of the country, as many more farmers have to be reached in one area than in another. As a measure of "average size of sale," I used average corn acres per farm reporting corn, X_3 .

The estimated slope coefficient, b, was used as a measure of the expected rate of acceptance in different areas. This assumes that producers were able to predict reasonably well the actual rate of acceptance.

There is no good way of estimating the relative costs of innovation. It is probably true that there are no substantial differences in the cost of developing a hybrid from scratch for any corn growing area of the country and, if there were some, they would be swamped by the large differences in returns. A difficulty arises, however, from the fact that a hybrid may be adaptable in more than one

TABLE III

CORRELATION COEFFICIENTS ON THE STATE LEVEL—N = 31

	X_1	X_3	b	X_4	X_{10}
Y	−.44	−.35	−.62	−.89	.82
X_1		.52	.77	.55	−.39
X_3			.46	.28	−.36
b				.68	−.51
X_4					−.79

Note:
    Y = Date of *origin*. The date an area reached 10 per cent, computed. See Tables I and II.
    X_1 = Market density. For states: average corn acreage 1937–46 times K, divided by land in farms in 1945. Similar for crop reporting districts but averaged over different periods, depending on the availability of data. Source: *Agricultural Statistics, Census of Agriculture*, and published and unpublished materials from state agricultural statisticians.
    X_3 = For states, average corn acres per farm, 1939. Source: *Census of Agriculture*. By crop reporting districts: the same average corn acreage as in X_1, divided by the 1939 or 1945 census number of farms reporting corn, depending on availability of data.
    b = The slope of the logistic transform, computed.
    X_4 = "Corn Beltliness." The proportion of all inbred lines accounted by "Corn Belt" lines in the pedigrees of recommended hybrids by areas. Source: C. B. Henderson, "Inbred Lines of Corn Released to Private Growers from State and Federal Agencies and Double Crosses Recommended by States," 2nd revision, Illinois Seed Producers Association, Champaign, April 15, 1956; and unpublished data from the Funk Bros. Seed Co., Bloomington, Ill.
    X_{10} = Earliest date of origin in the immediate neighborhood.

area, allowing the cost of innovation to be spread over several areas, and because the experiment stations have borne a substantial part of the innovation cost by developing and releasing inbred lines and whole hybrids. That is, the actual cost of innovating for an area will depend on whether or not hybrids which have already been developed for other areas prove adaptable in this area, and on whether or not the experiment stations have produced and released inbred lines or hybrids adaptable to this area.

Since most of the early research was done for the area known as the "Corn Belt," other areas benefitted from the availability of these research results to a varying degree, depending on the adaptability of Corn Belt inbred lines to those areas. A measure of the degree to which other areas are different from the Corn Belt with respect to the adaptability of Corn Belt lines can be approximated by taking the published pedigrees of the recommended hybrids in different areas in 1956 and computing the percentage of all inbred lines represented by "Corn Belt" lines. An index of "Corn Beltliness," X_4 was defined as the number of Corn Belt inbred lines in the pedigrees of the recommended hybrids for that area, divided by the total number of lines.[21]

To take other aspects of the "complementarity" problem into account, another variable, X_{10}, was defined as the earliest date of entry (origin) in the immediate (contiguous) neighborhood of the area under consideration.[22] X_{10} was introduced on the assumption that it may be cheaper, both from the point of view of the additional research needed and from the point of view of setting up a marketing organization, to enter an area contiguous to an area already entered even though the "market potential" there may be lower than in some other area farther away.

Using either the number of released inbred lines or hybrids or the reported research expenditures, several unsuccessful attempts were made to measure the relative contribution of the various experiment stations. To some extent, however, the impact of this variable is already accounted for by our measures of the "market." The contribution of the various experiment stations is strongly related to the importance of corn in the area. In the "good" corn areas the stations did a lot of work on hybrids and in the marginal areas, less.[23]

The simple correlation coefficients between these variables, on the state level and on the crop reporting district level, are presented in Tables III and IV respectively. All of the correlation coefficients with Y have the expected sign and

[21] On the state level, a published list of recommended hybrids and their pedigrees was used, with Iowa, Illinois, Indiana, Ohio, and Wisconsin lines defined as "Corn Belt" lines. See C. B. Henderson, "Inbred Lines of Corn Released to Private Growers from State and Federal Agencies and Double Crosses Recommended by States," Second Revision, Illinois Seed Producers Association, Champaign, April 15, 1956. On the crop reporting district level, I used unpublished data from the Funk Bros. Seed Co., listing their hybrids by "maturity groups" and giving coded pedigrees.

[22] This is analogous to the introduction of a lagged value of the dependent variable into the regression in time series analysis. Except that the "lag" here is spatial rather than a time lag.

[23] There are a few exceptions to this statement. In the North, Connecticut, Wisconsin, and Minnesota contributed more than their "share," and so did Texas and Louisiana in the South.

TABLE IV

CORRELATION COEFFICIENTS ON THE CROP REPORTING DISTRICT LEVEL—N = 132

	X_1	X_3	b	X_4	X_{10}
Y	$-.56$	$-.35$	$-.70$	$-.73$	$.95$
X_1		$.69$	$.73$	$.57$	$-.57$
X_3			$.54$	$.40$	$-.36$
b				$.67$	$-.73$
X_4					$-.76$

See *Note* at bottom of Table III.

most of them are also significantly different from zero. The inter-correlation among the independent variables, however, prevents us from successfully estimating their separate contributions from these data. Almost all sets and subsets of independent variables in these tables were tried without yielding more than one significant coefficient in each multiple regression.[24] These results are disappointing, particularly because the highest correlations are with the rather artificial variables X_4 ("Corn Beltliness") and X_{10} (the "spatial trend").[25] Hence, another approach to the problem was sought.

The trouble with the above approach is that it does nothing about the problem of the "right" geographic unit of analysis. Considering only the "market density" variable, it is obvious that it does not always measure what we want. Markets are continuous. While some areas are poor by themselves they may be a part of a larger market. Also an area may be entered because it is a springboard to other areas rather than on its own grounds. One way of taking these considerations into account is to define the "market potential" of an area as a weighted average of the "market densities" in *all* areas, densities in other areas weighted inversely to the distance from the area under consideration.[26] Given more than a few areas, however, the calculation of such a variable becomes impracticable.[27]

[24] Similar results were obtained when the logarithms rather than the actual values of the independent variables were used.

[25] The good performance of X_{10} is not surprising. The smaller the geographic unit of analysis, the better will be the relationship between Y and X_{10}. This can be seen by comparing the correlation coefficients on the state and crop reporting district levels. There is, however, another way of rationalizing the performance of X_{10}. See footnote 27.

[26] See W. Warnz, "Measuring Spatial Association with Special Consideration of the Case of Market Orientation of Production," *Journal of the American Statistical Association*, 51, December 1956, 597–604.

[27] It does suggest, though, a reason for the good performance of X_{10}. Consider a simple model in which the date of origin is a function of the "true" market measure, the "true" measure being a weighted average of the densities in all areas, weights declining with distance. This "true" measure can be approximated by the actual density in the area and the "true" measure in the immediate neighborhood. But the date of origin in the immediate neighborhood is a function of the "true" density there and can serve as its measure. This implies that X_{10} is another measure of the "market!" For a similar approach in a different context, see M. Nerlove, "Estimates of the Elasticities of Supply of Selected Agricultural Commodities," *Journal of Farm Economics*, 38, May 1956, 500–503.

The trouble with our geographic units arises because states are too large while crop reporting districts are too small and neither corresponds either to technical regions of adaptation of particular hybrids nor to the decision units of the private seed companies. It is possible, however, to ask a more modest question: What were the characteristics of the areas entered in a particular year as compared with the characteristics of areas entered in another year? It is possible to aggregate areas according to the year of entry and test the "market potential" hypothesis on these aggregates. I shall define areas according to the year of entry, i.e., all districts with the *origin* in 1939 will make up one such area, and aggregate the data by crop reporting districts into such areas. Given our "10 per cent" definition of *origin*, we have 16 such areas, 1935 to 1950. Alternatively, we would like to define areas according to the adaptability of particular hybrids. However, most hybrids overlap geographically and there are almost no data on the geographical distribution of particular hybrids, but there are breakdowns of the country into "maturity regions." A major seed company breaks down the U.S. and its line of hybrids into 11 "maturity groups," locating the areas of adaptation of these groups on a map. It is possible to aggregate the crop reporting districts into these "technical" regions and ask whether high market areas were entered earlier than others.

The results of these calculations are presented in Table V-A. In the aggregation by year of origin, to simplify the calculations, the actual "10 per cent or more" year rather than the calculated date from the logistic was used. For the technical regions the computed origins by districts were used, weighted by the average corn acreage in the district and adjusted for differences in ceilings. That is, aggregate $Y = \Sigma Y A K / \Sigma A K$, where A stands for average corn acres. Aggregate X_1 was defined as $\Sigma A K / \Sigma L$, where L stands for total land in farms. Because

TABLE V-A

CORRELATION COEFFICIENTS BETWEEN THE AGGREGATES OF Y, X_1, X_4 AND X_{10}

Aggregation by	X_1	X_4	X_{10}
"Date of Origin": All areas $N = 16$			
Y	$-.82$	$-.98$	$.95$
X_1		$.82$	$-.64$
X_4			$-.93$
"Date of Origin": All areas except the Southeast $N = 13$			
Y	$-.94$	$-.97$	$.96$
X_1		$.90$	$-.86$
X_4			$-.97$
"Technical Regions": $N = 12$			
Y	$-.69$	$-.82$	$.95$
X_1		$.90$	$-.59$
X_4			$-.78$

of the simplicity of the computations involved in this particular approach, 90 more crop reporting districts were added at this point to the analysis, raising the number of included districts to 222. Where separate logistic curves were not computed, Y was estimated by linear interpolation. As the technical regions overlap, each of the aggregates includes a few districts also included in the neighboring aggregates.[28]

To make the results comparable with those presented in Table IV, similar calculations were also performed on X_4 and X_{10}. For the aggregation procedure by "date of origin," X_{10} was defined as the earliest date of origin in the immediate neighborhood of the area defined by the procedure, and X_4 as a simple unweighted average for the districts included in the aggregate. For the aggregation by "technical regions," X_{10} was defined as the lowest weighted average date of origin among the neighboring "technical regions." No aggregation had to be performed on X_4, as it had been originally defined and computed for these regions.

The results presented in Table V-A indicate a strong association between the date of *origin* and average market density in the area, and suggesting that the market density variable is much more important than is indicated by the results in Tables III and IV. The association is higher if we exclude the Southeast from the aggregation procedure. This is explained by the relative lateness of the research contributions of the southeastern experiment stations and by the various obstacles put in the way of private seed companies there. Also, after we come down to a certain low level, it does not really pay to discriminate between areas on the basis of X_1 because the differences are too small, and other factors predominate. This is brought out when we ask the same question about the association of Y with X_1 within each technical region separately. When regressions of Y on log X_1 were computed for each of the technical regions separately, 9 had the expected sign and were significantly different from zero, while the other 3 were not significantly different from zero. This result is significant on a sign test alone. But more interestingly, the r^2's were .66 rank correlated with the mean value of X_1, indicating that the explanatory power of this variable declined for areas with low average X_1 values.

The aggregation procedure, besides indicating that X_1 is a better variable than is implied by Tables III and IV, also helps us with the collinearity problem. Before aggregation, the partial correlation coefficient of Y with X_1, holding X_{10} constant, was $-.24$ on the state level and only $-.08$ on the crop reporting district level. Now it becomes $-.90$ for the aggregates by date of origin, $-.84$ when we leave out the Southeast, and $-.64$ for the data by technical regions. The regressions of Y on X_1 and X_{10} are presented in Table V-B. The coefficient of X_1 has the expected sign and is significantly different from zero for the aggregates by "date of origin" and is almost twice the size of its standard error for the aggregates by technical region. This indicates that it is possible to separate the contributions of X_1 and X_{10} if we define our area units correctly.

[28] Because one of the "maturity" areas is much larger than the others, it was divided into two on a north-south basis. Hence, we have 12 technical regions in our analysis.

TABLE V-B

REGRESSIONS OF Y ON X_1 AND X_{10}

Aggregation by	Coefficients of		R^2
	X_1	X_{10}	
"Date of Origin": All areas	−17.8	1.02	.982
	(2.5)	(.07)	
"Date of Origin": All areas except the Southeast	−16.5	1.03	.977
	(3.4)	(.07)	
"Technical Region":	−10.5	.88	.925
	(5.6)	(.12)	

Note: Figures in parentheses are the calculated standard errors.

While these results may not be too conclusive, together with information gathered in conversations with executives in the industry and a graphical survey of the data, they leave little doubt in my mind that the development of hybrid corn was largely guided by expected pay-off, "better" areas being entered first, even though it may be difficult to measure very well the variables entering into these calculations.

4. THE RATE OF ACCEPTANCE

Differences in the *slope* or adjustment coefficient b will be interpreted as differences in the rate of adjustment of demand to the new equilibrium, and will be explained by variables operating on the demand side rather than by variables operating on the supply side.[29] Actually, the path traced out is an intersection of short-run supply and demand curves. It is assumed, however, that while shifts on the supply side determine the origin of the development, the rate of development is largely a demand, or "acceptance," variable.[30] The usefulness of this assumption is due to a very elastic long-run supply of seed and is supported by

[29] The dimension of b, the adjustment coefficient, may be of some interest. b indicates by how much the value of the logistic transform will change per time unit. A value of $b = 1.0$ implies that the development will go from, e.g., 12 to 27 to 50 to 73 to 88 per cent from year to year; i.e., the distance from 12 to 88 per cent will be covered in 4 years. A value of $b = 0.5$ would imply a path: 12, 18, 27, 38, 50, 62, 73, 82, 88, etc., i.e., it would take twice the time 8 years, to transverse the same distance. If one thinks in terms of the cumulative normal distribution positioned on a time scale, which is very similar to the logistic, then b is approximately proportional to $1/\sigma$. A low standard deviation implies that it will take a short time to go from, e.g., 10 to 90 per cent, while a higher standard deviation implies a longer period of adjustment.

[30] Implicitly, we have the following model: the potential adjustment path of supply is an exponential function, which after a few years rises quickly above the potential adjustment function of demand. The demand adjustment function has the form of the logistic. The actual path followed is the lower of the two, which, after the first few years, is the demand path.

the fact that only local and transitory seed shortages were observed. On the whole, the supply of seed was not the limiting factor.[31]

Differences in the rate of acceptance of hybrid corn, the differences in b, are due at least in part to differences in the profitability of the changeover from open pollinated to hybrid seed. This hypothesis is based on the general idea that the larger the stimulus the faster is the rate of adjustment to it.[32] Also, in a world of imperfect knowledge, it takes time to realize that things have in fact changed. The larger the shift the faster will entrepreneurs become aware of it, "find it out," and hence they will react more quickly to larger shifts.[33]

My hypothesis is that the rate of acceptance is a function of the profitability of the shift, both per acre and total. Per acre profitability may be defined as the increase in yield due to the use of hybrid seed, times the price of corn, and minus the difference in the cost of seed. As there is very little relevant cross-sectional variation in the price of corn, the seeding rate, or the price of seed, these will be disregarded and only differences in the superiority of hybrids over open-pollinated varieties taken into account.[34]

I shall use two measures of the superiority of hybrids over open pollinated varieties: (1) the average increase in yield in bushels per acre, based on un-published mail questionnaire data collected by the Agricultural Marketing Service, X_7, and (2) the long-run average pre-hybrid yield of corn, X_8. The latter measure was used on the basis of the widespread belief that the superiority of hybrids can be adequately summarized as a percentage increase.[35] A variation in pre-hybrid yields, given a percentage increase, will also imply a variation in the absolute superiority of hybrids over open pollinated varieties. Twenty per

[31] "Clearly it would have been physically impossible for a large percentage of operators to have planted hybrids in the early thirties. There simply was not enough seed. It seems likely, however, that this operated more as a potential than an actual limitation upon the will of the operator, and that rapidity of adoption approximated the rate at which farmers decided favorably upon the new technique." B. Ryan, "A Study in Technological Diffusion," *Rural Sociology*, 13, 1948, p. 273. Similar views were expressed to the author by various people closely associated with the developments in hybrid corn.

[32] E. g., "The greater the efficiency of the new technology in producing returns, . . . the greater its rate of acceptance."—"How Farm People Accept New Ideas," Special Report No. 15, Agricultural Extension Service, Iowa State College, Ames, November, 1955, p. 6.

[33] This is analogous to the situation in Sequential Analysis. The ASN (average sample number) is an inverse function of, among other things, the difference between the population means. That is, the larger the difference between the two things which we are testing, the sooner we will accumulate enough evidence to convince us that there is a difference. See A. Wald, *Sequential Analysis*, John Wiley & Sons, New York, 1947.

[34] The apparent cross-sectional variation in the average price of hybrid seed is largely due to differences in the mix of "public" versus "private" hybrids bought by farmers. The "public" hybrids sell for about $2.00 less per bushel. The rank correlation between the price of hybrid seed and the estimated share of "private" hybrids in 1956 was .73.

[35] The data from experiment station yield tests indicate that this is not too bad an assumption. See Sprague, *op. cit.*, and the literature cited there. It is unfortunate that these data are not comparable between states and, hence, cannot be used directly in this study.

cent is the figure quoted most often for this superiority.[36] Average corn acres per farm, X_3, were used to add the impact of total profits per farm.

As the value of b depends strongly on the ceiling K, to make them comparable between areas, the b's had to be adjusted for differences in K. Instead of b, $b' = bK$ was used as the dependent variable, translating the b's back into actual percentage units from percentage of ceiling units. Alternatively, one should have adjusted the independent variables to correspond only to that fraction of the acres which will eventually shift to hybrids. But there are no data for making such an adjustment; hence b was adjusted to imply the same actual percentage changes in different areas.[37]

Linear and log regressions were calculated for the data from 31 states and 132 crop reporting districts. The results are presented in Table VI.[38] The figures speak largely for themselves, indicating the suprisingly good and uniform results obtained. The log form and X_8 rather than X_7 did somewhat better but not significantly so. The similarity of the coefficients in comparable regression is striking. For example, compare the coefficients of X_8 and X_7 in the log regressions and all the coefficients in the similar regressions on the state and crop reporting district levels. These results were also similar to those obtained in preliminary analyses using b rather than b' as the dependent variable [39] (see Table VII).

An attempt was made to incorporate several additional variables into the analysis. Rural sociologists have suggested that socioeconomic status or level-of-living is an important determinant of the rate of acceptance of a new technique.[40] The United States Department of Agriculture level-of-living index for 1939,

---

[36] "If an average percentage increase in yield to be expected by planting hybrids as compared to open pollinated varieties were to be computed at the present it would probably be near 20 per cent. . . ." —J. T. Swartz, "A Study of Hybrid Corn Yields as Compared to Open Pollinated Varieties," Insurance Section, FCIC, Washington, April and May, 1942, unpublished manuscript.

"Experience in other corn-growing regions of the United States shows that increases of approximately 20 per cent over the open pollinated varieties may be expected from the use of adapted hybrids. Results so far in Texas are in general agreement with this figure," J. S. Rogers and J. W. Collier, "Corn Production in Texas," Texas Agricultural Experiment Station, Bulletin 746, February 1952, p. 7.

"Plant breeders conservatively estimate increase in yields of 15 to 20 per cent from using hybrid seed under field conditions. They expect about the same relative increases in both ow—and high—yielding areas," USDA, *Technology of the Farm*, Washington, 1940, p. 2.2

[37] This adjustment affects our results very little. See Table VII, below.

[38] X_7 was not used on the state level because it was felt that the aggregation error would be too large. We want an average of differences while I could only get a difference between averages. For some states this difference exceeded the individual differences in all the crop reporting districts within the state.

[39] These were calculated for subsamples of 65 and 32 crop reporting districts.

[40] See "How Farm People Accept New Ideas," *op. cit.*, and E. A. Wilkening, "The Acceptance of Certain Agricultural Programs and Practices in a Piedmont Community of North Carolina," unpublished Ph.D. thesis, University of Chicago, 1949, and "Acceptance of Improved Farm Practices in Three Coastal Plain Counties," Tech. Bull. No. 98, North Carolina Agricultural Experiment Station, May 1952.

TABLE VI
REGRESSIONS OF *SLOPES* ON "PROFITABILITY"
VARIABLES

Regression	Coefficients of			
	X_3	X_7	X_8	R^2
By states—N = 31:				
$b' = c_0 + c_3 X_3 + c_8 X_8$	.006		.017	.66
	(.002)		(.005)	
$\log b' = c_0 + c_3 \log X_3$	.30		.66	.67
$\quad + c_8 \log X_8$	(.08)		(.11)	
By crop reporting districts—				
N = 132:				
$b' = c_0 + c_3 X_3 + c_7 X_7$	.0073	.079		.57
	(.0008)	(.009)		
$b' = c_0 + c_3 X_3 + c_8 X_8$	.0076		.016	.61
	(.0007)		(.002)	
$\log b' = c_0 + c_3 \log X_3$	.44	.70		.61
$\quad + c_7 \log X_7$	(.04)	(.09)		
$\log b' = c_0 + c_3 \log X_3$	.44		.57	.69
$\quad + c_8 \log X_8$	(.03)		(.05)	

Notes:

Figures in parentheses are the calculated standard errors.

X_3—Average corn acres per farm reporting corn.

X_7—The average difference between hybrid and open pollinated yields by districts tabulated only from reports showing both and averaged over 4 to 10 years, depending on the overlap of the available data with the adjustment period (10 to 90 per cent). Based on unpublished AMS "Identicals" data.

X_8—Pre-hybrid average yield. Usually an average for the 10 years before an area reached 10 per cent in hybrids. Sometimes fewer years were used, depending on the available data. Source: for states, *Agricultural Statistics*; for crop reporting districts, various published and unpublished data from the AMS and from state agricultural statisticians.

TABLE VII
REGRESSIONS OF UNADJUSTED *SLOPES* ON "PROFITABILITY" VARIABLES

Regression	Coefficients of			
	X_3	X_7	X_8	R^2
$b = c_0 + c_3 X_3 + c_7 X_7$	.005	.06		.40
$(N = 65)$	(.001)	(.01)		
$b = c_0 + c_3 X_3 + c_8 X_8$	.005		.022	.75
$(N = 32)$	(.001)		(.002)	

when added to the regressions by states, had a negative coefficient in the linear form and a positive coefficient in the logarithmic form. In neither case was the coefficient significantly different from zero.

A measure of the "importance" of corn—the value of corn as a percentage of the value of all crops—was added in the belief that the rate of acceptance may be affected by the relative importance of corn within the farmer's enterprise. However, its coefficient was not significantly different from zero. Nor was the coefficient of total capital per farm significantly different from zero. The latter variable was introduced in an attempt to measure the impact of "capital rationing." [41]

The rate of acceptance may be also affected by the "advertising" activities of the extension agencies and private seed companies. There are no data, however, which would enable us to take this into account. There is also some evidence that the estimated rate of acceptance will be affected by the degree of aggregation and the heterogeneity of the aggregate. Heterogeneous areas imply different component growth curves and hence a lower aggregate slope coefficient. This is exhibited by the lower state values for b as compared to the values for the individual crop reporting districts within these states. No way has been found, however, to introduce this factor into the analysis.

Nevertheless, our results do suggest that a substantial proportion of the variation in the rate of acceptance of hybrid corn is explainable by differences in the profitability of the shift to hybrids in different parts of the country.

5. THE EQUILIBRIUM LEVEL OF USE

I am interpreting the *ceilings* as the long-run equilibrium percentages of the corn acreage which will be planted to hybrid seed. Differences in the percentage at which the use of hybrid seed will stabilize are the result of long-run demand factors. It is assumed that in the long run the supply conditions of seed are the same to all areas, the same percentage increase in yield over open pollinated varieties at the same relative price. However, this same technical superiority may mean different things in different parts of the country.

The ceiling is a function of some of the same variables which determine b, the rate of acceptance. It is a function of average profitability and of the distribution of this profitability. With the average above a certain value no farmer will be faced with zero or negative profitability of the shift to hybrids. With the average profitability below this level some farmers will be facing negative returns and hence will not switch to hybrids. In marginal corn areas, however, "average profitability" may become a very poor measure. Its components lose their connection with the concepts they purport to represent. Yield variability may overshadow the average increase from hybrids. The relevance of the published price of corn diminishes. In many marginal corn areas there is almost no market for corn off the farm. The only outlet for increased production is as an input in another production or consumption process on the farm. But on farms on which corn is a marginal enterprise, with little or no commercial livestock production, the use of corn is limited to human consumption, feed for draft animals, a cow and a few chickens. The farmer is interested in producing a certain amount of corn to fill his needs, having no use for additional corn. It will pay him to switch to hybrid corn only if he has alternative uses for the released land and other resources which would return him more than the extra cost of seed. But in many

[41] The failure of the last two variables is due largely to their strong intercorrelation with the included variables. "Importance" is highly correlated with average yield and capital with corn acres per farm. When used separately, these two variables did as well on the state level as yield and corn acres per farm.

of these areas corn is already on the poorest land and uses resources left over from other operations on the farm. Also, there may already be substantial amounts of idle land in the area. All these factors may tend to make hybrids unprofitable although they are "technically" superior. Similarly, in areas where capital rationing is important the recorded market rate of interest will be a poor measure of the opportunity costs of capital. While the returns to hybrid corn may be substantial, if corn is not a major crop, the returns to additional investments in other branches of the enterprise may be even higher.

Ceilings are not necessarily constant over time. Even without any apparent change in the profitability of the shift from open pollinated to hybrid corn, a change in the relative profitability of corn growing, an improvement in the functioning of the market for corn, or an increase in storage facilities may change them. Also, in areas where there are large year-to-year changes in the corn acreage, the percentage planted to hybrid seed may fluctuate as a result of the differential exit and entry in and out of corn of farmers using hybrid or open pollinated seed. These changes may occur without any "real" changes in the relative profitability of hybrids or in farmers' attitudes towards them. It is very difficult to deal statistically with a development composed of a series of adjustments to shifting equilibrium values.[42] As a first approximation I shall ignore this problem. Only in the marginal corn areas is this a problem of some importance. For most of the Corn Belt the assumption of an immediate ceiling of 100 per cent is tenable. In the fringe areas ceiling values somewhat lower than 100 per cent fit very well. There are some indications that in the South ceilings may have shifted over time, but I doubt that this is important enough to bias seriously our results.

In spite of all these reservations and the crudeness with which the ceilings were estimated in the first place, it is possible to explain a respectable proportion of their variation with the same "profitability" variables that were used in the analysis of *slopes*. Because there is a ceiling of 1.00 to the possible variation in K, the logistic function was used again, giving us logit $K = \log_e [K/(1 - K)]$ as our dependent variable. As there were a substantial number of areas with $K = 1.0$, a value not defined for the transform, two approximations were used. On the state level all values of $K = 1.0$ were set equal to .99, while on the crop reporting level, where there was no problem of degrees of freedom, these values were left out of the analysis. X_3, average corn acres per farm, and X_8, pre-hybrid yield, were used as "profitability" measures, and X_{11}, capital per farm, was added to take "capital rationing" into account. The results of these calculations are presented in Table VIII. They indicate that differences in measures of average profitability, differences in average corn acres and pre-hybrid yields, can explain a substantial proportion of the variation in *ceilings*, the long-run equilibrium level of hybrid seed use. The proportion of the variation explained on the state

---

[42] I am aware of only one attempt in the literature to deal with this kind of problem. See C. F. Roos and V. von Szelisky, "Factors Governing Changes in Domestic Automobile Demand," particularly the section on "The Concept of a Variable Maximum Ownership Level," pp. 36–38, in General Motors Corporation, *Dynamics of Automobile Demand*, New York, 1939.

TABLE VIII
REGRESSIONS OF LOGIT K ON "PROFITABILITY" VARIABLES

Regression	Coefficients of			
	X_3	X_8	X_{11}	R^2
By states—N = 31:				
$c_0 + c_3 X_3 + c_8 X_8$	.03	.11		.71
	(.01)	(.02)		
$c_0 + c_3 \log X_3 + c_8 \log X_8$	1.94	5.88		.71
	(.56)	(.80)		
$+ c_{11} \log X_{11}$	1.55	5.25	.71	.72
	(.84)	(1.30)	(1.14)	
By crop reporting districts—				
N = 86:				
$c_0 + c_3 \log X_3 + c_8 \log X_8$	1.09	2.22	1.35	.39
$+ c_{11} \log X_{11}$	(.48)	(.61)	(.64)	

Notes:
Figures in parentheses are the calculated standard errors.
X_3—Average corn acres per farm.
X_8—Pre-hybrid yield.
X_{11}—On the state level, value of land and buildings per farm, 1940. Source: *Statistical Abstract of the United States, 1948,* p. 600. On the crop reporting district level, total capital investment per farm, 1949. Computed from Table 11, E. G. Strand and E. O. Heady, "Productivity of Resources Used on Commercial Farms," USDA, Technical Bulletin No. 1128, Washington, November 1955, p. 45.

level is substantially higher, indicating that additional variables which may be at work at the crop reporting district level may cancel out at the state level. For example, the coefficient of capital investment per farm, a measure of "capital rationing," is significant at the crop reporting district level but not at the state level. Undoubtedly this analysis could be improved by the addition of other variables but I would not expect it to change the major conclusion appreciably.

6. LIMITATIONS, SUMMARY, AND CONCLUSIONS

The above analysis does not purport to present a complete model of the process of technological change. Rather the approach has been to break down the problem into manageable units and to analyze them more or less separately. I have concentrated on the longer-run aspects of technological change, interpreting differences in the pattern of development of hybrid corn on the basis of the long-run characteristics of various areas, and ignoring the impact of short-run fluctuations in prices and incomes. This limitation is not very important in the cases of hybrid corn because the returns from the changeover were large enough to swamp any short-run fluctuations in prices and other variables.[43] It might, however, become serious were we to consider other technical changes requiring substantial investments, and not as superior to their predecessors as was hybrid corn. Nor can we transfer the particular numerical results to the consideration of other developments. Nevertheless, a cursory survey of trends in the number of cornpickers and tractors on farms, and of trends in the use of fertilizer, does

[43] Estimates made for Kansas data indicate returns from 300 to 1000 per cent on the extra cost of seed.

indicate that it might also be possible to apply a version of our approach to their analysis.

I hope that this work does indicate that at least the process of innovation, the process of adapting and distributing a particular invention to different markets and its acceptance by entrepreneurs, is amenable to economic analysis. It is possible to account for a large share of the spatial and chronological differences in the use of hybrid corn with the help of "economic" variables. The lag in the development of adaptable hybrids for particular areas and the lag in the entry of seed producers into these areas can be explained on the basis of varying profitability of entry. Also, differences in both the long-run equilibrium use of hybrids and in the rate of approach to that equilibrium level are explainable, at least in part, by differences in the profitability of the shift from open pollinated to hybrid varieties.

Looking at the hybrid seed industry as a part of the specialized sector which provides us with technological change, it can be said that both private and public funds were allocated efficiently within that sector.[44] Given a limited set of resources, the hybrid seed industry expanded according to a pattern which made sense, allocating its resources first to the areas of highest returns.

The American farmer appears also to have adjusted rationally to these new developments. Where the profits from the innovation were large and clear cut, the changeover was very rapid. It took Iowa farmers only four years to go from 10 to 90 per cent of their corn acreage in hybrid corn. In areas where the profitability was lower, the adjustment was also slower. On the whole, taking account of uncertainty and the fact that the spread of knowledge is not instantaneous, farmers have behaved in a fashion consistent with the idea of profit maximization. Where the evidence appears to indicate the contrary, I would predict that a closer examination of the relevant economic variables will show that the change was not as profitable as it appeared to be.[45]

University of Chicago

[44] Some minor quibbles could be raised about the allocation of public funds, but the returns to these funds have been so high that the impact of the existing inefficiencies is almost imperceptible.

[45] In this context one may say a few words about the impact of "sociological" variables. It is my belief that in the long run, and cross-sectionally, these variables tend to cancel themselves out, leaving the economic variables as the major determinants of the pattern of technological change. This does not imply that the "sociological" variables are not important if one wants to know which *individual* will be first or last to adopt a particular technique, only that these factors do not vary widely cross-sectionally. Partly this is a question of semantics. With a little ingenuity, I am sure that I can redefine 90 per cent of the "sociological" variables as economic variables. Also, some of the variables I used, e.g., yield of corn and corn acres per farm, will be very highly related cross-sectionally to education, socio-economic status, level-of-living, income, and other "sociological" variables. That is, it is very difficult to discriminate between the assertion that hybrids were accepted slowly because it was a "poor corn area" and the assertion that the slow acceptance was due to "poor people." Poor people and poor corn are very closely correlated in the U.S. Nevertheless, one may find a few areas where this is not so. Obviously, the slow acceptance of hybrids on the western fringes of the Corn Belt, in western Kansas, Nebraska, South Dakota, and North Dakota was not due to poor people, but the result of "economic" factors, poor corn area.

Econometrica, Vol. 25, 4 (October 1957)

AN INTERNATIONAL COMPARISON OF HOUSEHOLD EXPENDITURE PATTERNS, COMMEMORATING THE CENTENARY OF ENGEL'S LAW[1]

By H. S. Houthakker

A comparison of elasticities for food, clothing, housing, and miscellaneous items with respect to total expenditure and family size, based on regression analyses of about 40 surveys from about 30 countries. The elasticities are found to be similar but not equal. Engel's law, formulated in 1857, is confirmed by all surveys.

Few dates in the history of econometrics are more significant than 1857. In that year Ernst Engel (1821–1896) published a study on the conditions of production and consumption in the Kingdom of Saxony [6], in which he formulated an empirical law concerning the relation between income and expenditure on food. Engel's law, as it has since become known, states that the proportion of income spent on food declines as income rises. Its original statement was mainly based on an examination of about two hundred budgets of Belgian laborers collected by Ducpétiaux. Since that date the law has been found to hold in many other budget surveys; similar laws have also been formulated for other items of expenditure.

With the formulation of Engel's law an important branch of econometrics took its start, though it was not until our days that consumption research was placed on a sound theoretical and statistical basis. It is proper that in this centennial year econometricians should pay tribute to one of their most illustrious precursors. His successful attempt to derive meaningful regularities from seemingly arbitrary observations will always be an inspiring example to the profession, the more so because in his day economic theory and statistical techniques were of little assistance in such an attempt. There can, I think, be no more fitting tribute to this enlightened empiricist than a further inquiry into the subject to which he devoted much of his life's work.

There is no need to go into details of Engel's analysis and of the developments that preceded it, for these matters have recently been discussed in the scholarly article by Stigler [13]. It should be enough to note that Engel was mainly influenced by two of his older contemporaries. One was the French engineer Frédéric Le Play, who had collected budgets from households all over Europe, mostly, it seems, from humanitarian interest. Engel had been Le Play's student at the École des Mines in Paris. The other main influence was the Belgian statistician Quételet, who was a firm proponent of the idea that human characteristics, at least in the average, were governed by laws as definite as those which govern

[1] This paper summarizes a part of the results of the Stanford Project for Quantitative Research in Economic Development, which is financed by the Ford Foundation. The author is greatly indebted to Andrew Goldner, Joseph Mensah, Charles Howe, Barbara Levine, and Mary Baird for their valuable help, and to individuals and government agencies in many countries for their assistance in providing data, but he takes full responsibility for the contents of the paper.

253

physical phenomena. Engel was, moreover, not entirely free of the materialism of his time, often epitomized in the phrase "Der Mensch ist was er isst"; he later wrote a monograph entitled "Der Kostenwerth des Menschen" (The Cost of Man). It should also be mentioned that Engel made the first empirical study of a demand curve.

The empirical study of consumption, it will be noted, had an international flavor from an early date. Le Play's observations covered many countries, and Engel himself had no hesitation in applying an inference drawn from Belgian data to his own country. As budget statistics in individual countries were improved, however, the interest in international comparisons diminished. The purpose of the budget surveys that were undertaken shifted gradually from the study of consumption for its own scientific interest to the construction of a cost-of-living index number. It was not until the 1930's that economists began to understand the significance of the results to be obtained from analysis of budget data. Allen and Bowley's *Family Expenditure* [1] marked the turning point in this respect, and it is noteworthy that it again deals with data from various countries.

The international comparison of expenditure patterns has recently acquired a new practical interest, which is actually quite similar to that which prompted Engel to use Belgian data. (He was concerned with the balance between production and consumption when population increases.) Many countries are now engaged in the construction of development programs and to do this adequately it is clearly necessary to have some idea about the changes in consumption that are likely to occur with rising income levels. In many underdeveloped countries, however, the data for estimating changes in consumption are unfortunately lacking. There is a real question concerning the extent to which data from one country are applicable to conditions in another country; it is one of the principal aims of the present investigation to clarify this point. In recent years the number of countries, both poor and rich, from which budget surveys are available has increased considerably and there is now enough material for, at the least, a first impression of the comparability of expenditure patterns.

It may be wise to deal at once with an objection which occurs to many people when they hear of an international comparison of expenditure patterns. They are willing to admit the possibility of comparison between countries, such as Holland and Belgium, which to them seem very similar. They become dubious, however, when conspicuously different countries, such as the United States and Ghana, or Brazil and Finland, are viewed under the same heading. Now it would be difficult to deny that these countries are in fact different in many ways, but this only makes it all the more interesting to see whether the same laws of expenditure apply to them also. The discovery of widely applicable generalizations is the principal aim of science. It will be shown, in fact, that there are meaningful propositions which appear to be valid in nearly all the countries considered, without reference to their climatic or cultural condition.

Because of limitations of data and resources it was decided to restrict the investigation to four major items of expenditure, namely food (not including al-

TABLE I

SURVEYS USED IN THE ANALYSIS

Country	Date	Sample Size	Type of Persons	Reference
Australia Queensland	1939640	450	Entire country	The Government Statistician, Brisbane. *The Queensland Year-book, 1945.* No. 6.
Austria	1954/55	6,023	City dwellers	Österreichisches Statistisches Zentralamt, *Der Verbrauch der Städtischen Bevölkerung Österreichs.* Vienna: 1956.
Belgium	1853	199	Industrial workers	Engel, Ernst, "Die Lebenskosten Belgischer Arbeiter Früher und Jetzt," *Bulletin de l'Institut International de Statistique,* IX (1895), pp. 38–39.
Brazil	1953	3,182	City dwellers	*Anuario Estatístico do Brasil,* XIV (Decembro, 1953), pp. 343–44.
Burma, Rangoon Hindustani	1927	768	Single workers	Bennison, J. J., "Report of an Enquiry into the Standard and Cost of Living of the Working Classes in Rangoon." Rangoon: 1928.
Tamils, Telugus, Uriyas	1927	1,599	Single workers	
Chittagonians	1927	654	Single workers	
Canada	1947/48	3,558	Non-farm population	Dominion Bureau of Statistics, "Canadian Non-farm Family Expenditures, 1947–48." Reference Paper No. 42. June, 1953.
Ceylon	1953	1,085	Rural and urban	Central Bank of Ceylon, Department of Economic Research. "Survey of Ceylon's Consumer Finances." Colombo: 1954.
China Peiping	1927	283	City dwellers	Gamble, S. D., *How Chinese Families Live in Peiping.* New York: Funk and Wagnalls Company, 1933.
Shanghai	1929/30	305	Laborers	The City Government of Greater Shanghai, Bureau of Social Affairs, "Standard of Living of Shanghai Laborers." Shanghai: 1934.
Cuba	1953	1,365	City dwellers	Central Bank of Cuba, Unpublished data.
Finland	1950/51	535	City dwellers	"Elinkustannustutkimus Helmikuu 1950-Tammikuu 1951," *Sosiaalisia Erikoistutkimuksia,* XXXII, No. 21 (1954).
France	1951	2,579	City dwellers	"Les Dépenses et les Consommations de Ménages à Paris, Rennes et dans 17 Grandes Villes de Province (Novembre–Decembre 1951)," *Bulletin Mensuel de Statistique,* Supplément 4 (October–December, 1953).

	Year	Group	Number	Source
Germany	1907	City dwellers	852	"Erhebung von Wirtschaftsrechnungen minderbemittelter Familien im Deutschen Reiche," 2. Sonderheft zum *Reichs-Arbeitsblatte*. Berlin: 1909.
	1928	Manual & clerical workers, Govt. officials	1,422	"Die Lebenshaltung von 2,000 Arbeiter-, Angestellten- und Beamtenhanshaltungen," *Einzelschrifter zur Statistik des Deutschen Reiches*, No. 22 (1932).
	1951	City dwellers	910	Statistisches Bundesamt, *Statistisches Jahrbuch für die Bundesrepublik Deutschland*. Wiesbaden: 1953.
Ghana (Gold Coast)				
Accra	1954	City dwellers	453	Government Statistician's Office, "1953 Accra Survey of Household Budgets." Statistical and Economic Papers No. 2. Accra: 1953.
Kumasi	1955	City dwellers	570	——, "Kumasi Survey of Population and Household Budgets." Statistical and Economic Papers No. 5. Accra: 1956.
Secondi-Takoradi	1955	City dwellers	546	——, "Sekondi-Takoradi Survey of Population and Household Budgets." Statistical and Economic Papers No. 4. Accra: 1956.
Akuse	1954	City dwellers	163	——, "1954 Akuse Survey of Household Budgets." Statistical and Economic Papers No. 3. Accra: 1595.
Guatemala				
Guatemala City	1947	City dwellers	179	Dirección General de Estadística, "Estudio sobre los Condiciones de Vida de 179 Familias en la Ciudad de Guatemala." Guatemala City: 1948.
India				
Bombay	1921	Single workers / Workers' families	603 / 597	Government of Bombay. Labour Office. *Report on an Enquiry into Working Class Budgets in Bombay*, by G. Findlay Shirras. Bombay: 1923.
Bhopal City	1951	Workers	360	Ministry of Labour, Labour Bureau, "Report on an Enquiry into the Family Budgets of Workers in Bhopal City." Delhi: 1954.
Punjab	1950	Industrial workers	465	Board of Economic Enquiry, Punjab, "An Economic Survey of Industrial Labour in Punjab," by Om Prakash. 1952.
Ireland	1951/52	City dwellers	2,880	Central Statistics Office, "Household Budget Inquiry, 1951-1952." Dublin: 1954.

TABLE I—*Continued*

Country	Date	Sample Size	Type of Persons	Reference
Italy	1952/53	1,574	Entire country	Cao-Pinna, V., "Contributo alla Preparazione dello Schema di Sviluppo dell'Occupazione e del Reddito in Italia nel Decennio 1955–1964" Rome: 1954. Additional data kindly supplied by the author.
Japan	1953 1955	21,964 885	Urban workers Urban workers	Bureau of Statistics, *Japan Statistical Yearbook.* 1954. ——, "Annual Report on the Family Income and Expenditure Survey." Tokyo: 1956.
Latvia	1936/37	170	Urban and rural workers	Davidsons, P., "Valsts statistika pārvalde: Gimeņu Budžeti 1936–37." Riga: 1940.
Libya	1950	35	Arab workers	Nicholson, J. L., "A Survey of the Living Conditions of Arab Families in Tripolitania in November–December, 1950," *Revue de l'Institut International de Statistique*, XXII, Nos. 1–3 (1954).
Mexico Mexico City	1931	970	City dwellers	Ferrocarriles Nacionales de México, Oficina de Estudios Económicos, "Un Estudio del Costo de la Vida en México." Estudio Número 2, Serie A. Mexico City: 1931.
Netherlands	1951	1,938	Manual and white collar workers	Centraal Bureau voor de Statistiek. "Nationaal budgetonderzoek 1951," Serie B 1, No. 4; B 2, No. 3. Utrecht: 1954.
Northern Rhodesia	1951	223	European mine employees	Central African Statistical Office. "Report on Northern Rhodesia Family Expenditure Survey 1951." Causeway, Southern Rhodesia: 1953.
Norway Oslo & Bergen	1952	197	City dwellers	Statistisk Sentralbyrå, "Forbruksundersøkelse 1952." Oslo: 1953.
Panama Panama City	1952	449	City dwellers	Dirección de Estadística y Censo, "Estudio de los Ingresos, Gastos y Costo de la Vida: Ciudad de Panamá 1952–1953," by P. Paro. 1954.
Philippines Manila	1954	923	City dwellers	Central Bank of the Philippines, Department of Economic Research. "Incomes and Expenditures of Metropolitan Manila Households." Manila: 1954.

Poland	1927	192	Working class	"Budżety Rodzin Robotniczych," *Statystyka Polski*, XL, Zeszyt I (1930).
Portugal Porto	1950/51	2,592	City dwellers	Instituto Nacional de Estatística, "Inquérito ao Custo de Vida na Cidade do Porto, 1950–1951." Estudos No. 27. Lisbon: 1955.
Puerto Rico San Juan	1950	278	Office workers	U. S. Department of Labor, Bureau of Labor Statistics, "Income and Expenditure of Office Workers' Families." Washington: 1953.
Whole Territory	1952	999	Working class	Puerto Rico Department of Labor, "Survey of Income and Expenditures of Wage Earners' Families in Puerto Rico in 1952." Preliminary Releases. San Juan: 1954–1956.
Sweden	1955	388	Entire country	Kungl. Socialstyrelsen, Sveriges Officiella Statistik, Priser och Konsumtion, "Levnadskostnaderna År 1952." Stockholm: 1956.
Switzerland	1919	277	Entire country	Bureau Fédéral de Statistique, "Comptes de Ménage de 277 Familles Suisses pour 1919." Berne: 1922.
United Kingdom Working Class	1937/38	2,219	Industrial workers	Prais, S. J. and H. S. Houthakker, *The Analysis of Family Budgets*. Cambridge: Cambridge University Press, 1955.
Middle Class	1938/39	1,361	Government officials and teachers	*Ibid.*
United States	1901	11,156	Industrial employees	*Eighteenth Annual Report of the United States Commissioner of Labor*. Washington, D. C.: 1903, pp. 582–83.
	1950	12,489	City dwellers	*Study of Consumer Expenditures, Incomes, and Savings*, Vol. II. Tabulated by the Bureau of Labor Statistics, U. S. Department of Labor for Wharton School of Finance and Commerce. Philadelphia: University of Pennsylvania, 1956.

coholic beverages), housing (including fuel and light), clothing (including foot-wear), and all other items. Food expenditure includes an imputed value for home-produced items wherever data were available, but since nearly all surveys covered urban consumers only, this component is normally small. No attempt was made to analyze the composition of these four items in different countries, and consequently it was not necessary to go into the difficulties associated with products that are peculiar to certain regions. The dependent variables, it should be emphasized, are expenditures (money amounts) rather than quantities bought. The elasticities calculated therefore reflect both the increase in physical quanti-ties and the increase in "quality" (average price per physical unit) associated with a rise in the level of living. The expenditure elasticity, in fact, is the sum of the quantity elasticity and the quality elasticity [12, p. 112]. Since the latter has been shown to be considerable in many cases [12, Ch. 8], [3], [5], our results can-not be immediately applied to the estimation of changes in physical quantities. The results for food, in particular, are not directly comparable with those obtained by Bennett [2] and Juréen [10] in their international comparisons.

The analysis also had to be simplified in other ways. Due to the lack of relevant data it was necessary to disregard prices as a factor determining differences in consumption patterns. The principal explanatory variable used in all cases was total expenditure (excluding direct taxes). Even on the theoretical level there are strong arguments for using this variable rather than current income, (cf., [12, p. 80–81]). On a more practical level the unambiguousness of total expendi-ture is particularly important when we have to deal with data of various origins whose exact nature is not always precisely described. One other variable, family size (defined as the number of persons), was introduced whenever possible.

A list of the surveys utilized is given in Table I. It will be noted that nearly all of them refer to urban households. As to the selection of data, an attempt was made to include all surveys conducted after World War II for which the results were available in sufficient detail. The search was facilitated by the bibliography in [16]. The minimal degree of detail that made a survey eligible for analysis was a one-way classification of the four major expenditure groups by income or total expenditure. Only the data for Brazil were of a different nature, as explained below. A few available surveys, particularly for European countries and the United States, were excluded because they would not have added sufficient variety. A number of older surveys were also analyzed both to provide some comparison over time and to improve coverage of the poorer countries for which information is least adequate.

The selection of families within each survey had been done by various methods, such as random sampling from lists, voluntary cooperation, taking every tenth house in the street, etc. Although in theory random sampling is the best method, in practice it does not always work out satisfactorily because of the low response rates commonly obtained in surveys which require considerable effort on the part of the respondent. The selection of households and the results obtained are therefore subject to various biases, which are more fully discussed in [12, Ch. 4]. No attempt has been made here to correct for those biases.

The principal criterion by which the similarity of expenditure patterns in different countries was judged was the elasticity of particular items of expenditure with respect to total expenditure. In what follows, this elasticity will often be referred to, briefly though inaccurately, as the "income elasticity." The fact that an elasticity is independent of the units of measurement of the variables it relates was especially important for the present purpose since the original data were always expressed in national currencies and since no attempt could be made to determine appropriate rates of exchange. The official exchange rates are of very limited usefulness in view of the many restrictions on international trade.

The choice of a mathematical form for the relation between particular expenditures and total expenditure was a matter of great concern. As Prais [11] has shown, calculated income elasticities depend on the type of function that has been fitted. Practical considerations limited the choice of function to three types: the linear, semi-logarithmic, and double-logarithmic. Linear functions were used by Allen and Bowley, but it is now generally recognized that they do not provide an adequate fit. Indeed the considerable variation between income elasticities which Allen and Bowley observed in their data may be partly due to their choice of an inappropriate function. The semi-logarithmic function is a stronger contender; it was recommended by Prais and Houthakker [12] for necessities. In the present inquiry, however, the double-logarithmic function was preferred. Its deciding advantages, in addition to those given in [8], are that it allows more freedom in dealing with multiple currencies and that it permits an easier introduction of the effects of family size. Interestingly enough, Engel himself also used a double-logarithmic approximation in his paper of 1857 (pp. 30–31).

The function fitted was accordingly as follows:

$$\log Y_i = \alpha_i + \beta_i \log X_1 + \gamma_i \log X_2 + \epsilon_i$$

where Y_i is expenditure on the ith group of items, X_1 is total expenditure, X_2 is family size, ϵ_i is a disturbance term, and α_i, β_i, and γ_i are constants to be estimated. The parameters were estimated by means of classical least squares regression, with observations weighted according to the number of households represented in each group average. The multiple regression coefficients, β_i and γ_i are the partial elasticities of the ith group of items with respect to total expenditure and family size respectively.

In household surveys income (or total expenditure) and family size tend to be rather strongly correlated, particularly if the households all belong to the same social class. The reason is that larger families usually contain more earners, so that family income is higher. Even if this factor is absent the head of a large household is more likely to be in the prime of his life and earning-power compared to the young head of a newly-formed and small household or the aged head of a household from which the children have departed. The implication is that if households are grouped by income or total expenditure it is impossible to obtain reliable estimates for β_i and γ_i in the above equation, because the two effects are inextricably intermingled. Multiple regressions can only be estimated if each of the predetermined variables has enough independent variation.

Reliable estimates can be obtained if the households are cross-classified by income (or total expenditure) and family size.[2] Unfortunately many surveys are published without cross-classifications; for those surveys a special procedure for estimating β_i (applied only to food) was necessary.

Before discussing this complication we give the results for cross-classified surveys in Table II. This table also contains results for Poland which are based on data for individual households rather than on group averages, and for France and Italy which are not based on cross-classifications by total expenditure and family size. In the latter two cases a regional and occupational breakdown, together with a one-way classification by total expenditure, was used which provided a sufficient variation in total expenditure and family size, provided the observed differences in expenditure items can indeed be attributed to those determinants. Since such an assumption is somewhat questionable the Italian and French elasticities deserve less confidence than the other ones. In the case of Mexico only estimates for food are given, the reason being that it was not possible to discover the number of households in each group average, so that an unweighted regression was computed although the numbers in the different groups apparently varied considerably. The correlation of food expenditure on total expenditure and family size was very high and the effect of weighting (had it been possible) would have been slight, but for the other items the correlation was somewhat lower and an unweighted regression might have been misleading. The regressions for Ireland were also unweighted, but this probably did not affect the results because the numbers in the groups appeared to be rather similar. Standard errors are given in brackets.

The data for Germany 1928, the Netherlands, and the United Kingdom were broken down according to the occupation of the head of the household. In order to derive combined figures it was assumed that the occupations had the same values of β_i and γ_i, but different values of α_i. This amounts to postulating that the occupations differ in their expenditure patterns by multiplicative "social-class factors," which represent effects other than those of total expenditure and family size. This technique is more fully discussed in [8, p. 17]; see also [12, Ch. 11].

Let us now look at the elasticities with respect to total expenditure in Table II. Those for food are all significantly less than one and therefore confirm Engel's law abundantly.[3] The range, however, is substantial, the highest figure being .731 for Poland and the lowest .344 for the British middle-class survey. Since

[2] Almost equally good results can be obtained if two one-way classifications *and* a joint frequency distribution of all households by income and family size are available. The appropriate procedure [9] was discovered too recently for use in the present analysis.

[3] Engel's law strictly speaking refers to income elasticities, but the latter are normally smaller than elasticities with respect to total expenditure (since the elasticity of total expenditure with respect to income is normally less than one), and the strict form of the law is therefore also confirmed. See [12, pp. 101–102].

ENGEL'S LAW

TABLE II
PARTIAL ELASTICITIES FOR FOUR EXPENDITURE GROUPS WITH RESPECT TO
TOTAL EXPENDITURE (b) AND FAMILY SIZE (c)

Country	Food		Clothing		Housing		Miscellaneous	
	b	c	b	c	b	c	b	c
Austria	.554	.351	1.767	−.350	.741	−.210	1.620	−.392
	(.019)	(.022)	(.055)	(.064)	(.038)	(.044)	(.022)	(.025)
Canadaᵃ	.647	.292	1.337	−.114	1.114	−.447	1.131	−.061
	(.008)	(.007)	(.092)	(.081)	(.043)	(.038)	(.036)	(.032)
Finland	.621	.272	1.622	−.310	.802	.008	1.445	−.367
	(.026)	(.019)	(.063)	(.047)	(.077)	(.056)	(.048)	(.036)
Franceᵇ	.483	.466	1.158	.232	1.098	−.652	1.656	−.536
	(.020)	(.029)	(.024)	(.034)	(.048)	(.068)	(.029)	(.041)
Germany 1907	.537	.261	1.498	.061	.913	−.154	1.604	−.358
	(.018)	(.015)	(.045)	(.038)	(.026)	(.022)	(.046)	(.039)
Germany 1927–28 manual workers	.598	.291	1.297	−.014	1.056	.476	1.474	−.481
	(.035)	(.019)	(.054)	(.029)	(.483)	(.262)	(.334)	(.181)
Germany 1927–28, clerical workers	.501	.274	1.035	.226	.881	−.052	1.469	−.298
	(.030)	(.025)	(.059)	(.049)	(.070)	(.058)	(.089)	(.074)
Germany 1927–28, government officials	.385	.319	.918	.149	.887	−.023	1.606	−.335
	(.027)	(.027)	(.079)	(.081)	(.054)	(.055)	(.069)	(.071)
Germany 1927–28, all three groupsᶜ	.473	.295	1.049	.102	.906	.196	1.447	.034
	(.020)	(.015)	(.047)	(.036)	(.045)	(.035)	(.082)	(.063)
Irelandᵍ	.597	.323	1.177	.009	.705	−.221	1.478	−.219
	(.019)	(.024)	(.307)	(.382)	(.021)	(.026)	(.025)	(.032)
Italyᵈ	.602	.346	1.042	−.733	ᵉ		ᵉ	
	(.096)	(.312)	(.196)	(.733)				
Japan 1955	.556	.309	1.593	−.051	.861	−.383	1.416	−.178
	(.025)	(.027)	(.119)	(.128)	(.023)	(.024)	(.040)	(.043)
Latviaᶠ	.430	.482	1.094	−.065	1.024	.002	1.567	−.516
	(.030)	(.033)	(.077)	(.084)	(.059)	(.062)	(.037)	(.040)
Mexicoᵍ	.657	.248	ᵉ		ᵉ		ᵉ	
	(.017)	(.014)						
Netherlands manual workers	.714	.237	1.634	−.110	.514	.021	1.273	−.241
	(.050)	(.014)	(.097)	(.027)	(.129)	(.036)	(.106)	(.029)
Netherlands white collar workers	.490	.304	1.059	.034	.619	−.016	1.403	−.157
	(.025)	(.019)	(.043)	(.034)	(.044)	(.035)	(.045)	(.036)
Netherlands both groupsᶜ	.502	.291	1.088	.001	.613	−.001	1.406	−.200
	(.022)	(.014)	(.045)	(.029)	(.036)	(.023)	(.041)	(.026)
Norwayʰ	.515	.131	1.266	−.044	.800	.031	1.524	−.296
	(.048)	(.030)	(.237)	(.149)	(.144)	(.091)	(.050)	(.032)
Polandⁱ	.731	.213	1.784	−.497	.662	−.068	1.774	−.534
	(.030)	(.027)	(.041)	(.036)	(.026)	(.022)	(.030)	(.026)
Sweden	.631	.311	1.119	.003	.803	−.008	1.446	−.269
	(.048)	(.048)	(.138)	(.138)	(.085)	(.084)	(.047)	(.046)
Switzerland	.460	.397	1.445	.044	.824	−.137	1.879	−.629
	(.036)	(.026)	(.075)	(.055)	(.242)	(.178)	(.118)	(.086)
United Kingdom, working class	.594	.294	1.042	.143	.553	−.072	1.793	−.390
	(.021)	(.019)	(.029)	(.026)	(.026)	(.023)	(.026)	(.023)
United Kingdom, middle class	.344	.386	1.342	−.111	.346	.145	1.488	−.221
	(.019)	(.021)	(.154)	(.169)	(.031)	(.034)	(.016)	(.018)
United Kingdom both groupsᶜ	.519	.330	1.096	.139	.477	−.045	1.640	−.358
	(.027)	(.032)	(.057)	(.067)	(.023)	(.027)	(.027)	(.032)
United States 1901ʰ	.712	.158	1.435	.016	.839	−.111	1.561	−.241
	(.004)	(.002)	(.019)	(.012)	(.016)	(.010)	(.045)	(.028)
United States 1950, large cities, North	.693	.224	1.399	.016	.764	−.155	1.367	−.111
	(.017)	(.016)	(.059)	(.054)	(.011)	(.010)	(.011)	(.010)

TABLE II—*Continued*

Country	Food		Clothing		Housing		Miscellaneous	
	b	c	b	c	b	c	b	c
United States 1950, sub-	.664	.280	1.303	.135	.978	−.236	1.255	−.125
urbs, North	(.029)	(.030)	(.090)	(.092)	(.115)	(.117)	(.108)	(.112)
United States 1950, small	.653	.258	1.367	.074	.810	−.237	1.370	−.068
cities, North	(.029)	(.028)	(.079)	(.076)	(.054)	(.052)	(.049)	(.047)
United States 1950, large	.685	.213	1.231	.134	.789	−.271	1.245	−.097
cities, South	(.015)	(.015)	(.055)	(.055)	(.040)	(.040)	(.021)	(.021)
United States 1950, sub-	.698	.190	1.147	.175	.974	−.292	1.178	−.090
urbs, South	(.037)	(.034)	(.062)	(.057)	(.085)	(.078)	(.036)	(.033)
United States 1950, small	.687	.235	1.068	.287	1.122	−.543	1.217	−.151
cities, South	(.031)	(.032)	(.055)	(.057)	(.081)	(.083)	(.033)	(.034)
United States 1950, large	.682	.193	1.410	−.111	.654	−.182	1.243	−.044
cities, West	(.023)	(.021)	(.048)	(.045)	(.032)	(.029)	(.011)	(.010)
United States 1950, sub-	.709	.225	1.285	.124	.933	−.401	1.081	−.111
urbs, West	(.031)	(.028)	(.067)	(.061)	(.031)	(.028)	(.010)	(.010)
United States 1950, small	.645	.292	1.195	.145	.766	−.292	1.286	−.187
cities, West	(.029)	(.029)	(.064)	(.063)	(.059)	(.059)	(.038)	(.038)
United States 1950, all	.692	.221	1.280	.080	.895	−.287	1.248	−.082
classes of cities	(.002)	(.002)	(.006)	(.006)	(.013)	(.012)	(.006)	(.006)

[a] Direct taxes (which are excluded from total and miscellaneous expenditure) estimated from other data in source.
[b] Based on breakdown by city (Paris, Rennes and 17 others combined) and total expenditure.
[c] Allowing for possible social-class differences in levels of Engel curves (see text).
[d] Based on breakdown by region (North vs. South), farm vs. non-farm, and total expenditure.
[e] Not computed because of insufficient data.
[f] Family size estimated from number of equivalent adults.
[g] Unweighted (see text).
[h] "Normal" families only, consisting of two adults and young children.
[i] Based on figures for individual households.

the standard errors are quite small the differences between the various estimates are mostly significant. The figures for Germany 1927–28, for the United Kingdom, and for the Netherlands, all of which refer to different social groups suggest that the elasticities for food may decrease with an increase in the general level of income, (see also [17, p. 271], though there is not much support for this thesis in the remainder of the table. It will be noted, for instance, that the elasticities for the United States and Canada are high compared to those of most European countries.

An explanation of the differences between the elasticities consequently seems difficult. It is conceivable, and indeed probable, that relative prices may influence the elasticities; thus it has sometimes been suggested that the income elasticity of a commodity is an increasing function of its price relative to other commodities. It is also possible that the income elasticity is determined not by the relative price of the item as a whole, but by relations among the prices of its components. No attempt can be made here to verify these ideas, but they may be fruitful for further research.

The elasticities for clothing with respect to total expenditure are all, with one statistically insignificant exception, greater than unity, and, with five exceptions, less than 1.5. In the technical sense clothing is therefore a luxury, though a moderate one. No particular pattern is apparent in the elasticities for different countries, and here again prices may have been an important determinant.

For housing (which includes fuel and light, but not furniture) the elasticities are mostly below one. Very small values are observed for the U.K., particularly in the middle-class survey. Even within the U.S. there are considerable differences in the elasticities; it appears that they are largest for suburbs (except in the South) and smallest in large cities. The reason might be that only persons who are prepared to spend a relatively large part of additional income on housing will move to the suburbs. Apart from this factor (whose importance for other countries has not been investigated) the pattern is again fairly random. Housing elasticities are presumably affected not only by international differences in rent, but also by the various types of rent control that exist in most countries. It appears, however, that on the whole housing is a necessity in the technical sense, a phenomenon known as Schwabe's law.[4]

The elasticities for miscellaneous expenditures are all well above one; indeed those for the Dutch manual workers, Canada, and the United States are the only ones below 1.4. In the latter two countries the larger share of transportation expenses, which are more of a necessity there, partly explains the low elasticity, though it should also be pointed out that the elasticities for the four commodity groups are not independent of each other. The sum of the four elasticities, each being weighted by the expenditure on the commodity concerned, must always equal unity (in formula, $\sum Y_i \beta_i = X_1$). As total expenditure rises, the share of the luxuries increases by definition, and to preserve the identity just mentioned it is necessary that some or all of the elasticities decline. In Canada and the United States, which have high average total expenditures, the elasticity for food is relatively high; those for clothing and housing are about average; hence the elasticity for miscellaneous items must be relatively low. A rather similar argument applies to the Dutch manual workers.

It also follows from this argument that the assumed constancy of elasticities can only be satisfied approximately and over limited ranges of total expenditure. This is a well-known defect of double-logarithmic Engel curves [12, p. 82 ff.], which has to be offset against their many advantages such as good fit, ease of computation, and automatic correction for heteroscedasticity. Perhaps one day a new type of Engel curve will be found which satisfies all theoretical requirements and fits the data adequately, though no doubt at the cost of increased computational difficulty. In the meantime various checks indicate that the above defect is numerically of minor importance.

Turning now to the elasticities with respect to family size in Table II we recall first that family size is measured by the number of persons, without any weighting according to age and sex. This measure is readily available in most surveys. A more correct treatment of family size is quite complicated, whereas blind application of an equivalent-adult scale intended for nutritional purposes to all commodities is probably worse than useless, not to speak of the difficulty of choosing between the many scales that have been proposed from Engel's days

---

[4] Those elasticities with respect to total expenditure that are greater than one would probably be below one if they were converted to income elasticities.

to our own. The procedure followed in the present paper is crude but flexible, and therefore suitable for the uniform analysis of several sets of data.

The coefficients γ_i in the equation on p. 539 actually represent a combination of two effects. The first or "specific" effect results from the increase in the "need" for various commodities when family size increases. The increase in need is usually less than proportional to the increase in size (no matter how the latter is measured) because of "economies of scale" in large households. Since an increase in family size does not increase the need for every commodity in the same proportion (and may indeed reduce the need for some), and since γ_i refers to the influence of family size when total expenditure is held constant, there is also what is metaphorically called an income effect: an increase in family size makes people relatively poorer. Although, for example, an increase in family size may increase a household's "need" for clothing, the simultaneously arising "need" for more food may force it to spend less for clothing on balance. In an adequate analysis these two opposing effects could be separated, but the coefficients γ_i fail to do so. If the specific effect is stronger than the income effect γ_i will be positive, otherwise it will be negative.

The elasticities with respect to family size are related to each other by an identity, just as the elasticities with respect to total expenditure were seen to be. Since the γ_i are partial elasticities the total effect of a change in family size on all expenditures must be zero, and hence $\sum Y_i \gamma_i = 0$. Consequently it is not possible for the γ_i to be all positive or all negative.

From Table II it appears that the partial elasticities for food with respect to family size are all significantly positive, and mostly between .2 and .35. The samples for which the lowest values were found, viz., Norway and the United States 1901, both consisted of "normal" families only, i.e., of families composed of two parents with varying numbers of young children. Since in such families an increase in family size necessarily means an increase in children rather than in adults, it is not surprising that γ is lower in those two cases than in surveys where an increase in family size will normally involve a certain proportion of adults. The use of a common unit-consumer scale for food in all surveys would have prevented this discrepancy, though it would have raised other problems and was in any case impracticable.[5]

The estimates of γ for clothing and housing illustrate previous remarks about the interaction of specific and "income" effects of family size. For both items the specific effects are no doubt positive (probably more strongly for clothing than for housing), but nevertheless many of the partial elasticities are negative. In the case of clothing it appears that the γ's are most likely to be negative in the surveys with the lowest average total expenditures. In those surveys the specific effect of family size on food was evidently strong enough to submerge the specific effect on clothing. Even in one of the U.S. city classes, however, γ is negative,

[5] On the basis of an analysis of a number of U. S. surveys (including some not analyzed here) Brady and Barber [4] arrived at a value of γ of $\frac{1}{3}$. This estimate has become known as the "cube-root law." Our calculations suggest that a value of $\frac{1}{3}$ is somewhat too high, particularly for the United States. The estimation procedure followed by these authors was apparently rather different from our own.

and so it is in Canada. In the latter two cases the rather high value of the elasticity of clothing with respect to total expenditure may be part of the explanation, for the income effect will be the stronger, the larger the "income elasticity" of the item concerned. The γ's for housing are mostly negative.

It is hard to say whether the specific effect of family size on miscellaneous expenditures as a whole is positive or negative. For items like entertainment and domestic help it is quite conceivably negative, but for other components (domestic appliances, furniture, transportation) it is probably positive. For the group as a whole the specific effect may therefore be small, and the γ's, which are all negative, would then be determined mostly by the income effect. Here again γ appears to be most negative where β is largest.

So far we have looked only at surveys for which separate estimates of the β's and γ's could be made. For the other surveys listed in Table I the information presented was not sufficient for that purpose. This is particularly unfortunate because the cross-classified surveys only refer to European and North American countries and to Japan, whereas countries elsewhere, with their lower income levels, are more interesting from the point of view of economic development. While the estimates from the latter countries are consequently less reliable than those from the countries with cross-classified data, they are by no means useless, because the information in Table II provides a basis for interpreting and adjusting them.

The unadjusted estimates in Table III are the gross elasticities for each of the four expenditure groups with respect to total expenditure, no allowance being made for variations in family size. Since family size and total expenditure are positively correlated, this means that the unadjusted b_i's in Table III overstate the effect of total expenditure when the effect of family size (as measured by γ_i) would have been positive. When γ_i would have been negative the unadjusted b_i's understate the effect of total expenditure.

The γ_i's appropriate to the surveys in Table III are of course unknown, but for food, at least, there is enough similarity in the γ_i's of Table II to warrant a crude adjustment. If we put γ_{food} equal to .28, for instance (which is approximately the mean for Table II), then the b's in Table III can be adjusted by reducing each by $.28 \sum w\tilde{x}_1\tilde{x}_2 / \sum w\tilde{x}_1^2$, where $\tilde{x}_1$ is the logarithm of total expenditure measured from its mean, $\tilde{x}_2$ is the logarithm of family size measured from its mean, w is the number of households in each group, and the summation extends over all groups in the survey.[6] The adjusted b's for food are also given in Table III.

It will be seen, then, that the adjusted estimates of β_{food} in Table III are not too dissimilar from those in Table II. In order to give an impression of the effect of the adjustment a few surveys already present in Table II have also been included in Table III (Austria, Canada, France, Germany 1928, Ireland, Sweden, and U.S. 1950); Italy, too, has been included, although no adjustment was pos-

---

[6] This formula can be easily verified by putting as the dependent variable not y (the logarithm of food expenditure) but $y - .28\, x_2$.

TABLE III
GROSS ELASTICITIES FOR FOUR EXPENDITURE GROUPS WITH RESPECT TO
TOTAL EXPENDITURE, AND ADJUSTED ELASTICITIES FOR FOOD

Country	Food		Clothing	Housing	Miscella-neous
	Unad-justed b	Adjusted b	Unad-justed b	Unad-justed b	Unad-justed b
Australia,	.390	a	1.025	1.180	1.323
Queensland	(.037)		(.043)	(.076)	(.087)
Austria	.732	.590	1.589	.634	1.422
	(.041)		(.063)	(.042)	(.046)
Belgium	.849	.849	1.338	.794	1.992
	(.010)		(.087)	(.014)	(.066)
Brazil	.802	.795	1.332	1.227	1.174
	(.028)		(.105)	(.136)	(.120)
Burma, Rangoon, Hindustani	.826	.826	.775	.947	1.465
	(.024)		(.069)	(.037)	(.073)
Burma, Rangoon, Tamils, Telugus, Uriyas	.847	.847	.658	1.316	1.430
	(.036)		(.049)	(.113)	(.042)
Burma, Rangoon, Chittagonians	.703	.703	1.448	1.031	1.630
	(.024)		(.101)	(.103)	(.096)
Canada	.867	.712	1.250	.777	1.085
	(.051)		(.069)	(.079)	(.028)
Ceylon	.856	.810	1.108	1.118	1.290
	(.037)		(.063)	(.168)	(.053)
China, Peiping	.651	.591	1.328	.940	1.489
	(.011)		(.054)	(.032)	(.041)
China, Shanghai	.769	.617	1.609	.714	1.440
	(.065)		(.045)	(.046)	(.100)
Cuba	.704	a	1.104	1.160	1.292
	(.020)		(.034)	(.061)	(.033)
France	.581	a	1.404	.781	1.621
	(.035)		(.062)	(.059)	(.033)
Germany 1928 (combined)	.532	.383	1.070	.946	1.454
	(.058)		(.050)	(.133)	(.082)
Germany 1951	.579	.526	1.436	.681	1.552
	(.034)		(.086)	(.024)	(.042)
Ghana, Accra	.952	.840	.967	.635	1.365
	(.024)		(.098)	(.062)	(.029)
Ghana, Kumasi	.954	.818	1.042	.618	1.495
	(.032)		(.091)	(.044)	(.084)
Ghana, Sekondi-Takoradi	.823	.654	1.289	.725	1.600
	(.037)		(.065)	(.065)	(.064)
Ghana, Akuse	.873	.791	.865	1.142	1.503
	(.037)		(.086)	(.099)	(.059)
Guatemala, Guatemala City	.750	.508	1.308	1.029	1.548
	(.036)		(.091)	(.087)	(.012)
India, Bombay Single workers	.709	.709	.486	1.475	1.538
	(.049)		(.050)	(.099)	(.103)
India, Bombay Workers' families	.837	.837	.775	.733	1.801
	(.015)		(.141)	(.068)	(.407)
India, Bhopal City	1.004	.821	.900	.730	1.223
	(.013)		(.045)	(.042)	(.060)

TABLE III—*Continued*

Country	Food		Clothing	Housing	Miscella-neous
	Unad-justed *b*	Adjusted *b*	Unad-justed *b*	Unad-justed *b*	Unad-justed *b*
India, Punjab	.943	.811	1.161	.764	1.394
	(.027)		(.252)	(.037)	(.024)
Ireland	.775	.621	1.224	.583	1.358
	(.052)		(.194)	(.038)	(.039)
Italy	.615	*a*	1.219		
	(.026)		(.034)		
Japan 1953	.648	.563	1.398	.906	1.387
	(.017)		(.149)	(.034)	(.011)
Libya	.895	.805	1.830	.900	1.403
	(.073)		(.165)	(.165)	(.329)
Northern Rhodesia	.514	.393	1.081	.229	1.308
	(.109)		(.093)	(.131)	(.040)
Panama, Panama City	.790	.717	1.226	.932	1.232
	(.055)		(.064)	(.072)	(.030)
Philippines, Manila	.810	.757	1.141	.874	1.312
	(.028)		(.037)	(.047)	(.026)
Portugal, Porto	.779	.623	1.296	.564	1.246
	(.047)		(.445)	(.301)	(.122)
Puerto Rico, San Juan	.699	.692	.957	1.049	1.177
	(.040)		(.026)	.083	(.076)
Puerto Rico, Whole Territory	.812	*a*	1.147	.963	1.315
	(.031)		(.055)	(.108)	(.019)
Sweden	.843	.652	1.139	.749	1.261
	(.092)		(.077)	(.061)	(.087)
United States 1950	.816	.642	1.336	.731	1.222
	(.025)		(.048)	(.273)	(.037)

a Adjustment not possible.

sible for lack of data. The adjustment evidently goes in the right direction, but it sometimes overshoots the mark.

The figures in Table III for surveys not included in Table II again lend some support to the suggestion made earlier that the elasticity for food with respect to total expenditure might be higher for the countries and time periods with lower average total expenditures, though the evidence is equivocal.[7] A very high elasticity is found, for instance, for data used by Engel in his original article (Belgium 1853, data originally collected by Ducpétiaux). In that survey no adjustment was necessary because all households were of the same size (two adult;

[7] It is also possible, however, that there is a statistical bias at work. Total expenditure is not strictly a predetermined variable, and it is conceivable that households have a high total expenditure because they happen to have a high food expenditure. This bias is more likely to be serious when food is a large fraction of the total, as it is in the poorer countries The effect of the bias is to raise the estimate of the elasticity of food with respect to total expenditure. It will be reduced if the households are classified by income (as is the case in most surveys) rather than by total expenditure. The author is indebted to Robert Summers and Jens Lübbert for bringing this point to his attention.

TABLE IV
SUPPLEMENTARY DATA

Country	Geometric mean of total expenditure in 1950 U.S.$	Geometric mean of family size	Food	Clothing	Housing	Misc.
Australia, Queensland	3,572	4.2	30	9	21	40
Austria	713	2.28	53	10	11	26
Belgium	200	6	64	14	14	8
Brazil	318	4.4	49	8	15	28
Burma, Rangoon, Hindustani	86	1	54	6	12	28
Burma, Rangoon, Tamils, etc.	114	1	61	9	16	14
Burma, Rangoon, Chittagonians	101	1	60	10	12	18
Canada	2,418	3.0	31	13	11	45
Ceylon	293	4.2	65	8	5	22
China, Peiping	268	4.5	47	7	21	26
China, Shanghai	156	4.6	54	7	15	24
Cuba	2,029		46	9	16	29
Finland	1,320	3.9	50	17	10	23
France	1,633	3.0	49	10	9	32
Germany 1907	1,700	4.3	45	10	20	25
Germany 1928, Manual	980	3.7	42	12	14	32
Germany 1928, Clerical	1,355	3.2	33	13	16	38
Germany 1928; Officials	1,454	3.5	33	14	17	36
Germany 1928, All	1,190	3.5	37	13	15	35
Germany 1951	1,887	3.6	42	15	15	28
Ghana, Accra	417	4.2	59	12	11	18
Ghana, Kumasi	381	4.1	58	14	14	14
Ghana, Sekondi-Takoradi	347	3.9	59	14	12	15
Ghana, Akuse	263	4.5	60	18	7	15
Guatemala, Guatemala City	1,129	5.0	52	10	21	17
India, Bombay, Single Workers	150	1	56	6	8	30
India, Bombay, Workers' Families	225	4	58	9	16	17
India, Bhopal City	186	4.9	61	8	13	18
India, Punjab	206	4.6	73	4	12	11
Ireland	1,327	4.1	40	13	15	32
Italy	1,237	4.5	46	15		
Japan 1953	567	4.8	50	8	12	30
Japan 1955	582	3.88	45	10	11	34
Latvia	670	2.9	34	15	15	36
Libya	196	5.4	70	6	11	13
Mexico, Mexico City	2,201	3.8	40			
Netherlands, Manual	900	3.91	39	13	14	34
Netherlands, White Collar	1,311	3.62	29	14	13	44
Netherlands, Both Groups	1,123	3.74	33	14	13	40
Northern Rhodesia	2,821	3.8	24	10	9	57
Norway	1,467	2.9	37	16	11	36
Panama, Panama City	1,758	4.9	38	12	17	33
Philippines, Manila	883	5.9	50	8	14	28
Poland	422	4.7	64	11	9	16
Portugal	580	4.4	58	7	15	20
Puerto Rico. Whole Territory	868		53	12	9	26
Sweden	1,267	2.2	37	12	16	35
Switzerland	1,602	4.1	46	10	17	27

TABLE IV—*Continued*

Country	Geometric mean of total expenditure in 1950 U.S.$	Geometric mean of family size	Proportion spent on			
			Food	Cloth-ing	Housing	Misc.
United Kingdom, Working Class	1,751	3.5	37	8	29	26
United Kingdom, Middle Class	3,887	3.0	25	12	19	44
United Kingdom, Both Groups	2,280	2.46	35	10	21	34
United States 1901	1,502	3.7	44	13	24	19
U.S. 1950, Large Cities, North	3,372	2.6	32	11	22	35
U.S. 1950, Suburbs, North	3,910	2.9	30	11	21	38
U.S. 1950, Small Cities, North	3,038	2.7	31	10	23	36
U.S. 1950, Large Cities, South	2,960	2.7	31	11	13	45
U.S. 1950, Suburbs, South	3,563	2.9	30	10	11	49
U.S. 1950, Small Cities, West	2,495	2.7	32	12	10	46
U.S. 1950, Large Cities, West	3,275	2.4	30	10	13	47
U.S. 1950, Suburbs, West	3,592	2.8	29	10	11	50
U.S. 1950, Small Cities, West	3,197	2.6	31	10	11	48
U.S. 1950, All Classes of Cities	3,290	2.6	31	11	16	42

and four children).[8] The elasticities for the three Indian surveys, which probably refer to the poorest households of all, are also very high, but those for China are about average. There is ample scope for further study here.

In the case of clothing, housing, and miscellaneous expenditures no adjustment has been made because the relevant estimates of γ in Table II are too variable and (for clothing and housing) often not significantly different from zero. It is likely that the relatively low values of b_i in Table III need to be adjusted upward and the relatively high ones adjusted downward, but Table II provides no guidance for doing so. The gross elasticities for "miscellaneous" no doubt require an upward adjustment, which is probably of the same absolute order of magnitude as the downward adjustment applied to the gross elasticities for food.

Table IV contains some data that may assist the reader in interpreting and elaborating the results of this paper. It gives first the geometric mean of total expenditure per household in U.S. dollars of 1950, obtained by converting the figure in local currency by the official dollar exchange rate during the year in which the survey was made,[9] and adjusting this to 1950 U.S. prices by means of the U.S. cost-of-living index. It should be stressed that *official* exchange rates were used, so that the figures in Table IV cannot be immediately used for international comparisons of real income;[10] moreover most of the surveys do not

[8] In the three surveys from Burma no adjustment was necessary either, because they covered single workers. These people sent a considerable part of their earnings to their families, but the remittances were not regarded as part of their expenditure. The same applies to the single workers in Bombay (India). Those families from Bombay that were included in the present analysis all consisted of two adults and two children, so the unadjusted and adjusted b again coincide.

[9] For countries with a multiple exchange system the lowest rate quoted was used.

[10] Such comparisons have been made by Gilbert and Kravis [7] for European countries *vs.* the United States and by Watanabe and Komiya [15] for Japan *vs.* the United States.

pretend to cover the whole country. Table IV also gives the geometric mean[11] of family size and the ratios which the geometric means of food, clothing, and miscellaneous expenditures bear to their total. The total of those four means does not necessarily equal the geometric mean of total expenditure, but the discrepancy is apparently nowhere more than two or three per cent.[12]

A question naturally raised by the data of Table IV is whether the differences in average expenditure on the four commodity groups among different countries can be explained in the same way as differences within one country can be explained. The answer is that variations in total expenditure and family size certainly account for a large part of the differences in composition, but since prices are also likely to be important such an explanation would be too one-sided to deserve much confidence. An analysis involving prices is outside the scope of this paper.

Some final comments are in order. What has been shown is mainly that the elasticities of the four main items of expenditure with respect to total expenditure are similar[13] but not equal, and that the elasticities with respect to family size are rather similar (but also unequal) for food and miscellaneous items, and irregular for clothing and housing. To return to the problem of development planning mentioned in the beginning of the paper: if no data on the expenditure patterns of a country are available at all, one would not be very far astray by putting the partial elasticity with respect to total expenditure at .6 for food, 1.2 for clothing, .8 for housing, and 1.6 for all other items combined, and the partial elasticity with respect to family size at .3 for food, zero for housing and clothing, and −.4 for miscellaneous expenditures. But it would be prudent not to use those guesses for wide extrapolations, and more prudent still to organize a survey and cross-classify the results.

Stanford University

REFERENCES

[1] ALLEN, R. G. D. AND A. L. BOWLEY: *Family Expenditure*. London: 1935.
[2] BENNETT, MERRILL K.: *The World's Food*. New York: 1954.
[3] BLACK, G.: "Variations in Prices Paid for Food by Income Level," *Journal of Farm Economics*, XXXIV (1952), p. 52.
[4] BRADY, D. S. AND H. A. BARBER: "The Pattern of Food Expenditures," *Review of Economics and Statistics*, XXX (1948), p. 198.
[5] BRISTOL, R.: Unpublished Ph.D. thesis at Yale University (1955).
[6] ENGEL, E.: "Die Productions- und Consumptionsverhältnisse des Königreichs

---

[11] Geometric means were used because of the constant elasticity assumption made in this paper. Strictly speaking they are weighted geometric means of arithmetic group means, for in most cases no individual data were available.

[12] These ratios are given merely to facilitate examination of the elasticity estimates of this paper. Those interested in the composition of private expenditures in different countries should consult [14, Table 164].

[13] By "similar" is meant that the estimates fall in a fairly narrow range without, however, differing merely by sampling deviations from a common "true" value. The partial elasticities for food, to take an example, range from .34 to .73 rather than (say) from −1 to +3.

Sachsen," originally in *Zeitschrift des Statistischen Bureaus des Königlich Sächsischen Ministerium des Inneren*, Nos. 8 and 9, November 22, 1857, reprinted in *Bulletin de l'Institut International de Statistique*, IX (1895).

[7] GILBERT, M. AND I. B. KRAVIS: *An International Comparison of National Products and the Purchasing Power of Currencies*. Paris: 1953.

[8] HOUTHAKKER, H. S.: "The Econometrics of Family Budgets," *Journal of the Royal Statistical Society Series A*, CXV (1952) p. 1.

[9] ———: "The Combined Use of Differently Grouped Observations in Least-Squares Regression," to be published in the *Journal of the American Statistical Association*.

[10] JURÉEN, L.: "Long-Term Trends in Food Consumption, a Multi-Country Study," *Econometrica*, XXIV (1956), p. 1.

[11] PRAIS, S. J.: "Non-linear Estimates of the Engel Curve," *Review of Economic Studies*, XX (1953), p. 87.

[12] PRAIS, S. J. AND H. S. HOUTHAKKER: *The Analysis of Family Budgets*. Cambridge (England): 1955.

[13] STIGLER, G. J.: "The Early History of Empirical Studies of Consumer Behavior," *Journal of Political Economy*, LXII (1954), p. 95.

[14] UNITED NATIONS. *Statistical Yearbook 1956*.

[15] WATANABE, T. AND R. KOMIYA: "International Price Comparison between Japan and the United States" (abstract, in Japanese), *Kokusai-Keizai*, 1955.

[16] WILLIAMS, F. M.: "International Comparisons of Patterns of Family Consumption" (unpublished).

[17] WOLD, H. IN ASSOCIATION WITH L. JURÉEN: *Demand Analysis*. Stockholm and New York: 1953.

Econometrica, Vol. 26, 1 (January 1958)

ESTIMATION OF RELATIONSHIPS FOR LIMITED DEPENDENT VARIABLES[1]

By James Tobin

"What do you mean, *less* than nothing?" replied Wilbur. "I don't think there is any such thing as *less* than nothing. Nothing is absolutely the limit of nothingness. It's the lowest you can go. It's the end of the line. How can something be less than nothing? If there were something that was less than nothing then nothing would not be nothing, it would be something—even though it's just a very little bit of something. But if nothing is *nothing*, then nothing has nothing that is less than *it* is."

E. B. White, *Charlotte's Web*
(New York: Harper, 1952) p. 28.

1. INTRODUCTION

IN ECONOMIC SURVEYS of households, many variables have the following characteristics: The variable has a lower, or upper, limit and takes on the limiting value for a substantial number of respondents. For the remaining respondents, the variable takes on a wide range of values above, or below, the limit.

The phenomenon is quite familiar to students of Engel curve relationships showing how household expenditures on various categories of goods vary with household income. For many categories—"luxuries"—zero expenditures are the rule at low income levels. A single straight line cannot, therefore, represent the Engel curve for both low and high incomes. If individual households were identical, except for income level, the Engel curve would be a broken line like OAB in Figure 1. But if the critical income level OA were not the same for all households, the average Engel curve for groups of households would look like the curve OB. A similar kind of effect occurs under rationing of a consumers' good. The ration is an upper limit; many consumers choose to take their full ration, but some prefer to buy less.[2]

[1] I am grateful to colleagues at the Cowles Foundation for Research in Economics at Yale University, in particular Tjalling Koopmans and Richard Rosett, for helpful advice and comments, and to Donald Hester for computational assistance. I am glad to acknowledge that the work represented in the paper was begun during tenure of a Social Science Research Council Faculty Fellowship and finished in the course of a research program supported by the Ford Foundation. I wish to thank also the Survey Research Center of the University of Michigan and the Board of Governors of the Federal Research System for the data from the Surveys of Consumer Finances used in the illustration. My interest in methods of analysis of survey data derives in large part from a semester I was enabled to spend at the Survey Research Center in 1953–54 by the hospitality of the Center under a program financed by the Carnegie Foundation.

It may be of interest that Mr. Rosett has programmed the iterative estimation procedure of this paper for the IBM Type 650 Data-Processing Machine and has applied the technique to a problem involving 14 independent variables.

[2] For a theoretical exposition of the effects on aggregate demand functions of lower or upper limits on individual expenditure in combination with differences in tastes among households, see [4] and [6] and the literature there cited.

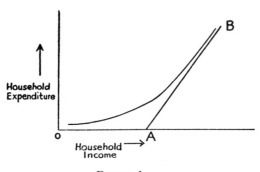

As a specific example, many—indeed, most—households would report zero expenditures on automobiles or major household durable goods during any given year. Among those households who made any such expenditure, there would be wide variability in amount.[3]

In other cases, the lower limit is not necessarily zero, nor is it the same for all households. Consider the net change in a household's holding of liquid assets during a year. This variable can be either positive or negative. But it cannot be smaller than the negative of the household's holdings of liquid assets at the beginning of the year; one cannot liquidate more assets than he owns.

Account should be taken of the concentration of observations at the limiting value when estimating statistically the relationship of a limited variable to other variables and in testing hypotheses about the relationship. An explanatory variable in such a relationship may be expected to influence both the probability of limit responses and the size of non-limit responses. If only the probability of limit and non-limit responses, without regard for the value of non-limit responses were to be explained, *probit analysis* provides a suitable statistical model. (See [2].) But it is inefficient to throw away information on the value of the dependent variable when it is available. If only the value of the variable were to be explained, if there were no concentration of observations at a limit, *multiple regression* would be an appropriate statistical technique. But when there is such concentration, the assumptions of the multiple regression model are not realized. According to that model, it should be possible to have values of the explanatory variables for which the expected value of the dependent variable is its limiting value; and from this expected value, as from other expected values, it should be possible to have negative as well as positive deviations.

A hybrid of probit analysis and multiple regression seems to be called for, and it is the purpose of this paper to present such a model.

2. THE MODEL

Let W be a limited dependent variable, with a lower limit of L. The limit may not be the same for all households in the population. Let Y be a linear combina-

---

[3] For figures on frequency of purchases and on the distribution of amounts spent among purchasers, see [1, Part II, Supplementary Tables 1, 5, and 10].

tion of the independent variables $(X_1, X_2, \cdots, X_m)$, to which W is by hypothesis related.

(1) $$Y = \beta_0 + \beta_1 X_1 + \beta_2 X_2 + \cdots \beta_m X_m.$$

Households differ from each other in their behavior regarding W for reasons for which differences in the independent variables X and the lower limit L do not fully account. Those other differences are taken to be random and to be reflected in ϵ, a random variable with mean zero and standard deviation σ, distributed normally over the population of households. Household behavior is then assumed to be as follows:

(2)
$$W = L \qquad\qquad (Y - \epsilon < L),$$
$$W = Y - \epsilon \qquad\qquad (Y - \epsilon \geqq L).$$

Let $P(x)$ represent the value of the cumulative unit-normal distribution function at x; let $Q(x) = 1 - P(x)$; let $Z(x)$ be the value of the unit-normal probability density function at x. The distribution of $W - L$ may be derived from the distribution of ϵ, as follows:

For given values of the linear combination Y and the limit L,

(3) $$Pr(W = L \mid Y, \ L) = Pr(\epsilon > Y - L) = Q\{(Y - L)/\sigma\}.$$

(4) $$Pr(W > x \geqq L \mid Y) = Pr(Y - \epsilon > x) = Pr(\epsilon < Y - x) = P\{(Y - x)/\sigma\}.$$

Consequently, the cumulative distribution function for W, for given Y and L, is:

(5)
$$F(x; Y, L) = 0 \qquad\qquad (x < L),$$
$$F(L; Y, L) = Q\{(Y - L)/\sigma\},$$
$$F(x; Y, L) = Q\{(Y - x)/\sigma\} \qquad\qquad (x > L).$$

The corresponding probability density function is:

(6) $$f(x; Y, L) = \frac{1}{\sigma} Z\{(Y - x)/\sigma\} \qquad\qquad (x > L).$$

The expected value of W for given values of Y and L is:

$$E(W; Y, L)$$

$$= LQ\{(Y - L)/\sigma\} + \int_L^\infty \frac{x}{\sigma} Z\{(Y - x)/\sigma\} \ dx$$

$$= LQ\{(Y - L)/\sigma\} + Y \int_{-\infty}^{(Y-L)/\sigma} Z(x) \ dx + \sigma \int_{-\infty}^{(Y-L)/\sigma} - xZ(x) \ dx.$$

Since $- xZ(x) = Z'(x) = dZ(x)/dx$, we have:

(7) $$E(W; Y, L) = LQ\{(Y - L)/\sigma\} + YP\{(Y - L)/\sigma\} + \sigma Z\{(Y - L)/\sigma\}.$$

3. THE MAXIMUM LIKELIHOOD SOLUTION

A sample includes q observations where W is at the limit L. Each observation consists of a limit L'_i, to which the dependent variable W'_i is equal, and a set of values of the independent variables $(X'_{1i}, X'_{2i}, \cdots, X'_{mi})$, where i is a subscript to denote the observation and runs from 1 to q. A sample also includes r observations for which W is above the limit L;[4] each one may be described as $(W_j, L_j, X_{1j}, X_{2j}, \cdots, X_{mj})$ where j runs from 1 to r.

Let $(a_0, a_1, a_2, \cdots, a_m, a)$ be estimates of $(\beta_0/\sigma, \beta_1/\sigma, \beta_2/\sigma, \cdots, \beta_m/\sigma, 1/\sigma)$. Let $I'_i = Y'_i a = a_0 + a_1 X'_{1i} + a_2 X'_{2i} + \cdots a_m X'_{mi}$ and let $I_j = Y_j a = a_0 + a_1 X_{1j} + a_2 X_{2j} + \cdots a_m X_{mj}$.

The likelihood of a sample is:

$$\phi(a_0, a_1, \cdots, a_m, a) = \prod_{i=1}^{q} F(L'_i ; Y'_i, L'_i) \cdot \prod_{j=1}^{r} f(W_j ; Y_j, L_j)$$

(8)
$$= \prod_{i=1}^{q} Q\left(\frac{Y'_i - L'_i}{1/a}\right) \cdot \prod_{j=1}^{r} aZ\left(\frac{Y_j - W_j}{1/a}\right)$$

$$= \prod_{i=1}^{q} Q(I'_i - aW'_i) \cdot \prod_{j=1}^{r} aZ(I_j - aW_j).$$

The natural logarithm of ϕ,

(9)
$$\ln \phi = \phi^*(a_0 a_1, \cdots, a_m, a)$$
$$= \sum_{i=1}^{q} \ln Q(I'_i - aW'_i) + r \ln a - \frac{r}{2} \ln 2\pi - \frac{1}{2} \sum_{j=1}^{r} (I_j - aW_j)^2.$$

Let X_0 and X'_0 be identically 1 for all i and j. Then setting the derivatives of ϕ^* equal to zero gives the following system of $m + 2$ equations.

(10)
$$\phi^*_k = \frac{\partial \phi^*}{\partial a_k} = \sum_{i=1}^{q} \frac{-Z(I'_i - aW'_i)X_{ki}}{Q(I'_i - aW'_i)} - \sum_{j=1}^{r} (I_j - aW_j)X_{kj} = 0$$

$$(k = 0, 1, 2, \cdots, m),$$

$$\phi^*_{m+1} = \frac{\partial \phi^*}{\partial a} = \sum_{i=1}^{q} \frac{Z(I'_i - aW'_i)W'_i}{Q(I'_i - aW'_i)} + \frac{r}{a} + \sum_{j=1}^{r} (I_j - aW_j)W_j = 0.$$

These equations are nonlinear. The quantity $-Z(x)/Q(x)$ is tabulated as $\Delta_{\min}$ in [2, pp. 185–88], where the argument for the table is $x + 5$.

The matrix of second derivatives, obtained by differentiating (10) is given by (11). Here $w'_{\min}(x)$ is the derivative of $-\Delta_{\min}(x)$, and may, like $\Delta_{\min}$, be found

---

[4] The value of L is assumed to be observable for the whole sample. I have made no investigation of the problems that would be presented by taking it as an unknown to be estimated.

by entering the tables of [2, pp. 185–188] with the argument $x + 5$.

$$\phi_{k,t}^* = \frac{\partial^2 \phi^*}{\partial a_k \partial a_t} = -\sum_{i=1}^{q} X_k' {}_{i} X_{t i}' w_{\min}'(I_i' - aW_i') - \sum_{j=1}^{r} X_{kj} X_{tj}$$

$$(k, t, = 0, 1, \cdots, m),$$

(11) $\quad \phi_{k,m+1}^* = \dfrac{\partial^2 \phi^*}{\partial a_k \partial a} = \displaystyle\sum_{i=1}^{q} W_i' X_{ki}' w_{\min}'(I_i' - aW_i') + \sum_{j=1}^{r} X_{kj} W_j$

$$(k = 0, 1, \cdots, m),$$

$$\phi_{m+1,m+1}^* = \frac{\partial^2 \phi^*}{\partial a^2} = -\sum_{i=1}^{q} W_i'^2 w_{\min}'(I_i' - aW_i') - \frac{r}{a^2} - \sum_{j=1}^{r} W_j^2.$$

Newton's method (see [3]) for iterative solution of (10), also known as the "method of scoring" (see [5]), may be applied as follows: Let

$$(a_0^{(0)}, a_1^{(0)}, \cdots, a_m^{(0)}, \cdots, a_{m+1}^{(0)})$$

be a trial solution, where, for notational convenience, a_{m+1} represents what has previously been written as simply a. (The choice of an initial trial solution will be discussed below.) New estimates

$$(a_0^{(0)} + \Delta a_0, a_1^{(0)} + \Delta a_1, \cdots, a_m^{(0)} + \Delta a_m, a_{m+1}^{(0)} + \Delta a_{m+1})$$

can be found by solving the set of $m + 1$ linear equations (12) for the Δa, where all the ϕ_k^* are assumed to be linear between the trial solution and the real solution.

$$\phi_k^*(a_0^{(0)} + \Delta a_0, \cdots, a_m^{(0)} + \Delta a_m, a_{m+1}^{(0)} + \Delta a_{m+1}) = \phi_k^*(a_0^{(0)}, a_1^{(0)}, \cdots, a_m^{(0)}, a_{m+1}^{(0)})$$

$$+ \sum_{t=0}^{m+1} \Delta a_t \phi_{kt}^*(a_0^{(0)}, a_1^{(0)}, \cdots, a_m^{(0)}, a_{m+1}^{(0)}) = 0 \qquad (k = 0, 1, 2, \cdots, m + 1).$$

(12) $\quad \displaystyle\sum_{t=0}^{m+1} \Delta a_t \phi_{kt}^*(a_0^{(0)}, a_1^{(0)}, \cdots, a_m^{(0)}, a_{m+1}^{(0)}) = -\phi_k^*(a_0^{(0)}, a_1^{(0)}, \cdots, a_m^{(0)}, a_{m+1}^{(0)}).$

The process may be repeated with the new estimates as provisional estimates until the Δa are negligible.

If the final estimates a_k are used to evaluate the matrix of second derivatives (11) at the point of maximum likelihood, the negative inverse of that matrix gives large-sample estimates of the variances and covariances of the estimates a_k around the corresponding population parameters.

4. TESTS OF HYPOTHESES

Hypotheses about the relationship of W to one or more of the independent variables X may be tested by the likelihood-ratio method. Consider for example, the hypothesis that $\beta_1 = \beta_2 = \cdots = \beta_m = 0$. This is the hypothesis that neither the probability nor the size of nonzero responses depends on the X's. According to the hypothesis, there remain only two parameters, β_0 and σ, to be estimated so as to maximize (9), which now becomes:

(13)
$$\phi^*(a_0, 0, 0, \cdots, 0, a) = \sum_{i=1}^{q} \ln Q(a_0 - aW_i')$$
$$- \frac{r}{2} \ln 2\pi + r \ln a - \frac{1}{2} \sum_{j=1}^{r} (a_0 - aW_j)^2.$$

The maximizing values of a_0 and a may be found by solving equations (10) similarly simplified by putting all other a_k equal to zero. If (13) is evaluated with these solutions, then the logarithm of the likelihood ratio λ is the difference between (13) and the value of (9) when it is maximized without the constraint of the hypothesis. The statistic $-2 \ln \lambda$ is for large samples approximately distributed by chi-square with m degrees of freedom. In similar fashion other hypotheses about subsets of the β's may be tested.

5. INITIAL TRIAL ESTIMATES

The speed of convergence of iteration by Newton's method depends, of course, on the choice of the initial trial estimates. The following procedure for finding initial estimates relies on a linear approximation of the function $-Z(x)/Q(x)$ or, in other words, on a quadratic approximation of $\ln Q(x)$. This approximation converts the first $m + 1$ equations of (10) into linear equations in the a_k for given a. These equations may be solved to give the a_k as linear functions of a. When

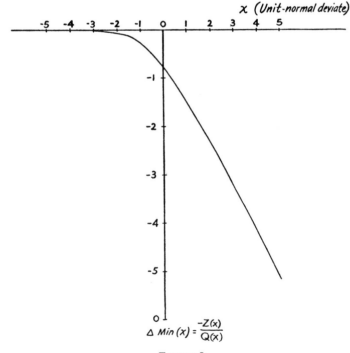

FIGURE 2

these solutions are substituted in the $m + 2$nd equation, it becomes a quadratic equation in a.

The function $\Delta_{\min}(x) = -Z(x)/Q(x)$ is graphed in Figure 2. Clearly it is not possible to approximate it linearly at all closely throughout its range. The important thing is to have a good approximation in the range where the sample observations are concentrated. There is no point in approximating well at $x = 4$ or $x = 5$ if the sample did not include constellations of the independent variables that made the probability of limit observations virtually nil. An easily computed estimate of the middle of the relevant range is x_o, the unit-normal deviate such that $Q(x_o) = q/(q + r)$, the proportion of cases in the sample for which the variable W takes on its limit-value. The tangent at x_o is one possible approximation, but not the best one, since it uniformly overestimates $\Delta_{\min}$ except at x_o itself.

Suppose that a linear approximation is fitted graphically:

$$(14) \qquad \Delta_{\min}(x) = A + Bx.$$

Substituting (14) in the first $m + 1$ equations of (10) gives

$$\sum_{i=1}^{q} (A X'_{ki} + B a_o X'_{oi} X'_{ki} + B a_1 X'_{1i} X'_{ki} + \cdots B a_m X'_{mi} X'_{ki} - B a W'_i X'_{ki})$$

$$- \sum_{j=1}^{r} (a_o X_{oj} X_{kj} + a_1 X_{1j} X_{kj} + a_m X_{mj} X_{kj} - a W_j X_{kj}) = 0,$$

$$(15) \quad a_o \left[\sum_{j=1}^{r} X_{oj} X_{kj} - B \sum_{i=1}^{q} X'_{oi} X'_{ki} \right] + a_1 \left[\sum_{j=1}^{r} X_{1j} X_{kj} - B \sum_{i=1}^{q} X'_{1i} X'_{ki} \right]$$

$$+ \cdots + a_m \left[\sum_{j=1}^{r} X_{mj} X_{kj} - B \sum_{i=1}^{r} X'_{mi} X'_{ki} \right]$$

$$= a \left[\sum_{j=1}^{r} W_j X_{kj} - B \sum_{j=1}^{q} W'_i X'_{ki} \right] + A \sum_{i=1}^{q} X'_{ki} \qquad (k = 0, 1, 2, \cdots, m).$$

Solving (15) gives numbers g_k and h_k such that:

$$(16) \qquad a_k = g_k + h_k a \qquad (k = 0, 1, 2, \cdots, m).$$

The final equation of (10) is, after using the approximation of (14):

$$\frac{r}{a} + a_o \left[\sum_{j=1}^{r} X_{oj} W - B \sum_{i=1}^{q} X'_{oi} W'_i \right]$$

$$(17) \qquad + \cdots + a_m \left[\sum_{j=1}^{r} X_{mj} W_j - B \sum_{j=1}^{q} X'_{mi} W'_i \right]$$

$$- a \left[\sum_{j=1}^{r} W_j^2 - B \sum_{i=1}^{q} W'^2_i \right] - A \sum_{i=1}^{q} W'_i = 0.$$

When (16) is substituted in (17), it becomes a quadratic equation in a. The solution of (17) may then be used in (16) to obtain initial trial estimates of all the coefficients.

6. AN EXAMPLE

For purposes of illustration, an example has been worked out using data from the reinterview portion of the 1952 and 1953 Surveys of Consumer Finances conducted by the Survey Research Center of the University of Michigan for the Board of Governors of the Federal Reserve System.[5]

The data refer to 735 primary nonfarm spending units[6] who were interviewed twice, once in early 1952 and once in early 1953. The frequencies, averages, and other statistics for the reinterview sample should not be taken as representative of the population of the United States. The Surveys of Consumer Finances do collect data on distributions of income, liquid assets, and durable goods purchases that are representative of that population; tables on these distributions may be found in [1]. But the reinterview sample, on which the calculations of this paper are based, fails to be representative insofar as it omits spending units who moved between the two surveys. Moreover, these calculations are based on simple counts of sampled spending units, without allowance for the fact that the sampling design gave some spending units greater probabilities of being included in the sample than others. The purpose of this example is not to estimate population frequency distributions, but only to examine the relationship of durable goods expenditure to age and liquid asset holdings within this sample. It is not necessary to consider here how the relationship exhibited in this sample differs from the one that would be exhibited in a complete enumeration. But it may well be that the sample gives unbiased estimates of the parameters of the relationship, even though it gives biased estimates of the separate frequency distribution of the variables.

The variables are as follows:

W, *the ratio of 1951–52 total durable goods expenditure to 1951–52 total disposable income.* Durable goods expenditure is the two-year sum of outlays, net of trade-ins or sales, for cars and major household appliances and furniture. Two-year dis-

---

[5] A brief general description of the concepts and methods of the annual Surveys of Consumer Finances is given in Board of Governors of the Federal Reserve System, "Methods of the Survey of Consumer Finances," *Federal Reserve Bulletin*, July, 1950. For a more complete treatment, see also Klein, L. R., editor, *Contributions of Survey Methods to Economics*, New York: Columbia University Press, 1954. Reports of the 1952 and 1953 Surveys are given in Board of Governors of the Federal Reserve System, *1952 Survey of Consumer Finances*, reprinted with supplementary tables from *Federal Reserve Bulletin*, April, July, August, and September, 1952, and Board of Governors of the Federal Reserve System, *1953 Survey of Consumer Finances*, reprinted with supplementary tables from *Federal Reserve Bulletin*, March, June, July, August, and September, 1952.

[6] Of the 1036 spending units in the reinterview sample, these 735 have been the subject for calculations for other purposes and are therefore a convenient group to use in this analysis. Excluded are all spending units who had one or more of the following characteristics: (a) farm; (b) secondary, i.e., not the owner or principal tenant of the dwelling; (c) total income for the two years 1951–52 zero or negative; (d) not ascertained as to age of head of spending unit, amount of expenditure on durable goods during 1951–52, or amount of liquid asset holdings in early 1951. In addition, one extreme observation was excluded, where the spending unit has such a low positive two-year income that the ratio of durable goods expenditure and, especially, liquid asset holdings to income were very high.

posable income is the sum of the two annual incomes reported by the spending unit less estimated federal income tax liabilities. Both expenditure and income were reported for 1951 in the interview in early 1952, and for 1952 in the second interview, in early 1953. Since expenditure is necessarily zero or positive, and since zero and negative incomes have been excluded, the ratio is necessarily zero or positive.

X_1 , *the age of the head of the spending unit*, as reported in 1953, on the following scale:

18–24 yrs...1
25–34 yrs...2
35–44 yrs...3
45–54 yrs...4
55–64 yrs...5
65 or more years..............................6

TABLE I
SUMS OF SQUARES AND CROSS PRODUCTS

	183 limit observations				552 non-limit observations			
	$X_0' = 1$	X_1'	X_2'	W'	$X_0 = 1$	X_1	X_2	W
$X_0' \equiv 1$	183				$X_0 \equiv 1$	552		
X_1'	824	4056			X_1	1976	8060	
X_2'	102.15	552.03	402.3333		X_2	168.06	751.54	255.6740
W'	0	0	0	0	W	61.449	207.598	20.559	13.113087

TABLE II
ITERATIVE ESTIMATION OF PARAMETERS

	a_0	a_1	a_2	a
Initial trial values	1.326	−.2200	.0330	7.984
First derivatives	−4.398	−21.759	−1.812	.898
Second derivatives a_0	−680.557			
a_1	−2542.416	−10,805.486		
a_2	−238.41	−1128.653	−535.223	
a	61.449	207.598	20.559	−21.772
Indicated changes	.0152	−.00507	.00199	.0376
Second trial values	1.3407	−.2251	.0350	8.022
First derivatives	−.047	.292	.064	.002
Second derivatives a_0	−680.260			
a_1	−2540.666	−10,795.522		
a_2	−238.26	−1,127.900	−535.893	
a	61.449	207.598	20.559	−21.688
Indicated changes	−.0015	.00037	.00001	−.00064
Final estimates	1.3392	−.2247	.0350	8.022
Standard errors	(.118)	(.0295)	(.0495)	(.252)

TABLE III

ITERATIVE ESTIMATION OF PARAMETERS ASSUMING THAT $\beta_2 = 0$

	a_0	a_1	a
Initial trial values	1.337	−.219	8.040
First derivatives	−2.841	−16.124	−.001
Second derivatives: a_0	−680.419		
a_1	−2541.428	10,799.12	
a	61.449	207.598	−21.652
Indicated changes	.010	−.004	−.010
Second trial values	1.347	−.223	8.030
First derivatives	−.456	−2.017	+.116
Second derivatives: a_0	−680.179		
a_1	−2539.988	−10,790.472	
a	61.449	207.598	−21.674
Indicated changes	.001	.0003	−.005
Final estimates	1.347	−.223	8.030
Standard errors	(.117)	(.028)	(.252)

X_2, the ratio of liquid asset holdings at the beginning of 1951 to 1951–52 total disposable income. Liquid asset holdings include bank deposits, savings and loan association shares, postal savings, and government saving bonds.

In this example, the lower limit L is zero for all cases. Table I shows the basic data.

Table II presents the estimates of the parameters obtained by the initial approximation and reports the successive iterations leading to the maximum likelihood estimates. Estimates are shown also in Table III, on the assumption that there is no relation between W and liquid asset holdings X_2.

In the approximation used to obtain initial trial values, the function $-Z(x)/Q(x)$ was approximated by the tangent at the point $x_o = .67$, so that $Q(x_o) = .25$,

TABLE IV

ESTIMATED VARIANCES AND COVARIANCES OF PARAMETER ESTIMATES

	a_0	a_1	a_2	a
a_0	+.0139			
a_1	−.00318	+.000867		
a_2	+.000880	−.000454	+.00245	
a	+.00987	−.00115	+.000470	+.0635

On assumption that $\beta_2 = 0$:

	a_0	a_1	a	
a_0	+.0136			
a_1	−.00302	+.000784		
a	+.00970	−.00106	+.0635	

TABLE V

CALCULATION OF EXPECTED VALUES

	$X_2 = 0$				$X_2 = 2$			
X_1	$I = 1.3392$ $- .2247 X_1$	Calculated probability of buying $P(I)$	$Z(I)$	Calculated expected value $E(W) = (IP +$ $Z)/8.022$	$I = 1.4092$ $- .2247 X_1$	Calculated probability of buying $P(I)$	$Z(I)$	Calculated expected value $E(W) = (IP$ $+ Z)/8.022$
0	1.3392	.910	.163	.172	1.4092	.921	.148	.180
1	1.1145	.867	.214	.147	1.1845	.882	.197	.155
2	.8898	.813	.267	.123	.9598	.832	.252	.131
3	.6651	.747	.319	.102	.7351	.768	.304	.108
4	.4404	.670	.362	.082	.5104	.695	.350	.088
5	.2157	.585	.390	.064	.2857	.612	.383	.070
6	− .0090	.497	.399	.049	.0610	.524	.398	.054
7	− .2337	.408	.388	.037	− .1637	.435	.393	.040
8	− .4584	.323	.359	.026	− .3884	.350	.370	.029

the proportion of nonzero cases in the sample. Thus the constants A and B in (15) and (17) were equal to − .76003 and − .75771 respectively.

Estimates of the variances and covariances of the parameter estimates can be obtained from the negative of the inverse of the final matrix of second derivatives. These are shown in Table IV. The corresponding standard errors of the coefficients are given in the final rows of Tables II and III.

The size of the standard error of a_2 indicates that the hypothesis that $\beta_2 = 0$, that there is no net relationship between expenditure and liquid asset holding, cannot be rejected. This hypothesis can also be tested, with the same conclusion, by the likelihood-ratio method. At the point of maximum likelihood, unrestricted by this hypothesis, ϕ^* in (9) has the value $722.5 - (552/2) \ln 2\pi$. The final estimates in Table III correspond to the point of maximum likelihood restricted by the hypothesis that $\beta_2 = 0$. At this point ϕ^* has the value $721.8 - (552/2) \ln 2\pi$. The statistic $- 2 \ln \lambda$ is thus equal to 1.4, which is not a significant value of chi-square with one degree of freedom.

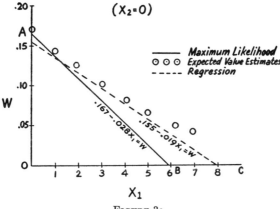

FIGURE 3a

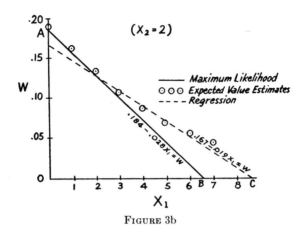

FIGURE 3b

A test of the hypothesis that neither age nor liquid asset holding has any effect on expenditure on durable goods may also be made by the likelihood-ratio method. Assume, in accordance with the hypothesis that $\beta_1 = \beta_2 = 0$, that the values of a_o and a that maximize (13) are found to be .4839 and 7.720. For these values, $\phi^* + 552/2 \ln 2\pi$ is equal to 692.7. Hence $-2 \ln \lambda$ is equal to 59.6, a significant chi-square for two degrees of freedom. The hypothesis must be rejected. Thus this test, as well as the size of the estimated standard error of a_1, indicates a significant relationship of durable goods expenditure to age.

The relationship of W to X_1 and X_2, as estimated in Table II, is shown in Figure 3, as the broken line ABC. The expected value of W implied by this relationship may be computed from (7) in the manner illustrated in Table V. These points are also shown in Figure 3. For comparison, the least squares multiple regression of W on X_1 and X_2 has also been plotted. The estimated effect of liquid asset holding X_2 has been illustrated by drawing two graphs relating W to X_1, the first (Figure 3-a) on the assumption that $X_2 = 0$ and the second (Figure 3-b) on the assumption that $X_2 = 2$. Observed proportions buying and average values of W at various levels of X_1, without regard to X_2, are shown in Table VI.

The expected value locus, estimated by the method of this paper, is nonlinear.

TABLE VI
OBSERVED VALUES
(all values of X_2)

X_1	Proportion buyng	Observed average value of W
1	.812	.124
2	.884	.118
3	.862	.098
4	.751	.083
5	.664	.145
6	.516	.047

It is always above the broken line ABC, asymptotic to AB at the left where the probability of not buying ($W = 0$) approaches zero, and asymptotic to BC at the right where the probability of buying ($W > 0$) approaches zero. Multiple regression approximates this nonlinear locus with a linear relationship. As Figure 3 shows, the approximation is fairly close for the central range of values of the sample. But outside the central range there can be large discrepancies. There are indeed conceivable values of the independent variables for which multiple regression would give negative estimates of the expected value of W. It is true that the absence of negative observations in the sample tends to keep the regression above the axis until extreme values of the independent variables are reached. But this protection is purchased at the cost of making the regression line so flat that expenditure is underestimated at the opposite end. These discrepancies could be important in predicting expenditure for extreme cases or for aggregates which include extreme cases.

Yale University

REFERENCES

[1] BOARD OF GOVERNORS OF THE FEDERAL RESERVE SYSTEM: *1953 Survey of Consumer Finances*, reprinted with supplementary tables from *Federal Reserve Bulletin*, March, June, July, August, and September, 1953.
[2] CORNFIELD, J., AND N. MANTEL: "Some New Aspects of the Application of Maximum Likelihood to the Calculation of the Dosage Response Curve," *Journal of the American Statistical Association*, 45 (1950), 181–210.
[3] CROCKETT, J. B., AND H. CHERNOFF: "Gradient Methods of Maximization," *Pacific Journal of Mathematics*, 5 (1955), 33–50. (Reprinted as Cowles Commission New Series Paper No. 92.)
[4] FARRELL, M. J.: "Some Aggregation Problems in Demand Analysis," *Review of Economic Studies*, 21 (1954), 193–204.
[5] RAO, C. R.: *Advanced Statistical Methods in Biometric Research* (New York: John Wiley & Sons, 1952), 165–172.
[6] TOBIN, J.: "A Survey of the Theory of Rationing," *Econometrica*, 20 (1952), 521–553.

Econometrica **27** (1959) 245-256

SIMULTANEOUS EQUATIONS AND CANONICAL CORRELATION THEORY[1]

By John W. Hooper

This paper uses a topic from multivariate analysis, i.e., canonical correlation theory, in the development of a generalized correlation coefficient for simultaneous equation systems. Canonical correlation theory within the framework of simultaneous equations is first presented and then the generalized correlation coefficient (the trace correlation) is developed from these results. The asymptotic variances of this statistic are presented and an application to a simultaneous equation system is given.

1. INTRODUCTION

THE PURPOSE OF this paper is twofold. The first purpose is to contribute towards the understanding of simultaneous equations estimation as a specific part of the more general theory of multivariate analysis. This is accomplished by integrating the econometric analysis of simultaneous equations with certain elements of classical multivariate analysis. The second purpose may best be explained by analogy to single-equation systems. In single-equation systems there are regression coefficients which measure systematic relationships between the variable to be explained and the explanatory variables; and there are also correlation coefficients which measure the extent to which these systematic relationships do, in fact, explain the fluctuations in the variable to be explained. For simultaneous equations, only the former aspect has been developed and it is the second purpose of this paper to develop a generalized correlation coefficient which measures the extent to which the systematic relationships explain the fluctuations in the set of all jointly dependent variables.

2. CANONICAL CORRELATION THEORY APPLIED TO JOINTLY DEPENDENT AND PREDETERMINED VARIABLES

Canonical correlation theory is concerned with the relations between two sets of variables. For our purpose these two sets are the jointly dependent variables of an equation system $y_1,\ldots,y_M$, and the predetermined variables $x_1,\ldots,x_A$. It is assumed that T observations on each of these variables are available, so that the aggregate set of data can be written in the form of two matrices, viz., a $T \times M$ matrix $Y = [y_\mu(t)]$ and a $T \times A$ matrix $X =$

---

[1] The author is very much indebted to Professor H. Theil for his helpful suggestions on the substance and form of this paper. Any errors which remain are the sole responsibility of the author. This study was done under the terms of a Fulbright grant while the author was a member of the Econometric Institute, Netherlands School of Economics.

$[x_\lambda(t)]$.[2] Canonical correlation theory then shows that there exist linear transformations of $y_1,\dots,y_M$ and $x_1,\dots,x_\Lambda$ into the variates $\eta_1,\dots,\eta_M$ and $\xi_1,\dots,\xi_\Lambda$ such that

(i) All ξ's and η's have zero mean and unit sum of squares.

(ii) Every ξ is uncorrelated with all other ξ's and every η is uncorrelated with all other η's.

(iii) The correlation between any ξ and η is zero except for Λ or M correlations (Λ if $\Lambda \leq M$, M if $\Lambda \geq M$) $r_1, r_2,\dots$, which may be regarded as the correlations between ξ_1 and η_1, ξ_2 and η_2, etc.

The ξ's and η's are called the canonical variates and $r_1, r_2,\dots$ the canonical correlations.[3] To determine the latter we consider a particular pair of canonical variates

(2.1) $$Yk = \eta; \quad Xh = \xi,$$

where ξ and η are column vectors of T observations on the two canonical variates and h and k are coefficient vectors of Λ and M elements respectively. Since the sums of squares are unity, we have

(2.2) $$\eta'\eta = k'Y'Yk = 1; \quad \xi'\xi = h'X'Xh = 1.$$

The correlation between η and ξ is then

(2.3) $$r = \xi'\eta = h'X'Yk,$$

which should be stationary for variations in h and k. So we consider the unconditional stationary value of

(2.4) $$h'X'Yk - \tfrac{1}{2}\lambda_1 (h'X'Xh - 1) - \tfrac{1}{2}\lambda_2 (k'Y'Yk - 1),$$

where the λ's are scalar Lagrange multipliers. This leads by differentiating (2.4) with respect to h and k, to

(2.5)
$$X'Yk - \lambda_1 X'Xh = 0,$$
$$Y'Xh - \lambda_2 Y'Yk = 0.$$

Premultiply the first set of equations by h' and the second by k'; then, by virtue of (2.2) and (2.3), we obtain

(2.6) $$\lambda_1 = \lambda_2 = r.$$

Combining the first set of (2.5) with (2.6), we have

$$h = \frac{1}{r}(X'X)^{-1}X'Yk$$

[2] It is also assumed that Y has rank M and X rank Λ, and that all variables are measured as deviates from their means so that the sums of the T rows of Y and X are zero row vectors.

[3] Cf. Harold Hotelling [2] and Gerhard Tintner [8, pp. 114-121]. Tintner seems to define the canonical correlation as the largest r and thus obtains a unique pair of canonical variates. For our purposes the more general definition is preferable.

and combining this with the second set gives

(2.7) $[(Y'Y)^{-1}Y'X(X'X)^{-1}X'Y - r^2I]\, k = 0,$

which implies that the squares of the canonical correlations are the latent roots of the matrix $(Y'Y)^{-1}Y'X(X'X)^{-1}X'Y$. If we consider Y and X as matrices of sample values derived from a certain universe with finite moments of the second order, then the corresponding parent canonical correlations $\varrho_1, \varrho_2, \ldots$ are found by solving the determinantal equation

(2.8) $|\{E(Y'Y)\}^{-1}\, E(Y'X)\, \{E(X'X)\}^{-1}\, E(X'Y) - \varrho^2 I| = 0,$

where E is the expected-value operator.

These are the usual results of canonical correlation theory; but we can proceed further by making use of some of the special properties of simultaneous equations. Assume now that X and Y are connected by a complete system of linear stochastic relations:

(2.9) $YB + X\Gamma = U,$

B and Γ being parameter matrices (of which B is square and nonsingular) and U a $T \times M$ matrix of disturbances. The reduced form of this system is

(2.10) $Y = -X\Gamma B^{-1} + UB^{-1} = X\Pi + \bar{V},$

where Π is the matrix of parent reduced-form coefficients and $\bar{V} = [\bar{v}_\mu(t)]$ the matrix of parent reduced-form disturbances. Estimating the reduced form by least-squares, we obtain

(2.11) $Y = XP + V,$

where $P = (X'X)^{-1}\, X'Y$, from which it easily follows that

(2.12) $(Y'Y)^{-1}\, P'X'XP = (Y'Y)^{-1}\, Y'X(X'X)^{-1}\, X'Y = I - D$, say,

where I is the unit matrix of order M, and D is considered below in (2.14). This implies that the matrix whose latent roots are considered in (2.7) is simply the inverse of the estimated moment matrix of the jointly dependent variables postmultiplied by the moment matrix of the systematic part of the estimated reduced form XP:

(2.13) $|(Y'Y)^{-1}\, P'X'XP - r^2I| = 0$ or $|(I-D) - r^2I| = 0.$

Since $X'V = 0$, we have

$$Y'Y = P'X'XP + V'V,$$

so that

(2.14) $(Y'Y)^{-1}\, V'V = D.$

When this is combined with (2.13) we obtain

(2.15) $|(Y'Y)^{-1}\, V'V - (1-r^2)I| = 0$ or $|D - (1-r^2)I| = 0.$

The matrix $(Y'Y)^{-1} V'V = D$ may be regarded as the matrix generalization of the ratio of the estimated variance of the disturbances to the estimated variance of the single dependent variable in single-equation systems; and this ratio is (as is well known) equal to $1 - R^2$, where R is the coefficient of multiple correlation. However, it follows from (2.15) that the latent roots of D are equal to $1 - r^2$, where r represents a canonical correlation between the y's and the x's. So we find that there is not only a matrix generalization of $1 - R^2$ in the case of simultaneous equations, i.e., the matrix D, but also a vector generalization, i.e., the vector $[1 - r_\mu^2]$ of M elements, which is the vector of the latent roots of D.[4] In a similar manner the matrix $(Y'Y)^{-1} P'X'XP = I - D$ may be regarded as the matrix generalization of R^2 in a single-equation system; and the vector of latent roots of $I - D$, i.e., $[r_\mu^2]$, may be interpreted as the vector generalization. Finally, we can deal with populations instead of samples. For the population values we write

$$(2.16) \quad \Delta = \{E(Y'Y)\}^{-1}(E\bar{V}'\bar{V}) \quad \text{and} \quad I - \Delta = \{E(Y'Y)\}^{-1}\Pi'E(X'X)\Pi,$$

(where we assume $E(X'\bar{V}) = 0$), and we find that the parent canonical correlations of (2.8) satisfy

$$(2.17) \qquad |\Delta - (1-\varrho^2)I| = 0 \quad \text{and} \quad |(I-\Delta) - \varrho^2 I| = 0.$$

3. VECTOR CORRELATION AND VECTOR ALIENATION COEFFICIENTS

It is sometimes considered desirable to describe the degree to which the systematic part of the equation system accounts for the variation of the jointly dependent variables in a scalar fashion, i.e., not in terms of a matrix or a vector. It will appear in Section 5 that this desire is all the more justifiable, because the latent roots of (2.13) and (2.15) are uncorrelated under appropriate assumptions; and thus, by combining the latent roots in an adequate scalar manner, we will be able to arrive at a measure which is characterized by relatively small sampling variability.

Two attempts which have been made by Hotelling [2] will be described and analyzed in this section. As a measure of the independence between the y- and x-variables we have the vector alienation coefficient, defined as the positive square root of z, where

$$3.1) \qquad z = \frac{\begin{vmatrix} Y'Y & Y'X \\ X'Y & X'X \end{vmatrix}}{|Y'Y| \quad |X'X|}.$$

---

[4] It should be observed that when there are fewer predetermined variables than jointly dependent variables some of the r's must vanish because the number of non-zero r's does not exceed Λ.

The numerator of (3.1) may be written (by making use of $Y'X = P'X'X$) as

$$\begin{vmatrix} P'X'XP + V'V & P'X'X \\ X'XP & X'X \end{vmatrix}.$$

If we multiply the last Λ rows of the numerator by $-P'$ and add this product to the first M rows (leaving the value of the determinant unchanged) we find that

$$(3.2) \qquad z = \frac{|\,V'V\,|}{|\,Y'Y\,|}.$$

This result shows that this measure of independence is identical to $|D|$; and so it is also a measure of the unexplained generalized variance of the jointly dependent variables.[5] In order to see the relationship between the alienation coefficient and canonical correlation it has only to be noticed that a determinant can be expressed as the product of its latent roots. So from (2.15) we have

$$(3.3) \qquad z = |\,D\,| = \prod_{\mu=1}^{M} (1 - r_{\mu}^{2}),$$

where the r_{μ}'s are the canonical correlations. Thus a z of unity, representing complete independence of the y's and x's, can only be obtained if all canonical correlations are zero.

As a measure of the dependence between the y's and the x's we have the vector correlation coefficient q defined as the positive square root of

$$(3.4) \qquad q^2 = (-1)^M \frac{\begin{vmatrix} 0 & Y'X \\ X'Y & X'X \end{vmatrix}}{|Y'Y|\ |X'X|}.$$

When we substitute $Y'X = P'X'X$ in the numerator, multiply the last Λ rows by $-\Pi'$, and add this product to the first M rows, we obtain

$$(3.5) \qquad q^2 = (-1)^M \frac{|\,P'X'XP\,|}{|\,Y'Y\,|} = |\,(Y'Y)^{-1}\,P'X'XP\,| = |\,I - D\,|.$$

Expressing $|I - D|$ as a product of latent roots we have from (2.13) that

$$(3.6) \qquad q^2 = |I - D| = \prod_{\mu=1}^{M} r_{\mu}^{2}.$$

Thus the vector correlation coefficient q will be unity only if all canonical correlations are unity, and zero if any of the canonical correlations are zero.

[5] Various properties of this measure, which is called the coefficient of simultaneous correlation, are discussed by H. Theil [7, chap. VI].

4. THE TRACE CORRELATION

Several objections may be raised against the use of the vector alienation and correlation coefficients in econometric equation systems. First, it is easily seen that the vector correlation coefficient vanishes if $\Lambda < M$ because then at least one canonical correlation is zero.[6] Second, both coefficients tend to zero when M is large, because each of them is derived by multiplying M quantities of a monotonically decreasing sequence between zero and one. This can be remedied by taking Mth roots:

$$(4.1) \qquad \sqrt[M]{|D|} = \sqrt[M]{\prod_{\mu=1}^{M} (1-r_\mu^2)}; \quad \sqrt[M]{|I-D|} = \sqrt[M]{\prod_{\mu=1}^{M} r_\mu^2},$$

which means that we consider the geometrical means of $1 - r_\mu^2$ and r_μ^2. However, as will be shown below, these measures do not satisfy the requirement that they sum to unity:

$$(4.2) \qquad \sqrt[M]{|D|} + \sqrt[M]{|I-D|} \neq 1.$$

This is indeed a very natural requirement, because the first term to the left of (4.2) is a measure for the unexplained part of the variance of the jointly dependent variables, and the second term is a measure for the explained part, and we should expect them to sum to unity, just as $1 - R^2$ and R^2 do in single-equation systems.

A measure which has none of these defects is what we shall term the *trace correlation*,[7] $\bar{r}$, defined as the positive square root of

$$(4.3) \qquad \bar{r}^2 = \frac{1}{M} \operatorname{tr}(I - D) = \frac{1}{M} \sum_{\mu=1}^{M} r_\mu^2.$$

On comparing this with

$$(4.4) \qquad 1 - \bar{r}^2 = \frac{1}{M} \operatorname{tr} D = \frac{1}{M} \sum_{\mu=1}^{M} (1-r_\mu^2),$$

we conclude that $\bar{r}^2$ can be naturally interpreted as that part of the total variance of the jointly dependent variables that is accounted for by the systematic part of the reduced form, and $1 - \bar{r}^2$ as the unexplained part.[8]

---

[6] This objection does not apply against the definition of Hotelling [2, pp. 332-333], who by placing the less numerous set of variables first assures that the vector correlation coefficient does not vanish identically. However this case is possible in econometric equation systems.

[7] The trace of a matrix is defined as the sum of its diagonal elements. The trace is also equal to the sum of the latent roots.

[8] The trace correlation also possesses the properties that $\bar{r}^2 + (1-\bar{r}^2) \equiv 1$, $0 \leq \bar{r}^2 \leq 1$, and $\bar{r}^2$ is invariant to the units in which the variables are measured. The first property is obvious and the last two follow from the fact that $\bar{r}^2$ is an arithmetic mean of squared canonical correlations, each of which is between zero and one, and are themselves invariant; see Hotelling [2, pp. 326-336].

This implies that we use the arithmetic means of the r_μ^2 and $1 - r_\mu^2$, contrary to the geometrical means considered in (4.1). Since geometrical means of nonnegative numbers are always less than arithmetic means (except for the trivial case when these numbers are all equal), we can replace the inequality sign of (4.2) by a $<$ sign.

So far, we have considered only the explanation of the y's in terms of the x's and not of the x's in terms of the y's. There is indeed much to say in favor of this asymmetry because of the very nature of econometric equation systems. Nevertheless, it is interesting to note that there is a simple relationship between the trace correlation corresponding to the y's as explained by the x's ($\bar{r}_{yx}$, say) and the trace correlation of the x's as explained by the y's ($\bar{r}_{xy}$). Consider the matrix

$$(4.5) \qquad I - D^* = (X'X)^{-1} X'Y(Y'Y)^{-1} Y'X,$$

which is obtained by interchanging X and Y in (2.12); the I to the left is now the unit matrix of order Λ. Then, by virtue of the lemma which states that $\operatorname{tr} AB = \operatorname{tr} BA$ for any matrices A and B (such that AB and BA both exist),

$$(4.6) \qquad \begin{aligned} \operatorname{tr} (I - D^*) &= \operatorname{tr} (X'X)^{-1} X'Y(Y'Y)^{-1} Y'X \\ &= \operatorname{tr} (Y'Y)^{-1} Y'X(X'X)^{-1} X'Y = \operatorname{tr} (I - D), \end{aligned}$$

from which it follows that,

$$(4.7) \qquad \Lambda \bar{r}_{xy}^2 = M \bar{r}_{yx}^2.$$

If $\Lambda = M$, both trace correlations are equal. If $\Lambda = M = 1$, they are ordinary zero-order correlations (disregarding sign). If $\Lambda > M = 1$, $\bar{r}_{yx}$ is the multiple correlation coefficient, and the squared trace correlation $\bar{r}_{xy}^2$, which describes the x's as "explained" by the single y, is $1/\Lambda$ times the square of this multiple correlation.

5. ASYMPTOTIC SAMPLING VARIANCES

In order to test the significance of a particular trace correlation computed from a sample, it is desirable to have at least the asymptotic sampling variance. We shall derive this variance under two different conditions. First, we shall assume that each of the T rows of $[X \ Y]$ are independent random drawings from a $(\Lambda + M)$-dimensional normal parent distribution with zero means. Second, we shall assume that X is a nonstochastic matrix, but that Y is normally distributed with mean $X\Pi$, the rows of Y being mutually independent. In both cases[9] we assume that there are no multiple roots in the population (except possibly zero multiple roots caused by the fact that $\Lambda < M$, which are allowed).

[9] These cases are, of course, but special cases of a more general situation, viz., that of "mixed variates." Cf. Hooper [1].

From (4.4) we have

(5.1)
$$M \bar{r} d\bar{r} = \sum_{\mu=1}^{M} r_{\mu} dr_{\mu},$$

$d\bar{r}$ and dr_{μ} being sampling differentials. On squaring and taking expected values, we find for large samples:

(5.2)
$$M^2 \bar{\varrho}^2 \operatorname{var} \bar{r} = \sum_{\mu,\mu'} \varrho_{\mu} \varrho_{\mu'} \operatorname{cov}(r_{\mu}, r_{\mu'}),$$

$\bar{\varrho}^2 = (1/M) \operatorname{tr}(I - \varLambda)$ being the square of the parent trace correlation.

This result holds under both alternative assumptions. If we then suppose that $[X\ Y]$ is normal, we have[10]

(5.3)
$$\operatorname{var} r_{\mu} = \frac{1}{T}(1 - \varrho_{\mu}^2)^2; \quad \operatorname{cov}(r_{\mu}, r_{\mu'}) = 0 \quad \text{for } \mu \neq \mu',$$

terms of higher order of smallness than T^{-1} being neglected. So

(5.4)
$$\operatorname{var} \bar{r} = \frac{1}{TM^2 \bar{\varrho}^2} \sum_{\mu=1}^{M} \varrho_{\mu}^2 (1 - \varrho_{\mu}^2)^2$$

to our degree of approximation.[11] Furthermore, since $\operatorname{var} \bar{r}^2 = 4\bar{\varrho}^2 \operatorname{var} \bar{r}$, we also have

(5.5)
$$\operatorname{var} \bar{r}^2 = \frac{4}{TM^2} \sum_{\mu=1}^{M} \varrho_{\mu}^2 (1 - \varrho_{\mu}^2)^2.$$

The variances and covariances of the canonical correlations under the alternative assumption that the X's are "fixed variates" are unknown in the literature and will be derived here. Write then

(5.6)
$$X'X = [\sigma_{\lambda\lambda'}]; \quad Y'Y = [s_{\mu\mu'}]; \quad X'Y = [c_{\lambda\mu}].$$

We can then write (2.2) and (2.3) in the form,

(5.7)
$$\sum_{\lambda,\lambda'} \sigma_{\lambda\lambda'} h_{\lambda} h_{\lambda'} = \sum_{\mu,\mu'} s_{\mu\mu'} k_{\mu} k_{\mu'} = 1; \quad \sum_{\lambda,\mu} c_{\lambda\mu} h_{\lambda} k_{\mu} = r.$$

Taking differentials (and remembering that $\sigma_{\lambda\lambda'}$ is fixed), we find

(5.8)
$$\sum_{\lambda,\lambda'} \sigma_{\lambda\lambda'} h_{\lambda} dh_{\lambda'} = 0; \quad 2\sum_{\mu,\mu'} s_{\mu\mu'} k_{\mu} dk_{\mu'} + \sum_{\mu,\mu'} k_{\mu} k_{\mu'} ds_{\mu\mu'} = 0;$$
$$\sum_{\lambda,\mu} c_{\lambda\mu} h_{\lambda} dk_{\mu} + \sum_{\lambda,\mu} c_{\lambda\mu} k_{\mu} dh_{\lambda} + \sum_{\lambda,\mu} h_{\lambda} k_{\mu} dc_{\lambda\mu} = dr.$$

Without loss of generality we may assume that our variates are in canonical form. This means that all h's and k's vanish except for one pair, h_1 and k_1

---

[10] Cf. Hotelling [**2**, p. 340]. Note that the variance expression of (5.3) holds only if $\varrho_{\mu} \neq 0$. If a $\varrho_{\mu} = 0$ because $\varLambda < M$, then the corresponding $r_{\mu} \equiv 0$, so that var $r = 0$. It will appear in footnote 11 below that this does not affect the final result. It should be remembered that the covariance of (5.3) is always zero, even if one of the correlations involved (or both) correspond to (multiple) zero roots in the population.

[11] Note that this expression remains valid in the case of zero parent roots caused by $\varLambda < M$, because the contribution of such a root to the right-side of (5.4) is zero.

say, which are both equal to 1. Then (taking account of $s_{11} = 1$, $c_{11} = r_1$) we can simplify as follows:

(5.9) $\quad dh_1 = 0; \quad 2dk_1 + ds_{11} = 0; \quad r_1 dk_1 + r_1 dh_1 + dc_{11} = dr_1;$

from which we find,

(5.10) $\qquad\qquad\qquad\qquad dr_1 = dc_{11} - \tfrac{1}{2} r_1 ds_{11}.$

Some algebraic rearrangements are sufficient to show that

$$E(dc_{11})^2 = E\{\,\Sigma X_1(t)\bar{v}_1(t)\,\}^2 = \frac{1}{T}\,(1 - \varrho_1^2);$$

$$E(ds_{11})^2 = E\{2\varrho_1 \Sigma X_1(t)\bar{v}_1(t) + \Sigma \bar{v}_1(t)^2 - (1 - \varrho_1^2)\}^2 = \frac{2}{T}\,(1 - \varrho_1^2)\,(1 + \varrho_1^2);$$

$$E(dc_{11}ds_{11}) = E\{[2\varrho_1\Sigma X_1(t)\bar{v}_1(t) + \Sigma \bar{v}_1(t)^2]\,[\Sigma X_1(t)\bar{v}_1(t)]\} = \frac{2}{T}\,\varrho_1\,(1 - \varrho_1^2),$$

so that

(5.11)
$$\begin{aligned} \text{var } r_1 &= E(dc_{11})^2 + \frac{1}{4}\,\varrho_1^2\,E(ds_{11})^2 - \varrho_1 E(dc_{11}ds_{11}) = \\ &= 1/2T\,(1 - \varrho_1^2)^2(2 - \varrho_1^2). \end{aligned}$$

In the same way it can be shown that the covariance of different canonical correlations vanishes to the order of T^{-1}. Thus it follows that

(5.12) $\qquad\qquad \text{var } \bar{r} = \dfrac{1}{2TM^{2-2}\varrho}\sum_{\mu=1}^{M}\varrho_\mu^2(1 - \varrho_\mu^2)^2(2 - \varrho_\mu^2),$

and

(5.13) $\qquad\qquad \text{var } \bar{r}^2 = \dfrac{2}{TM^2}\sum_{\mu=1}^{M}\varrho_\mu^2(1 - \varrho_\mu^2)^2(2 - \varrho_\mu^2).$

It is interesting to note that these are always equal to or less than the corresponding expressions in (5.4) and (5.5).[12,13]

6. SOME SPECIAL PROBLEMS IN RELATION TO ECONOMETRIC EQUATION SYSTEMS

There are certain special problems that arise in the application of trace and canonical correlations to econometric equation systems. One such

---

[12] The case of zero canonical correlations can be handled in the manner indicated in footnotes 10 and 11 above.

[13] There seems to be an interesting relationship between Hotelling's T_0^2 [3] and the squared trace correlation, $\bar{r}^2$ since both are functions of the sums of latent roots of certain determinantal equations. If the precise form of this relationship could be determined, it would be useful since many properties of T_0^2 are known. In connection with this problem the reader may find Pillai [5, 6] useful. I am indebted to one of the referees of this paper for suggesting this relationship, and to Dr. A. Madansky for several helpful discussions concerning this problem.

problem occurs when there are nonstochastic equations (definitional equations) in the structural equation system. Such equations can be used to eliminate some of the jointly dependent variables. Which of the variables is eliminated is, to some extent, arbitrary; and the trace correlation (or the vector alienation and correlation coefficients) are not, in general, invariant as to which variables are eliminated. This can be seen from the following simple equation system:

$$(6.1) \qquad y_1 = \gamma x + u,$$

$$(6.2) \qquad y_2 = y_1 + x.$$

If we eliminate y_2 and consider (6.1) only, which is in the reduced form, we find that the correlation between y_1 and x is determined by

$$(6.3) \qquad \frac{\varrho^2}{1 - \varrho^2} = \frac{\gamma^2 \mathrm{var}\, x}{\mathrm{var}\, \mu}.$$

But if we eliminate y_1 so that the equation for y_2 becomes $y_2 = (1 + \gamma) x + u$, then the corresponding correlation of y_2 and x is determined by

$$(6.4) \qquad \frac{\varrho'^2}{1 - \varrho'^2} = \frac{(1 + \gamma)^2 \mathrm{var}\, x}{\mathrm{var}\, \mu},$$

so that $\varrho \neq \varrho'$. This is a very simple case in which the alternative equation systems after elimination are single-equation systems; hence the trace correlation coincides with the simple correlation. It is clear, however, that we arrive in general at the same negative result when we consider larger systems.

A second consideration is that, when a method of estimation is used which takes account of all the restrictions[14] in the structural equation system (e.g., full-information maximum-likelihood), a different and presumably more efficient set of estimates will be obtained. However, it is also true that these estimates are, in general, not such that the corresponding estimated disturbances in the reduced form are uncorrelated with the predetermined variables in the sample. This affects the derivation of Section 2, since we made use there of this absence of correlation. The best procedure is presumably to define D in accordance with (2.14), V being interpreted as the matrix of estimated disturbances corresponding to the estimation method under consideration, and to disregard the definition of $I - D$ as $P'X'XP$ (P being the estimated coefficient matrix in the reduced form).

---

[14] These restrictions imply that certain elements of B and Γ in (2.9) should be zero; see, e.g., Koopmans, Rubin, and Leipnik [4].

7. AN EXAMPLE

In this section we shall apply the results obtained in the previous sections to an econometric model in order to illustrate these results. For this purpose we shall use Tintner's model[15] of the American meat market which consists of the following two equations:

$$(7.1) \qquad\qquad y_1 = \beta y_2 + \gamma_1 x_1 + u_1,$$

$$(7.2) \qquad\qquad y_1 = \beta' y_2 + \gamma_2 x_2 + \gamma_3 x_3 + u_2,$$

where (7.1) is the demand equation, (7.2) the supply equation, y_1 is per capita consumption of meat in pounds, y_2 the retail price of meat, x_1 is real per capita disposable income in dollars, x_2 the cost of processing meat, and x_3 the cost of producing agricultural products. All observations are annual and cover the years 1919—1941. From the data presented by Tintner we obtain,

$$(7.3) \qquad\qquad Y'Y = \begin{bmatrix} 1{,}369.54 & -352.55 \\ & 1{,}581.49 \end{bmatrix}$$

and

$$(Y'Y)^{-1} = \begin{bmatrix} .00077460 & .00017268 \\ & .00067080 \end{bmatrix}.$$

The matrix of reduced-form, least-squares residuals is,

$$(7.4) \qquad\qquad V'V = \begin{bmatrix} 694.117 & -560.188 \\ & 643.563 \end{bmatrix}$$

and so

$$(7.5) \qquad D = \begin{bmatrix} .44093 & -.32279 \\ -.25591 & .33497 \end{bmatrix} \text{ and } I - D = \begin{bmatrix} .55907 & .32279 \\ .25591 & .66503 \end{bmatrix}.$$

The canonical correlations are obtained from

$$(7.6) \qquad\qquad |(I - D) - r^2 I| = 0$$

and this results in $r_1^2 = .90432$ and $r_2^2 = .31979$.

We have for the square of the vector correlation coefficient,

$$(7.7) \qquad\qquad q^2 = |I - D| = .28919 \quad \text{and} \quad q = .5378.$$

The square of the vector alienation coefficient is

$$(7.8) \qquad\qquad z = |D| = .065091 \quad \text{and} \quad \sqrt{z} = .2551,$$

and in this case where $M = 2$, q and $\sqrt{z}$ are the respective geometric means.

---

[15] Cf. Tintner [8, pp. 169-172] for a complete description of this model.

For the squared trace correlation we find

(7.9) $$\bar{r}^2 = \frac{1}{M}\,\mathrm{tr}\,(I - D) = .61205 \quad \text{and} \quad \bar{r} = .7823,$$

and also

(7.10) $$1 - \bar{r}^2 = \frac{1}{M}\,\mathrm{tr}\,D = .38795 \quad \text{and} \quad \sqrt{1 - \bar{r}^2} = .6229.$$

The estimated variance of the trace correlation under the assumption that the x's are normal random variables is

(7.11) $$\mathrm{var}\,\bar{r}^2 = \frac{4}{TM^2}\sum_{\mu=1}^{2} r_\mu^2\,(1 - r_\mu^2)^2 = .0067933,$$

and under the assumption that the x's are "fixed variates" we obtain

(7.12) $$\mathrm{var}\,\bar{r}^2 = \frac{2}{TM^2}\sum_{\mu=1}^{2} r_\mu^2\,(1 - r_\mu^2)^2(2 - r_\mu^2) = .0056018.$$

One interpretation of the results in (7.9) is that approximately 3/5 of the generalized variance of the set of jointly dependent variables has been accounted for by the regression relationship and that approximately 2/5 remains "unexplained." The significance of the trace correlation may then be tested by the results given in (7.11) and (7.12).

The RAND Corporation

REFERENCES

[1] HOOPER, JOHN W.: "The Sampling Variation of Correlation Coefficients Under Assumptions of Fixed and Mixed Variates," *Biometrika*, Vol. 45 (1958).

[2] HOTELLING, H.: "Relations Between Two Sets of Variates," *Biometrika*, Vol. 28 (1936), pp. 321-377.

[3] ———: "A Generalized T Test and Measure of Multivariate Dispersion," *Proceedings of The Second Berkeley Symposium on Mathematical Statistics and Probability*, edited by J. NEYMAN, Berkeley: The University of California Press, 1951, Press, 1951, pp. 23-41.

[4] KOOPMANS, T. C., H. RUBIN, AND R. B. LEIPNIK: "Measuring The Equation Systems of Dynamic Economics, " Chap. II in *Statistical Inference in Dynamic Economic Models*, edited by T. C. KOOPMANS, New York: John Wiley and Sons, 1950.

[5] PILLAI, K. C. S.: "Some New Test Criteria in Multivariate Analysis," *Annals of Mathematical Statistics*, Vol. 26 (1955), pp. 117-121.

[6] ———: "Some Results Useful in Multivariate Analysis," *Annals of Mathematical Statistics*, Vol. 27 (1956), pp. 1106-1114.

[7] THEIL, H.: *Economic Forecasts and Policy*, Amsterdam: North-Holland Publishing Co., (forthcoming).

[8] TINTNER, G.: *Econometrics*, New York: John Wiley and Sons, 1952.

Econometrica, Vol. 27, 4 (October 1959)

THE DYNAMIC PROPERTIES OF THE KLEIN-GOLDBERGER MODEL

By Irma Adelman and Frank L. Adelman[*]

The authors examine the dynamic properties of the Klein-Goldberger model of the United States economy by extrapolating the exogenous variables and solving the equations on the IBM 650 for one hundred years. In this process no indication was found of oscillatory behavior. The introduction of random impulses of a reasonable order of magnitude, however, generates cycles which are comparable in their properties to those of the United States economy.

1. INTRODUCTION

ONE OF THE MOST vexing of the unsolved problems of dynamic economic analysis is that of constructing a model which will reproduce adequately the cyclical behavior of a modern industrial community. None of the schemes so far advanced have (yet) offered a satisfactory endogenous explanation of the persistent business fluctuations so characteristic of Western capitalism. It is true that there exist theories which lead to oscillatory movements, but, except under·very special assumptions, these swings either die down, or else they are explosive in nature.[1] In the latter case, appeal is usually made to externally imposed constraints in order to limit the fluctuations of the system,[2] while, in the former case, exogenous shocks must be introduced from time to time to rejuvenate the cyclical movement.[3] Since recourse to either of these devices is rather artificial, it is of interest to seek a more satisfactory mechanism for the internal generation of a persistent cyclical process.

While it is desirable for an economic model (or any other model, for that matter) to be as simple as possible, it is almost certain that an adequate explanation of the business cycle cannot be found through approaches as idealized as those usually suggested. It may be of interest, therefore, to examine, from this point of view, the most complicated econometric description of the United States published in recent years—the 1955 forecast-

* The authors are, respectively, Acting Assistant Professor of Economics at Stanford University and physicist at the Livermore branch of the University of California Lawrence Radiation Laboratory. They are grateful to the Computation Division of the Radiation Laboratory for the use of their facilities. Also, they wish to express their appreciation to Arthur Goldberger for his helpful discussion of this paper.

[1] P. A. Samuelson, "The Interaction of the Accelerator and the Multiplier," *Review of Economic Statistics*, vol. XXI (1939), pp. 75–78.

[2] J. R. Hicks, *A Contribution to the Theory of the Trade Cycle* (Oxford, 1939.)

[3] R. Frisch, "Propagation Problems and Impulse Problems in Dynamic Economics," *Economic Essays in Honor of Gustav Cassel* (London, 1933), pp. 171–205.

ing scheme of Klein and Goldberger.[4] This structure, which consists of 25 difference equations[5] in a corresponding number of endogenous variables, is nonlinear in character, and includes lags up to the fifth order. By its very nature it constitutes a description of a dynamic world, rather than a portrayal of comparative statics. Not only are the endogenous variables in each period functions of exogenous inputs, but also of lagged endogenous quantities and of stock variables. Thus, even if all the exogenous magnitudes were held constant, the economy represented by these equations would still vary with time.

But, while this model has been applied to yearly projections of economic activity in this country with some success, its dynamic properties have been analyzed only under highly simplifying assumptions.[5a] In particular, it would be interesting to find out whether this construct really offers an endogenous explanation of a persistent cyclical process. We should like to learn whether the system is stable when subjected to single exogenous shocks, what oscillations (if any) accompany the return to the equilibrium path, and what is the reponse of the model to repeated external and internal shocks.

The purpose of this paper, then, is to investigate these issues in some detail. There are perhaps two major reasons which indicate why this work has not previously been done. First of all, the fact that Klein and Goldberger used observed quantities as inputs for their annual forecasts, rather than values generated by the model from earlier data, prevented them from studying, at the same time, the type of dynamic paths which would be traversed by the system in the absence of external interference. Secondly, the complexity of the model requires the use of modern high-speed computers for the long-run solution of the system in a reasonable length of time. Since the problem is about the right size for the IBM 650 calculator, and since the appropriate computing facilities exist at the University of California Radiation Laboratory, we programmed the equations for that machine.

2. THE MODEL

The Klein-Goldberger econometric model of the United States[6] is a system of 25 difference equations in as many endogenous variables. Some

[4] L. R. Klein and A. S. Goldberger, *An Econometric Model of the United States, 1929–1952* (Amsterdam, 1955).

[5] Including 5 tax equations.

[5a] In the December, 1957 meeting of the Econometric Society, A. S. Goldberger and J. Cornwall presented the results of their (independent) investigations of their respective linearized versions of the Klein-Goldberger model. (The abstracts appear in *Econometrica*, vol. 26 (1958), pp. 620, 621.) At the same meeting one of us (I.A.) gave a discussion paper on these studies, including in it the material of Sections I–V of the present paper.

[6] For an excellent, more detailed description of this model, see C. F. Christ, "Aggregate Econometric Models," *American Economic Review* ,vol. XLVI (1956), pp. 385–408.

of the equations are accounting identities, while others, behavioral in nature, were derived from statistical fits to empirical data. Generally speaking, each equation describes some significant feature of the economy. The real sector of the model includes, in addition to the usual consumption and investment relationships, a production function, a corporate profits equation, and a corporate savings function. Also taken into account are private employee compensation, farm income, imports,and depreciation. The monetary sector consists of two liquid asset functions, two interest rate equations, a wage adjustment relationship, and an agricultural price equation. There are also five tax equations, which represent the impact of government tax policies upon the economy, and five accounting identities. Of the exogenous variables, the most important (aside from time) are government expenditures, population size, and the distribution of the labor force among the several sectors of the economy. All these equations are given in Appendix A, together with the definitions of the symbols used.

For this study of the Klein-Goldberger system several changes were introduced into the most recent Klein-Goldberger model, some for convenience and some for consistency or logic. First, whenever the standard error of estimate of a regression coefficient was more than twice as large as the coefficient itself, we dropped the corresponding term from the equations. The justification for so high a level of significance is that, for our purposes, we felt it less serious an error to ascribe to a zero coefficient a nonzero value than to ignore a regression coefficient which has an economic existence. The alterations made in accordance with this criterion are indicated in Appendix B, Section 1. In principle, of course, one should correct the equations for these omissions. However, since we were not interested in accurate prediction, but, rather, in the dynamic performance of the model, we felt that the required modifications were small[7] and would not add to the value of the study.

A second departure from the original system was to delete the import equation. This was done because, during the sample period, the calculated quantities of imports constituted a poor approximation to the values observed.[8] After imports had been dropped from the list of endogenous variables, it seemed reasonable also to omit both imports and exports from the model. For, since both would now be exogenous, and since their difference contributes only a small amount to GNP, it is difficult to see how their exclusion could alter the dynamic character of the system.

A modification of quite another sort was made in the form of the tax equations. Since those given by Klein and Goldberger were not intended

[7] Indeed, in all cases, the quantitative changes which would have been required lay within the standard errors of the constants to be altered.

[8] Cf. Klein-Goldberger, *op. cit.*, p. 95 and Figure 29, p. 102.

to be applicable for more than a few years,[9] we had to re-estimate all the tax relationships. Therefore, at the suggestion of A. Goldberger,[10] we adopted a new set of tax functions, which assumed that the tax policies of 1952, interpreted as relationships between real variables, would continue indefinitely into the future. These are incorporated into the tax equations which appear in Appendix B.1.

We were also forced to alter the interest rate equations. Since the excess bank reserves, R_t, are taken as exogenous, the short term interest rate $(i_S)_t$ and the long term rate $(i_L)_t$ can both be computed without reference to the rest of the system. With the small values of R_t typical of the postwar period, it is evident from the short-term interest rate equation [Eq. (15)] that $(i_S)_t$ will double (roughly) every decade. And yet there is no restoring force within the system to keep this quantity at a reasonable value! Similarly, $(i_L)_t$ will, ultimately, become equal to about $0.7(i_S)_t$. In view of the fact that such a projection would eventually result in economic nonsense, we decided to suppress the interest rate equations and to fix (arbitrarily) the short term rate at 2.5% and the long term rate at 3.5%.

Lastly, the agricultural price equation was re-evaluated, using only the postwar data. The reason for this alteration was the admittedly unsatisfactory behavior of the form used by Klein and Goldberger.[11]

We were still not in a position to follow the long-term development of this system, however, as it was necessary to extrapolate the exogenous variables far into the future. This was done, in some instances, by fitting a least-squares straight line to the postwar data. But, in the case of governmental expenditures, the discontinuity because of the Korean War and the subsequent intensification of military preparedness, imparted a trend to the postwar data much steeper than could reasonably be expected to continue. Therefore, we estimated the rate of increase of government expenditures by fitting a straight line to both the prewar and the postwar points, omitting only those of 1951 and 1952. The level was chosen to coincide, more or less, with that of those latter two years. With this procedure we found that our extrapolation leads to numbers which appear to be consistent with current experience.

On the other hand, agricultural subsidy income and the number of farm operators have a declining trend. For these quantities it seemed more appropriate to use a fit of the form

$$X = a + \frac{b}{t - a},$$

in order that they never become negative. Finally, since there was no obvious

[9] Klein-Goldberger, *op. cit.*, pp. 96–102.
[10] Private communication.
[11] Klein-Goldberger, *op. cit.*, p. IX and Fig. 31, p. 105.

trend, during the postwar period, for the index of hours worked and the index of farm exports, both were taken as constant. The extrapolations of all the exogenous quantities appear in Appendix B. 2. The initial values of the lagged variables are listed in Appendix B. 3.

3. CALCULATIONAL PROCEDURE

The modified Klein-Goldberger model to be investigated thus consists of a set of 22 simultaneous equations in a corresponding number of endogenous variables. What we must do in order to evaluate the magnitudes of the endogenous variables for the year t is to insert into these equations the values for the $(t-1)$st and preceding years, as required, along with appropriate exogenous numbers, and solve the equations simultaneously. Using the newly found endogenous quantities for the tth year plus the required exogenous magnitudes, we can then solve the system for the endogenous variables of the $(t+1)$st period. This process is continued until we have traveled sufficiently far into the future to satisfy our curiosity.

At first glance the system we wish to analyze would appear to be highly nonlinear. The substitution of $q = 1/p$ as a variable, however, instead of the price level p itself, leaves us with only a single nonlinear equation (18), the wage and salary identity. Of course, it is much easier to solve a set of simultaneous *linear* equations than it is to evaluate a nonlinear system. For this reason it was decided to "linearize"[12] (18), and then to utilize a successive approximation procedure to find the solution of the nonlinear set to the desired degree of accuracy. Our criteria for an acceptable solution were that the value of each variable appearing in the nonlinear equation must differ from its previous approximation by less than 1/2% and that the original form of that equation also be satisfied to that accuracy. Since convergence was quite rapid, even when the initial guess was poor, our criteria appear to be sufficiently stringent to assure convergence to the economically relevant solution of the system (in case there is more than one solution).

Before actually programming the equations for the IBM 650, however, it was possible, by appropriate algebraic substitutions, to reduce the 22 equations down to a set of four simultaneous equations in four unknowns. The investment relation (2) could be evaluated from exogenous and lagged data, while the equations remaining after the completion of the algebra could be solved *seriatim* as soon as the answers to the first five were available. This procedure was advantageous, if not actually necessary, because the computation time required for the solution of a simultaneous linear system by matrix inversion is proportional to the cube of the rank of the matrix.

---

[12] To do this, we wrote the equation in terms of differences from initial (extrapolated) guesses, which must be consistent with the integral form of the equation.

After all the preceding considerations were taken into account, it turned out that neither memory space nor running time was a serious limitation on the use of the IBM 650. Therefore, the problem was coded for the machine in a straightforward manner. As a matter of interest, the computations for one year could be made during an operating time of about one minute.[13]

4. THE DYNAMIC NATURE OF THE MODEL

Now, we are finally in a position to study some of the problems raised in the Introduction. First of all, what is the dynamic nature of the Klein-Goldberger model? That is, what sort of time path will these equations generate in the absence of additional external constraints or shocks? A priori, it is conceivable that the long-run extrapolation of this short-run

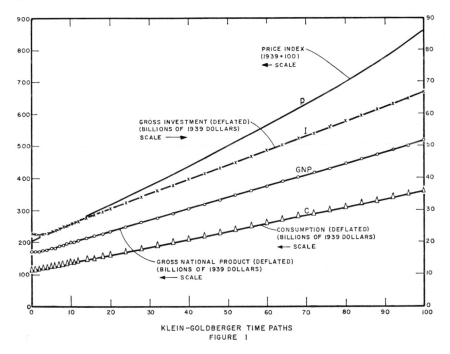

KLEIN–GOLDBERGER TIME PATHS
FIGURE I

predictive system will indicate that the economy so described is subject to a business cycle more or less analogous to that observed in modern industrialized societies. On the other hand, it is also possible that this model cannot offer even a qualitative picture of the economic growth process in the real world.

[13] The actual time depends on the number of iterations required for convergence; in the linear part of the time path, the first guess is adequate.

Our first machine data decided the issue unequivocally. After a brief "settling-down" period, the system is quite monotonic and essentially linear. These is no hint whatever of any internally generated business cycle, and, indeed, even in the first few years, the shock of start-up is not sufficient to induce more than a single turning point in any variable. Of course, since most of the exogenous trends are fitted by straight lines, it is not surprising that the overall character of the solution is linear, rather than, say, quadratic, but the absence of oscillations is less obvious (a priori) and more significant.

The time paths of several of the more important quantities are depicted in Figure 1. The several curves in Figure 1 represent the projections of the price index and of the real values of GNP, consumer expenditures, and gross private investment, respectively. The approximate behavior of the rest of the variables may be inferred from the information in Table I.[14]

In an attempt to see whether the qualitative properties of the solution are at all sensitive to the starting conditions, we reduced the magnitudes of all but seven[15] of the initial values of the real quantities by 10 per cent. The results of this calculation possessed the same general character as had been observed previously. As might have been anticipated, the new ordinates were invariably lower, and, except for corporate savings, the slopes of the curves tended to be the same or smaller. The linearity was even more marked with the reduced inputs; indeed, only two variables showed any turning points at all. These were corporate savings and corporate surplus, both of which were actually negative for several periods. Since, in view of these results, it was felt that small variations in our input would not lead to significant differences in the *nature* of our solution, a more detailed investigation of the influence of initial values upon the operation of the model was postponed to a future date.

The implications of these results are quite clear. Since the economic variables in the Klein-Goldberger model grow almost linearly with time, it is apparent that this scheme does not contain an intrinsic explanation of a persistent oscillatory process. That is, the complete lack of even a broad hint of cyclical behavior in the absence of shocks precludes the application of the Klein-Goldberger analysis to economies in which oscillations are presumed to develop spontaneously. The conclusions one may draw from this observation lie anywhere between the two extreme positions which follow. On the one hand, if one wishes to retain the hypothesis that periodic cumulative movements are self-generated in the course of the growth

[14] The authors will be happy to furnish, upon request, the detailed results of their computations.

[15] The ones excluded were N_W, h, N_E, N_F, N_G, N, N_P (for explanation of symbols, see Appendix A).

TABLE I

BEHAVIOR OF KLEIN-GOLDBERGER MODEL THROUGH TIME

Variable* (years)	24 (first year)	30	60	90	120
$Y + T + D$	171.5	186.0	291.1	396.3	501.5
$\Delta(Y+T+D)$	.294	3.42	3.51	3.51	3.51
C	115.1	125.1	199.3	273.9	348.7
ΔC	.015	2.42	2.48	2.49	2.49
W_1	80.6	86.7	137.5	188.4	239.3
ΔW_1	—.046	1.64	1.70	1.70	1.70
A_1	9.0	9.5	12.6	15.9	19.2
ΔA_1	.008	.100	.108	.109	.110
I	22.9	24.0	37.9	51.5	64.9
ΔI	—.289	.434	.455	.450	.448
K	45.9	65.3	163.0	260.8	357.1
ΔK	3.75	3.05	3.24	3.23	3.20
D	18.5	21.0	34.6	48.2	62.2
ΔD	.396	.429	.458	.452	.448
P_C	14.9	15.4	22.5	29.6	36.8
ΔP_C	—.454	.245	.233	.237	.240
P	33.1	33.8	44.3	54.7	65.3
ΔP	—.667	.361	.343	.349	.353
S_P	.44	.57	2.17	2.85	3.16
ΔS_P	—.192	.082	.032	.015	.007
B	.63	2.96	48.80	125.71	216.51
ΔB	.250	.65	2.20	2.86	3.16
N_W	54.2	53.6	64.7	75.7	86.9
ΔN_W	—1.06	.352	.365	.370	.373
L_1	70.5	71.7	80.6	89.6	98.7
ΔL_1	.037	.288	.299	.301	.301
L_2	40.8	45.9	79.4	112.7	146.0
ΔL_2	1.40	1.00	1.12	1.11	1.11
w	344	443	1043	1817	2776
Δw	15.9	17.3	22.9	29.0	35.2
p	206	238	412	604	825
Δp	4.1	5.8	6.0	6.9	7.9
p_A	318	363	604	871	1179
Δp_A	5.7	8.1	8.3	9.6	11.0
T	14.5	15.8	25.5	35.3	45.0
ΔT	.028	.315	.324	.324	.324
T_W	7.6	9.0	19.2	29.3	39.5
ΔT_W	.069	.329	.338	.339	.339
T_A	.47	.49	.65	.82	.99
ΔT_A	.0003	.0050	.0055	.0056	.0056
T_C	9.4	9.6	12.9	16.0	19.3
ΔT_C	—.204	.110	.105	.108	.108
T_P	12.9	13.2	19.4	26.0	32.8
ΔT_P	—.268	.198	.212	.225	.231

* For any quantity Q, $\Delta Q = Q_{t+1} - Q_t$.

process in a realistic economy, one may contend that the Klein-Goldberger model is fundamentally inadequate, and hence that it is inapplicable to further business cycle theory. On the other hand, one may hold that, to the extent that the behavior of this system constitutes a valid qualitative approximation to that of a modern capitalist society, the observed solution of the Klein-Goldberger equations implies that one must look elsewhere for the origin of business fluctuations. Under the latter assumptions, cyclical analysis would be limited to an investigation of the reaction of the economic system to various perturbations. And, since the Klein-Goldberger model does present a more or less detailed description of the interactions among the various sectors of the economy, it could itself be utilized in the examination of the mechanism of response to shocks. Actually, as we shall see, exploitation of the latter alternative can prove extremely profitable.

5. STABILITY OF THE SYSTEM

It is apparent from the preceding discussion that, under ordinary conditions, the Klein-Goldberger model is non-oscillatory in nature. It remains to be seen whether the economy described by this system is stable under large exogenous displacements.

In order to study this point, we solved the equations as in the preceding section, until the system was essentially on its long-run equilibrium path (about 8 years). Then, in the ninth period, we suddenly reduced the real magnitude of federal outlays from its extrapolated level of 37.5 to the much lower figure of 10; in the succeeding years government expenditures were returned to the values they would have had in the absence of external interference.

While it is obvious that such a discontinuity in an exogenous variable is basically equivalent to a change in initial conditions, it is equally obvious that the response of a dynamic system to large displacements may be quite different from its behavior under small perturbations.[16]

Figure 2 presents some of the calculated results of this extremely severe shock to the economy.[17] As is evident from these curves, the community was immediately thrown into a very deep depression by the sudden drop in federal outlays. The restoration of a normal governmental budget during the following year alleviated the situation only slightly, but, by the second year after the dip, the business world had more than recovered. The

---

[16] E.g., consider a marble trapped in a horizontal saucer. If the disturbance is not large enough to cause the marble to cross the saucer rim, the system is stable. However, once the marble crosses the rim, it will not return to the saucer without the application of external forces. See also, P. A. Samuelson, *Foundations of Economic Analysis* (Harvard, 1953), pp. 200–262.

[17] More data are, of course, available for this case, and will be provided upon request.

next period saw the return of national income, farm receipts, and total employment to their pre-shock trends. However, it was not until the fourth year after the disturbance that real private employee compensation achieved its unperturbed level, as the price index rose more rapidly than the wage rate. Meanwhile, possibly as a result of the fact that consumer expenditures lagged yet another period, there was a mild business recession

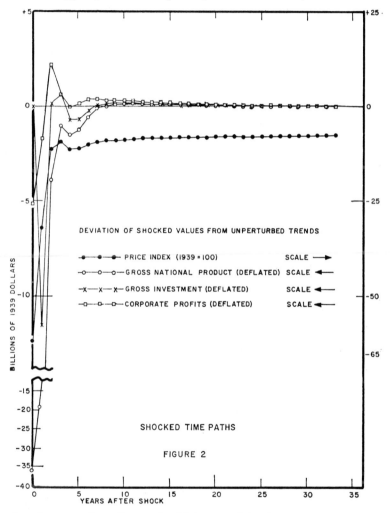

DEVIATION OF SHOCKED VALUES FROM UNPERTURBED TRENDS

●—●—● PRICE INDEX (1939 = 100)   SCALE ⟶
—o—o—o—GROSS NATIONAL PRODUCT (DEFLATED) SCALE ◀—
—x—x—x—GROSS INVESTMENT (DEFLATED)   SCALE ◀—
—□—□—□—CORPORATE PROFITS (DEFLATED)   SCALE ◀—

BILLIONS OF 1939 DOLLARS

SHOCKED TIME PATHS

FIGURE 2

YEARS AFTER SHOCK

in the fourth year, the effects of which were felt throughout the rest of the economy for the next two periods. The subsequent boom reached its peak (with respect to its unperturbed trend) about eight years later, and then tapered off extremely slowly over an additional 22 years or so. While calculations were not continued beyond this point, it appears that, after this 34 year cycle, the economy has essentially returned to its basic equilibrium path, except for the price and wage indices[18] and for the cumulative corporate surplus (all of which remained lower). While the details of the response of a Klein-Goldberger economy to a strong shock will depend on the nature of the perturbation, it would appear likely from this calculation that even a very strong shock will not permanently distort the long-run path of the economy. In other words, the Klein-Goldberger system is stable. Nevertheless, a sharp disturbance does suffice to create a business cycle of depth comparable to that which one would expect in an actual economy under a corresponding inpulse. And, while the duration of the cyclical movement is much longer than that normally observed in practice, it is probable that the later stages of such a cycle, if it really existed, would be obscured by the intervention of new exogenous shocks.

6. INTRODUCTION OF RANDOM SHOCKS

So far, we have studied the dynamic properties of the Klein-Goldberger system by treating it as if it were composed of a set of exact functional relationships. That is to say, we have abstracted from the random elements which are inherent in the statistical specification of the equations. Furthermore, we have used smooth extrapolation procedures for predicting the magnitudes of the exogenous variables. We saw that under those assumptions the Klein-Goldberger equations are inadequate as an explanation of the cyclical behavior of our economy.

We cannot yet assess the validity of the Klein-Goldberger equations, however, as a representation of the United States economy over a long period of time because we must still analyze the time path of their system under the impact of random shocks.[19] After all, as was pointed out by Haavelmo,[20] a model which differs from empirical fact by comparatively small and nonsystematic external factors may still be useful. It is therefore of great interest to see whether or not the introduction of relatively minor uncorrelated perturbations into the Klein-Goldberger structure will generate cyclical fluctuations analogous to those observed in practice.

With these considerations in mind, we exposed the Klein-Goldberger system to two distinct varieties of random impulses. First of all, random

---

[18] The real wage rate, however, does return to its equilibrium trend by the end of the cycle.

[19] The idea that economic fluctuations may be due to random shocks was first suggested in 1927 by E. Slutzky, "The Summation of Random Causes as the Source of Cyclical Processes," translated into English in *Econometrica*, Vol. 5 (1937), pp. 105 ff. It was also suggested independently by R. Frisch, *op. cit.*

[20] T. Haavelmo, "The Inadequacy of Testing Dynamic Theory by Comparing Theoretical Solutions and Observed Cycles," *Econometrica*, Vol. 8 (1940), p. 312.

shocks were superimposed upon the extrapolated values of the exogenous quantities (shocks of type I). Secondly, random perturbations were introduced instead into each of the empirically fitted Klein-Goldberger equations (shocks of type II). In addition we made a set of calculations in which both kinds of disturbances were present.

7. SHOCKS OF TYPE I

Shocks of type I arise logically whenever exogenous quantities are projected in a smooth manner over long periods of time, for, while it is convenient to extrapolate these variables in a continuous fashion, even a cursory glance at the data over a period of a few years shows that these magnitudes tend to jump more or less erratically with respect to any smooth curve one might draw. It is, of course, obvious that a system that incorporates such statistical fluctuations may not be completely satisfactory for quantitative purposes. On the other hand, it may still prove fruitful to compare with economic experience the frequency of occurrence and the amplitudes of whatever cycles may arise.

We shall therefore modify our method of extrapolation of the exogenous variables in order to see what effects these random perturbations may have. For this purpose we define the value of an exogenous variable y_t at time t as its trend value $\bar{y}_t$ plus the shock term δy_t, and assume that δy_t has a Gaussian distribution[21] with a mean of zero. In order that the shocks inflicted upon the system be of a more or less realistic magnitude at all times, we evaluate the standard deviation of δy_t over that portion of the data for which our least squares fit was made,[22] and, for our subsequent calculations, we maintain the ratio of the standard deviation of δy_t to y_{t-1} at a value independent of time. It is interesting to note that these standard deviations (see Appendix B. 4) are, in general, quite small; in fact, only three of them exceed 10 per cent of the trend value of the corresponding variable.

In examining the behavior of the twelve exogenous variables[23] over the sample period, it becomes evident that there exists a high degree of correlation between the long- and the short-term interest rates, and between the size of government payrolls and the number of government em-

---

[21] This assumption also underlies the principle of least squares fits.

[22] It will be recalled that we used data from 1946–1952 for our least squares extrapolations of all exogenous variables except government expenditures, G; for G, data for 1929–1940 and 1946–1950 were used.

[23] These variables, it will be recalled, are the short-term i_S and long term interest rates i_L, the index of hours worked h, government employee compensation W_2, government expenditures G, the index of agricultural exports F_A, agricultural subsidies A_2 and five population and labor force variables (N_P, N, N_E, N_F, and N_G).

ployees.[24] It is therefore appropriate to assume that these pairs of variables move together and that the determination of a shock on one variable of each pair automatically sets the size of the corresponding shock on the other. Hence we are left with a set of ten random exogenous shocks, whose magnitudes and signs are to be established.

The technique employed for this purpose was to divide the normal curve of error into 100 regions of equal area. To each region we assigned both the normal deviate associated with the midpoint of its interval and a previously unassigned integer between 00 and 99, inclusive. Then selecting a two-digit random number, we effectively chose at random a specific region of the Gaussian distribution and the corresponding normal deviate. Multiplying this deviate by the standard deviation of δy_t, we found the magnitude and direction of a shock on the variable y at time t. Since the selection of an interval in this manner was thus purely random, and since all intervals defined the same area under the curve, this method produced a normally distributed[25] *random* shock upon the variable in question. By repeating this

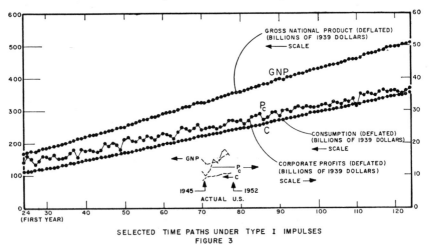

SELECTED TIME PATHS UNDER TYPE I IMPULSES
FIGURE 3

procedure for each of the exogenous variables and adding the calculated shocks to the appropriate trend values, we arrived at a set of shocked exogenous quantities to use as inputs for the tth period. The values of the endogenous variables for this period were then found, of course, as before.

Some of the results obtained with shocks of type I are summarized in Figure 3. The solid lines in this graph portray the computed time paths

[24] The correlation coefficient between government payrolls W_2 and government expenditures G for the sample years 1946–52 is 0.97 and that between the interest rates is 0.89.

[25] Since we have divided the normal curve into discrete intervals, we actually have only a (good) approximation to a normal distribution.

of GNP, consumption, and corporate profits, while the dotted lines represent actual time paths of these variables for the postwar portion of the sample period.[26] From this figure, it would seem that the introduction of forces of type I into the model generates 3 to 4 year swings in the variables of the system. However, the same graph also reveals that the average amplitude of the "cycles" induced by random shock on exogenous quantities is unrealistically small. It would appear, then, that type I perturbations of reasonable magnitude superimposed upon the Klein-Goldberger model will not produce the sort of cyclical behavior observed in the actual economy. We shall therefore proceed to see whether shocks of type II will prove more promising.

8. SHOCKS OF TYPE II

To understand the origin of shocks of type II, one should recall that, in the process of fitting their empirical data, Klein and Goldberger endowed each of their behavioral equations with a random error term.[27] At least three sources of irregularity could produce this term. In the first place, simplifying assumptions are inevitable whenever one wishes to construct a concrete model of a realistic economy. Some of these abstractions are made for convenience, others because the precise equations of motion of an economic system are not yet known. Variables which in practice exert a direct influence upon the solution may be suppressed from several of the equations, made exogenous, or omitted entirely; similarly, relationships which are an integral part of the description may be lost in the process of approximation. Moreover, in predictive models, inherently nonlinear relationships are often treated in a linear approximation for the sake of expediency. In view of these considerations, it is reasonable to expect that the inexactness of the functional form of the Klein-Goldberger equations as a representation of the economic behavior of our society contributes to the size of the random error term.

Secondly, even if the Klein-Goldberger relationships did have a functional form derived from indisputable theory, the fact that the coefficients are based upon empirical data would imply a random error term, as a result of the usual sampling fluctuations. These include, for example, the uncertainty of the degree to which the sample is representative of the universe, as well as the changes in accounting practices, coverage, and reporting techniques which generally occur in the collection of data over a long period of time.

---

[26] The data for the actual time paths are taken from Klein-Goldberger, *op. cit.*, pp. 131–133.

[27] This is standard econometric procedure; cf. Klein-Goldberger, *op. cit.*, pp. 42–46.

A third potential contributor to the size of shocks of type II is of quite
a different character. It arises from the possibility that some of the economic
relationships which compose the Klein-Goldberger system may *never* be
valid as exact equations. This situation will result if the aggregation of
microeconomic quantities into macroeconomic variables is not a legitimate
procedure. For example, if the value of total consumption depends upon
the distribution of income as well as on its magnitude, a precise macro-
economic relationship between overall consumption and aggregate income
will not exist. A similar effect, which will also be reflected in the size of the
random error term, would occur if decision functions are probabilistic
rather than single-valued.

It is therefore evident from the above discussion that the residuals of the
several empirically fitted equations included in the Klein-Goldberger
model can be attributed to a number of different types of irregularity.
Since there would appear to be no a priori correlation among the many
individual sources of fluctuation, the random error terms can be assumed
for all practical purposes to be distributed in a Gaussian manner. We
therefore postulate that each error term is distributed normally about a
mean of zero, and we evaluate its standard deviation, just as in the case
of shocks of type I, from the standard errors observed for the sample period
(see Appendix B. 5).

In order to introduce perturbations of type II into the Klein-Goldberger
model, we added a random error term to the right-hand side of each of the
original non-definitional relationships.[28] Then the same process of algebraic
substitution which was used in the simplification of the unshocked system
was applied to this new group of equations. These operations left us with a
set of equations in which the several error terms appear as parameters,
analogous to the exogenous and the lagged variables. Once the sizes and
directions of these endogenous shocks are determined (by the selection of
two-digit random numbers, as in the case of type I impulses), the system is
solved as before. A similar procedure can be used to investigate the behavior
of the Klein-Goldberger equations when both shocks of type I and shocks
of type II are present simultaneously.

Some of the results of the computation with shocks of type II are plotted
in Figure 4. As in Figure 3, the solid lines represent the calculated behavior
of GNP, consumption, and corporate profits, respectively, while the dotted
lines depict the time paths traversed by the same quantities during the
postwar period in the United States.[26] As before, we see that the shocked
Klein-Goldberger system produces oscillatory movements with periods of
3 to 4 years. But, unlike the behavior of the model under the action of forces

---

[28] The equations involved are (1) – (8) and (10) – (13) of Appendix A.

of type I, the swings generated here compare favorably in magnitude with those experienced by the United States economy after World War II. Thus, the superposition of impulses of type II upon the Klein-Goldberger equations leads to cycles whose gross properties are reasonably realistic.

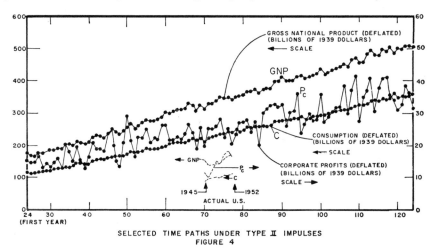

SELECTED TIME PATHS UNDER TYPE II IMPULSES
FIGURE 4

Since the effects of shocks of type II are much larger than those of type I disturbances, the same statement can be made for a system in which both kinds of perturbations are present. And, in view of the fact that, on a priori grounds, either type of shock may be present in an actual economy, it would seem appropriate to carry out our more detailed analysis for the case in which both forces are present.

9. ANALYSIS OF COMPUTED CYCLES

It is encouraging, of course, to find that the amplitudes and the periods of the oscillations observed in this model are roughly the same as those which are found in practice. But, this much agreement is merely a necessary condition for an adequate simulation of the cyclical fluctuations of a real industrial economy. We must investigate further to find out whether or not a shocked version of the Klein-Goldberger system really produces business cycles in the technical sense.[29] Specifically, how nearly all-pervasive are the cumulative movements which arise? How are the various oscillations correlated? Is there any consistent phase relationship among the

---

[29] R. A. Gordon, for example, defines business cycles in the following manner: "Business cycles consist of recurring alternations of expansion and contraction in aggregate economic activity, the alternating movements in each direction being self-reinforcing and pervading virtually all parts of the economy." *Business Fluctuations* (Harpers, 1952), p. 214.

several economic series? Do the time paths of the individual variables of the model correspond to those observed in the United States economy? In other words, if a business cycle analyst were asked whether or not the results of a shocked Klein-Goldberger computation could reasonably represent a United States-type economy, how would he respond?

To answer these questions we shall apply to the data techniques developed by the National Bureau of Economic Research (NBER)[30] for the analysis of business cycles.

One property of cyclical fluctuations in an industrial economy is a marked tendency for a clustering of peaks and troughs of individual economic time series about particular reference dates. It is, in fact, precisely this characteristic of business cycles that Burns and Mitchell use as their criterion for the dating of turning points in the United States economy.[31] And, inasmuch as the oscillations in the Klein-Goldberger model occur in response to random (i.e., noncorrelated) perturbations, a study of the simultaneity of occurrence of peaks (and troughs) will provide us with quite a stringent test of the validity of the model.

As in the normal NBER procedure,[32] we first date the specific cycles;[33] i.e., we determine all the turning points of each of the several time series. Then, to establish the reference dates[33] for the turning points of the *overall* business cycle, we examine the data for bunching (in time) of specific cycle peaks and troughs.[34]

Table II is a summary of some of the relevant characteristics of the business cycles observed in our shocked Klein-Goldberger economy. In examining this table, one should recall that intervals and dates can have

[30] The methods and results of the NBER work are summarized in A. F. Burns and W. C. Mitchell, *Measuring Business Cycles* (National Bureau, 1946) and in W. C. Mitchell, *What Happens During Business Cycles* (National Bureau, 1951).

[31] Mitchell, *op. cit.*, pp. 10–11.

[32] See Burns and Mitchell, *op. cit.*, Ch. 2.

[33] In the rest of this paper we will need the definitions of several quantities prevalent in the literature of business cycles. See, for example, Mitchell, *op. cit.*, pp. 9–11, or Gordon, *op. cit.*, p. 232.

(1) Reference dates are those dates which mark the turning points of overall business activity in the economy.

(2) A reference cycle of an economic variable V represents the behavior of V between the reference dates marking two consecutive minima of overall business activity.

(3) A specific cycle of V represents the behavior of V between the dates marking two consecutive minima of V itself.

[34] Our procedure corresponds to that of the NBER (cf. Mitchell, *op. cit.*, pp. 10–12). As a basis for establishing the reference dates we used all the Klein-Goldberger endogenous quantities except the 5 tax variables. A reference peak (trough) was said to occur (in our data) during any year in which the modal number of specific cycle peaks occurs, provided that at least 10 peaks (troughs) are found in a two-year period which includes the model year.

TABLE II

REFERENCE DATING FOR SHOCKED KLEIN-GOLDBERGER MODEL

Reference Dates		Elapsed Time (Years)		Number of Series at Peaks Which:			Number of Series at Troughs Which:		
Trough (T)	Peak(P)	T→P	P→T	Lag One Year	Coincide	Lead One Year	Lag One Year	Coincide	Lead One Year
–	27	–	2	–	–	–	–	–	–
29	31	2	1	2	8	6	1	6	4
32	37	5	1	1	8	5	4	7	4
38	42	4	1	1	10	0	1	13	1
43	45	2	1	2	7	4	0	10	0
46	51	5	2	2	11	1	3	8	3
53	54	1	2	4	12	1	2	10	4
56	59	3	1	1	10	1	1	11	4
60	63	3	1	2	7	6	4	6	2
64	68	4	2	6	6	3	5	7	1
70	72	2	1	2	7	3	1	13	1
73	74	1	1	2	9	1	2	8	2
75	77	2	1	2	8	4	0	10	2
78	79	1	1	2	8	2	3	9	3
80	83	3	2	2	12	1	1	7	3
85	86	1	2	4	12	2	2	11	2
88	90	2	1	2	12	2	1	11	4
91	94	3	2	3	10	1	3	11	3
96	98	2	4	5	8	3	1	9	3
102	106	4	1	3	12	2	3	10	2
107	109	2	1	4	9	1	5	11	2
110	113	3	1	2	11	4	5	7	1
114	116	2	1	5	7	4	3	13	0
117	119	2	1	1	8	8	4	9	3
120	–	–	–	–	–	–	–	–	–
Totals		59	34	60	212	65	55	217	54
Average per cycle		2.56	1.48	2.61	9.22	2.82	2.39	9.43	2.34
Percent of Specific Cycles Represented		–	–	14.5	51.2	15.7	13.3	52.4	13.0

significance only to the nearest year, inasmuch as the Klein-Goldberger computation was made on a year-to-year basis. The first two columns give the reference dates for the peaks and troughs, respectively. Since one can identify 23 complete business cycles (measured either from trough to trough or from peak to peak) occurring in the 93 years included in our calculation, the average length of a cycle is 4.0 years. This result is in startling agreement with the 4 year post-World War II cycles in the United States economy, as well as with the mean length of American peacetime business cycles since 1854.[35]

The Klein-Goldberger cycles are broken down, in columns 3 and 4, to indicate the duration of the expansion and contraction phases of each cycle. The average expansion covered 2.6 years, while the normal contraction occupied only 1.5. The agreement with the observed figures for the United States (2.1 and 1.8, respectively)[36] is surprisingly good when one considers the fact that the length of a single business cycle stage in our Klein-Goldberger computation can be estimated only to an integral number of years.

The validity of this comparison of United States and Klein-Goldberger business cycles is dependent, of course, upon the degree of reliability with which the reference dates have been determined. One criterion which can be used is the extent to which specific cycle peaks (troughs) tend to cluster at times coincident with the maxima (minima) of the overall business cycles. In our Klein-Goldberger data, 51 per cent of the individual series, on the average, have maxima coincident with an upper turning point of general business activity, and 52 per cent have minima which coincide with a reference trough. The corresponding figures for the United States economy are 58 per cent and 52 per cent respectively.[36] In addition, the proportions of specific cycles which lead or lag the business cycle in our computed data is quite similar to the analogous figure[37] for the United States economy. Our numbers are given in the last line of Table II.

All in all, it would appear that there is a remarkable correspondence between the characteristics of fluctuations generated by the superposition of random shocks upon the Klein-Goldberger system and those of the business cycles which actually occur in the United States economy. The resemblance is not restricted to qualitative parallelism, but is, indeed,

[35] Computed from the NBER dating for the period 1854–1949, reproduced in Gordon, *op. cit.*, p. 216. We omitted from our averages the Civil War cycle and those corresponding to the two World Wars.

[36] These percentages were estimated from Chart 3 (pp. 16–17) of G. H. Moore, *Statistical Indicators of Cyclical Revivals and Recessions* (National Bureau Occasional Paper 31, 1950). Moore's graph was presented on a monthly basis and included the years 1885–1940.

[37] Mitchell, *op. cit.*, Table 15, pp. 154–155, Table 16, pp. 159–167, and Table 42, pp. 312–325.

TABLE III
COMPARISON OF KLEIN-GOLDBERGER AND NBER SPECIFIC CYCLES

Variable	Frequencies and Other Properties at Peaks								Frequencies and Other Properties at Troughs								Remarks
	One Year Lead	Coincide	One Year Lag	Other	K-G Classification	NBER Classification	K-G Index of Conformity (%)	NBER Index of Conformity (%)	One Year Lead	Coincide	One Year Lag	Other	K-G Classification	NBER Classification	K-G Index of Conformity (%)	NBER Index of Conformity (%)	Remarks
$Y+T+D$	1	21	1	1	Coincident	Coincident	+100	*+100	2	21	0	1	Coincident	Coincident	+92	*+50	
Y	1	21	1	1	Coincident	Coincident	+100	*+100	1	22	0	1	Coincident	Coincident	+100	*+50	
C	1	8	3	0	Coincident	Coincident	+100	*+100	5	5	1	1	Leading-Coincident	Coincident	−17	*+50	
I	4	20	0	3	Coincident	Coincident	+100	*+100	0	23	1	3	Coincident	Coincident	+100	*+100	
W_1	2	10	3	2	Coincident	Coincident	+83	*+83	1	10	3	3	Coincident	Concident	+8	*+50	
A_1	6	8	7	7	Irregular	Coincident	−4	+60	8	5	5	10	Irregular	Coincident	−33	+12	
P	4	19	0	4	Coincident	Coincident	+91	—	0	22	1	4	Coincident	Coincident	+100	—	
N_w	4	18	2	2	Coincident	Coincident	+91	+100	3	19	2	2	Coincident	Coincident	+100	+100	
P_c	4	20	0	4	Coincident	Coincident	+100	*+100	3	20	1	4	Coincident	Coincident	+92	+100	
S_P	4	16	0	4	Coincident	Coincident	+83	+100	0	17	4	3	Coincident	Coincident	+100	*+100	
B	0	5	1	1	Coincident	—	+100	—	1	5	1	0	Coincident	—	−42	—	
K	1	9	6	0	Coincident	—	+87	—	0	11	3	1	Coincident	—	+33	—	
D	10	6	3	6	Leading	—	+22	—	10	7	4	5	Leading	—	−25	—	
L_1	14	4	5	3	Leading	—	+13	—	5	6	9	5	Lagging-Irregular	—	+8	—	
L_2	4	15	0	4	Coincident	—	−65	—	2	17	3	1	Coincident	—	−83	—	Inverse
p	3	17	2	0	Coincident	Coincident	+100	+64	0	20	2	0	Coincident	Coincident	+83	+82	
p_A	4	17	2	5	Coincident	Coincident	+100	+50	6	14	4	4	Coincident	Coincident	+42	+60	
w	0	1	9	1	Lagging	Lagging	+83	+100	0	4	7	0	Lagging	Coincident	−67	−50	
w/p	2	17	1	5	Coincident	—	−74	—	0	21	0	4	Coincident	—	−100	—	Inverse
K/Y	4	19	1	4	Coincident	—	−100	—	5	19	1	3	Coincident	—	−100	—	Inverse

317

quantitative, in the sense that the duration of the cycle, the relative length of the expansion and contraction phases, and the degree of clustering of peaks and troughs are all in numerical agreement (within the accuracy of measurement) with empirical evidence. Therefore, we shall study the Klein-Goldberger cycles in more detail.

Table III summarizes, for the shocked Klein-Goldberger model, some of the significant features of the specific cycle patterns observed in the endogenous variables. As can be seen from columns 6, 7, 14, and 15, the segregation of the Klein-Goldberger economic variables into leading, coincident, and lagging series is quite similar to the division of the analogous quantities in the United States economy by the NBER. (Columns 2 – 5 and 10 – 13 give the data which lead to our grouping; the NBER separation into categories is taken from Mitchell.[37]) Of the 20 series listed, 12 are classified as coincident series at both peaks and troughs. These are gross national product $(Y + T + D)$, national income Y, gross investment I, private employee compensation W_1, non-wage non-farm income P, employment N_W, corporate profits P_C, corporate savings S_P, corporate surplus B, capital stock K, the general price index p, and the index of agricultural prices p_A. In addition, consumption C coincides at peaks, but has a tendency to lead at troughs. All of these results are in accord with NBER experience (when available), except that the United States specific cycles for consumption coincide, rather than lead at the troughs.

Three additional variables (corporate liquid assets L_2, real wages w/p, and the capital-output ratio K/Y) are in inverse coincidence with the business cycle, in the sense that their troughs tend to occur at reference peaks and vice versa. Unfortunately, we were unable to find the identical items among the NBER data; however, on both theoretical and empirical grounds, these inverse relationships are eminently reasonable. As far as L_2 is concerned, for example, both transactions demand and investment opportunities are reduced as business activity falls and therefore liquid surpluses should begin to accumulate.[38] Indeed, the NBER has some experimental data to support the proposition that the cash component of L_2, at least, tends to rise as the downturn develops (and vice versa).[39]

With respect to the capital-output ratio, it too should fall in times of expansion and climb during a contraction. From a theoretical point of view, as shown by Duesenberry,[40] a non-decreasing capital-output ratio during a business expansion would imply a rising marginal efficiency of investment. But the marginal efficiency of investment cannot increase unless

---

[38] An excellent description of this process can be found in Gordon, *op. cit.*, p. 270–271.

[39] Mitchell, *op. cit.*, p. 148.

[40] J. S. Duesenberry, *Business Cycles and Economic Growth* (McGraw-Hill, 1958), p. 112.

the capital-output ratio drops. Therefore, the capital-output ratio must fall during the boom phase. Furthermore, the time required for the formation and depletion of the capital stock exceeds the time lag inherent in the production of consumer goods; this too implies that the capital-output ratio will move in a direction opposite to that of the general level of economic activity.

With regard to w/p, both Marshall[41] and Keynes[42] suggested that real wages tend to vary inversely with the level of output and employment. This theorem, which has been thoroughly discussed in the literature,[43] is consistent with our observations. In addition, experimental data concerning the movement of real wages in industrial economies,[44] while somewhat inconclusive, tend to confirm the calculated inverse behavior of this variable.

Of the remaining four quantities, the NBER considers farm income A_1 to concur with the general business cycle and money wage rates w to coincide at troughs and to lag at peaks. We, on the other hand, find the former series to be irregular and the latter to lag everywhere. But, as is evident from Table III, the NBER data for agricultural incomes do not show a very high degree of conformity to the overall business cycle (especially at the troughs), and farm output itself (in real terms) tends to have a higher correlation with metereological cycles than with business cycles.[45] For wages, the disagreement between the behavior of the shocked Klein-Goldberger model at the troughs and the NBER analysis may simply be a reflection of the fact that the Klein-Goldberger equations do not appear to allow enough interaction between unemployment and wage rates.[46]

[41] A. Marshall, *Principles of Economics*, 8th ed. (Macmillan, 1947), p. 620.

[42] J. M. Keynes, *The General Theory of Employment, Interest and Money* (Harcourt Brace, 1935), p. 10.

[43] See, e.g., J. T. Dunlop, "The Movement of Real and Money Wage Rates, "*Economic Journal*, Vol. 48 (1938), pp. 413–34; L. Tarshis, "Changes in Real and Money Wages," *Economic Journal*, Vol. 49 (1939), pp. 150–154; R. Ruggles, "The Relative Movements of Real and Money Wage Rates," *Quarterly Journal of Economics*, Vol. 55 (1940), pp. 130–149; S. C. Tsiang, *The Variations of Real Wages and Profit Margins in Relation to the Trade Cycle* (London, 1947), pp. 10–12; and K. W. Rotschild, *The Theory of Wages* (New York, 1956), pp. 128–131.

[44] Roughly speaking, statistical evidence seems to support the proposition if we take account of *product wages* (i.e., money wages deflated by an index of wholesale prices) (see Tsiang, *op. cit.*, Ch. III) and to undermine it if we consider money wages deflated by a cost of living index (see Dunlop, *op. cit.*, and Tarshis, *op. cit.*). It should be noted that the deflator used for real wages in our computations is the implicit deflator for GNP, and therefore that our (w/p) is closer to the product wage rate than to the measure of real wages analyzed by Dunlop and Tarshis.

[45] Mitchell, *op. cit.*, p. 56 and Gordon, *op. cit.*, pp. 347–350.

[46] D. Creamer and M. Bernstein, *Behavior of Wage Rates During Business Cycles* (National Bureau Occasional Paper 34) applied the NBER method to British and American statistics and found an average lag of wages behind general business activity of about 7 months at the major turning points, and longer for the minor ones.

In our study personal liquid assets L_1 tend to lead at peaks and to lag somewhat irregularly at troughs. We have not encountered comparable NBER series. However, one might attribute a lead in personal liquidity at a peak to the de facto financing of the last stages of the boom by dishoarding on the part of overoptimistic consumers, and the lag at a trough to the satisfaction of pent-up demand in the light of renewed income prospects.

Finally, depreciation D leads, in our calculations, at both troughs and peaks. While Fabricant[47] has found that depreciation charges tend to show much less cyclical fluctuation than corporate gross income or physical output, our computations do not exhibit this behavior. But, it should be noted that, first of all, the Klein-Goldberger depreciation is deflated and more complicated than that of Fabricant, and, secondly, that Fabricant's data cover only the first fourteen years immediately following World War I. We feel, therefore, that existing empirical work is inconclusive on this point, especially in view of the complex nature of any realistic measure of depreciation.

Columns 8 – 9 and 16 – 17 of Table III present the indices of conformity[48] of the specific cycles to the expansions and contractions of the business cycles of both the Klein-Goldberger data and the NBER statistics.[49] These indices measure the correlation between the direction of movements in the individual series which comprise the business cycle and that of the overall economic fluctuations which result. In evaluating the data, one should note that those NBER indices which are preceded by an asterisk in the table are based upon only four complete cycles and therefore that they can assume no numerical values other than 0, $\pm$ 50, and $\pm$ 100. While, by definition, an index of $+$ 100 denotes perfect concurrence in direction of specific cycles with the general business cycle for all four cycles, an index of $+$ 50 for these data states merely that, in exactly three out of the four cases examined, the series expanded during the reference expansion (or contracted during the reference contraction).

As can be seen from this table, there is reasonably good agreement

[47] S. Fabricant, *Capital Consumption and Adjustment* (NBER, 1938), p. 197.

[48] The index of conformity of a set of specific cycles to the expansion of the overall business cycle is the percentage of conforming movements minus the percentage of non-conforming movements. A conforming movement occurs when the value of the variable at a reference peak is higher than its value at the preceding trough. If the two values are equal, the movement does not contribute to the index (although it is counted as an event in computing the percentages). A non-conforming movement is a movement opposite in direction to a conforming movement. The index of conformity to reference contractions is defined in an analogous manner.

[49] The NBER data are taken from Mitchell, *op. cit.*, Table 15, pp. 154–155, Table 16, pp. 159–167, and Table 42, pp. 312–325.

between the Klein-Goldberger indices of conformity and those of the NBER, especially during expansions.[50] A major discrepancy appears, however, in agricultural incomes A_1, where the tendency for irregular behavior of the Klein-Goldberger series observed in the classification process is confirmed by the low values of the conformity indices; the NBER conformity is somewhat higher. We also find that the Klein-Goldberger total payrolls W_1 do not conform as well to business contractions as the NBER data would suggest they should. This is probably due primarily to the failure of money wages w to contract sufficiently in the model. This tendency for rigidity in money wages during contractions, however, is confirmed in the NBER data. Finally, Klein-Goldberger consumption C appears to have little or no tendency to fall during business contractions. This behavior, which agrees with post-World War II United States experience, may be due to the fact that a strong upward trend in consumption expenditures (and in the economic variables in general) has been built into our extrapolation of the Klein-Goldberger model. It is, however, conceivable that there exists a real difference in consumption patterns since World War II, as compared with the prewar era (from which the NBER data were taken). Such a shift would be reflected, at least partially, in the Klein-Goldberger statistical fits.

Generally speaking, then, the specific cycles generated in the Klein-Goldberger model by random shocks thus bear an obvious resemblance to those of cycles found in the United States economy. The division of the Klein-Goldberger data into leading, lagging, and coincident series is almost identical to that of the NBER (when available), and is in accord with theoretical expectations. Similarly, the indices of conformity to the business cycle are reasonably consistent with those given by Mitchell[51] for the United States economy.

10. CONCLUSIONS

Our investigation into the dynamic nature of the econometric model of Klein and Goldberger suggests that their equations do not offer an immediate explanation of an internally generated cyclical process. For, in the absence of perturbations, the time paths of the economic variables are monotonic and essentially linear in character. Furthermore, the behavior of the model is remarkably stable, as evidenced by the fact that

[50] In an economy with a prevalent upward trend, conformity to expansions is more regular than conformity to contractions. Therefore, for the Klein-Goldberger data, a conformity index of +60 to expansions is fairly low. However, since the rising trend also tends to weaken the conformity to expansion of series with inverted timing, a conformity —60 to expansions is high.

[51] Mitchell, *op. cit.*, pp. 154–55, 159–167, and 312–325.

the solution resumes its unperturbed equilibrium growth trend even after a strong exogenous disturbance.

On the other hand, when random shocks of a realistic order of magnitude are superimposed upon the original form of the Klein-Goldberger equations, the cyclical fluctuations which result are remarkably similar to those described by the NBER as characterizing the United States economy. The average duration of a cycle, the mean length of the expansion and contraction phases, and the degree of clustering of individual peaks and troughs around reference dates all agree with the corresponding data for the United States economy. Furthermore, the lead-lag relationships of the endogenous variables included in the model and the indices of conformity of the specific series to the overall business cycle also resemble closely the analogous features of our society. All in all, it would appear that the shocked Klein-Goldberger model approximates the behavior of the United States economy rather well.

In view of these results, it is not unreasonable to suggest that the gross characteristics of the interactions among the real variables described in the Klein-Goldberger equations may represent good approximations to the behavioral relationships in a practical economy. There are, of course, a number of significant defects in the detailed workings of the Klein-Goldberger system. For example, the treatment of the monetary quantities and the interconnections between them and the real sector both need improvement. Nevertheless, the representation would seem to offer a good working basis for the investigation of cyclical fluctuations, especially if the deficiencies mentioned above are corrected.

But, the behavior of the Klein-Goldberger system under random perturbations is also suggestive from another point of view. Ever since the path-breaking article of Frisch on the propagation of business cycles, the possibility that the cyclical movements observed in a capitalistic society are actually due to random shocks has been seriously considered by business cycle theorists. The results we have found in this study tend to support this possibility. For, the agreement between the data obtained by imposing uncorrelated perturbations upon a model which is otherwise non-oscillatory in character is certainly consistent with the hypothesis that the economic fluctuations experienced in modern, highly developed societies are indeed due to random impulses.

Of course, these random impulses are not necessarily synonymous with an exogenous theory of the business cycle. For, as we saw in Section 8 above, it was primarily shocks of type II which led to agreement between the cyclical behavior of the model and that of the United States economy. And, the reader will recall, these shocks may reflect inexactness in the model, statistical inaccuracies in the fits, or inherent randomness in the decision functions of the economic units themselves. While none of these factors is, strictly speaking, endogenous to the particular Klein-Goldberger system investigated, this does not imply that the type of perturbations actually responsible for the observed cyclical behavior are exogenous to economic theory in general.

In conclusion, we should like to emphasize that, while we have shown that the shocked Klein-Goldberger model offers excellent agreement with economic fact, we have not proved either that the Klein-Goldberger model itself is a good representation of the basic interactions among the several sectors of our economy or that random shocks are the prime cause of business cycles. In view of the remarkable quantitative correspondence with reality, however, we are very tempted to suggest that the second of these hypotheses is true and that, in addition, the Klein-Goldberger system is, except for the deficiencies discussed, not very far wrong.

Berkeley, California

APPENDIX A

1. Explanation of Symbols

$Y + T + D$	Gross national product, 1939 dollars
C	Consumer expenditures, 1939 dollars
I	Gross private domestic capital formation, 1939 dollars
G	Government expenditures for goods and services, 1939 dollars
p	Price index of gross national product, 1939: 100
F_E	Exports of goods and services, 1939 dollars
F_I	Imports of goods and services, 1939 dollars
W_1	Private employee compensation, deflated
W_2	Government employee compensation, deflated
D	Capital consumption charges, 1939 dollars
P_C	Corporate profits, deflated
S_P	Corporate savings, deflated
T	Indirect taxes less subsidies, deflated
T_W	Personal and payroll taxes less transfers associated with wage and salary income, deflated
T_P	Personal and corporate taxes less transfers associated with nonwage nonfarm income, deflated
T_C	Corporate income taxes, deflated
T_A	Taxes less transfers associated with farm income, deflated
K	End-of-year stock of private capital, 1939 dollars from arbitrary origin
F_A	Index of agricultural exports, 1939: 100
p_A	Index of agricultural prices, 1939: 100
p_I	Index of prices of imports, 1939: 100
N_P	Number of persons in the United States
N	Number of persons in the labor force
N_W	Number of wage-and-salary-earners
N_G	Number of government employees
N_F	Number of farm operators
N_E	Number of nonfarm entrepreneurs

h Index of hours worked per year, 1939: 100
w Index of hourly wages, 1939: 122.1
P Nonwage nonfarm income, deflated
A_1 Farm income, deflated
A_2 Government payments to farmers, deflated
i_L Average yield on corporate bonds, per cent
i_S Average yield on short term commercial paper, per cent
R Excess reserves of banks as a percentage of total reserves
L_1 End-of-year liquid assets held by persons, deflated
L_2 End-of-year liquid assets held by businesses, deflated
t Time trend, years, $t = 1$ is 1929
B End-of-year corporate surplus, deflated, from arbitrary origin

2. Klein and Goldberger's Equations

(1)* $\quad C_t = -22.26 + 0.55(W_1 + W_2 - T_W)_t + 0.41(P - T_P - S_P)_t$
$$+ 0.34(A_1 + A_2 - T_A)_t + 0.26C_{t-1} + 0.072(L_1)_{t-1} + 0.26(N_P)_t$$

(2)* $\quad I_t = -16.71 + 0.78(P - T_P + A_1 + A_2 - T_A + D)_{t-1} - 0.073K_{t-1}$
$$+ 0.14(L_2)_{t-1}$$

(3)* $\quad (S_P)_t = -3.53 + 0.72\,(P_C - T_C)_t + 0.076\,(P_C - T_C - S_P)_{t-1} - 0.028\,B_{t-1}$

(4)* $\quad (P_C)_t = -7.60 + 0.68P_t$

(5)* $\quad D_t = 7.25 + 0.10\,\dfrac{K_t + K_{t-1}}{2} + 0.044(Y + T + D - W_2)_t$

(6)* $\quad (W_1)_t = -1.40 + 0.24(Y + T + D - W_2)_t + 0.24(Y + T + D - W_2)_{t-1} + 0.29t$

(7)* $\quad (Y + T + D - W_2)_t = -26.08 + 2.17[h(N_W - N_G) + N_E + N_F]_t$
$$+ 0.16\,\dfrac{K_t + K_{t-1}}{2} + 2.05t$$

(8)* $\quad w_t - w_{t-1} = 4.11 - 0.74(N - N_W - N_E - N_F)_t + 0.52(p_{t-1} - p_{t-2}) + 0.54t$

(9)* $\quad (F_I)_t = 0.32 + 0.0060(W_1 + W_2 - T_W + P - T_P + A_1 + A_2 - T_A)_t$
$$+ 0.81(F_I)_{t-1}$$

(10)* $\quad (A_1)_t\dfrac{p_t}{(p_A)_t} = -0.36 + 0.054(W_1 + W_2 - T_W + P - T_P - S_P)_t\dfrac{p_t}{(p_A)_t}$
$$- 0.007(W_1 + W_2 - T_W + P - T_P - S_P)_{t-1}\dfrac{p_{t-1}}{(p_A)_{t-1}} + 0.012(F_A)_t$$

(11)* $\quad (p_A)_t = -131.17 + 2.32p_t$

(12)* $\quad (L_1)_t = 0.14(W_1 + W_2 - T_W + P - T_P - S_P + A_1 + A_2 - T_A)_t$
$$+ 76.03(i_L - 2.0)_t^{-0.84}$$

(13)* $\quad (L_2)_t = -0.34 + 0.26(W_1)_t - 1.02(i_S)_t - 0.26(p_t - p_{t-1}) + 0.61(L_2)_{t-1}$

(14)* $\quad (i_L)_t = 2.58 + 0.44(i_S)_{t-3} + 0.26(i_S)_{t-5}$

(15)* $\quad 100\,\dfrac{(i_S)_t - (i_S)_{t-1}}{(i_S)_{t-1}} = 11.17 - 0.67R_t$

$$(16) \qquad C_t + I_t + G_t + (F_E)_t - (F_I)_t = Y_t + T_t + D_t$$

$$(17) \qquad (W_1)_t + (W_2)_t + P_t + (A_1)_t + (A_2)_t = Y_t$$

$$(18) \qquad h_t \frac{w_t}{p_t} (N_W)_t = (W_1)_t + (W_2)_t$$

$$(19) \qquad K_t - K_{t-1} = I_t - D_t$$

$$(20) \qquad B_t - B_{t-1} = (S_P)_t$$

$$(21) \qquad T_t = 0.0924(Y + T + D)_t - \frac{275.4}{p_t}$$

$$(22) \qquad (T_W)_t = 0.1549(W_1)_t + 0.1310(W_2)_t - \frac{1398.1}{p_t}$$

$$(23) \qquad (T_C)_t = 0.4497(P_C)_t + \frac{548.2}{p_t}$$

$$(24) \qquad (T_P)_t = 0.248(P - T_C - S_P)_t + 0.2695 \frac{p_{t-1}}{p_t} (P - T_C - S_P)_{t-1} +$$

$$+ 0.4497(P_C)_t - \frac{1162.1}{p_t}$$

$$(25) \qquad (T_A)_t = \frac{50.0}{p_t}$$

APPENDIX B

1. The equations that, for the actual calculations, replaced their counterparts of Appendix A

$$(3) \qquad (S_P)_t = -3.53 + 0.72(P_C - T_C)_t - 0.028B_{t-1}$$

$$(9) \qquad (F_I)_t = (F_E)_t$$

$$(10) \qquad (A_1)_t \frac{p_t}{(p_A)_t} = 0.054(W_1 + W_2 - T_W + P - T_P - S_P)_t \frac{p_t}{(p_A)_t} + 0.012(F_A)_t$$

$$(11) \qquad (p_A)_t = 1.39p_t + 32.0$$

$$(13) \qquad (L_2)_t = 0.26(W_1)_t - 1.02(i_S)_t - 0.26(p_t - p_{t-1}) + 0.61(L_2)_{t-1}$$

$$(14) \qquad (i_L)_t = 3.5$$

$$(15) \qquad (i_S)_t = 2.5$$

$$(16) \qquad C_t + I_t + G_t = Y_t + T_t + D_t$$

$$(21) \qquad T_t = 0.0924(Y + T + D)_t - 1.3607$$

$$(22) \qquad (T_W)_t = 0.1549(W_1)_t + 0.131(W_2)_t - 6.9076$$

$$(23) \qquad (T_C)_t = 0.4497(P_C)_t + 2.7085$$

(24) $(T_P)_t = 0.248(P - T_C - S_P)_t + 0.2695 \dfrac{p_{t-1}}{p_t} (P - T_C - S_P)_{t-1}$
$$+ 0.4497(P_C)_t - 5.7416$$

(25) $(T_A)_t = 0.0512(A_1 + A_2)_t$

2. Extrapolations

$$(W_2)_t = 1.82 + .578t$$

$$(N_E)_t = 3.70 + .118t$$

$$(N_F)_t = 4.01 + \frac{2.12}{t-15}$$

$$(N_G)_t = 2.01 + .321t$$

$$(N_P)_t = 97.39 + 2.589t$$

$$N_t = 44.53 + .964t$$

$$h_t = 1.062$$

$$G_t = 19.892 + .567t$$

$$(A_2)_t = .108 + \frac{.0746}{t-16}$$

$$(F_A)_t = 171.86$$

3. Initial values used in calculations

Endogenous Variables	1951 $(t-2)$	1952 $(t-1)$	Exogenous Variables	1952 $(t-1)$	1953 (t)
$Y + T + D$	—	172.0	h	—	1.062
C	—	111.4	W_2	15.12	15.70
W_1	—	78.65	G	—	33.5
A_1	—	7.3	A_2	0.1187	0.1173
I	—	24.3	F_A	—	171.86
K	—	41.5	N_P	—	159.6
D	—	19.35	N	—	67.63
P_C	—	16.51	N_E	—	6.53
P	—	35.17	N_F	—	4.25
S_P	—	1.9	N_G	—	9.71
B	—	.19	i_S	2.5	2.5
N_W	—	56.0	i_L	3.5	3.5
L_1	—	95.2			
L_2	—	38.1			
w	—	326.2			
p	197.5	202.4			
p_A	—	303.0			
T	—	14.51			
T_W	—	8.63			
T_A	—	.38			
T_C	—	10.14			
T_P	—	13.72			

4. Standard deviations used for Type I shocks (upon exogenous variables)

Variable	$\sigma_{\delta y_t}$	$\dfrac{\sigma_{\delta y_t}}{y_{t-1}}$
i_S	.512	.20
i_L	.146	.0423
h	.0185	.018
W_2	1.77	.123
G	.88	.026
A_2	.0192	.16
F_A	12.2	.071
N_P	.086	.00054
N	.125	.0018
N_E	.114	.017
N_F	.234	.055
N_G	.975	.10

5. Standard deviations used for Type II shocks (upon equations)

Variable	Equation	$\sigma_{\delta y_t}$	$\dfrac{\sigma_{\delta y_t}}{y_{t-1}}$
C	(1)*	.958	.0086
I	(2)*	2.946	.12
S_P	(3)	5.428	.29
P_C	(4)*	.700	.044
D	(5)*	.699	.036
W_1	(6)*	1.0325	.013
$Y + T + D$	(7)*	2.319	.013
w	(8)*	4.861	.015
A_1	(10)	.955	.13
L_1	(12)*	.017575	.00059
L_2	(13)	1.2911	.034
p_A†	(11)	15.716	.052

† Based on residuals from our re-estimated equation for p_A for the years 1946–52.

Econometrica, Vol. 28, 2 (April 1960)

THE DURABILITY OF CONSUMERS' DURABLE GOODS

By RICHARD STONE AND D. A. ROWE

This paper illustrates the results obtained by adapting the model proposed by the authors in an earlier paper [6] to incorporate the method of estimating durability proposed by Nerlove [3]. It is found that in the cases examined the estimates of durability obtained in this way are very low. Possible reasons for these results are briefly indicated but are not examined empirically.

1. INTRODUCTION

IN ANALYSING THE demand for durable goods it is desirable to allow for the possibility of adaptive behaviour which takes time, a difficulty which is not so obviously present in dealing with the demand for food and similar perishables. In two earlier papers [6, 7], the present authors set out a simple dynamic model of consumers' demand which takes account explicitly of (i) the differences in durability between goods, and (ii) the differences in the speed with which consumers try to reestablish equilibrium in their consumption when circumstances change. This model can be applied to data in the form of time-series and, in its initial form, it appeared that it would usually be necessary to assume a value for the parameter associated with durability. In some cases an extraneous estimate of this parameter can be made without too great difficulty, as, for instance, where there is a well organised second-hand market [2] or where detailed records of consumers' inventories are available [4]. But these cases are exceptional. In general, a reasonable guess has to be made, based perhaps on the current practice of valuers or tax assessors. A way round this difficulty has recently been indicated by Nerlove [3]. He has shown that, subject to certain reasonable restrictions, a direct estimate of the parameter associated with durability can be made from the time-series themselves, in conjunction with the other parameters of the demand function. This is likely to be an advantage, partly because it provides an additional basis of estimation and partly because the values obtained in this way should be more consistent with the model than any estimates determined extraneously.

Some results from the application of this method to British data are presented in the later sections of this paper. It will be convenient to give first a brief statement of the model and the derivation of the basic regression equation.

2. THE MODEL

The formulation of the model is given here in terms of a period analysis, since this is best adapted for applications to actual data. There is a parallel formulation in continuous form which leads to closely similar results.

The quantity of a commodity purchased in any period, q, is the sum of replacement demand, equal to the depreciation or consumption of the period, u, and net investment, v. That is

$$(1) \qquad q = u + v.$$

Consumption is assumed to be a continuous process which uses up the existing stock at a constant proportionate rate. This is equivalent to depreciation as calculated by the reducing balance method. In any period, therefore, consumption will consist of a certain proportion, $1/n$, say, of the initial stock, s, *plus* a further, generally smaller, fraction, $1/m$, of the purchases of the period:

$$(2) \qquad u = \frac{s}{n} + \frac{q}{m}.$$

Net investment constitutes a net addition to the stock during the period and is therefore equivalent to the difference between the opening and closing stocks of the period. In symbols

$$(3) \qquad v = Es - s$$

where E is the shift operator such that $E^{\theta}x(t) = x(t + \theta)$.

Combining these three equations gives

$$(4) \qquad q = \frac{s}{n} + \frac{q}{m} + Es - s = \frac{m}{m-1} \left\{ Es - \left(\frac{n-1}{n} \right)s \right\}$$
$$= k\{1 + (n-1)\Delta\}Es$$

where $k = m/n(m-1)$ and $\Delta = 1 - E^{-1}$; so that

$$(5) \qquad \Delta q = k\{1 + (n-1)\Delta\}v = k\Omega v,$$

say. It is assumed further that adjustment to a new level of stocks (and consumption) is normally spread over more than a single period and, specifically, that

$$(6) \qquad v = r(s^* - s)$$

where s^* represents the level of stocks which consumers would eventually wish to hold at current levels of income and prices. With the parameter r equal to some positive fraction, the net investment of the period is only sufficient partially to bridge the gap between the desired level, s^*, and the stock held at the beginning of the period, s. In effect, equation (6) specifies a distributed lag of exponential form in investment behaviour.

Associated with the equilibrium level of stocks, s^*, there is an equilibrium level of purchases, q^*, which is wholly replacement demand and just sufficient to maintain stocks constant at the desired level. From (4) it is evident that

$$(7) \qquad q^* = ks^*.$$

The usual assumptions of static demand theory may be invoked to specify the determinants of q^*. It is desirable, however, that the form of the equation be essentially linear in the determining variables. For the present applications it has been assumed that

(8) $$q^* = a + \beta \, (\mu/p) + \gamma(\pi/p)$$

where μ is total expenditure, p is own price and π is an index of all other prices. This equation will be recognised as a version of the linear expenditure function [5] and the parameters a, β and γ may be interpreted in accordance with that formulation.

The required regression equation may be obtained by applying the operator $k\Omega$ from (5) to both sides of (6) and substituting from (4), (5), (7), and (8); this yields

(9) $$\Delta q = ra + r\beta\Omega(\mu/p) + r\gamma\Omega(\pi/p) - rE^{-1}q .$$

Although the parameters of the model do not enter linearly in this equation, the estimation procedure, as Nerlove has shown, is quite straightforward. For a given value of n, the transformed variables $\Omega(\mu/p)$ and $\Omega(\pi/p)$ can be computed. With these variables and the series for q, the parameters in (9) can be estimated. The calculations are repeated for different values of n and that value is chosen which maximises the multiple correlation coefficient, R^2. Estimates of the individual parameters r, a, β, and γ are readily obtained from the coefficients of the regression equation. This procedure could be carried out easily on a fully automatic computer. For the applications reported here an ordinary desk calculating machine was used.

With the usual assumptions as regards residuals, the estimates obtained in this way are maximum likelihood estimates. Although identical estimates would be obtained if q were taken as the dependent variable in the regression equation, it is likely that in practice the use of Δq will give a better indication of the degree of explanation achieved.

No difficulty arises in dealing with a purely perishable good. It is only necessary to set $n = 1$ in equation (9). The parameters are then derived from the coefficients of the equation

(10) $$\Delta q = ra + r\beta(\mu/p) + r\gamma(\pi/p) - rE^{-1}q .$$

Similarly, no more than one regression would be required if q^* were a function of a single variable, ϱ, real income, say. For then equation (9) could be written

(11) $$\Delta q = ra + r\beta\varrho + r\beta(n - 1)\Delta\varrho - rE^{-1}q$$

and the parameters determined directly from the regression coefficients. This form might be used whenever the contribution of relative prices and other factors is known to be comparatively small.

3. SOME APPLICATIONS

The method set out in the preceding section may be applied equally to annual or quarterly data, and both have been used here. The annual data relate to two groups of household durable goods in the interwar period. These two groups, furniture and hardware, include most of the larger durables bought by households, apart from motor vehicles. The furniture group includes certain soft furnishing goods as well as furniture and floor coverings, radios and gramophones. Electrical appliances other than radios are included in the hardware group together with most kinds of domestic equipment. The basic series used [8] were: expenditure per family on furniture (or hardware) at constant (1938) prices, q; total expenditure per family at current prices, μ; an index of furniture (or hardware) prices, $1938 = 1.000$, p; and an index of the prices of all other consumer goods, $1938 = 1.000$, π. From these series the variables specified in equation (9) were constructed for the period 1922—38, with values of $n = 1, 2, 3, 4$, and 5, and the coefficients were estimated by the method of least squares. The results are shown in Table I.

TABLE I
REGRESSION ESTIMATES FOR HOUSEHOLD DURABLES, 1922—38
(annual data)

n	5	4	3	2	1
Furniture, etc:					
R^2	0.716	0.729	0.750	0.781	0.769
αr	—1.09	—1.67	—2.65	—4.54	—8.29
	(0.91)	(0.98)	(1.07)	(1.21)	(1.65)
$\beta r \times 10^2$	0.66	0.80	1.01	1.39	2.32
	(0.28)	(0.35)	(0.48)	(0.74)	(1.84)
γr	0.19	0.42	0.89	1.92	3.78
	(1.07)	(1.33)	(1.74)	(2.50)	(4.96)
r	0.11	0.12	0.15	0.20	0.33
	(0.05)	(0.05)	(0.05)	(0.06)	(0.11)
Hardware, etc.:					
R^2	0.891	0.892	0.899	0.924	0.928
αr	2.86	2.79	2.39	0.93	0.20
	(0.87)	(0.97)	(1.13)	(1.26)	(1.34)
$\beta r \times 10^2$	1.55	1.98	2.69	3.81	4.86
	(0.21)	(0.25)	(0.31)	(0.36)	(0.63)
γr	—5.15	—6.38	—8.21	—10.44	—12.28
	(0.59)	(0.73)	(0.93)	(1.27)	(2.43)
r	0.54	0.57	0.60	0.66	0.87
	(0.10)	(0.10)	(0.10)	(0.10)	(0.11)

In this table there are given for each regression, the value of the multiple correlation coefficient, R^2, and the net regression coefficients, with their "standard errors" in parentheses. These standard errors were calculated by the conventional formulae, with no allowance for the error arising from the assumed value of n, and they cannot be regarded as specifying precise confidence limits. They are nevertheless useful as a rough guide to whether the variable concerned makes any real contribution to the explanation.

It can be seen that in all cases the degree of explanation obtained is reasonably high, particularly when it is remembered that the dependent variable is in first-difference form. The slightly lower values of R^2 for the furniture group are accompanied by some implausible coefficients. Neither the implied negative sign for the parameter a nor the positive sign for γ is theoretically acceptable, but it is very doubtful whether either is significant. The variation in R^2 between the different regressions is very slight for both groups and the indication of the best value of n seems hardly decisive. Such as it is, it suggests low values for both commodity groups: 2 for furniture and 1 for hardware. This result is somewhat surprising. It might have been expected that a value in the region of $n = 4$ would have been most likely. This would imply a period of about 8 years to use up all but 10 per cent of the initial value of a purchase. As it is, the results obtained here suggest that hardware is treated very much as a perishable in this respect and that furniture is used up only a little less rapidly.

It is evident from Table I that the estimate of r is not wholly independent of the value assumed for n, but tends to increase as n approaches unity. Nevertheless there is a marked difference in level between the two commodity groups. The rate of adjustment is much lower for furniture than for hardware. This difference may be due to the higher proportion of large durables in the furniture group. It is with respect to large purchases such as furniture and carpets that the longest delays in adjustment might be expected. The hardware group, on the other hand, includes many small items of kitchen equipment and ironmongery for which any appreciable lag in adjustment seems much less likely.

The dynamic formulation of demand adopted here gives rise to both short-term and long-term elasticities. The short-term elasticities vary with the rate of adjustment and the length of the unit period considered. The long-term elasticities which are given here depend only on the equilibrium level of purchases. The gross elasticities with respect to total expenditure and prices are defined in the following way

$$(12) \qquad \eta_\mu^* = \frac{\mu}{q^*}\frac{dq^*}{d\mu} = \frac{\beta\mu}{pq^*},$$

$$(13) \qquad \eta_p^* = \frac{p}{q^*}\frac{dq^*}{dp} = -\frac{\beta\mu + \gamma\pi}{pq^*},$$

and

(14)
$$\eta_\pi^* = \frac{\pi}{q^*} \frac{dq^*}{d\pi} = \frac{\gamma\pi}{pq^*}.$$

Similarly, the price (substitution) elasticities, with real expenditure held constant, are

(15)
$$\sigma_p^* = \frac{pq^*}{\mu} \; \eta_\mu^* + \eta_p^* = \beta - \frac{\beta\mu + \gamma\pi}{pq^*},$$

and

(16)
$$\sigma_\pi^* = \left(1 - \frac{pq^*}{\mu}\right) \eta_\mu^* + \eta_\pi^* = \frac{\beta\mu + \gamma\pi}{pq^*} - \beta = -\sigma_p^*.$$

The estimates of these values for an average level of q^* are set out in Table II. No confidence limits are given for these estimates but it is probable that in many cases they will be fairly wide.

TABLE II
ESTIMATED ELASTICITIES FOR HOUSEHOLD DURABLES, 1922—38
(annual data)

n	η_μ^*	η_p^*	η_π^*	σ_p^*
Furniture, etc.:				
1	2.04	—3.04	1.00	—2.97
2	1.99	—2.82	0.83	—2.75
3	1.89	—2.39	0.50	—2.32
4	1.74	—2.01	0.27	—1.95
5	1.59	—1.73	0.14	—1.67
Hardware, etc.:				
1	3.94	—0.95	—2.99	—0.89
2	4.15	—0.74	—3.41	—0.68
3	3.22	—0.26	—2.96	—0.22
4	2.54	—0.09	—2.45	—0.05
5	2.09	—0.02	—2.07	0.01

A second application of the method was made to quarterly data for a comparable range of commodities in the postwar period 1953—58. The two groups, somewhat more narrowly defined than for the interwar period, are furniture and floor coverings, and radio and electrical goods. For the short period of six years covered it was not thought necessary to deflate the series for population changes. Accordingly the series used [1] were: expenditure on furniture and floor coverings (or radio and electrical goods) at constant (1954) prices (q); total consumers' expenditure at current prices (μ); an index of prices for the particular commodity group (p) and for all other consumer goods (π), both $1954 = 1.000$. Each series was seasonally corrected by removing a constant seasonal pattern. As before, a series of regressions in the form of equation (9) was calculated for different values of n. The results are shown in Table III. The values of n chosen are for quarterly

TABLE III

REGRESSION ESTIMATES FOR HOUSEHOLD DURABLES, 1953—58

(quarterly data)

n	20 (5.4)	15 (4.1)	10 (2.9)	5 (1.7)	4 (1.46)	3 (1.25)	2 (1.07)	1.5 (1.01)	1 (1)
Furniture and floor coverings:									
R^2	0.534	0.547	0.571	0.619	0.631	0.637	0.613	...	0.478
αr	11.91	13.84	17.72	27.52	30.32	31.14	21.99	...	—5.53
	(13.10)	(13.74)	(15.33)	(21.38)	(24.65)	(30.19)	(41.05)	...	(64.56)
$\beta r \times 10^3$	4.48	6.04	9.21	18.27	22.13	27.21	32.86	...	35.08
	(1.25)	(1.65)	(2.39)	(4.32)	(5.13)	(6.34)	(8.32)	...	(11.93)
γr	—11.67	—15.81	—24.14	—46.24	—53.89	—60.27	—54.24	...	—19.29
	(7.17)	(9.46)	(13.87)	(25.89)	(31.36)	(39.98)	(55.75)	...	(88.32)
r	0.17	0.20	0.26	0.44	0.52	0.64	0.80	...	0.96
	(0.13)	(0.13)	(0.13)	(0.14)	(0.14)	(0.15)	(0 18)	...	(0.25)
Radio and electrical goods:									
R^2	0.301	0.314	0.339	0.403	0.426	0.451	0.464	0.454	0.421
αr	17.06	17.60	18.69	21.67	22.84	24.04	22.84	17.34	3.30
	(12.02)	(12.47)	(13.53)	(17.65)	(20.09)	(24.56)	(34.16)	(42.86)	(52.72)
$\beta r \times 10^3$	3.23	4.41	6.87	14.41	17.89	22.77	28.52	29.99	27.71
	(1.39)	(1.84)	(2.71)	(5.10)	(6.18)	(7.86)	(10.91)	(13.51)	(16.64)
γr	—8.19	—11.10	—17.06	—34.75	—42.58	—52.95	—61.65	—56.90	—33.48
	(5.70)	(7.60)	(11.38)	(22.69)	(28.36)	(37.94)	(57.28)	(74.54)	(94.98)
r	0.28	0.30	0.34	0.46	0.52	0.61	0.72	0.77	0.80
	(0.16)	(0.16)	(0.16)	(0.16)	(0.17)	(0.17)	(0.19)	(0.20)	(0.22)

rates of consumption reasonably comparable with the annual rates used previously, with additional values in the neighbourhood of the apparent maximum of R^2; the corresponding annual values are shown in parentheses in this and the following table.

The values of R^2 obtained are considerably lower than for the annual data. By contrast the maxima are more clearly determined. The results, however, confirm the relatively low values of n found in the analysis of the interwar annual data.

The coefficients, in all but one case, are acceptable as regards sign. The decline in the size of the "standard errors" with increasing n, which was also apparent with the annual data, is most likely a reflection of the increasing variance of the constructed series $\Omega(\mu/p)$ and $\Omega(\pi/p)$.

The rates of adjustment are much the same for the two groups, especially for the lower values of n. The level in both groups is also consistently higher than in the interwar period, when allowance is made for the difference between annual and quarterly rates. These changes may be partly accounted for by the altered coverage of the series. Certainly the two postwar groups are more nearly alike in containing only the larger durable goods. The more rapid rate of adjustment may indicate a real change in attitude.

The elasticities shown in Table IV also suggest some change in behaviour patterns in the postwar period, when compared with the corresponding figures of Table II. A much more precise analysis, however, would be required to confirm this.

TABLE IV

ESTIMATED ELASTICITIES FOR HOUSEHOLD DURABLES, 1953—58

(quarterly data)

n	η^*_μ	η^*_p	η^*_π	σ^*_p
Furniture and floor coverings:				
1 (1)	1.30	—1.07	—0.23	—1.03
2 (1.07)	1.47	—0.68	—0.79	—0.64
3 (1.25)	1.53	—0.43	—1.10	—0.39
4 (1.46)	1.53	—0.32	—1.21	—0.28
5 (1.7)	1.50	—0.27	—1.23	—0.23
10 (2.9)	1.31	—0.21	—1.10	—0.17
15 (4.1)	1.12	—0.17	—0.95	—0.14
20 (5.4)	1.00	—0.16	—0.84	—0.13
Radio and electrical goods:				
1 (1)	1.54	—0.94	—0.60	—0.91
1.5 (1.01)	1.75	—0.68	—1.07	—0.64
2 (1.07)	1.80	—0.54	—1.26	—0.50
3 (1.25)	1.71	—0.42	—1.29	—0.38
4 (1.46)	1.57	—0.36	—1.21	—0.33
5 (1.7)	1.43	—0.32	—1.11	—0.29
10 (2.9)	0.94	—0.19	—0.75	—0.17
15 (4.1)	0.68	—0.12	—0.56	—0.11
20 (5.4)	0.54	—0.10	—0.44	—0.09

4. CONCLUSION

In assessing the results presented in the preceding section, due allowance must be given to both the defects of the data and the limitations of the model.

The deficiencies of much of the basic data will be generally appreciated. There are many difficulties involved in the compilation of time series of consumers' expenditure, whether on an annual or a quarterly basis, and the figures are subject to both systematic and random errors. It is also certain that some discrepancy must arise from the use of aggregates combining many commodities that are far from homogeneous.

The differences in coverage preclude any precise comparison between the results obtained for the interwar and postwar periods. But it is not without interest to compare the long-term elasticities set out in Tables II and IV. While the expenditure elasticity for the furniture group is substantially the same in the two periods, there is a marked fall in the case of radio and electrical goods. The postwar elasticity is less than half the interwar figure. In view of the greatly increased ownership of many items of household electrical equipment (vacuum cleaners, washing machines, television sets, etc.) since the war, this change may be interpreted in terms of a saturation effect. A comparable shift may be observed in the price elasticities, though the wide margins of error attaching to the coefficients render this much less certain.

Apart from the quality of the data, the limitations of the model must also contribute to the uncertainty of the results. Important factors may have been omitted from the formulation adopted. The relatively low degree of explanation achieved in the postwar analyses suggests the need for further enquiry. It seems likely that some influence should be attributed to the effect of changing hire purchase regulations during this period. But to accommodate factors of this kind in the model would probably require the adjustment rate, r, and perhaps also n, to vary with changing circumstances. The estimation problem then becomes very much more complicated.

The importance of the dynamic formulation is generally borne out in the analyses by an estimate of r significantly different from unity. It is also evident, however, that the estimates of both r and the long-term elasticities are systematically dependent on the value assumed for n. A reason for this may be seen by rewriting equation (9) in the form

$$(17) \qquad \Delta q = r(q^* - E^{-1}q) + r(n - 1)\Delta q^*.$$

In this equation the terms Δq and $(q^* - E^{-1}q)$ may be assumed to be of a similar order of magnitude. If, therefore, an excessively large value is chosen for n, the otherwise overwhelming effect of the final term must be neutralised by a diminution of r or of Δq^*. An overestimate of n will produce a corresponding underestimate of r and of the elasticities of q^* with respect to income and prices. The determination of the correct value of n is of crucial importance.

In the original conception of the model the parameter n was thought of primarily in terms of the average service life of a durable good. The relatively low values of n which emerge from the present analysis suggest that this interpretation needs to be modified. First, with regard to goods of this kind, it is probable that most consumers put a high premium on newness, and this is particularly likely to be so in the case of commodity groups in which newness is accompanied by the novelty of a continuous stream of new products. The scanty evidence of secondhand prices certainly suggests that these goods are depreciated much more rapidly than the decline in their usefulness would warrant. Second, it must be recognised that the concept of maintenance embodied in the model presupposes that buyers are interested in holding constant the total number of years of use that can still be extracted from their stock. An alternative model could be based on a renewal rather than a depreciation method, but this has not been considered. Finally, as was suggested by Wold at the Amsterdam meeting, the model may suffer from a concentration on first sales to the exclusion of any detailed consideration of the second-hand market. With the further development of analysis in this field it is likely that the essential concepts of durability and consumption will lose much of their apparent simplicity. But these problems must stand over for future investigation.

University of Cambridge and
National Institute of Economic and Social Research

REFERENCES

[1] CENTRAL STATISTICAL OFFICE: *Monthly Digest of Statistics*, H. M. Stationery Office.
[2] CRAMER, J. S.: "The Depreciation and Mortality of Motor-cars," *Journal of the Royal Statistical Society, Series A*, Volume 121, Part 1, 1958, pp. 18–59.
[3] NERLOVE, MARC: "The Market Demand for Durable Goods: A Comment," *Econometrica*, Volume 28, No. 1,1960, pp. 132–142.
[4] PENNOCK, JEAN L., AND CAROL M. JAEGER: "Estimating the Service Life of Household Goods by Actuarial Methods," *Journal of the American Statistical Association*, Volume 52, No. 278, 1957, pp. 175–85.
[5] STONE, RICHARD: "Linear Expenditure Systems and Demand Analysis: An Application to the Pattern of British Demand," *The Economic Journal*, Volume LXIV, No. 255, 1954, pp. 511–27.
[6] STONE, RICHARD, AND D. A. ROWE: "The Market Demand for Durable Goods," *Econometrica*, Volume 25, No. 3, 1957, pp. 423–43.
[7] ———: "Dynamic Demand Functions: Some Econometric Results," *The Economic Journal*, Volume LXVIII, No. 269, 1958, pp. 256–70.
[8] ———: "The Measurement of Consumers' Expenditure and Behaviour in the United Kingdom, 1920–1938," Volume II. *Cambridge University Press* (to be published).

Econometrica, Vol. 28, 4 (October 1960)

UNDERIDENTIFICATION, STRUCTURAL ESTIMATION, AND FORECASTING

By Ta-Chung Liu[1]

Since the publication of Haavelmo's well-known papers on simultaneous equation estimation in 1943–44, the literature on this subject has dealt mainly with overidentified relationships. Practically all the econometric models estimated by the simultaneous equation approach are overidentified, the contention being that economic theory or a priori information would require the exclusion of a sufficient number of variables from a given relationship so that it becomes overidentified. It is argued in this paper that the contrary is true and that economic theory would require the inclusion of many more variables than those found in the existing econometric models so that the structural relationships included in these models are likely to be underidentified. Apparently "reasonable" overidentified structures have been obtained probably only because the specification errors arising from omission of relevant variables have cancelled one another. A consequence of the prevalence of underidentified structures is that the least squares reduced from equations are likely to be the best forecasting equations.

A STRUCTURAL RELATIONSHIP in a system of simultaneous linear equations is identifiable if and only if the following condition is met:[2]

$$\text{Rank } [\Pi_{\Delta, **}] = G^{\Delta} - 1 \, ,$$

where $[\Pi_{\Delta, **}]$ is the matrix of the regression coefficients, in the reduced forms, of the jointly dependent variables included in the given relationship (G^{Δ} in number) on the predetermined variables included in the structure but excluded from the given relationship (K^{**} in number). For this condition to be fulfilled, it is necessary that:[3]

$$K^{**} \geqslant G^{\Delta} - 1 \, .$$

---

[1] The author has benefited greatly from suggestions by Marc Nerlove and Edwin Kuh who, however, may be in disgreement with the main position presented here.

[2] The notations used here are taken from the well-known Koopmans-Hood article. See [6, especially p. 138].

[3] It is possible to question whether this condition is really necessary and whether the underidentified relationships are more unidentifiable than the overidentified ones. In the overidentified case (where $K^{**} > G^{\Delta} - 1$), the number of equations (i.e., the number of columns of the $[\Pi_{\Delta, **}]$ matrix) available for the determination of the structural coefficients is larger than the number of the structural coefficients themselves. Solutions for the structural coefficients are obtained only by imposing linear restrictions upon the $[\Pi_{\Delta, **}]$ matrix in such a way that the "surplus" equations cause no trouble. In the underidentified case (where $K^{**} < G_{\Delta} - 1$), the number of equations is smaller than that of the structural coefficients to be determined. It is on this ground that the underidentified relationships are considered unidentifiable. The number of equations, however, can be increased by making assumptions about

Although necessary for identification, this condition is apparently unimportant. For it has been found to be satisfied in all the existing statistical estimates of structural relationships. This is rather surprising. The original premise underlying the simultaneous equation approach and the universal fulfillment of the necessary condition of identification in the empirical models, taken together, present us with an interesting situation: Economic variables are considered by econometricians as mutually dependent, but the degree of simultaneity is recognized only to the extent that it does not prevent the structural coefficients from being identified. But is there any logical reason why the degree of simultaneity must always stop short of causing real troubles? The answer given in the literature is that economic theory or a priori information often requires us to exclude from a given structural relationship a sufficient number of variables so that it becomes overidentified. It is suggested in this note that, quite to the contrary, economic theory requires the inclusion of a much larger number of variables than those included in the existing models of economic structures. The complexity of modern economic society makes it much more likely that the true structural relationships are underidentified rather than overidentified. That the existing empirical structural relationships are all overidentified may very well be the result of unconscious but determined efforts to obtain "significant" structural estimates. Statistical difficulties (mainly high intercorrelations between explanatory variables) which have plagued econometricians for decades, rather than economic theory or a priori information, are probably responsible for the tendency toward oversimplification of structural relationships and hence overidentification. The misleading nature of this kind of so-called structural estimate will be demonstrated. A more positive conclusion of this discussion is that the least squares reduced forms are likely to be better forecasting equations than the reduced forms obtained by solving the overidentified structural relationships. The rather doubtful prospects of overidentifying an otherwise underidentified structural relationship by resorting to more finely divided time periods or by disaggregating the variables are also discussed.

1

To demonstrate the oversimplification of the existing overidentified statistical models, one inevitably refers to the Klein-Goldberger model of the United States economy [5], the most ambitious empirical model ever

---

the disturbances and by imposing a priori restrictions on the coefficients themselves (other than the excluded-included variables). It may not be more arbitrary to make assumptions about the disturbances than to impose linear restrictions on the Π coefficients. But we shall not pursue this point further here.

fitted by the simultaneous estimation technique. All the Klein-Goldberger fitted equations are overidentified. For example, out of a total of twenty endogenous variables and fifteen predetermined variables, personal consumption is specified to be a function of only six variables, and investment of only three. In the case of the investment function, the authors did acknowledge that the equation is primarily an "empirical" one. The authors, however, have "experimented with" only two other variables (current profits and the long term interest rate), and have not found it possible to include them.[4] Even if these two variables are included, there would still be only five explanatory variables in the investment function. It might be thought that five or six explanatory variables is not a small number. The *habit* of fitting even more oversimplified relationships has been so deeply and firmly implanted in us that we may consider even six variables to be an extraordinarily large number. Suppose, however, we do not undertake the task of deriving a statistical investment function with "reasonable" and "significant" regression coefficients. Instead, let us attempt merely to enumerate a reasonably complete list of variables which, according to economic theory, would be expected to have had an important influence on aggregate investment in the United States during the period 1929–52. In this way, we may shake off the habit of clinging to a small number of variables and face up to the fact that investment is not determined by only five or six variables. Even restricting ourselves to the variables included in the Klein-Goldberger model itself, we can easily count at least seventeen variables that ought to have been included in the aggregate investment function. Needless to say, such an enlarged investment function is hopelessly underidentified.[5]

[4] See [5, pp. 66–68]. Klein and Goldberger have attributed the lack of statistical evidence of the effects of interest rates on investment to the heavily aggregated nature of their investment variable. The bearing of disaggregation on structural estimation is briefly discussed in Section 2. It is suggested below, however, that their failure to obtain reasonable magnitudes for the coefficients of the interest rate variables in the investment function may very well have been the result of the omission of other important variables from the function. See pp. 656–657 and especially footnote 8.

[5] It should be pointed out here that a large number of the predetermined variables in the Klein-Goldberger model are lagged endogenous variables. Seven out of the fifteen fitted equations of the Klein-Goldberger model, however, are associated with error terms having significant serial correlation. Three more have residuals in which the degree of serial correlation is very nearly significant. (See [5, pp. 90–92]). The existence of serial correlation precludes the use of lagged endogenous variables as predetermined variables. When these variables are excluded from the predetermined category, there are very few predetermined variables left in the Klein-Goldberger model and, as a consequence, their structural equations are probably all underidentified even if additional variables are not included in them.

We shall not take advantage of this fact, however. Instead, let us assume that

The criterion used by Klein and Goldberger for the selection or rejection of explanatory variables throws a great deal of light on the principles that have guided them in specifying the structure. These principles are, in fact, responsible for the overidentification of the Klein-Goldberger structural relationships. Essentially, a relevant explanatory variable is excluded if inclusion would result in a significantly unreasonable magnitude for its own coefficient or for some other structural coefficients.[6] Diligent experiments with alternative combinations of a smaller and smaller number of explanatory variables would, of course, eventually lead to a set of "significant" and "reasonable" coefficients.[7] The result so obtained, however, is anything but an estimate of the structure. It is important to realize that unreasonable magnitudes (or signs) of the structural coefficients of the included variables can be removed by *adding* relevant explanatory variables as well as by *dropping* variables.[8] When a "reasonable" structural relationship could

serial correlation is absent from all the Klein-Goldberger structural equations. There are strong a priori grounds for believing that all the following variables (represented in the Klein-Goldberger notation), in addition to the three included in the Klein-Goldberger function itself, had significant influences over aggregate investment in the United States during the period 1929–52: $(P + A + D - T_p - T_A)_t$, L_{2t}, i_{Lt}, $(i_L)_{t-1}$, i_{st}, $(i_s)_{t-1}$, $t, p_t - p_{t-1}$, $p_{t-1} - p_{t-2}$, $(G + F_E)$ and $(G + F_E)_{t-1}$—e.g., though the effect of defense expenditure on private investment in plant and equipment, and all the six explanatory variables included in the Klein-Goldberger consumption function (through their bearing on the demand for residential housing construction). Only six of the fifteen variables, given by Klein and Goldberger as predetermined variables, are now excluded from this list of explanatory variables.

[6] Or if the inclusion results in structural coefficients with "wrong" signs and with magnitudes significantly different from zero. Klein-Goldberger used the word "unstable" instead of "unreasonable." The latter seems to be a better description, because in some situations a coefficient may be reasonably expected to be "explosive." See [5, p. 68].

[7] As explained in footnote 8 below, specification errors resulting from omission of many relevant variables could compensate for each other in such a way that the remaining variables take on "reasonable" magnitudes in spite of the specification errors.

[8] This point, while it is a familiar experience for all practicing econometricians, can be vividly brought home by using the technique for analyzing specification errors recently developed by Theil. (See [13] and, for a lucid exposition of this technique, see Nerlove [10]). Klein and Goldberger have attempted to combine interest rate with other explanatory variables in the investment function, but have found the results unreasonable. Assume that one of the alternatives they have experimented with is as follows (with x_1 representing profits; x_2, year-end capital stock; x_3, business liquid assets; and x_4, an interest rate variable):

(1) $$I = b_0 + b_1 x_1 + b_2 x_2 + b_3 x_3 + b_4 x_4 .$$

Suppose, contrary to a priori expectations, b_2 and b_4 turned out to be positive. x_4, the interest rate variable, was then dropped; and the investment function given in their book was obtained as follows: (See [5, p. 90] .)

(2) $$I = b_0' + b_1' x_1 + b_2' x_2 + b_3' x_3$$

be obtained either by dropping variables from, or adding variables to, an over-simplified relationship, the complexity of the modern economy ensures that the "enlarged" estimate is a closer approximation to reality than the two simpler ones.[9] Obviously, the high intercorrelations of the larger number of explanatory variables so included would almost certainly result in large standard errors or even wrong signs for some of the estimated structural coefficients. When this happens, the only legitimate conclusion

where $b_0' = -16.71$, $b_1' = 0.78$, $b_2' = -0.073$ and $b_3' = 0.14$. These magnitudes appear to be fairly reasonable. Let us assume, however, for the sake of argument that the "true" investment function is as follows:

(3) $$I = a_0 + a_1 x_1 + a_2 x_2 + a_3 x_3 + a_4 x_4 + a_5 x_5$$

where x_5 represents, say, the rate of change of the price level. (For the present purpose there is no need to write out fully the "true" investment function as is done in footnote 5.) Theil has shown that the expected values of the b coefficients in equation (1) and those of the b' coefficients in equation (2) can be expressed as functions of the "true" coefficients (the a's) as follows:

$$\mathscr{E}\begin{bmatrix} b_1 \\ b_2 \\ b_3 \\ b_4 \end{bmatrix} = \begin{bmatrix} a_1 + p_{51}a_5 \\ a_2 + p_{52}a_5 \\ a_3 + p_{53}a_5 \\ a_4 + p_{54}a_5 \end{bmatrix}, \quad \text{and} \quad \mathscr{E}\begin{bmatrix} b_1' \\ b_2' \\ b_3' \end{bmatrix} = \begin{bmatrix} a_1 + \pi_{41}a_4 + \pi_{51}a_5 \\ a_2 + \pi_{42}a_4 + \pi_{52}a_5 \\ a_3 + \pi_{43}a_4 + \pi_{53}a_5 \end{bmatrix},$$

where p_{5j}, $j = 1, 2, 3, 4$, are multiple regression coefficients of x_5 on x_1, x_2, x_3 and x_4; and π_{ij}, $i = 4, 5$ and $j = 1, 2, 3$ are the multiple regression coefficients respectively of x_4 and x_5 on x_1, x_2 and x_3. Probably a_5 is positive and so also is p_{54}. If $a_5 p_{54} > |a_4|$, $\mathscr{E}(b_4)$ is likely to be positive. Moreover, $\mathscr{E}(b_2)$ could be similarly "sabotaged" into a positive magnitude. (These are the unreasonable results assumed to have been obtained by Klein and Goldberger.) On the other hand, by dropping x_4 (i.e., by fitting equation (2) instead of (1)), $\mathscr{E}(b_2')$ would have a good chance of taking on the negative (and the "right") sign if both π_{42} and π_{52} are positive. Moreover, the positive specification error $\pi_{52}a_5$ may be roughly canceled by the negative specification error $\pi_{42}a_4$ so that $\mathscr{E}(b_2')$ may fall within the "reasonable" range of magnitude for a_2. This can easily happen. For the "reasonable" range, as determined on a priori grounds, is inevitably quite large.

Thus, in spite of the fact that equation (1) has specified the explanatory variables more nearly correctly than equation (2), the regression coefficients of the former may turn out to be "less reasonable" than those of the latter. The procedure used by Klein and Goldberger is apparently to drop x_4 from equation (1) so that the highly misleading equation (2) would be the final equation obtained. Our position is the opposite one of recognizing the reality that both x_4 and x_5 (and, in fact, many others) are also explanatory variables even if "significant" estimates cannot be obtained for the structural coefficients.

[9] It would be most helpful if there were satisfactory statistical tests which could be employed to decide upon the specification when there are a large number of alternate hypotheses. The trouble is that such a test is not yet available. (The Anderson-Rubin test, for instance, does not serve this purpose.) Moreover, even when such a test has been worked out theoretically, data limitations are so severe that the test is not likely to be conclusive.

we can draw is that the complexity of economic reality and the nature of the basic data are such that the structural coefficients are really indeterminate. The temptation to omit relevant variables until a seemingly reasonable and significant "structural estimate" is obtained must be resisted.

The bearing of this discussion on the technique of forecasting is obvious. The current practice of making forecasts from the reduced form equations, obtained by solving the artificially overidentified (i.e., over-simplified) structural relationships for the jointly dependent variables in terms of the predetermined variables, must be rejected as both theoretically unsound and computationally burdensome. The following simple procedure may be suggested. First, we should write out the structural relationships *fully* to include all important variables which, according to economic theory, are relevant without regard to whether the structural coefficients can be identified or not. Needless to say, I do not suggest the foolish extreme of specifying that every variable is a function of all other variables. It is sufficient if we do not omit any variable that might have been included except for the fear (or the realization through experimentation) that their inclusion would "sabotage" the signs or magnitudes of the structural coefficients. Such fully specified structural relationships tend to be underidentified. The next step is simply to obtain the single equation least squares regressions of the jointly dependent variables on the predetermined variables (i.e., the least squares reduced forms) and use these equations for forecasting purposes.[10]

In fact, if we succeed in freeing ourselves from the pretention of estimating structure,[11] we can go further in the following two directions which we otherwise would have to avoid: (a) Separate predicting variables into groups with high within-group intercorrelations, and select a "representative variable" from each group to include in the forecasting equation. (b) Include jointly dependent variables in the predictors whenever possible. An illustration will make point (a) clear. Suppose, in attempting to fit a

[10] For an underidentified structure, the single equation least squares estimates of the reduced forms are identical with those obtained by solving the structural relationships for the jointly dependent variables in terms of the predetermined variables. (Note, however, that in the underidentified case the structural relationships cannot in fact be obtained.)

[11] Just to avoid misunderstanding, I should hasten to add that no econometrician can be an anti-structural estimationist. Our ultimate aim is naturally to estimate economic structures, but it is not our job to derive "structural" relationships by artificially overidentifying the structure and thereby getting around data limitations. When structural estimates cannot be derived by the techniques now in our possession because of underidentification and data limitations, it would be a better allocation of resources if efforts were directed toward straightforward forecasting and to the development of techniques for identifying the underidentified relationships. For a discussion of the fact that the underidentified relationships are not really more unidentifiable than the overidentified ones, see footnote 3.

forecasting equation for current consumption, it is found that, among the predictors, lagged personal income and lagged household liquid assets are more highly correlated with each other than with other predictors. Only one of them need then be included;[12] the other would be left out to make room for other predicting variables, in spite of the strong likelihood that both these variables have a more important bearing, in the structural sense, on personal consumption than do the other predictors. In any actual forecasting problem, it is likely that many such groups of predictors can be formed and that each group will contain more than just two variables. By selecting only one "representative variable" from each group, the number of predictors can be reduced to manageable proportions and the combined effect of a change in the magnitude of a group of highly correlated variables on the predicand may become measurable. Point (b) concerns a possibility worth looking into if the current magnitude of a jointly dependent variable might, for any reason, become known before the prediction is made, or if some hypothetical magnitudes may be reasonably or purposefully assumed. Since our aim is not to make structural estimates, we need not worry about least squares biases in the regression coefficients of the jointly dependent variables. On the other hand, the inclusion of a jointly dependent variable in the forecasting equation will improve the efficiency of the equation.[13] Neither the grouping of variables nor the use of a jointly dependent variable as an "independent" variable in a single-equation least squares estimate is a legitimate procedure if we insist upon making structural estimates.

A last point about the suggested procedure. It has been said that the least squares reduced forms cannot be used for making forecasts under a changed structure. When the structure itself cannot be identified, however, either

---

[12] In so doing, it is of course assumed that these two variables will move together in more or less the same way as in the past. In fact, whether two variables are likely to move together in the future on the past pattern should be an important consideration (in addition to the actual intercorrelation observed for the past) in deciding whether to put them in the same group. The econometrician's own more or less intuitive and arbitrary judgment is bound to enter such a consideration. No suggestion is therefore made here to apply mechanically any of the standard statistical techniques for the separation of the predictors into groups. In all candor one must admit that, at the present stage of development, any attempt to construct a forecasting model necessarily involves a great deal of intuitive judgment. The same is true (and perhaps even more so) with regard to structural estimation.

[13] This conclusion was obtained by Foote and Waugh through a Monte Carlo experiment. (See [2]). The validity of this point can be seen as follows. The disturbances of reduced forms (v_t) are functions of the disturbances of the structural relationships (u_t). Using the Koopmans-Hood notations, $v'_t = \beta^{-1} u'_t$; (See [6, p. 125].) Since the jointly dependent variables are correlated with u'_t, they are also correlated with v'_t. The inclusion of the jointly dependent variables in the reduced forms will therefore reduce the variance of v_t.

because of underidentification or because of data limitations, there is literally no rigidly defined statistical model that can be used for forecasting under a changed structure. Moreover, changes in structural coefficients are not the only way to take care of changes in structure. Most of the structural changes we have in mind are changes in public policy variables (e.g., tax rates). These variables can be included in the structure as exogenous variables if we have past experience with them. Forecasting under changed structure then becomes forecasting under an unchanged structure with changed magnitudes for exogenous variables.[14]

2

The likelihood of achieving identification is probably greater in quarterly models than in annual models. Because of resorting to more finely divided sub-periods, it is necessary that more lags be brought into the system. Some of the variables that are jointly dependent in longer periods may become "predetermined" in shorter periods. Other things being equal, the greater the number of predetermined variables, the more likely are the structural relationships to be identifiable. The evidence we have so far, however, can perhaps support some optimism but not complacency. For it **is** precisely in quarterly models that serial correlation in the disturbance terms tends to be so strong that lagged endogenous variables cannot legitimately be considered as predetermined variables. If serial correlation is not removed from the disturbance terms, using data pertaining to shorter periods of time would not help identification at all.

Klein and Barger have attempted to solve this difficulty by randomizing the disturbance terms through autoregressive schemes (See [4]). To consider an autoregressive scheme for an error term as a part of structural estimation is clearly unsatisfactory. For the use of such a scheme amounts to a confession that an economic explanation for a systematic (nonrandom) part of the movement in the variable to be explained has not been found.

The omission of relevant variables is an important, if not the main, reason for the existence of serial correlation in the estimated residuals.[15] Economic variables tend to be serially correlated. When relevant explanatory variables are omitted from a structural equation, their effects on the dependent variable are left with the unexplained residuals. As a result, the residuals are also serially correlated. A serious attempt to deal with this difficulty would thus require, quite in line with the argument presented in Section 1,

[14] Thus, changes in tax rates have been included in a simple forecasting model for the U.S. as changes in predetermined variables. Even wartime restrictions have been dealt with in a similar manner. See [8, pp. 438–39].
[15] See Orcutt [12].

the inclusion of more explanatory variables in the structural relationship. The question is whether to include more current variables or more lagged variables. On the basis of a most interesting analysis of adaptive expectations and of the interactions of long- and short-run responses, Nerlove and Addison have found that the inclusion of the lagged quantity of a given commodity in its demand and supply functions not only is theoretically sound but also reduces serial correlation in the estimated residuals to insignificant levels.[16] These findings are important, especially in the case of supply functions for agricultural products in which lagged variables probably play a more important part than current variables.[17] More empirical research along this line will add significantly to our knowledge.[18] In the case of demand functions, however, it is doubtful whether a number of current variables, such as current prices of competitive and complementary products, are not at least as important as the lagged quantity as explanatory variables, and whether they would not *also* significantly reduce serial correlation in the estimated residuals.

The attractive features of the lagged variables are also reasons for caution in using them. The lagged variables fit well with the current variables, especially with the current magnitudes of the same variables; they help to identify the structure; and they reduce serial correlation in the estimated residuals. The apparently satisfactory estimates obtained (including high multiple correlation coefficients) preclude the inclusion of equally relevant current variables, and can result in the over-simplification of reality. Unless very strong theoretical grounds justify it,[19] a predominant use of lagged variables would make structural relationships rigid in the sense that, given the past, the present is more or less unchangeable.[20] It should also be realized that an exclusive reliance upon lagged variables, such as in the recursive models used by Barger and Klein (See [4]), is a fundamental reversal of the position underlying the simultaneous equation approach. One may wonder whether we will ever have economic data pertaining to periods so short that simultaneity would be less important than recursiveness.

[16] See [11, pp. 877–879].

[17] For instance, once the crops are planted, the possibility of not harvesting them due to post-planting considerations still exists but is probably not important. For an interesting analysis of abandonment of planted acreage, see Nerlove [9, pp. 112–121].

[18] Nerlove's models are fitted to annual data for agricultural products. It would be interesting to see how his approach would work in quarterly models for non-agricultural commodities.

[19] Such grounds exist in the case of Nerlove's supply functions.

[20] In more or less uneventful periods, these "rigid" relationships may turn out to be as good or as bad as others. In more troublesome periods, however, economic variables are notoriously sensitive to current endogenous and exogenous changes. Examples of this kind of sensitivity can be found during the recent recession.

Similarly to the division of time periods into shorter intervals, disaggregation of variables might also appear to be helpful in identifying the structure. The strength of the argument lies in the assumption that, as the variables are disaggregated, the number of jointly dependent variables belonging to a given relationship declines relative to the predetermined ones. Whether this assumption is valid can be seen by examining the available sector structural estimates dealing with disaggregated variables and using the simultaneous approach. The agricultural econometricians are again research pioneers in this area. Take the well-known study by Hildreth and Jarrett as an example. Variables are defined as predetermined often with difficulty, and current (and important) jointly dependent variables are excluded from the model rather arbitrarily. The authors themselves have questioned the validity of specifying the quantity of feeds produced as being predetermined to the livestock market.[21] They have also quoted from an unpublished paper by Koopmans to the effect that the treatment of such general variables as total disposable income and the general price level as predetermined in models dealing with small sector markets may result in biases in structural estimates.[22] In addition, one would seriously doubt that the demand for meat could be unrelated to the demand for seafood, cheese and other dairy products, eggs, and for that matter, vegetables, fruits, and cereal products.[23] Indeed, there does not appear to be any convincing reason at all why disaggregation would reduce the ratio of the number of jointly dependent variables to the number of predetermined variables. The disaggregation of food consumption into n components, for instance, immediately adds $n—1$ relative price terms to each of the new structural relationships, thus increasing the number of jointly dependent variables.[24] Yet, as Koop-

[21] See [3, p. 24].

[22] See [3, p. 25, footnote 20]. The important and surprising aspect of this point is that the mere smallness of a sector market (say, meat consumption in total personal consumption) is neither a necessary nor a sufficient reason for expecting a small percentage bias in the estimated coefficient.

[23] The same criticism is applicable to more recent sector estimates for agricultural products using the simultaneous approach. For instance, see [1].

[24] Take the Klein-Goldberger investment function as another example. The disaggregation of aggregate investment into the four components of residential housing construction, changes in inventory, plant and equipment immediately adds three jointly dependent variables to each of the four disaggregated investment functions. (Can we imagine an increase in investment in plants that would not directly increase the demand for equipment to be installed in them, or the demand for more inventory of construction materials, or the demand for residential housing in the neighborhood of the new plants?) At the same time, not many variables enumerated in footnote 5 can be omitted from the disaggregated functions. Moreover, as the variables to be explained are disaggregated, the explanatory variables must also be disaggregated, thus again expanding the number of relevant variables. It has been pointed out by Koopmans

mans has shown, it may not be possible to re-specify some of the jointly dependent variables as predetermined without resulting in biases in the estimated structural coefficients.[25] The likelihood of achieving identification through disaggregation does not appear to be great.

Cornell University

REFERENCES

[1] FISHER, M.: "A Sector Model—The Poultry Industry of the U.S. A.," *Econometrica,* Vol. 26 (1958), pp. 37–66.

[2] FOOTE, R. J., AND F. V. WAUGH: "Results of an Experiment to Test the Forecasting Merits of Least Squares and Limited Information Equations," *Econometrica,* Vol. 26 (1958), pp. 607–608.

[3] HILDRETH, C., AND F. G. JARRETT: *A Statistical Study of Livestock Production and Marketing,* New York: John Wiley and Sons, 1955.

[4] KLEIN, L. R., AND H. BARGER: "A Quarterly Model for the U.S. Economy," *Journal of American Statistical Association,* 1954.

[5] KLEIN, L. R., AND A. S. GOLDBERGER: *An Econometric Model of the United States,* 1929–1952, Amsterdam: North-Holland Publishing Company, 1955.

[6] KOOPMANS, T. C., AND W. C. HOOD: "The Estimation of Simultaneous Linear Economic Relationships," in *Studies in Econometric Method,* New York: John Wiley and Sons, 1953, pp. 112–199.

[7] KOOPMANS, T. C.: "Identification Problems in Economic Model Construction," in *Studies in Econometric Method,* New York: John Wiley and Sons, 1953, pp. 27–48.

[8] LIU, T. C.: "A Simple Forecasting Model for the U.S. Economy," *Staff Papers,* International Monetary Fund, Vol. IV (1955), pp. 434–466.

[9] NERLOVE, M.: *The Dynamics of Supply,* Baltimore: The Johns Hopkins Press, 1958.

[10] NERLOVE, M.: "On the Nerlove Estimate of Supply Elasticity: A Reply," *Journal of Farm Economics,* August, 1958, pp. 723–28.

[11] NERLOVE, M., AND W. ADDISON: "Statistical Estimation of Long-Run Elasticities of Supply and Demand," *Journal of Farm Economics,* November, 1958, pp. 861–880.

[12] ORCUTT, G. H.: "A Study of the Autoregressive Nature of the Time Series Used for Tinbergen's Model of the Economic System of the United States, 1919–1932," *Journal of the Royal Statistical Society (Supplement),* Vol. 111 (1948) pp. 1–52.

[13] THEIL, H.: *Economic Forecasting and Policy,* Amsterdam: North-Holland Publishing Company, 1958.

(See [7, p. 44]) that disaggregation helps identification only when it introduces specific explanatory variables applicable to some but not all components of the aggregate variable. This point should be qualified by adding that the specific explanatory variables introduced must not be of the jointly dependent type. Otherwise, identification would be made more difficult by disaggregation.

[25] See footnote 22.

Econometrica, Vol. 29, 2 (April 1961)

ON THE COST OF APPROXIMATE
SPECIFICATION IN SIMULTANEOUS EQUATION ESTIMATION[1]

By Franklin M. Fisher

This paper considers the question of whether simultaneous equation estimation is possible in view of the fact that specification errors are always
made in the construction of models which are supposed only to hold approximately. It is shown that, so far as consistency is concerned, good approximations give good results, but that different estimators have different sensitivities
to specification errors of the types considered. It follows that the choice of an
estimator may depend crucially on its properties in such situations.

The problem leads naturally to a consideration of the positions of T. C.
Liu and H. Wold on the prevalence of underidentification and recursiveness,
respectively. The concept of recursiveness is generalized as is the Proximity
Theorem, and it is shown that a position intermediate between the two just
mentioned is highly tenable, such a position permitting the use of simultaneous equation estimators. The whole problem turns out to be related to the
question of almost unilateral coupling of dynamic systems and some conjectures are presented on the possibility of generalizing the recent aggregation
and partition theorem of H. Simon and A. Ando.

1. T. C. LIU'S OBJECTIONS TO SIMULTANEOUS EQUATION METHODS

IN RECENT years, there has been growing discussion of the techniques and
problems of simultaneous equation estimation.[2] Most of this discussion has
been concerned primarily with the techniques of estimation in the overidentified case. An important exception to this, however, is the work of T. C. Liu.

In a 1955 article[3] Liu advanced a disturbing argument which he has
vigorously maintained ever since.[4] This argument is disturbing because
its premises apparently cannot be doubted and because its conclusions, if
accepted, imply that the hope of structural estimation by any techniques
whatsoever is forlorn indeed.

It is perhaps best to emphasize immediately that this paper *only* takes
issue with the very general and most disturbing form of Liu's position. The

---

[1] I am indebted to Paul A. Samuelson for suggesting this study. This paper was
written while I was a member of the University of Chicago Department of Economics
and was supported in part by the Ford Foundation Econometrics Workshop of that
department.

[2] See, for example, Sargan [10], and Theil [16, Chapter 6].

[3] Liu [7, pp. 436–437, 464–466].

[4] For example, in his contribution to the Roundtable Discussion of Simultaneous
Estimation Techniques at the Chicago Meeting of the Econometric Society, December,
1958 published as [9]. Liu has also given his detailed argument in [8]. A partial but
still inadequate reply along the lines of the present paper is given in S. Valavanis
[18, pp. 130–132].

fact that I argue that such a *general* position is largely untenable should not be taken to mean that I think the problems to which Liu calls attention are not important in many particular instances. Some of these Liu has pointed out.

The argument is as follows. Econometric models are only approximations to reality. Of necessity, they abstract from the real world by limiting the number of variables included in each equation and in the system as a whole. In fact, however, there are always more variables "really" in each equation —either variables included in other equations of the model or variables excluded altogether therefrom—than are assumed in the practical approximations. Furthermore, the equations stated in the model are not a complete set of equations. In fact, other, outside equations always exist, either relating variables in the model alone or relating them to unincluded variables.

Now, Liu goes on to argue, these points have serious consequences which are of three types. First, the usual form of *a priori* restriction used for identification—the restriction that some parameters in a structural equation are zero, that is, that some variables included elsewhere in the system do not enter into that equation—is likely to be incorrect. Such restrictions, at best, will only hold approximately, and approximately is not good enough. If the variables in question really belong in the equation being studied, then that equation is underidentified and its parameters cannot be estimated by any reasonable technique.

Secondly, the existence of other variables in the equation that are not included elsewhere in the system, together with the existence of unincluded equations relating those variables to the included ones or relating the included variables to each other, means that the number of equations in the system has been understated so that the necessary order condition for identifiability[5]—which runs in terms of the number of *a priori* restrictions and the number of equations—is not satisfied in fact. Finally, few variables are truly exogenous to the complete system; to count only the explicitly stated equations is to treat endogenous variables as exogenous. Once again it follows that identification and, *a fortiori*, overidentification is the unusual case and underidentification the usual one.

Therefore, says Liu, the current emphasis on techniques of estimation in overidentified systems is entirely misplaced. Structural estimation is generally not possible in simultaneous systems, and only reduced forms can be obtained. Furthermore, unrestricted least squares estimation of the reduced form is the appropriate method, for restricting the reduced form by

---

[5] See Koopmans, Rubin and Leipnik [5, p. 79 and pp. 81–82]. Actually, Liu generally states the order condition in terms of the number of endogenous variables included in and the number of exogenous variables excluded from a given equation, which is an equivalent statement.

the *a priori* restrictions not only adds no more information, it is positively harmful, as it adds *mis*information. Forecasting should therefore always be done with the unrestricted reduced form which, as is well known, has smallest error variance for the sample observations, as there is no reason to expect mistakenly oversimplified and restricted models to do as well or better.

Now, this is a powerful and disturbing argument. There can be no doubt that econometric models do in fact abstract from reality in the way described by Liu and thus that *a priori* restrictions which exclude variables from equations are frequently misspecified. Further, there can be no doubt that Liu is largely correct in stating that the treatment of certain variables as exogenous is also likely to be misspecification. The economic system even considered as a whole is embedded in a far larger socio-physical framework. If Liu is right in his conclusions, then there must be serious doubt as to the possibility of structural estimation.

Nor do two counter-observations which might be advanced here seem very helpful in a direct way. The first of these is that it has now been shown that *a priori* restrictions of a far more general kind than those considered by Liu may be used for identification.[6] The usual case is certainly the one which Liu considers, and even the use of inequalities (which are common restrictions) will not directly help very much.

The second observation is that variables need not be exogenous to the system as a whole to be exogenous with respect to some subset of equations. It is therefore not sufficient to argue that few variables are exogenous to the complete system; one must also hold that there are excluded equations specifically providing some "feedback" effect (however weak) from endogenous to assumed exogenous variables or connecting the latter with variables influencing the error terms. Otherwise, the system may be what we shall define below as "block recursive." However, since the existence of such excluded equations cannot be denied in general—especially equations connecting the variables in the error terms of the original system and the exogenous variables—this remark is also not directly helpful save as a reservation to Liu's argument in special cases.

While these counter-arguments are, however, not of much help directly, they do provide aid in an indirect way, for they indicate that the problem may not be quite so dichotomous as Liu makes it. Thus, in the next section, we use the above mentioned results on general restrictions to show that the proper question is not whether certain parameters assumed to be zero are in fact so; the issue is rather whether they are in some sense sufficiently small—whether the restriction that the corresponding variables do not appear is or is not a good approximation. We show that the problem is not

---

[6] See Fisher [2].

the discontinuous one of just or overidentification if the restrictions hold exactly and underidentification if they do not, but rather one of diminishing estimation inconsistency as the restrictions are better and better approximations.

Similarly, in later sections, we go on to consider the problems of omitted variables and of exogenous variables and show that the issue is not whether a variable assumed exogenous is "really" so, or whether omitted variables "really" have zero coefficients but rather whether these things are sufficiently so in an approximate sense. We thus justify the practice of breaking down a complete system into parts by assuming certain variables exogenous that are only approximately so, and by assuming certain variables absent that truly appear with very small coefficients.

These results have several consequences. First, of course, structural estimation is seen to be entirely possible in general, so that discussion and criticism must be directed toward the goodness or badness of the approximate assumptions in a particular case and not toward the truth or falsity thereof.

Secondly (and this is a somewhat different way of looking at the matter), we may say that whereas, hitherto, estimation techniques required the knowledge or assumption that certain things (parameters, covariances, and so forth) were zero, the results here presented allow estimation with negligible inconsistency provided only that such things are known (or assumed) to be small. Since the latter kind of knowledge is easier to come by than the former and the assumption involved is likely to be held with greater confidence, this is a reassuring and perhaps not insignificant result.

Thirdly, even if it is considered obvious that small errors have small consequences,[7] it is always of interest to know exactly where errors must be small and thus to clarify assumptions.

Finally, an objection to simultaneous equation estimation somewhat better known than that of Liu is the position of H. Wold[8] which states that the real world is not truly simultaneous at all, but that causation is unilateral and that true systems are always recursive. Part of the Liu objection, on the other hand, can be crudely put as the argument that the real world is always more simultaneous than we think—that no economic model ever fully states the true simultaneity—and therefore that estimation is impossible since the world is truly underidentified. It would seem at first glance as though no middle ground between these two positions is possible, that once the possibility of simultaneous causation is admitted, one cannot stop short

---

[7] That the obvious is not always true in this area has been shown by R. H. Strotz who has recently provided us with an example of a case where the limit of the maximum likelihood estimator as specification error goes to zero is *not* the maximum likelihood estimator of the limit. See [14].

[8] [19, chapter 2], for example.

of an explicit statement of the total set of equations explaining the socio-physical universe. We shall see, however, that this is not the case; a position intermediate between Wold and Liu is indeed possible, for systems—and highly plausible systems at that—do exist in which simultaneity is present but not completely overriding. Estimation of the usual simultaneous type is thus entirely possible.[9]

2. MISSPECIFICATION IN THE *a priori* RESTRICTIONS

We first consider in isolation the problem of the misspecification of the *a priori* restrictions. Throughout this section it will be assumed that the system is correctly specified save for the *a priori* restrictions. We shall remove this assumption below.

Consider the system of equations:

$$(2.1) \qquad u(t) = Ax(t)$$

where $u(t)$ is an $(m+1)$ dimensional column vector of disturbances, A is an $(m+1) \times (n+1)$ matrix of coefficients with first row A_1, and $x(t)$ is an $(n+1)$ dimensional column vector of variables. Without loss of generality we may renumber the variables so that

$$(2.2) \qquad x(t) = \begin{bmatrix} y(t) \\ \hline z(t) \end{bmatrix}$$

where $y(t)$ is an $(m+1)$ dimensional column vector of endogenous variables and $z(t)$ an $(n-m)$ dimensional column vector of exogenous variables. Then A may be partitioned accordingly into:

$$(2.3) \qquad A = [B \mid G]$$

where B is a square nonsingular matrix of rank $m+1$. We further assume that there are no linear identities connecting the exogenous variables.

Now, let ϕ' be a matrix with K columns and $n+1$ rows, where $n \geq K \geq m$. Each column of ϕ' is to contain precisely one unit element and have all other elements zero.[10] Impose (incorrectly) the *a priori* restrictions on A_1:

$$(2.4) \qquad A_1 \phi' = 0 ,$$

---

[9] Although, of course, this does not remove the possibility that either Liu or Wold is correct; the real world may be constructed as one of them describes it. The point is that it need not be so constructed and that it is very plausible that it should not.

[10] In fact, ϕ' can be any constant matrix so that all remarks and theorems apply *mutatis mutandis* to any consistent set of misspecified linear homogeneous restrictions. The case given in the text is the usual one of excluding variables from equations and is thus of greatest interest. Linear but inhomogeneous restrictions could obviously be handled with but a slight change in notation. Nonlinear restrictions present certain formal complexities which would unduly obscure the discussion, but the basic theorem is always the same. For a general treatment of the latter two types of restrictions see Fisher [2].

and assume that the rank of the matrix $A\phi'$ is m, so that the necessary and sufficient conditions for unique identifiability of A_1 are satisified if (2.4) holds. Select some endogenous variable not excluded from the first equation of (2.1) by (2.4)—of course, such must exist—and normalize by setting the corresponding element of A_1 equal to unity.[11] Without loss of generality, we may assume that it is the first variable which is thus treated. Extend the definition of ϕ' by adding to it a new first column which has a one at the top and zeros elsewhere. ϕ' now has $K+1$ columns and (2.4) is replaced by

$$(2.4') \qquad\qquad A_1\phi' = (1,0,\ldots,0) \ .$$

It is easy to see that the new $A\phi'$ must have rank $m+1$.

We now assume that (2.4) and hence (2.4') are misspecified so that the variables excluded from the first equation of (2.1) are really in that equation, so that (2.4) is only approximately true at best. Let the *true a priori* restrictions corresponding to (2.4') be

$$(2.5) \qquad\qquad A_1\phi' = (1 \ \bar{\eta})$$

where $\bar{\eta}$ is a K-dimensional row vector.

It will be convenient at this stage to rewrite the first equation of (2.1). Let $y_1(t)$ be the first variable. Let $y^1(t)$ be the vector of endogenous variables whose coefficients in the first equation are not specified by (2.5); similarly, let $z^1(t)$ be the vector of exogenous variables whose coefficients in the first equation are not specified by (2.5). Let B_1^1 and G_1^1 be the corresponding vectors of true coefficients. Finally, let $w(t)$ be the vector of variables (other than $y_1(t)$) whose coefficients are specified by (2.5). Then the first equation of (2.1) can be written:

$$(2.6) \qquad\qquad y_1(t) + B_1^1 y^1(t) + G_1^1 z^1(t) + \bar{\eta}w(t) = u_1(t) \ .$$

Now, let $a_{1j}(\eta,\bar{\eta})$ be the probability limit—if it exists—of the estimate of A_{1j} obtained by imposing

$$(2.7) \qquad\qquad A_1\phi' = (1 \ \eta)$$

when (2.5) is true and using one of the standard estimation techniques.[12] Thus, $a_{1j}(0,\bar{\eta})$ is the probability limit—if it exists—of the estimate of A_{1j} obtained by imposing (2.4') and using one of the standard techniques.

---

[11] By Fisher [2, Lemmas 4 and 5, pp. 436–437], this is always possible no matter what ϕ' is, so long as the rank condition holds.

[12] It is shown in what follows that two different estimation techniques (in particular, two-stage least squares and limited information) for both of which $a_{1j}(0,0) = A_{1j}$ (in general, $a_{1j}(\bar{\eta},\bar{\eta}) = A_{1j}$), may have different $a_{1j}(\eta,\bar{\eta})$ for $\eta \neq \bar{\eta}$. We shall discuss this below; however, it would unduly complicate the notation to take explicit account of it here.

Similarly, $a_{1j}(\bar{\eta},\bar{\eta})$ is the probability limit—if it exists—of the estimate of A_{1j} obtained by imposing the true restrictions.

In what follows, we restrict our attention to estimators of Theil's k-class.[13] This class includes two-stage least squares and limited information, maximum likelihood as well as other estimators. Similar theorems could obviously be proved for estimators not in the k-class, save that for full information, maximum likelihood misspecifications elsewhere in the system must be assumed to go to zero.

Now, choose a set of T values for $u(t)$ and for those predetermined variables which are not lagged endogenous variables; further, choose a set of initial values for those predetermined variables which are lagged endogenous variables. The values of the endogenous variables are then completely determined by the matrix A. We shall assume that all asymptotic variances and covariances (between variables or between variables and residuals) are finite.

Next, fix all rows of A other than the first and all elements of B_1^1 and G_1^1. Consider an infinite sequence of equation systems differing only in $\bar{\eta}$, such that $\bar{\eta}$ converges to the zero vector as we move along the sequence. We shall assume that there exists a neighborhood of the zero vector, such that all systems in the sequence for which $\bar{\eta}$ lies within that neighborhood are stable.

This assumption requires some discussion. We shall show that it is a sufficient condition for $a_{1j}(0,\bar{\eta})$ to approach A_{1j} as a limit as $\bar{\eta}$ goes to zero, and hence that it implies that simultaneous equation estimators are only negligibly inconsistent for all elements of $\bar{\eta}$ sufficiently small (i.e., for (2.4′) a good enough approximation to (2.5)). The assumption may not be necessary, however; indeed, it seems quite clear that the theorem in question holds provided that there exists a neighborhood of zero for which consistent estimation is possible under correct specification (provided that identifiability is present). Whether there exist unstable systems for which the usual estimators are not consistent under correct specification is as yet an open question save in special cases. Our assumption should be regarded as a declaration that we are not here concerned with answering this question, but that we are dealing with only one problem at a time.[14]

---

[13] [16, pp. 227–229, 334–336].

[14] I am indebted to H. Uzawa for calling this problem to my attention by pointing out the incompleteness of an earlier proof that ignored it and to J. D. Sargan for helpful discussion of the present proof. The stability assumption is implicitly made in all later theorems.

In general, the proof given will be valid for the non-stable consistent estimator case if T can be replaced by some $f(T)$ such that the required probability limits exist and are nonzero. We should ordinarily expect this, provided that the estimator involved is consistent under correct specification for $\bar{\eta}$ in some neighborhood of the zero vector.

THEOREM 1.

$$\lim_{\bar{\eta}\to 0} |a_{1j}(0,\bar{\eta}) - A_{1j}| = 0 \ \textit{for all } j = 1,\ldots, n+1 \ .$$

Proof: It is shown in [**2**, Theorem 13, p. 444] that a necessary and sufficient condition for the identifiability of A_1 under (2.5) is that the rank of $A\phi'$ be $m + 1$. We have already observed that this is the case for $\bar{\eta} = 0$; it must therefore also be the case for $\bar{\eta}$ sufficiently close to zero, for the elements of $A\phi'$ are either constant or continuous functions of $\bar{\eta}$ and the value of a determinant is a continuous function of its elements. Hence, for $\bar{\eta}$ sufficiently close to zero, A_1 is identifiable under (2.5).

Now, the theorem is trivially true for those elements of A_1 which are also elements of $\bar{\eta}$. We may therefore restrict our attention to the elements of B_1^1 and G_1^1.

Following Theil,[15] define a new endogenous variable, $q(t)$, as:

(2.8) $$q(t) \equiv y_1(t) + \bar{\eta}w(t)$$

and rewrite (2.6) as:

(2.9) $$q(t) + B_1^1 y^1(t) + G_1^1 z^1(t) = u_1(t) \ .$$

We call the system of equations formed by (2.8) and (2.1) with the first equation of the latter set replaced by (2.9) the *auxiliary* system to (2.1). It is evident that (2.1) and its auxiliary system are equivalent and that the inhomogeneous restrictions (2.5) corresponding to (2.1) have been replaced with equivalent restrictions of the usual zero-coefficient type in the auxiliary system. Further, observe that the variables that are included in $y^1(t)$ and $z^1(t)$ do not depend on the value of $\bar{\eta}$ or on statements about that value. That is, the auxiliary equation (2.9) differs from the original equation (2.6) with the misspecified restrictions $\bar{\eta} = 0$ imposed only in that $q(t)$ and not $y_1(t)$ appears.

Now consider an estimator of the k-class. Let $a_1^1(\eta,\bar{\eta})$ be the column vector of those $a_{1j}(\eta,\bar{\eta})$ corresponding to the elements of B_1^1 and G_1^1. Let V be a matrix of observations on the residuals from the least squares estimates of the reduced form equations explaining the elements of $y^1(t)$. Let all other capital letters denote the observation matrices of the corresponding lower case variables. Then the typical k-class estimator of (2.9) is given by:

(2.10) $$\begin{bmatrix} (Y^1)'Y^1 - kV'V & (Y^1)'Z^1 \\ (Z^1)'Y^1 & (Z^1)'Z^1 \end{bmatrix}^{-1} \begin{bmatrix} (Y^1 - kV)'Q \\ (Z^1)'Q \end{bmatrix} .$$

Letting H be the matrix whose inverse is taken, this may be rewritten:

(2.11) $$(TH^{-1})(1/T\begin{bmatrix} (Y^1 - kV)'Q \\ (Z^1)'Q \end{bmatrix})$$

15 [**16**, pp. 341–342].

and, under the stability and identifiability assumptions made, the probability limit of (TH^{-1}) exists for $\bar{\eta}$ sufficiently close to zero, as does the probability limit of the second factor. Further, the probability limit of the product is $a_1^1(\bar{\eta},\bar{\eta})$ and

$$(2.12) \qquad a_1^1(\bar{\eta},\bar{\eta}) = \begin{bmatrix} (B_1^1)' \\ (G_1^1)' \end{bmatrix}$$

provided that the probability limit of k is one.

There are now two cases to consider. The first case is that in which the probability limit is independent of η—that is, independent of our misspecification. This is the case of two-stage least squares (k identically equal to one) and of certain other members of the k-class.[16] The case in which the probability limit of k does depend on $\bar{\eta}$ is exemplified by limited information, maximum likelihood, and we shall restrict our attention in the second case to this example.

Suppose now that the probability limit of k is independent of η. Form the k-class estimator of (2.6) on the assumption that $\bar{\eta} = 0$—i.e., under misspecification. This estimator can be written as:

$$(2.13) \qquad (TH^{-1})(1/T \begin{bmatrix} (Y^1 - kV)'\, Y_1 \\ (Z^1)'\, Y_1 \end{bmatrix}) \ .$$

The crucial point here is that H is unaltered by the misspecification; hence the probability limit of (TH^{-1}) exists as does the probability limit of the second factor which involves only asymptotic moment matrices. The probability limit of the product is $a_1^1(0,\bar{\eta})$, and we have:

$$(2.14) \qquad a_1^1(\bar{\eta},\bar{\eta}) - a_1^1(0,\bar{\eta}) = \operatorname{Plim}\left\{(TH^{-1})\,(1/T \begin{bmatrix} (Y^1 - kV)'\, W \\ (Z^1)'\, W \end{bmatrix}) \, (\bar{\eta}')\right\},$$

and this clearly approaches zero as a limit as $\bar{\eta}$ goes to zero, thus proving the theorem in this case in view of (2.12).

The case of limited information, maximum likelihood is similar, save that here k is not independent of η, since it is equal to $(1+\varrho)$ where ϱ is the smallest root of the determinantal equation

$$(2.15) \qquad |M_1 - (1 + \varrho)\, M| = 0$$

where M_1 and M are different for the auxiliary and the misspecified systems. For the auxiliary system, they are the moment matrices of the estimated residuals in the least squares regressions of $q(t)$ and the elements of $y^1(t)$ on the elements of $z^1(t)$ and on all the exogenous variables, respectively. For the misspecified system, on the other hand, they are the same with $y_1(t)$ in place of $q(t)$. Of course, the two coincide for $\bar{\eta} = 0$.

---

[16] For example, where k depends only on the number of variables in $y^1(t)$ and $z^1(t)$ and on the total number of exogenous variables in the system. See [**16**, p. 229].

The probability limits of M_1 and M and hence of ϱ and k exist in either case. It is clear, moreover, that the two cases differ only in the first rows and columns of M_1 and M. As $\bar{\eta}$ approaches zero, these first rows and columns approach each other, in view of (2.8), as do the probability limits of the corresponding k's. For $\bar{\eta}$ sufficiently close to zero, therefore, the probability limit of k in the misspecified system will be sufficiently close to that in the auxiliary system (unity) to insure the existence of the probability limit of (TH^{-1}) when H is computed using the k corresponding to the misspecified system. The proof now proceeds as before.

Some remarks are now in order. First, it is clear that the theorem could easily be generalized to the case where $\bar{\eta}$ approaches η for given η. We should then merely have $(\bar{\eta} - \eta)'$ in place of $\bar{\eta}'$ on the extreme right of (2.14). Moreover, the same generalization shows that the theorem remains true if we allow η to approach $\bar{\eta}$ for fixed $\bar{\eta}$, that is, allow our statement to approach the truth rather than (as above) allowing the truth to approach our statement. (We have adopted the latter course because of the context of the problem.)

Secondly, we have now shown that it is not the case that the use of *a priori* restrictions which only hold approximately necessarily leads to the abandonment of simultaneous equation methods of estimation. It is true that such use leads to inconsistency in the estimates, but, provided the approximations involved are good enough, such inconsistencies will be negligible.

What is involved in deciding whether particular approximations are "good enough" is an interesting but complex and difficult question. It has been answered by Theil[17] for the case of a single equation with misspecified *a priori* restrictions. The answer for simultaneous equations is far more difficult to obtain and is a fit subject for further work, especially in view of the fact (brought out in the above proof) that different estimators may have different sensitivities to this kind of misspecification. We shall return to this below. Here we are concerned only to show that some "good enough" approximation does exist, so that simultaneous equation methods need not be discarded simply because restrictions are only approximate. It may indeed be true that many or all *a priori* restrictions actually used are not "good enough" approximations (in the sense that they lead to inconsistencies too large to be tolerated); however, this must be decided on a case by case basis and no general *a priori* argument can be made to this effect.

Thirdly, it follows from our theorem and discussion that Liu is wrong in claiming that the unrestricted least squares estimates of the reduced form should be used for prediction because the use of *a priori* restrictions adds only misinformation. The reduced form matrix is a continuous transformation

---

[17] [**16**, pp. 331–333].

of the coefficient matrix of the system; it follows that as inconsistencies in the estimates of the elements of the latter go to zero, so do inconsistencies in the estimates of the reduced form coefficients. The use of *a priori* restrictions which are approximate thus leads to negligible inconsistencies in such estimates also—for good enough approximations. It follows that the restricted estimates of the reduced form obtained from structural equation estimates converge more rapidly to probability limits that differ slightly or negligibly from the true reduced form coefficients than the unrestricted least squares reduced form estimates converge to the true reduced form parameters. Here is a case in which a slightly or negligibly inconsistent estimator is more efficient than a consistent estimator. In applying the restrictions in the estimation of the reduced form, one trades consistency for efficiency. Such a trade of precise accuracy for convenient closeness is always the price of approximate assumptions. Provided the approximations are close enough, the efficiency properties of simultaneous equation estimators will more than compensate for their inconsistency. Here again, there is no general *a priori* argument that approximations will not be "close enough"; this can only be decided in particular cases.

3. BLOCK RECURSIVE SYSTEMS: OMITTED VARIABLES

The last section considered the effect of misspecification in the *a priori* restrictions alone. Throughout this section, unless otherwise stated, we assume that the *a priori* restrictions are correctly specified and turn to the next type of approximate misspecification considered by Liu.

It will be convenient to alter our notation somewhat and to define some new concepts. A triangular matrix is a square matrix with zeros everywhere below the main diagonal. As is well known, an equation system whose matrix is triangular is a recursive system; its equations may be treated singly or sequentially rather than simultaneously and may be estimated by least squares. The equations of the system form a unilateral causal chain.[18]

We now generalize these concepts in the following way. For any matrix, M, let $r(M)$ be the number of rows of M and $c(M)$ be the number of columns. Consider a square matrix

$$(3.1) \qquad W = \begin{bmatrix} R^1 & S^1 & & & \\ 0^{21} & R^2 & S^2 & & \\ 0^{31} & 0^{32} & R^3 & S^3 & \\ . & . & . & . & \\ . & . & . & . & . \\ . & . & . & . & . \\ 0^{N1} & 0^{N2} & 0^{N3} & . & . & R^N \end{bmatrix}$$

---

[18] See H. Wold in association with L. Juréen [19, pp. 14, 49–53, and elsewhere].

where the R^i are nonsingular (and hence square) matrices and the S^i are matrices which may or may not be zero. The 0^{ij} are zero matrices; clearly,

(3.2)
$$r\,(0^{ij}) = r\,(R^i)\,,$$
$$c\,(0^{ij}) = c\,(R^j) = r\,(R^j) \qquad (i,j = 1,\ldots,N)\,.$$

Such a matrix is said to be *block triangular*; it is triangular in blocks rather than in single elements.[19] The reason for imposing nonsingularity on the R^i is one of convenience and will be apparent shortly.

Observe that each of the submatrices:

$$R^N,\ \begin{bmatrix} R^{N-1} & S^{N-1} \\ 0^{NN-1} & R^N \end{bmatrix},\ \begin{bmatrix} R^{N-2} & S^{N-2} & \\ 0^{N-1N-2} & R^{N-1} & S^{N-1} \\ 0^{NN-2} & 0^{NN-1} & R^N \end{bmatrix},\ \ldots,\ W$$

is square and nonsingular and is block triangular (the last property holding in an empty sense for R^N which has only one block).

Now consider the equation system

(3.3) $u = Ax\,.$

(We have dropped the time argument for convenience; it is to be understood.) As in the last section, partition A and x to correspond to endogenous and exogenous variables, the endogenous variables coming first. Thus rewrite (3.3) as:

(3.4) $u = [B\ \ G]\begin{bmatrix} y \\ z \end{bmatrix}\,.$

Now assume that B is block triangular with N blocks and partition u and y into N corresponding blocks, thus:

(3.5)
$$u = \begin{bmatrix} u^1 \\ u^2 \\ u^3 \\ \vdots \\ u^N \end{bmatrix};\ \ y = \begin{bmatrix} y^1 \\ y^2 \\ y^3 \\ \vdots \\ y^N \end{bmatrix}\,.$$

We call an equation such as (3.3) in which the part of the coefficient matrix corresponding to the endogenous variables is block triangular, *block*

[19] The term is evidently a natural one. Since first using it, it has been pointed out to me by Jerome Rothenberg that "block triangularity" has already been suggested by Walter Jacobs and used by George Dantzig to describe rather similar matrices occurring in linear programming. (See Dantzig [1, p. 176]). Save for the requirement that the R^i be nonsingular, my block triangularity property is the same as the well-known property of decomposability (See Solow [13]), a fact that will be of interest below.

recursive. Any equation system (block recursive or not) which has a square coefficient matrix (in our notation, where G is null) will be called *self-contained.*

Block recursive systems have the property that—given the exogenous variables, if any—the variables in y^N are (stochastically) determined solely by the equations corresponding to B^N; the variables in y^{N-1} are then determined by the exogenous variables, the variables in y^N, and the equations corresponding to B^{N-1}; and so forth. Accordingly, it is clear that if all the equations that involve the variables have been included in the system and the system itself correctly specified, the parameters of the subset of equations with u^j as left hand member (say the jth subset) may be estimated with regard only for the equations in that subset and without regard for the existence of the remaining equations.[20] The variables in any y^i may clearly be considered exogenous to the jth subset of equations provided that $i > j$, or to any union of such subsets as may be seen by solving (3.4) for y in terms of z and u. It is clear that ordinary recursive systems are special cases of block recursive systems with the B^i single rows and the 0^{ij} single elements.

The analysis of causation for self-contained block recursive systems has been given by H. Simon.[21] He argues (considering more general systems as well) that the variables in y^N can plausibly be regarded as "causing" the variables in y^{N-1} in such a case; the variables in y^N and y^{N-1} can be regarded as "causing" the variables in y^{N-2}; and so forth, a concept of causality which Strotz and Wold have aptly termed "vector causality."[22] The dynamic properties of block recursive systems are obviously closely related to those of unilaterally coupled systems considered by R. Goodwin;[23] indeed, block

---

[20] This assumes that the elements of any u^i are independent of the elements of any u^j for $j \neq i$. Actually, since we shall be explicitly investigating the effects of all omitted variables, we could well assume that all elements of u are independent of each other. This is an innocuous assumption since any dependence here can always be expressed in terms of some variable wrongly omitted from two or more equations (and thus present in the error term). Of course, this assumption is only meant to apply to cases where explicit account is taken of all omitted variables. Aside from being innocuous, however, this strong assumption is unnecessary; all that is needed for the results is the assumption in the first sentence of this footnote for block recursive systems and for systems supposed to be block recursive. A similar problem arises with ordinary recursive systems, and a similar assumption is always made in practice —although without the explicit sufficient justification given here, since omitted variables are not excluded from the error term. See Wold and Juréen [19, pp. 52–53]. Of course, the theorems given below provide justification for this practice when the specification of no omitted variables is approximately correct.

[21] [11]. The question of whether any system is really part of a self-contained system is a metaphysical one which need not concern us here.

[22] [15, pp. 421–422].

[23] [3]. See also Solow [13].

recursive systems are the generalization of unilaterally coupled systems to more than two markets. We shall have something to say about such dynamic properties in a later section.

We turn now to the second issue of specification error raised by Liu, that of the incorrect or only approximately correct omission of relevant variables from the whole system of equations being studied. As observed above, Liu argues that such omitted variables are likely to be connected with the included variables by equations other than those explicitly included. It will be convenient both now and later to frame our discussion (which is quite general) in terms of block recursive systems.

Consider the system of equations explicitly under investigation:

$$(3.6) \qquad u^2 = [D^{21}\ B^2\ G^2] \begin{bmatrix} x^1 \\ y^2 \\ z^2 \end{bmatrix}$$

where B^2 is square and nonsingular; G^2 and D^{21} are rectangular; and the reason for the superscripts will appear shortly. In (3.6), y^2 is a vector of explicitly endogenous and z^2 a vector of explicitly assumed exogenous variables. x^1, on the other hand, is a vector of variables assumed absent from the system. In other words, D^{21} is incorrectly assumed to be a zero matrix.

In what follows we shall assume that the specification of z^2 as a vector of exogenous variables is correct, leaving the alternative case to a later section. We further suppose that sufficient *a priori* restrictions of the usual type have been imposed on the first equation of the system to identify it when D^{21} is in fact zero, that is (where ϕ' is, as before, the transposed matrix of the coefficients of the restrictions), we suppose that the rank of the matrix $[B^2\ G^2]\phi'$ is $r(B^2)-1$. For the present we continue to assume that all such *a priori* restrictions are true ones so that the problems studied in the last section do not arise.

We now consider all equations relating the variables of x^1 to the included variables of y^2 and z^2. We do this in the following way: consider equations explaining each of the elements of x^1 (y^2 is explained by (3.6) and z^2 is exogenous). If such equations involve variables not in (3.6) expand the definition of x^1 and hence of D^{21} to include all such variables. Continue this process until either there are as many new independent equations as there are variables in the expanded x^1, or until all variables left unexplained in the expanded x^1 are exogenous to the entire system. (There may be very many equations in the result.) Now partition x^1 into a vector of variables endogenous to the complete system, y^1, and a vector (possibly null) of variables exogenous to the complete system, z^1. Correspondingly, partition D^{21} into E^{21} and F^{21}. The complete system of which (3.6) is a part is thus:

(3.7)
$$\begin{bmatrix} u^1 \\ u^2 \end{bmatrix} = \left[\begin{array}{c|c|c} B^1 & H^1 & G^1 \\ \hline E^{21} & F^{21} & B^2 \mid G^2 \end{array} \right] \begin{bmatrix} y^1 \\ z^1 \\ y^2 \\ z^2 \end{bmatrix}$$

where B^1 is square and corresponds to y^1. We shall assume B^1 to be non-singular for the present. It is easily seen that $r(E^{21}) = r(B^2)$ and $c(E^{21}) = r(B^1)$. It is thus clear (if you like, reshuffle columns to put all exogenous variables together) that the assumption that $E^{21} = 0$ is the assumption that the system (3.7) is block recursive so that the subsystem (3.6) can be estimated in isolation. Of course, the assumption that $F^{21} = 0$ is the additional assumption that all exogenous variables that appear in (3.7) have been explicitly included in (3.6).

Let n be the total number of variables and m be the total number of equations in (3.7). Let:

(3.8)
$$A = [D^{21}\, B^2\, G^2] = [E^{21}\, F^{21}\, B^2\, G^2]$$

and consider the problem of estimating the first row of A, as before, A_1. Let the probability limit of the estimate of A_{1j} obtained by assuming that $D^{21} = 0$ and applying a standard technique[24] be $\alpha_{1j}(0, D^{21})$. As in the previous section, choose an indefinitely large set of values for u^1 and u^2 and for those elements of z^1 and z^2 that are not lagged endogenous variables; choose a set of initial values for all lagged endogenous variables in z^1 and z^2. Now fix B^1, H^1, G^1, B^2 and G^2, and consider a collection of systems differing only in D^{21}. Consider an infinite sequence of such systems such that D^{21} approaches the zero matrix. We prove that the inconsistency involved in assuming D^{21} zero—that is, in omitting x^1 from the equations—goes to zero as D^{21} goes to zero, as the approximation involved gets better and better.

THEOREM 2.

$$\lim_{D^{21} \to 0} |\alpha_{1j}(0, D^{21}) - A_{1j}| = 0 \text{ for all } j = 1, \ldots, n .$$

Proof: We prove the theorem by showing it to be a special case of Theorem 1. Estimation of A_1 on the assumption that $D_1^{21} = 0$ is estimation applying as many new (though incorrect) *a priori* restrictions as there are elements in D_1^{21}, i.e., as many restrictions as there are variables in x^1. By assumption, however, there are already available at least $r(B^2) - 1$ restrictions on the other elements of A_1; hence the necessary order condition for the identifiability of A_1 *considered as a part of* (3.7) *rather than just of* (3.6) is certainly satisfied when $D_1^{21} = 0$ since

(3.9) $r(B^2) - 1 + c(D^{21}) \geqslant r(B^2) - 1 + c(E^{21}) = r(B^2) + r(B^1) - 1 = m - 1.$

[24] A similar remark to that made in footnote 12 above applies here.

If F^{21} is not null, there are more restrictions than necessary (as there may also be if there were more than $r(B^2)-1$ original restrictions).

We must now show that the necessary and sufficient rank condition is also satisfied when $D_1^{21} = 0$. Arrange the restrictions $D_1^{21} = 0$ so that the coefficients thereof form a unit matrix with $c(D^{21})$ rows and columns. The rank condition will be satisfied if the rank of the matrix:

$$(3.10) \quad \left[\begin{array}{c|c|c|c} B^1 & H^1 & G^1 \\ \hline E^{21} & F^{21} & B^2 & G^2 \end{array}\right]\left[\begin{array}{c|c} I & 0 \\ \hline 0 & \phi' \end{array}\right] = \left[\begin{array}{c|c|c} B^1 & H^1 & G^1\phi' \\ \hline E^{21} & F^{21} & (B^2\ G^2)\phi' \end{array}\right]$$

is $m-1$.

To see that this is the case for D^{21} sufficiently close to zero, strike out the row of the above product matrix that corresponds to A_1, denoting the result by the use of lower case instead of upper case letters. Further, select $r(B^2)-1$ independent columns from ϕ' and assume (for convenience only) that these are the only columns in ϕ'. Consider the following submatrix of the above matrix:

$$(3.11) \qquad\qquad \left[\begin{array}{c|c} B^1 & G^1\phi' \\ \hline e^{21} & (b^2\ g^2)\phi' \end{array}\right] = W(e^{21}), \quad \text{say}.$$

This is $(m-1) \times (m-1)$. Now consider $W(0)$, and suppose that it were singular. Then a nonzero row vector, say, λ, would exist such that $\lambda W(0) = 0$. Partition λ into $(\lambda^1\ \lambda^2)$ corresponding to the two rows of blocks in $W(0)$. Singularity of $W(0)$ then implies that

$$(3.12) \qquad\qquad (\lambda^1\ \lambda^2)\left[\begin{array}{c|c} B^1 & G^1\phi' \\ \hline 0 & (b^2\ g^2)\phi' \end{array}\right] = 0$$

and hence that

$$(3.13) \qquad\qquad \lambda^1 B^1 + \lambda^2 0 = \lambda^1 B^1 = 0$$

which is impossible unless $\lambda^1 = 0$, since B^1 was assumed nonsingular. It thus follows that

$$(3.14) \qquad\qquad \lambda^1 G^1\phi' + \lambda^2(b^2\ g^2)\phi' = \lambda^2(b^2\ g^2)\phi' = 0.$$

This is impossible, however, unless $\lambda^2 = 0$, for $(b^2\ g^2)\phi'$ is also nonsingular by assumption. Hence $\lambda = 0$ and $W(0)$ must be nonsingular. It now follows immediately that $W(e^{21})$ must also be nonsingular for D^{21} (and hence e^{21}) sufficiently close to zero, for the determinant of a matrix is a continuous function of its elements. Therefore the product matrix in (3.10) has rank $m-1$ for D^{21} sufficiently close to zero and the rank condition is satisfied.

This being the case, estimation of A_1 on the assumption that $D_1^{21} = 0$ is estimation which involves incorrect *a priori* restrictions; however, for the remaining rows of D^{21} sufficiently close to zero, identification of A_1 is present when the restrictions are actually correct. *This is just the situation considered in Theorem* 1, *however*;[25] hence as *all* rows of D^{21} (including the first) approach zero, $\alpha_{1j}(0,D^{21})$ and A_{1j} approach each other for all j, by Theorem 1. *Q.E.D.*

It is thus the case that, when the specification that the variables in x^1 do not appear in the system (3.6) is a "good enough" approximation, the inconsistency involved in applying it will be negligible in estimating any equation of (3.6) which is otherwise identified. (Once again, it is far more difficult precisely to define "good enough.") Moreover, a more important result than this is readily available.

The theorem just proved dealt with the estimation of one equation on the assumption that *all* specification errors approached zero—that not only were the omitted variables nearly absent from the equation in question, but that they were nearly absent from the system (3.6)—that is, that *all* rows of D^{21} approached zero, not just the first. It is easy to show, however, that the negligibility of inconsistencies in the estimation of A_1 almost never depends on the closeness to zero of the last $r(B^2)-1$ rows of D^{21}. To see this, observe that the only use made of such closeness in the proof of the theorem was to show that $W(e^{21})$ was nonsingular, and hence that the rank condition was satisfied for the last rows of D^{21} close enough to zero. *The necessary order condition is always satisfied regardless of the value of D^{21}*, in view of (3.9). Furthermore, the closeness to zero of the last rows of D^{21} is a sufficient, but by no means a necessary condition for the rank condition to hold; $W(e^{21})$ can be nonsingular for other configurations. Indeed, since a determinant is a linear function of any element and of the elements in any row, and since $W(0)$ is known to be nonsingular, $W(e^{21})$ must be nonsingular for all points in the space of the elements of e^{21}, save for a set of measure zero. Hence the rank condition is satisfied almost everywhere in the space of the elements of the last $r(B^2)-1$ rows of D^{21} and we have:

THEOREM 3 (*Limited Effects of Other Errors Theorem*).

$$\lim_{\substack{D^{21}_1 \to 0}} |\, \alpha_{1j}(0,D^{21}) - A_{1j}\,| = 0 \text{ for all } j = 1,\ldots, n$$

almost always regardless of the last $r(B^2)-1$ rows of D^{21}. [26]

---

[25] It is necessary to add that in the present case, V in (2.10) refers to residuals from regressions on the elements of z^2 only, rather than on all exogenous variables. A similar remark applies to the interpretation of M_1 and M in (2.15). This amounts to using the elements of z^2 as instrumental variables and the remainder of the proof follows as before.

[26] This is a special case of the general remark made in Koopmans, Rubin, and Leipnik [**5**, p. 83].

This is an important theorem, for it shows that the mistaken omission of nonnegligible variables from a given structural equation generally affects only the estimates of the parameters of that equation and not the estimates of parameters of other equations in the system. Specification errors of this type are thus of limited effect, and the estimates of the parameters of a given equation can be judged with regard only for the question of the goodness of approximation in the specification of that equation.

Some further remarks are now in order. If F^{21} and H^1 are not null, i.e., if some of the omitted variables are exogenous to (3.7), then it can easily happen that even when e^{21} is such as to make $W(e^{21})$ singular, the rank condition holds, so that the preceding theorem is slightly stronger. Secondly, the assumption that B^1 is nonsingular seems an innocuous one. It can be discarded, however, and replaced with the statement that $W(0)$ (and hence $W(e^{21})$ for small e^{21}) will be nonsingular almost everywhere in the space of the elements of B^1. As before, the rank condition can hold even with singularity of $W(e^{21})$ if there are omitted exogenous variables so that H^1 is not null.

Finally, we observe that the proofs of Theorems 2 and 3 do not depend on the truth or falsity of the original *a priori* restrictions. If those restrictions only hold approximately, it suffices to observe that the rank of $(b^2 \ g^2)\phi'$ will be $r(B^2)-1$ almost everywhere in the space of the elements of $(b^2 \ g^2)$ and must be $r(B^2)-1$ if the original *a priori* restrictions are close enough approximations (this follows as in the proof of Theorem 1). Hence we may treat all *a priori* restrictions—the original ones and the restrictions that $D_1^{21} = 0$—together. Let $(B_1^2 \ G_1^2)\phi' = \bar{\eta}$ as in the preceding section. Denote by $\tilde{a}_{1j}(0,\bar{\eta};0,D^{21})$ the probability limit of the estimate of A_{1j} is obtained on the assumption that $D^{21} = 0$ and $(B_1^2 \ G_1^2)\phi' = 0$. Consider the same sequence of systems as described before Theorem 2, save that B_1^2 and G_1^2 are only fixed in those elements not determined by the *a priori* restrictions. We have:

COROLLARY TO THEOREMS 1 AND 2:

$$\lim_{\substack{\bar{\eta}\to 0 \\ D^{21}\to 0}} | \tilde{a}_{1j}(0,\bar{\eta};0,D^{21}) - A_{1j}| = 0 \quad \text{for all} \quad j = 1,\ldots,n \; ;$$

and

COROLLARY TO THEOREMS 1 AND 3:

$$\lim_{\substack{\bar{\eta}\to 0 \\ D_1^{21}\to 0}} |\tilde{a}_{1j}(0,\bar{\eta};0,D^{21}) - A_{1j}| = 0$$

for all $j = 1,\ldots,n$ almost always regardless of the last $r(B^2)-1$ rows of D^{21}.

Thus as approximations of both kinds so far considered get better and better, the inconsistency of estimates goes to zero. It follows that for good enough approximations—both in the *a priori* restrictions and in the omission of variables—such inconsistencies will be negligible. The effects of the assumption of block recursiveness and of approximate *a priori* restrictions are thus independent in this regard.

All this has been on the assumption that all variables assumed exogenous really are. We shall investigate the consequences of misspecification in this area after further discussion in the next section of the effects of omitted variables.

4. GENERALIZATION OF PROXIMITY THEOREM I

In the last section, we established conditions under which the inconsistency of the structural parameter estimates is negligible, even though variables are mistakenly or approximately excluded from the equation system studied. Those conditions were essentially that the coefficients of the excluded variables in the true system be very close to zero. In this section, we ask a somewhat different question. Suppose that the true coefficients of the omitted variables are not very close to zero. Under what conditions can the coefficients of the included variables be estimated with negligible inconsistency? In other words, let $J^2 = [B^2 \ G^2]$ and rewrite (3.6) as:

$$(4.1) \qquad u^2 = [D^{21} \ J^2] \begin{bmatrix} x^1 \\ x^2 \end{bmatrix}.$$

Continue to assume that the rank of $J^2\phi'$ is $r(J^2)-1$, where ϕ' is the coefficient matrix of true linear homogeneous *a priori* restrictions, $J_1^2\phi' = 0$. We wish to ascertain the conditions under which J_1^2, the first row of J^2, can be estimated with negligible inconsistency when D^{21} is assumed zero, but is in fact *not* very close to zero.[27]

Now, define a new residual vector, v, as

$$(4.2) \qquad v \equiv u^2 - D^{21}x^1 = J^2x^2 .$$

---

[27] The question may be raised of why estimation of J_1^2 is desirable in these circumstances. Since we shall show below that the estimates obtained are estimates of the gross effect of the variables in x^2 (both their direct effect and their effect through the variables in x^1), are not such estimates to be desired for all purposes? The answer here is the same as in the case of reduced form versus structural estimation (indeed, the question is a special case of that question): Measurement of such gross effects may indeed be helpful for prediction, but in the event of a partial structural break that disturbs the relation between the included and the (mistakenly) omitted variables, the use of gross estimates leads to serious error, whereas true structural knowledge can still be used. An example would be the imposition of a tax on one of the variables.

Estimation of J^2 on the assumption that $D^{21} = 0$ is thus seen to be estimation of (4.2) on the assumption that the elements of v are distributed independently of the exogenous variables z^2. Leaving the interpretation of what follows in terms of a complete system such as (3.7) to later discussion, suppose that in fact v is related to x^2 by:

(4.3) $v = Px^2 + u^2 + \mu = Ly^2 + Qz^2 + u^2 + \mu \,,$

that is, the relations between the excluded and included variables are such that $D^{21}x^1 = -Px^2 + \mu$. We continue to assume that the true residuals —the elements of $(u^2 + \mu)$—are in fact distributed independently of the elements of z^2. It is easy to see, however, that this cannot generally be the case with the elements of v unless some rows of P are zero, since eliminating y^2 from (4.2) and (4.3) gives:

(4.4) $v = [I - L(B^2)^{-1}]^{-1}[Q - L(B^2)^{-1}G]z^2 + [I - L(B^2)^{-1}]^{-1}(u^2 + \mu) \,.$

An element of v can thus only be independent of the elements of z^2 if some row of the matrix $[Q - L(B^2)^{-1}G]$ is zero. This will be the case if the corresponding row of $P = [L \; Q]$ is zero; otherwise, it can only happen (on a set of measure zero) if the effects of z^2 on v directly are exactly cancelled by the indirect effects through y^2.[28]

As before, choose an indefinitely large number of values for u^2 and μ and for such elements of z^2 as are not lagged endogenous variables, choosing initial conditions for the remaining elements of z^2. Fix J^2 and consider systems differing only in P. Let $j_1(0,P)$ be the vector of the probability limits of the estimates of J_1^2 obtained for given P by wrongly assuming that $P = 0$ and applying one of the standard simultaneous equation techniques.[29] *Note that this may, but need not be, the mistaken assumption that no variables have been omitted* (the assumption of the last section). We shall discuss this below. We prove:

---

[28] Should this exceptional case occur, in particular, should it be the first element of v that is distributed independently of z^2, it may happen that the first equation of (4.2) is underidentified unless there are more than enough *a priori* restrictions to begin with. This is so because the first row of (4.3) will be indistinguishable in form from the first row of (4.2). (This does not otherwise arise because of the dependence of the elements of v and of z^2.) The exceptional case is of no importance; one could never know that it was present in any practical problem. The possibility of its existence does not substantially affect our discussion, save as a curiosity, since we are concerned with the more interesting case where rows of P are near zero. The possible existence of the exceptional case, however, does mean that we are stating sufficient but not always necessary conditions for negligible inconsistency.

[29] A similar remark to that given in footnote 12, above, applies here.

THEOREM 4 (*Generalized Proximity Theorem I*).

(a) $\lim\limits_{P\to 0} j_1(0,P) = \lim\limits_{P\to 0} (J_1^2 - P_1) = J_1^2$;

(b) $\lim\limits_{P_1\to 0} j_1(0,P) = \lim\limits_{P_1\to 0} (J_1^2 - P_1) = J_1^2$

almost always regardless of the last $r(P) - 1$ rows of P.

Proof:
Solve (4.2) and (4.3) for $(u^2 + \mu)$, obtaining

(4.5) $\qquad\qquad (u^2 + \mu) = (J^2 - P) x^2$.

This system of equations is in the same form as (4.2), and $(u^2 + \mu)$ meets the assumptions made about (4.2)—its elements are distributed independently of z^2. Hence some linear combination of the rows of (4.2) will be estimated. It remains to be shown that as P goes to zero, that estimate approaches $(J_1^2 - P_1)$. Consider the vector $(J_1^2 - P_1)\phi'$. As P approaches zero, this must approach $J_1^2\phi' = 0$ by assumption. Therefore, as P approaches zero, $(J_1^2 - P_1)$ comes closer and closer to satisfying the *a priori* restrictions. Furthermore, as P approaches zero, the matrix $(J^2 - P)\phi'$ approaches $J^2\phi'$. The determinant of a matrix, however, is a continuous function of its elements; hence, for P close enough to zero, the rank of $(J^2 - P)\phi'$ and of $J^2\phi'$ will be the same, namely, $r(J^2) - 1$. It now follows that $j_1(0,P)$ is an estimate satisfying all the conditions of Theorem 1, for P sufficiently close to zero, and statement (a) of the Theorem has been proved.

Statement (b) now follows as in the last section by observing that the rows of P other than the first only enter in the above proof in consideration of the rank of $(J^2 - P)\phi'$.

Before going on to discuss the reason for naming the theorem as we have, some remarks are in order regarding its consequences. Let us return to the notation of the last section (of (3.7) in particular). Here, however, we make one change. Previously we agreed to expand x^1 until all its elements were either explained or exogenous; now we must expand it until all its elements are either explained or distributed independently of z^2. This is not the same thing, for functions of exogenous variables are themselves exogenous. We suppress all such independent variables (and also H^1 and F^{21}) by writing them as functions of x^1 with zero coefficients, and thus including them in y^1. From (3.7):

(4.6) $\qquad\qquad y^1 = -(B^1)^{-1}G^1x^2 + (B^1)^{-1}u^1$.

Hence

(4.7) $\quad v = u^2 - D^{21}x^1 = u^2 - E^{21}y^1 = E^{21}(B^1)^{-1}G^1x^2 + u^2 - E^{21}(B^1)^{-1}u^1$, and this is precisely (4.3) with

(4.8)
$$P = E^{21}(B^1)^{-1}G^1 ,$$
$$\mu = -E^{21}(B^1)^{-1}u^1 .$$

It follows that the conditions of the second part of the theorem will be satisfied if the first row of $E^{21}(B^1)^{-1}G^1$ goes to zero; hence inconsistencies will be negligible in the estimation of J_1^2 if all elements in that first row are sufficiently close to zero. Let us ask what this means.

In the first place, observe that the row in question will be near zero if the first row of E^{21} is near zero. This is scarcely surprising. If that is the case, then clearly inconsistencies in the estimation of E_1^{21} on the assumption that the latter is zero will be negligible. Combined with the results of Theorem 4, this gives us Theorems 2 and 3 as a special case.[30]

Secondly, the row in question will be near zero if G^1 and thus $(B^1)^{-1}G^1$ is near zero. It is the second matrix which is of most interest. This is a quasi-reduced form matrix showing the full effects of the included variables on the omitted ones. Clearly, if all such effects are near zero, inconsistencies will be negligible.[31]

Finally, we can make a general statement covering all cases. Inconsistencies will be negligible if to each nonnegligible element of E_1^{21}, say E_{1k}^{21}, there corresponds a negligible row of $(B^1)^{-1}G^1$, the kth row. In other words, inconsistencies will be negligible provided that the only omitted variables that enter into the first equation with nonnegligible coefficients are those variables on which the influence of the included variables is slight.

We have called Theorem 4 a generalization of the Proximity Theorem. The latter theorem is due to Wold[32] and applies to a single equation. It states that the least squares regression coefficients of a single equation will be nearly unbiased either if the residuals from that equation are small or if they are nearly uncorrelated with the explanatory variables. The two effects reinforce each other. In the case of omitted variables, where only one equation is involved (i.e., $r(J^2) = 1$), it is easy to see that this is essentially the same as our theorem with unbiasedness substituted for consistency.[33]

---

[30] A special case which was worth proving separately, nonetheless, because of the way in which the omission of variables enters as providing just sufficient *a priori* restrictions.

[31] Note that this is equivalent to the statement that the system can be put in block-recursive form (possibly with three blocks) by an appropriate renumbering of equations and variables.

[32] [**19**, Theorem 12.1.3, p. 189. Also see pp. 37–38]; more precise results have been obtained by Wold and P. Faxér [**20**].

[33] We can only deal with consistency in general because simultaneous equation estimators are not generally unbiased under correct specification.

Clearly, in this case, the single row of P will be negligible if and only if the zero order least squares regression coefficients of $D^{21}x^1$ on the included variables x^2 are all zero. These regression coefficients are, however, the products of correlation coefficients and the ratio of the variance of $D^{21}x^1$ to the variance of the variable in question. P will therefore be close to zero if either all the correlations are near zero or if the variance of $D^{21}x^1$ is near zero; and the two effects reinforce each other (they multiply). Hence our theorem essentially reduces to the Proximity Theorem in the single equation case. This is not the only generalization of the Proximity Theorem to the simultaneous equations case, however. Another such will be given in the next section.[34]

We may emphasize that the regression coefficients and not simply the correlations of the residual with the explanatory variables are important here.[35] Even if all such correlations were perfect, if the effects on the residual of moving the explanatory variables were very small, relative to the direct effects of such movement on the dependent variable, the inconsistency involved would be very slight. A similar statement holds for the simultaneous equation case.[36]

Finally, we observe that Theorem 4 and Theorem 1 can hold at the same time, that is, all inconsistencies in the estimation of J^2 will go to zero as P_1 goes to zero and as the *a priori* restrictions become better approximations. Thus such inconsistencies will be negligible if P_1 is close to zero and all *a priori* restrictions are good enough approximations.

5. GENERALIZATION OF PROXIMITY THEOREM II

Thus far we have assumed that all variables assumed to be exogenous actually are so. The time has now come to remove that restriction. Until further notice, we shall assume that all *a priori* restrictions are correctly specified and that no variables have been omitted from the system. More general cases will be considered below.

[34] It is interesting to observe that taken together the results of the two sections imply that the conditions of the Proximity Theorem imply that the system being studied is nearly recursive or block-recursive, with the equation being estimated forming one block. It follows that a defense of least squares based on the Proximity Theorem differs in degree but not fundamentally in kind from the defense that the real world is recursive. (An exception to this occurs when there are no omitted variables and the variance of the true structural residual is near zero.)

[35] Although useful results may be obtained in the single equation case using the the correlation coefficients alone, see A. C. Harberger [4].

[36] A clear statement of the theorem in the single equation case in terms of omitted variables and regression coefficients has been given by J. Lintner [6, Ch. II]. As usual in this area of analysis H. Theil has proved a general theorem (for a single equation) of which this is a special case. [17, p. 43].

Consider the system of equations:

(5.1) $$u^1 = A^1 x = [B^1 \ G^1] \begin{bmatrix} x^1 \\ x^2 \end{bmatrix}$$

where, as usual, B^1 is assumed nonsingular. Here x^1 is assumed endogenous and x^2 is (incorrectly) assumed exogenous. We further assume that, were those assumptions correct, A_1^1 would be identified, that is, that there exist *a priori* restrictions, $A_1^1 \phi' = 0$ and that the rank of $A^1 \phi'$ is $r(A^1) - 1$.

Now, suppose that in reality (5.1) is part of a larger system:

(5.2) $$\begin{bmatrix} u^1 \\ u^2 \end{bmatrix} = \begin{bmatrix} B^1 & G^1 \\ E^{21} & B^2 \end{bmatrix} \begin{bmatrix} x^1 \\ x^2 \end{bmatrix}.$$

For simplicity, we assume that B^2 is square and nonsingular, i.e., that no additional variables are needed to explain x^2. In short, we assume that (5.2) is self-contained. More complex and realistic cases will be considered below.

We have already investigated the effect of assuming that $E^{21} = 0$ on the estimates of the second block of equations in (5.2). We now consider the effect of the same assumption on the estimates of the first block. Note once more that this assumption is that of block recursiveness. Should we prove that the effects of the assumption are here negligible for E^{21} sufficiently close to zero, we shall be in a position to speak strongly about the effects of separating total systems for partial analysis.

Let the coefficient matrix of (5.2) be A, rewrite (5.2) as:

(5.3) $$u = Ax .$$

Then (assuming A to be nonsingular, which it must be for E^{21} sufficiently close to zero):

(5.4) $$x = A^{-1} u .$$

However,

(5.5) $A^{-1} =$
$$\left[\begin{array}{c|c} (B^1 - G^1(B^2)^{-1}E^{21})^{-1} & -(B^1 - G^1(B^2)^{-1}E^{21})^{-1}G^1(B^2)^{-1} \\ \hline -(B^2 - E^{21}(B^1)^{-1}G^1)^{-1}E^{21}(B^1)^{-1} & (B^2 - E^{21}(B^1)^{-1}G^1)^{-1} \end{array} \right]$$

which reduces when $E^{21} = 0$ to:

(5.6) $$A^{-1} = \left[\begin{array}{c|c} (B^1)^{-1} & -(B^1)^{-1}G^1(B^2)^{-1} \\ \hline 0 & (B^2)^{-1} \end{array} \right]$$

so that, in the latter case, x^2 depends only on u^2 and not on u^1. It follows that only when $E^{21} = 0$ is the assumption that x^2 consists of variables exogenous to (5.1) correct.

Now, as usual, choose an indefinitely large set of values for the elements of u. Fix B^1, G^1, and B^2. Consider a sequence of systems differing only in E^{21} and allow the latter matrix to go to zero. Note that (in view of (5.5)) the values of x^1 and x^2, and hence all estimates, are continuous functions of the elements of E^{21}. Clearly, we can prove a theorem analogous to Theorem 1 if we can show that all estimates are continuous functions of the *assumed* value of E^{21} also.

This, however, is not hard to do. It will prove instructive to transform the problem slightly. Denote the true asymptotic variance-covariance matrix of the elements of u^1 by $\bar{M}_{u^1u^1}$[37] and the asymptotic covariance matrix of the elements of x^2 and u^1 by $\bar{M}_{x^2u^1}$, the rows corresponding to the elements of x^2 and the columns to the elements of u^1. Let Q be the matrix in the left-hand lower corner of A^{-1} in (5.5). Then, from (5.4) and the remarks in footnote 20 above,

$$(5.7) \qquad \bar{M}_{x^2u^1} = Q\bar{M}_{u^1u^1} \, .$$

Furthermore, observe that given $\bar{M}_{x^2u^1}$ and $\bar{M}_{u^1u^1}$, Q is determined by (5.7) (we assume $\bar{M}_{u^1u^1}$ to be nonsingular; we are choosing u^1). Given B^1, G^1, and B^2, it is easy to show that E^{21} is determined by Q. It follows that with everything else fixed, E^{21}—and hence the values of the elements of x—is determined as a continuous function of $\bar{M}_{x^2u^1}$; further, that function is such that E^{21} is zero if and only if $\bar{M}_{x^2u^1}$ is zero.

The assumption that the elements of x^2 are exogenous with respect to (5.1) is precisely the assumption that $\bar{M}_{x^2u^1} = 0$. It is clear, however, that this is but a limiting assumption—one out of an infinite number that might be made. Given *any* value assumed for $\bar{M}_{x^2u^1}$, and a method of estimation consistent for $\bar{M}_{x^2u^1} = 0$, and making an appropriate stability assumption, estimates of A_1^1 will exist. Indeed, the latter estimates generally depend only on the first column of $\bar{M}_{x^2u^1}$. If the true value of $\bar{M}_{x^2u^1}$ and the assumed value coincide, such estimates will be consistent. This is most clearly seen in the case of the method of instrumental variables, where the covariances in question appear explicitly. Since limited information, maximum likelihood and two stage least squares estimators are equivalent to the method of instrumental variables for appropriate choices of instruments,[38] the same properties obviously hold for them. Such properties also hold for the full information, maximum likelihood method.

Let the assumed value of $\bar{M}_{x^2u^1}$ be $M_{x^2u^1}$. Let the vector of the probability limits of the estimates of the elements of A_1^1 obtained by making that

---

[37] By the strong assumption in footnote 20 above, this is a diagonal matrix. Equation (5.7) below follows from the weak assumption in footnote 20; it allows us to forget u^2 in computing covariances, which is all that is necessary.

[38] See J. D. Sargan [**10**, p. 393] and H. Theil [**16**, p. 336].

assumption and applying one of the standard methods[39] be $a_1^1 (M_{x^2u^1},$ $\bar{M}_{x^2u^1})$. It is clear that each element of the latter vector is a continuous function of both (matrix) arguments. It now follows exactly as in the proof of Theorem 1 that:

THEOREM 5 (*Generalized Proximity Theorem II*):

$$\lim_{\bar{M}_{x^2u^1} \to 0} a_1^1 (0, \bar{M}_{x^2u^1}) = A_1^1 .$$

Further, since $\bar{M}_{x^2u^1}$ and E^{21} are in a one-to-one relation and so are the assumed values thereof, we have (where the notation is obvious):

COROLLARY TO THEOREM 5:

$$\lim_{E^{21} \to 0} \alpha_1^1 (0, E^{21}) \equiv \lim_{E^{21} \to 0} a_1^1 (0, \bar{M}_{x^2u^1}) = A_1^1 .$$

It thus follows that inconsistencies in the estimation of A_1^1 will be negligible for E^{21} close enough to zero—for the variables in x^2 "nearly" exogenous to (5.1).

We have called Theorem 5 another generalization of the Proximity Theorem discussed in the last section. That it is so may be seen as follows. In the case of a single equation, $\bar{M}_{x^2u^1}$ consists of a single row, the vector of covariances between the single residual and the assumed exogenous variables. Any such covariance, however, may be written as the product of the corresponding correlation coefficient, the standard error of the residual, and, the standard error of the variable in question. Hence $\bar{M}_{x^2u^1}$ will go to zero in this case as both the correlations between the independent variables and the residual and the variance of the residual go to zero, the two effects reinforcing each other.[40]

We may now remove the assumption that (5.2) is self-contained. To begin with, it is clear that no problem whatsoever is created by the appearance of variables exogenous to (5.1) in the equations explaining x^2; we shall not include them explicitly to avoid unduly complicating our notation.

A problem does arise, however, when variables appear in the equations explaining x^2 which are not truly exogenous to (5.1). Call the vector of all such variables x^0; it is to be thought of as expanded to include variables

---

[39] A remark similar to that made in footnote 12 above applies here.

[40] It is truly the variance of the residual and not just its standard error that is important here since, other residual variances remaining equal, the variance of the independent variable involved is a linear function of the variance of the residual in question, by the remarks in footnote 20, above.

explaining x^2, variables explaining such variables, and so forth, until either a self-contained system is reached or all remaining unexplained variables are truly exogenous to (5.1). (As just stated, we may assume the first of these alternatives for simplicity.) Suppose that, instead of (5.2), (5.1) is a subsystem of:

$$(5.8) \qquad \begin{bmatrix} u^0 \\ u^1 \\ u^2 \end{bmatrix} = \begin{bmatrix} B^0 & E^{01} & E^{02} \\ 0^{10} & B^1 & G^1 \\ E^{20} & E^{21} & B^2 \end{bmatrix} \begin{bmatrix} x^0 \\ x^1 \\ x^2 \end{bmatrix}$$

where B^0 is assumed nonsingular. Note the appearance of 0^{10}; we are still assuming that there are no omitted variables in (5.1) and that A_1^1 is identified under true *a priori* restrictions.

By an analysis similar to that just given it is not hard to show that all inconsistencies in estimating A_1^1 on the assumption that the elements of x^2 are exogenous will go to zero as both the matrices E^{21} and $E^{20}(B^0)^{-1}E^{01}$ go to zero. The interpretation of this condition is as follows: E^{21}, as before, represents the direct effects of x^1 on x^2. Negligible inconsistency clearly requires that these effects be close to zero. The matrix $E^{20}(B^0)^{-1}E^{01}$, however, represents the indirect effects of x^1 on x^2 by way of the effects of x^1 on x^0 and x^0 on x^2. For negligible inconsistency, these effects must be close to zero also.[41] The latter condition may be interpreted further.

Assume that $E^{21} = 0$. If $E^{20} = 0$, (5.8) is block recursive as it stands and we have (5.2), the case already considered. In this case, we already know that $E^{21} = 0$ is a sufficient condition for consistency of all estimates. Now suppose that $E^{20} \neq 0$ but that $E^{01} = 0$. In this case, the system is block recursive also, but x^0 and x^2 must be written in the same block. This is the case mentioned above, where the additional variables explaing x^2 are exogenous to (5.1). Finally, $E^{20}(B^0)^{-1}E^{01}$ can be near zero, even if E^{20} and E^{01} both contain nonnegligible elements. The full condition for this is that the jth column of E^{20} can be nonnegligible only if the jth row of E^{01} is negligible. In other words, any variable in x^0 which has nonnegligible influence on the variables in x^2 must be influenced only negligibly by all variables in x^1.[41a]

We observe that, as usual, nothing in the above analysis would be affected if the *a priori* restrictions held only approximately. We conclude that inconsistencies will be near zero if all *a priori* restrictions are sufficiently close approximations *and* the above conditions hold.

We may now remove the last restriction and consider the general case where there are variables omitted from (5.1). Without loss of generality,

---

[41] Actually, inconsistencies can be negligible if the indirect and direct effects just cancel out, that is, if $(E^{21} - E^{20}(B^0)^{-1}E^{01}) = 0$. This could only happen by accident if the conditions named in the text are not satisfied; moreover, one could never tell whether it were nearly the case in practice. We thus disregard it.

[41a] Note that the full condition also implies that the system is nearly block recursive.

we may expand x^0 to include such variables and all variables explaining them and so forth until either a self-contained system is reached or all unexplained variables are exogenous to (5.1). For simplicity, we continue to assume the first of these alternatives.[42] x^0 now contains all variables needed to explain x^1 and x^2 and all variables needed to explain such variables, and to forth. Replacing 0^{10} in (5.8) by E^{10}, we have the *perfectly general* system:[43]

$$
(5.9) \qquad
\begin{bmatrix} u^0 \\ u^1 \\ u^2 \end{bmatrix}
=
\begin{bmatrix} B^0 & E^{01} & E^{02} \\ E^{10} & B^1 & G^1 \\ E^{20} & E^{21} & B^2 \end{bmatrix}
\begin{bmatrix} x^0 \\ x^1 \\ x^2 \end{bmatrix}.
$$

We continue to assume the B^i nonsingular; this is the general case.

It is easy to show that the conditions given for the near exogeneity of x^2 to the second block of equations in (5.9) and hence for negligible inconsistencies are unchanged. They are the same as those just discussed in the case of (5.8) (of course, the magnitudes of the inconsistencies involved may be different; the point is that the limit—zero— is the same in both cases). Further, as observed above, all inconsistencies will go to zero as both those conditions are satisfied *and* as all *a priori* restrictions are better approximations. It was shown in Section 3, above, however, that estimation of the first equation of the second block of (5.9) on the assumption that $E_1^{10} = 0$, that is, on the erroneous omission of x^0, is in general equivalent to estimation with erroneous *a priori* restrictions, and hence that as E_1^{10} goes to zero, so do the effects of this misspecification. It follows that all our theorems hold concurrently (a similar statement holds for Theorem 4). Thus, inconsistencies in the estimation of the first row of the second block of equations in (5.9) will be negligible if all of the following conditions hold:

(1) All *a priori* restrictions are close approximations.

(2) E_1^{10} is close to zero; that is, omitted variables have small coefficients (this is sufficient save on a space of measure zero).[44]

(3) E^{21} is near zero—that is, the endogenous variables have negligible direct effects on the assumed exogenous variables.

(4) $E^{20}(B^0)^{-1}E^{01}$ is close to zero—that is, the endogenous variables have negligible indirect effects on the assumed exogenous variables.

---

[42] The additional remarks necessary if the second alternative holds are given in Section 3, above.

[43] Perfectly general, save for the self-contained feature just discussed.

[44] Alternatively, if only estimates of B_1^1 and G_1^1 are required (greatly inconsistent estimates of E_1^{10} are acceptable), we might have:

(2′) The first row of the matrix $E^{10}(B^0)^{-1}[E^{01} \ E^{02}]$ is near zero, that is, any omitted variable with a nonnegligible coefficient is only negligibly influenced by the included variables.

If in addition, the other rows of E^{10} are near zero, so that all coefficients of omitted variables in the block of equations investigated are small, then conditions 2–4 imply that the system is nearly block recursive either as it stands or as rewritten with the first and third blocks of equations grouped together. In either case, analysis of the second block of equations is possible without explicit reference to the total system of which it is a part. *It is the existence of situations such as this which permits estimation of partial economic models*, indeed, which permits estimation of general economic models which are in turn embedded in models of the socio-physical universe. Liu's objections to simultaneous equation estimation are thus not generally damning. They cannot be taken as general objections, but as highly important criticisms which must be considered case by case in the light of how good the approximations involved are, not in the light of whether such approximations are exactly true or not.

Having said this much, however, we must go on to inquire whether the four conditions named above are easily fulfilled in practice. It seems clear that the first three are likely to be; any reasonably attentive investigator will pay fairly close attention to them. The fourth condition, on the other hand, is not so easily disposed of. It is very easy to overlook the possibility that the endogenous variables may have sizeable effects on the assumed exogenous variables by way of effects on a third set, which set may be exceedingly large. Therefore this is the point to which close attention must be paid in practice.

Finally, we may draw a further conclusion. Liu's objections, though not valid as stated, point to a redirection of some current work. The theorems in this paper speak only of consistency. They have no bearing on the variance of estimators nor on the small sample properties thereof. We have seen that different estimators can have different probability limits under misspecifications of the types discussed here. It is likely that their asymptotic variances are different and almost certain that their small sample properties are different. Even if the approximations involved in such misspecifications are very good (as they must be for negligible inconsistencies) one estimator may do better than another. That is, one estimator may be less sensitive than another to errors of this kind. The choice among estimators may therefore depend on their behavior under approximative misspecification, even though negligible inconsistencies are assured for all. To put it slightly differently, the goodness of a "good enough" approximation may depend, particularly in small samples, on the estimator used. Since the situations envisaged by Liu arise commonly (as he convincingly argues) it follows that, even though his specific conclusions are wrong, it is imperative that work be done along the lines indicated. In particular, a good deal of future work in Monte Carlo experiments should be directed towards discovering the small sample properties of various estimators under the types of approximative misspecification pointed out by Liu and discussed here.

6. CONJECTURES ON DYNAMICS

A good deal of this paper has been concerned with estimation problems in equation systems that are close to being block recursive. We have seen that such closeness is a sufficient condition to permit estimation of the usual kind to take place despite Liu's objections. Since such closeness is also a necessary condition, in general, it seems clear that a large part of the profession implicitly believes the world to be constructed in this way. Indeed, it is interesting that, considered from this point of view, Liu's objections to simultaneous equation estimation lie at the other extreme from the better known objections of Wold. Wold has insisted that the real world is recursive in the ordinary sense. Liu's objections, if they are to hold, must imply that the real world is not generally recursive in any sense. As just observed, the middle ground that the real world is nearly block recursive is implicitly held by those practicing simultaneous equation methods.

If the real world is nearly block recursive, however, it becomes interesting to consider the dynamics of block recursive systems. A first step in this direction is the consideration of the dynamics of a first degree difference or differential equation whose matrix is block triangular. Explicitly, consider the equation system:

$$(6.1) \qquad x(t) \equiv \begin{bmatrix} x^1(t) \\ x^2(t) \\ \vdots \\ x^N(t) \end{bmatrix} = \begin{bmatrix} B^1 & G^1 & & & \\ 0^{21} & B^2 & G^2 & & \\ \vdots & \vdots & \vdots & \ddots & \\ 0^{N1} & 0^{N2} & 0^{N3} & \cdots & B^N \end{bmatrix} \begin{bmatrix} x^1(t-1) \\ x^2(t-1) \\ \vdots \\ x^N(t-1) \end{bmatrix} \equiv Ax(t-1)$$

where the B^i are nonsingular. Clearly, the subsystems obtained by dropping the first k rows and columns of matrices and the corresponding x^i have the property that their dynamic properties may be investigated without regard for the remainder of the system.

Now consider matrices that are nearly block triangular, that is, matrices such as:

$$(6.2) \qquad A(\eta) = A + \eta D$$

where η is a positive scalar and D is any matrix with finite elements. We are interested in the dynamic properties of systems with such matrices for small η.

Now, a special case of (6.1) arises when all the G^i are zero. In this case, A is completely decomposable, and $A(\eta)$ is nearly completely decomposable for small η. For nearly completely decomposable matrices, H. Simon and A. Ando have proved an important theorem.[45] Crudely interpreted, this theorem states that equilibrium in a system with a nearly completely decomposable matrix (for small η) is approached in three stages. During the first stage the variables within each $x^i(t)$ adjust to reach equilibrium positions that are related to each other according to the limiting completely decomposable system—to the B^i. Following this, in the second stage, maintaining such equilibrium at all times, the variables adjust *en bloc*—the variables with each $x^i(t)$ moving together—until at the final stage, as in any linear system, the variables approach the rate of growth corresponding to the largest latent root. These properties permit Leontief-Hicks type aggregation of the variables within each $x^i(t)$ during and after the second stage.

It is clear that nearly completely decomposable matrices are a special case of nearly block triangular matrices. Indeed, the latter are far more apt to arise in practice. It follows that all our theorems about estimation inconsistency apply to nearly completely decomposable matrices. Further, it seems clear that the problem of estimation inconsistency and the problem of equilibrium adjustment are related here. Both the Simon-Ando Theorem and the theorems proved in this paper concern the strength of feed-back effects. It seems likely that this relationship is not accidental. We therefore offer the following conjectures for further investigation:

(1) The Simon-Ando Theorem holds, *mutatis mutandis*, for nearly block triangular and not just for nearly completely decomposable systems.[46]

(2) If the first conjecture is true, there exists a direct proof thereof which depends on the theorems on estimation here proved.

(3) If the first two conjectures are true, a general theorem exists concerning the relationship between negligible inconsistency for negligible misspecification on the one hand and the equilibrium properties of closely related systems on the other.

Since block triangular systems may be fairly generally encountered, the first conjecture alone is an important one. If linkages are far stronger one way than another between related markets, for example, this conjecture, if true, would provide valuable information about the dynamic properties of the whole system of markets considered and would allow easier handling of the solution of the system.

Massachusetts Institute of Technology

---

[45] [12].

[46] Since this was written, Professor Ando and I have proved that this conjecture is indeed correct. The precise theorem and proof will be given in a later paper.

380 FRANKLIN M. FISHER

REFERENCES

[1] DANTZIG, G. B.: "Upper Bounds, Secondary Constraints, and Block Triangularity in Linear Programming," *Econometrica*, Vol. 23, No. 2 (April, 1955), pp. 174–183.

[2] FISHER, F. M.: "Generalization of the Rank and Order Conditions for Identifiability," *Econometrica*, Vol. 27, No. 3 (July, 1959), pp. 431–447.

[3] GOODWIN, R. M.: "Dynamical Coupling with Especial Reference to Markets Having Production Lags," *Econometrica*, Vol. 15, No. 3 (July, 1947), pp. 181–204.

[4] HARBERGER, A. C.: "On the Estimation of Economic Parameters," Cowles Commission Discussion Paper: Economics No. 2088, 1953 (unpublished).

[5] KOOPMANS, T. C., H. RUBIN, AND R. B. LEIPNIK: "Measuring the Equation Systems of Dynamic Economics," Chapter II in *Statistical Inference in Dynamic Economic Models* (T. C. Koopmans, ed.), New York, John Wiley and Sons, 1950 (Cowles Commission Monograph No. 10).

[6] LINTNER, J.: "Dividends, Earnings and Retained Earnings, Common Stock Prices and Expectations," forthcoming supplement to the *Review of Economics and Statistics*.

[7] LIU, T. C.: "A Simple Forecasting Model for the U.S. Economy," International Monetary Fund, *Staff Papers*, Aug., 1955, pp. 434–466.

[8] ———: "Structural Estimation and Forecasting: A Critique of the Cowles Commission Method," *Tsing Hua Journal*, forthcoming.

[9] ———: "Underidentification, Structural Estimation, and Forecasting," *Econometrica*, Vol. 28, No. 4 (Oct., 1960), pp. 855–865.

[10] SARGAN, J. D.: "The Estimation of Economic Relationships Using Instrumental Variables," *Econometrica*, Vol. 26, No. 3 (July, 1958), pp. 393–415.

[11] SIMON, H. A.: "Causal Ordering and Identifiability," Chapter 3 in *Studies in Econometric Method* (W. C. Hood and T. C. Koopmans, eds.), New York, John Wiley and Sons, 1953 (Cowles Commission Monograph No. 14); reprinted as Chapter 1 in H. A. Simon, *Models of Man*, New York, John Wiley and Sons, 1957.

[12] SIMON, H. A., AND A. ANDO: "Aggregation of Variables in Dynamic Systems," *Econometrica*, this issue.

[13] SOLOW, R. M.: "On the Structure of Linear Models," *Econometrica*, Vol. 20, No. 1 (Jan., 1952), pp. 29–46.

[14] STROTZ, R. H.: "Interdependence As a Specification Error," *Econometrica*, Vol. 28, No. 2 (April, 1960), pp. 428–442.

[15] STROTZ, R. H., AND H. WOLD: "Recursive *Vs.* Nonrecursive Systems: An Attempt at Synthesis," *Econometrica*, Vol. 28, No. 2 (April, 1960), pp. 417–427.

[16] THEIL, H.: *Economic Forecasts and Policy*, Amsterdam, North-Holland Publishing Co., 1958.

[17] ———: "Specification Errors and the Estimation of Economic Relationships," *Review of the International Statistical Institute*, Vol. 25, 1957, pp. 41–51.

[18] VALAVANIS, S.: *Econometrics*, New York, McGraw-Hill Book Company, 1959.

[19] WOLD, H., in association with L. JURÉEN: *Demand Analysis*, New York, John Wiley and Sons, 1953.

[20] WOLD, H., AND P. FAXÉR: "On the Specification Error in Regression Analysis," *Annals of Mathematical Statistics*, Vol. 28, No. 1 (Mar., 1957) pp. 265–267.

Econometrica, Vol. 30, No. 1 (January, 1962)

THREE-STAGE LEAST SQUARES:
SIMULTANEOUS ESTIMATION OF SIMULTANEOUS EQUATIONS

By Arnold Zellner and H. Theil

1. INTRODUCTION

In simple though approximate terms, the two-stage least squares method of estimating a structural equation consists of two steps, the first of which serves to estimate the moment matrix of the reduced-form disturbances and the second to estimate the coefficients of one single structural equation after its jointly dependent variables are "purified" by means of the moment matrix just mentioned. The three-stage least squares method, which is developed in this paper, goes one step further by using the two-stage least squares estimated moment matrix of the structural disturbances to estimate all coefficients of the entire system simultaneously. The method has full-information characteristics to the extent that, if the moment matrix of the structural disturbances is not diagonal (that is, if the structural disturbances have nonzero "contemporaneous" covariances), the estimation of the coefficients of any identifiable equation gains in efficiency as soon as there are other equations that are over-identified. Further, the method can take account of restrictions on parameters in different structural equations. And it is very simple computationally, apart from the inversion of one big matrix.

The order of discussion is as follows. The essential ideas of the method are explained in Section 2, after which the asymptotic moment matrix of the estimator is derived in Section 3. When there are just-identified equations in the system, the computations can be simplified; this is explained in Section 4. Section 5 contains a numerical example as well as a directory of computations.

Section 6 gives some concluding remarks. The reader who is interested in results only is advised to read Section 4.2 immediately after Section 2, and then to proceed to Section 5.

2. THE THREE-STAGE LEAST SQUARES METHOD

2.1. *Description of the System.* It will be assumed throughout that we are dealing with a complete system of M linear stochastic structural equations in M jointly dependent variables and Λ predetermined variables; furthermore, that this system can be solved for the jointly dependent variables (so that the reduced form exists); finally, that the disturbances of the structural equations (the structural disturbances) have zero mean, are serially independent, and are "homoscedastic" in the sense that their variances and "contemporaneous" covariances are finite and constant through time. This contemporaneous covariance matrix will be supposed to be nonsingular.[1]

Let T be the number of observations. Then any structural equation, say the μth, can be written in the following form for all observations combined:

$$(2.1) \qquad y_\mu = Y_\mu \gamma_\mu + X_\mu \beta_\mu + u_\mu = Z_\mu \delta_\mu + u_\mu .$$

where y_μ is the column vector of observations on one of the jointly dependent variables occurring in that equation (usually we write the variable "to be explained" on the left); Y_μ is the $T \times m_\mu$ matrix of values taken by the explanatory dependent variables of that equation; γ_μ is the corresponding coefficient vector; X_μ is the $T \times l_\mu$ matrix of values taken by the explanatory predetermined variables; β_μ is its coefficient vector; u_μ is the column vector of T structural disturbances; and

$$(2.2) \qquad Z_\mu = [Y_\mu \quad X_\mu] ; \qquad \delta_\mu = \begin{bmatrix} \gamma_\mu \\ \beta_\mu \end{bmatrix} .$$

Further, we write X for the $T \times \Lambda$ matrix of values taken by all (Λ) predetermined variables, and we shall suppose that its rank is Λ. Our objective is to estimate the parameter vectors δ_μ, and for this purpose it will be supposed that all equations are identifiable.[1] This implies

$$(2.3) \qquad \Lambda \geqslant n_\mu = m_\mu + l_\mu \qquad\qquad (\mu = 1, \ldots, M) ,$$

where n_μ is the total number of coefficients to be estimated in the μth equation.

2.2. *Two-Stage Least Squares Applied to a Single Equation.* Premultiplying (2.1) by X', we obtain

$$(2.4) \qquad X'y_\mu = X'Z_\mu \delta_\mu + X'u_\mu ,$$

---

[1] See Section 4 for a generalization.

which is a system of Λ equations involving n_μ parameters (δ_μ) and a "disturbance vector" $(X'u_\mu)$ with zero mean. In the special case $\Lambda = n_\mu$ (just-identification) it is customary to estimate δ_μ according to

$$(2.5) \qquad d_\mu = (X'Z_\mu)^{-1}X'y_\mu \ ;$$

that is, one replaces δ_μ by its estimator d_μ in (2.4), and simultaneously $X'u_\mu$ by its expectation.[2] In the more usual case where $\Lambda > n_\mu$, we can also use (2.4) but in a slightly more complicated manner. Assuming that the predetermined variables are all "fixed" variables, we find for the covariance matrix of the disturbance vector $X'u_\mu$:

$$(2.6) \qquad V(X'u_\mu) = E(X'u_\mu u'_\mu X) = \sigma_{\mu\mu}X'X \ ,$$

where $\sigma_{\mu\mu}$ is the variance of each of the T disturbances of the μth structural equation. Then, applying Aitken's method of generalized least squares to (2.4),[3] we obtain

$$(2.7) \qquad Z'_\mu X(\sigma_{\mu\mu}X'X)^{-1}X'y_\mu = Z'_\mu X(\sigma_{\mu\mu}X'X)^{-1}X'Z_\mu d_\mu \ ,$$

from which we derive the two-stage least squares estimator

$$(2.8) \qquad d_\mu = [Z'_\mu X(X'X)^{-1}X'Z_\mu]^{-1}Z'_\mu X(X'X)^{-1}X'y_\mu \ ,$$

which reduces to (2.5) in the special case when $X'Z_\mu$ is square and nonsingular. The covariance matrix of d_μ is

$$(2.9) \qquad V(d_\mu) = \sigma_{\mu\mu}[Z'_\mu X(X'X)^{-1}X'Z_\mu]^{-1} + o(1/T) \ ,$$

where $o(1/T)$ stands for terms of higher order of smallness than $1/T$.

2.3. *Three-Stage Least Squares Applied to a Complete System.* The crucial

[2] It is perhaps useful to add that (2.5) is a far simpler method of computing the point estimates of the coefficients in the just-identified case than the method which is sometimes recommended and which involves estimation of reduced-form coefficients, followed by transformations from the reduced form to the structure. The only thing one has to do is to compute the second-order moments of the predetermined variables of the system on the one hand and the variables of the equation on the other, followed by the inversion of $X'Z_\mu = [X'Y_\mu \ X'X_\mu]$ and postmultiplication by $X'y_\mu$.

[3] Aitken's method [1] works as follows. Let $r = R\theta + \varepsilon$ be the equation whose coefficient vector θ has to be estimated, r being a column vector of observations on the dependent variable, R the matrix of values taken by the explanatory variables, and ε the disturbance vector. Let $E(\varepsilon) = 0$ and $V(\varepsilon) = \Omega$ where Ω is a positive-definite matrix, than $\hat\theta = (R'\Omega^{-1}R)^{-1}R'\Omega^{-1}r$ is the generalized least squares estimator of θ according to Aitken, and $V(\hat\theta) = (R'\Omega^{-1}R)^{-1}$ if the elements of R are fixed. In the present case $r = X'y_\mu$, $R = X'Z_\mu$, $\theta = \delta_\mu$, $\varepsilon = X'u_\mu$, $\Omega = \sigma_{\mu\mu}X'X$. It is not true here that the elements of $R = X'Z_\mu$ are fixed (due to the presence of Y_μ in Z_μ); which is the reason why $(R'\Omega^{-1}R)^{-1}$ yields only the asymptotic covariance matrix (see (2.9)).

idea of three-stage least squares is that (2.4) can be written in the following form for all equations combined:

$$(2.10) \quad \begin{bmatrix} X'y_1 \\ X'y_2 \\ \cdot \\ \cdot \\ \cdot \\ X'y_M \end{bmatrix} = \begin{bmatrix} X'Z_1 & 0 & \ldots & 0 \\ 0 & X'Z_2 & \ldots & 0 \\ \cdot & \cdot & & \cdot \\ \cdot & \cdot & & \cdot \\ \cdot & \cdot & & \cdot \\ 0 & 0 & \ldots & X'Z_M \end{bmatrix} \begin{bmatrix} \delta_1 \\ \delta_2 \\ \cdot \\ \cdot \\ \cdot \\ \delta_M \end{bmatrix} + \begin{bmatrix} X'u_1 \\ X'u_2 \\ \cdot \\ \cdot \\ \cdot \\ X'u_M \end{bmatrix},$$

which is a system of ΛM equations involving

$$(2.11) \qquad n = \sum_{\mu=1}^{M} n_\mu$$

parameters. Let us write δ for the n-element column vector of parameters on the right of (2.10). Then we can apply generalized least squares to (2.10) to estimate all elements of δ simultaneously. For this purpose we need the covariance matrix of the disturbance vector of (2.10):

$$(2.12) \quad V \begin{bmatrix} X'u_1 \\ X'u_2 \\ \cdot \\ \cdot \\ \cdot \\ X'u_M \end{bmatrix} = \begin{bmatrix} \sigma_{11}X'X & \sigma_{12}X'X & \ldots & \sigma_{1M}X'X \\ \sigma_{21}X'X & \sigma_{22}X'X & \ldots & \sigma_{2M}X'X \\ \cdot & \cdot & & \cdot \\ \cdot & \cdot & & \cdot \\ \cdot & \cdot & & \cdot \\ \sigma_{M1}X'X & \sigma_{M2}X'X & \ldots & \sigma_{MM}X'X \end{bmatrix},$$

where $\sigma_{\mu\mu'}$ is the contemporaneous covariance of the structural disturbances of the μth and the μ'th equation:

$$(2.13) \qquad E(u_\mu u'_{\mu'}) = \begin{bmatrix} \sigma_{\mu\mu'} & 0 & \ldots & 0 \\ 0 & \sigma_{\mu\mu'} & \ldots & 0 \\ \cdot & \cdot & & \cdot \\ \cdot & \cdot & & \cdot \\ 0 & 0 & \ldots & \sigma_{\mu\mu'} \end{bmatrix} = \sigma_{\mu\mu'} I,$$

I being the unit matrix of order T. Also, we need the inverse of the covariance matrix (2.12):

$$(2.14) \quad V^{-1} \begin{bmatrix} X'u_1 \\ X'u_2 \\ \cdot \\ \cdot \\ \cdot \\ X'u_M \end{bmatrix} = \begin{bmatrix} \sigma^{11}(X'X)^{-1} & \sigma^{12}(X'X)^{-1} & \ldots & \sigma^{1M}(X'X)^{-1} \\ \sigma^{21}(X'X)^{-1} & \sigma^{22}(X'X)^{-1} & \ldots & \sigma^{2M}(X'X)^{-1} \\ \cdot & \cdot & & \cdot \\ \cdot & \cdot & & \cdot \\ \cdot & \cdot & & \cdot \\ \sigma^{M1}(X'X)^{-1} & \sigma^{M2}(X'X)^{-1} & \ldots & \sigma^{MM}(X'X)^{-1} \end{bmatrix},$$

where $\sigma^{\mu\mu'}$ is an element of the inverse of the contemporaneous covariance matrix of the structural disturbances:

$$(2.15) \qquad [\sigma^{\mu\mu'}] = [\sigma_{\mu\mu'}]^{-1}.$$

A straightforward application of generalized least squares gives then the following result: the two-stage column vector $Z'_\mu X(\sigma_{\mu\mu}X'X)^{-1}X'y_\mu$ on the left of (2.7) is replaced by

$$\begin{bmatrix} \sigma^{11}Z_1'X(X'X)^{-1}X'y_1 & +\ldots+ & \sigma^{1M}Z_1'X(X'X)^{-1}X'y_M \\ \hdotsfor{3} \\ \sigma^{M1}Z_M'X(X'X)^{-1}X'y_1 + & \ldots + & \sigma^{MM}Z_M'X(X'X)^{-1}X'y_M \end{bmatrix};$$

and the two-stage $n_\mu \times n_\mu$ matrix $Z_\mu'X(\sigma_{\mu\mu}X'X)^{-1}X'Z_\mu$ on the right of (2.7) is replaced by the $n \times n$ matrix,

$$\begin{bmatrix} \sigma^{11}Z_1'X(X'X)^{-1}X'Z_1 & \ldots & \sigma^{1M}Z_1'X(X'X)^{-1}X'Z_M \\ \vdots & & \vdots \\ \sigma^{M1}Z_M'X(X'X)^{-1}X'Z_1 & \ldots & \sigma^{MM}Z_M'X(X'X)^{-1}X'Z_M \end{bmatrix}.$$

These matrices involve σ's which are generally unknown. We recommend that they be replaced by their two-stage least squares estimates, to be denoted by $s^{\mu\mu'}$. Thus, the three-stage least squares estimator is defined as

$$(2.16) \quad \hat{\delta} = \begin{bmatrix} s^{11}Z_1'X(X'X)^{-1}X'Z_1 & \ldots & s^{1M}Z_1'X(X'X)^{-1}X'Z_M \\ \vdots & & \vdots \\ s^{M1}Z_M'X(X'X)^{-1}X'Z_1 & \ldots & s^{MM}Z_M'X(X'X)^{-1}X'Z_M \end{bmatrix}^{-1}$$

$$\times \begin{bmatrix} \sum s^{1\mu}Z_1'X(X'X)^{-1}X'y_\mu \\ \vdots \\ \sum s^{M\mu}Z_M'X(X'X)^{-1}X'y_\mu \end{bmatrix},$$

where the summations in the right hand column vector extend over $\mu = 1$, ..., M. As will be shown in Section 3, the moment matrix of $\hat{\delta}$ is

$$(2.17) \quad V(\hat{\delta}) = \begin{bmatrix} s^{11}Z_1'X(X'X)^{-1}X'Z_1 & \ldots & s^{1M}Z_1'X(X'X)^{-1}X'Z_M \\ \vdots & & \vdots \\ s^{M1}Z_M'X(X'X)^{-1}X'Z_1 & \ldots & s^{MM}Z_M'X(X'X)^{-1}X'Z_M \end{bmatrix}^{-1} + o(1/T).$$

It will be observed that there is a gain in asymptotic efficiency compared with two-stage least squares only if $[\sigma_{\mu\mu'}]$ is not diagonal; if it is diagonal, two-and three-stage least squares are identical, because the non-diagonal blocks of (2.17) are then zero and $\sigma^{\mu\mu} = 1/\sigma_{\mu\mu}$.

3. THE ASYMPTOTIC MOMENT MATRIX OF THREE-STAGE LEAST SQUARES

3.1. *Derivation of the Moment Matrix.* The three-stage least squares estimator $\hat{\delta}$ as defined in (2.16) differs in two respects from a straightforward application of Aitken's procedure. First, $\hat{\delta}$ is based on the $s^{\mu\mu'}$, which are the two-stage least squares estimates of the $\sigma^{\mu\mu'}$ which we would really need for this procedure. Secondly, some of the "explanatory variables" of the relation (2.10) to which this procedure is applied are correlated with the disturbances of that relation. This is so because each $X'Z_\mu$ contains a $X'Y_\mu$ as a submatrix, and the Y_μ of this product is correlated with the u's which enter into the disturbance vector of (2.10).

To handle these two difficulties we shall employ a special notation (which will be used in this section only). We shall write (2.10) and (2.12) in the form:

$$(3.1) \qquad v = W\delta + \varepsilon \; ; \qquad E(\varepsilon\varepsilon') = \Omega \, ,$$

where v is the left hand column vector of (2.10), W the $\Lambda M \times n$ matrix on the right, ε the disturbance vector of (2.10), and Ω its covariance matrix as specified in (2.12). It is easily verified that the elements Ω are of $O(T)$, and those of v and W are of $O(T)$ in probability. Since Ω is unknown due to the σ's on which it depends, it is replaced in the three-stage procedure by

$$(3.2) \qquad \Omega_e = \Omega + \Lambda_1 \, ,$$

where the Ω_e-elements are of $O(T)$ and those of Λ_1 are of $O(T)^{\frac{1}{2}}$ in probability. The last statement follows from the fact that the two-stage least squares estimates, $s^{\mu\mu'}$, on which Ω_e is based, differ from the corresponding $\sigma^{\mu\mu'}$ by an amount which is of $O(T^{-\frac{1}{2}})$ in probability. The $\sigma^{\mu\mu'}$ themselves being of $O(T^0) = O(1)$.

In the present notation, the three-stage least squares estimator takes the form[4]

$$\delta = (W'\Omega_e^{-1}W)^{-1}W'\Omega_e^{-1}v \, ,$$

from which we see immediately that its sampling error is

$$(3.3) \qquad \hat\delta - \delta = (W'\Omega_e^{-1}W)^{-1}W'\Omega_e^{-1}\varepsilon \, .$$

Applying (3.2), we find that the inverse Ω_e^{-1} can be written as

$$(3.4) \qquad \Omega_e^{-1} = (\Omega + \Lambda_1)^{-1} = \Omega^{-1} + \Lambda_2 \, ,$$

where Λ_2 is of $O(T^{-1\frac{1}{2}})$ in probability because Ω is of $O(T)$ and Λ_1 is of $O(T^{\frac{1}{2}})$ in probability.

Next, we consider W, the matrix of values taken by the "explanatory variables" of (2.10). Each of its diagonal blocks ($X'Z_\mu$, say) can be decomposed into a part involving predetermined variables only ($X'X_\mu$) and a part containing jointly dependent variables ($X'Y_\mu$). Hence, if we write $\bar W$ for the conditional expectation of W (given the X-elements), and write

$$(3.5) \qquad W = \bar W + \Lambda_3 \, ,$$

[4] Note that $(W'C^{-1}W)\,W'C^{-1}v$ defines a linear class of estimators. With $C = I$, we have the two-stage least squares estimator, and, with $C = \Omega_e$, we obtain the three-stage least squares estimator which, as is shown below, is linear in v to within an error which is of $O(T^{-1})$ in probability.

then $\varDelta_3$ is a matrix which consists largely of zeros except that it contains submatrices in the diagonal blocks of the type X' multiplied by the matrix of reduced-form disturbances corresponding to Y_μ. Hence the $\varDelta_3$-elements are of $O(T^{\frac{1}{2}})$ in probability, as against the $\bar{W}$-elements which are of $O(T)$. Combining (3.4) and (3.5), we then find

$$(3.6) \qquad W'\Omega_e^{-1} = (\bar{W} + \varDelta_3)'(\Omega^{-1} + \varDelta_2) = \bar{W}'\Omega^{-1} + \varDelta_4 ,$$

where $\bar{W}'\Omega^{-1}$ is of $O(1)$ and $\varDelta_4$ is of $O(T^{-\frac{1}{2}})$ in probability. Similarly:

$$W'\Omega_e^{-1}W = (\bar{W}'\Omega^{-1} + \varDelta_4)(\bar{W} + \varDelta_3) = \bar{W}'\Omega^{-1}\bar{W} + \varDelta_5 ,$$

where $\bar{W}'\Omega^{-1}\bar{W}$ is of $O(T)$ and $\varDelta_5$ is of $O(T^{\frac{1}{2}})$ in probability. Hence:

$$(3.7) \qquad (W'\Omega_e^{-1}W)^{-1} = (\bar{W}'\Omega^{-1}\bar{W} + \varDelta_5)^{-1} = (\bar{W}'\Omega^{-1}\bar{W})^{-1} + \varDelta_6 ,$$

where $(\bar{W}'\Omega^{-1}\bar{W})^{-1}$ is of $O(T^{-1})$ and $\varDelta_6$ is of $O(T^{-1\frac{1}{2}})$ in probability. On combining (3.6) and (3.7) we find

$$(W'\Omega_e^{-1}W)^{-1}W'\Omega_e^{-1} = [(\bar{W}'\Omega^{-1}\bar{W})^{-1} + \varDelta_6](\bar{W}'\Omega^{-1} + \varDelta_4)$$
$$= (\bar{W}'\Omega^{-1}\bar{W})^{-1}\bar{W}'\Omega^{-1} + \varDelta_7 ,$$

where $(\bar{W}'\Omega^{-1}\bar{W})^{-1}\bar{W}'\Omega^{-1}$ is of $O(T^{-1})$ and $\varDelta_7$ is of $O(T^{-1\frac{1}{2}})$ in probability. On combining this with (3.3), we finally obtain the following expression for the sampling error of $\hat{\delta}$:

$$(3.8) \qquad \hat{\delta} - \delta = (\bar{W}'\Omega^{-1}\bar{W})^{-1}\bar{W}'\Omega^{-1}\varepsilon + \varDelta_7\varepsilon .$$

The proof of the covariance result (2.17) is now virtually complete, for the first term on the right of (3.8) is the leading term of the sampling error and of $O(T^{-\frac{1}{2}})$ in probability (due to the fact that ε is a vector of random variables which are of $O(T^{\frac{1}{2}})$ in probability, ε having zero mean and covariance matrix Ω which is of $O(T)$), and the second term is of $O(T^{-1})$ in probability.[5] If we then postmultiply the sampling error by its own transpose, the leading term is

$$(\bar{W}'\Omega^{-1}\bar{W})^{-1}\bar{W}'\Omega^{-1}\varepsilon\varepsilon'\Omega^{-1}\bar{W}(\bar{W}'\Omega^{-1}\bar{W})^{-1} ,$$

the expectation of which is $(\bar{W}'\Omega^{-1}\bar{W})^{-1}$. This is of $O(T^{-1})$ and all other terms are of higher order of smallness. Hence $(\bar{W}'\Omega^{-1}\bar{W})^{-1}$ is the asymptotic covariance matrix of $\hat{\delta}$. In (2.17) the expression $(W'\Omega_e^{-1}W)^{-1}$ has been in-

---

[5] Since $T^{\frac{1}{2}}(\bar{W}'\Omega^{-1}\bar{W})^{-1}\bar{W}'\Omega^{-1}\varepsilon$ is asymptotically normally distributed under rather general stochastic conditions and since plim $T^{\frac{1}{2}}\varDelta_7\varepsilon = 0$, the asymptotic distribution of $T^{\frac{1}{2}}(\hat{\delta} - \delta)$ is normal; see the convergence theorem in [2, p. 254]. A similar argument can be employed to establish the asymptotic normality of the two-stage least squares estimator.

troduced as the leading term, but it follows immediately from (3.7) that these two matrices are identical to $O(T^{-1})$.[6]

3.2. *What Do We Gain?* The mere fact that two-stage least squares is not identical with three-stage least squares implies that the former method is less efficient. It is instructive, however, to obtain an explicit expression for the gain in efficiency obtained by the three-stage method. Since we have only an illustrative purpose in mind, we shall confine ourselves to a two-equation system, in which case the covariance matrix of three-stage least squares is equal to the inverse of

$$
(3.9) \qquad
\begin{bmatrix}
\sigma^{11} Z_1' X (X'X)^{-1} X' Z_1 & \sigma^{12} Z_1' X (X'X)^{-1} X' Z_2 \\
\sigma^{21} Z_2' X (X'X)^{-1} X' Z_1 & \sigma^{22} Z_2' X (X'X)^{-1} X' Z_2
\end{bmatrix}
$$

(apart from higher-order terms), whereas the covariance matrix of the two-stage least squares estimator of the first equation is equal to the inverse of

$$
(3.10) \qquad (1/\sigma_{11}) Z_1' X (X'X)^{-1} X' Z_1
$$

(again, apart from higher-order terms). Hence our objective is to compare the inverse of (3.10) with the leading $n_1 \times n_1$ submatrix of the inverse of (3.9), this submatrix being the moment matrix of the three-stage estimator of the coefficient vector of the first equation.

Since X has rank Λ, there exists a matrix K which is square of order and rank Λ such that $K'K = (X'X)^{-1}$. We can then write (3.9) and (3.10) in the form

$$
\begin{bmatrix}
\sigma^{11} A_1' A_1 & \sigma^{12} A_1' A_2 \\
\sigma^{21} A_2' A_1 & \sigma^{22} A_2' A_2
\end{bmatrix}
\quad \text{and} \quad (1/\sigma_{11}) A_1' A_1 ,
$$

respectively, where $A_\mu = KX' Z_\mu$ for $\mu = 1, 2$. Hence A_1 is of order $\Lambda \times n_1$ and rank n_1, and A_2 of order $\Lambda \times n_2$ and rank n_2. Furthermore, we write the $\sigma_{\mu\mu'}$-matrix in the form

$$
\begin{bmatrix}
\sigma_1^2 & \varrho \sigma_1 \sigma_2 \\
\varrho \sigma_1 \sigma_2 & \sigma_2^2
\end{bmatrix} ,
$$

[6] Note that this proof is so straightforward only because the number of rows and columns of the fundamental matrices involved (W, Ω, and ε) is independent of T. If these numbers would depend on T, the situation becomes entirely different: the elements of a product such as AB then have an order of magnitude in T which is no longer determined by the orders of the A- and B-elements, but also by the number of columns of A (or rows of B), which then depends on T, too.

so that its inverse becomes

$$
\begin{bmatrix}
\dfrac{1}{\sigma_1^2(1-\varrho^2)} & \dfrac{-\varrho}{\sigma_1\sigma_2(1-\varrho^2)} \\[2ex]
\dfrac{-\varrho}{\sigma_1\sigma_2(1-\varrho^2)} & \dfrac{1}{\sigma_2^2(1-\varrho^2)}
\end{bmatrix}.
$$

If we apply the notation of the preceding paragraph to (3.9) and (3.10), we observe, first, that (3.10) becomes $Q = (1/\sigma_1^2)A_1'A_1$. Hence, the moment matrix of two-stage least squares is $Q^{-1} = \sigma_1^2(A_1'A_1)^{-1}$. Secondly, we note that (3.9) becomes

$$
\begin{bmatrix}
\dfrac{1}{\sigma_1^2(1-\varrho^2)}A_1'A_1 & \dfrac{-\varrho}{\sigma_1\sigma_2(1-\varrho^2)}A_1'A_2 \\[2ex]
\dfrac{-\varrho}{\sigma_1\sigma_2(1-\varrho^2)}A_2'A_1 & \dfrac{1}{\sigma_2^2(1-\varrho^2)}A_2'A_2
\end{bmatrix},
$$

so that the leading $n_1 \times n_1$ submatrix of its inverse is itself the inverse of

$$
(3.11) \qquad Q^* = \frac{1}{\sigma_1^2(1-\varrho^2)}A_1'A_1 - \frac{\varrho^2}{\sigma_1^2(1-\varrho^2)}A_1'A_2(A_2'A_2)^{-1}A_2'A_1 .
$$

Thus, the three-stage moment matrix of the first equation is Q^{*-1}, whereas the two-stage moment matrix is $Q^{-1} = \sigma_1^2(A_1'A_1)^{-1}$.

Suppose now that the second equation is just-identified. This implies $\varLambda = n_2$, so that A_2 is square. Supposing that it is also nonsingular, we can write

$$
A_1'A_2(A_2'A_2)^{-1}A_2'A_1 = A_1'A_2A_2^{-1}A_2'^{-1}A_2'A_1 = A_1'A_1 ,
$$

from which it follows that (3.11) can be simplified to $Q^* = (1/\sigma_1^2)A_1'A_1 = Q$. In words, this means that if the second equation is just-identified, the three-stage moment matrix of the first equation is identical with its two-stage moment matrix. Hence we gain nothing for the first equation in this case.

But suppose that the second equation is over-identified, so that $\varLambda > n_2$ in which case A_2 has more rows than columns. In that case we can write

$$
A_1'A_2(A_2'A_2)^{-1}A_2'A_1 = A_1'A_1 - A^* .
$$

A^* is a positive semi-definite matrix, for the left hand matrix product can be interpreted as the matrix of sums of squares and products of the "systematic part" of the least squares regression of A_1 on A_2, while $A_1'A_1$ is the matrix of sums of squares and products of the "dependent variables" (arranged in the A_1-matrix) themselves; and, therefore, A^* is the matrix of sums of squares and products of the corresponding least squares residuals. It follows that (3.11) can be written in the form

$$(3.12) \qquad Q^* = \frac{1}{\sigma_1^2} A_1' A_1 + \frac{\varrho^2}{\sigma_1^2(1-\varrho^2)} A^* = Q + \frac{\varrho^2}{\sigma_1^2(1-\varrho^2)} A^*.$$

This shows that Q^* is obtained by adding a positive semi-definite matrix to Q. Since Q and Q^* are symmetric and Q is positive-definite, this implies that the determinant of Q^* is larger than or equal to that of Q.[7] Hence the determinant of Q^{*-1} is smaller than (or equal to) that of Q^{-1}. But the determinants of Q^{*-1} and Q^{-1} are the generalized variances of the three-stage and two-stage least squares estimators, respectively; therefore, the former generalized variance is smaller than the latter except when $\varrho = 0$ or $A^* = 0$, in which case the two are equal.[8]

4. PROBLEMS OF IDENTIFICATION AND RELATED ISSUES

4.1. *Analysis.* It has been assumed that the matrix $[\sigma_{\mu\mu'}]$ is nonsingular; but when there are definitional equations or identities or, more generally, equations that hold exactly with disturbances that are identically zero, this assumption is no longer tenable since each such equation causes one row and one column of $[\sigma_{\mu\mu'}]$ to be zero. This is not a serious problem, however, because the coefficients of such equations are in general known (usually 1, —1, or 0), so that there is no need to estimate them. The recommendation is simply to delete such equations in the three-stage procedure.[9]

Another problem is that of the under-identified equations. Their two-stage least squares estimates do not exist, and, therefore, each such equation implies that one row and one column of $[\sigma_{\mu\mu'}]$ cannot be estimated. Our recommendation is to delete such equations and to confine the three-stage procedure to identifiable equations.[10]

Furthermore, it is useful to distinguish between just and over-identified equations. The analysis of Section 3.2 shows for the two-equation case that the estimation of the coefficients of one equation is improved if the other equation is over-identified, and is not improved if the latter is just-identified; and a result of this kind holds in fact more generally. Let us write p for the number of over-identified equations and hence $M-p$ for that of the just-

---

[7] See, e.g., Rao [**4**, p. 26].

[8] In a similar way, it can be shown that the variances of the three-stage coefficient estimators are smaller than the corresponding two-stage variances.

[9] It is sometimes recommended that such equations be eliminated by a substitution of variables. This is superfluous and makes the computations more complicated than necessary.

[10] But see Section 6 under (2).

identified equations. Further, let us arrange them such that the former equations have numbers $1, \ldots, p$ and the latter $p+1, \ldots, M$; for reasons of typographical simplification we write q for $p+1$. Then the moment matrix of the three-stage least squares estimates for all M equations combined can be written in partitioned form:

$$(4.1) \qquad \begin{bmatrix} G_1 & G_3 \\ G_3' & G_2 \end{bmatrix}^{-1} = \begin{bmatrix} H_1 & H_3 \\ H_3' & H_2 \end{bmatrix},$$

where the index 1 refers to the set of over-identified equations, 2 to the just-identified equations, and 3 to a mixture of both sets:

$$\begin{aligned} G_1 &= \begin{bmatrix} \sigma^{11} A_1' A_1 & \ldots & \sigma^{1p} A_1' A_p \\ \cdots\cdots\cdots\cdots\cdots\cdots\cdots \\ \sigma^{p1} A_p' A_1 & \ldots & \sigma^{pp} A_p' A_p \end{bmatrix}, \quad G_2 = \begin{bmatrix} \sigma^{qq} A_q' A_q & \ldots & \sigma^{qM} A_q' A_M \\ \cdots\cdots\cdots\cdots\cdots\cdots\cdots\cdots \\ \sigma^{Mq} A_M' A_q & \ldots & \sigma^{MM} A_M' A_M \end{bmatrix}, \\[2mm] &\qquad\qquad G_3 = \begin{bmatrix} \sigma^{1q} A_1' A_q & \ldots & \sigma^{1M} A_1' A_M \\ \cdots\cdots\cdots\cdots\cdots\cdots\cdots \\ \sigma^{pq} A_p' A_q & \ldots & \sigma^{pM} A_p' A_M \end{bmatrix}, \end{aligned}$$

(4.2)

the A_μ being equal to $KX'Z_\mu$ where K is square and such that $K'K = (X'X)^{-1}$ as in Section 3.2. By partitioned multiplication we obtain from (4.1):

$$(4.3) \qquad \begin{aligned} H_1 &= (G_1 - G_3 G_2^{-1} G_3')^{-1} \ ; \\ H_3' &= - G_2^{-1} G_3' H_1 \ ; \\ H_2 &= G_2^{-1} + G_2^{-1} G_3' H_1 G_3 G_2^{-1} \ . \end{aligned}$$

Our first objective will be H_1, which is the moment matrix of the three-stage coefficients of the over-identified equations. We shall show that *we shall arrive at precisely the same moment matrix if the three-stage estimation procedure is confined to this group of over-identified equations*, i.e., if the estimation is carried out under complete disregard of the just-identified equations. Consider then G_2^{-1}, which plays a role in the H_1-equation of (4.3). Taking account of the fact that all A_μ are square for $\mu \geqslant q$, we find

$$(4.4) \qquad G_2^{-1} = \begin{bmatrix} \tau_{qq} A_q^{-1} A_q'^{-1} & \ldots & \tau_{qM} A_q^{-1} A_M'^{-1} \\ \cdots\cdots\cdots\cdots\cdots\cdots\cdots\cdots \\ \tau_{Mq} A_M^{-1} A_q'^{-1} & \ldots & \tau_{MM} A_M^{-1} A_M'^{-1} \end{bmatrix},$$

where

$$(4.5) \qquad [\tau_{\mu\mu'}] = \begin{bmatrix} \sigma^{qq} & \ldots & \sigma^{qM} \\ \cdots\cdots\cdots\cdots \\ \sigma^{Mq} & \ldots & \sigma^{MM} \end{bmatrix}^{-1}.$$

By postmultiplying G_2^{-1} by G_3' we obtain

$$(4.6) \qquad G_2^{-1} G_3' = \begin{bmatrix} v_{q1} A_q^{-1} A_1 & \cdots & v_{qp} A_q^{-1} A_p \\ \cdots\cdots\cdots\cdots\cdots\cdots \\ v_{M1} A_M^{-1} A_1 & \cdots & v_{Mp} A_M^{-1} A_p \end{bmatrix},$$

where

$$(4.7) \qquad [v_{\mu\mu'}] = \begin{bmatrix} \sigma^{qq} & \cdots & \sigma^{qM} \\ \cdots\cdots\cdots\cdots \\ \sigma^{Mq} & \cdots & \sigma^{MM} \end{bmatrix}^{-1} \begin{bmatrix} \sigma^{q1} & \cdots & \sigma^{qp} \\ \cdots\cdots\cdots\cdots \\ \sigma^{M1} & \cdots & \sigma^{Mp} \end{bmatrix}.$$

We go on in this way by premultiplying $G_2^{-1} G_3'$ by G_3 and subtracting the re-sulting product from G_1. According to (4.3), this gives the inverse of H_1:

$$(4.8) \qquad H_1^{-1} = \begin{bmatrix} \varphi_{11} A_1' A_1 & \cdots & \varphi_{1p} A_1' A_p \\ \cdots\cdots\cdots\cdots\cdots\cdots \\ \varphi_{p1} A_p' A_1 & \cdots & \varphi_{pp} A_p' A_p \end{bmatrix},$$

where

$$(4.9) \qquad [\varphi_{\mu\mu'}] = \begin{bmatrix} \sigma^{11} & \cdots & \sigma^{1p} \\ \cdots\cdots\cdots\cdots \\ \sigma^{p1} & \cdots & \sigma^{pp} \end{bmatrix}$$

$$- \begin{bmatrix} \sigma^{1q} & \cdots & \sigma^{1M} \\ \cdots\cdots\cdots\cdots \\ \sigma^{pq} & \cdots & \sigma^{pM} \end{bmatrix} \begin{bmatrix} \sigma^{qq} & \cdots & \sigma^{qM} \\ \cdots\cdots\cdots\cdots \\ \sigma^{Mq} & \cdots & \sigma^{MM} \end{bmatrix}^{-1} \begin{bmatrix} \sigma^{q1} & \cdots & \sigma^{qp} \\ \cdots\cdots\cdots\cdots \\ \sigma^{M1} & \cdots & \sigma^{Mp} \end{bmatrix}.$$

We proceed to consider the τ's, v's and φ's in more detail. They are all ob-tained by multiplying and inverting submatrices of $[\sigma^{\mu\mu'}]$, and it is easily seen that more convenient expressions are available. Let us write

$$(4.10) \qquad \begin{bmatrix} \sigma^{11} & \cdots & \sigma^{1p} & \sigma^{1q} & \cdots & \sigma^{1M} \\ \vdots & & \vdots & \vdots & & \vdots \\ \sigma^{p1} & \cdots & \sigma^{pp} & \sigma^{pq} & \cdots & \sigma^{pM} \\ \sigma^{q1} & \cdots & \sigma^{qp} & \sigma^{qq} & \cdots & \sigma^{qM} \\ \vdots & & \vdots & \vdots & & \vdots \\ \sigma^{M1} & \cdots & \sigma^{Mp} & \sigma^{Mq} & \cdots & \sigma^{MM} \end{bmatrix} = \begin{bmatrix} R_1 & R_3 \\ R_3' & R_2 \end{bmatrix} = \begin{bmatrix} S_1 & S_3 \\ S_3' & S_2 \end{bmatrix}^{-1}.$$

Then we have

$$(4.11) \qquad [\tau_{\mu\mu'}] = R_2^{-1}; \qquad [v_{\mu\mu'}] = R_2^{-1} R_3'; \qquad [\varphi_{\mu\mu'}] = R_1 - R_3 R_2^{-1} R_3',$$

so that $[\varphi_{\mu\mu'}] = S_1^{-1}$. But S_1 is nothing else than the moment matrix of the disturbances of the over-identified equations; hence

$$(4.12) \qquad [\varphi_{\mu\mu'}] = \begin{bmatrix} \sigma_{11} & \cdots & \sigma_{1p} \\ \cdots\cdots\cdots\cdots \\ \sigma_{p1} & \cdots & \sigma_{pp} \end{bmatrix}^{-1}.$$

On combining (4.8) and (4.12) and remembering that H_1 is the moment matrix of the three-stage least squares estimates of the over-identified equations, we find that it is indeed true that this matrix is the same as the one which is obtained when the three-stage procedure is confined to the set of over-identified equations. The latter method is preferable because it is computationally efficient, since the matrix to be inverted to obtain the estimates is of smaller order.

Let us now write $\hat{\delta}_A$ for the three-stage estimator when referring to the over-identified equations, and $\hat{\delta}_B$ for the just-identified equations. Assume that $\hat{\delta}_A$ has been computed as indicated above. Disregarding for a moment the differences between the σ's and the s's, we can write the estimation equations corresponding to (2.16) in the following form:

$$\begin{bmatrix} G_1 & G_3 \\ G_3' & G_2 \end{bmatrix} \begin{bmatrix} \hat{\delta}_A \\ \hat{\delta}_B \end{bmatrix} = \begin{bmatrix} A_1' KX' \, \Sigma \, \sigma^{1\mu} y_\mu \\ \vdots \\ A_M' KX' \, \Sigma \, \sigma^{M\mu} y_\mu \end{bmatrix},$$

so that the coefficient vector $\hat{\delta}_B$ of the just-identified equations can be written as

$$(4.13) \qquad \hat{\delta}_B = G_2^{-1} \begin{bmatrix} A_q' KX' \, \Sigma \, \sigma^{q\mu} y_\mu \\ \vdots \\ A_M' KX' \, \Sigma \, \sigma^{M\mu} y_\mu \end{bmatrix} - G_2^{-1} G_3' \hat{\delta}_A .$$

Hence $\hat{\delta}_B$ is the sum of two vectors. Applying (4.4) and (4.5), we find that the first can be written as

$$\begin{bmatrix} A_q^{-1} KX' \, \sum_{r=q}^{M} \sum_{\mu=q}^{M} \tau_{qr} \sigma^{r\mu} y_\mu \\ \vdots \\ A_M^{-1} KX' \, \sum_{r=q}^{M} \sum_{\mu=q}^{M} \tau_{Mr} \sigma^{r\mu} y_\mu \end{bmatrix} = \begin{bmatrix} A_q^{-1} KX' y_q \\ \vdots \\ A_M^{-1} KX' y_M \end{bmatrix} = \begin{bmatrix} (X'Z_q)^{-1} X' y_q \\ \vdots \\ (X'Z_M)^{-1} X' y_M \end{bmatrix} = d_B ,$$

i.e., the two-stage least squares estimator of the coefficients of the just-identified equations. For the second vector on the right of (4.13) we find, by applying (4.6),

$$G_2^{-1} G_3' \hat{\delta}_A = \begin{bmatrix} v_{q1} A_q^{-1} A_1 \ldots v_{qp} A_q^{-1} A_p \\ \cdots\cdots\cdots\cdots\cdots\cdots\cdots \\ v_{M1} A_M^{-1} A_1 \ldots v_{Mp} A_M^{-1} A_p \end{bmatrix} \hat{\delta}_A = \begin{bmatrix} (X'Z_q)^{-1} X' \, \Sigma \, v_{q\mu} X' Z_\mu \hat{\delta}_\mu \\ \vdots \\ (X'Z_M)^{-1} X' \, \Sigma \, v_{M\mu} X' Z_\mu \hat{\delta}_\mu \end{bmatrix},$$

where the summation on the right extends over $\mu = 1, \ldots, p$. Hence the three-stage least squares estimator for the just-identified equations is

$$(4.14) \qquad \hat{\delta}_B = d_B - \begin{bmatrix} (X'Z_q)^{-1} X' \sum_1^p v_{q\mu} X'Z_\mu \hat{\delta}_\mu \\ \vdots \\ (X'Z_M)^{-1} X' \sum_1^p v_{M\mu} X'Z_\mu \hat{\delta}_\mu \end{bmatrix},$$

which shows that the three-stage estimate is obtained by adding to the two-stage estimate a linear combination of the three-stage estimates of the over-identified equations. The v's can be derived from (4.7); but it is computationally more efficient to obtain them from

$$(4.15) \qquad [v_{\mu\mu'}] = -S_3'S_1^{-1} = - \begin{bmatrix} \sigma_{q1} & \cdots & \sigma_{qp} \\ \cdots\cdots\cdots\cdots\cdots \\ \sigma_{M1} & \cdots & \sigma_{Mp} \end{bmatrix} \begin{bmatrix} \sigma_{11} & \cdots & \sigma_{1p} \\ \cdots\cdots\cdots\cdots \\ \sigma_{p1} & \cdots & \sigma_{pp} \end{bmatrix}^{-1},$$

(see (4.10) and (4.11)).

The three-stage moment matrix of the just-identified equations is H_2, as defined in (4.3). It is the sum of two matrices, the first of which is G_2^{-1}, as specified in (4.4). It is useful to write matrices such as $A_q^{-1} A_q'^{-1}$ in the form

$$(A_q' A_q)^{-1} = (Z_q' X K' K X' Z_q)^{-1} = (X'Z_q)^{-1} X' X (Z_q' X)^{-1}.$$

The second matrix on the right of (4.3) is H_1 premultiplied by $G_2^{-1} G_3'$ and postmultiplied by $G_3 G_2^{-1}$. Now H_1 is available when the computations for the over-identified equations are completed, and $G_2^{-1} G_3'$ is specified in (4.6). But it is useful to write such matrices as $A_q^{-1} A_1$ in the form

$$(K X' Z_q)^{-1} K X' Z_1 = (X'Z_q)^{-1} K^{-1} K X' Z_1 = (X'Z_q)^{-1} X' Z_1.$$

Hence the three-stage moment matrix of the just-identified equations is

$$(4.16) \quad H_2 = \begin{bmatrix} \tau_{qq}(X'Z_q)^{-1} X' X (Z_q' X)^{-1} & \cdots & \tau_{qM}(X'Z_q)^{-1} X' X (Z_M' X)^{-1} \\ \cdots\cdots\cdots\cdots\cdots\cdots\cdots\cdots\cdots\cdots\cdots\cdots\cdots\cdots \\ \tau_{Mq}(X'Z_M)^{-1} X' X (Z_q' X)^{-1} & \cdots & \tau_{MM}(X'Z_M)^{-1} X' X (Z_M' X)^{-1} \end{bmatrix}$$

$$+ \begin{bmatrix} v_{q1}(X'Z_q)^{-1} X' Z_1 & \cdots & v_{qp}(X'Z_q)^{-1} X' Z_p \\ \cdots\cdots\cdots\cdots\cdots\cdots\cdots\cdots \\ v_{M1}(X'Z_M)^{-1} X' Z_1 & \cdots & v_{Mp}(X'Z_M)^{-1} X' Z_p \end{bmatrix}$$

$$\times H_1 \begin{bmatrix} v_{1q} Z_1' X (Z_q' X)^{-1} & \cdots & v_{1M} Z_1' X (Z_M' X)^{-1} \\ \cdots\cdots\cdots\cdots\cdots\cdots\cdots\cdots \\ v_{pq} Z_p' X (Z_q' X)^{-1} & \cdots & v_{pM} Z_p' X (Z_M' X)^{-1} \end{bmatrix},$$

where the v's are specified in (4.15) and the τ's in (4.5). A more convenient expression for the τ's is:

$$(4.17) \quad [\tau_{\mu\mu'}] = S_2 - S_3'S_1^{-1}S_3 = S_2 + [v_{\mu\mu'}]S_3 = \begin{bmatrix} \sigma_{qq} & \cdots & \sigma_{qM} \\ \cdots\cdots\cdots\cdots \\ \sigma_{Mq} & \cdots & \sigma_{MM} \end{bmatrix}$$

$$- \begin{bmatrix} \sigma_{q1} & \cdots & \sigma_{qp} \\ \cdots\cdots\cdots\cdots \\ \sigma_{M1} & \cdots & \sigma_{Mp} \end{bmatrix} \begin{bmatrix} \sigma_{11} & \cdots & \sigma_{1p} \\ \cdots\cdots\cdots\cdots \\ \sigma_{p1} & \cdots & \sigma_{pp} \end{bmatrix}^{-1} \begin{bmatrix} \sigma_{1q} & \cdots & \sigma_{1M} \\ \cdots\cdots\cdots\cdots \\ \sigma_{pq} & \cdots & \sigma_{pM} \end{bmatrix},$$

because this does not require inversion of the complete matrix $[\sigma_{\mu\mu'}]$ of all equations. In the same way, the "cross-moment" matrix of the just- and over-identified equations is

$$(4.18) \quad H_3' = - \begin{bmatrix} v_{q1}(X'Z_q)^{-1}X'Z_1 & \cdots & v_{qp}(X'Z_q)^{-1}X'Z_p \\ \cdots\cdots\cdots\cdots\cdots\cdots\cdots\cdots\cdots\cdots\cdots \\ v_{M1}(X'Z_M)^{-1}X'Z_1 & \cdots & v_{Mp}(X'Z_M)^{-1}X'Z_p \end{bmatrix} H_1.$$

In conclusion, we observe that if $[\sigma_{\mu\mu'}]$ is block-diagonal, so that it can be written in the form

$$(4.19) \quad [\sigma_{\mu\mu'}] = \begin{bmatrix} \Sigma_1 & 0 & \cdots & 0 \\ 0 & \Sigma_2 & \cdots & 0 \\ \cdots\cdots\cdots\cdots\cdots \\ 0 & 0 & \cdots & \Sigma_k \end{bmatrix},$$

the three-stage estimation procedure can be conveniently carried out block by block; i.e., the estimation of any structural equation is then essentially based only on the over-identifying restrictions of the equations whose disturbances are correlated with its own disturbances. It will be noted that the procedure recommended for systems containing definitions (see the first paragraph of this section) is a special case of (4.19).

4.2. *Summary of Rules.* The results derived in Section 4.1 can be summarized as follows:

(1) If the system contains definitional equations (and possibly other equations whose coefficients are known and whose disturbances are zero), then these are to be disregarded, i.e., the M of (2.16) and (2.17) is to be interpreted as the total number of equations excluding this category.

(2) If the system contains under-identified equations, these are to be disregarded too.[11]

(3) If the system contains just-identified as well as over-identified equations, it is computationally efficient to apply the three-stage procedure sep-

[11] But see Section 6 under (2).

arately to these two groups. For the over-identified equations, one should proceed in the manner described in Section 2 but interpret the M of (2.16) and (2.17) as the number of these equations, i.e., the total number of equations excluding the definitions and the just- and under-identified equations. (If there is only one over-identified equation, this procedure does of course not lead to additional efficiency beyond that of two-stage least squares, so that it is not to be applied in that case.)

(4)   For just-identified equations one proceeds as follows. Suppose that the system contains at least one over-identified equation (if there is no such equation, the procedure does not lead to additional efficiency). Write $\mu = 1$, ..., p for the over-identified equations and $\mu = q, \ldots, M$ for the just-identified group, where $q = p + 1$. Then the three-stage least squares estimator of the coefficient vector of the just-identified equations is $\hat{\delta}_B$ as specified in (4.14), where on the right d_B is the two-stage least squares estimator of this vector and $\hat{\delta}_1, \ldots, \hat{\delta}_p$ is the three-stage least squares estimators of the over-identified equations (which are computed as stated under (3)). The asymptotic covariance matrix of $\hat{\delta}_B$ is H_2 as given in (4.16), and the matrix of the asymptotic covariances of δ_B, on the one hand, and $\delta_1, \ldots, \delta_p$, on the other, is H'_3 as given in (4.18), where H_1 is the asymptotic covariance matrix of $\hat{\delta}_1, \ldots, \hat{\delta}_p$ and is computed as indicated under (3). The τ's and v's occurring in these expressions are given in (4.17) and (4.15), respectively. For the actual calculation one should replace the σ's of these formulae (the variances and covariances of the structural disturbances) by corresponding s's (their two-stage least squares estimates).

(5) If the covariance matrix of the structural disturbances is block-diagonal as in (4.19), the three-stage estimation procedure should be carried out separately for each group of equations corresponding with such a block.

5. AN EXAMPLE; DIRECTORY OF COMPUTATIONS[12]

5.1. *Some Computational Simplifications.* There are two groups of numerical results which we need. One of them deals with such matrices as $Z'_1 X(X'X)^{-1}$ $X'Z_1$, $Z'_1 X(X'X)^{-1}X'y_1$, etc., and the other with the elements $s^{\mu\mu'}$ of the inverse of the two-stage least squares estimated contemporaneous covariance matrix of the structural disturbances. Starting with the former group, we observe that it is useful to introduce the partitioned matrix

(5.1) $Z = [Y \quad X]$,

where Y is the matrix of values taken by all relevant jointly dependent

---

[12] The example contains no just-identified equations; reference is made to point (4) of Section 4.2 for the appropriate calculations when there are such equations.

variables in such a way that y_μ, Y_μ are all submatrices of Y. It is then easy to see that the matrices $Z_1'X(X'X)^{-1}X'Z_1$, $Z_1'X(X'X)^{-1}X'y_1$, etc., are all submatrices of the symmetric matrix

$$(5.2) \qquad Z'X(X'X)^{-1}X'Z = \begin{bmatrix} Y'X(X'X)^{-1}X'Y & Y'X \\ X'Y & X'X \end{bmatrix}.$$

Proceeding to the $s^{\mu\mu'}$, we start by writing the M equations (2.1) in the form

$$(5.3) \quad [y_1\ y_2 \ldots y_M] = [Y_1\ Y_2 \ldots Y_M]\begin{bmatrix} \gamma_1 & 0 & \cdots & 0 \\ 0 & \gamma_2 & \cdots & 0 \\ \vdots & \vdots & & \vdots \\ 0 & 0 & \cdots & \gamma_M \end{bmatrix}$$

$$+ [X_1\ X_2 \ldots X_M]\begin{bmatrix} \beta_1 & 0 & \cdots & 0 \\ 0 & \beta_2 & \cdots & 0 \\ \vdots & \vdots & & \vdots \\ 0 & 0 & \cdots & \beta_M \end{bmatrix} + [u_1\ u_2 \ldots u_M].$$

Let us write Y_L for the matrix of values taken by the left hand jointly dependent variables and similarly Y_R, X_R for those referring to the right hand dependent and predetermined variables respectively:

$$(5.4) \qquad \begin{aligned} Y_L &= [y_1\quad y_2\ \cdots\ y_M], \\ Y_R &= [Y_1\quad Y_2\ \cdots\ Y_M], \\ X_R &= [X_1\quad X_2\ \cdots\ X_M]. \end{aligned}$$

Then the two-stage least squares estimate of (5.3) takes the form

$$(5.5) \qquad Y_L = Y_RC + X_RB + \hat{U},$$

where $\hat{U}$ is the $T \times M$ matrix of two-stage least squares estimated structural disturbances, and

$$(5.6) \qquad C = \begin{bmatrix} c_1 & 0 & \cdots & 0 \\ 0 & c_2 & \cdots & 0 \\ \vdots & \vdots & & \vdots \\ 0 & 0 & \cdots & c_M \end{bmatrix}, \quad B = \begin{bmatrix} b_1 & 0 & \cdots & 0 \\ 0 & b_2 & \cdots & 0 \\ \vdots & \vdots & & \vdots \\ 0 & 0 & \cdots & b_M \end{bmatrix},$$

the c's and b's being two-stage least squares coefficient estimates.

The separation in terms of Y_R and X_R is chosen because it is useful to take account of the condition, $X_R'\hat{U} = 0$. Doing so, we find

$$(5.7)\ [Ts_{\mu\mu'}] = \hat{U}'\hat{U} = Y_L'Y_L - Y_L'Y_RC - C'Y_R'Y_L + C'Y_R'Y_RC - B'X_R'X_RB.^{[12a]}$$

The first matrix on the right $(Y_L'Y_L)$ is simply a submatrix of Y', Y and is

[12a] [In footnote 13, section 6, of their paper, reprinted in this volume, Rothenberg and Leenders point out that this equation is invalid since X'_RU is not necessarily zero for finite samples. The typographical error noted in that footnote has also been corrected. Corrections to Tables III, page 76, and IV, page 77, below have been made by the authors.—The Editors.]

derived as such. The second is computed by postmultiplying such submatrices by $c_1, c_2, \ldots$, giving

$$(5.8) \qquad Y'_L Y_R C = [Y'_L Y_1 c_1 \quad Y'_L Y_2 c_2 \quad \ldots \quad Y'_L Y_M c_M].$$

The third matrix on the right of (5.7) is the transpose of the second. The fourth is a symmetric matrix which can be partitioned as follows:

$$(5.9) \qquad C' Y'_R Y_R C = \begin{bmatrix} c'_1 Y'_1 Y_1 c_1 & \ldots & c'_1 Y'_1 Y_M c_M \\ \vdots & & \vdots \\ c'_M Y'_M Y_1 c_1 & \ldots & c'_M Y'_M Y_M c_M \end{bmatrix},$$

which implies that we have to premultiply such matrices as $Y'_1 Y_2$ by c'_1 and postmultiply by c_2. The last matrix on the right of (5.7) is completely analogous:

$$(5.10) \qquad B' X'_R X_R B = \begin{bmatrix} b'_1 X'_1 X_1 b_1 & \ldots & b'_1 X'_1 X_M b_M \\ \vdots & & \vdots \\ b'_M X'_M X_1 b_1 & \ldots & b'_M X'_M X_M b_M \end{bmatrix}.$$

5.2. *Klein's Model I.* The example which we shall use is Klein's Model I [3], which consists of three behavioral equations and three definitions. The former category includes a consumption function which describes consumption (C) linearly in terms of profits (Π), profits lagged one year (Π_{-1}), and the total wage bill ($W_1 + W_2$), where W_1 refers to the private wage bill and W_2 to the government wage bill. Thus,

$$(5.11) \qquad C = \alpha_0 + \alpha_1 \Pi + \alpha_2 (W_1 + W_2) + \alpha_3 \Pi_{-1} + u_1.$$

Furthermore, there is an investment equation describing net investment (I) linearly in terms of profits, lagged profits, and capital stock at the beginning of the year (K_{-1}):

$$(5.12) \qquad I = \beta_0 + \beta_1 \Pi + \beta_2 \Pi_{-1} + \beta_3 K_{-1} + u_2.$$

Finally, there is a demand-for-labor equation which describes the private wage bill linearly in terms of national income (Y) plus indirect taxes (T) minus the government wage bill, the same variable lagged one year, and time (measured in calendar years):

$$(5.13) \qquad W_1 = \gamma_0 + \gamma_1 (Y + T - W_2) + \gamma_2 (Y + T - W_2)_{-1} + \gamma_3 t + u_3.$$

The system is completed by three definitions:

$$(5.14) \qquad \begin{aligned} Y + T &= C + I + G, \\ Y &= W_1 + W_2 + \Pi, \\ K &= K_{-1} + I, \end{aligned}$$

where G is government expenditure on goods and services.

The system (5.11)-(5.14) is a complete one in six jointly dependent variables (C, Π, W_1, I, Y, K) and eight predetermined variables $(W_2, T, G, t, \Pi_{-1}, K_{-1}, (Y+T-W_2)_{-1}$, and the variable corresponding to the constant terms). Our objective is to estimate the α's, β's, and γ's on the basis of American data for the period 1921–1941.

5.3. *Computations.* The three definitions (5.14) are to be disregarded according to point (1) of Section 4.2. Furthermore, the three behavioral equations are all over-identified, hence we should proceed along the lines of Section 2 for $M = 3$. The detailed steps are as follows:

STEP ONE: *Arranging the variables.* Arrange the jointly dependent variables falling under y_μ, Y_μ for $\mu = 1,\ldots,M$ into the matrix Y; similarly, arrange all predetermined variables under X and form the partitioned matrix $Z = [Y\ X]$, see (5.1).

For Klein's Model I the arrangement of Table I is convenient. It defines one variable for $W_1 + W_2$ because this has one single coefficient in (5.11). This variable is a mixture of jointly dependent and predetermined variables and therefore listed as dependent (because it is not independent of the disturbances). The same applies to $Y + T - W_2$. The variable representing the constant term is indicated by $x_8 \equiv 1$.

TABLE I

ARRANGEMENT OF VARIABLES

Jointly dependent variables					
y_1	y_2	y_3	y_4	y_5	y_6
C	I	W_1	Π	$W_1 + W_2$	$Y + T - W_2$

Predetermined variables							
x_1	x_2	x_3	x_4	x_5	x_6	x_7	x_8
W_2	T	G	t	Π_{-1}	K_{-1}	$(Y+T-W_2)_{-1}$	1

STEP TWO: *Computing the moments.* Compute the sums of squares and products of all variables listed in Step One: $Y'Y$, $X'X$, $X'Y$, and also $Y'X(X'X)^{-1}X'Y$ (which is the matrix of the sums of squares and products of the computed value of Y in its regression on X).

These four matrices in our numerical case are specified in Table II.[13]
STEP THREE: *Computing the two-stage least squares estimates.* Select the variables falling under y_μ, Y_μ, X_μ (and hence $Z_\mu = [Y_\mu\ X_\mu])$ for each

---

[13] All data are taken from [3, Appendix, p. 135].

TABLE II

MOMENT MATRICES USED IN 3SLS ESTIMATION OF KLEIN'S MODEL I

A. *Jointly dependent, $Y'Y^*$:*

	y_1	y_2	y_3	y_4	y_5	y_6
y_1	62166.63	1679.01	42076.78	19566.35	48054.11	69501.99
y_2		286.02	1217.92	726.10	1321.72	2104.42
y_3			28560.86	13296.61	32604.93	47173.09
y_4				6347.25	15117.72	22049.39
y_5					37275.87	53827.54
y_6						77998.58

B. *Predetermined, $X'X^*$:*

	x_1	x_2	x_3	x_4	x_5	x_6	x_7	x_8
x_1	626.87	789.27	1200.19	238.00	1746.22	21683.18	6364.43	107.50
x_2		1054.95	1546.11	176.00	2348.48	28766.25	8436.53	142.90
x_3			2369.94	421.70	3451.86	42026.14	12473.50	208.20
x_4				770.00	−11.90	590.60	495.60	0.00
x_5					5956.29	69073.54	20542.22	343.90
x_6						846132.70	244984.77	4210.40
x_7							72200.03	1217.70
x_8								21.00

C. *Jointly dependent–predetermined, $Y'X^*$:*

	x_1	x_2	x_3	x_4	x_5	x_6	x_7	x_8
y_1	5977.33	7858.86	11633.68	577.70	18929.37	227767.38	66815.25	1133.90
y_2	103.80	160.40	243.19	−105.60	655.33	5073.25	1831.13	26.60
y_3	4044.07	5315.62	7922.46	460.90	12871.73	153470.56	45288.51	763.60
y_4	1821.11	2405.53	3578.05	18.90	6070.13	70946.78	21030.44	354.70
y_5	4670.94	6104.89	9122.65	698.90	14617.95	175153.74	51652.94	871.10
y_6	6654.45	8776.10	13046.62	655.80	21290.34	253183.59	74755.48	1261.20

D. *"Calculated" jointly dependent, $Y'X(X'X)^{-1}X'Y$:*

	y_1	y_2	y_3	y_4	y_5	y_6
y_1	**	**	**	19507.721	48010.448	69399.702
y_2		**	**	681.203	1283.799	2021.602
y_3			**	13255.034	32564.923	47091.507
y_4				6285.300	15076.144	21945.864
y_5					37235.862	53745.956
y_6						77813.470

* Klein's data are given accurately to one decimal place; thus these moments have two places beyond the decimal point.
** These moments are not needed in computing 3SLS estimates.

equation and compute the two-stage least squares estimates by using the formula

$$(5.15) \quad d_\mu = \begin{bmatrix} Y'_\mu X(X'X)^{-1} X' Y_\mu & Y'_\mu X_\mu \\ X'_\mu Y_\mu & X'_\mu X_\mu \end{bmatrix}^{-1} \begin{bmatrix} Y'_\mu X(X'X)^{-1} X' y_\mu \\ X'_\mu y_\mu \end{bmatrix}.$$

In our case this means:

$$\begin{bmatrix} a_1 \\ a_2 \\ a_3 \\ a_0 \end{bmatrix} = \begin{bmatrix} 6285.300 & 15076.144 & \vdots & 6070.13 & 354.70 \\ 15076.144 & 37235.862 & \vdots & 14617.95 & 871.10 \\ \hdotsfor{5} \\ 6070.13 & 14617.95 & \vdots & 5956.29 & 343.90 \\ 354.70 & 871.10 & \vdots & 343.90 & 21.00 \end{bmatrix}^{-1} \begin{bmatrix} 19507.721 \\ 48010.448 \\ \hdotsfor{1} \\ 18929.37 \\ 1133.90 \end{bmatrix} = \begin{bmatrix} 0.017 \\ 0.810 \\ \hdotsfor{1} \\ 0.216 \\ 16.555 \end{bmatrix},$$

$$\begin{bmatrix} b_1 \\ b_2 \\ b_3 \\ b_0 \end{bmatrix} = \begin{bmatrix} 6285.300 & \vdots & 6070.13 & 70946.78 & 354.70 \\ \hdotsfor{5} \\ 6070.13 & \vdots & 5956.29 & 69073.54 & 343.90 \\ 70946.78 & \vdots & 69073.54 & 846132.70 & 4210.40 \\ 354.70 & \vdots & 343.90 & 4210.40 & 21.00 \end{bmatrix}^{-1} \begin{bmatrix} 681.203 \\ \hdotsfor{1} \\ 655.33 \\ 5073.25 \\ 26.60 \end{bmatrix} = \begin{bmatrix} 0.150 \\ \hdotsfor{1} \\ 0.616 \\ -0.158 \\ 20.278 \end{bmatrix},$$

$$\begin{bmatrix} c_1 \\ c_2 \\ c_3 \\ c_0 \end{bmatrix} = \begin{bmatrix} 77813.470 & \vdots & 74755.48 & 655.80 & 1261.20 \\ \hdotsfor{5} \\ 74755.48 & \vdots & 72200.03 & 495.60 & 1217.70 \\ 655.80 & \vdots & 495.60 & 770.00 & 0.00 \\ 1261.20 & \vdots & 1217.70 & 0.00 & 21.00 \end{bmatrix}^{-1} \begin{bmatrix} 47091.507 \\ \hdotsfor{1} \\ 45288.51 \\ 460.90 \\ 763.60 \end{bmatrix} = \begin{bmatrix} 0.439 \\ \hdotsfor{1} \\ 0.147 \\ 0.130 \\ 1.500 \end{bmatrix}.$$

STEP FOUR: *Estimating the moment matrix of the structural disturbances.* Form the matrices needed to calculate the matrix products in (5.7). For Klein's model we have

$$Y_L = [y_1 \ y_2 \ y_3],$$
$$Y_R = [Y_1 \ Y_2 \ Y_3] = [y_4 \ y_5 \ y_4 \ y_6],$$
$$X_R = [X_1 \ X_2 \ X_3]$$
$$\quad = [x_5 \ x_8 \ x_5 \ x_6 \ x_8 \ x_7 \ x_4 \ x_8].$$

(Check twice!) Then the following matrices are employed in calculating $[Ts_{\mu\mu'}]$ from (5.7):

$$Y'_L Y_L = \begin{bmatrix} 62166.63 & 1679.01 & 42076.78 \\ & 286.02 & 1217.92 \\ & & 28560.86 \end{bmatrix},$$

$$Y'_L Y_R = \begin{bmatrix} 19566.35 & 48054.11 & 19566.35 & 69501.99 \\ 726.10 & 1321.72 & 726.10 & 2104.42 \\ 13296.61 & 32604.93 & 13296.61 & 47173.09 \end{bmatrix},$$

$$Y'_R Y_R = \begin{bmatrix} 6347.25 & 15117.72 & 6347.25 & 22049.39 \\ & 37275.87 & 15117.72 & 53827.54 \\ & & 6347.25 & 22049.39 \\ & & & 77998.58 \end{bmatrix},$$

$$X'_R X_R = \begin{bmatrix} 5\,956.29 & 343.90 & 5\,956.29 & 69\,073.54 & 343.90 & 20\,542.22 & -11.90 & 343.90 \\ & 21.00 & 343.90 & 4\,210.40 & 21.00 & 1\,217.70 & 0.00 & 21.00 \\ & & 5\,956.29 & 69\,073.54 & 343.90 & 20\,542.22 & -11.90 & 343.90 \\ & & & 846\,132.70 & 4\,210.40 & 244\,984.77 & 590.60 & 4\,210.40 \\ & & & & 21.00 & 1\,217.70 & 0.00 & 21.00 \\ & & & & & 72\,200.03 & 495.60 & 1\,217.70 \\ & & & & & & 770.00 & 0.00 \\ & & & & & & & 21.00 \end{bmatrix},$$

$$C = \begin{bmatrix} -0.0173 & 0 & 0 \\ 0.8102 & 0 & 0 \\ 0 & 0.1502 & 0 \\ 0 & 0 & 0.4389 \end{bmatrix}, \quad B = \begin{bmatrix} 0.2162 & 0 & 0 \\ 16.5548 & 0 & 0 \\ 0 & 0.6159 & 0 \\ 0 & -0.1578 & 0 \\ 0 & 20.2782 & 0 \\ 0 & 0 & 0.1467 \\ 0 & 0 & 0.1304 \\ 0 & 0 & 1.5003 \end{bmatrix}.$$

With these matrices the right hand side of (5.7) can be computed to yield

$$[T s_{\mu\mu'}] = \begin{bmatrix} 21.926 & 9.966 & -5.758 \\ & 29.047 & -4.156 \\ & & 10.005 \end{bmatrix}.$$

Then by inverting $[s_{\mu\mu'}]$ we obtain

$$[s^{\mu\mu'}] = \begin{bmatrix} 1.272 & -0.353 & 0.585 \\ & 0.867 & 0.157 \\ & & 2.503 \end{bmatrix}.$$

STEP FIVE: *Calculating 3SLS estimates.* Form the matrices in (2.16) by selecting appropriate submatrices from Table II and multiplying their elements by elements of $[s^{\mu\mu'}]$. It is to be remembered that on the right side of (2.16) Z_μ represents the partitioned matrix $[Y_\mu \quad X_\mu]$. Then the first matrix in (2.16) is inverted. On comparing (2.16) and (2.17), it is seen that this inverse, given in Table III, is the estimated covariance matrix of 3SLS estimators. The vector appearing in (2.16) is then calculated. In our case we have

TABLE III

Estimated Covariance Matrix of 3SLS Coefficient Estimators for Klein's Model ($\times 10^4$)

	a_1	a_2	a_3	a_0	b_1	b_2	b_3	b_0	c_1	c_2	c_3	c_0
a_1	116.9	-11.7	-80.6	-17.0	60.9	-49.4	-.0	-15.7	-13.5	13.9	6.4	.8
a_2		14.4	-5.6	-30.7	8.9	-8.6	3.0	-62.1	-3.7	-.1	-5.2	2.8
a_3			100.9	-5.6	-59.0	63.4	-2.9	54.7	8.8	-14.0	4.4	28.6
a_0				170.2	-43.0	15.3	-7.3	169.5	9.9	-.0	3.4	-61.5
b_1					262.1	-223.5	32.7	-732.2	.0	-.0	4.9	-1.7
b_2						233.9	-30.4	604.5	1.8	.7	-6.6	-14.8
b_3							10.6	-217.6	-2.1	2.1	1.8	.0
b_0								4615.5	37.9	-44.8	-33.0	27.7
c_1									10.1	-9.1	-2.8	-7.9
c_2										11.7	.5	-12.9
c_3											7.8	14.1
c_0												124.5

$$
\begin{bmatrix}
\sum_\mu s_1^{1\mu} Z_1' X (X'X)^{-1} X' y_\mu \\
\sum_\mu s^{2\mu} Z_2' X (X'X)^{-1} X' y_\mu \\
\sum_\mu s^{3\mu} Z_3' X (X'X)^{-1} X' y_\mu
\end{bmatrix}
=
\begin{bmatrix}
32\,335.954 \\
79\,687.291 \\
31\,384.947 \\
1\,880.124 \\
-4\,212.733 \\
-4\,091.236 \\
-51\,886.945 \\
-257.212 \\
158\,827.353 \\
152\,771.080 \\
1\,475.328 \\
2\,579.466
\end{bmatrix}.
$$

This vector is then premultiplied by the matrix given in Table III to yield 3SLS coefficient estimates which are presented in Table IV along with their 2SLS counterparts and also with estimated variances of coefficient estimators.

TABLE IV

THREE-STAGE AND TWO-STAGE LEAST SQUARES ESTIMATES OF PARAMETERS IN KLEIN'S MODEL I

Equation	Coefficient of	3SLS		2SLS	
		Coefficient estimate	Variance of coefficient estimator	Coefficient estimate	Variance of coefficient estimator
Consumption	Π	0.1249	0.01169	0.0173	0.013936
	$W_1 + W_2$	0.7901	0.00144	0.8102	0.001620
	Π_{-1}	0.1631	0.01009	0.2162	0.011506
	1	16.44	0.01702	16.5548	1.745
Investment	Π	−0.0131	0.02621	0.1502	0.030084
	Π_{-1}	0.7557	0.02339	0.6159	0.026499
	K_{-1}	−0.1948	0.00106	−0.1578	0.001305
	1	28.18	0.46155	20.2782	56.892
Demand for labor	$Y + T - W_2$	0.4005	0.00101	0.4389	0.001270
	$(Y + T - W_2)_{-1}$	0.1813	0.00117	0.1467	0.001508
	t	0.1497	0.00078	0.1304	0.000849
	1	1.80	0.01245	1.5003	1.317

6. CONCLUDING REMARKS

(1) When there are linear a priori restrictions on coefficients of different structural equations (e.g., $\alpha_1 = \frac{1}{2}\beta_1$ in (5.11)–(5.12)), one proceeds as follows. Write the three-stage least squares estimation equations in the form (3.1), $v = W\delta + \varepsilon$, and write the restrictions in the form $R\delta = r$, where R and r are matrices with known elements. The number of rows of R and r equals the number of a priori restrictions, and the number of their columns in n and 1, respectively. Then apply constrained generalized least squares (see Theil [5, Appendix to Chapter 8]).

(2) When the μth equation is under-identified, (2.4) is a system of $\Lambda < n_\mu$ equations. But if there is some a priori knowledge about the components of δ_μ which can be written in linear stochastic form (and which may therefore be uncertain knowledge), this raises effectively the number of estimation equations. This is the method of mixed linear estimation (see Theil and Goldberger [6]).

(3) The three-stage least squares estimator $\hat{\delta}$ implies in general a new estimator of $[\sigma_{\mu\mu'}]$ which differs from $[s_{\mu\mu'}]$. One can set up a new stage based on this estimator rather than $[s_{\mu\mu'}]$ and proceed iteratively. No reports on this method can be made as yet, but we hope to come back to it in the future.

University of Wisconsin and the Netherlands School of Economics

REFERENCES

[1] AITKEN, A. C.: "On Least-Squares and Linear Combination of Observations," *Proceedings of the Royal Society of Edinburgh*, vol. 55 (1934–35), pp. 42–48.
[2] CRAMER, H.: *Mathematical Methods of Statistics*, Princeton, Princeton University Press, 1946.
[3] KLEIN, L. R.: *Economic Fluctuations in the United States, 1921–1941*, New York, John Wiley and Sons, 1950.
[4] RAO, C. R.: *Advanced Statistical Methods in Biometric Research*, New York, John Wiley and Sons, 1952.
[5] THEIL, H.: *Economic Forecasts and Policy,* Second Edition, Amsterdam, North-Holland Publishing Company, 1961.
[6] THEIL, H., AND A. S. GOLDBERGER: "On Pure and Mixed Statistical Estimation in Economics," Report 6009 of the Econometric Institute of the Netherlands School of Economics (1960). To be published in the *International Economic Review*.

Econometrica, Vol. 32, No. 1–2 (January–April, 1964)

EFFICIENT ESTIMATION OF SIMULTANEOUS EQUATION SYSTEMS

By T. J. Rothenberg and C. T. Leenders[1]

The asymptotic covariance matrix of the full-information maximum-likelihood estimator is derived. The paper then compares the asymptotic efficiency of three estimators: full-information maximum likelihood, three-stage least squares, and linearized maximum likelihood. It is shown that all three are efficient if the covariance matrix of the contemporaneous structural disturbances is unknown. If, however, some elements of this covariance matrix are known a priori, then three-stage least squares is no longer efficient.

1. INTRODUCTION

A number of methods for estimating the parameters in simultaneous equation models have been proposed. The full-information maximum-likelihood (FIML) approach is known to be asymptotically most efficient under very general conditions but unfortunately it is impractical because of the difficult computations required. It is desirable, therefore, to find an estimator that is both efficient and relatively easy to compute.

The present paper has three purposes. First, it gives a new derivation of the FIML estimator and also an explicit expression for its asymptotic covariance matrix. Second, it suggests a new estimator, called linearized maximum-likelihood (LML), which has the same optimal large sample properties as FIML, but which is much simpler to compute. Third, the paper compares the efficiency of LML and FIML with that of the three-stage least-squares (3SLS) estimator. It is shown that 3SLS is as efficient as FIML or LML if nothing is assumed about the covariance matrix of the contemporaneous structural disturbances. If, on the other hand, some elements of the covariance matrix are known a priori (e.g., if it is assumed that the structural disturbances from different equations are independently distributed), then 3SLS is inefficient.

The order of presentation is as follows: the assumptions underlying the analysis are given in Section 2. The FIML estimator is derived in Section 3 and its covariance matrix in Section 4. In Section 5 the newly proposed LML estimator is introduced. Section 6 discusses the asymptotic efficiency of various estimators under a number of different assumptions. Finally, a numerical example is given in Section 7.

2. THE MODEL

We shall consider a complete system of M linear stochastic structural equations

---

[1] The authors are indebted to Professor H. Theil for his many helpful suggestions. This study was made while the first author was a Fulbright Visitor at the Econometric Institute, Netherlands School of Economics.

406

in M jointly dependent variables and Λ predetermined variables.[2] The sample consists of T observations on these M plus Λ variables. Then the μth structural equation can be written in the following form for all observations combined:

$$(2.1) \qquad y_\mu = Y_\mu \gamma_\mu + X_\mu \beta_\mu + u_\mu = Z_\mu \delta_\mu + u_\mu \,, \qquad (\mu = 1, \ldots, M)$$

where y_μ is a $T \times 1$ matrix of sample observations on one of the jointly dependent variables, Y_μ is a $T \times m_\mu$ matrix of values taken by the explanatory dependent variables in the equation, X_μ is a $T \times l_\mu$ matrix of observations on the predetermined variables in the equation, and u_μ is a $T \times 1$ matrix of structural disturbances; γ_μ and β_μ are column vectors of population parameters; Z_μ and δ_μ are defined as

$$(2.2) \qquad Z_\mu = [Y_\mu \quad X_\mu]\,, \qquad \delta_\mu = \begin{bmatrix} \gamma_\mu \\ \beta_\mu \end{bmatrix}.$$

The M sets of equations of (2.1) may be combined to form

$$(2.3) \qquad y = Z\delta + u \,,$$

where

$$(2.4) \qquad y = \begin{bmatrix} y_1 \\ y_2 \\ \vdots \\ y_M \end{bmatrix}; \quad Z = \begin{bmatrix} Z_1 & 0 & \cdots & 0 \\ 0 & Z_2 & \cdots & 0 \\ \vdots & \vdots & & \vdots \\ 0 & 0 & \cdots & Z_M \end{bmatrix}; \quad \delta = \begin{bmatrix} \delta_1 \\ \delta_2 \\ \vdots \\ \delta_M \end{bmatrix}; \quad u = \begin{bmatrix} u_1 \\ u_2 \\ \vdots \\ u_M \end{bmatrix}.$$

Thus δ is the vector of all the regression coefficients that need to be estimated; the number of coefficients is

$$(2.5) \qquad n = \sum_{\mu=1}^{M} n_\mu \equiv \sum_{\mu=1}^{M} (m_\mu + l_\mu)\,.$$

We shall assume that there are no a priori restrictions on the value of δ. The a priori restrictions based on the exclusion of variables from an equation are, of course, already built into (2.3).

The statistical assumptions on the model represented by (2.3) are as follows:

(a) Each equation is identifiable by the a priori restrictions. This implies that $n_\mu \leq \Lambda$ for all μ.

(b) The $T \times \Lambda$ matrix X of all predetermined variables has the property that plim $(1/T)X' u_\mu = 0$ for all μ. Furthermore, plim $(1/T)Z'_\mu Z_{\mu'}$ is finite for all μ and μ'. Finally, X has rank Λ, and Z has rank n with probability one.

(c) The MT dimensional disturbance vector u has a multivariate normal distribution with mean zero and positive definite covariance matrix Ψ.

(d) The disturbances at different observation points are uncorrelated; the contemporaneous disturbances are homoscedastic.

----

[2] The notation in this paper follows that of Zellner and Theil [10].

The last two assumptions can be summarized by the statement that u is normally distributed with

(2.6) $E(u)=0$ and $E(uu')=\Psi=\Sigma\otimes I$,

where Σ is an $M\times M$ positive definite matrix,[3] $\otimes$ represents the Kronecker product,[4] and I is a $T\times T$ identity matrix.

Under these assumptions the joint density function of the MT disturbances may be written as

(2.7) $f(u)=(2\pi)^{-\frac{1}{2}MT}\det^{-\frac{1}{2}}\Psi\exp\{-\frac{1}{2}u'\Psi^{-1}u\}$.

The logarithmic likelihood function is then defined as

(2.8) $L(u,\Psi)=\dfrac{1}{T}\log f(u)=k+\dfrac{1}{2T}\log\det\Psi^{-1}-\dfrac{1}{2T}u'\Psi^{-1}u$.

Equation (2.3) may now be considered as a transformation of variables where y replaces u as the random variable. The likelihood function (2.8) now becomes

(2.9) $L(y,\Psi,\delta,Z)$

$$=k+\frac{1}{T}\log|J|+\frac{1}{2T}\log\det\Psi^{-1}-\frac{1}{2T}(y-Z\delta)'\,\Psi^{-1}(y-Z\delta),$$

where $|J|$ is the absolute value of the Jacobian of the transformation, that is,

(2.10) $J=\det\left[\dfrac{\partial u_i(t)}{\partial y_j(t')}\right]$,

where $u_i(t)$ and $y_j(t')$ represent typical (scalar) elements of u and y. The value of this Jacobian is not readily computed from (2.3) because some of the elements of Z are also elements of y. But (2.3) may be rewritten as

(2.11) $\displaystyle\sum_{j=1}^{M}\gamma_{ij}\,y_j(t)+\sum_{\lambda=1}^{\Lambda}\beta_{i\lambda}x_\lambda(t)=u_i(t)$ $(i=1,\ldots,M;\,t=1,\ldots,T)$

where the coefficients γ_{ij} and $\beta_{i\lambda}$ are either elements of δ (apart from sign) or fixed a priori. Then

(2.12) $\dfrac{\partial u_i(t)}{\partial y_j(t')}=\begin{cases}0 & \text{if } t<t',\\ \gamma_{ij} & \text{if } t=t'.\end{cases}$

The value of (2.12) when $t>t'$ may be nonzero if any of the X's are lagged endogen-

---

[3] The assumption that Σ is nonsingular implies that the system (2.3) contains no identities. Hence (2.3) should be interpreted as the system after all identities have been solved out. See, however, Section 7 for a generalization.

[4] The Kronecker product $A\otimes B$, where A is an $n\times n$ matrix and B is an $m\times m$ matrix, is the $nm\times nm$ matrix with typical submatrix $a_{ij}B$. For some relevant theorems on Kronecker products, see, e.g., Anderson [1, pp. 347–8].

ous variables. This last possibility does not affect the value of $|J|$. Ordering the equations of (2.11) in groups from the same observation point

$$(2.13) \quad J = \det \left[\frac{\partial u_i(t)}{\partial y_j(t')} \right] = \det \begin{bmatrix} \Gamma & * & \dots & * \\ 0 & \Gamma & \dots & * \\ \vdots & \vdots & & \vdots \\ 0 & 0 & \dots & \Gamma \end{bmatrix} = \det{}^T \Gamma .$$

where $\Gamma = [\gamma_{ij}]$ and where the upper part of the matrix (represented by $*$) is determined by the lag structure of the endogenous variables. We now require the further assumption

(e) The $M \times M$ matrix Γ is nonsingular.

Using (2.13) and the fact that

$$(2.14) \quad \det \Psi^{-1} = \det(\Sigma^{-1} \otimes I) = \det{}^T \Sigma^{-1} ,$$

the likelihood function (2.9) becomes

$$(2.15) \quad L(\delta, \Sigma, y, Z)$$
$$= k + \log |\det \Gamma| + \tfrac{1}{2} \log \det \Sigma^{-1} \; - \; \frac{1}{2T} (y - Z\delta)' \Psi^{-1} (y - Z\delta) .$$

This function is the basis for the maximum-likelihood approach to estimating parameters in multi-equation systems. It is essentially identical to equation (5.52) of Hood and Koopmans [4, p. 160]. Our derivation differs from theirs in that it incorporates explicitly the a priori restrictions into the likelihood function. The present approach will prove to be very convenient in what follows.

3. MAXIMUM-LIKELIHOOD ESTIMATES

3.1. *Unrestricted Σ-Matrix*
To obtain full-information maximum-likelihood estimates we must differentiate (2.15) with respect to δ and Σ, set the resulting functions equal to zero, and solve these equations for δ and Σ. Because of the particular form of (2.15), we can conveniently carry out this process in two steps.[5] First we differentiate with respect to the elements of Σ^{-1}, obtaining

$$(3.1)$$
$$\frac{\partial L}{\partial \sigma^{ij}} = \sigma_{ij} - \frac{1}{T}(y_i - Z_i \delta_i)'(y_j - Z_j \delta_j), \qquad \text{for } i \neq j ,$$

$$\frac{\partial L}{\partial \sigma^{ii}} = \tfrac{1}{2}\sigma_{ii} - \frac{1}{2T}(y_i - Z_i \delta_i)'(y_i - Z_i \delta_i), \qquad \text{for } i = j .$$

---

[5] This stepwise maximization of the likelihood function is discussed in detail by Hood and Koopmans [4, pp. 156–8].

Thus, at the maximum the following condition must hold:

$$(3.2) \qquad \sigma_{ij} = \frac{1}{T}(y_i - Z_i\delta_i)'(y_j - Z_j\delta_j) \equiv s_{ij} \qquad (i, j = 1, \ldots, M)$$

where s_{ij} is defined by the second equality sign. Substituting (3.2) into (2.15), the likelihood function becomes

$$(3.3) \qquad L^*(\delta, y, Z) = k + \log|\det \Gamma| - \tfrac{1}{2} \log \det S - \frac{1}{2T} u'(S^{-1} \otimes I)u,$$

where $S = [s_{ij}]$. But the last term

$$(3.4) \qquad \frac{1}{2T} u'(S^{-1} \otimes I)u = \frac{1}{2T} \sum_{i=1}^{M} \sum_{j=1}^{M} u_i' u_j s^{ij} = \tfrac{1}{2} \sum_{i=1}^{M} \sum_{j=1}^{M} s_{ij} s^{ij} = \frac{M}{2}$$

is a constant; thus the "concentrated" likelihood function is

$$(3.5) \qquad L^*(\delta, y, Z) = k' + \log|\det \Gamma| - \tfrac{1}{2} \log \det S,$$

where both Γ and S are functions of δ.

The maximum-likelihood estimating equations are obtained by differentiating (3.5) with respect to δ and equating the result to zero. Defining the n-dimensional vectors $p(\delta)$ and $q(\delta)$ by

$$(3.6) \qquad p(\delta) \equiv \frac{\partial \log|\det \Gamma|}{\partial \delta}, \qquad q(\delta) \equiv -\tfrac{1}{2} \frac{\partial \log \det S}{\partial \delta},$$

the estimating equations are

$$(3.7) \qquad p(\delta) + q(\delta) = 0.$$

The equations (3.7) are nonlinear in δ and cannot be solved easily.[6] Iteration methods, however, are available and have been successfully used [4, Chapter 10]. Nonetheless, the computational problems of FIML estimation are formidable.

3.2. Restricted Σ-Matrix

The derivation in the previous subsection was based on the assumption that both δ and Σ are unknown parameters to be estimated. The a priori restrictions on the regression coefficients have already been incorporated in the definition of δ. It is also possible, however, that there exists some a priori information concerning Σ. Two such restrictions will be discussed in this subsection.

First let us examine the case where Σ is known to be a diagonal matrix. Equation (3.2) now becomes

$$\sigma_{ii} = \frac{1}{T}(y_i - Z_i\delta_i)'(y_i - Z_i\delta_i) \equiv s_{ii} \qquad (i = 1, \ldots, M),$$

$$\sigma_{ij} = 0 \equiv s_{ij}, \qquad i \neq j.$$

---

[6] To insure that a solution of (3.7) is the true maximum, the second order conditions must be satisfied. Even these conditions only insure a relative maximum. For the relationship between uniqueness and identifiability, see Section 4.2 below, especially footnote 10.

The "concentrated" likelihood function (3.5) is still correct, but may be conveniently rewritten as

$$L^*(\delta, y, Z) = k' + \log |\det \Gamma| - \tfrac{1}{2} \sum_{i=1}^{M} \log s_{ii}.$$

The estimating equations remain in the form (3.7) but $q(\delta)$ is now of a simplier form. In the special case where $p(\delta)$ is zero, the maximum-likelihood approach produces the least squares equations

$$(3.8) \qquad q_\mu(\delta) = Z'_\mu(y_\mu - Z_\mu \delta_\mu) = 0 \qquad (\mu = 1, \ldots, M).$$

This is the case in the so-called recursive system where Γ is triangular and Σ diagonal.

As a second possible restriction on Σ, let us examine the case where Σ is completely known. In that case, equation (2.15) is directly maximized with respect to δ. Again the estimating equations may be written in the form (3.7) but with a different $q(\delta)$ vector. In the special case where $p(\delta) = 0$, the maximum-likelihood approach produces the "generalized" least-squares equations

$$(3.9) \qquad q(\delta) = Z' \Psi^{-1}(y - Z\delta) = 0.$$

4. THE ASYMPTOTIC COVARIANCE MATRIX OF THE FIML ESTIMATOR

4.1. *Some Lemmas*

In the previous section the maximum-likelihood estimating equations were derived. Because these equations are nonlinear, however, the FIML estimator itself cannot be explicitly given. Nonetheless, we can derive the large-sample properties of the estimator by means of a well-known general theorem on maximum-likelihood estimators:[7]

Let $L(\theta, x)$ be $1/T$ times the logarithm of the joint density function of a sample x and parameter vector θ. Then, under certain regularity conditions, the maximum-likelihood estimator $\hat{\theta}$ tends to a multivariate normal distribution with mean θ and covariance matrix $\bar{R}^{-1}$, where

$$(4.1) \qquad \bar{R} = T \lim_{T \to \infty} E\left[- \frac{\partial^2 L}{\partial \theta \, \partial \theta'} \right].$$

The likelihood function for our regression system is given by (2.15). Under the assumptions of Section 2, the necessary regularity conditions are satisfied.[8] Thus the full covariance matrix of the maximum-likelihood estimator $(\hat{\delta}, \hat{\Sigma})$ is the inverse of

---

[7] See, for example, Kendall and Stuart [5, pp. 54–5] or Koopmans [8, pp. 149–53].
[8] For a detailed analysis, see Koopmans [8, pp. 133–148].

$$(4.2) \quad -T \lim_{T\to\infty} E \begin{bmatrix} \dfrac{\partial^2 L}{\partial\delta\,\partial\delta'} & \dfrac{\partial^2 L}{\partial\delta\,\partial(\text{vec }\Sigma)'} \\[2ex] \dfrac{\partial^2 L}{\partial(\text{vec }\Sigma)\partial\delta'} & \dfrac{\partial^2 L}{\partial(\text{vec }\Sigma)\partial(\text{vec }\Sigma)'} \end{bmatrix} = \begin{bmatrix} \bar{R}_1 & \bar{R}_2 \\[2ex] \bar{R}'_2 & \bar{R}_3 \end{bmatrix} = \bar{R},$$

where vec Σ is the vector formed from the elements of Σ. In this paper, we shall be interested only in the covariances among the δ's, that is, in the submatrix of $\bar{R}^{-1}$ corresponding to $\bar{R}_1$. Denoting this submatrix by R^{-1}, we may express the desired matrix as

$$(4.3) \quad R^{-1} = (\bar{R}_1 - \bar{R}_2\,\bar{R}_3^{-1}\,\bar{R}'_2)^{-1}.$$

In the case where Σ is unrestricted, it has been proved [8, pp. 151–53] that R, as defined in (4.3), is equivalent to

$$(4.4) \quad R = -T \lim_{T\to\infty} E\left[\frac{\partial^2 L^*}{\partial\delta\,\partial\delta'}\right],$$

where L^* is the concentrated likelihood function (3.5). The algebra will be easier if we use (4.4) rather than (4.3).

The first derivatives of (3.5) have already been defined in (3.6) as $(p+q)$. Defining the matrices $P \equiv \partial p/\partial\delta'$ and $Q \equiv \partial q/\partial\delta'$, the desired covariance matrix is the inverse of

$$(4.5) \quad R = -T \lim_{T\to\infty} E[P+Q] = -T \text{ plim } [P+Q],$$

assuming the probability limit exists.

The following facts will be useful in deriving an expression for R:[9]

(I) If $A = [a_{ij}]$ is a nonsingular matrix with inverse $A^{-1} = [a^{ij}]$, then

$$\frac{\partial \log |\det A|}{\partial a_{ij}} = a^{ji}$$

and

$$\frac{\partial a^{ij}}{\partial a_{hk}} = -a^{ih}a^{kj}.$$

(II) If $C = [c_{ij}]$ is a matrix whose elements are rational functions of the stochastic variables x_k and if plim $x_k = \bar{x}_k$ is finite for all k, then plim $C(x) = C(\bar{x})$. Moreover, plim (AB) equals (plim A)(plim B) if A and B are matrices with finite probability limits.

(III) Plim $S = \Sigma$.

(IV) Any endogenous variable y_η may be written in its reduced form,

---

[9] For the proof of I see Anderson [1, pp. 346–9]; for II, Cramér [2, pp. 254–5]. The results III and IV are easily obtained from the assumptions given in Section 2.

$$(4.6) \quad y_\eta = -\sum_{\mu=1}^{M}\sum_{\lambda=1}^{\Lambda} \gamma^{\eta\mu}\beta_{\mu\lambda}x_\lambda + \sum_{\mu=1}^{M}\gamma^{\eta\mu}u_\mu \equiv \sum_{\lambda=1}^{\Lambda}\pi_{\eta\lambda}x_\lambda + v_\eta \equiv \bar{y}_\eta + v_\eta \, ,$$

where x_λ is a column of the matrix X and $\gamma^{\eta\mu}$ is an element of Γ^{-1}. Furthermore,

$$\operatorname{plim} \frac{1}{T}\, \bar{y}'_\eta u_\mu = 0 \qquad \text{for all } \eta \text{ and } \mu.$$

4.2. The Derivation: Σ Unrestricted

Using the rule (I) for differentiating functions of matrices, it is seen that a typical (scalar) element of p is

$$(4.7) \quad p_i = \frac{\partial \log |\det \Gamma|}{\partial \delta_i} = \begin{cases} 0 & \text{if } \delta_i \text{ is a } \beta \, , \\ -\gamma^{kh} & \text{if } \delta_i \text{ is } -\gamma_{hk} \, , \end{cases}$$

and a typical (scalar) element of P is

$$(4.8) \quad P_{ij} = \frac{\partial p_i}{\partial \delta_j} = \begin{cases} 0 & \text{if either } \delta_i \text{ or } \delta_j \text{ or both are } \beta\text{'s,} \\ -\gamma^{kh'}\gamma^{k'h} & \text{if } \delta_i \text{ is } -\gamma_{hk} \text{ and } \delta_j \text{ is } -\gamma_{h'k'}. \end{cases}$$

The derivation of q is done most easily if we consider subvectors of the form

$$q_\mu = -\tfrac{1}{2}\frac{\partial \log \det S}{\partial \delta_\mu} \qquad (\mu = 1, \ldots, M) \, ,$$

where δ_μ is the vector of unknown coefficients appearing in the μth structural equation. Using (I) and the definition of S as given in (3.2),

$$(4.9) \quad q_\mu = -\tfrac{1}{2}\sum_{i=1}^{M}\sum_{j=1}^{M}\frac{\partial \log \det S}{\partial s_{ij}}\cdot\frac{\partial s_{ij}}{\partial \delta_\mu}$$

$$= \frac{1}{2T}\left(\sum_{i=1}^{M} s^{\mu i}Z'_\mu u_i + \sum_{j=1}^{M} s^{j\mu}Z'_\mu u_j\right) = \frac{1}{T}\sum_{i=1}^{M} s^{\mu i}Z'_\mu u_i \, .$$

In matrix notation, the full q-vector can be expressed as

$$(4.10) \quad q = \frac{1}{T}\, Z'(S\otimes I)^{-1}u \, .$$

The matrix Q consists of M^2 submatrices $Q_{\mu\mu'}$:

$$(4.11)$$
$$Q_{\mu\mu'} = \frac{\partial q_\mu}{\partial \delta'_{\mu'}} = \frac{1}{T}\sum_{i=1}^{M} s^{\mu i}\frac{\partial Z'_\mu u_i}{\partial \delta'_{\mu'}} + \frac{1}{T}\sum_{i=1}^{M} Z'_\mu u_i\sum_{j=1}^{M}\sum_{k=1}^{M}\frac{\partial s^{\mu i}}{\partial s_{jk}}\cdot\frac{\partial s_{jk}}{\partial \delta'_{\mu'}}$$

$$= -\frac{1}{T}\, s^{\mu\mu'}Z'_\mu Z_{\mu'} + \frac{1}{T^2}\sum_i\sum_j (s^{\mu j}s^{\mu' i} + s^{\mu\mu'}s^{ij})Z'_\mu u_i u'_j Z_{\mu'} \, .$$

The notation may be simplified by defining the $M \times M$ matrix

(4.12) $F_{\mu\mu'} = [s^{\mu j} s^{\mu' i} + s^{\mu\mu'} s^{ij}]$

and the $T \times M$ matrix of disturbances

(4.13) $U = [u_1 \dots u_M]$.

Then (4.11) becomes

(4.14) $Q_{\mu\mu'} = - \dfrac{1}{T} s^{\mu\mu'} Z'_\mu Z_{\mu'} + \dfrac{1}{T^2} Z'_\mu U F_{\mu\mu'} U' Z_{\mu'}$.

We must now evaluate plim $(P+Q)$. Since the γ's are not stochastic, plim $P = P$. However, plim Q is much more complicated since the u's, the s's, and the y-components of Z are all stochastic. We shall consider plim $Q_{\mu\mu'}$ as the typical submatrix. It will prove convenient to partition $Q_{\mu\mu'}$ according to endogenous and predetermined variables. Thus

(4.15)
$$\text{plim } Q_{\mu\mu'} = \text{plim} \left(- \frac{s^{\mu\mu'}}{T} \begin{bmatrix} Y'_\mu Y_{\mu'} & Y'_\mu X_{\mu'} \\ \\ X'_\mu Y_{\mu'} & X'_\mu X_{\mu'} \end{bmatrix} \right.$$
$$\left. + \frac{1}{T^2} \begin{bmatrix} Y'_\mu U F_{\mu\mu'} U' Y_{\mu'} & Y'_\mu U F_{\mu\mu'} U' X_{\mu'} \\ \\ X'_\mu U F_{\mu\mu'} U' Y_{\mu'} & X'_\mu U F_{\mu\mu'} U' X_{\mu'} \end{bmatrix} \right) = \text{plim} \begin{bmatrix} Q_1 & Q_2 \\ Q_3 & Q_4 \end{bmatrix}$$

Evaluating in reverse order,

(4.16)
$$\text{plim } Q_4 = -\sigma^{\mu\mu'} \text{plim} \frac{1}{T} X'_\mu X_{\mu'} + (\text{plim} \frac{1}{T} X'_\mu U)(\text{plim } F_{\mu\mu'})(\text{plim} \frac{1}{T} U' X_{\mu'})$$
$$= -\sigma^{\mu\mu'} \text{plim} \frac{1}{T} X'_\mu X_{\mu'} ,$$

(4.17)
$$\text{plim } Q_3 = -\sigma^{\mu\mu'} \text{plim} \frac{1}{T} X'_\mu (\overline{Y}_{\mu'} + V_{\mu'}) + (\text{plim} \frac{1}{T} X'_\mu U)(\text{plim } F_{\mu\mu'})$$
$$\times (\text{plim} \frac{1}{T} U' Y_{\mu'}) = -\sigma^{\mu\mu'} \text{plim} \frac{1}{T} X'_\mu \overline{Y}_{\mu'} ,$$

and, similarly,

(4.18) $\text{plim } Q_2 = -\sigma^{\mu\mu'} \text{plim} \dfrac{1}{T} \overline{Y}'_\mu X_{\mu'}$.

The final part, plim Q_1, is more complicated. We shall consider, therefore, typical elements y_1 of Y_μ and y_2 of $Y_{\mu'}$. Then one element of plim Q_1 is

(4.19)
$$\text{plim } Q_1^{(1,2)} = -\sigma^{\mu\mu'} \text{plim} \frac{1}{T} (\overline{y}_1 + v_1)' (\overline{y}_2 + v_2)$$
$$+ (\text{plim} \frac{1}{T} y'_1 U)(\text{plim } F_{\mu\mu'})(\text{plim} \frac{1}{T} U' y_2) .$$

The first of the two terms on the right of (4.19) is

$$-\sigma^{\mu\mu'} \operatorname{plim} \frac{1}{T} \bar{y}_1' \bar{y}_2 - \sigma^{\mu\mu'} \operatorname{plim} \frac{1}{T} \sum_{i=1}^{M} \sum_{j=1}^{M} \gamma^{1i} u_i' u_j \gamma^{2j}$$

$$= -\sigma^{\mu\mu'} \operatorname{plim} \frac{1}{T} \bar{y}_1' \bar{y}_2 - \sigma^{\mu\mu'} \sum_{i=1}^{M} \sum_{j=1}^{M} \gamma^{1i} \gamma^{2j} \sigma_{ij}.$$

The second of the terms on the right of (4.19) is

$$\sum_{i=1}^{M} \sum_{j=1}^{M} (\sigma^{\mu j} \sigma^{\mu' i} + \sigma^{\mu\mu'} \sigma^{ij})(\operatorname{plim} \frac{1}{T} v_1' u_i)(\operatorname{plim} \frac{1}{T} v_2' u_j)$$

$$= \sum_{i=1}^{M} \sum_{j=1}^{M} (\sigma^{\mu j} \sigma^{\mu' i} + \sigma^{\mu\mu'} \sigma^{ij})\left(\sum_{k=1}^{M} \gamma^{1k} \operatorname{plim} \frac{1}{T} u_k' u_i\right)\left(\sum_{l=1}^{M} \gamma^{2l} \operatorname{plim} \frac{1}{T} u_l' u_j\right)$$

$$= \sum_{i=1}^{M} \sum_{j=1}^{M} (\sigma^{\mu j} \sigma^{\mu' i} + \sigma^{\mu\mu'} \sigma^{ij})\left(\sum_k \sum_l \gamma^{1k} \gamma^{2l} \sigma_{ki} \sigma_{lj}\right)$$

$$= \sigma^{\mu\mu'} \sum_{k=1}^{M} \sum_{l=1}^{M} \gamma^{1k} \gamma^{2l} \sigma_{lk} + \gamma^{1\mu'} \gamma^{2\mu}.$$

Combining these terms, (4.19) becomes

$$(4.20) \qquad \operatorname{plim} Q^{(1,2)} = -\sigma^{\mu\mu'} \operatorname{plim} \frac{1}{T} \bar{y}_1' \bar{y}_2 + \gamma^{1\mu'} \gamma^{2\mu}.$$

From (4.8) we see that a similar partitioning of $\operatorname{plim} P_{\mu\mu'}$ yields the zero matrices P_2, P_3, and P_4; and $\operatorname{plim} P_1^{(1,2)} = -\gamma^{1\mu'} \gamma^{2\mu}$.

The results in (4.19) and (4.20) are easily generalized for the whole matrix Q_1. Thus, on combining (4.15)–(4.20),

$$(4.21) \qquad R_{\mu\mu'} = -T \operatorname{plim} [P_{\mu\mu'} + Q_{\mu\mu'}] = T \sigma^{\mu\mu'} \operatorname{plim} \frac{1}{T} \begin{bmatrix} \bar{Y}_\mu' \bar{Y}_{\mu'} & \bar{Y}_\mu' X_{\mu'} \\ X_\mu' \bar{Y}_{\mu'} & X_\mu' X_{\mu'} \end{bmatrix}.$$

Defining

$$(4.22) \qquad Z = \begin{bmatrix} \bar{Y}_1 & X_1 & 0 & 0 & \dots & 0 & 0 \\ 0 & 0 & \bar{Y}_2 & X_2 & \dots & 0 & 0 \\ \vdots & & & & & & \vdots \\ 0 & 0 & 0 & 0 & \dots & \bar{Y}_M & X_M \end{bmatrix} = \begin{bmatrix} Z_1 & 0 & \dots & 0 \\ 0 & Z_2 & \dots & 0 \\ \vdots & & & \vdots \\ 0 & 0 & \dots & Z_M \end{bmatrix},$$

we may write the general result

$$(4.23) \qquad R = -T \operatorname{plim} [P + Q] = T \operatorname{plim} \frac{1}{T} Z' \Psi^{-1} Z.$$

But

$$(4.24) \qquad Z_\mu = [\bar{Y}_\mu \quad X_\mu] = [X \Pi_\mu \quad X_\mu] = X[\Pi_\mu \quad D_\mu] \equiv X W_\mu,$$

where Π_μ is the $\Lambda \times m_\mu$ matrix of reduced form coefficients corresponding to Y_μ; D_μ is a matrix of 1's and 0's such that the (i, j)th element is 1 if the jth column of X_μ is the ith column of X, and zero otherwise. Defining

$$(4.25) \quad W = \begin{bmatrix} W_1 & 0 & \cdots & 0 \\ 0 & W_2 & \cdots & 0 \\ \vdots & \vdots & & \vdots \\ 0 & 0 & \cdots & W_M \end{bmatrix},$$

equation (4.23) becomes

$$(4.26) \quad R = T \operatorname{plim} \frac{1}{T} W'[\Sigma^{-1} \otimes (X'X)]W = TW'(\Sigma^{-1} \otimes \mathcal{M})W,$$

where $\mathcal{M} = \operatorname{plim}(1/T) X'X$. Thus the asymptotic covariance matrix of the FIML estimator when Σ is unrestricted is

$$(4.27) \quad \frac{1}{T} [W'(\Sigma^{-1} \otimes \mathcal{M})W]^{-1}.$$

The inverse will exist if and only if the rank of W is n. Since $\rho(W) = \sum_{\mu=1}^{M} \rho(W_\mu)$, W_μ must have rank n_μ. Since W_μ is a $\Lambda \times n_\mu$ matrix, a necessary condition is the well-known order condition of identifiability[10] $\Lambda \geq n_\mu$.

4.3. *The Derivation*: Σ *Restricted*

The derivation in Section 4.2 assumed that there existed no a priori knowledge about the matrix Σ. Suppose, however, that some of the elements of Σ are restricted (by economic theory or by other empirical evidence) to known values. Two examples of such restrictions were given in Section 3.2. How does this added certainty affect the sampling variation of the maximum-likelihood estimator?

A very general answer can be given on the basis of the theory presented in Section 4.1. Let A be the matrix on the right of (4.2). Suppose that the last row and column of A represent an element of Σ that is now known a priori. Let B be the matrix obtained by deleting this row and column. If the a priori information is ignored, the covariance matrix for the ML estimator $\hat{\delta}$ is a submatrix of A^{-1}. However, if the information is used, the covariance matrix of the new estimator $\tilde{\delta}$ is the corresponding submatrix of B^{-1}. Let

$$A^{-1} = \begin{bmatrix} B & c \\ c' & d \end{bmatrix}^{-1} = \begin{bmatrix} \bar{B} & \bar{c} \\ \bar{c}' & \bar{d} \end{bmatrix}$$

[10] See Hood and Koopmans [4, p. 174]. The matrix to be inverted in (4.27) is also the probability limit of the Hessian matrix of our maximization problem. Thus the identification condition is necessary to insure that the equations in (3.7) are independent.

where $(c'\ d)$ is the deleted row. Since it is a nonsingular covariance matrix, A is positive definite (and therefore so are B, $\bar{B}$, d, and $\bar{d}$). But a little algebra yields $\bar{B} - B^{-1} = \bar{c}\bar{c}'/\bar{d}$ which is positive semidefinite. As long as $\bar{c}$ is not zero, $\bar{B}$ is "more" positive definite than B^{-1} and the same is true for all principle submatrices. We may therefore conclude that estimation under correct a priori information yields a "smaller" covariance matrix.[11]

Returning to the examples of Section 3.2, consider first the case where Σ is known to be a diagonal matrix. The vector p and the matrix P remain unchanged, but q becomes

$$(4.28) \qquad q_\mu = \frac{1}{T\sigma_{\mu\mu}} Z'_\mu u_\mu ,$$

and Q takes the form

$$(4.29) \qquad Q_{\mu\mu'} = \begin{cases} 0 & \text{if } \mu \neq \mu' , \\ \dfrac{1}{-Ts_{\mu\mu}} Z'_\mu Z_\mu + \dfrac{2}{T^2 s^2_{\mu\mu}} Z'_\mu u_\mu u'_\mu Z_\mu & \text{if } \mu = \mu'. \end{cases}$$

Finally, $R = -T \operatorname{plim}(P+Q)$ takes the form

$$(4.30) \qquad R_{\mu\mu'} = \begin{cases} -TP_{\mu\mu'} & \text{if } \mu \neq \mu' , \\ T \operatorname{plim} \dfrac{1}{T\sigma_{\mu\mu}} Z'_\mu Z_\mu + TP_{\mu\mu} & \text{if } \mu = \mu' . \end{cases}$$

In the second example where Σ is known completely,

$$(4.31) \qquad Q = -\frac{1}{T} Z' \Psi^{-1} Z ,$$

and

$$(4.32) \qquad R = -TP + T \operatorname{plim} \frac{1}{T} Z' \Psi^{-1} Z .$$

In both cases the a priori knowledge changes the covariance matrix of the $\hat{\delta}$ estimator. Only under the very special assumptions that $P = 0$ and $Z = \bar{Z}$ will the added restrictions not increase the efficiency of estimation. These special assumptions reduce the model (2.3) to the case of classical "non-simultaneous" estimation. Thus, contrary to classical regression, in simultaneous equation models knowledge about variances increases the efficiency of the ML estimator of the means.

5. AN ALTERNATIVE ESTIMATOR

5.1. *A General Theorem*
We now suggest a simpler estimator which is closely related to the maximum-

---

[11] Klein [7, pp. 224–9] presents a similar result. See also Section 6 below.

likelihood estimator. This "linearized maximum-likelihood" estimator is motivated by the following general theorem:[12]

Let $L(\theta, x)$ be $1/T$ times the logarithm of the likelihood function of a sample x and an n-dimensional parameter vector θ. It is assumed that all the partial derivatives of $L(\theta)$ up to the third order are continuous functions of θ, are bounded for all values of θ, and have finite probability limits. Let θ^0 be some consistent estimator of θ with sampling variance $O(T^{-\frac{1}{2}})$. Let θ^M be the maximum-likelihood estimator. Finally, let the linearized ML estimator be defined as

$$(5.1) \qquad \theta^L = \theta^0 - \left[\frac{\partial^2 L}{\partial \theta_i \partial \theta_j}\right]^{-1}_{\theta=\theta^0} \left[\frac{\partial L}{\partial \theta_i}\right]_{\theta=\theta^0}.$$

Then, θ^L has the same asymptotic distribution as θ^M.

PROOF: The ML estimator θ^M satisfies, by definition, the equations

$$(5.2) \qquad \frac{\partial L}{\partial \theta_r}\bigg|_{\theta=\theta^M} = 0 \qquad\qquad (r=1, \ldots, n).$$

The rth equation may be rewritten as

$$(5.3) \qquad \frac{\partial L}{\partial \theta_r}\bigg|_{\theta=\theta^0} + \sum_{i=1}^{n} (\theta_i^M - \theta_i^0)\left(\frac{\partial^2 L}{\partial \theta_r \partial \theta_i}\right)_{\theta=\theta^0}$$
$$+ \tfrac{1}{2}\sum_i\sum_j(\theta_i^M - \theta_i^0)(\theta_j^M - \theta_j^0)\left(\frac{\partial^3 L}{\partial \theta_r \partial \theta_i \partial \theta_j}\right)_{\theta=\theta^*} = 0,$$

where θ^* is between θ^0 and θ^M. From (5.1), an element of θ^L is

$$(5.4) \qquad \theta_s^L = \theta_s^0 - \sum_r g_{sr}\left(\frac{\partial L}{\partial \theta_r}\right)_{\theta=\theta^0},$$

where g_{sr} is an element of $\left[\dfrac{\partial^2 L}{\partial \theta_s \partial \theta_r}\right]^{-1}_{\theta=\theta^0}$. Combining (5.3) and (5.4),

$$\theta_s^L = \theta_s^M + \tfrac{1}{2}\sum_i\sum_j(\theta_i^M - \theta_i^0)(\theta_j^M - \theta_j^0)\sum_r g_{sr}\left(\frac{\partial^3 L}{\partial \theta_r \partial \theta_i \partial \theta_j}\right)_{\theta=\theta^*}$$
$$= \theta_s^M + (\theta^M - \theta^0)' A_s(\theta^M - \theta^0) \equiv \theta_s^M + \varDelta_s.$$

By our assumptions, plim A_s is finite. In addition $(\theta^M - \theta^0)$ is of the order $T^{-\frac{1}{2}}$ in probability since both θ^M and θ^0 are consistent and of that order. Hence $\varDelta_s$ is of the order T^{-1} in probability. The vector θ^L may then be written as $\theta^L = \theta^M + \varDelta$, where $\varDelta$ is of the order T^{-1} in probability.

Under regularity conditions, $T^{\frac{1}{2}}\theta^M$ has an asymptotic normal distribution.

[12] Professor E. Parzen has called to our attention a similar theorem stated, without proof, by Ferguson [3, pp. 1049–50]. The idea is not new; it probably originates with R. A. Fisher.

Clearly $T^{\frac{1}{2}}\varDelta$ converges to zero as T approaches infinity. Thus, by a simple convergence theorem (Cramér [2, pp. 254–55]), $T^{\frac{1}{2}}\theta^L$ converges to the same distribution as $T^{\frac{1}{2}}\theta^M$ as T approaches infinity.

5.2. *The LML Estimating Equations*

While deriving the FIML sampling covariances in Section 4 we produced all the equations necessary for the linearized estimator. Hence we may summarize as follows: Let δ^0 be some consistent estimate of δ, such that $\delta^0 - \delta$ is of the order $T^{-\frac{1}{2}}$ in probability. One possible choice is the two-stage least-squares estimator [10, p. 56]:

(5.7) $\delta_\mu^0 = [Z_\mu' X (X'X)^{-1} X'Z_\mu]^{-1} Z_\mu' X (X'X)^{-1} X'y_\mu$.

Let $u_\mu^0 = (y_\mu - Z_\mu \delta_\mu^0)$ and $T\sigma_{\mu\mu'}^0 = u_\mu^{0'} u_{\mu'}^0$. Then the LML estimator is of the form

(5.8) $\hat{\delta} = \delta^0 - (P_0 + Q_0)^{-1} (p_0 + q_0)$.

The vector p and the matrix P are defined in (4.7) and (4.8). The vector q is given in (4.10). The matrix Q is determined as follows:
   1. When Σ is unrestricted

(5.9) $Q_0 = -\dfrac{1}{T} Z' \Psi_0^{-1} Z + \dfrac{1}{T^2} Z' G_0 Z$,

where

(5.10) $G = [G_{\mu\mu'}] = [U F_{\mu\mu'} U']$.

   2. When Σ is a diagonal matrix, Q_0 remains of the form (5.9) but with

(5.11) $G = [G_{\mu\mu'}] = [2\sigma^{\mu\mu'} \sigma^{\mu\mu'} u_\mu u_{\mu'}']$.

   3. When Σ is a known matrix

(5.12) $Q_0 = -\dfrac{1}{T} Z' \Psi^{-1} Z$.

These equations may be interpreted as follows: the matrix $Z' \Psi^{-1} Z$ is the matrix of generalized least squares estimation. The matrix P adjusts for the endogenous variables in Z. The second part of Q is due to the fact that Σ must be estimated also.

6. EFFICIENT ESTIMATION UNDER ALTERNATIVE MODELS

In Sections 3 and 5 two estimators of the parameter vector δ (FIML and LML) have been presented. Both are "full information" estimators in the sense that all the a priori restrictions on the model are taken into account. Recently Zellner and

Theil [10][13] have proposed another full information estimator, three-stage least squares (3SLS). In another article Zellner [9] has applied a similar approach to the special case where the matrix Z of (2.3) is entirely nonstochastic. The 3SLS approach can be described as follows. If Z is uncorrelated with u, generalized least squares may be applied to (2.3). This yields the estimator

(6.1) $\hat{\delta} = (Z' \Psi^{-1} Z)^{-1} Z' \Psi^{-1} y$.

Since Ψ is generally unknown, a consistent estimator (based on single equation least squares) is used. If Z contains current endogenous variables, generalized least squares is not consistent. In this case Zellner and Theil propose to "purify" Z by means of the X-matrix. The estimator in the general case is

(6.2) $\hat{\delta}_3 = [Z'\{\hat{\Sigma}^{-1} \otimes X(X'X)^{-1} X'\}Z]^{-1} Z'(\hat{\Sigma}^{-1} \otimes X(X'X)^{-1} X')y$,

where $\hat{\Sigma}$ is some consistent estimator of Σ. Zellner and Theil show that $\hat{\delta}_3$ is asymptotically normal with mean δ and covariance matrix

(6.3) $\text{plim}[Z'\{\Sigma^{-1} \otimes X(X'X)^{-1} X'\}Z]^{-1}$.

A priori information about Σ does not change this asymptotic covariance matrix. Since $Z_\mu = XW_\mu$, (6.3) may be rewritten as

(6.4) $\text{plim}[W'\{\Sigma^{-1} \otimes (X'X)\}W]^{-1} = \dfrac{1}{T}[W'(\Sigma^{-1} \otimes \mathcal{M})W]^{-1}$

We now have described three different estimating methods: FIML, LML, and 3SLS. All yield estimates of δ which are asymptotically unbiased and normally distributed. We can then compare them on the basis of their asymptotic covariance matrices. We shall use the following definition of efficiency in our comparison:

Let δ_i be a consistent and asymptotically normally distributed estimator with covariance matrix Ω_i. Then δ_0 is *efficient* if and only if $\Omega_i - \Omega_0$ is positive semidefinite, that is,

$c' \Omega_0 c \leqq c' \Omega_i c$

for all vectors c and for all other estimators δ_i.

This definition is equivalent to Cramér's [2, p. 493] definition which is in terms of concentration ellipses.

We then can state the following result: *The FIML and LML approaches yield efficient estimates of δ as long as the a priori information upon which they are based is*

---

[13] Professor Dale Jorgenson has pointed out an error on page 66 of the Zellner and Theil paper. In the equation below (4.13) μ should be summed from 1 to M, not q to M. This error does not affect the results. However, another error on page 70 invalidates the numerical example of Section 5.2. Equation (5.7) is wrong since $X_R'\hat{U}$ is not necessarily zero for finite samples. We have recomputed their example and present it in Section 7. Finally, a printing error in Table II: the $y_1 x_8$ moment should read 1133.90.

correct. The proof for the general maximum likelihood approach is given by Cramér [2, 498–504]. Rubin and others[14] have shown that the regularity assumptions of the general theorem are valid for the model described in Section 2. The theorem of Section 5.1 proves the result for LML.

Our comparison of LML, FIML, and 3SLS then comes down to the question: under what conditions does the covariance matrix of the 3SLS estimator equal those of LML and FIML? The answer can be seen from equation (6.4), (4.27), and the discussion in Section 4.3. It can be summarized in the statements:

1. Three-stage least squares is efficient when there are no a priori restrictions on Σ.
2. In the special case where Z contains no current endogenous variables, three-stage least squares is equivalent to the method proposed by Zellner [9, pp. 2–5]. This method is efficient even if Σ is restricted.
3. Three-stage least squares is inefficient when Σ is restricted as long as Z contains current endogenous variables.

Computationally, 3SLS is the easiest of the three methods; the most difficult is clearly FIML. Thus it seems reasonable (on the basis of large-sample theory) to use 3SLS when Σ is unrestricted and LML when Σ is restricted. In the case of exact identification, all three methods give the same results.

7. AN EXAMPLE [15a]

In the model presented in Section 2, it was assumed that all M equations of (2.3) are stochastic. Thus any identities must have already been "solved out." This assumption, however, was introduced only to simplify the derivation; in actual computations, there is no need to reduce the system algebraically.

Suppose that the system contains M stochastic equations and M' identities. We assume that there are no unknown parameters in the identities. The system (2.11) may be written as

$$(7.1) \quad \Gamma_1 y_1(t) + \Gamma_2 y_2(t) + B_1 x(t) = u(t),$$

$$(7.2) \quad \Gamma_3 y_1(t) + \Gamma_4 y_2(t) + B_2 x(t) = 0,$$

where $y_1(t)$ is a vector of M of the dependent variables, $y_2(t)$ is a vector of the remaining M' dependent variables, $x(t)$ is the vector of all Λ predetermined variables, and $u(t)$ is the M-dimensional vector of disturbances.[15] Supposing Γ_4 is nonsingular,

$$(7.3) \quad y_2(t) = -\Gamma_4^{-1}\Gamma_3 y_1(t) - \Gamma_4^{-1} B_2 x(t).$$

[14] See [4, p. 147; 8, pp. 133–145] and the works cited there.

[15] The notation introduced here is used only in equations (7.1) to (7.6).

[15a] For more accurate computations, see A. Zellner and H. Thornber, "Computational Accuracy and Estimation of Simultaneous Equation Econometric Models," *Econometrica*, Vol. 34 (July, 1966), pp. 727–729.

The derivation of Section 2 may be applied by considering (7.1) as a transformation of $u(t)$ to $y_1(t)$. The only term in (2.9) which is affected by the presence of $y_2(t)$ is $\log |\det J|$. In the present case

(7.4) $\dfrac{\partial u(t)}{\partial y_1'(t)} = \dfrac{\partial u(t)}{\partial y_1'(t)} + \dfrac{\partial u(t)}{\partial y_2'(t)} \dfrac{\partial y_2(t)}{\partial y_1'(t)} = \Gamma_1 - \Gamma_2 \Gamma_4^{-1} \Gamma_3$.

But[16]

(7.5) $\det(\Gamma_1 - \Gamma_2 \Gamma_4^{-1} \Gamma_3) = \det \Gamma \cdot \det \Gamma_4^{-1}$,

where Γ is the matrix (of order $M + M'$) of all endogenous coefficients. Therefore,

(7.6) $\log |\det(\Gamma_1 - \Gamma_2 \Gamma_4^{-1} \Gamma_3)| = \log |\det \Gamma| + \text{constant}$.

The above analysis suggests the following rule for FIML and LML estimation: when forming $q(\delta)$ and $Q(\delta)$ completely ignore the identities. When forming $p(\delta)$ and $P(\delta)$ use the elements of Γ^{-1}, the full matrix including identities.

We shall now use the LML method to estimate Klein's Model I of the U.S. economy [6, pp. 58–80]. The system consists of a consumption equation, an investment equation, a demand for labor equation, and three identities:

$$
\begin{aligned}
C &= \delta_1 \Pi + \delta_2(W_1 + W_2) + \delta_3 \Pi_{-1} + \delta_4 + u_1 , \\
I &= \delta_5 \Pi + \delta_6 \Pi_{-1} + \delta_7 K_{-1} + \delta_8 + u_2 , \\
W_1 &= \delta_9(Y + T_a - W_2) + \delta_{10}(Y + T_a - W_2)_{-1} + \delta_{11} t + \delta_{12} + u_3 , \\
Y + T_a &= C + I + G , \\
Y &= W_1 + W_2 + \Pi , \\
K &= K_{-1} + I .
\end{aligned}
$$

The T-dimensional vectors C, I, W_1, Y, Π, and K are the time series for the current endogenous variables. Therefore,

$$
\Gamma =
\begin{bmatrix}
1 & 0 & -\delta_2 & 0 & -\delta_1 & 0 \\
0 & 1 & 0 & 0 & -\delta_5 & 0 \\
0 & 0 & 1 & -\delta_9 & 0 & 0 \\
-1 & -1 & 0 & 1 & 0 & 0 \\
0 & 0 & 1 & -1 & 1 & 0 \\
0 & -1 & 0 & 0 & 0 & 1
\end{bmatrix} .
$$

The Z-matrix, defined in (2.4), is formed from the matrices

$$
\begin{aligned}
Z_1 &= [\Pi \quad W_1 + W_2 \quad \Pi_{-1} \quad 1] , \\
Z_2 &= [\Pi \quad \Pi_{-1} \quad K_{-1} \quad 1] ,
\end{aligned}
$$

and

$$
Z_3 = [(Y + T_a - W_2) \quad (Y + T_a - W_2)_{-1} \quad t \quad 1] ,
$$

---

[16] See, for example, Anderson [1, p. 344].

where 1 represents a vector of unity elements.

The LML estimate of δ, under no prior restrictions on Σ, is

$$\delta^L = \delta^0 - (TP + TQ)^{-1}(Tp + Tq).$$

The matrices P and Q and the vectors p and q are, of course, functions of the initial estimates δ^0 and Σ^0. For these estimates we shall use the two-stage least squares results, as given in Zellner and Theil [10, pp. 74–5]:[17]

$$\delta_0 = \begin{bmatrix} \delta_1 \\ \delta_2 \\ \delta_3 \\ \delta_4 \\ \delta_5 \\ \delta_6 \\ \delta_7 \\ \delta_8 \\ \delta_9 \\ \delta_{10} \\ \delta_{11} \\ \delta_{12} \end{bmatrix} = \begin{bmatrix} 0.0173 \\ 0.8102 \\ 0.2162 \\ 16.5548 \\ 0.1502 \\ 0.6159 \\ -0.1578 \\ 20.2782 \\ 0.4389 \\ 0.1467 \\ 0.1304 \\ 1.5003 \end{bmatrix} ; \quad \Sigma_0 = \begin{bmatrix} -1.0441 & 0.4379 & -0.3850 \\ & 1.3832 & 0.1926 \\ & & 0.4764 \end{bmatrix}.$$

From these estimates we may form

$$\Gamma_0^{-1} = \begin{bmatrix} -1.6636 & 0.6636 & 1.2193 & 0.6636 & 0.1285 & 0 \\ 0.1531 & 1.1531 & -0.0518 & 0.1531 & 0.1759 & 0 \\ 0.7973 & 0.7973 & 1.5124 & 0.7973 & 0.1336 & 0 \\ 1.8167 & 1.8167 & 1.1675 & 1.8167 & 0.3043 & 0 \\ 1.0194 & 1.0194 & -0.3448 & 1.0194 & 1.1708 & 0 \\ 0.1531 & 1.1531 & -0.0518 & 0.1531 & 0.1759 & 1 \end{bmatrix}$$

and

$$\Sigma_0^{-1} = \begin{bmatrix} 2.1596 & -0.9819 & 2.1422 \\ & 1.2126 & -1.2838 \\ & & 4.3492 \end{bmatrix}.$$

As an example of the calculation of p, take the first element p_1. This element represents δ_1, which appears in Γ as $-\gamma_{15}$. Thus, according to (4.7), p_1 equals $-\gamma^{51}$ or 1.0194. Similarly, let us take P_{19} as an example of the calculation of P. This element represents δ_1 and δ_9, which appear in Γ as $-\gamma_{15}$ and $-\gamma_{34}$. By (4.8), P_{19} equals $-\gamma^{53}\gamma^{41}$ or 0.6264.

For the computation of q and Q we shall need the nine vectors

$$Z'_\mu u_i = Z'_\mu y_i - Z'_\mu Z_i \delta_i \qquad (\mu, i = 1, 2, 3).$$

---

[17] We have recalculated the Σ-matrix (see footnote 13). We present the 2SLS estimates to four decimal places. In the actual calculations more places were used to avoid rounding errors.

TABLE I

ESTIMATES OF THE PARAMETERS IN KLEIN'S MODEL I

Equation	Coefficient	Coefficient of	2SLS Coefficient estimate	2SLS Var. of coeff. estimator	3SLS Coefficient estimate	3SLS Var. of coeff. estimator	LML Coefficient estimate	LML Var. of coeff. estimator
Consumption	δ_1	Π	0.0173	0.0139	0.1232	0.0117	0.1237	0.0099
	δ_2	$W_1 + W_2$	0.8102	0.0016	0.7819	0.0015	0.7756	0.0014
	δ_3	Π_{-1}	0.2162	0.0115	0.1695	0.0101	0.2004	0.0083
	δ_4	1	16.5548	1.745	16.6913	1.7259	16.4510	1.6454
Investment	δ_5	Π	0.1502	0.0301	-0.1073	0.0289	-0.1953	0.0245
	δ_6	Π_{-1}	0.6159	0.0265	0.8343	0.0252	0.8967	0.0213
	δ_7	K_{-1}	-0.1578	0.0013	-0.2227	0.0013	-0.2243	0.0012
	δ_8	1	20.2782	56.892	34.0981	56.6364	34.8503	52.3102
Demand for Labor	δ_9	$Y + T - W_2$	0.4389	0.0013	0.4052	0.0010	0.3324	0.0014
	δ_{10}	$(Y + T - W_2)_{-1}$	0.1467	0.0015	0.1757	0.0012	0.2403	0.0015
	δ_{11}	t	0.1304	0.0008	0.1454	0.0008	0.1823	0.0008
	δ_{12}	1	1.5003	1.317	1.8149	1.2576	2.4624	1.2848

TABLE II

ESTIMATED COVARIANCE MATRIX OF LML COEFFICIENT ESTIMATORS FOR KLEIN'S MODEL I

col 1	col 2	col 3	col 4	col 5	col 6	col 7	col 8	col 9	col 10	col 11	col 12
0.009888	-0.001406	-0.006119	-0.008478	0.001282	-0.000943	-0.000705	0.135263	-0.001614	0.001539	0.000920	0.007706
	0.001446	-0.000427	-0.029242	0.000922	-0.000866	0.000368	-0.075127	0.000085	-0.000109	-0.000587	0.001238
		0.008284	-0.014602	-0.002818	0.003769	0.000009	-0.015892	0.000860	-0.001339	0.000341	0.026012
			1.645379	-0.013780	-0.009836	-0.003490	1.114676	0.009669	0.000464	0.003238	-0.626100
				0.024516	-0.020427	0.003490	-0.779573	0.002603	-0.002240	-0.000618	-0.026522
					0.021336	-0.003104	0.618108	-0.002000	0.001962	0.000294	0.006417
						0.001183	-0.245320	0.000345	-0.000254	-0.000082	-0.005995
							52.310152	-0.080432	0.056720	0.021984	1.554446
								0.001388	-0.001250	-0.000429	-0.010932
									0.001474	0.000180	-0.010438
										0.000849	0.015317
											1.3_____

These may be calculated from the moments given in Table II of [10] and from the 2SLS estimates of δ given above. Then

$$Tq_\mu = \sum_{i=1}^{3} Z'_\mu u_i \sigma^{\mu i} \quad (\mu = 1, 2, 3),$$

and

$$TQ_{\mu\mu'} = -Z'_\mu Z_{\mu'} \sigma^{\mu\mu'} + \frac{1}{T} \sum_{i=1}^{3} \sum_{j=1}^{3} Z'_\mu u_i u'_j Z_{\mu'} (\sigma^{\mu\mu'} \sigma^{ij} + \sigma^{\mu j} \sigma^{\mu' i})$$
$$(\mu, \mu' = 1, 2, 3).$$

The LML, 2SLS, and 3SLS estimates are given in Table I. Also presented in that table are the estimated variances of these estimates. Finally, the complete matrix of the LML covariances is consistently estimated by $-(TP + TQ)^{-1}$. This matrix appears in Table II.

Northwestern University and The Netherlands School of Economics

REFERENCES

[1] ANDERSON, T. W.: *An Introduction to Multivariate Statistical Analysis*, New York, John Wiley and Sons, 1957.

[2] CRAMÉR, H.: *Mathematical Methods of Statistics*, Princeton, Princeton University Press, 1946.

[3] FERGUSON, T. S.: "A Method of Generating Best and Asymptotically Normal Estimates with Application to the Estimation of Bacterial Densities," *Annals of Mathematical Statistics*, Vol. 29, No. 4 (1958), pp. 1046–1062.

[4] HOOD, W. C., AND T. C. KOOPMANS: *Studies in Econometric Method*, New York, John Wiley and Sons, 1953.

[5] KENDALL, M. G., AND A. STUART: *Advanced Theory of Statistics*, Vol. 2, London, Griffin & Co., 1961.

[6] KLEIN, L. R.: *Economic Fluctuations in the United States, 1921–1941*, New York, John Wiley and Sons, 1950.

[7] ———: "The Efficiency of Estimation in Econometric Models" in *Essays in Economics and Econometrics*, Chapel Hill, University of North Carolina Press, 1960.

[8] KOOPMANS, T. C.: *Statistical Inference in Dynamic Economic Models*, New York, John Wiley and Sons, 1950.

[9] ZELLNER, A.: "An Efficient Method of Estimating Seemingly Unrelated Regressions and Tests for Aggregation Bias," *Journal of the American Statistical Association*, Vol. 57, (1962), pp. 348–368.

[10] ZELLNER, A., AND H. THEIL: "Three-Stage Least Squares: Simultaneous Estimation of Simultaneous Equations," *Econometrica*, Vol. 30 (1962), pp. 54–78.

Econometrica, Vol. 32, 3 (July 1964)

SPECTRAL ANALYSIS OF SEASONAL ADJUSTMENT PROCEDURES*

BY MARC NERLOVE

This paper discusses one of the uses to which two powerful techniques of modern time series analysis may be put in economics: namely, the study of the precise effects of seasonal adjustment procedures on the characteristics of the series to which they are applied. Since most economic data appearing at intervals of less than a year are to a greater or lesser extent "manufactured" from more basic time series, the problem of assessing the effects of the "manufacturing" processes upon the essential characteristics of the raw material to which they are applied is not unimportant. Perhaps the most common type of adjustment applied to raw economic time series is that designed to eliminate so-called seasonal fluctuations. The precise nature of seasonality is not easy to define, but an attempt is made in Section 2.1 below.

The techniques employed to study the effects of seasonal adjustment procedures are those of *spectral* and *cross-spectral* analysis. In somewhat oversimplified terms the basic idea behind these types of analysis is that a stochastic time series may be decomposed into an infinite number of sine and cosine waves with infinitesimal random amplitudes. Spectral analysis deals with a single time series in terms of its frequency "content"; cross-spectral analysis deals with the relation between two time series in terms of their respective frequency "contents." The two techniques are discussed in both theoretical and practical terms.

Spectral analyses have been made for about seventy-five time series of United States employment, unemployment, labor force, and various categories thereof. Cross-spectral analyses have been made of the relations between these series and the corresponding series as seasonally adjusted by the procedures used by the Bureau of Labor Statistics. Two major conclusions regarding the effects of the BLS seasonal adjustment procedures emerge from these analyses. First, these procedures remove far more from the series to which they are applied than can properly be considered as seasonal. Second, if the relation between two seasonally adjusted series in time is compared with the corresponding relation between the original series in time, it is found that there is a distortion due to the process of seasonal adjustment itself. Both defects impair the usefulness of the seasonally adjusted series as indicators of economic conditions, but, of the two, temporal distortion is the more serious defect. Examples of some of these results are discussed below in Section 3.3.

1. THE NATURE OF SPECTRAL ANALYSIS

1.1. *Description of a Time Series in the Time Domain*

THE QUESTION of assessing the effects of a method of seasonal adjustment, or any other adjustment procedure, may be answered in terms of an accurate description of the original series, the modified series, and the relation between the two. In order to implement this approach, one must have a statistical theory of the description of cyclical time series. Interest in formal techniques of describing time series

---

* For author's acknowledgements and some additional references to the literature, see page 284.

goes back to the early years of this century. The periodogram and the correlogram are examples of techniques which were employed very early. Let $x(t)$ be a time series, with zero mean, observed at points in time $t = \ldots, -2, -1, 0, 1, 2, \ldots$. We generally suppose that $x(t)$ is actually a continuous function of time, although we observe it at discrete intervals. The *autocovariance* of $x(t)$, if it exists, is

$$(1.1) \qquad \gamma(t, \tau) = \mathscr{E}x(t)x(t+\tau) \qquad (\tau = 0, \pm 1, \pm 2, \ldots).$$

In general, γ will be a function of t as well as of the lag τ. But if $x(t)$ is what is known as a covariance-stationary stochastic process, the autocovariance will be a function of the lag alone and not of the point in time at which x is measured.[1] For such a process, we may normalize the autocovariances by dividing each by the variance, $\gamma(0)$; the result is the *autocorrelation*. If $x(t)$ is covariance stationary, we may estimate the autocovariance for lag τ, $\gamma(\tau)$, by the mean lagged product

$$(1.2) \qquad C(\tau) = \frac{1}{2T} \sum_{t=-T+1+M}^{T-M} \{x(t-\tau)x(t) + x(t)x(t+\tau)\},$$

where we assume we have a finite number of observations $2T$ and where $\tau = 0, 1, \ldots, M$, M being the maximal lag autocovariance computed.[2] The estimated autocorrelation for lag τ is then

$$(1.3) \qquad R(\tau) = \frac{C(\tau)}{C(0)} \qquad (\tau = 1, \ldots, M).$$

A plot of $R(\tau)$ as a function of τ is called the *correlogram* of the time series. One way to describe a time series statistically is to compute and plot its correlogram or its estimated autocovariance function.[3]

An example of an estimated autocovariance function for an economic time series is graphed in Figure 1. The function for the weighted second difference of total United States unemployment, based on data for July, 1947, through December, 1961, is plotted as the solid line; the function for the same series seasonally adjusted is plotted as the dashed line. The weighted second differences of both series were of the form

---

[1] The term "covariance stationarity" is used by Parzen [18]. Doob [5] and others use such terms as "weak stationarity," "stationarity in the wide sense," or "second-order stationarity." Note that covariance stationarity implies that $\gamma(\tau) = \gamma(-\tau)$.

[2] Blackman and Tukey [2] suggest adjusting the divisor, 2T, for loss of degrees of freedom; unfortunately, although this procedure leads to unbiased estimates under general conditions, it appears to have unfortunate consequences in the estimation of power spectra. The estimate (1.2) is used to avoid these difficulties. This estimate was suggested orally by E. Parzen. The particular form of (1.2), based on numbering the observations from $-T+1$ to T rather than from 0 to T and using both positive and negative lags, is introduced in order to facilitate a comparison with the definitions of cross-lag-covariances presented in Section 3.2 below.

[3] Alternatively, of course, one might "describe" the time series by plotting the values $x(t)$ against time. Such a graph, called the *trace* of the series, does not involve abstracting any of the essential properties of the series and is not highly useful for the purpose here envisaged.

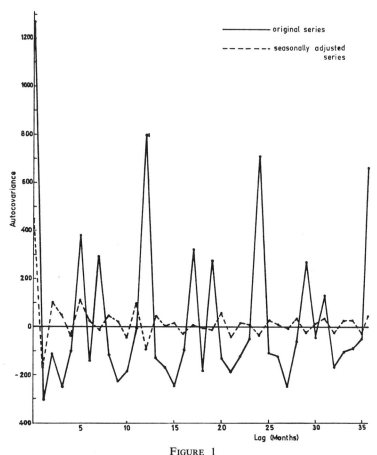

FIGURE 1
Autocovariance Function, U.S. Unemployment, Weighted Second Differences

$$(1.4) \qquad x(t) - 1.5x(t-1) + 0.5625x(t-2) \ .$$

The reasons for applying this particular differencing scheme are discussed more fully below. The sharp spikes at lags of 12 months, 24 months, and 36 months in the autocovariance function of the original series are due to seasonal effects, as are some of the other regularities. Some of the latter are also due to the differencing procedure which was applied. This is clearly not the place for an extensive discussion of the properties and uses of the autocovariance function of economic time series.[4] Suffice it to say that such a description is of considerable use if we wish to determine an autoregressive scheme or test for randomness; however, as will soon appear, it is not as useful in the analysis of adjustment procedures as an alternative description of the time series in terms of its frequency content.

[4] Some of the practical difficulties involved in interpreting autocovariance functions are illustrated in Kendall [11] and Quenouille [21]. Wold [27] is the classic work on the subject.

1.2. *Description of a Time Series in the Frequency Domain*

Let us begin by considering a simple deterministic function of time:

(1.5) $x(t) = A \sin \lambda t$.

Except for its origin in time (phase) this function is completely described by a pair of numbers, namely the amplitude A and the frequency λ. An alternative, but much more complicated, description of the same function is in terms of its *average lag product function*:[5]

$$
\begin{aligned}
(1.6) \quad & \lim_{T \to \infty} \frac{1}{2T} \int_{-T}^{T} x(t) x(t+\tau) \, dt \\
& = \lim_{T \to \infty} \frac{A^2}{2T} \int_{-T}^{T} \sin \lambda t \, \sin \lambda(t+\tau) \, dt \\
& = \lim_{T \to \infty} \frac{A^2}{2T} \left\{ \cos \lambda\tau \int_{-T}^{T} \sin^2 \lambda t \, dt + \sin \lambda\tau \int_{-T}^{T} \sin \lambda t \, \cos \lambda t \, dt \right\} \\
& = \lim_{T \to \infty} \frac{A^2}{2\pi} \left\{ \cos \lambda\tau \int_{-\pi}^{\pi} \sin^2 mt' \, dt' + \sin \lambda\tau \int_{-\pi}^{\pi} \sin mt' \, \cos mt' \, dt' \right\} \\
& = \frac{A^2}{2} \cos \lambda\tau ,
\end{aligned}
$$

where $t' = \pi t/T$ and $m = \lambda T/\pi$. The average lag product function is quite analogous to the autocovariance function introduced in the previous section. Of the two descriptions it is apparent that the one in terms of the pair (λ, A) is by far the simpler and more revealing.

The above considerations lead one to ask whether or not it might also be possible to describe stochastic time functions in such terms as frequency and amplitude. The answer is indeed yes; to see how and why, it is useful to take up a particular case of a Gaussian, or normal, time series.[6]

A time series, $x(t)$, is called Gaussian if for any n and every choice of times $t_1 < t_2 < \ldots < t_n$, the values of the function $x(t_1), \ldots, x(t_n)$ have an n-variate normal distribution. To simplify, let the means in this distribution all be zero. In this case, as is well known, the distribution, i.e., the probability law governing the process, is specified by the autocovariances, $\mathscr{E} x(t_i) x(t_k)$, $i, k = 1, \ldots, n$. If the process is stationary in addition,[7] these autocovariances will depend only on the time difference $\tau = t_i - t_k$. Thus zero-mean, stationary Gaussian time series have probability structures which are entirely described by their autocovariance functions $\gamma(\tau)$ defined earlier.

As an example of a zero-mean Gaussian random process consider the following:

---

[5] This might loosely be called an autocovariance function. To use such an expression here, however, would be improper as we are dealing with a non-stochastic function.

[6] The discussion which follows in the next three paragraphs is based in part on Goodman [8, pp. 221–23].

[7] For Gaussian processes, covariance stationarity implies strict stationarity. The latter, of course, implies the former in all cases.

Let $0 \leqslant \lambda_1 < \ldots < \lambda_N \leqslant \pi$ be N discrete frequencies, and let a_i and b_i, $i = 1, \ldots, N$ be $2N$ independent, zero-mean, normal variates with common variance σ_i^2 for each i, i.e.,

$$(1.7) \qquad \mathcal{E} a_i a_k = \mathcal{E} b_i b_k = \begin{cases} \sigma_i^2 & \text{if} \quad i = k, \ i = 1, \ldots, N \\ 0 & \text{if} \quad i \neq k \end{cases}$$

$$\mathcal{E} a_i b_k = 0, \qquad i, k = 1, \ldots, N .$$

The time series

$$(1.8) \qquad x(t) = \sum_{i=1}^{N} (a_i \cos \lambda_i t + b_i \sin \lambda_i t)$$

is a zero-mean, stationary Gaussian process.

Since $x(t)$ is a linear combination of normal variates, it is itself normal. Indeed the variables $x(t_k)$, $k = 1, \ldots, n$, have a multivariate normal distribution. The means are obviously zero. We have only to prove the process is stationary, i.e., to show $\mathcal{E} x(t) x(t+\tau)$ depends only on τ and not on t. Using (1.7), we find

$$(1.9) \qquad \mathcal{E} x(t) x(t+\tau) = \mathcal{E} \left\{ \sum_{i=1}^{N} \sum_{k=1}^{N} [a_i a_k \cos \lambda_i t \cos \lambda_k(t+\tau) + \right.$$
$$a_i b_k \cos \lambda_i t \sin \lambda_k(t+\tau) + a_k b_i \cos \lambda_k(t+\tau) \sin \lambda_i t +$$
$$\left. + b_i b_k \sin \lambda_i t \sin \lambda_k(t+\tau)] \right\}$$

$$= \sum_{i=1}^{N} \sigma_i^2 [\cos \lambda_i t \cos \lambda_i(t+\tau) + \sin \lambda_i t \sin \lambda_i(t+\tau)]$$

$$= \sum_{i=1}^{N} \sigma_i^2 \cos \lambda_i \tau .$$

Thus the process $x(t)$ is stationary with autocovariance function $\gamma(\tau)$ equal to the above.

The variance σ_i^2, as a function of frequency (i.e., of the index i), is called the *spectrum* of the time series $x(t)$. The autocovariance function, by (1.9) is just the Fourier cosine transform of the spectrum and, from the theory of such transforms, it follows that, conversely, the spectrum may be represented as

$$(1.10) \qquad \sigma_i^2 = \frac{1}{\pi} \int_{-\pi}^{\pi} \gamma(\tau) \cos \lambda_i \tau \, d\tau .^{[8]}$$

[8] Since

$$\frac{1}{\pi} \int_{-\pi}^{\pi} \gamma(\tau) \cos \lambda_k \tau \, d\tau = \frac{1}{\pi} \int_{-\pi}^{\pi} \left\{ \sum_{k=1}^{N} \sigma_i^2 \cos \lambda_i \tau \cos \lambda_k \tau \right\} d\tau$$

$$= \frac{1}{\pi} \sum_{k=1}^{N} \sigma_i^2 \left\{ \int_{-\pi}^{\pi} \cos \lambda_i \tau \cos \lambda_k \tau \, d\tau \right\}$$

$$= \frac{1}{\pi} \sum_{k=1}^{N} \sigma_i^2 \begin{cases} \pi, & \text{for} \quad \lambda_i = \lambda_k \\ 0, & \text{for} \quad \lambda_i \neq \lambda_k \end{cases} = \sigma_i^2 .$$

Thus the spectrum and the autocovariance function are Fourier transform pairs; one may just as well consider one as the other.

Since the process $x(t)$ is assumed to be Gaussian either $\gamma(\tau)$ or σ_i^2, $i=1, \ldots, N$, gives us a complete description of the probability law of the process: the autocovariance function describes it in the time domain; the spectrum describes it in the frequency domain.[9] If the coefficients a_i and b_i in (1.8) had not been assumed to be normal, of course $x(t)$ would not be a Gaussian process; nevertheless, the spectrum and the autocovariance function are still descriptions of the process, albeit imperfect ones, and each contains exactly the same information as the other.

It is natural at this point to ask whether any stationary random process can be equally well described in frequency and time domains as above. The answer for stationary processes is again in the affirmative provided we do not restrict ourselves to finite parameter schemes such as (1.8). It can be shown that any covariance stationary random process $x(t)$ can be expressed in the form

$$(1.11) \quad x(t) = \int_0^\infty \cos \lambda t\, dU(\lambda) + \int_0^\infty \sin \lambda t\, dV(\lambda) ,$$

where $dU(\lambda)$ and $dV(\lambda)$ are random variables with properties described below.[10] The reason for using a Stieltjes rather than an ordinary integral will become apparent in a moment. Regarding the integrals as sums and the variables $dU(\lambda)$ and $dV(\lambda)$ as amplitudes, however, we see that (1.11) shows that the time series $x(t)$ is "decomposed" into a superposition of sine and cosine waves of different frequencies and random amplitudes $dU(\lambda)$ and $dV(\lambda)$. No special economic significance should be attached to the various sinusoidal variations; they are merely components of a description of the time series $x(t)$ in the frequency domain.

The random variables $dU(\lambda)$ and $dV(\lambda)$, by means of which (1.11) expresses the stochastic time series $x(t)$, have particularly simple properties. First, they are orthogonal; that is, their covariances at different frequencies vanish:

$$(1.12) \quad \mathscr{E}\, dU(\lambda)\, dU(\lambda') = \mathscr{E}\, dV(\lambda)\, dV(\lambda') = 0 , \quad \text{all} \quad \lambda \neq \lambda' ,$$

where "$\lambda \neq \lambda'$" means "λ and λ' belong to non-overlapping intervals." Second, the variables $dU(\lambda)$ and $dV(\lambda)$ are orthogonal at any frequencies:

$$(1.13) \quad \mathscr{E}\, dU(\lambda)\, dV(\lambda') = 0 , \quad \text{all } \lambda \text{ and } \lambda'.$$

And third, the random variables $dU(\lambda)$ and $dV(\lambda)$ have a common variance at the same frequency:

$$(1.14) \quad \mathscr{E}[dU(\lambda)]^2 = \mathscr{E}[dV(\lambda)]^2 = dF(\lambda) .$$

The function $dF(\lambda)$ is often called the *power spectrum* of $x(t)$, and $F(\lambda)$ the *cumulative*

---

[9] As Tukey [25] points out, estimation of the spectrum of a time series is analogous to components-of-variance analysis in more classical applications of statistics.

[10] See Doob [5, pp. 481–86].

power spectrum. $F(\lambda)$ is a monotonically increasing function which can be written in the form

(1.15) $F(\lambda) = F_1(\lambda) + F_2(\lambda) + F_3(\lambda)$,

where F_1, F_2, and F_3 are nondecreasing functions of frequency. F_1 is an absolutely continuous function with derivative $f(\lambda)$; F_2 is a step function, and F_3 is the continuous singular component of F (i.e., a function which is constant almost everywhere in the mathematical sense).[11] In economic applications, the component F_3 may be neglected. The interpretation of the step function is simple in the case of the time series defined in (1.8); in this case, the cumulated power spectrum consists of a step function with steps of σ_i^2 at frequency λ_i. The function $F_2(\lambda)$ thus corresponds to a component of the time series which is perfectly periodic (although not for that reason perfectly deterministic).[12] The component $F_1(\lambda)$ is the most interesting from an economic point of view. It is absolutely continuous and we may write $dF_1(\lambda)/d\lambda = f(\lambda)$.[12a] It is, however, the possibility of components F_2 that leads us to write (1.11) in Stieltjes integral form.

The *spectral representation* of the time series $x(t)$ given by (1.11) is a representation in the frequency domain of the stochastic process. The great simplicity of the properties of the random variables $dU(\lambda)$ and $dV(\lambda)$ suggests that in many types of problems involving time series it will be more useful to consider these variables and their properties than to consider the statistical properties of the time series itself.[13] The Gaussian or normal time series defined earlier in this section has a particularly simple definition in terms of the spectral representation of a process. The time series $x(t)$ is Gaussian if and only if the random variables $dU(\lambda)$ and $dV(\lambda)$ are distributed as independent univariate normal variables with common variance at the same frequency. In this case, the probability law governing $x(t)$ is completely specified by specifying the power spectrum $dF(\lambda)$; i.e., the common variances of $dU(\lambda)$ and $dV(\lambda)$ at every frequency; or, alternatively, by specifying the auto-covariance function $\gamma(\tau)$.

Note, as before, that the spectral representation of a time series suppresses all information concerning its origin in time, i.e., all *phase* information; however, if the process is stationary this information is irrelevant.

Since, in the case of a Gaussian process, either the power spectrum or the auto-

[11] Doob [5, p. 488].

[12] We argue below that it is most unlikely that any realistic economic time series will possess such a component.

[12a] Hannan [9, p. 12].

[13] For example, in regression problems involving serial correlation in the residuals, properties of various estimates may be better described in terms of the spectrum of the residuals than in terms of their autocovariance function. The point is that the spectral representation takes serial dependence as central, whereas in the time domain lack of independence is essentially a complication.

covariance function completely specifies the probability law, they both contain exactly the same information about the process. This is true irrespective of whether the process is Gaussian or not, since it may be shown that the power spectrum and the autocovariance function form a Fourier transform pair and are therefore uniquely related to one another.[14] This fact is simply derived making use of the properties (1.12–1.14) of the random variables $dU(\lambda)$ and $dV(\lambda)$:

$$(1.16) \quad \gamma(\tau) = \mathscr{E} x(t) x(t+\tau)$$

$$= \mathscr{E} \left\{ \int_0^\infty \int_0^\infty \cos \lambda t \cos \lambda'(t+\tau) dU(\lambda) dU(\lambda') \right.$$

$$+ \int_0^\infty \int_0^\infty \cos \lambda t \sin \lambda'(t+\tau) dU(\lambda) dV(\lambda')$$

$$+ \int_0^\infty \int_0^\infty \cos \lambda'(t+\tau) \sin \lambda t \, dU(\lambda') dV(\lambda)$$

$$+ \left. \int_0^\infty \int_0^\infty \sin \lambda t \sin \lambda'(t+\tau) dV(\lambda) dV(\lambda') \right\}$$

$$= \int_0^\infty \{\cos \lambda t \cos \lambda(t+\tau) + \sin \lambda t \sin \lambda(t+\tau)\} dF(\lambda)$$

$$= \int_0^\infty \cos \lambda \tau \, dF(\lambda) .$$

A particularly important special case of (1.16) occurs when τ is set equal to zero; for in this case we have

$$(1.17) \quad \gamma(0) = \int_0^\infty (\cos 0) dF(\lambda) = \int_0^\infty dF(\lambda) ,$$

where $\gamma(0)$ is just the variance of $x(t)$. *Thus the spectrum of a time series may be thought of as a decomposition of the variance at different frequencies.* Equation (1.17) expresses the variance of $x(t)$ as the "sum" of variances at different frequencies.

Equation (1.11) gives a representation of a real time series in terms of a super-position of cosines and sines, real numbers, with random amplitudes, also real numbers. The entire expression may be represented in complex form more compactly. The complex form is also convenient for other reasons, as will become clear. As we know

$$e^{j\lambda t} = \cos \lambda t + j \sin \lambda t ,$$

where $j = \sqrt{-1}$. Thus

$$\cos \lambda t = \frac{e^{j\lambda t} + e^{-j\lambda t}}{2} ,$$

$$\sin \lambda t = \frac{e^{j\lambda t} - e^{-j\lambda t}}{2j} .$$

[14] Doob [5, pp. 473–76]; Wilks [26, pp. 517–21].

Substituting in (1.11)

$$(1.18) \quad x(t) = \int_0^\infty \left(\frac{e^{j\lambda t}+e^{-j\lambda t}}{2}\right) dU(\lambda) + \int_0^\infty \left(\frac{e^{j\lambda t}-e^{-j\lambda t}}{2j}\right) dV(\lambda)$$

$$= \int_{-\infty}^\infty \tfrac{1}{2}e^{j\lambda t}\,dU(\lambda) - \int_{-\infty}^\infty \tfrac{1}{2}e^{j\lambda t}j\,dV(\lambda) = \int_{-\infty}^\infty e^{j\lambda t}\,dZ(\lambda),$$

where $dZ(\lambda)$ is the complex random variable

$$(1.19) \quad dZ(\lambda) = \tfrac{1}{2}[dU(\lambda) - j\,dV(\lambda)],$$

and where we define $dU(\lambda)$ and $dV(\lambda)$ for negative frequencies by

$$(1.20) \quad \begin{aligned} dU(\lambda) &= dU(-\lambda), \\ -dV(\lambda) &= dV(-\lambda). \end{aligned}$$

If the variance of a complex random variable is defined as the expected value of its squared modulus we have from (1.14):

$$(1.21) \quad \mathscr{E}\,dZ(\lambda)\,\overline{dZ(\lambda)} = \tfrac{1}{2}dF(\lambda),$$

where the bar denotes the complex conjugate. There are two possible covariances for a complex random variable, $\mathscr{E}\,dZ(\lambda)\,\overline{dZ(\lambda')}$ and $\mathscr{E}\,\overline{dZ(\lambda)}\,dZ(\lambda')$, but by (1.12) and (1.13) these are both zero.

It is now possible to write the autocovariance of $x(t)$ in most suggestive form: From (1.16)

$$(1.22) \quad \gamma(\tau) = \int_0^\infty \cos \lambda\tau\,dF(\lambda) = \int_0^\infty \frac{e^{j\lambda\tau}+e^{-j\lambda\tau}}{2}\,dF(\lambda) = \int_{-\infty}^\infty e^{j\lambda\tau}\frac{dF(\lambda)}{2},$$

since by (1.20) and (1.21) $dF(-\lambda) = \overline{dF(\lambda)} = dF(\lambda)$. Thus the autocovariance function is just the complex Fourier transform of the spectrum. By the theory of such transforms,[15] the spectrum in turn is

$$(1.23) \quad dF(\lambda) = \frac{1}{\pi}\int_{-\infty}^\infty e^{-j\lambda\tau}\gamma(\tau)\,d\tau.$$

Thus the autocovariance function and the power spectrum are just a Fourier transform pair; knowledge of one is equivalent to knowledge of the other. The values of the spectrum (as estimated) will, however, normally have simpler statistical properties since they are essentially variances of normal independent variables in the case of Gaussian processes.

It should be noted that real stationary time series have a spectrum which is symmetric about the origin. For such time series it is possible to prove an important theorem: a necessary and sufficient condition that the spectrum of a time series equal a constant, i.e., be "flat," is that all autocovariances except that for $\tau = 0$ be

---

[15] Stuart [**24**, p. 46].

zero.[16] Thus if successive values of $x(t)$ are independent, all the autocovariances except at $\tau = 0$ will be zero, and the spectrum of $x(t)$ will be flat. Conversely, if $x(t)$ is a Gaussian time series and has a flat spectrum then successive values of $x(t)$ are independent. Stationary time series with flat spectra are called *white noise*.

1.3. *Practical Problems in the Estimation of Spectra*

One problem in practical spectral analysis of economic time series is what has been called *aliasing*.[17] Economic time series, though they may be continuous in theory, are in fact observed only at discrete intervals of time. This means that harmonic components of the series with periods shorter than twice the period of observation, or with frequencies greater in absolute value than $\frac{1}{2}$ cycles per period, cannot be directly discerned. Such harmonic components will, however, be reflected in the estimated power spectrum, since the effects of such components will be combined with the effects of harmonics of lower frequencies which are observed directly. The rationale behind this observation is illustrated in Figure 2. The solid

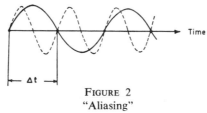

FIGURE 2
"Aliasing"

line is a sine wave with period exactly twice the period of observation; the dashed line is a sine wave with half this period, or twice the frequency; if the two waves are observed only at intervals Δt, they will be indistinguishable. The frequency of $\frac{1}{2}$ cycles per period is called the *Nyquist folding frequency*. Let this be λ_N and let λ be a frequency in the interval, or frequency band $[-\lambda_N, \lambda_N]$; then frequencies $\lambda \pm \lambda_N$, $\lambda \pm 2\lambda_N$, $\lambda \pm 3\lambda_N$, etc., are the aliases of λ.[18] The contributions of harmonic components at all these frequencies will be confounded with the effects of the harmonic component of frequency λ. Thus, in the interpretation of a spectral analysis of an economic time series, one must be careful not to identify the effects at an observed frequency necessarily with that frequency alone. However, in the analyses reported below, aliasing does not appear to have been a severe problem.[19]

[16] See Wilks [**26**, p. 521].

[17] Blackman and Tukey [**2**, pp. 31–33, 117–20].

[18] From this point onward in this section, frequency will be expressed in terms of cycles per unit time rather than in fractions of 2π.

[19] The practical significance of aliasing is that peaks in the power spectrum at frequencies less than $\frac{1}{2}$ cycles per unit time may be due to causes operating well above the observable frequency range. The only criterion one can use to decide whether aliasing is a problem is whether observed peaks have plausible explanations; if not, one may have to seek an explanation at higher frequencies. Since all peaks in the analyses reported below had one simple explanation, seasonality, there appeared to be no problem.

A second problem in the analysis of economic time series is the severe limitation on the number of observations available. When I first began to explore the possibilities of using spectral techniques in economics, I had in mind that they might be applied in the study of livestock cycles. Livestock inventory figures are available, for example, annually since 1867. Thus somewhat under 100 observations are available for analysis, which would seem to be a large number. However, a complete cattle cycle takes between 13 and 17 years, which means that less than seven such cycles have been observed. The effective number of observations, then, for cycles of this length is, at most, seven, a small number indeed for any sort of statistical analysis! It follows that, in the study of economic time series, the power of discrimination at low frequencies is severely limited by the length of the record. Note that this is true regardless of how short the unit observation period; while we can increase the maximum observable frequency by reducing the interval between observations, we cannot improve discrimination at low frequencies by such means. Not all fluctuations in economic time series of interest, however, are of such long duration. In particular, most of the operations performed on quarterly, monthly, or weekly economic time series are designed to remove high frequency components and to make these series more usful for short term economic forecasts or for assessment of the current economic situation. Whether or not existing procedures perform this function adequately is a problem of some importance. Furthermore, it is a problem in which high frequency components are of special interest, and, therefore, in which the short length of most economic time series does not pose a severe handicap on the use of spectral techniques.

Suppose that we have $2T$ observations on a particular time series available. How do we go about estimating the power spectrum of the series? First note that if $2T$ is the total number of observations, autocovariances of, at most, order $M = 2T - 1$ can be computed. Indeed, we shall generally wish to make M much less than $2T$ in order to increase the statistical reliability of the estimated autocovariances of high order. The general rule of thumb that has been adopted in the analyses reported below is that the maximal lag should be no more than about 20 per cent of the total number of observations available. Suppose, then, that we have computed M autocovariances according to 1.2; the next step is to make use of the discrete analogue of equation (1.23) above. This turns out to be

$$(1.23')\quad I_M(\lambda_i) = \frac{1}{\pi}[c(0) + 2 \sum_{\tau=1}^{M} \cos 2\pi\lambda_i \tau c(\tau)],$$

where $\lambda_i = i/2M$, $i = 0, 1, \ldots, M$.[20] Note that we can measure the power only at

[20] Since

$$\sum_{\tau=-M}^{M} e^{-j2\pi\lambda_i\tau} c(\tau) = \sum_{\tau=1}^{M} (\cos 2\pi\lambda_i\tau - j \sin 2\pi\lambda_i\tau) c(\tau)$$

$$+ \sum_{\tau=-M}^{1} (\cos 2\pi\lambda_i\tau - j \sin 2\pi\lambda_i\tau) c(\tau) + c(0) = c(0) + 2 \sum_{\tau=1}^{M} \cos 2\pi\lambda_i\tau c(\tau),$$

since $\sin i\pi = 0$ and $\sin(-x) = -\sin x$. It is usual to make the end correction which gives $c(M)$ half the weight of $c(\tau)$, $0 < \tau < M$.

certain frequencies equal in number to the number of lags which have been chosen. Since all economic time series are real, their spectra will be symmetric about the origin; hence, we need only consider positive frequencies. When the frequencies are equally spaced, as they are in (1.23'), the expression is just the classical periodogram due to Schuster.[21]

The classical periodogram, as described in the preceding paragraph, is the technique one would normally use for investigating the harmonics of fixed, known frequencies under the assumption that the time series under consideration is strictly periodic, repeating itself exactly every M periods. If this were the case, the true cumulative power spectrum would be a pure step function; i.e., we would have only F_2 in the decomposition (1.15). If the time series is not strictly periodic, however, it will have a continuous power spectrum. The most that one can hope to do with a finite number of observations is to measure the average power, in some sense, in a band about the frequencies λ_i. These averages may be defined in a variety of ways by specifying weights in either the time domain or the frequency domain. As the number of observations, and hence the number of lags, is increased, it would be possible to reduce the width of the band and so obtain finer discrimination of frequencies and better measurement of the power at each frequency. It can be shown, however, that as the width of the frequency band over which average power is measured is reduced, the variance of any estimate of this power is increased, *no matter how many observations are taken.*[22] The limiting case where one attempts to measure power at a particular frequency is precisely the classical periodogram analysis applied to time series which are not strictly periodic, and no series of relevance in economics is strictly periodic.

Although it can be shown that the periodogram ordinates are asymptotically unbiased estimators of the power spectrum at corresponding frequencies for non-strictly periodic time series, it can also be shown that they are not consistent estimators; indeed the variance of the periodogram ordinates tends to $[\gamma(0)f(\lambda_i)]^2$, where, assuming $F_2(\lambda) \equiv 0$, $dF(\lambda_i)/d\lambda = f(\lambda_i)$.[23] It is this fact, for example, which in part accounts for the spiked appearance of a periodogram estimated from a finite sample of white noise (which should have a flat spectrum). Consequently, use of the classical periodogram in economics is not only inappropriate but will lead to results which are nearly impossible to interpret. Perhaps it is this that has led to the disrepute into which harmonic analysis of economic time series has fallen.

Rather, then, than estimate the power spectrum at a specific frequency, it is necessary, in order to achieve results which are statistically consistent, to estimate average power about the frequency in question. Naturally, we would like to estimate an average which reflects most heavily the power at frequencies near the one at which we center the estimate. Thus, we consider weighted averages of power in

[21] Schuster [23]
[22] Parzen [17, p. 180].
[23] Jenkins [10, p. 150]; Hannan [9, pp. 52–55].

the frequency domain; these averages correspond to weighting the raw auto-covariances of the time series before computing the spectral estimates. In the frequency domain a particular weighting scheme is called a *spectral window*; the inverse Fourier transform of a spectral window is a weighting scheme in the time domain for the raw autocovariances and is called a *lag window*. Ideally, one would like to choose a spectral window that would weight power equally at all fre-quencies $\pm\frac{1}{2}$ the distance from the chosen frequency point to the next frequency point (assuming the centers of our averages to be equally spaced) and give power at frequencies outside this interval a zero weight. Unfortunately, it is mathe-matically impossible to find a finite lag window corresponding to this spectral window. Consequently, a great deal of the literature of spectral analysis deals with alternative choices of spectral and lag windows and with the statistical properties of the resulting estimates.[24]

It would serve no useful function in this paper to go into the technical details of different sorts of windows and their statistical properties. Suffice it to say that in the analyses reported below a window recommended by Parzen has been used. This corresponds to forming weighted averages of the raw autocovariances

$$(1.24) \quad C(\tau) = \sum_{k=1}^{M} w(k) c(k),$$

where the weights are given by

$$(1.25) \quad w(k) = \begin{cases} 1 - 6\dfrac{k^2}{M^2}\left(1 - \dfrac{k}{M}\right), & 0 \leqslant k \leqslant \dfrac{M}{2}, \\ 2\left(1 - \dfrac{k}{M}\right)^3, & \dfrac{M}{2} \leqslant k \leqslant M, \\ 0, & M < k. \end{cases}$$

M is the maximal lag. Alternatively, in the frequency domain, the lag window (1.25) corresponds to the spectral window

$$(1.26) \quad A(\omega) = \frac{3}{4\pi M^3}\left[\frac{\sin 2\pi \dfrac{M(\lambda-\omega)}{4}}{\sin 2\pi \dfrac{(\lambda-\omega)}{4}}\right]^4. [25]$$

Thus, the estimates obtained are of spectral averages about a series of designated

---

[24] Blackman and Tukey [2]; Jenkins [10]; Parzen [17].

[25] Parzen [17, p. 176, eq. 5.10]. One of the reasons for using Parzen's window is that it is everywhere positive. Another window, due to Tukey, has small negative side lobes. Thus, the high power at low frequencies present in most economic time series can actually produce *negative* estimates of the spectrum at higher frequencies. Since the spectrum is essentially a variance, negative estimates are not easy to interpret. See the discussion of leakage below.

frequencies λ; as one can see from the form of the window (1.26), they are averages of the power at all frequencies, but the main weight of the average is concentrated in the close vicinity of the designated frequency. The window is symmetric about the frequency λ. A graph of this function for $M = 36$ and positive values of $\lambda - \omega$ is plotted in Figure 3. Fewer lags would have produced a window less sharply focused on the designated frequency; more lags, a window of lesser width.

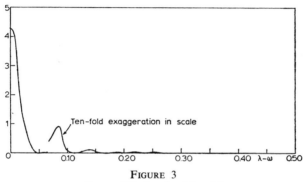

FIGURE 3
Parzen Window for $M = 36$

The fact that only spectral averages have the statistical property of consistency, and that, therefore, we must look at the spectrum of a time series through a window, has important consequences for the estimation of spectra. The issue is closely connected with the problem of the non-stationarity of many economic time series. The window through which we look at a spectrum does concentrate its main weight very near a designated frequency, but not all the weight is concentrated there; there is some weight, however small, at all other frequencies. This means that very high power at some frequencies will distort spectral estimates at other frequencies, some of them distant from those at which high power is present. This phenomenon might be called "leakage through the edges of the window." Two important forms of non-stationarity in time series that are Gaussian, or nearly so, are: (a) a variance that changes with time, and (b) a mean that changes with time. Changing variance has not appeared to be a serious problem in those time series studied here.[26] Changes in the mean with time are better known under the designation "trends." In any finite realization of a process, trends will be indistinguishable from very low frequency components. Indeed, the sample mean itself may be regarded as a cycle of zero frequency or infinite period. Thus, since most

[26] Various devices, such as dividing the observations by a moving sample variance, could be employed if variance non-stationarity appeared to be present. Over short periods of under 200 observations, however, it would be difficult to detect changes in variance. Changing variance may present problems in longer economic time series.

Other, more complicated, forms of non-stationarity are, of course, possible, e.g., trending autocovariances. However, it is most improbable that such forms would occur without a trending variance.

economic time series do show trends of one sort or another, the power spectrum of a typical economic time series will show very high power concentrated at frequencies near zero, and gradually diminishing power at higher frequencies. This shape is illustrated in Figure 4 by the power spectrum of the Federal Reserve Board Index of Industrial Production.[27]

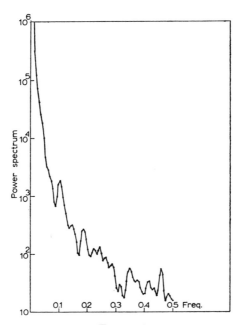

FIGURE 4
Spectral Density, Federal Reserve Board Index of Industrial Production

Because economic time series have high power concentrated at low frequencies (the power at frequencies near zero in the FRB index is 10,000 times as great as the power near $\frac{1}{2}$), the problem of leakage is a particularly severe one in any attempt to analyse even their high frequency components. This problem is compounded because of the limited number of observations available for analysis, for this limitation limits the number of lags which can be taken and, hence, the degree to which the width of the window may be reduced. To circumvent this difficulty, it is necessary to "filter" out some of the power at low frequencies. In communications or electrical engineering, in connection with which much of the theory of spectral analysis has been developed, filters are often actual physical entities. For our purposes, however, a filter may be defined as any series of arithmetical operations

[27] The estimates were computed on the basis of 486 monthly observations. These were differenced, for reasons to be described. An estimate of the power spectrum for the undifferenced series was recovered from an estimate of that of the differenced series by a procedure called "recoloring." The seasonally adjusted FRB Index of Industrial Production is an unusually smooth series which accounts for the very great concentration of power at the low end of the frequency scale.

used to transform the data prior to its analysis. The use of such operations to filter out power at low frequencies is called *prewhitening*.[28]

Many sorts of arithmetical operations could be employed to remove low frequency components; for example: (a) fit a polynomial in time of low degree to the data and subtract the appropriate calculated value from each observation; (b) subtract a weighted or unweighted moving average from each observation, or (c) difference the series. Filters of types (b) or (c) are all of the general form

$$(1.27) \quad y(t) = \sum_{i=-p}^{q} \delta_i x(t+i),$$

where the δ_i are constants independent of time. The series $x(t)$ is the original, or *input*, series; $y(t)$ is the transformed, or *output*, series. For example, for ordinary first differences of the input, we have $\delta_0 = 1$, $\delta_{-1} = -1$, and $\delta_i = 0$ for all $i \neq 0, -1$; for a centered, three-term, unweighted, moving average, we have $\delta_1 = \frac{1}{3}$, $\delta_0 = \frac{1}{3}$, $\delta_{-1} = \frac{1}{3}$, $\delta_i = 0$, $i \neq 1$, 0, -1. Filters of the general form given in (1.27) are called time-invariant *linear filters*. Subtraction of a polynominal trend, determined by a regression, from the original series is a non-time invariant filter.[29] Any one of the standard methods of seasonal adjustment is a nonlinear filter, and usually not time invariant as well. The importance of linear filters in spectral analysis arises because the spectrum of the output of a linear filter is very simply related to the spectrum of the input series. Let u be the shift operator such that

$$(1.28) \quad \begin{aligned} ux(t) &= x(t+1) \\ u^i x(t) &= x(t+i). \end{aligned}$$

Then (1.27) may be written as

$$(1.29) \quad y(t) = \sum_{i=-p}^{q} \delta_i u^i x(t).$$

The frequency response function of a linear filter, which is discussed at greater length below, is obtained by setting the input equal to $e^{-j2\pi 0}$ (recall that $j = \sqrt{-1}$):

$$(1.30) \quad l(\lambda) = \sum_{i=-p}^{q} \delta_i e^{-j2\pi\lambda i}. \quad [30]$$

The frequency response function is generally a complex-valued function of frequency; the square of its modulus at each frequency is called the transfer function of the filter and denoted by $|l(\lambda)|^2$. It can be shown that the spectrum of an output from a linear filter, $g(\lambda)$, is related to the spectrum of the input, $f(\lambda)$, by

$$(1.31) \quad g(\lambda) = |l(\lambda)|^2 f(\lambda). \quad [31]$$

---

[28] Blackman and Tukey [2, pp. 39–43].

[29] A fitted *moving* polynomial would fall into the category of time invariant linear filters, since the "time" in the polynomial is then essentially an index different from real time.

[30] Lanning and Battin [13, pp. 192–93]; see also Section 3.2 below.

[31] Bartlett [1, p. 174].

Thus, an estimate of the power spectrum of a series which has been prewhitened by application of a linear filter can be obtained from the estimate of the power spectrum of the prewhitened series by dividing the latter, at each frequency, by the transfer function of the filter. Although the term does not appear in general usage, I have called such a procedure "recoloring", and the resulting estimate the *recolored power spectrum*.

To minimize the effects of leakage through the edges of a spectral window, one would ideally like to prewhiten the series in such a way that the power spectrum of the result was as flat as possible. Of course, if one could do this perfectly, it would be tantamount to perfect knowledge of the spectrum of the original series and so quite unnecessary. Some leakage effects are thus unavoidable. As far as economic time series are concerned, it would seem that the best practice is to remove considerable power only at the lowest frequencies. However, care must be taken not to remove so much that much higher power occurs at high frequencies than at low, for then leakage of this power would seriously distort our estimates at the lower frequencies. In order to eliminate trends and consequent high power at low frequencies, repeated differences of the form

(1.32) $\Delta_k x(t) = x(t) - k\, x(t-1)$

were employed.[32] In the case $k=1$, the effect is to give first-, second-, or higher-order differences as the operation defined in (1.32) is repeated. When, however, ordinary first or second differences were applied to the series discussed below, it was found that too much power was removed near the zero frequency. The resulting estimated spectra tended to have high power concentrated in the upper frequencies and relatively little at lower frequencies, which meant that estimates at some of the lower frequencies of interest were likely to have been distorted. For want of a better term, I call differences of the form (1.32) "quasi-differences" when $k \neq 1$.

This result appeared to dictate a choice of k different from one. But what other value? In particular, should k be less or greater than one? It can be shown that the transfer function for the pth quasi-difference is

(1.33) $|l(\lambda)|^2 = [1 - 2k \cos 2\pi\lambda + k^2]^p .$[33]

[32] Durbin [6] gives several reasons for preferring difference filters to moving averages or trend elimination by the subtraction of a polynomial in time.

[33] By equation (1.28) the first-order quasi-difference may be written as $(1 - ku^{-1})x(t)$. Hence, the pth order quasi-difference of this form is $(1 - ku^{-1})^p x(t)$ which may be expanded as

(i) $(1 - ku^{-1})^p x(t) = \sum_{i=0}^{p} \binom{p}{i} (-k)^i u^{-i} x(t) .$

Inserting this result in (1.30), we obtain

(ii) $l(\lambda) = \sum_{i=0}^{p} \binom{p}{i} (-k)^i e^{j2\pi\lambda i} = \sum_{i=0}^{p} \binom{p}{i} (-k)^i [e^{j2\pi\lambda}]^i = [1 - ke^{j2\pi\lambda}]^p .$

Thus

(iii) $|l(\lambda)|^2 = [1 - ke^{-j2\pi\lambda}]^p [1 - ke^{j2\pi\lambda}]^p = [(1 - ke^{-j2\pi\lambda})(1 - ke^{j2\pi\lambda})]^p$

           $= [1 - k(e^{j2\pi\lambda} + e^{-j2\pi\lambda}) + k^2]^p = [1 - 2k \cos 2\pi\lambda + k^2]^p .$

At frequencies near zero this function is approximately $(1-k)^{2p}$; and, at frequencies near $\frac{1}{2}$, it is approximately $(1+k)^{2p}$. It follows that by making k less than one we shall raise power at higher frequencies less and also lower power at lower frequencies by a smaller amount. Beyond this observation, however, there seems to be no very good method of determining k.[34] Hence, it was decided to try a number of different values of k and p and to choose that combination yielding the flattest estimated spectrum. In all the analyses performed $k=0.75$ and $p=1, 2,$ or 3 proved to give satisfactory results. Thus the procedure employed amounted to setting $k=0.75$, computing power spectra of the series differenced one, two, or three times according to (1.32), selecting the flattest spectrum, then recoloring the estimates at each frequency by dividing by the transfer function at that frequency for the appropriate value of p.[35]

2. SEASONALITY AND SEASONAL ADJUSTMENT

2.1. The Nature of Seasonality

When one examines a number of economic time series observed at quarterly, monthly, or even weekly intervals, one is particularly struck by the highly regular within-year movements in many series. For example, the regular swing of the monthly time series of U.S. employment from a low point in midwinter to a peak in midsummer is one of the most persistent and characteristic features of this

---

[34] In an oral discussion, Parzen suggested prewhitening by means of autoregressive schemes estimated by least squares. This would mean estimating the appropriate values for δ_i in (1.27) directly. In some ways this technique would appear to produce results similar to those obtained by the procedure actually employed. Unfortunately it has not been possible to date to explore the potentialities of Parzen's suggestion.

[35] I am indebted to H. Rosenblatt for pointing out that the suggestion for using a quasi-difference, rather than an ordinary first difference, to avoid difficulty at zero frequency occurs in Blackman and Tukey [2, pp. 52–3], where a value, $k = 0.6$, is given. What seems to be novel in the present approach is the use of higher order differences and iteration until the estimated spectrum becomes flat.

It may be that this approach has wider implications. For example, in the estimation of seasonal factors it is necessary first to remove trend. This is usually accomplished by deducting a moving average of the series from itself. When such a procedure is followed, however, it is not immediately clear that all the trend has been removed. (It is this difficulty which in the BLS method leads to the iterations there employed.) If a time series is regarded as trend-cycle plus seasonal plus white noise, then any filter which reduces the series to white noise plus seasonal (see below for a definition of seasonal) clearly removes the undesired trend-cycle. What more natural way is there to determine this point empirically?

Durbin has pointed out that quasi-differencing amounts to removal, over a finite period, of an exponentially damped polynomial and that, therefore, the beginning and end of the series are treated asymmetrically. For this reason, he suggests $(1 - ku^{-1})(1 - ku)x(t) = -kx(t+1) + (1 + k^2)x(t) - kx(t-1)$, which is a more symmetrical filter. I have not had an opportunity to explore this suggestion.

series.[36] Almost all economic time series contain such regular movements to a greater or lesser degree. These movements are perhaps most prominent in agricultural series, less so in some financial series, but surprisingly widespread in series covering every facet of economic life.[37] Their very regularity suggests that, in the main, they are due to the round of the climatic seasons, conventional holidays, and repetitive institutional practices, if not directly affecting the particular series under consideration, then indirectly through other related economic phenomena. However, these movements, which we call seasonal, are not perfectly regular, i.e., do not repeat themselves exactly from year to year. The pattern of weather is never exactly the same from one year to another; the dating of conventional holidays, the number of weekends in a month, institutional conventions and economic relationships change, sometimes gradually and systematically, sometimes abruptly and irregularly.

It is the close but not perfect approach to regularity which renders the precise definition of seasonality so difficult. If there were no regularity at all, there would be no problem; on the other hand, if such movements were perfectly regular, seasonality could be defined as precisely those regularities. The notion of the power spectrum of a time series enables us to give a more precise definition of seasonality even in the presence of irregularity and systematic change.

Suppose first that some part of the time series is perfectly periodic within a one year period. The strict periodicity need not rule out a stochastic series, however. Such a series may be represented by a finite sum of sine and cosine terms with random amplitudes. If the fundamental period of the series is one year and monthly observations (1/12 of the fundamental period) are taken, it suffices to include precisely eleven such terms in addition to a constant representing the mean of the series. The representation is thus

$$(2.1) \qquad y(t) = \alpha_0 + \sum_{i=1}^{6} (\alpha_i \cos 2\pi\lambda_i t + \beta_i \sin 2\pi\lambda_i t),$$

where $\lambda_i = i/12$. Note that since $\sin (2\pi \cdot 6/12)t = 0$ for all t, the last sine term in the sum vanishes identically, so that there are only eleven α's and β's in addition to the constant term required to determine a particular annual pattern.[38] The frequencies λ_i and the corresponding periods of their cycles are shown in the accompanying table. The frequencies λ_i listed below may be called *seasonal frequencies*.[39]

---

[36] [19, p. 162].

[37] Kuznets [12]; Moore [14, pp. 517–51]; [16, pp. 185–92].

[38] That is, β_6 is perfectly arbitrary.

[39] It is rather important not to attach any particular meaning to the individual seasonal frequencies. All six frequencies are required to represent an arbitrary twelve month pattern as the sum of sinesoidal variations. If fewer are required or if, for example, the variance of α_i and β_i is much larger for one particular frequency than for all the others, it simply means that the twelve month pattern is quite like a sine wave of that frequency.

(1) Frequency (cycles/month)	(2) Period (months)	(3) Number of times a cycle is completed in one year
0.0833	12	1
0.1667	6	2
0.2500	4	3
0.3333	3	4
0.4167	2.4	5
0.5000	2	6

Suppose that $\alpha_1, \ldots, \alpha_6$ and $\beta_1, \ldots, \beta_6$ are independent random variables with zero means and variances:

$$(2.2) \qquad \mathscr{E}\alpha_i^2 = \mathscr{E}\beta_i^2 = \sigma_i^2 \qquad (i=1, \ldots, 6) .$$

The constant α_0 may be any sort of stationary process so long as it is independent of α_i and β_i, $i=1, \ldots, 6$. Then, as we saw in Section 1.2, the cumulative spectrum of the term in the summation in (2.1) consists of a series of jumps at the seasonal frequencies λ_i equal in height to the variances σ_i^2. The spectrum of the process $y(t)$ is thus the superposition of six spectral "lines" on the spectrum of α_0, where the "lines" are such that the integrated power spectrum has jumps of σ_i^2 at the seasonal frequencies λ_i.[40] In this simple and rather unrealistic case a precise definition of seasonality can be given: it is just that part of the series which gives rise to the spectral lines at the seasonal frequencies. Note that the seasonal part is regular without being deterministic, i.e., nonstochastic.

It is doubtful whether seasonal variations found in economic time series, however, conform to the simple model outlined above. Instead we must expect that the amplitudes and phases of the harmonic terms in (2.1) will be subject to some systematic as well as random changes over time. We may immediately dispose of systematic phase changes since they may always be translated into corresponding changes in the amplitudes of the sine and cosine terms at the same frequency. Let us consider, then, what effect systematic, but still stochastic, changes in amplitude and perfectly random phase shifts will have on the spectrum of the process (2.1). We may do this effectively by considering the following simple process:

$$(2.3) \qquad y(t)=x(t) \cos (\lambda t+\varphi) ,$$

where $x(t)$ is a stationary process with zero mean, autocovariance function $\gamma_x(\tau)$, and continuous spectrum

$$(2.4) \qquad f_x(\lambda) = \frac{1}{\pi}\int_{-\infty}^{\infty} e^{-j\lambda\tau}\gamma_x(\tau)\,d\tau .$$

---

[40] If the spectrum of α_0 is continuous, the spectrum of $y(t)$ is said to be *mixed*. The analysis of processes with mixed spectra has been extensively discussed by Priestley [20].

For simplicity we suppose that φ is a random variable, independent of $x(t)$ and uniformly distributed in the interval $[-\pi, \pi]$.[41] We may suppose that the spectrum of $x(t)$ is roughly the same shape as that of, say, the Federal Reserve Board index of industrial production pictured in Figure 4; that is, it is symmetric about the origin with high power at and near zero frequency, the power falling off rapidly in either direction away from zero frequency.

Since $x(t)$ and φ are independent and $x(t)$ has zero mean, it is easily seen that $y(x)$ has zero mean. Furthermore, $y(t)$ is a stationary process with autocovariance function

$$(2.5) \qquad \gamma_y(\tau) = \mathscr{E}\, y(t)\, y(t+\tau)$$

$$= \frac{\gamma_x(\tau)}{2\pi} \int_{-\pi}^{\pi} [\cos \lambda t \cos \varphi - \sin \lambda t \sin \varphi] \times$$

$$[\cos \lambda(t+\tau) \cos \varphi - \sin \lambda(t+\tau) \sin \varphi]\, d\varphi$$

$$= \frac{\gamma_x(\tau)}{2\pi} \pi [\cos \lambda t \cos \lambda(t+\tau) + \sin \lambda t \sin \lambda(t+\tau)] = \tfrac{1}{2}\gamma_x(\tau) \cos \lambda\tau .$$

Writing $\cos \lambda\tau$ in complex form, we may easily show that the spectrum of $y(t)$ is

$$(2.6) \qquad f_y(\mu) = \frac{1}{\pi} \int_{-\infty}^{\infty} e^{-j\mu\tau} \gamma_y(\tau)\, d\tau$$

$$= \frac{1}{\pi} \int_{-\infty}^{\infty} e^{-j\mu\tau} \left(\frac{e^{j\lambda\tau}+e^{-j\lambda\tau}}{2}\right) \frac{\gamma_x(\tau)}{2}\, d\tau$$

$$= \tfrac{1}{4} \left\{ \frac{1}{\pi} \int_{-\infty}^{\infty} [e^{-j(\mu-\lambda)\tau}\gamma_x(\tau) + e^{-j(\mu+\lambda)\tau}\gamma_x(\tau)]\, dt \right\}$$

$$= \tfrac{1}{4}\{f_x(\mu-\lambda) + f_x(\mu+\lambda)\} .$$

Thus the spectrum of $y(t)$ is approximately the spectrum of $x(t)$ with origin shifted to the frequency λ and attenuated by a factor of 4.[42]

Given the supposed shape of the spectrum of the random amplitudes α_i and β_i in (2.1), it is easily seen that the spectrum of $y(t)$ will no longer consist of a series of spectral lines superimposed on the continuous spectrum of α_0 at the frequencies λ_i, but rather of a series of more or less broad peaks at those frequencies. The narrower the peaks, the more pronounced and regular will be the seasonal variation.[43]

---

[41] $\cos(\lambda t + \varphi)$ is stationary if and only if φ has the rectangular distribution on the interval $[-\pi, \pi]$, so that if this were not assumed, $y(t)$ could not be treated as a stationary series.

[42] Processes of this sort are called *narrow band* processes; see Davenport and Root [4, p. 158]. Note that $f_x(\mu + \lambda)$ will be small compared with $f_x(\mu - \lambda)$ if the power in $x(t)$ is concentrated near the origin.

[43] In the limiting case in which $x(t)$ tends to a constant $\bar{x}$ (a non-zero mean for $x(t)$ would have added a spectral line at the origin in (2.6)), $y(t)$ becomes

$$\bar{x} \cos(\lambda t + \varphi) = (\bar{x} \cos \varphi) \cos \lambda t + (-\bar{x} \sin \varphi) \sin \lambda t$$
$$= a_i \cos \lambda t + b_i \sin \lambda t .$$

Under the assumption that φ is uniformly distributed in $[-\pi, \pi]$ we have $\mathscr{E}\, a_i = \mathscr{E}\, b_i = 0$, $\mathscr{E}\, a_i b_i = 0$, $\mathscr{E}\, a_i^2 = \mathscr{E}\, b_i^2 = \bar{x}^2/2$, precisely the characteristics specified for α_i and β_i in (2.1), apart from normality.

In the more general case, then, we may define seasonality as that characteristic of a time series that gives rise to spectral peaks at seasonal frequencies.

Two series with exceedingly marked seasonal variations are the monthly series of federally inspected hog and cattle slaughter which go back to 1907. Graphs of the estimated positive halves of the spectra of these two series, based on recolored second quasi-differences of the form described in Section 1.3, are given in Figures 5 and 6. Both series exhibit extremely marked peaks at the frequency 0.0833 corre-

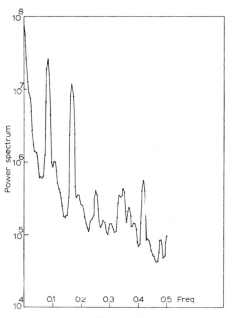

FIGURE 5
Spectral Density, Hog Slaughter

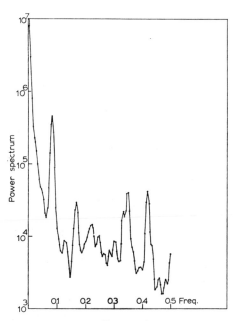

FIGURE 6
Spectral Density, Cattle Slaughter

sponding to a twelve month cycle. The hog slaughter series has in addition a very marked peak at 0.1667 corresponding to a six month cycle. There are smaller peaks at all the other seasonal frequencies, the ones at 0.3333 in both series being largely obscured by a nearby peak at or near 0.3500.[44] Thus, the definition given above appears to correspond well with intuition.

[44] In their forthcoming book, Granger and Hatanaka give an example which probably contains the explanation for this peak: "Taking into account leap years, the average number of days in a month is 30.437 and so there are 4.348 weeks in the average month. If a . . . series . . ., measured every month, contained an important weekly cycle, it would thus correspond to the frequency 0.348." Thus since slaughter occurs only on working days, which have more or less a weekly cycle, we would expect a peak at the point nearest 0.348 at which the average power spectrum is measured. Essentially, then, this peak occurs because of the cycle in the number of working days per month.

2.2. *Seasonal Adjustment*

In many economic time series, for example, the monthly series on United States unemployment, that part of the month to month variation that can be called seasonal is so important as to obscure other movements in the series. It is probably true that the single most important—or, at least, politically most important—statistic published by the Federal Government is the seasonally adjusted unemployment rate. The reason that the seasonally adjusted rate, and not the rate as estimated directly from the Bureau of the Census Current Population Survey, is most important is not hard to explain. During the mild recession of 1961 it was exceedingly important to the President and his advisors to assess correctly the general movement of unemployment, to know, for example, whether the change from May to June, 1961, could reasonably have been attributed to the sort of factors which normally cause unemployment to rise between May and June, or whether the general tendency of unemployment was up, which could be interpreted as a deepening of the recession calling for remedial actions. It would, of course, have been easy enough to compare the unemployment rates in May and June with those of the year before, but that would not have revealed whether unemployment rates had *risen* to their then high levels or *fallen* to them from still higher levels in the past few months. In terms of the concepts introduced in the previous section, the high power at seasonal frequencies was making interpretation of the information contained in the series difficult. The process of seasonal adjustment which was applied to the series in order to make it more readily interpretable was designed to smooth the series by filtering out some of the high power at seasonal frequencies.[45]

In one sense, the whole problem of seasonal adjustment of economic time series is a spurious one. Seasonal variations have causes (for example, variations in the weather), and insofar as these causes are measurable they should be used to explain changes that are normally regarded as seasonal. Indeed, seasonality does not occur in isolated economic series, but seasonal and other changes in one series are related to those in another. Hence, ideally one should formulate a complete econometric model in which the causes of seasonality are incorporated directly in the equations. Even if one cannot measure all the causes of seasonality, it may be possible to allow for seasonal shifts in economic relationships through the use of shift variables. To implement the sort of approach to seasonality consistent with this point of view would require the formulation and estimation of a monthly econometric model, and this is subject to a number of practical and conceptual

---

[45] Alternatively one might argue that the only *new* information in an observation on an economic time series is that part which could not have been predicted on the basis of past knowledge of the series. Since unemployment "usually" rises in June, the fact that it does is not news. Seasonal adjustment can then be viewed as a kind of prediction designed to remove a certain type of "non-information" from the series.

difficulties.[46] On the practical side the problems include the lack of availability of many relevant series, the non-measurability of key items, and the lack of appropriate statistical methodology for estimation of simultaneous equation systems relating highly temporally disaggregated series. In addition, the precise structure of the model will very much affect the analysis of seasonal effects, i.e., the results will be much affected by specification error in the model. On the conceptual side the problem is basically one of continuing structural change, which is essentially the sort of thing which causes seasonality to show up in the form of spectral peaks rather than spectral lines.

Considering these difficulties, the more simple-minded approach of attempting to find a filter which will remove spectral peaks at seasonal frequencies and alter the remaining characteristics of the series as little as possible makes considerable practical sense. It is not my purpose here to develop such filters, by no means an easy task, but rather to analyze the extent to which existing procedures succeed in this task with particular reference to the U.S. employment and unemployment statistics.

While a considerable number and variety of seasonal adjustment methods have been proposed, the vast bulk of those in current use are very closely related to the technique used by the Bureau of Labor Statistics to adjust the monthly series of employment and unemployment estimates issued by that agency.[47] As a detailed description of this method has been given elsewhere [19, Appendix G], it is only necessary to present a bare and incomplete outline here. The model underlying this method is the familiar one, each value of a series being the product (or sum)[48] of three factors: (1) trend-cycle, (2) seasonal, and (3) irregular. The problem is to disentangle these three components, then to eliminate the seasonal by division (or subtraction). In the terminology introduced earlier in this paper, trend-cycle consists largely of the low frequency components of the time series; seasonal of components at seasonal frequencies; and irregular of all the rest.

The first step in the procedure is an attempt to isolate the components at seasonal frequencies. This is done by computing a twelve month moving average of the series and finding the ratio of series for each month to the average centered on that month. The forming of ratios to moving average is a highly nonlinear filter designed to remove the low frequency components, leaving only the higher frequency seasonal and irregular components.

[46] T. C. Liu is attempting to construct a monthly model of the U. S. economy. Not only does this involve a formidable amount of interpolation but, for a variety of reasons, the model must be constructed with seasonally *adjusted* data, thus rendering it inapplicable for the purpose of seasonal adjustment.

[47] A comprehensive survey of proposed methods and those in use has been made by S. N. Marris [16, pp. 35–78].

[48] Multiplicative models can always be converted into additive ones by transforming the data to logarithms; conversely an additive model can be converted to a multiplicative one by taking exponentials.

The next step in the procedure attempts to separate seasonal components from the other high frequency components with which they are mixed. This is done in the BLS method by computing a five term moving average of the ratios to moving average for each month (i.e., five Januaries, five Februaries, etc.). The reason a five term moving average is used rather than a longer one (in the extreme all the ratios available) is to allow for the possibility of slowly varying seasonals (the narrow band versus the spectral line nature of seasonality). The length of the average reflects a judgment on the speed of this variation; the shorter the average, the faster the seasonal factor may vary and the broader the band of frequencies attributed to seasonality is supposed to be.

At this point in the procedure there is available a series of estimates of the seasonal component of the time series. If this is now divided into the original series, the result will be an estimate of the trend-cycle and irregular components, i.e., a preliminary seasonally adjusted series. However, the procedure does not stop with this preliminary adjustment, because it is felt that the original attempt to remove the low frequency components, without distorting the higher frequency ones by the formation of ratios to moving average, may not have been completely successful. Consequently, the resulting estimate of the trend-cycle and irregular components is again averaged, this time with a weighted seven term formula, in order to arrive at a new estimate of the trend-cycle component. If the ratios of the original series to this new estimate of the trend-cycle component are formed, the result will be a new estimate of the seasonal and irregular components. The second step in the procedure can then be repeated to arrive at a new estimate of the seasonal components, and so on indefinitely. The BLS procedure, however, is to repeat this operation only twice more after the initial estimate of the trend-cycle components by means of a twelve-month moving average.

The most recent complete set of seasonal factors obtained by the method is used to filter the series for the current year.

The above description does not attempt to do justice to the details of the procedure, which often involve considerable sophistication in the treatment of outliers, end-point corrections, and so forth. One further detail, however, peculiar to the U.S. employment and unemployment statistics, deserves special mention. The employment, unemployment, and labor force series, as estimated from a sample survey, actually consist of a large number of components. Distinctions are made on the basis of age and sex, major industry attachment (agricultural *versus* non-agricultural), and, in recent years, color. In the unemployment statistics there is also a classification on the basis of length of unemployment. Thus, in seasonally adjusting these series, it is possible either to adjust them all individually, including such major aggregates as total unemployment, employment, and labor force, or to adjust certain components, deriving seasonally adjusted values for the aggregates by implication. In the published series for the U.S. all aggregates and components are adjusted for seasonality separately except total unemployment. This series is seasonally adjusted by adjusting four major age-sex categories of unemployed (male and female, age 14–19, and age 20 and over) and summing the resulting four seasonally adjusted components to arrive at the adjusted total. The reason for this refinement is not hard to explain. If one examines the power spectra of the four categories presented in Figures 8–11, one finds that the degree of seasonality, as measured by the height of the peaks at seasonal frequencies, is much greater for males and females under 20 than it is for the older unemployed. The seasonal patterns, either as conventionally measured or by implication of the power spectra, are also quite different for the four groups. Since the relative contribution of the four groups to the total volume of unemployment has been changing over time, separate adjustment is a way of narrowing the frequency bands about seasonal frequencies in which the seasonal adjustment procedure must reduce power in the aggregate series, and thereby increasing the supposed accuracy of the adjustment.[49] It is this same idea, turned on its head so to speak, which provides the rationale for the so-called "residual" method of obtaining the seasonally adjusted total unemployment series.[50] According to this rationale, the way to obtain the seasonally adjusted unemployment series is first to adjust total employment and total labor force by the usual BLS procedure and then to derive the adjusted unemployment series by subtraction. There is a variety of reasons adduced for preferring this procedure to the one actually employed; closer examination does not suggest any strong a priori reason for preferring it to the one in use. In Sections 3.1 and 3.3 the effects of the residual method and those of the standard method are compared; the results suggest that, in terms of the criteria developed below, neither method is significantly superior to the other.

3. ANALYSIS OF THE EFFECTS OF SEASONAL ADJUSTMENT PROCEDURES

3.1. *Comparison of Power Spectra*

Existing methods of seasonal adjustment, of which the BLS method described above is typical, are non parametric in character. There are no statistically adequate tests for removal of seasonal effects or for the changes in the seasonal patterns which are induced by averaging the monthly ratios to moving averages for only a

---

[49] Examination of the spectra of other components of unemployment and of various components of employment and labor force also reveals some striking differences in the degree and pattern of seasonality. As the relative contributions of these components to the corresponding aggregates has also been changing over time, it would also seem that some such component by component analyses should be incorporated in the seasonal adjustment of other aggregates. However, this is not done by the BLS. Too fine a disaggregation would of course tend to increase the sampling variability of both adjusted and unadjusted estimates, which provides some reason for not attempting to build up estimates from a very large number of components.

[50] Although this idea had been discussed in government circles some years previously, it appears to have been first brought to public attention by Brittain [3]. For its advocacy in a more political context see Samuelson [22].

few past years. Furthermore, all these methods are highly nonlinear filters, so that it is difficult to specify a priori what the effects of seasonal adjustment on the series will be; possible effects include: (a) removal of more than strictly seasonal components; (b) introduction of non-seasonal movements; and (c) distortion of the relationship between the seasonally adjusted series and other related series. Although it is possible, at least in a partial way, to assess effects (a) and (b) by comparing the power spectrum of a series with its seasonally adjusted counterpart, it is not possible to assess effect (c). The reason, as has already been mentioned in Section 1, is that both the spectrum and the autocovariance function of a time series suppress all phase information. Such information is, of course, neither interesting nor relevant when considering a single stationary time series, but it is both when two such time series are considered.

Figures 7–16 give the estimated power spectra for total unemployment and unemployment in the four major age-sex categories. The spectrum of the original series is given as a solid line. The dashed line in Figures 7–11 shows the estimated power spectrum of the corresponding seasonally adjusted series as computed by the ordinary BLS procedure; the dashed line in Figures 12–16 shows the power spectrum of the corresponding seasonally adjusted series as computed by the residual method, i.e., by subtracting seasonally adjusted employment from seasonally adjusted labor force. Figures 7 and 12 are the spectra for total U.S. unemployment estimated from monthly data July, 1947–December, 1961. The remaining four figures in each group refer to the major age-sex categories of unemployment. In order, males, 14–19 years of age; males, 20 years of age and over; females, 14–19 years of age; and females, 20 years of age and over. The data from which the spectra for the categories have been estimated cover the period July, 1948–December, 1961.

Perhaps the most striking finding is the great loss in power which occurs at all frequencies in the seasonally adjusted unemployment of both sexes regardless of whether the ordinary BLS method or the residual method is used; in all four cases the power spectra of the seasonally adjusted series lie well below the corresponding spectra for the original series. For the older age groups and the aggregate figure, the loss of power at non-seasonal frequencies is less marked, though still quite noticeable, especially at frequencies between 0.0833 and 0.3333 where a large amount of power is present in the original series. It is also apparent that in no case does the use of the residual method improve the situation much, if at all.[51]

[51] It is possible to construct asymptotic confidence intervals based on the chi-square distribution for the individual points on the power spectrum. The degrees of freedom are based on considerations related to the "width" of the spectral window used. Connecting these points, however, does not give a confidence bound for the spectrum as a whole. Furthermore, in order to test whether the estimated spectrum for the seasonally adjusted spectrum lies significantly below the estimated spectrum for the original series we would need *joint* confidence bands. These have not been developed, though confidence bounds for the *gain*, to be introduced below, are available for one type of spectral window.

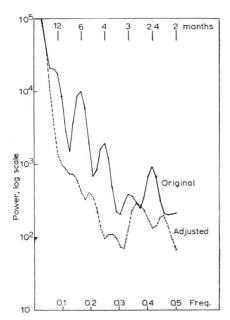

FIGURE 7
Spectral Densities: Total Unemployment, Original and BLS Adjusted

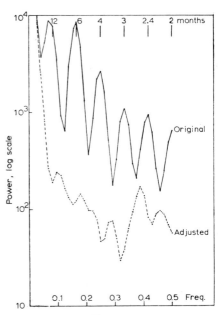

FIGURE 8
Spectral Densities: Unemployment,
Male 14–19, Original and BLS
Adjusted

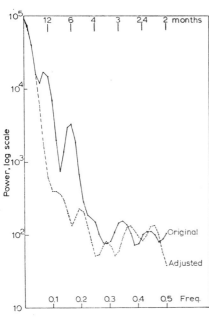

FIGURE 9
Spectral Densities: Unemployment,
Male 20+, Original and BLS Adjusted

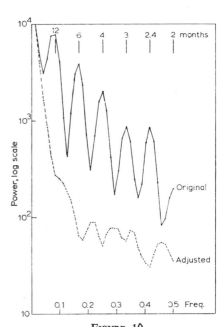

FIGURE 10
Spectral Densities: Unemployment,
Female 14–19, Original and BLS
Adjusted

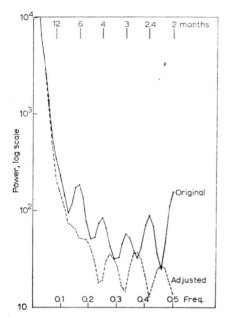

FIGURE 11
Spectral Densities: Unemployment,
Female 20+, Original and BLS
Adjusted

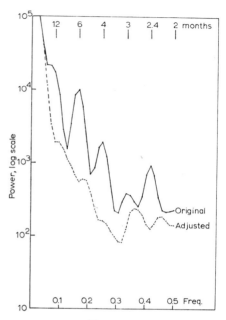

FIGURE 12
Spectral Densities: Unemployment,
Original and Residually Adjusted

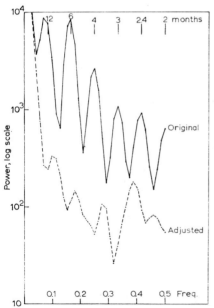

FIGURE 13
Spectral Densities: Unemployment,
Male 14–19, Original and
Residually Adjusted

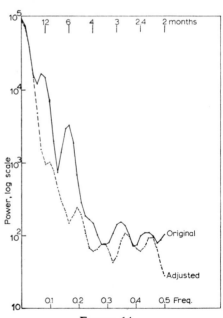

FIGURE 14
Spectral Densities: Unemployment,
Male 20+, Original and
Residually Adjusted

FIGURE 15   FIGURE 16

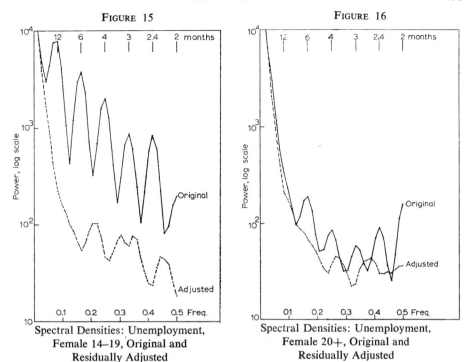

Spectral Densities: Unemployment,
Female 14–19, Original and
Residually Adjusted

Spectral Densities: Unemployment,
Female 20+, Original and
Residually Adjusted

The conclusion which may be drawn from the relation between the pairs of estimated spectra is that either technique of seasonal adjustment removes more than strictly seasonal components. There is no evidence that non-seasonal components have actually been introduced by either method. The fact that more than strictly seasonal components are removed is due perhaps to the great flexibility of the seasonal factors as computed by the BLS. This flexibility arises from the use of relatively short, five term, moving averages to separate the seasonal from the irregular component in the second step of each iteration in the procedure. This high degree of flexibility is most serious when the seasonal patterns are most regular, as in the case of the two younger age groups, for the BLS seasonal factors then tend to incorporate more of the randomness as supposed, but actually nonexistent, change. Comparison of the power spectra of the original and seasonally adjusted series for other categories of unemployment, employment, and labor force tends to support this conclusion but also suggests that other factors in the make-up of the series, such as the relative amount of power at low and high frequencies, may play a role in determining whether or not seasonal adjustment will remove excessive power at non-seasonal frequencies.[52]

[52] One of the referees has pointed out that in drawing this conclusion I tacitly assume that the spectrum of the time series free of seasonality will be a smooth function of frequency free of dips at seasonal frequencies. There are two reasons for this assumption, one theoretical, the other empirical.

Theoretically, it is reasonable to regard the time series as composed of a trend-cycle component,

The preceding conclusions are drawn in a rather rough fashion from visual comparison. To achieve a more quantitative measure of the loss of power at non-seasonal frequencies, as well as to answer the question of whether any temporal distortions (phase shifts) have been introduced by the adjustment processes, it is necessary to make use of another technique known as cross-spectral analysis.

3.2. Filters, Frequency Response Functions, and Cross-Spectra

In Section 1.3 we defined a linear, time-invariant filter in connection with the discussion of prewhitening. The frequency response function of a filter was defined, and the transfer function of the filter was defined as the squared modulus of the frequency response function. This discussion was couched in discrete terms, however, and the continuous formulation is easier to work with. In the continuous formulation, the linear, time-invariant filter L is defined by

$$(3.1) \qquad y(t) = Lx(t) = \int_{-\infty}^{\infty} K(\tau) x(t - \tau) d\tau ,$$

which includes the discrete case as a special case when the weights, $K(\tau)$, are appropriately defined.[53] The weight function, $K(\tau)$, is called the *kernel* of the filter

---

a seasonal component, and white noise. Thus, the spectrum is built up out of a flat piece corresponding to the white noise, a series of narrow band peaks at seasonal frequencies, and the spectrum of the trend-cycle component. The assumption is thus essentially that all frequencies are needed to represent the trend-cycle component, and that although the power at low frequencies may be very high, this power as a function of frequency does not drop abruptly to zero at some point below the lowest seasonal frequency. If one assumes that the trend-cycle component can be approximated by some auto-regressive scheme, then precisely this conclusion emerges. For example, suppose that the pth order quasi-differences of the series $x(t)$, as defined in the previous section, are white noise, i.e., that the auto-regression is

$$\sum_{i=0}^{p} \binom{p}{i} (-k)^i x(t - i) = \varepsilon(t) ,$$

where

$$\mathscr{E}\varepsilon(t) = 0 ; \quad \mathscr{E}\varepsilon(t)\varepsilon(t') = \sigma^2 , \quad \text{if} \quad t = t' , \quad \text{and} \quad = 0 , \quad \text{if} \quad t \neq t' .$$

Then the spectrum of $x(t)$ is just

$$f_x(\lambda) = \frac{1}{[1 - 2k \cos 2\pi\lambda + k^2]^p} ,$$

which has exactly the shape which (we argued above) is typical of economic time series: it has high power at low frequencies, and low at high frequencies, but it has some power everywhere in the interval $[-\frac{1}{2}, \frac{1}{2}]$.

The empirical reason for the tacit assumption that the spectrum of a seasonality-free time series does not have dips at seasonal frequencies is that spectra of precisely this sort are produced when more reasonable methods of seasonal adjustment, such as that suggested by Hannan, are employed.

[53] For example, as $a\delta(\tau_1 - \tau_2)$ where $\delta(\tau_1 - \tau_2)$ is the Dirac delta function such that

$$\int_{-\infty}^{\infty} \delta(\tau_1 - \tau_2) d\tau_2 = 1, \quad \delta(\tau_1 - \tau_2) = 0 \qquad \text{for} \quad \tau_1 \neq \tau_2 .$$

L which operates on the input $x(t)$ to produce the output $y(t)$. The *frequency response function* of the filter, $l(\lambda)$, is the Fourier transform of the kernel:

$$(3.2) \quad l(\lambda) = \int_{-\infty}^{\infty} K(\tau)e^{-j\lambda\tau}d\tau = u(\lambda) + jv(\lambda),$$

and is, in general, a complex-valued function of frequency. We have already introduced the notion of the transfer function of a filter, the squared modulus of $l(\lambda)$, and indicated the relation between the input and output power spectra in terms of this function in (1.31). A more complete description of the relationship between the input and output of a linear, time-invariant filter is given by the frequency response function of the filter. For linear filters, we have

$$(3.3) \quad Le^{j\lambda t} = \int_{-\infty}^{\infty} K(\tau)e^{j\lambda(t-\tau)}d\tau = \left[\int_{-\infty}^{\infty} K(\tau)e^{-j\lambda\tau}d\tau\right]e^{j\lambda t} = l(\lambda)e^{j\lambda t}$$
$$= [u(\lambda) + jv(\lambda)][\cos \lambda t + j \sin \lambda t] = [u(\lambda) \cos \lambda t - v(\lambda) \sin \lambda t]$$
$$+ j[u(\lambda) \sin \lambda t + v(\lambda) \cos \lambda t].$$

Since $Le^{j\lambda t} = L \cos \lambda t + jL \sin \lambda t$, we see that the real part of $Le^{j\lambda t}$ is the output resulting from the input of a cosine wave of frequency λ and unit amplitude; the imaginary part is the output resulting from the input of a sine wave of frequency λ and unit amplitude.

Let the angle $\varphi(\lambda)$ be defined as

$$(3.4) \quad \varphi(\lambda) = \arg [u(\lambda) + jv(\lambda)] = \arctan \frac{v(\lambda)}{u(\lambda}),$$

so that

$$(3.5) \quad \cos \varphi(\lambda) = \frac{u(\lambda)}{\sqrt{u(\lambda)^2 + v(\lambda)^2}},$$

$$\sin \varphi(\lambda) = \frac{y(\lambda)}{\sqrt{u(\lambda)^2 + v(\lambda)^2}}.$$

Thus the effect of L on a sine wave of frequency λ and unit amplitude is to transform it to

$$(3.6) \quad L \sin \lambda t = u(\lambda) \sin \lambda t + v(\lambda) \cos \lambda t$$
$$= [u(\lambda)^2 + v(\lambda)^2]^{\frac{1}{2}}[\cos \varphi(\lambda) \sin \lambda t + \sin \varphi(\lambda) \cos \lambda t]$$
$$= [u(\lambda)^2 + v(\lambda)^2]^{\frac{1}{2}} \sin [\lambda t + \varphi(\lambda)],$$

that is, another sine wave with amplitude $[u(\lambda)^2 + v(\lambda)^2]^{\frac{1}{2}}$ and non-zero phase $\varphi(\lambda)$. The filter thus increases or attenuates the amplitude by a factor of $[u(\lambda)^2 + v(\lambda)^2]^{\frac{1}{2}}$ and shifts the origin of the sine wave in time by $\varphi(\lambda)/\lambda$. Similarly

(3.7) $L \cos \lambda t = u(\lambda) \cos \lambda t - v(\lambda) \sin \lambda t$
$$= [u(\lambda)^2 + v(\lambda)^2]^{\frac{1}{2}} [\cos \varphi(\lambda) \cos \lambda t - \sin \varphi(\lambda) \sin \lambda t]$$
$$= [u(\lambda)^2 + v(\lambda)^2]^{\frac{1}{2}} \cos [\lambda t + \varphi(\lambda)] .$$

These effects on sine and cosine waves can be conveniently summarized, in terms of the frequency response function, for this, in polar form, is just

(3.8) $l(\lambda) = G(\lambda) e^{j\varphi(\lambda)} ,$

where $G(\lambda) = [u(\lambda)^2 + v(\lambda)^2]^{\frac{1}{2}}$ is called the *gain* of the filter and $\varphi(\lambda)$ its *phase angle*.

We are now in a position to show that the operation of a linear, time-invariant filter on any time series can be completely described in terms of its frequency response function. Let $x(t)$ be such a time series; then by (1.18) we can write

(3.9) $Lx(t) = \int_{-\infty}^{\infty} K(\tau) x(t-\tau) d\tau = \int_{-\infty}^{\infty} K(\tau) \left[\int_{-\infty}^{\infty} e^{j\lambda(t-\tau)} dZ_x(\lambda) \right] d\tau$
$$= \int_{-\infty}^{\infty} e^{j\lambda t} \int_{-\infty}^{\infty} K(\tau) e^{-j\lambda\tau} d\tau \, dZ_x(\lambda) = \int_{-\infty}^{\infty} e^{j\lambda t} l(\lambda) dZ_x(\lambda) .$$

Thus if we write

(3.10) $y(t) = \int_{-\infty}^{\infty} e^{j\lambda t} dZ_y(\lambda) ,$

we see that the new random variables $dZ_x(\lambda)$ and $dZ_y(\lambda)$ into which the input and output series of the filter can be decomposed are simply related by

(3.11) $dZ_y(\lambda) = l(\lambda) dZ_x(\lambda) .$

Multiplying on both sides by the complex conjugate of $dZ_x(\lambda)$ and taking expected values, we have

(3.12) $l(\lambda) = \dfrac{\mathscr{E} \, dZ_y(\lambda) \overline{dZ_x(\lambda)}}{\mathscr{E} \, dZ_x(\lambda) \overline{dZ_x(\lambda)}} .$

Thus, $l(\lambda)$ is the slope of the regression line between the complex random variables $dZ_y(\lambda)$ and $dZ_x(\lambda)$.

The interpretation of the values of a frequency response function as a series of regression slopes, one for each frequency in the representation of the input and output series of a filter, suggests an interesting application. In ordinary statistical work on economic time series we frequently relate two variables by means of a least squares regression line even though we know the relation between the two variables is not truly linear; the idea is to obtain some measure of the "average" relationship. In the same way, even though we know a filter is not truly linear or time-invariant, we can relate the input and output series by means of (3.12); then the regression slope obtained at each frequency represents the "average" frequency response function. In other words, if we take a sample input and output series

from any filter and form an estimate of the quantity on the right hand side of
(3.12), this will estimate the frequency response function of a linear, time-invariant
filter *which is an approximation to the actual filter valid over the range of the random
amplitudes which characterize the input series as it occurred in the sample*. The
results then give a way of characterizing any filter in terms of gain and phase angle
at frequencies for which the estimates are made.

But how do we form estimates of the complex quantities, i.e., the "regression
slopes,"

$$\frac{\mathscr{E}\, dZ_y(\lambda)\, \overline{dZ_x(\lambda)}}{\mathscr{E}\, dZ_x(\lambda)\, \overline{dZ_x(\lambda)}}\ ?$$

The denominator is easily recognized by (1.21) as 1/2 the power spectrum at
frequency λ of the input series $x(t)$. In Section 1.2 we showed this was the complex
Fourier transform of the autocovariance function $\gamma_x(\tau)$ of the input series. Since
this autocovariance function is even, it followed that its power spectrum $f_{xx}(\lambda)$
could be represented by a cosine transform of the autocovariance function. Thus
we formed an estimate of the power spectrum by taking, essentially, the finite cosine
transform of weighted averages of the sample autocovariance of $x(t)$.[54]

The numerators of our "regression slopes" are covariances of the complex
random variables $dZ_y(\lambda)$ and $dZ_x(\lambda)$ at the same frequency. Twice these covariances
as a function of frequency are called the *cross-spectrum* of the two time series $x(t)$
and $y(t)$, and denoted by

$$(3.13) \quad dF_{xy}(\lambda) = dC_{xy}(\lambda) - j\, dQ_{xy}(\lambda) = 2\mathscr{E}\, dZ_y(\lambda)\, d\overline{Z_x(\lambda)}\ .$$

The real part of the cross-spectrum (which is generally a complex valued function)
is $dC_{xy}(\lambda)$; it is called the co-spectrum of $x(t)$ and $y(t)$. The complex part of the
cross-spectrum, $dQ_{xy}(\lambda)$, is called the *quadrature spectrum*. The meaning of these
two parts of the cross-spectrum becomes clearer if we rewrite the two series in real
form, following (1.11):

$$(3.14) \quad \begin{aligned} x(t) &= \int_0^\infty \cos \lambda t\, dU_x(\lambda) + \int_0^\infty \sin \lambda t\, dV_x(\lambda)\ , \\ y(t) &= \int_0^\infty \cos \lambda t\, dU_y(\lambda) + \int_0^\infty \sin \lambda t\, dV_y(\lambda)\ . \end{aligned}$$

Since

$$(3.15) \quad \begin{aligned} \mathscr{E}\, dZ_y(\lambda)\, d\overline{Z_x(\lambda)} &= \tfrac{1}{4}\mathscr{E}\{[dU_y(\lambda) - j\, dV_y(\lambda)][dU_x(\lambda) + j\, dV_x(\lambda)]\} \\ &= \tfrac{1}{4}[\mathscr{E}\, dU_x(\lambda)\, dU_y(\lambda) + \mathscr{E}\, dV_x(\lambda)\, dV_y(\lambda)] \\ &\quad - \tfrac{j}{4}[\mathscr{E}\, dU_x(\lambda)\, dV_y(\lambda) - \mathscr{E}\, dU_y(\lambda)\, dV_x(\lambda)]\ , \end{aligned}$$

---

[54] Equation (1.23') with autocovariances modified by (1.25).

we see that $dC_{xy}(\lambda)$ is essentially the covariance of the amplitudes of the *in phase* components of $x(t)$ and $y(t)$; and $dQ_{xy}(\lambda)$ is essentially the covariance of amplitudes of cosines with sines which are 90° out of phase or *in quadrature*.

To see how to estimate the cross-spectrum we must first show that the covariance of the complex random variables $dZ_x(\lambda)$ and $dZ_y(\lambda)$ is zero at different frequencies; we already know from Section 1.2 that

(3.16) $\mathscr{E} \, dZ_x(\lambda) \, d\overline{Z_x(\lambda')} = 0 = \mathscr{E} \, dZ_y(\lambda) \, d\overline{Z_y(\lambda')}$,

for λ and λ' in non-overlapping bands, i.e., "$\lambda \neq \lambda'$." What we wish to show is that

(3.17) $\mathscr{E} \, dZ_x(\lambda') \, d\overline{Z_y(\lambda)} = 0 = \mathscr{E} \, d\overline{Z_x(\lambda')} \, dZ_y(\lambda)$,

for "$\lambda \neq \lambda'$," for all $l(\lambda) \neq 0$.

Unfortunately, it is not in general true that (3.17) holds for two arbitrary stationary processes; it will hold if and only if the two series are *jointly* stationary in the weak sense used throughout this paper; i.e., if and only if the lag covariance function is independent of time.[55] It is, however, easily seen that it is sufficient for joint stationarity that $x(t)$ be stationary and that $y(t)$ be the output of a linear, time-invariant filter applied to $x(t)$. For then (3.11) holds; multiplying by $d\overline{Z_x(\lambda')}$ and taking expected values, we have

(3.18) $\mathscr{E} \, dZ_y(\lambda) \, d\overline{Z_x(\lambda')} = l(\lambda) \mathscr{E} \, dZ_x(\lambda) \, d\overline{Z_x(\lambda')} = 0,$ for "$\lambda \neq \lambda'$" and $l(\lambda) \neq 0$.

Similarly,

(3.19) $\mathscr{E} \, d\overline{Z_y(\lambda)} \, dZ_x(\lambda') = \overline{l(\lambda)} \mathscr{E} \, dZ_x(\lambda) \, d\overline{Z_x(\lambda')} = 0$,   for "$\lambda \neq \lambda'$" and $l(\lambda) \neq 0$.

Conversely, it can be shown that if $x(t)$ is stationary and $y(t)$ is the output of a linear time-invariant filter applied to $x(t)$, then $\mathscr{E}x(t) \, y(t+\tau)$ will be independent of t. From this it also follows that (3.18) and (3.19) hold.[56] Joint stationarity is a very

---

[55] I am indebted to W. M. Gorman for pointing out my earlier mistake in this respect. He gave as a counterexample the two series,

$$x(t) = a_1 \cos t + b_1 \sin t + a_2 \cos 2t + b_2 \sin 2t ,$$
$$y(t) = a_2 \cos t + b_2 \sin t + a_1 \cos 2t + b_1 \sin 2t ,$$

which are each stationary if

$$\mathscr{E}a_i^2 = \sigma_i^2 = \mathscr{E}b_i^2 ,$$

and

$$\mathscr{E}a_i b_i = 0, \quad \mathscr{E}a_i a_j = 0 \quad \text{if} \quad i \neq j \quad \text{and} \quad \mathscr{E}b_i b_j = 0 \quad \text{if} \quad i \neq j ,$$

but not jointly stationary since

$$\mathscr{E}x(t)y(t+\tau) = \sigma_1^2 \cos [t + 2\tau] + \sigma_2^2 \sin [3t + \tau] \text{ is not independent of } t.$$

[56] Doob [5, pp. 596–98].

strong condition. Nonetheless, it is clear that it is an entirely reasonable one when dealing with linear, time-invariant filters.

Equations (3.18) and (3.19) may be used to show that the cross-spectrum is the complex Fourier transform of the lag covariance function $\mathscr{E} y(t) x(t-\tau)$. For

$$(3.20) \quad \mathscr{E} y(t) x(t-\tau) = \mathscr{E}\, y(t)\overline{x(t-\tau)}$$

$$= \int_{-\infty}^{\infty} \int_{-\infty}^{\infty} e^{j(\lambda-\lambda')t} e^{j\lambda'\tau} \mathscr{E}\, dZ_y(\lambda)\, \overline{dZ_x(\lambda')}$$

$$= \int_{-\infty}^{\infty} e^{j\lambda\tau} \frac{dF_{xy}(\lambda)}{2},$$

since $\mathscr{E}\, dZ_y(\lambda)\overline{dZ_x(\lambda')}=0$ for $\lambda\neq\lambda'$ by (3.18), and $=dF_{xy}(\lambda)/2$ for $\lambda=\lambda'$ by (3.13). It therefore follows that $\mathscr{E} y(t) x(t-\tau)$ and $dF_{xy}(\lambda)/2$ are Fourier transform pairs and

$$(3.21) \quad dF_{xy}(\lambda) = \frac{1}{\pi} \int_{-\infty}^{\infty} e^{-j\lambda\tau}[\mathscr{E}\, y(t) x(t-\tau)]\, d\tau .$$

Equation (3.21) enables us to derive a way of estimating the real and complex parts of the cross-spectrum.

Just as before, the function F_{xy} has the classical decomposition in terms of three functions: the first absolutely continuous, the second a step function, and the third a singular function. If the last two are ruled out as essentially irrelevant for economic time series, we may write

$$(3.22) \quad dF_{xy}(\lambda)=f_{xy}(\lambda)\, d\lambda=c_{xy}(\lambda)\, d\lambda-jq_{xy}(\lambda)\, d\lambda .$$

The discrete analogue of (3.21) for a finite number M of lags is then

$$(3.23) \quad f_{xy}(\lambda) = c_{xy}(\lambda)-jq_{xy}(\lambda) = \frac{1}{\pi} \sum_{\tau=-M}^{M} e^{-j\lambda\tau} \mathscr{E}\, y(t) x(t-\tau)$$

$$= \frac{1}{\pi} \sum_{\tau=-M}^{M} (\cos \lambda\tau -j \sin \lambda\tau)\mathscr{E}\, y(t) x(t-\tau)$$

$$= \frac{1}{\pi} \left\{ \mathscr{E}\, y(t) x(t) + \sum_{\tau=1}^{M} \cos \lambda\tau\, \mathscr{E}[y(t) x(t-\tau)+y(t) x(t+\tau)] \right.$$

$$\left. -j \sum_{\tau=1}^{M} \sin \lambda\tau\, \mathscr{E}[y(t) x(t-\tau)-y(t) x(t+\tau)] \right\} .$$

Note that if $y(t)$ is set equal to $x(t)$, the complex part vanishes and the expected values in the first and second terms become, respectively, $\gamma(0)$ and $2\gamma(\tau)$ so that (3.23) represents a generalization of (1.23′).

Let

$$(3.24) \quad R_{xy}(\tau) = \frac{1}{2T} \sum_{t=-T+1+M}^{T-M} \{y(t) x(t-\tau)+y(t) x(t+\tau)\}$$

and

$$(3.25) \quad S_{xy}(\tau) = \frac{1}{2T} \sum_{t=-T+1+M}^{T-M} \{y(t)x(t-\tau) - y(t)x(t+\tau)\}$$

be the sample estimates of the expected values occurring in (3.23); then replacing the expected values by their sample estimates and equating real part to real part and complex part to complex part, we have estimates of the co- and quadrature spectra of $x(t)$ and $y(t)$

$$(3.26) \quad \begin{aligned} \hat{c}_{xy}(\lambda) &= \frac{1}{\pi} \left\{ R(0) + \sum_{\tau=1}^{M} \cos \lambda\tau \, R_{xy}(\tau) \right\}, \\ \hat{q}_{xy}(\lambda) &= \frac{1}{\pi} \left\{ \sum_{\tau=1}^{M} \sin \lambda\tau \, S_{xy}(\tau) \right\}. \end{aligned}$$

These estimates, however, are not consistent.[57] To obtain consistent estimates, suitably weighted averages of the raw sample estimates $R_{xy}(\tau)$ and $S_{xy}(\tau)$ are employed; i.e., a lag window is used. In the results reported below, the window (1.25), which was used for spectral estimation, was also employed. In addition, both series were prewhitened by the quasi-difference method described in Section 1.3. The same order of quasi-differences was used to prewhiten both the original and seasonally adjusted series; after estimation of the cross-spectra, the estimates were recolored by dividing at each frequency by the transfer function of the quasi-difference filter.[58]

Given estimates $\hat{c}_{xy}(\lambda)$, $\hat{q}_{xy}(\lambda)$, and $\hat{f}_{xy}(\lambda)$ of the co-spectrum and quadrature spectrum of the input and output series, and the spectrum of the input series, the frequency response function is estimated by

$$(3.27) \quad \hat{l}(\lambda) = \frac{\hat{c}_{xy}(\lambda)}{\hat{f}_{xx}(\lambda)} - j \frac{\hat{q}_{xy}(\lambda)}{\hat{f}_{xx}(\lambda)}.$$

Consequently, estimates of its gain and phase angle are given by

$$(3.28) \quad \begin{aligned} \hat{G}(\lambda) &= \frac{\sqrt{\hat{c}_{xy}(\lambda)^2 + \hat{q}_{xy}(\lambda)^2}}{\hat{f}_{xx}(\lambda)}, \\ \hat{\varphi}(\lambda) &= \arctan\left[-\frac{\hat{q}_{xy}(\lambda)}{\hat{c}_{xy}(\lambda)} \right]. \end{aligned}$$

[57] Murthy [15].

[58] The asymptotic distribution of the cross-spectrum and spectra of two series as estimated using a different lag window than the one used here has been worked out by Goodman [7]. Goodman shows how simultaneous confidence intervals may be obtained and works out several for combinations of the estimates such as the gain and phase angle of a filter. Unfortunately, in addition to being based on a different window, application of Goodman's results requires an a priori knowledge of the coherency between the two series which is analogous to a squared correlation coefficient and which is defined, for two series, as the squared modulus of the cross-spectrum divided by the product of the spectra. Since the procedure replacing the actual coherency by its estimated value seems somewhat doubtful, confidence intervals have not been given for the estimates presented below.

3.3. *Estimated Gains and Time Lags for Seasonal Filters*

The estimated gains and phase angles divided by frequency (to give an estimated time lag) are plotted for the five unemployment series and the BLS and residual methods of seasonal adjustment in Figures 17–26.

The gains which are graphed at the top of each chart give a picture entirely consistent with, but more accurate than, the comparisons of the spectra of the original and seasonally adjusted series which were made in Section 3.1. Except in the case of unemployed males, 20 and over, in which the gain is slightly and insignificantly larger than one at a few frequencies for the BLS method of adjustment, the estimated gains are uniformly between zero and one; and, of course, they tend to be lowest at seasonal frequencies. However, whereas before we were only able to note excessive removal of power at nonseasonal frequencies, we can now measure the extent of power removal at different frequencies in the same series and at the same frequency in different series. The first important point to be noted is that in the cases of both unemployed males and females over 20, which as already noted do not have as well defined seasonals as the two younger groups, power removal at different seasonal frequencies is highly uneven. There does not appear to be a consistent frequency pattern in the effectiveness of the seasonal adjustment, and the residual method offers no improvement on this score. The removal of excessive power at non-seasonal frequencies shows up in an exceedingly clear fashion in the gains. Cross-comparisons of the gains of the BLS and residual filters for seasonal adjustment at the same frequencies again yield no clearcut pattern and tend to support the contention that the effects of either method are about equally bad.

In comparing the spectra of the original and seasonally adjusted series, all information about phase shifts induced by the filter was suppressed. The possibility of phase shifts, however, particularly at low frequencies which contain the bulk of a series' information on the state of the economy, is a very serious one. Perhaps the most important finding of this paper is contained in the lower halves of Figures 17–26 in which the time lags (phase angle divided by frequency) have been plotted.[59] These show that the seasonal adjustment filters produce strong phase shifts particularly at low frequencies.[60] If all economic time series had the same harmonic

---

[59] Before computation of the time lags all negative phase angles were converted into positive ones by the addition of 2π (i.e., 360°). The rationale behind this adjustment is as follows: a positive phase angle of $\varphi(\lambda)$ at a frequency λ means that $\cos[\lambda t + \varphi(\lambda)]$ and $\sin[\lambda t + \varphi(\lambda)]$ are shifted *backward* in time by $\varphi(\lambda)/\lambda$. A negative phase angle of $\varphi(\lambda)$, however, means that they are shifted *forward*. Now $\cos[\lambda t + 2\pi + \varphi(\lambda)] = \cos[\lambda t + \varphi(\lambda)]$ and $\sin[\lambda t + 2\pi + \varphi(\lambda)] = \sin[\lambda t + \varphi(\lambda)]$. Thus a forward shift of $\varphi(\lambda)/\lambda$ is precisely equivalent to a backward shift of $2\pi/\lambda + \varphi(\lambda)/\lambda$ when $\varphi(\lambda)$ is negative. From the standpoint of the use of the seasonally adjusted values of a time series to indicate turning points and other major fluctuations, it is only backward shifts which make sense.

[60] It can easily be seen that any one-sided linear filter (i.e., one which operates only on past values of the data) must produce some phase shifts. For, in order that no phase shifts occur, the frequency response function *(See further p. 282)*

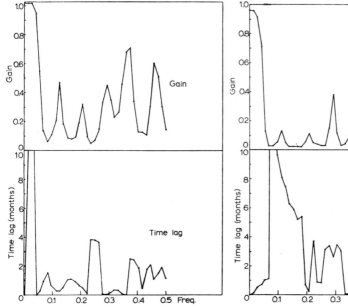

FIGURE 17
Total Unemployment,
Original and BLS Adjusted

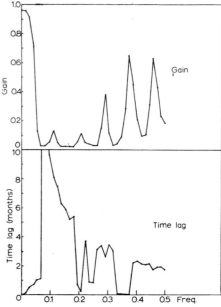

FIGURE 18
Unemployment, Males 14–19,
Original and BLS Adjusted

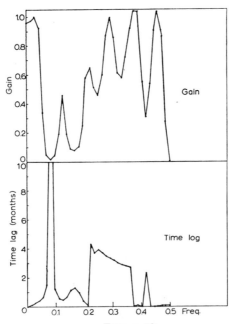

FIGURE 19
Unemployment, Male 20+,
Original and BLS Adjusted

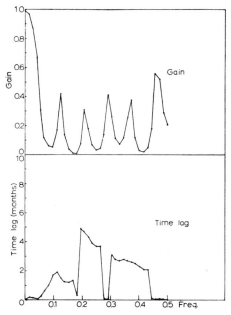

FIGURE 20
Unemployment, Female 14–19,
Original and BLS Adjusted

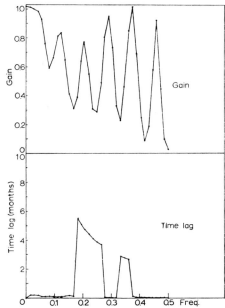

FIGURE 21
Unemployment, Female 20+,
Original and BLS Adjusted

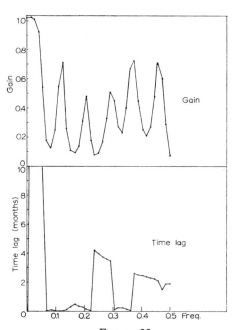

FIGURE 22
Total Unemployment,
Original and Residually Adjusted

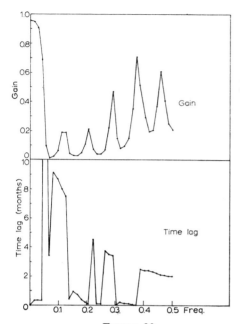

FIGURE 23
Unemployment, Male 14–19,
Original and Residually Adjusted

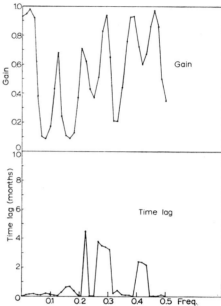

FIGURE 24
Unemployment, Male 20+,
Original and Residually Adjusted

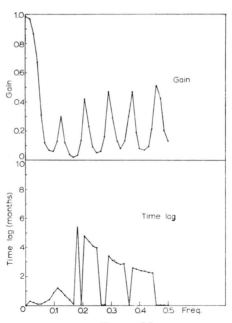

FIGURE 25
Unemployment, Female 14–19,
Original and Residually Adjusted

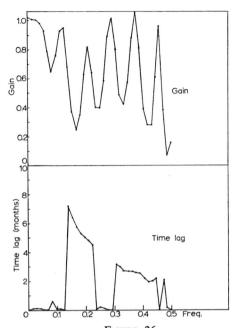

FIGURE 26
Unemployment, Female 20+,
Original and Residually Adjusted

content and if the filters employed to remove seasonality produced exactly the same phase shifts at the same frequency, this phenomenon would be of little significance. It is apparent, however, from the analyses presented in this paper that both of these assumptions lie very far from the truth. Thus, the fact that different series have quite different harmonic compositions and that ordinary methods of seasonal adjustment produce severe and different phase shifts at different frequencies, means, in effect, that these methods of adjustment distort the lead-lag relationships which exist among the original series to which they are applied. Consequently, doubt is cast upon the standard practice of seasonally adjusting key economic indicators by the usual methods, although I would not argue with the position that some form of allowance for seasonality is necessary if the data are to be used with any intelligence.

$$I(\lambda) = \int_{-\infty}^{\infty} K(\tau)\, e^{-j\lambda\tau} d\tau = u(\lambda) + jv(\lambda)$$

must be real, i.e., $v(\lambda) = 0$, and this can only occur when $K(\tau)$ is symmetric about $\tau = 0$. Of course the BLS and residual filters are not linear, but they are one-sided, which is a plausible reason for the phase shifts which they produce. It would seem desirable in future research to attempt to design filters that would minimize phase shifts or, at least, confine large phase shifts to higher frequencies.

4. CONCLUSIONS

In this article I have attempted to show that description of economic time series in the frequency domain is an exceptionally fruitful way of looking at them. Many have been discouraged about the prospects of using spectral techniques in economics because of the very large numbers of observations required and because of the obviously non-stationary character of economic time series. Two important conclusions of this article, however, are, first, that the number of observations available to economists does not prevent satisfactory analysis of the high frequency components, and, second, that much of the supposed non-stationary character of economic time series may simply be treated as high power at low frequencies and allowed for by prewhitening. The method of prewhitening which has been used does not appear to have been discussed in the available literature; it is to take weighted quasi-differences of a series until the estimated spectrum of the series appears relatively flat.

Among the high frequency components of economic time series which may successfully be studied by spectral techniques are those produced by seasonality. It is shown in this article that a slowly changing and stochastic seasonal pattern will reveal itself in the spectrum of an economic time series by a series of peaks at certain frequencies. The breadth of these peaks depends essentially on the regularity of the seasonal pattern, being narrower and more pronounced the more regular the pattern.

A practical problem of considerable significance which may be treated by means of spectral techniques is that of assessing quantitatively the effects of a seasonal adjustment procedure. Seasonal adjustment may produce three types of effects in addition to the elimination of seasonality: (1) elimination of components that are not seasonal; (2) introduction of components that are not seasonal; and (3) distortion of temporal relations among series. Apart from the methods here proposed, there do not seem to be satisfactory methods of measuring these possible effects. Many time series of U.S. employment, unemployment, labor force, and components thereof have been analyzed. The results for total unemployment and its four major age-sex categories are reported here. Two methods of seasonal adjustment have been considered, the one currently in use by the Bureau of Labor Statistics, and the so-called "residual" method. In the analysis of any sort of filtering operation, such as seasonal adjustment, it is found that an estimated frequency response function, derived from estimates of the spectrum of the original series and the cross-spectrum between the original and seasonally adjusted series, provides the most useful method of analysis.

The major substantive conclusion of this article is that both the BLS and residual methods of seasonal adjustment eliminate far more than can properly be called seasonal and produce severe phase shifts at lower frequencies, but neither appears to introduce non-seasonal components. The presence of strong phase shifts at low frequencies casts considerable doubt on the ability of these series as seasonally adjusted by current techniques to serve as sensitive indicators of underlying economic conditions.

Stanford University

ACKNOWLEDGEMENT

I am especially indebted to George S. Fishman for assistance in carrying out the research which underlies this paper. He has not only been responsible for all programming and supervision of the computations, but his suggestions have been important to the whole formulation of the approach taken. During the course of the study numerous helpful suggestions were also received from K. J. Arrow, R. Dorfman, J. Durbin, C. W. J. Granger, W. M. Gorman, Z. A. Lomnicki, E. Parzen, M. B. Priestley, H. Rosenblatt, J. Tukey, and H. Wold, although I regret to say they cannot be held responsible for my errors and omissions. D. Hulett, B. Mitchell, and H. Oniki also helped with programming, computations, and the graphing of results.

The bulk of the research which this paper reports was carried out under Grant NSF G 16114 from the National Science Foundation to Stanford University. Although the initial writing was completed during the first three months of my tenure as Fellow of the John Simon Guggenheim Memorial Foundation and Fulbright Research Grantee at the Econometric Institute, Rotterdam, certain rewriting was accomplished under NSF GS-142. Additional funds for computations were received from the President's Committee to Appraise Employment and Unemployment Statistics, and some of the results reported here were reported more briefly in the Committee's report [19, pp. 175–75]. I am indebted to the National Science Foundation and to the chairman of the President's Committee, R. A. Gordon, for the funds with which to carry out this research.

Miss Margaret E. Martin of the Bureau of the Budget supplied many unpublished figures and much helpful advice on how to interpret them.

This paper appeared originally as Report 6227 of the Econometric Institute, Netherlands School of Economics (December 4, 1962), and in this connection typing and clerical assistance in the preparation of the charts were supplied and are much appreciated. Since this time, I have learned of a number of other applications of spectral techniques to economic problems: Especially not to be overlooked is the forthcoming volume, *Analysis of Economic Time Series* by C. W. J. Granger and M. Hatanaka, Chapter 3 of which contains a first-rate introduction to spectral theory. An exposition of the theory, with applications to a number of problems including the determination of lead-lag relationships between series, may be found in J. Cunnyngham, "The Spectral Analysis of Economic Time Series," Working Paper No. 14, U. S. Bureau of the Census (Washington, D. C.: 1963). In a paper presented at the meetings of the American Statistical Association, September 4, 1963, in Cleveland, Ohio, "Spectral Analysis and Parametric Methods for Seasonal Adjustment of Economic Time Series," H. Rosenblatt of the Bureau of the Census tests a method of parametric seasonal adjustment due to Hannan (*Australian Journal of Statistics*, 2: 1–15, April, 1960) by methods similar to those employed here. Finally, in an unpublished Master's thesis at the Australian National University, Canberra, N. F. Nettheim has treated the problem of seasonal adjustment analytically by means of spectral theory.

REFERENCES

[1] BARTLETT, M. S.: *An Introduction to Stochastic Processes*. Cambridge University Press, Cambridge, 1955.

[2] BLACKMAN, R. B., AND J. W. TUKEY: *The Measurement of Power Spectra*. Dover, New York, 1958.

[3] BRITTAIN, J. A.: "A Bias in the Seasonally Adjusted Unemployment Series and a Suggested Alternative," *Review of Economics and Statistics*, Vol. 41 (1959), pp. 405–411.

[4] DAVENPORT, W. B., AND W. L. ROOT: *An Introduction to the Theory of Random Signals and Noise*. McGraw-Hill, New York, 1958.

[5] DOOB, J. L.: *Stochastic Processes*. John Wiley and Sons, New York, 1953.

[6] DURBIN, J.: "Trend Elimination by Moving Average and Variate Difference Filters," *Bulletin de l'Institut International de Statistique*, Vol. 39 (1961), pp. 130–141, 2e livraison.

[7] GOODMAN, N. R.: "On the Joint Estimation of the Spectra, Cospectrum, and Quadrature Spectrum of a Two-Dimensional Stationary Gaussian Process." Technical Report No. 8, Nonr-285 (17), David Taylor Model Basin (March, 1957).

[8] ———: "Some Comments on Spectral Analysis of Time Series," *Technometrics*, Vol. 3 (1961), pp. 221–228.

[9] HANNAN, E. J.: *Time Series Analysis*. Methuen, London, 1960.

[10] JENKINS, G. M.: "General Considerations in the Analysis of Spectra," *Technometrics*, Vol. 3 (1961), pp. 133–166.

[11] KENDALL, M. G.: *Contributions to the Study of Oscillatory Time-Series*. Cambridge University Press, Cambridge, 1946.

[12] KUZNETS, S.: *Seasonal Variations in Industry and Trade*. National Bureau of Economic Research, New York, 1933.

[13] LANNING, J. H., AND R. H. BATTIN: *Random Processes in Automatic Control*. McGraw-Hill, New York, 1956.

[14] MOORE, GEOFFREY H., EDITOR: *Business Cycle Indicators*, Vol. I. Princeton University Press, Princeton, 1961.

[15] MURTHY, V. K.: "Estimation of the Cross-Spectrum," Technical Report No. 11, DA ARO(D)31-124-G91, Applied Math. and Stat. Labs., Stanford University (May, 1962).

[16] ORGANIZATION FOR ECONOMIC COOPERATION AND DEVELOPMENT: *Seasonal Adjustment on Electronic Computors*. O.E.C.D., Paris, 1961.

[17] PARZEN, E.: "Mathematical Considerations in the Estimation of Spectra," *Technometrics*, Vol. 3 (1961), pp. 167–190.

[18] ———: *Stochastic Processes*. Preliminary edition. Holden-Day, San Francisco, 1961.

[19] PRESIDENT'S COMMITTEE TO APPRAISE EMPLOYMENT AND UNEMPLOYMENT STATISTICS: *Measuring Employment and Unemployment*. U.S. Government Printing Office, Washington, 1962.

[20] PRIESTLEY, M. B.: "On the Analysis of Stationary Processes with Mixed Spectra." Unpublished Ph.D. thesis, University of Manchester (1959).

[21] QUENOUILLE, M. H.: *The Analysis of Multiple Time-Series*. Charles Griffin and Co., London, 1957.

[22] SAMUELSON, P. A.: "Letter to the Editor," *New York Times*, November 12, 1961.

[23] SCHUSTER, A.: "The Periodogram of the Magnetic Declination as Obtained from the Records of the Greenwich Observatory During the Years 1811–1895," *Transactions of the Cambridge Philosophical Society*, Vol. 18 (1899), pp. 107ff.

[24] STUART, R. D.: *An Introduction to Fourier Analysis.* Methuen, London, 1961.

[25] TUKEY, J. W.: "Discussion Emphasizing the Connection between Analysis of Variance and Spectrum Analysis," *Technometrics,* Vol. 3 (1961), pp. 1–29.

[26] WILKS, S. S.: *Mathematical Statistics.* New York, 1962.

[27] WOLD, H.: *A Study in the Analysis of Stationary Time Series.* Second edition. Almqvist and Wiksell, Stockholm, 1953. First edition, 1938.

Econometrica, Vol. 32, No. 4 (October, 1964)

A COMPARISON OF ALTERNATIVE ESTIMATORS FOR SIMULTANEOUS EQUATIONS

By Gregory C. Chow[1]

A natural generalization of least squares is proposed to estimate parameters in simultaneous linear equations. Full-information maximum likelihood is shown to be identical with this generalization. The extent to which other estimators deviate from the generalization is discussed. A paradox of Strotz is resolved, and application of canonical correlation theory to structural equations is indicated.

1. SUMMARY

This PAPER compares various estimators of the parameters of linear simultaneous equations in terms of the following generalization of the method of least squares. To explain one (column) vector y by a set of vectors $Z=(z_1, \ldots, z_K)$, the method of least squares minimizes the variance of the difference $y\beta' - Z\gamma'$, with respect to the scalar β' and the column vector γ', subject to the restriction that the variance of $y\beta'$ equals any positive constant c. To explain a linear combination $Y\beta'$ of a set of vectors $Y=(y_1, \ldots, y_G)$ by a set of vectors $Z=(z_1, \ldots, z_K)$, the method of least squares minimizes the variance of the difference $Y\beta' - Z\gamma'$, with respect to the column vectors β' and γ', subject to the restriction that the variance of $Y\beta'$ equals c. To explain many linear combinations $Y\beta'_1, Y\beta'_2, \ldots, Y\beta'_G$ of a set of vectors Y respectively by the linear combinations $Z\gamma'_1, Z\gamma'_2, \ldots, Z\gamma'_G$ of a set of vectors Z, a natural generalization of least squares is to minimize the generalized variance of the differences $Y\beta'_1 - Z\gamma'_1, \ldots, Y\beta'_G - Z\gamma'_G$, subject to the restriction that the generalized variance of $Y\beta'_1, \ldots, Y\beta'_G$ equals c, and other restrictions imposed for identification.

This generalization essentially results from (a) replacing the variable y to be explained in ordinary least squares by *linear combinations* of the variables Y, and (b) replacing the variances in ordinary least squares by their corresponding *generalized variances*, as will be discussed in Section 2. The method of full-information maximum likelihood is precisely the above generalization of the method of least squares (Section 3). All other methods deviate from this generalization. Limited-information maximum likelihood (Section 4) adheres to the linear combination aspect (a), but, since identifying restrictions on the coefficients (β_i γ_i) of other equations are ignored, it cannot deal with the generalized variance (b) of $Y\beta'_1 - Z\gamma'_1, \ldots, Y\beta'_G - Z\gamma'_G$. Two-stage least squares (Section 5) deviates from both aspects (a) and (b) of the above generalization; so does Theil's k-class (Section 6).

[1] Without committing them, I would like to thank Jacques Drèze, Robert Strotz, and the referees for helpful suggestions leading to revisions of the original IBM Research Report, RC-781, dated September, 1962.

Three-stage least squares (Section 7) follows the principle of generalized variance, but not linear combination.

Among the byproducts of this comparison are a solution to the Paradox of Strotz [23], a derivation of the method of three-stage least squares by minimizing a generalized variance, and a generalization of canonical correlations for the structure of simultaneous equations.

2. A GENERALIZATION OF THE METHOD OF LEAST SQUARES

2.1. *Relation Between One Variable and a Set of Variables*

The method of least squares as applied to the model of multiple linear regression can be briefly stated. Let y_t $(t = 1, \ldots, T)$ be the sum of a linear function of K fixed variates $z_{t1}, \ldots, z_{tK}$, and a random term u_t drawn independently (of the z's and of u_τ, $\tau \neq t$) from a distribution with mean zero and variance σ^2. Let y be the column vector of T observations on the dependent variable, $z_1, \ldots, z_K$ be column vectors of the K explanatory variables, and the matrix Z be $(z_1, \ldots, z_K)$. To estimate the column vector γ' of coefficients in the linear regression by least squares, one minimizes the sum of squares $(y - Z\gamma')'(y - Z\gamma') \equiv \|y - Z\gamma'\|^2$, i.e., the squared length of the vector $y - Z\gamma'$, with respect to γ'. Since the squared length of $y - Z\gamma'$ is proportional to the variance, one can speak of minimizing the variance of $y - Z\gamma'$.

Consider a symmetrical expression $y\beta' - Z\gamma'$, where symmetry is introduced by the scalar β' multiplying the vector y. One will immediately note that the direction for minimizing its squared length is determined by a normalization rule. The method of least squares just stated is to minimize the squared length of $y\beta' - Z\gamma'$, with respect to all the coefficients β' and γ', subject to the normalization $\beta' = 1$. This minimization amounts to finding the orthogonal projection of the vector y on the space $\{Z\}$ spanned by the vectors Z.

It is important to note that the above normalization $\beta' = 1$ accomplishes two distinct functions of normalization. One function is to fix the direction of minimizing the sum of squares, to be called *direction-normalization*. The other is to fix the scale for the coefficients, to be called *scale-normalization*. These two functions can best be set forth by posing the following constrained minimization problem with two steps. In the first step, minimize $\|y\beta' - Z\gamma'\|^2$ subject to $\|y\beta'\|^2 = c$. For any positive constant c, this step determines the direction of minimization since it projects a multiple of the vector y, with given squared length c, on the space $\{Z\}$. After the coefficients β' and γ' are estimated by this step, one may wish to take a second step to rescale them, preserving their ratios. For example, if one wishes to set the coefficient of y equal to one, he will divide all estimated coefficients by the estimate of β'. This will give the same estimates as in the last paragraph. Note that the *scale-normalization* $\beta' = 1$ in Step 2 of this constrained minimization does not determine the direction of minimization, which is governed by the *direction-normalization* $\|y\beta'\|^2 = c$ in Step 1. Had the direction normalization, say $\|z_1 \gamma_1'\|^2 =$

c, been used in Step 1, the resulting estimates could still be scaled to make $\beta'=1$. However, the direction of projection would be from the vector z_1 onto a space spanned by $y, z_2, z_3, \ldots, z_K$, and would not be the direction desired.

Besides formulating the method of least squares by the above constrained minimization, one can choose to minimize the ratio of the residual variance to the total variance to be explained, i.e., $\|y\beta'-Z\gamma'\|^2/\|y\beta'\|^2$. Whatever the solution for β' and γ' happens to be, or whatever the value c of $\|y\beta'\|^2$ happens to be, this ratio is minimized if and only if its numerator $\|y\beta'-Z\gamma'\|^2$ is minimized for $\|y\beta'\|^2$ equal to that value c. Thus, the minimization of this ratio itself determines the direction. No matter what scale-normalization, such as $\beta'=1$ or $\gamma_1'=1$, is introduced in minimizing this ratio, the direction is assured. To summarize, using the constrained minimization of $\|y\beta'-Z\gamma'\|^2$, one determines the direction by the constraint (or direction-normalization) $\|y\beta'\|^2=c$. Using the minimization of the ratio, one determines the direction by its denominator $\|y\beta'\|^2$. In both cases further scale-normalization can be introduced.

In the multiple regression model of this Section 2.1, there is no question concerning which direction to minimize the sum of squares $\|y\beta'-Z\gamma'\|^2$. In the population, the vector y is assumed to be the sum of two parts, its mean vector $Z\gamma'$ in the space $\{Z\}$, and a random vector u orthogonal to (independent of) the vectors Z. Accordingly, in the sample, the mean vector $Z\gamma'$ is estimated by the orthogonal projection of y on the space $\{Z\}$, as we have stated algebraically.

If the random term u_t in this model is further assumed to be normally distributed, it is well known that the least-squares estimator is identical with the maximum-likelihood estimator. Normality of the residuals need not be assumed in the models that follow, since the rationale for various generalizations of least squares does not require normality. Some generalizations will be identical with maximum likelihood if normality is assumed, as will be noted.

2.2. Relation between Two Sets of Variables in One Equation

Let there be G variables, denoted by $y_{t1}, \ldots, y_{tG}$, for the tth observation $(t=1, \ldots, T)$. Assume that a linear function of these variables is generated by a linear function of the fixed variates $z_{t1}, \ldots, z_{tK}$, plus a random term u_t drawn independently (of the z's and of u_τ, $\tau \neq t$) from a population with mean zero and variance σ^2:

$$\beta_1 y_{t1} + \ldots + \beta_G y_{tG} = \gamma_1 z_{t1} + \ldots + \gamma_K z_{tK} + u_t \qquad (t=1, \ldots, T).$$

Geometrically this model assumes that a linear combination $Y\beta'$ of the vectors $Y=(y_1, \ldots, y_G)$ is the sum of a mean vector $Z\gamma'$ in the space $\{Z\}$ spanned by the vectors $Z=(z_1, \ldots, z_K)$, and a random vector u independent of (orthogonal to) $z_1, \ldots, z_K$.

To estimate the coefficients of this model by least squares, one would correspondingly find the orthogonal projection of a linear combination $Y\beta'$ of the vectors Y

on the space $\{Z\}$, either by minimizing $\|Y\beta' - Z\gamma'\|^2$ subject to $\|Y\beta'\|^2 = c$ or by minimizing the ratio $\|Y\beta' - Z\gamma'\|^2/\|Y\beta'\|^2$. Either will guarantee that the projection is directed from a linear combination $Y\beta'$ of a given length to the space $\{Z\}$.

Once the direction-normalization is accomplished by either method, one is free to choose a scale-normalization such as $\beta_1 = 1$ or $\gamma_1 = 1$. Let it be emphasized that when an arbitrary scale-normalization is adopted one should not discard the constraint $\|Y\beta'\|^2 = c$ in the constrained minimization, or the denominator $\|Y\beta'\|^2$ in the ratio minimization, which is essential for setting the direction. If the scale-normalization, say $\beta_1 = 1$, is introduced in the constrained minimization formulation, one should first use the constraint $\|Y\beta'\|^2 = c$ in minimizing $\|Y\beta' - Z\gamma'\|^2$. The estimated coefficients can then be scaled to make $\beta_1 = 1$. Were the restriction $\beta_1 = 1$ used in place of $\|Y\beta'\|^2 = c$ in minimizing $\|Y\beta' - Z\gamma'\|^2$, the vector y_1 alone would be projected on the space spanned by $y_2, \ldots, z_1, \ldots, z_K$. This projection would be appropriate for the model where y_1 is the sum of a mean vector in the space $\{y_2, \ldots, z_1, \ldots, z_K\}$ and a random vector orthogonal to $y_2, \ldots, z_1, \ldots, z_K$. If a scale-normalization is introduced in the ratio minimization formulation, the appropriate expression $\|Y\beta'\|^2$ must be kept in the denominator.

The model of this section is closely related to, but is different from, the model of Harold Hotelling in his classic paper [15] "Relations between Two Sets of Variates." Hotelling considers two sets of variates $y_{t1}, \ldots, y_{tG}$ and $z_{t1}, \ldots, z_{tK}$, both of which are normally distributed, while we treat one set $z_{t1}, \ldots, z_{tK}$ as fixed. If each u_t in our model is further assumed to be normal, then Hotelling's model will imply ours as it implies that the conditional distribution of $\beta_1 y_{t1} + \ldots + \beta_G y_{tG}$, given $z_{t1}, \ldots, z_{tK}$, is normal, with a mean equal to a linear function of the z's. However, Hotelling is interested in the correlation problem between linear functions of two sets of variates, while we are interested in the regression problem of estimating the coefficients of the linear functions of y's and z's.

In introducing his closely related problem, Hotelling did have in mind applications to economics. He wrote [15, p. 322],

> Much attention has been given to the effects of the crops of various agricultural commodities on their respective prices, with a view to obtaining demand curves. The standard errors associated with such attempts, when calculated, have usually been found quite excessive. One reason for this unfortunate outcome has been the large portion of the variance of each commodity price attributable to crops of other commodities. Thus the consumption of wheat may be related as much to the prices of potatoes, rye, and barley as to that of wheat. The like is true of supply functions. It therefore seems appropriate that studies of demand and supply should be made by groups rather than by single commodities. . . . It is logically as well as empirically necessary to replace the classical one-commodity type of analysis, relating for example to the incidence of taxation, utility, and consumer's surplus, by a simultaneous treatment of a multiplicity of commodities.

In this example, Hotelling appeared to be thinking of the relations between prices y of related agricultural commodities and their quantities demanded or supplied, z.

The algebra of the method of least squares applied to our problem is similar to that of Hotelling's problem. We propose to

(2.2.1)   minimize $(\beta Y' - \gamma Z')(Y\beta' - Z\gamma') = \beta Y'Y\beta' - 2\beta Y'Z\gamma' + \gamma Z'Z\gamma'$,
subject to $\beta Y'Y\beta' - c = 0$,

whereas Hotelling's correlation problem maximizes the covariance $\beta Y'Z\gamma'$ between $Y\beta'$ and $Z\gamma'$ subject to the two constraints $\beta Y'Y\beta' = 1$ and $\gamma Z'Z\gamma' = 1$, or, equivalently, minimizes the same expression $(\beta Y' - \gamma Z')(Y\beta' - Z\gamma')$ as ours, subject to an additional constraint, $\gamma Z'Z\gamma' = 1$.

We form the Lagrange expression

(2.2.2) $L = (\beta Y' - \gamma Z')(Y\beta' - Z\gamma') - \lambda(\beta Y'Y\beta' - c)$,

and, first, set its derivative with respect to γ' equal to zero,

(2.2.3) $\dfrac{\partial L}{\partial \gamma'} = -2Z'Y\beta' + 2Z'Z\gamma' = 0$,

obtaining an equation for the unknown vector γ',

(2.2.4) $\gamma' = (Z'Z)^{-1}Z'Y\beta'$.

Thus, however β' is estimated, γ' is obtained by applying least squares to the regression of $Y\beta'$ on Z.

Substituting (2.2.4) for γ in L, we have the concentrated Lagrange expression

(2.2.5) $L^{\bullet} = \beta Y'[I - Z(Z'Z)^{-1}Z'][I - Z(Z'Z)^{-1}Z']Y\beta' - \lambda(\beta Y'Y\beta' - c)$.

Let the idempotent matrix $I - Z(Z'Z)^{-1}Z'$ be denoted by M, and (2.2.5) becomes

(2.2.6) $L^{\bullet} = \beta Y'MY\beta' - \lambda(\beta Y'Y\beta' - c) = \beta Y'(M - \lambda I)Y\beta' + \lambda c$.

Equation (2.2.6) will now be differentiated with respect to β' and to λ, yielding

(2.2.7) $\dfrac{\partial L^{\bullet}}{\partial \beta'} = 2Y'(M - \lambda I)Y\beta' = 0$,

and

(2.2.8) $\dfrac{\partial L^{\bullet}}{\partial \lambda} = -\beta Y'Y\beta' + c = 0$.

Premultiplying (2.2.7) by β yields

(2.2.9) $\beta Y'MY\beta' = \lambda \beta Y'Y\beta'$,

which implies

(2.2.10) $L^{\bullet} = \lambda c$.

Therefore our minimization problem amounts to finding the smallest λ satisfying (2.2.7), or satisfying the determinantal equation

(2.2.11) $|Y'(M - \lambda I)Y| = |Y'MY - \lambda Y'Y| = |Y'MY(Y'Y)^{-1} - \lambda I| \cdot |Y'Y| = 0$.

Thus λ is the smallest characteristic root of the matrix $Y'MY(Y'Y)^{-1}$; β is the characteristic vector corresponding to that root.

We have gone through this algebra, already familiar from Hotelling's work, partly to show that other estimators can be obtained by changing the direction-normalization in the above minimization problem. The direction-normalization in (2.2.1) and (2.2.2) is the restriction $\beta Y'Y\beta' - c = 0$. Had another normalization involving only β' been introduced in (2.2.2), we easily see that (2.2.3), (2.2.4), and the first term of (2.2.5) and (2.2.6) would still follow. However, the normalization $\beta Y'Y\beta' - c = 0$ implies (2.2.7); a violation of (2.2.7) thus also violates the above direction-normalization.

For values of λ other than a characteristic root of $Y'MY(Y'Y)^{-1}$, the matrix $Y'(M-\lambda I)Y$ would be nonsingular, (2.2.7) would be satisfied only by $\beta' = 0$, or (2.2.7) would not be satisfied by any $\beta' \neq 0$. Thus, our minimization problem subject to the above direction-normalization requires finding a characteristic root. Nevertheless, consider finding a vector $\beta' \neq 0$ other than the characteristic vector corresponding to the smallest characteristic root λ, and requiring that β' violates (2.2.7) "not too severely." One way to do so is to partition the matrix Y into its first column y_1 and the rest Y_1, and the row vector β into its first element β_1 and the rest $\bar{\beta}$, so that equations (2.2.7) can be written in two parts.

(2.2.12) $\quad \begin{pmatrix} y_1' \\ Y_1' \end{pmatrix} (M - \lambda I)(y_1 \ Y_1) \begin{pmatrix} \beta_1 \\ \bar{\beta}' \end{pmatrix} = 0$,

or

(2.2.12a) $y_1'(M - \lambda I)(y_1\beta_1 + Y_1\bar{\beta}') = 0$,
(2.2.12b) $Y_1'(M - \lambda I)(y_1\beta_1 + Y_1\bar{\beta}') = 0$.

Let us ignore the first part (2.2.12a), and concentrate on the second part:

(2.2.13) $\quad Y_1'(M - \lambda I)Y_1\bar{\beta}' = (-\beta_1)Y_1'(M - \lambda I)y_1$.

Provided that $Y_1(M - \lambda I)Y_1$ is nonsingular, (2.2.13) can be solved for $\bar{\beta}'$:

(2.2.14) $\quad \bar{\beta}' = (-\beta_1)[Y_1'(M - \lambda I)Y_1]^{-1} Y_1'(M - \lambda I)y_1$

after a normalization on β_1 such as $\beta_1 = -1$. In brief, the estimator $\bar{\beta}'$ of (2.2.14) is obtained by changing the characteristic root problem of (2.2.7) involving a $G \times G$ matrix to a problem of solving $G-1$ linear equations from (2.2.7) while ignoring one of them (2.2.12a).

The estimator (2.2.14) can be given an interpretation familiar in the econometrics literature. Let $V_1^* = MY_1$ be the matrix of residuals in the sample regression of Y_1 on Z. Then

$$\bar{\beta}' = [Y_1' M Y_1 - \lambda Y_1' Y_1]^{-1} [Y_1' M - \lambda Y_1'] y_1$$

$$(2.2.15) \quad = (-\lambda)^{-1} \left[\frac{-1}{\lambda} Y_1' M M Y_1 + Y_1' Y_1 \right]^{-1} (-\lambda) \left[\frac{-1}{\lambda} Y_1' M + Y_1' \right] y_1$$

$$= \left[Y_1' Y_1 - \frac{1}{\lambda} V_1^{*'} V_1^* \right]^{-1} \left[Y_1' - \frac{1}{\lambda} V_1^{*'} \right] y_1 .$$

Defined by (2.2.15), the estimator $\bar{\beta}'$ is obtained not by least squares $[Y_1' Y_1]^{-1} Y_1' y_1$ applied to the regression of the normalized variable y_1 on the other Y_1, but rather by correcting the variables Y_1 (or the cross product $Y_1' Y_1$) by a fraction $k = 1/\lambda$ of the residuals V_1^* (or the cross product $V_1^{*'} V_1^*$) in the sample regression of Y_1 on Z. In other words, (2.2.15) results from applying Theil's idea on the k-class estimators [27, Chapter 6] to the model of this section. Note that, although the estimator obtained by the direction-normalization $\beta Y Y' \beta' - c = 0$ can be viewed as a special case of (2.2.15), this estimator is the only one that satisfies both (2.2.12a) and (2.2.12b); no other member of the class (2.2.15) satisfies (2.2.7), or satisfies the direction-normalization suggested in this section. Note also that the idea of two-stage least squares applied to this section would yield the estimator (2.2.15) with $k = 1/\lambda = 1$, but, in this case, the $(G-1) \times (G-1)$ matrix

$$Y_1' Y_1 - V_1^{*'} V_1^* = Y_1' Y_1 - Y_1' M Y_1 = Y_1'(I - M) Y_1 = Y_1' Z(Z' Z)^{-1} Z' Y_1$$

has an inverse only if the rank of Z is at least $G-1$.

2.3. *Relations between Two Sets of Variables in a System of Equations*

Let the model of Section 2.2 be generalized to G equations. The ith equation is

$$\beta_{i1} y_{t1} + \ldots + \beta_{iG} y_{tG} = \gamma_{i1} z_{t1} + \ldots + \gamma_{iK} z_{tK} + u_{ti} \quad \begin{matrix} (t = 1, \ldots, T; \\ i = 1, \ldots, G) \end{matrix}$$

or

$$Y \beta_i' = Z \gamma_i' + u_i \quad (i = 1, \ldots, G) .$$

The whole system can be written as

$$Y(\beta_1' \ldots \beta_G') = Z(\gamma_1' \ldots \gamma_G') + (u_1 \ldots u_G) ,$$

or, in obvious notation,

$$Y B' = Z \Gamma' + U .$$

It is assumed that, for the ith equation, a certain linear combination $Y \beta_i'$ of a specified subset of the vectors Y is the sum of a vector $Z \gamma_i'$ in a specified subspace of $\{Z\}$ and a random vector u_i orthogonal to $\{Z\}$. (The "specified subset" and the "specified subspace" in this assumption, which amount to setting some specified coefficients in the ith equation equal to zero, are for identification.) The random variables $u_{t1}, \ldots, u_{tG}$ have a G-variate distribution with means zero and covariance matrix Σ, and are independent of all z's and of $u_{\tau 1}, \ldots, u_{\tau G}$ $(\tau \neq t)$. This is the statistical model proposed by the Cowles Commission [12, 19] for studying economic relationships.

In the following we shall confine our discussion to the Cowles Commission model as stated in the last paragraph. As a member of the Cowles Commission has stressed [11, pp. 847–8], this model is not the only model to be used in economic statistics. Even among models of linear simultaneous equations, other formulations have been proposed, e.g., [23], [24], and [29]. We will not add to the discussion on model formulations, although the discussion cannot be avoided completely. Since in the writings on the alternative estimators to be discussed no other statistical assumptions than the above have been explicitly stated, the authors must have referred to this same model. We will follow them in this regard.

When there is only one equation, as in Section 2.2, the method of least squares minimizes the squared length, or variance, of the difference $Y\beta' - Z\gamma' = u$, subject to the restriction that the squared length, or variance, of $Y\beta'$ equals c. There are G equations in the present model. We propose to generalize the method of least squares by minimizing the squared volume of the parallelotope formed by, or the generalized variance of, the G differences $Y\beta_1' - Z\gamma_1' = u_1, \ldots, Y\beta_G' - Z\gamma_G' = u_G$, subject to the restriction that the squared volume similarly formed by, or the generalized variance of, $Y\beta_1', \ldots, Y\beta_G'$ equals c. Algebraically, we minimize the squared volume, i.e., the determinant,

$$|(Y\beta_1' - Z\gamma_1', \ldots, Y\beta_G' - Z\gamma_G')'(Y\beta_1' - Z\gamma_1', \ldots, Y\beta_G' - Z\gamma_G')| =$$
$$= |(YB' - Z\Gamma')'(YB' - Z\Gamma')|$$

subject to

$$|(Y\beta_1' \ldots Y\beta_G')'(Y\beta_1' \ldots Y\beta_G')| = |(YB')'(YB')| = c,$$

or, equivalently, the ratio of the former determinant to the latter. The possibility of using the trace, rather than the determinant, for the generalization will be commented on later in this section.

As compared with the method of least squares for the model of multiple linear regression in Section 2.1, our generalization (a) replaces one vector y in one equation by the linear combination $Y\beta_i$ in the ith equation, and (b) replaces the variances by their corresponding generalized variances. Although this is not the unique generalization of least squares, we do claim that it is a natural generalization. Furthermore, we feel that the replacements (a) and (b) are more reasonable for the present model than any other candidates which have been suggested.

Regarding (a), the linear combination aspect of the generalization, one may ask: why treat $Y\beta_i'$ as one composite dependent variable in the ith equation, and not simply treat y_i, for example, as the dependent variable? Suppose that the first equation is a demand equation relating quantity y_1 and price y_2 to other variables. Should y_1 not be treated differently from y_2 when the parameters are being estimated? Our answer to this is that the assumptions in the statistical model provide no ground for such asymmetrical treatment of the dependent variables in the estimation stage. Since the model states that a linear combination $Y\beta_i'$ is generated by a linear combination $Z\gamma_i'$ and a vector u_i orthogonal to the z's, all the y's in the combination should be treated symmetrically for estimation purposes. This paper is confined to the estimation problem arising from the model specified above. If one favors some asymmetry in treating the dependent variables in the estimation stage, he has to introduce asymmetry into the statistical models first, before asymmetrical treatment in an estimation procedure can be justified.

Regarding (b), the generalized variance aspect of the generalization, one may point out that it is the most widely used generalization of the variance in statistics. As one example, applied to a system of G linear regressions $Y - Z\Pi' = V = (v_1, \ldots, v_G)$, where Π' consists of columns of coefficients and $v_{t1}, \ldots, v_{tG}$ are drawn at random from a G-variate normal distribution with a certain covariance matrix, the method of least squares can be derived from minimizing the squared volume $|(Y - Z\Pi')'(Y - Z\Pi')|$ with respect to Π (e.g. [1, p. 228, Exercise 5]).[2] Recent applications of the generalized variance include the works of Kiefer and Wolfowitz [16, 18] on optimum designs in regression problems, and of Kiefer [17] on optimum experimental designs. One may consider using the trace of the matrix $(YB' - Z\Gamma')'(YB' - Z\Gamma')$, rather than its determinant, but this would imply ignoring the covariances among the residuals or the "simultaneity" in the equations. In fact, we shall show that the "simultaneity" in the estimation by three-stage least squares results from minimizing a similar generalized variance (except for normalization).

3. FULL-INFORMATION MAXIMUM LIKELIHOOD

The above generalization of least squares can be put in the form of a constrained minimization, or of minimization of a ratio. In the first form, we minimize the determinant,

$$|(YB' - Z\Gamma')'(YB' - Z\Gamma')|, \quad \text{subject to} \quad |BY'YB'| = c.$$

As long as the constraint (direction-normalization) is respected, we can arbitrarily impose scale-normalizations such as $\beta_{ii} = 1$ $(i = 1, \ldots, G)$. Computationally, when G is larger than 1, the constraint alone will not determine numerical estimates. Numerical estimates can be obtained by simultaneously imposing $G - 1$ scale-normalizations together with the constraint. The remaining scale-normalization can be applied afterwards as in the case $G = 1$.

In the ratio form, we minimize

$$|(YB' - Z\Gamma')'(YB' - Z\Gamma')|/|BY'YB'|.$$

Here, as long as the denominator is retained, one can introduce G scale-normaliza-

---

[2] Normalization for $|Y'Y|$ does not involve unknown coefficients and is therefore not binding.

tions simultaneously with the minimization of the ratio, as in the case $G=1$. Note again that the G scale-normalizations alone, without the denominator, will not be sufficient for providing direction-normalization.

It is easy to show that our generalization of least squares, expressed in ratio form, is precisely the method of full-information maximum likelihood when the G-variate distribution of the u's is assumed to be normal. Since

$$|BY'YB'|=|B|\cdot|Y'Y|\cdot|B'|=|B|^2|Y'Y|,$$

where the elements of Y are given data, minimizing the above ratio is equivalent to maximizing

$$|B|^2/|(BY'-\Gamma Z')(YB'-Z\Gamma')|$$

which is indeed (except for a constant factor) the square of the likelihood function for the structure of simultaneous equations (Koopmans and Hood [**12**, p. 161, Equation 5.58]).

Our formulation of least squares also provides a solution to the paradox of Strotz [**23**, pp. 429–31]. Strotz considers the recursive model

(I) $\qquad B_0 y'(t)+B_1 y'(t-\theta)+\Gamma z'(t)=u'(t),$

where B_0 is triangular, with one's on the principle diagonal for scale-normalization, and points out two ways of applying maximum likelihood as θ approaches 0. One is to take first the limit form of the above model as θ approaches 0, i.e.,

(II) $\qquad By'(t)+\Gamma z'(t)=u^{*\prime}(t),$

where $B=B_0+B_1$. Then apply maximum likelihood to this limit form, or maximize the ratio

(L. II) $\quad |B|^2/|(BY'+\Gamma Z')(YB'+Z\Gamma')|.$

We agree completely with this approach but we would like to add that, since the matrix B_0 is now only a part of the sum B, scale-normalizations of B, such as $\beta_{ii}=1$, have to be introduced to obtain numerical estimates in maximizing the above ratio.

The second approach is to take first the likelihood of Model (I), i.e.,

(1.2) $\quad |B_0|^2/|[B_0\,Y'(t)+B_1\,Y'(t-\theta)+\Gamma Z'(t)][Y(t)B_0'+Y(t-\theta)B_1'+Z(t)\Gamma']|.$

Strotz then argues that, since $|B_0|=1$ *from the given scale-normalizations, only the denominator of* (1.2), *or the numerator in our formulation of least squares, remains.* Now take the limit of this denominator as θ approaches 0, and obtain

(L. I) $\quad |(BY'+\Gamma Z')(YB'+Z\Gamma')|^{-1}.$

The maximization of (L. I) is said to be different from the maximization of (L. II) because, "otherwise, of the two terms

(1.5) $\quad |B|^2$ and $\quad |(BY'+\Gamma Z')(YB'+Z\Gamma')|^{-1}$

the second must attain a maximum for the same values of B at which the first attains a stationary value, and this would be highly special."

We disagree with Strotz's execution of the approach. The scale-normalizations on the diagonals of B_0, implying $|B_0| = 1$, are sufficient to support the maximization of the ratio (1.2), or the minimization of its reciprocal. When used in conjunction with the ratio, they complete direction-normalization also. It is the ratio, however, which assures correct direction-normalization. Thus, the numerator of (1.2), or the denominator of our ratio formulation, cannot be discarded without appropriate replacement. As in the first approach, we need here some scale-normalizations such as $\beta_{ii} = 1$. These scale-normalizations have to be applied to a ratio, as given by (L. II). To comment on the last quoted statement, we say that $|(BY' + \Gamma Z')(YB' + Z\Gamma')|^{-1}$ must indeed attain a maximum for the same values of B at which $|B|^2$ attains a stationary value, and this should be the case for the purpose of direction-normalization.

4. LIMITED-INFORMATION MAXIMUM LIKELIHOOD

Our generalization of least squares also provides a convenient setting for the discussion of other methods of estimating parameters in simultaneous equations. The limited-information maximum likelihood estimator of Anderson and Rubin [2] will first be discussed.

In Section 2.2, it was pointed out that to find a linear combination $Y\beta'$ of the dependent variables which is best explained by a linear combination $Z\gamma'$ of the predetermined variables, we minimize the squared length $\|Y\beta' - Z\gamma'\|^2$ subject to $\|Y\beta'\|^2 = 1$. One equation, say the first, in a system of simultaneous equations is used to explain a linear combination $Y\beta_1'$ (where some elements of β_1' may be zero) of a subset of dependent variables by a linear combination $Z\gamma_1'$ (where some elements of γ_1' may be zero) of a subset of predetermined variables in the system.

Let the coefficients $(\beta_1 \gamma_1)$ in the first equation be partitioned as $(\beta\ 0\ \gamma\ 0)$. Let the matrix $(Y\ Z)$ be accordingly partitioned as $(Y_\Delta Y_{\Delta\Delta} Z_1 Z_{**})$. Following Section 2.2 one might be tempted to minimize $\|Y_\Delta \beta' - Z_1 \gamma'\|^2$ subject to $\|Y_\Delta \beta'\|^2 = 1$. Such a method is invalid, however, since the random variables Y_Δ are determined not only by the predetermined variables Z_1 in the first equation, but also by the other predetermined variables Z_{**} in the system of simultaneous equations. Specifically, in addition to the first equation,

$$(4.1) \qquad Y_\Delta \beta' = Z_1 \gamma' + u_1 ,$$

the model specifies the reduced-form equations explaining Y_Δ by Z_1 and Z_{**},

$$(4.2) \qquad Y_\Delta = Z_1 \Pi_{11}' + Z_{**} \Pi_{12}' + V_\Delta .$$

Postmultiplying (4.2) by β' gives

$$(4.3) \qquad Y_\Delta \beta' = Z_1 \Pi_{11}' \beta' + Z_{**} \Pi_{12}' \beta' + V_\Delta \beta' .$$

Equation (4.3) provides a link between the reduced-form equations (4.2) and the structural equation (4.1); it also provides an appropriate restriction for the minimization of $\|Y_A\beta' - Z_1\gamma'\|^2$. If (4.1) were treated in isolation, one would simply minimize the sum of squares $u_1'u_1 = \|Y_A\beta' - Z_1\gamma'\|^2$ of the estimated residuals subject to the restriction $\beta Y_A' Y_A \beta' = c$ as given in Section 2.2. When (4.2) or (4.3) is also present, however, it seems natural to minimize the above sum of squares $\|Y_A\beta' - Z_1\gamma'\|^2$ relative to the sum of squares of the estimated residuals of (4.3). Let V_A^* be the residuals of (4.2) estimated by a regression of Y_A on both Z_1 and $Z_{\bullet\bullet}$. Then the sum of squares of the estimated residuals of (4.3) will be $\beta V_A^{*\prime} V_A^* \beta'$, which provides a restriction in the minimization of $\|Y_A\beta' - Z_1\gamma'\|^2$. The method of limited-information maximum likelihood is to

(4.4)   minimize $(\beta Y_A' - \gamma Z_1')(Y_A\beta' - Z_1\gamma')$ subject to $\beta V_A^{*\prime} V_A^* \beta' = c$,

or, equivalently, to minimize with respect to β the ratio

$$l(\beta) = \frac{\min_{\gamma}\|Y_A\beta' - Z_1\gamma'\|^2}{\min_{\gamma_1}\|Y_A\beta' - Z\gamma_1'\|^2} ,$$

called the variance ratio by Koopmans and Hood [12, p. 168].

Geometrically, we project a vector $Y_A\beta'$ in the subspace $\{Y_A\}$ of $\{Y\}$ on the subspace $\{Z_1\}$ of $\{Z\}$, and the same vector $Y_A\beta'$ on the entire space $\{Z\}$, with the coefficients β' so chosen that the squared distance from $Y_A\beta'$ to $\{Z_1\}$ be smallest as compared to the squared distance from $Y_A\beta'$ to $\{Z\}$. Since we are comparing two squared distances from the same vector $Y_A\beta'$, the length of $Y_A\beta'$ is indeterminate, and the restriction on $\beta V_A^{*\prime} V_A^* \beta'$ takes the place of normalization on the squared length $\|Y_A\beta'\|^2$.

The algebra for problem (4.4) is the same as for problem (2.2.1) and will not be repeated. The Lagrange expression corresponding to (2.2.2) is

(4.5) $L = (\beta Y_A' - \gamma Z_1')(Y_A\beta' - Z_1\gamma') - \lambda(\beta V_A^{*\prime} V_A^* \beta' - c)$.

The solution of γ' in terms of β' is, as in (2.2.4),

$\gamma' = (Z_1' Z_1)^{-1} Z_1' Y_A\beta'$.

The concentrated Lagrange expression is

(4.6) $L^* = \beta Y_A' M_1 Y_A \beta' - \lambda(\beta V_A^{*\prime} V_A^* \beta' - c)$,

where $M_1 = I - Z_1(Z_1' Z_1)^{-1} Z_1'$.

Differentiating (4.6) with respect to β', we have

(4.7) $\dfrac{\partial L^*}{\partial \beta'} = 2(Y_A' M_1 Y_A - \lambda V_A^{*\prime} V_A^*)\beta' = 0$.

As in Section 2.2, the minimum of L is obtained by finding the smallest root λ satisfying the determinantal equation $|Y'_\Delta M_1 Y_\Delta - \lambda V^{*\prime}_\Delta V^*_\Delta|$, and the vector β' corresponding to that root.

We have seen that limited-information maximum likelihood is an application of least-squares, in the sense that the ratio of two squared distances from the same vector to two vector spaces is minimized, or in the sense that the squared length of the residuals $\|Y_\Delta \beta' - Z_1 \gamma'\|^2$ in (4.1) is minimized subject to the restriction $\beta V^{*\prime}_\Delta V^*_\Delta \beta' = c$, where V^*_Δ is from (4.2). The limited-information maximum likelihood method utilizes the information that the variables Z_1 appear in the first equation and other variables Z_{**} appear in the system, or this method utilizes (4.1) and (4.2) only but does not utilize the a priori restrictions on other equations in the system. As Koopmans and Hood [12, p. 176] remark, "In general, the more (valid) over-identifying information [concerning the other equations] is used in deriving maximum-likelihood estimates, the more efficient the estimates will be, at least asymptotically and presumably also for finite samples." In so far as a model of simultaneous structural equations is correctly specified, the method of this section and those of Sections 5 and 6 are limited-information methods, and are subject to the same limitation of using only a part of the model specifications.

5. TWO-STAGE LEAST SQUARES

The method of two-stage least squares suggested by Theil [26] and Basmann [3] applies least squares, in the first stage, to estimate each dependent variable

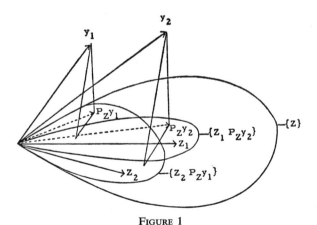

FIGURE 1

by all predetermined variables, and, after one particular dependent variable is chosen (on independent grounds) in each equation in the second stage, applies least squares to explain that dependent variable by the previously estimated values of the other dependent variables and by the predetermined variables in that equation.

Geometrically, as illustrated in Figure 1, the first stage is to project each of the vectors $y_1, y_2, \ldots$ on the space $\{Z\}$ spanned by the vectors $z_1, \ldots, z_K$; the estimated vectors representing the dependent variables are the projections $P_Z y_1, P_Z y_2, \ldots$. Let y_1 be the dependent variable chosen for the first equation, y_2 be the dependent variable chosen for the second equation, etc. Let $Z_1, Z_2, \ldots$, respectively, be the sets of vectors in the first, second, ..., equations. The second stage is to project y_1 on the space $\{Z_1 \ P_Z y_2 \ldots\}$, y_2 on the space $\{Z_2 \ P_Z y_1 \ldots\}$, etc. Note that the projection of y_1 on $\{Z_1 P_Z y_2 \ldots\}$ is the same as the projection of $P_Z y_1$ on the same space since the latter is a subspace of $\{Z\}$.

The first observation that would make one uneasy about the method of two-stage least squares is that the choice of a dependent variable, say y_1, for the first equation, etc., in the second stage seems arbitrary. The estimates will differ according to the choice made. In other words, one has not yet specified in which directions the sums of squares should be minimized in the second stage. We shall show that by applying an appropriate symmetric normalization in the second stage, the limited-information maximum likelihood estimate will result. In the second stage for the first equation, with $Y_A^* = Z(Z'Z)^{-1}Z'Y_A$, we

(5.1) $\quad$ minimize $(\beta Y_A^{*'} - \gamma Z_1')(Y_A^* \beta' - Z_1 \gamma')$.

An appropriate normalization, as pointed out in Section 4, is $\beta V_A^{*'} V_A^* \beta' = c$, whereas two-stage least squares sets one element of β' equal to a constant. Using the symmetric constraint and setting the partial derivative of the Lagrange expression with respect to γ' equal to zero,

(5.2) $\quad \gamma' = (Z_1' Z_1)^{-1} Z_1' \ Y_A^* \beta' = (Z_1' Z_1)^{-1} Z_1' \ Y_A \beta'$.

The concentrated Lagrangean is

(5.3) $\quad L^* = \beta Y_A^{*'} M_1 \ Y_A^* \beta' - \lambda (\beta V_A^{*'} V_A^* \beta' - c)$.

Setting its derivative with respect to β' equal to zero,

(5.4) $\quad \dfrac{\partial L^*}{\partial \beta'} = 2(Y_A^{*'} M_1 \ Y_A^* - \lambda V_A^{*'} V_A^*)\beta' = 0$.

Since

(5.5) $\quad Y_A^{*'} M_1 \ Y_A^* = (Y_A' - V_A^{*'}) M_1 (Y_A - V_A^*) = Y_A' M_1 \ Y_A - 2V_A^{*'} M_1 \ Y_A + V_A^{*'} V_A^*$
$\quad\quad\quad\quad\quad\quad = Y_A' M_1 \ Y_A - V_A^{*'} \ V_A^*$,

(5.4) can be written as

(5.6) $\quad \dfrac{\partial L^*}{\partial \beta'} = 2(Y_A' M_1 \ Y_A - (1+\lambda)V_A^{*'} V_A^*)\beta' = 0$,

which is the same as (4.7) for limited-information maximum likelihood, except for a change in notation for the root from λ to $1+\lambda$. Two-stage least squares fails to adopt a symmetric normalization in the second stage appropriate for the symmetric statistical model of the Cowles Commission given in Section 2.3; its proponents do not spell out a set of asymmetrical *statistical* assumptions in the model to justify asymmetry in the estimation method.

In the Cowles Commission model it is further specified that the differences $Y\beta_i' - Z\gamma_i' = u_i$ between the sets of linear combinations have a G-variate normal distribution. The second criticism of the limited-information methods of Sections 4, 5, and 6 is that they do not adequately take into account the interdependence (or simultaneity) of the u_i in different equations. This criticism was made by Zellner and Theil in their article "Three-Stage Least Squares: Simultaneous Estimation of Simultaneous Equations" [30]. We shall return to this second criticism in Section 7.

6. THEIL'S k-CLASS ESTIMATORS

Our first criticism of two-stage least squares was that, under the assumptions of the Cowles Commission on simultaneous equations, it is not justified in the second stage to project the vectors $P_Z y_1, \ldots, P_Z y_G$ in the subspaces spanned by some other $P_Z y_j$ (in the ith equations) and by some Z_k, all subspaces of the space $\{Z\}$. The idea of k-class estimators [27, Chapter 6] is to free the above restriction of performing all projections in the space $\{Z\}$.

Let Y_i be the matrix whose $G_i - 1$ columns are T observations on the dependent variables, other than y_i, appearing in the ith equation. Let Z_i be the matrix of observations on the K_i predetermined variables in the ith equation. In the first stage we estimate the dependent variables Y from the predetermined variables Z by least squares:

$$P_Z Y = Y^* = Z(Z'Z)^{-1} Z' Y .$$

Let $V = Y - Y^*$ be the matrix of differences (residuals) between the observed Y and the estimated Y^*; let $V_i = Y_i - Y_i^*$ and let $v_i = y_i - y_i^*$ for the dependent variables in the ith equation. In the second stage we project $y_i^* = y_i - v_i$ (with the somewhat inappropriate normalization $\beta_{ii} = 1$) on the subspace $\{Y_i^* Z_i\} = \{Y_i - V_i \ Z_i\}$ of the space $\{Z\}$, and obtain the estimated coefficients $(\bar{b}_i \bar{c}_i)_1$ in the ith equation (with subscript 1 denoting two-stage, and the bar denoting the omission of zeros and of $b_{ii} = 1$ in $\bar{b}_i$):

$$(6.1) \qquad (\bar{b}_i \ \bar{c}_i)_1' = \left[\begin{pmatrix} Y_i' - V_i' \\ Z_i' \end{pmatrix} (Y_i - V_i \ Z_i) \right]^{-1} \begin{bmatrix} Y_i' - V_i' \\ Z_i' \end{bmatrix} [y_i - v_i] .$$

Since $Y'V = (Y^* + V)'V = Y^{*'}V + V'V = V'V$, i.e., the residuals V are uncorrelated with the estimated Y^*, and since $V'Z = 0$, we can write

$$(6.2) \qquad (\bar{b}_i \ \bar{c}_i)_1' = \begin{bmatrix} Y_i' Y_i - V_i' V_i \ Y_i' Z_i \\ Z_i' Y_i & Z_i' Z_i \end{bmatrix}^{-1} \begin{bmatrix} Y_i' - V_i' \\ Z_i' \end{bmatrix} y_i .$$

Now, rather than projecting $y_i - v_i$ on $\{Y_i - V_i \; Z_i\}$ in the second stage, we project $y_i - qv_i$ on $\{Y_i - qV_i \; Z_i\}$, q being a scalar to be chosen, and obtain the estimated coefficients $(\bar{b}_i \bar{c}_i)_k$ for the ith equation:

$$
(6.3) \quad (\bar{b}_i \; \bar{c}_i)'_k = \left[\begin{pmatrix} Y'_i - qV'_i \\ Z'_i \end{pmatrix} (Y_i - qV_i \; Z_i) \right]^{-1} \left[\begin{array}{c} Y'_i - qV'_i \\ Z'_i \end{array} \right] [y_i - qv_i]
$$

$$
= \left[\begin{array}{cc} Y'_i \, Y_i + (q^2 - 2q)V'_i V_i & Y'_i Z_i \\ Z'_i Y_i & Z'_i Z_i \end{array} \right]^{-1} \left[\begin{array}{c} Y'_i + (q^2 - 2q) V'_i \\ Z_i \end{array} \right] y_i .
$$

This is Theil's k-class estimators [27, p. 227 (1958)], with the scalar k replacing $(q^2 - 2q)$, although Theil's motivation in proposing it was somewhat different.

Using Figure 1 again, we can point out the essential idea of k-class estimators simply. Instead of using the vectors $y_i - v_i = P_Z y_i = y_i^*$ for projections in the second stage, we use the vectors $y_i - qv_i$. Geometrically we no longer limit our projections in the (subspaces of the) space $\{Y - V, \; Z\}$, or the space $\{Z\}$ since $\{Y - V\}$ is in $\{Z\}$. We lift the subspace $\{Y - V\}$ out of $\{Z\}$ by performing our projections in the subspace $\{Y - qV\}$. Since the scalar q can be chosen, with $q = 1$ ($k = 1$) to represent two-stage least squares as a special case, Theil's k-class estimators should be at least as good as two-stage. In fact, using approximating distributions, Nagar [20] has found two estimators in the k-class, one unbiased and the other having a minimum second moment around the true parameter, both to the degree of his approximation.

Algebraically, as the reader may have anticipated from Section 2.2, the k-class estimators can be derived from changing the determinantal-equation problem (4.7) of limited-information maximum likelihood to a linear-equations problem by ignoring one equation in (4.7), thus violating a symmetrical normalization restriction. Partition all the dependent variables Y_A in the first equation, say, into $(y_1 \; Y_1)$, and partition V_A^* into $(v_1^* \; V_1^*)$. The equations (4.7) become

$$
(6.4) \quad \left[\begin{pmatrix} y'_1 \\ Y'_1 \end{pmatrix} M_1 (y_1 \; Y_1) - \lambda \begin{pmatrix} v_1^{*\prime} \\ V_1^{*\prime} \end{pmatrix} (v_1^* \; V_1^*) \right] \begin{bmatrix} \beta_{11} \\ \beta \end{bmatrix} = 0 .
$$

Written separately, they are

$$
(6.5\text{a}) \quad [y'_1 M_1 (y_1 \; Y_1) - \lambda v_1^{*\prime}(v_1^* \; V_1^*)] \begin{bmatrix} \beta_{11} \\ \beta \end{bmatrix} = 0 ,
$$

$$
(6.5\text{b}) \quad [Y'_1 M_1 (y_1 \; Y_1) - \lambda V_1^{*\prime}(v_1^* \; V_1^*)] \begin{bmatrix} \beta_{11} \\ \beta \end{bmatrix} = 0 .
$$

Ignore the first equation and solve the remaining $G_1 - 1$ equations

$$
(6.6) \quad [Y'_1 M_1 \, Y_1 - \lambda V_1^{*\prime} V_1^*]\bar{\beta} = (-\beta_{11})[Y'_1 M_1 y_1 - \lambda V_1^{*\prime} v_1^*] ,
$$

which, as can easily be checked, will give the k-class estimator. Although limited-information maximum likelihood can be considered as a member of the k-class, it is the only member satisfying all G_1 equations (6.4) which are implied by the symmetric restriction $\beta V_A^{*\prime} V_A^* \beta' = c$. One may say that the k-class estimators are alterations of a determinantal-equation problem (6.4) into linear-equations problems by omitting one equation; only the original problem of limited-information maximum likelihood does not involve an omission.

7. THREE-STAGE LEAST SQUARES

One criticism of the above three limited-information methods was that they fail to account for the simultaneity of the structural equations. In the second stage of the k-class estimators the projections are performed equation by equation, whereas the model is one of simultaneous equations. This criticism does not apply to three-stage least squares suggested by Zellner and Theil [30]. We will show that this method can be derived from minimizing the determinant of a covariance matrix of the residuals in the G equations.

After the projections of all y_i on $\{Z\}$ have been completed in the first stage, i.e., after the estimation of

$$(7.1) \qquad Y^* = P_Z Y = Z(Z'Z)^{-1}Z'Y = Y - V,$$

we consider each difference $u_i^* = y_i^* - (Y_i^* \bar{\beta}_i + Z_i \bar{\gamma}_i)$ between the estimated y_i^* and a linear combination of the estimated y_j^* and z_k appearing in the ith equation, and minimize the generalized variance of the G differences. Note that the use of the generalized variance gives the method of three-stage least squares its "simultaneity"; instead of minimizing the squared length of each vector u_i^* individually as by the method of two-stage least squares, we now minimize the squared volume of the parallelotope formed by the set of G vectors u_i^*. Thus we minimize the determinant of a $G \times G$ matrix Σ^*

$$(7.2) \qquad |\Sigma^*| = |U^{*\prime} U^*| = |(u_1^* \ldots u_G^*)'(u_1^* \ldots u_G^*)|,$$

with respect to $(\bar{\beta}_i \ \bar{\gamma}_i)$, $i = 1, \ldots, G$. Let the ith row $(\beta_i \ \gamma_i)$ of (B Γ) be composed of the element $\beta_{ii} = 1$, the elements of $-\bar{\beta}_i$, the elements of $\bar{\gamma}_i$, and some zero elements appropriately located. We can write

$$(7.3) \qquad U^* = Y^* \mathrm{B}' - Z\Gamma' = (y_1^* - Y_1^* \bar{\beta}_1 - Z_1 \bar{\gamma}_1 \ldots y_G^* - Y_G^* \bar{\beta}_G - Z_G \bar{\gamma}_G).$$

Differentiate the determinant $|\Sigma^*|$ with respect to the vector $(\bar{\beta}_i \ \bar{\gamma}_i)'$, denoting the cofactor of its $g-h$ element σ_{gh}^* by the scalar Σ_{gh}^* :

$$(7.4) \qquad \frac{\partial |\Sigma^*|'}{\partial(\bar{\beta}_i \ \bar{\gamma}_i)'} = \sum_{g,h}^{G} \Sigma_{gh}^* \frac{\partial \sigma_{gh}^*}{\partial(\bar{\beta}_i \ \bar{\gamma}_i)'},$$

where

$$(7.5) \qquad \sigma_{gh}^* = \left[y_g^{*\prime} - (\bar{\beta}_g \ \bar{\gamma}_g) \binom{Y_g^{*\prime}}{Z_g'} \right] \left[y_h^* - (Y_h^* \ Z_h) \binom{\bar{\beta}_h'}{\bar{\gamma}_h'} \right]$$

and

$$(7.6) \qquad \frac{\partial \sigma_{gh}^*}{\partial(\bar{\beta}_i \ \bar{\gamma}_i)'} \begin{cases} = 0, & i \neq g \quad \text{and} \quad i \neq h, \\ = \begin{pmatrix} Y_i^{*'} \\ Z_i' \end{pmatrix} y_h^* - \begin{pmatrix} Y_i^{*'} \\ Z_i' \end{pmatrix} (Y_h^* \ Z_h) \begin{pmatrix} \bar{\beta}_h' \\ \bar{\gamma}_h' \end{pmatrix}, & i = g, \\ = \begin{pmatrix} Y_i^{*'} \\ Z_i' \end{pmatrix} y_g^* - \begin{pmatrix} Y_i^{*'} \\ Z_i' \end{pmatrix} (Y_g^* \ Z_g) \begin{pmatrix} \bar{\beta}_g' \\ \bar{\gamma}_g' \end{pmatrix}, & i = h. \end{cases}$$

Hence,

$$(7.7) \qquad \frac{\partial |\Sigma^*|}{\partial(\bar{\beta}_i \ \bar{\gamma}_i)'} = 2 \sum_h^G \Sigma_{ih}^* \left[\begin{pmatrix} Y_i^{*'} \\ Z_i' \end{pmatrix} y_h^* - \begin{pmatrix} Y_i^{*'} \\ Z_i' \end{pmatrix} (Y_h^* \ Z_h) \begin{pmatrix} \bar{\beta}_h' \\ \bar{\gamma}_h' \end{pmatrix} \right] \qquad (i = 1, \ldots, G).$$

Since the cofactor Σ_{ih}^* equals the element σ^{*hi} of Σ^{*-1} times the determinant $|\Sigma|$, we have, setting the above derivatives equal to zero and denoting the solution vectors for $(\bar{\beta}_i \ \bar{\gamma}_i)$ by $(\bar{b}_i \ \bar{c}_i)_{(3)}$:

$$(7.8) \qquad \sum_h \sigma^{*hi} \begin{pmatrix} Y_i^{*'} \\ Z_i' \end{pmatrix} y_h^* = \sum_h \sigma^{*hi} \begin{pmatrix} Y_i^{*'} \\ Z_i' \end{pmatrix} (Y_h^* \ Z_h) \begin{pmatrix} \bar{b}_h' \\ \bar{c}_h' \end{pmatrix}_{(3)} \qquad (i = 1, \ldots, G).$$

The above is an equality between each of two column vectors of $G_i - 1 + K_i$ elements (rows).

We may consider the vector $(\bar{b}_1, \bar{c}_1, \ldots, \bar{b}_G, \bar{c}_G)_{(3)}$ of $\Sigma_{i=1}^G (G_i - 1 + K_i)$ unknown coefficients, and express the right side of the above equality as

$$(7.9) \qquad \begin{bmatrix} Y_i^{*'} \\ Z_i' \end{bmatrix} [\sigma^{*1i}(Y_1^* \ Z_1) \ldots \sigma^{*Gi}(Y_G^* \ Z_G)] \begin{bmatrix} \bar{b}_1' \\ \bar{c}_1' \\ \cdot \\ \cdot \\ \cdot \\ \bar{b}_G' \\ \bar{c}_G' \end{bmatrix}_{(3)}.$$

By vertically piling up the above G equalities, we obtain the following set of $\Sigma_{i=1}^G (G_i - 1 + K_i)$ equations in the same number of unknown coefficients.

$$(7.10) \qquad \begin{bmatrix} \sigma^{*11} \begin{pmatrix} Y_1^{*'} \\ Z_1' \end{pmatrix} (Y_1^* \ Z_1) \ldots \sigma^{*G1} \begin{pmatrix} Y_1^{*'} \\ Z_1' \end{pmatrix} (Y_G^* \ Z_G) \\ \cdot \qquad \qquad \cdot \\ \cdot \qquad \qquad \cdot \\ \sigma^{*1G} \begin{pmatrix} Y_G^{*'} \\ Z_G' \end{pmatrix} (Y_1^* \ Z_1) \ldots \sigma^{*GG} \begin{pmatrix} Y_G^{*'} \\ Z_G' \end{pmatrix} (Y_G^* \ Z_G) \end{bmatrix} \begin{bmatrix} \bar{b}_1' \\ \bar{c}_1' \\ \cdot \\ \cdot \\ \bar{b}_G' \\ \bar{c}_G' \end{bmatrix} = \begin{bmatrix} \sum_h \sigma^{*h1} \begin{pmatrix} Y_1^{*'} \\ Z_1' \end{pmatrix} y_h^* \\ \cdot \\ \cdot \\ \sum_h \sigma^{*hG} \begin{pmatrix} Y_G^{*'} \\ Z_G' \end{pmatrix} y_h^* \end{bmatrix}.$$

This is the set of normal equations for three-stage least squares. To check it with the set given by Zellner and Theil [30, (2.16), p. 58], one may note that our $(Y_i^* \; Z_i) = Z(Z'Z)^{-1}Z'(Y_i \; Z_i)$ is their $X(X'X)^{-1}X'Z_\mu$, and, again, that

$$\begin{pmatrix} Y_i^{*'} \\ Z_i' \end{pmatrix} y_h^* = \begin{pmatrix} Y_i^{*'} \\ Z_i' \end{pmatrix} y_h - \begin{pmatrix} Y_i^{*'} \\ Z_i' \end{pmatrix} v_h = \begin{pmatrix} Y_i^{*'} \\ Z_i' \end{pmatrix} y_h .$$

The method of three-stage least squares, by minimizing the determinant $|\Sigma^*|$, has corrected the lack of simultaneity in two-stage least squares. However, our first criticism of two-stage least squares and of the k-class, namely, the wrong directions for minimizing the sum of squares, has not been answered. This criticism remains as long as we fail to adopt a direction-normalization on the linear combinations $Y\beta_i'$, either as a constraint or as the denominator of a ratio.

8. CANONICAL CORRELATIONS APPLIED TO STRUCTURE OF SIMULTANEOUS EQUATIONS

Hooper, [13 and 14], has applied canonical correlation theory to the reduced form of simultaneous equations. Since the reduced form is a system of linear regression equations, canonical correlation theory applies, except that the coefficients in the reduced form are subject to nonlinear restrictions (from identification) which are often ignored by econometricians in estimating the coefficients. It is interesting to apply canonical correlation theory to the structure of simultaneous equations itself, as follows.

Hotelling [15] derives canonical correlations by maximizing the covariance of two linear combinations $Y\beta'$ and $Z\gamma'$ of the two sets of variables Y and Z, subject to normalizations on the squared lengths $\beta Y'Y\beta' = 1$ and $\gamma Z'Z\gamma' = 1$. This is equivalent to minimizing the variance of the difference $Y\beta' - Z\gamma'$ subject to the same normalization restrictions. For the simultaneous equations structure we can minimize the general variance $|(BY' - \Gamma Z')(YB' - Z\Gamma')|$ subject to the restrictions on the squared volumes $|BY'YB'| = 1$ and $|\Gamma Z'Z\Gamma'| = 1$.

For the case of two sets of (the same number of) variables $Y = (y_1 y_2 \ldots)$ and $Z = (z_1 z_2 \ldots)$, the squared vector correlation coefficient is defined as the ratio $|Y'Z|^2 / |Y'Y| \cdot |Z'Z|$. For our case of two sets of linear combinations of variables $YB' = (Y\beta_1' \ldots Y\beta_G')$ and $Z\Gamma' = (Z\gamma_1' \ldots Z\gamma_G')$, a squared vector-combination correlation coefficient can be defined as the ratio $|BY'Z\Gamma'|^2 / |BY'YB'| \cdot |\Gamma Z'Z\Gamma'|$. Similarly,

$$\frac{\begin{vmatrix} BY'YB' & BY'Z\Gamma' \\ \Gamma Z'YB' & \Gamma Z'Z\Gamma' \end{vmatrix}}{|BY'YB'| \cdot |\Gamma Z'Z\Gamma'|}$$

can be defined as a vector-combination coefficient of alienation, as a generalization of the vector coefficient of alienation.

9. CONCLUDING REMARKS

We will conclude by commenting briefly on the criteria for choosing among alternative estimators. Assuming the model of Section 2.3 (including a priori restrictions) to be correctly specified and without considering computational costs, which method would be preferred? The answer depends on one's view on statistical inference. From the classical (non-decision, non-Bayesian) viewpoint, an estimator is judged by its sampling distribution in relation to the fixed, but unknown, parameters. The sampling distribution of an estimator may be derived explicitly, or general theorems on optimum sampling properties of a method of estimation may be relied upon. As examples of the latter, the method of maximum likelihood has been shown to yield efficient (in an exact sense) estimates under certain conditions, and asymptotically efficient estimates under a weaker set of conditions [10, pp. 482–506].

As far as large sample properties of the estimators for simultaneous equations are concerned, full-information maximum likelihood estimates are known to be asymptotically efficient. About small-sample properties, there have been Monte Carlo studies by Wagner [28], Summers [25], Brown [9], and Nagar [21], and mathematical derivations of distributions by Basmann [4, 5] and Nagar [20], but no definite preference for one estimator can be claimed. Although large-sample properties may not be regarded as conclusive, one probably would not discard them completely. If one were to rely solely on exact sampling distributions, he would have no reason for preferring two-stage to single-stage least squares, or for preferring three-stage to two-stage least squares. Furthermore, most of the estimators which have been proposed are explicitly justified by certain principles of estimation such as "the natural generalization of least squares" and maximum likelihood for limited-information, and Aitken's method for both two-stage and three-stage least squares. While the exact sampling distribution may be a more definitive criterion, both the asymptotic sampling distribution of an estimator and the principle by which it is derived serve as criteria for judging an estimator. By these criteria full-information maximum likelihood seems preferable.

Some would consider a certain basic principle in statistical inference paramount. According to the likelihood principle recently expounded by Birnbaum [6, 7, and 8], "The evidential meaning of any outcome x of any experiment E is characterized fully by giving the likelihood function $cf(x, \theta)$ (which need be described only up to an arbitrary positive constant factor), without other reference to the structure of E" [8, p. 271]. The method of full-information maximum likelihood utilizes only the likelihood function, and can be justified by the likelihood principle.

The question was posed in the beginning of this section with two qualifications. We will not add any comments on specification errors in the model, but will point out that full-information maximum likelihood estimates are not more difficult to compute than three-stage least squares strictly defined. The normal equations (7.10) for three-stage least squares are nonlinear in (B Γ) as they involve σ^{*hi}. Zellner and Theil [30] recommended using two-stage least squares to estimate the nonlinear terms σ^{*hi} first, and then take them as given in solving the resulting linear equations. The normal equations for full-information maximum likelihood, derived from differentiating $|\Sigma|$ subject to a different normalization $|BY'YB'| = |W|$ in the denominator, are similar to (7.10), with nonlinear terms σ^{hi} and w^{hi} (elements of W^{-1}).[3] If the same recommendation for treating the nonlinear terms were accepted, the resulting linear equations would be as easy to solve.[4] If not, both methods would require iterations. One iterative procedure is to recompute the nonlinear terms after the linear equations are solved each time. This procedure for maximum likelihood can easily be shown to be the P method given in Chernoff and Divinsky [12, p. 254].

International Business Machines Corporation

REFERENCES

[1] ANDERSON, T. W.: *Introduction to Multivariate Statistical Analysis*, John Wiley & Sons, Inc., 1958.

[2] ANDERSON, T. W., AND H. RUBIN: "Estimation of the Parameters of a Single Equation in a Complete System of Stochastic Equations," *Annals of Mathematical Statistics*, Vol. 20 (1949), pp. 46–63.

[3] BASMANN, R. L.: "A Generalized Classical Method of Linear Estimation of Coefficients in a Structural Equation," *Econometrica*, Vol. 25, No. 1 (1957), pp. 77–83.

[4] ———: *On the Exact Finite Sample Distributions of Generalized Classical Linear Structural Estimators*. (SP-91) Santa Barbara: Technical Military Planning Operations, General Electric Company, July 1, 1960.

[5] ———: "A Note on the Exact Finite Sample Frequency Functions of Generalized Classical Linear Estimators in Two Leading Over-Identified Cases," *Journal of the American Statistical Association*, Vol. 56, No. 295 (1961), pp. 619–636.

[6] BIRNBAUM, A.: "On the Foundations of Statistical Inference Binary Experiments," *Annals of Mathematical Statistics*, Vol. 32, No. 2 (1961), pp. 414–435.

[7] ———: "Another View of the Foundations of Statistics," *American Statistician*, Vol. 16, No. 1 (1962) pp., 17–21.

[8] ———: "On the Foundations of Statistical Inference," *Journal of the American Statistical Association*, Vol. 57, No. 298 (1962), pp. 269–306, with discussion by others, pp. 307–326.

[9] BROWN, T. M.: "Simplified Full Maximum Likelihood and Comparative Structural Estimates," *Econometrica*, Vol. 27, No. 4 (1959), pp. 638–653.

[10] CRAMER, H.: *Mathematical Methods of Statistics*, Princeton: Princeton University Press, 1946.

---

[3] This remark is now elaborated in another paper, "Two Methods of Computing Full-Information Maximum Likelihood Estimates in Simultaneous Stochastic Equations," IBM Research Report, RC-1116, February, 1964. *International Economic Review*, Vol. 9, No. 1 (1968), pp. 100–112.

[4] Since this paper was submitted for publication, I have come across an interesting paper by Rothenberg and Leenders [22] on linearizing full-information maximum likelihood estimates.

[11] HILDRETH, C.: "Simultaneous Equations: Any Verdict Yet?" *Econometrica*, Vol. 28, No. 4 (1960), pp. 846–854.

[12] HOOD, W. C., AND T. C. KOOPMANS (EDITORS): *Studies in Econometric Method*, Cowles Commission for Research in Economics, Monograph 14, New York: John Wiley & Sons, Inc., 1953.

[13] HOOPER, J. W.: "Simultaneous Equations and Canonical Correlation Theory," *Econometrica*, Vol. 28, No. 2 (1959), pp. 245–256.

[14] ———: "Partial Trace Correlations," *Econometrica*, Vol. 30, No. 2 (1962), pp. 324–331.

[15] HOTELLING, HAROLD: "Relations Between Two Sets of Variates," *Biometrika*, Vol. 28 (1936), pp. 321–377.

[16] KIEFER, J.: "Optimum Designs in Regressions Problems, II," *Annals of Mathematical Statistics*, Vol. 32, No. 1 (1961), pp. 298–325.

[17] ———: "Two More Criteria Equivalent to D-Optimality of Designs," *Annals of Mathematical Statistics*, Vol. 33, No. 2 (1962), pp. 792–796, and References [5] and [7] thereof.

[18] KIEFER, J., AND J. WOLFOWITZ: "Optimum Designs in Regression Problems," *Annals of Mathematical Statistics*, Vol. 30, No. 2 (1959), pp. 271–294.

[19] KOOPMANS, T. C. (EDITOR): *Statistical Inference in Dynamic Economic Models*, Cowles Commission for Research in Economics, Monograph 10, New York: John Wiley & Sons, Inc. 1950.

[20] NAGAR, A. L.: "The Bias and Moment Matrix of the General k-Class Estimators of the Parameters in Simultaneous Equations," *Econometrica*, Vol. 27, No. 4 (1959), pp. 575–595.

[21] ———: "A Monte Carlo Study of Alternative Simultaneous Equation Estimators," *Econometrica*, Vol. 28, No. 3 (1960), pp. 573–590.

[22] ROTHENBERG, T., AND C. T. LEENDERS: "Efficient Estimation of Simultaneous Equation Systems," *Econometrica*, Vol. 32, No. 3 (1964).

[23] STROTZ, R. H.: "Interdependence as a Specification Error," *Econometrica*, Vol. 28, No. 2 (1960), pp. 428–442.

[24] STROTZ, R. H., AND H. O. A. WOLD: "Recursive *vs.* Nonrecursive Systems: An Attempt at Synthesis," *Econometrica*, Vol. 28, No. 2 (1960), pp. 417–427.

[25] SUMMERS, ROBERT: "A Strategy for Appraising Various Simultaneous Equation Estimating Methods by Means of Sampling Experiments" (mimeographed), January, 1959.

[26] THEIL, H.: *Estimation and Simultaneous Correlation in Complete Equation Systems*, The Hague: Centraal Planbureau, 1953.

[27] ———: *Economic Forecasts and Policy*, Amsterdam: North-Holland Publishing Company (1958 and 1961).

[28] WAGNER, H. M.: "A Monte Carlo Study of Estimates of Simultaneous Linear Structural Equations," *Econometrica*, Vol. 26, No. 1 (1958), pp. 117–133.

[29] WOLD, H. O. A.: "A Generalization of Casual Chain Models," *Econometrica*, Vol. 28, No. 2 (1960), pp. 443–463.

[30] ZELLNER, ARNOLD, AND H. THEIL: "Three-Stage Least Squares: Simultaneous Estimation of Simultaneous Equations," *Econometrica*, Vol. 30, No. 1 (1962), pp. 54–78.

INDEX

Acceleration principle, 62, 179–206
Addison, W., 346, 348
Aftalion, A., 53
Agriculture, U.S., and technological change, 231–252
Aitchison, J., 233
Aitken, A. C., 225, 227, 383–405
Allen, R. G. D., 254, 260, 271
Analysis
  demand, 44–69
  dynamic, 298–337. *See also* Time series.
  multiple regression, 274–285
  multivariate, 286–297
  probit, 274–285
  sequential, 246
  time series: individual trend, 17–31
Anderson, R. L., 71
Anderson, T. W., 136, 214, 223, 230, 408, 412, 422, 425, 480, 482, 492
Anderson–Rubin test, 342
Ando, A., 379, 380
Arrow, K. J., 469
Asymptotic
  covariance matrix, 406–425
  sampling variances, 292–294

Baird, M., 253
Barber, H. A., 265, 271
Barger, H., 154–158, 345–348
Bartlett, M. S., 441, 470
Basmann, R. L., 484, 491, 492
Battin, R. H., 441, 470
Bennett, M. K., 259, 271
Berkson, J., 234
Bickerdike, F., 53
Birnbaum, A., 491, 492
Black, G., 259, 271
Blackman, R. B., 427, 435, 438, 441, 443, 470
Bobkoski, F., 224
Bowley, A. L., 254, 260, 271
Brady, D. S., 265, 271
Bridgman, P. W., 44
Bristol, R., 259, 271
Brittain, J. A., 451, 470
Bronfenbrenner, J., 215, 223. *See also* Crockett
Brown, J. A. C., 233
Brown, T. M., 491, 492
Brown, W. L., 232
Burns, A. F., 314
Bush, R. R., 235

Capacity principle, 196–204
  overcapacity, 179–206
Carver, T. N., 53
Cassell, G., 53
Chawner, L., 154–158
Chenery, H. B., 180, 182, 187
Chernoff, H., 215, 223, 230, 277, 285, 492, 493
Chow, G. C., 492
Christ, C. F., 299
Clark, J. M., 53, 62, 192
Clark, P., 186
Coefficients
  estimation of, 224–230
  vector, 289–291
Collier, J. W., 247
Consumer behavior, 207–223
Consumer goods
  durable, 58–63, 328–337
  enterprises, 47–69
Cornfield, J., 274, 277, 285
Cornwall, J., 299
Correlations
  canonical, 286–297, 473, 490
  time series data, 17–31
Crabb, A. R., 232
Cramér, H., 229, 387, 405, 412, 420, 425, 491, 492
Cramer, J. S., 328, 337
Crockett, J. B., 277, 285. *See also* Bronfenbrenner
Cunnyngham, J., 469

Dantzig, G. B., 360, 380
Davenport, W. B., 446, 470
Davis, H. T., 234
Demand
  capital goods, 63–122
  consumer goods, 60–63, 207–223
  durable goods, 44–69
  function, 49–52, 58–113
  and investment, 132–142
Derksen, J. B. D., 173, 178
Dirks, F., 149–158
Divinsky, N., 230, 492, 493
Doob, J. L., 71, 427, 431–433, 460, 470
Dorfman, R., 469
Dow, C. H., 6–8
Dow theory, 6–8
Drèze, J., 472
Duesenberry, J. S., 210–223, 318
Dunlop, J. T., 319
Durbin, J., 442, 443, 469, 470